Christianity and Developmental Psychopathology

Foundations and Approaches

Edited by
Kelly S. Flanagan and Sarah E. Hall

An imprint of InterVarsity Press
Downers Grove, Illinois

There's a difference between knowing an idea and knowing an experience.
I dedicate this book to my grandparents, who helped me experience
the ideas in this book. I also dedicate it to my children,
Aidan, Quinn and Caitlin—I hope I can pass
that legacy on to you. —KSF

To my husband, Ryan, and my parents, Bruce and Judy,
for your love and support. —SEH

InterVarsity Press
P.O. Box 1400, Downers Grove, IL 60515-1426
World Wide Web: www.ivpress.com
Email: email@ivpress.com

©2014 by Kelly S. Flanagan and Sarah E. Hall

InterVarsity Press® is the book-publishing division of InterVarsity Christian Fellowship/USA®, a movement of students and faculty active on campus at hundreds of universities, colleges and schools of nursing in the United States of America, and a member movement of the International Fellowship of Evangelical Students. For information about local and regional activities, write Public Relations Dept., InterVarsity Christian Fellowship/USA, 6400 Schroeder Rd., P.O. Box 7895, Madison, WI 53707-7895, or visit the IVCF website at www.intervarsity.org.

All Scripture quotations, unless otherwise indicated, are taken from THE HOLY BIBLE, NEW INTERNATIONAL VERSION®, NIV® Copyright © 1973, 1978, 1984, 2011 by Biblica, Inc.™ Used by permission. All rights reserved worldwide.

While all stories in this book are true, some names and identifying information in this book have been changed to protect the privacy of the individuals involved.

The Twelve Thriving Indicator Wheel in figure 7.1 is used courtesy of Thrive Foundation for Youth.

Cover design: Cindy Kiple
Interior design: Beth Hagenberg
Images: jpa1999/Getty Images

ISBN 978-0-8308-2855-5 (print)
ISBN 978-0-8308-9587-8 (digital)

Printed in the United States of America ∞

Library of Congress Cataloging-in-Publication Data
A catalog record for this book is available from the Library of Congress.

P	24	23	22	21	20	19	18	17	16	15	14	13	12	11	10	9	8	7	6	5	4	3	2	1
Y	35	34	33	32	31	30	29	28	27	26	25	24	23	22	21	20	19	18	17	16	15	14		

Contents

128628

The King will reply, "Truly I tell you,
whatever you did for one of the least of these
brothers and sisters of mine, you did for me."

MATTHEW 25:40

Because each child brings a different story to the tapestry of creation,
there is no way to describe the totality of childhood. Yet one
response to the God who creates in freedom is to listen
to as many of their stories as possible, to be changed
by their different refrains and opened
to those children anew.

JENSEN, 2005, P. 129

THE TASK OF INTEGRATING ONE'S CHRISTIAN FAITH with one's clinical work can be challenging; adding to the challenge for clinicians who work with children and adolescents is the dearth of thoughtful, in-depth integrative writing that directly addresses therapeutic work with youth and their families. As we have worked with families in clinical settings and taught students in academic settings over the past decade, the need for further integrative child clinical literature has become more and more apparent to us. We embarked on this book in an effort to organize our own thinking about the integration of our faith with our work as child clinicians as well as to contribute to the sparse literature. As we have worked on the book, we have been grateful for valuable resources upon which to draw and build. In teaching child psychology classes each semester to undergraduate and graduate students, we have utilized material from numerous resources and past integrative writing (e.g., *Journal of Psychology and Christianity, 22,* 2003) to help us and our students think about how to integrate psychological theory and practice with our faith, our experience with children and our own childhoods, and our particular, personal journeys in integration (Moriarty, 2010; Tan, 2001). We have learned so much from our students and class discussions. We have been lucky to come across excellent writings by theologians who care deeply about children and adolescents and their families that have informed our thinking. We feel blessed to have been "raised" by developmental psychopathologists (in academia and in clinical settings) who value understanding the multifaceted nature of the stories that children bring to us in our clinical work. What wonderfully created beings, what diversity within God's creation, and what a calling to work with the "least of these"! In proposing this book, we desired to synthesize and share some of this rich learning and perspective with readers.

Therefore, the purpose of this book is to integrate a Christian viewpoint with developmental understandings of child psychopathology in order to provide a theoretically and empirically sound background to help developing and practicing Christian mental health professionals work competently with children, adolescents and families. Integrative approaches for understanding the development of psychopathology in children from a Christian perspective are lacking, despite strong integrative work focused on psychological disorders and treatments in adults (e.g., Jones & Butman, 2011; McMinn & Campbell, 2007; Yarhouse, Butman & McRay, 2005) and calls over the past decade for increased attention to this underserved population (Canning, Case & Kruse, 2001; Hathaway, 2003; Sisemore & Moore, 2002; Yangarber-Hicks et al., 2006).

In a recent "look ahead" at the future of applied integration with children and adolescents, Walker (2012) describes the status of this integrative work as being "in its infancy." In response to the nascent status of this field, we agree that applied integrative efforts should "combine spirit led, Biblically based theology with high quality empirical psychological science" to include what both theology and psychology can offer (p. 138). However, we also believe that these approaches must be informed by a thoughtful and coherent theoretical foundation that is developmentally sensitive; Flanagan and Canning (in Yangarber-Hicks et al., 2006) have argued that developmental psychopathology provides such a framework. We hope that this book will be useful to practicing Christian therapists, faculty and students, and researchers by providing a Christian perspective on a major guiding theoretical framework for work with children and families. We aim to integrate current research and thought within child clinical psychology with theological explorations of childhood and "the child" in order to provide guidance for a more holistic conceptualization of children's and families' presenting problems and their etiology.

The first chapter of this book provides an overview of developmental psychopathology and defines its guiding principles and concepts. Developmental psychopathology represents a holistic theoretical framework that incorporates consideration of biological, sociocultural and psychological influences on the development of health and disorder over time. Since its introduction in the early 1980s, developmental psychopathology has become one of the most influential frameworks within child clinical psychology; however, no work of which we are aware has integrated this framework with a Christian approach to psychopathology. As we will demonstrate, developmental psychopathology provides a holistic framework in which children are understood as having individual characteristics that interact with influences in their particular environments, such as family, peer and school, and broader cultural contexts. Exploring the effects of these contexts on children's development, particularly in light of the concepts of pathways and mechanisms across time, is crucial to our understanding of the development of psychopathology as well as children's current functioning and presentation within clinical settings. The crucial role of these developmental influences makes the study of psychopathology in childhood qualitatively different from that in adulthood.

In addition, we introduce the three integrative themes that are explored by the authors of each subsequent chapter. These themes, derived from theological and biblical ideas and writings, are (1) children are to be valued as divine gifts, (2) children are to be respected as persons, and (3) children are to be viewed as agentic beings (Bunge, 2001a, 2008; Jensen, 2005; Mercer, 2005; Miller-McLemore, 2003). The requisite to *value children as divine gifts* is presented in light of Jesus' affirmations of children's worth and his teachings to welcome, honor and care for children. The obligation to *respect children as persons* who are created in God's image and given full personhood suggests that children deserve esteem, empathy and human rights (in contrast to causing them to stumble) and that they possess God-given capacities for spiritual and moral growth and experience. The need to *view children as moral and spiritual agents* forces us to contend with the ideas of children's mutuality in relationship with adults, capable of participating in grace and reconciliation, a source of God's revelation and hope to others, and persons in their own right who are experiencing and learning how to be in God's world. Exploration of the topics within this book utilize theory, empirical research and theology to fully integrate each chapter's core concepts with a Christian worldview.

Based on the foundational ideas of developmental psychopathology, this book explores the influence and interaction of several core intrapersonal and interpersonal aspects of development across both normal and abnormal trajectories. These aspects of development have been chosen because of their centrality to a full understanding of children's current healthy and problematic functioning as well as how disorder develops. In section one of the book, "Intrapersonal Influences," the chapters provide a focus on two psychological, biological and emotional within-person aspects of development—temperament (Mezulis, Harding and Hudson) and emotion regulation (Hall)—selected for their central role in children's development. First, the normal development of these intrapersonal influences is explored, along with the factors that promote healthy development in consideration of temperament and emotion regulation. Second, the authors describe abnormal developmental trajectories, including the risk processes that influence maladaptation and the ways in which the abnormal development of this characteristic affects other aspects of the child's development.

Section two of the book, "Interpersonal Influences," focuses on the multiple bidirectional influences on children within the specific contexts of family and peers. Specifically, these three chapters—covering the marital dyad (Clements, Guarino and Bartos), the parent-child relationships (Seegobin) and peer relations (Flanagan, Kelly and Peeler)—each begin with a section discussing research on trajectories of normal development across childhood and adolescence. The authors then provide a review of abnormal trajectories and the risk factors associated with such trajectories. Specific examples of abnormal development are presented to explicate these processes and their relation to child psychopathology. Research on specific childhood disorders and difficulties is utilized to illustrate the main concepts of developmental psychopathology.

As Walker (2012) noted, there are few resources for applied clinical integration with children and adolescents, although a recent volume from the American Psychological Association provides some promising spiritual interventions with children and adolescents (Walker & Hathaway, 2013). Thus, section three of this book, "Prevention and Treatment," includes two chapters broadly addressing the promotion of resilience and the prevention and treatment of childhood disorders from an integrative developmental psychopathology framework to inform the crucial task of translating theory into practice. The authors of the chapters in this section focus specifically on Christian considerations of applied developmental science. First, from a strengths-based approach, King and Clardy explore the general implications of a developmental psychopathology framework for resilience and positive youth development. Second, Canning, Flanagan, Hailey and de la O broadly discuss a developmentally informed and evidence-based approach to intervention with at-risk and disordered children. Both chapters underscore the following: "As we do the work of care and learn about the gifts, the needs, and the care of the most vulnerable children among us, we will deepen our understanding of care for less vulnerable persons and the environments in which they live. We will find new connections between caring for children and caring for families, communities, nations, the world, and the earth" (Couture, 2000, p. 13).

The fourth section of this book, "Application from Theoretical Orientations," provides an overview of four theoretical orientations and explores how the principles of integrative developmental psychopathology can inform clinical practice from these orientations. Because developmental psychopathology is not a theoretical orientation but rather a framework that can guide our understanding of the origins of psychopathology, it is an approach that can benefit clinicians from a variety of theoretical orientations. In order to illustrate these varied applications, the authors in this section explore how an understanding of developmental psychopathology can contribute to effective treatment from psychodynamic (Pressley and Vanden Hoek), behavioral (Blackburn, Weisgerber and Shelley), cognitive-behavioral (Walker, Whitesell, Montes, Partridge and Hall), and family systems (Rueger and Van Dyke) approaches in working with youth and their families. First, each chapter provides an overview of the orientation, its theoretical background and its applications for clinical practice with youth. Second, and of particular importance for readers, the implications of developmental psychopathology for both theoretical and practical applications of the orientation is explored. Third, an integrative case study is presented and discussed to provide an example of a holistic treatment approach combining the orientation, the principles of developmental psychopathology and a Christian worldview. In the context of the case study, implications of the three integrative themes (children respected as persons, valued as gifts and viewed as agents) are considered.

We pray that this book will challenge you to a more nuanced view of the children and families with whom you work and a greater appreciation of the richness of their stories. Further, through a review of research and clinical approaches, the provision of practical suggestions, and exploration of the three integrative themes, we pray that this book might encourage a more integrated approach to treatment.

1

Overview of
Developmental Psychopathology
and Integrative Themes

Kelly S. Flanagan and Sarah E. Hall

For you created my inmost being;
you knit me together in my mother's womb.
I praise you because I am fearfully and wonderfully made;
your works are wonderful,
I know that full well.

PSALM 139:13-14

[A] developmental perspective invites [us] to see each human life as a
unique person emerging through common aspects that can be
observed, measured, and evaluated, yet in essence a
human soul, a soul with spiritual reality
at core, alive through God's
redemptive grace.

WARD, 1995, P. 16

Start children off on the way they should go,
and even when they are old they will not turn from it.

PROVERBS 22:6

ADVANCES OVER THE PAST FEW DECADES within child clinical psychology and Christian theology reflect complex views of children and the need to attend to the multifaceted nature of their cognitive, emotional, social, moral and spiritual development. We contend that the parallel process within these two disciplines that has resulted in greater recognition of the complex and dynamic nature of children and their growth leads us to a nexus of integration. We also contend that child clinical psychology and theology have the potential to inform each other. For example, our understanding of child development (e.g., attachment relationships, prevention, child effects on parenting) can impact theological themes, such as the nature of faith, spiritual development, the human condition and church practice (Bunge, 2001a). In turn, theological understandings of children also affect how we understand their psychological well-being and conceptualize psychopathology.

Both developmental psychopathology and contemporary theological views of children challenge us to respect children and treat them with esteem and concern. Advocacy and care for the least of these is apparent throughout both disciplines (e.g., Couture, 2007; Tseng, 2012). Yet it is not always easy to be in relationship with children, a fact that we encounter in our clinical work and perhaps also our personal lives. In writing about her experience raising three children, Miller-McLemore (2007) describes parenting as a spiritual practice of "contemplation in the midst of chaos"; interactions with children cause us to face our own inner chaos (e.g., anger, fear, joy, love, humility and frustration) as well as learn to be with them in the external chaos that their personalities, activity level, desires and needs may instigate. We have a significant role when in relationship with children and thus must have an informed understanding of their world and their unique paths, which include both struggles and growth. Our relationships with children affect their understanding and perceptions of God (Yust, 2004), and likewise, the therapeutic alliance is crucial to work with children and their families (Shirk, Karver & Brown, 2011).

The need to recognize and accept the complexity of children and their world has been identified within Christianity (Miller-McLemore, 2003; Mercer, 2005). There are deep theological roots for attending to children. The care of children is founded on Jesus' call to love one's neighbor, to serve others and to heal the sick (Mk 10:23-25; Acts 4:30; Jas 5:16), and on his example to welcome children and not neglect them or cause them to stumble (Mt 18:1-6). Gundry-Volf (2001) explains that welcoming children necessitates the practice of service and hospitality and the recognition that children are paradoxically blessed in their powerlessness in the kingdom of God (Lk 9:46-48; Mt 18:3-4). Though a call to action to serve children was espoused by some theologians in the past (e.g., Wesley, Francke), within the past decade, numerous theologians have called their colleagues to attend to children so that children do not remain marginalized within contemporary theology (e.g., Bunge, 2001a, 2008; Couture, 2007; Jensen, 2005; Mercer, 2005; Miller-McLemore, 2003). Theologians who emphasize care for the young reflect on children in consideration of *who* the child is (personhood) within her *context* (Bunge, 2001b). The complexity of children is represented in the Bible, with contradictory portrayals of children throughout Scripture, including children as signs of God's blessing and as sources of joy (Gen 17) but also foolish, impulsive (Prov 22:15) and in need of discipline (Prov 29:15); as occupying low social status but privileged by Christ (Mk 10:13-16); as models of faith in their vulnerability and dependency but also needing guidance and discipline (Deut 6:6-9; Mt 18:1-6) (Gundry-Volf, 2001). Further, the moral and religious complexity of children is acknowledged through honest appraisals of the multifaceted and multilayered representations of children and their nurture in the Bible (Bunge, 2008).

Within the discipline of psychology, the field of developmental psychopathology has helped clinicians and researchers to view children in a more complex light and to better understand their needs and the interface between development and psychopathology. Scientific insights from the field of developmental psychopathology can shape our clinical work via an informed view of the role of the development process and its impact on later functioning. Yet, we also do not want to reduce our science to merely identification of the right tools and prevention or intervention efforts for "optimal" development. Therefore, our scientific and clinical efforts must be continually grounded in a biblical and theological view of children.

The interface of psychology and Christianity regarding children has a sometimes difficult history, as described by Miller-McLemore (2003), and yet it is crucial in determining how we view children and interact with them. Certain religious practices or theological views might portray mental illness in less than helpful ways, and religion/spirituality has often been ignored within psychology (Yarhouse, Butman & McRay, 2005). Sometimes the nature of how we view psychology and theology may lead us to rely on psychology to the neglect of spiritual values, or likewise, certain views may lead us to distrust psychology as self-focused and spiritually bereft. For example, if we place decreasing importance on the role of sin, parents might turn primarily to secular experts for the difficult task of ensuring their children's well-being and "improved functioning" (Miller-McLemore, 2003; Yarhouse et al., 2005). Yet our work with children inherently involves soul care as much as external reinforcement of desirable behavior, cognitive reappraisals, systems changes or the provision of insight. We must consider the multifaceted processes that shape the well-being of the whole child as a spiritual and bodily being. Parents should be guided by their moral values and, in the case of Christian parents, be informed by their faith in Christ and by the Holy Spirit's leading. Likewise, spiritual and moral development should be a major focus for children's growth and should not be pushed aside for a focus on achievement, self-fulfillment and happiness as an end in itself. In addition, an understanding of development can help us understand children's capacities and how to walk with them in our mutual spiritual journey (e.g., Stonehouse & May, 2010; Yust, 2004) just as an informed perspective on abnormal development can help us to understand how to serve children and families who are suffering and ameliorate difficulties.

We need to wrestle with how our theology may affect our clinical work and our interactions with children (as well as how we may mistakenly set it aside when we work in what we see as a separate arena). Likewise, we need to wrestle with how our experiences with children in our clinical work and our scientific knowledge may affect our theological views. The purpose of this book is to integrate complex theological and clinical views of children and childhood to inform mental health research and practice. In general, the integrative approach the chapters will take is that of theology and psychology informing each other—theological doctrines influencing our views of children's health and pathology, and psychological truths about child development and psychopathology influencing our theological views of childhood. Given historical influences on theological approaches to childhood, we do not believe that theology has a complete understanding of child development and psychopathology (see Bunge, 2001a); in fact, it has been noted that theologians have most often written about children only in relation to another issue, such as the doctrine of salvation and the baptism of infants (Mercer, 2005), rather than attending to children and childhood in its own right. Neither do we think that developmental and child clinical psychology have a holistic view of the child that considers her a spiritual being created in God's image and placed in his world to be in relationship with him. Both disciplines must inform each other in order to present a more nuanced and complex understanding of the child and his or her development, which we believe children deserve. This book seeks to provide guidance to more appropriately understand and support children by examining how developmental psychopathology and Christian theology can complement each other to promote a respectful and open stance toward children.

OVERVIEW OF DEVELOPMENTAL PSYCHOPATHOLOGY

Developmental psychopathology has been identified as a scientific discipline with distinct theoretical tenets and components that differentiate it from other disciplines (Cicchetti, 1989). In 1984, a special issue of the journal *Child Development* was published that gave voice to this emerging field. The following definition provided in this publication continues to direct the field: "*the study of the origins and course of individual patterns of behavioral maladaptations,* whatever the age of onset, whatever the causes, whatever the transformations in behavioral manifestation, and however complex the course of the developmental pattern may be" (Sroufe & Rutter, 1984, p. 18). More recently, developmental psychopathology has succinctly been described as "an evolving scientific discipline whose predominant focus is elucidating the interplay among the biological, psychological, and social-contextual aspects of normal and abnormal development" (Cicchetti, 2006, p. 1).

The view of psychopathology within this framework emphasizes its malleable and context-based nature; that is, psychopathology is "probabilistic rather than predetermined," with the interaction between the individual and the environment over time resulting in multiple pathways of development. This perspective underscores the integrated nature of development. We are reminded that "our patterns of adaptation and maladaptation, our particular liabilities and strengths, whether and how we are vulnerable or resilient—all are complex products of a lengthy developmental process" (Sroufe, 2009, p. 179). Thus, a lifespan perspective on development is crucial for researchers and clinicians who work from within this framework. Cicchetti (1989) reviewed the theoretical principles of differentiation, organization and hierarchical integration that govern development as crucial influences on the emergence of this discipline. For example, theories regarding the successive integration of stages of development into later growth in a hierarchical, cumulative fashion lead to the perspective that early development and experience remain a part of a person as she continues to develop. Given the intrapersonal, interpersonal and environmental influences on development, simplistic, linear thinking regarding causality is abandoned. Similarly, treatment and intervention approaches within this framework seek to understand and address the distinct developmental processes that have led to a unique individual's current functioning.

As such, developmental psychopathology is an inherently multidisciplinary approach that combines principles from the study of development with understandings of health and maladaptation (Cicchetti, 2006). This creates a unique perspective on both development and disorder by combining research and perspectives from developmental and clinical psychology as well as an increasing breadth of other fields (e.g., cultural psychology, cognitive psychology, biology, epigenetics and sociology). Further, rather than merely drawing from multiple disciplines, developmental psychopathology aims to integrate information across disciplines to create a unique, complex, truly multisystemic perspective for understanding functioning. The multidisciplinary nature of developmental psychopathology is also highlighted in the view that multiple levels of analysis are necessary to understand any developmental process (Cicchetti, 2008). A child's functioning at any point in time can be explored on several different levels, including biological (e.g., genetic, biochemical, physiological), psychological (cognitive, affective, experiential), social (e.g., intrafamilial, interpersonal), and cultural (e.g., socioeconomic, ethnic/racial, gendered). Developmental psychopathologists argue that multilevel analysis is not only beneficial but *required* to fully understand the development and adaptation of complex human beings. Practically speaking, then, developmental psychopathology is neither a theory of development nor a therapeutic orientation (such as psychodynamic and behavioral approaches are) but is rather a broad approach to understanding the complexities of human development that can inform theory and research within a variety of therapeutic approaches.

Several terms and concepts are central to a developmental psychopathology–based approach to the study of disorder. These include the ideas of normalcy and abnormality, the importance of context, a focus on pathways (including equifinality, multifinality, continuity and discontinuity), risk, protection, resilience, and prevention and intervention.

Normalcy and Abnormality

A central tenet of developmental psychopathology is that understandings of normal and abnormal development inform one another and are both necessary in the study of disorder (Cicchetti, 2006). On a basic level, how can we know what is abnormal if we do not know what is normal? How can we understand and identify autism, for example, without a good understanding of normal socioemotional development? Might we mislabel anxiety as pathological if we do not understand the typical development of children's fears or separation anxiety? Therefore, developmental psychopathologists find value in the study of the mechanisms and processes that produce normal or typical developmental outcomes as well as those that produce pathology. In addition, health and disorder are viewed as existing along a continuum, with individuals ranging from more to less healthy in a particular realm rather than in the clearly distinguishable categories of "disordered" or "nondisordered." All points along the continuum are significant, not merely cut-off points or the end points, as (1) the line between adaptation and maladaptation is often unclear, and (2) all degrees of competence offer value to researchers exploring the interplay of development and (mal)adaptation. Thus, developmental psychopathologists are interested in nondisordered populations, pathological populations, at-risk populations and high-risk nondisordered (resilient) populations.

It is important to clarify the meaning of the terms *normal* and *abnormal.* These are loaded terms, and the assumptions of a developmental psychopathology approach are better captured by the concepts of adaptation and maladaptation. Behaviors or outcomes that are adaptive are those that promote positive functioning in one's various contexts (e.g., relationships, work, school); maladaptation, in contrast, occurs when an individual's behavior interferes with optimal functioning. For example, the ability to sit quietly at one's desk during a test even when one is anxious or distressed would be considered adaptive, whereas disrupting one's classmates by storming out of the room or complaining angrily about the test is generally maladaptive. Clinical psychology's focus on identifying the line between normal and abnormal is reinforced by its diagnostic system as outlined in the *Diagnostic and Statistical Manual of Mental Disorders,* 5th edition (APA, 2013). There have been some positive changes in the most recent edition of the *DSM,* including an attempt to incorporate dimensional approaches into the categorical system, and to account for the course of illness over development with specific symptom considerations for different age groups and a developmental organization of disorders within categories; however, complaints about this diagnostic system abound, several of which are particularly relevant for child psychopathology. For example, with regard to questions of normalcy versus abnormality, the diagnostic criteria in the current categorization system (*DSM-5*) do not include an etiological component for understanding or diagnostic decision making. Disorders are defined by their symptoms, with little regard for the interaction between symptom and environment. In this approach, there is no opportunity to understand behavior as an adaptation to the demands of the environment. Along similar lines, the individualistic focus of the *DSM-5* is inappropriate for children (and perhaps even adults). Symptoms are identified based on the client's emotions and behaviors without accounting for the role of context. A teenager whose depression develops in the absence of any clear situational risk factors and one who displays symptoms of depression after years of abuse would be indistinguishable by current diagnostic criteria, even though their different developmental pathways are crucial to understand in conceptualizing the case.

It is important to note that all behaviors are, in some way, adaptations to the demands of the environment. A teenager who is aggressive toward his peers because the effectiveness of aggression has been modeled by his parents is attempting to function in his environment by soliciting attention from others and fulfill his need for interaction in the only way he has observed to be effective. A young child who dissociates as a reaction to sexual abuse is adapting to the demands of a situation that overwhelm her ability to consciously cope with severe danger and trauma. However, when we consider whether a behavior is truly adaptive or maladaptive, normal or abnormal, we must consider both its short- and long-term consequences. If the child who dissociates during a traumatic incident experiences a dissociative episode in class, her academic performance is likely to suffer. If dissociation becomes an automatic defense mechanism for coping with stress, her behavior will be maladaptive over the course of her development because such psychological distancing and withdrawal inhibits the ability to fully engage with a situation and make adaptive behavioral choices. For example, an adolescent who dissociates during an intense argument with a friend will likely not be capable of behaving in ways that resolve the conflict and preserve the relationship.

We must also recognize the role of societal factors in defining normalcy. The idea of normal is suspended within time and context; without placing a behavior in a particular setting at a particular point in history, we cannot determine whether it is normal (Trommsdorff & Cole, 2011). For example, in some cultures, striving hard for individual achievement and success is highly valued; in others, the effect of an individual's behavior on others is more strongly emphasized than individual success. There is also wide cultural variation in views of masculinity and its defining characteristics (Gilmore, 1990). In a culture in which aggression is considered an important part of masculinity, a young man who displays violent behavior toward peers might be viewed as healthy, whereas in a setting in which violence is viewed negatively, such aggression would represent problematic behavior and maladaptive functioning. Furthermore, cultures are not homogenous; views of masculinity among men of the same national and cultural background show a fair amount of variation (Torres, Solberg & Carlstrom, 2002). Therefore, we must be deliberate in our assessment of the broader cultural influences on judgments of behavior while leaving room for the unique context of each individual.

Importance of Context

Context is a crucial component in our understanding of behavior for multiple reasons (Cicchetti & Aber, 1998). As addressed in the previous section, we cannot determine whether a behavior is adaptive or normative outside of its context. Jumping up and down and yelling is appropriate at a football game but not in the classroom, for instance. Furthermore, the context in which a child develops—including family, neighborhood, school, peers and culture—is an extremely important influence on development, an idea first popularized in ecological theory (Bronfenbrenner, 1979). Consistent with a multiple-levels-of-analysis approach, developmental psychopathology embraces the idea that each of these levels of contextual influence must be considered in developmental and clinical applications (e.g., Mian, Wainwright, Briggs-Gowan & Carter, 2011). As discussed throughout the chapters in this book, research consistently highlights the role of parental, sibling, peer, classroom, neighborhood, and cultural influences on children's health and well-being,

Building on the idea of reciprocal determinism, in which the environment affects and is affected by an individual (Bandura, 1986), developmental psychology takes a transactional view of the development of children that occurs within multiple systems (Sameroff, 1975; Sameroff & Chandler, 1975; Lerner, 2002). A transactional view of development assumes that individuals are not only affected by their environments but also change and select their environments in both incidental and purposeful ways. A child is not a passive recipient of the influences of her classroom; rather, her behavior shapes the classroom environment itself, potentially impacting elements such as the emotional tone

of the class, peer interactions, and even the physical set-up of the room. Furthermore, especially as children grow older, they select environments that fit
their preferences and abilities in a phenomenon known as niche picking (Scarr,
1993); a teenager not only behaves in ways that affect her classrooms and peers
but also chooses whether to take advanced math and whether to spend time
with delinquent neighbors, actively shaping the influences to which she is exposed. The importance of recognizing children's agency in their own development is highlighted by these ideas.

In a transactional view, not only is the person-environment interaction reciprocal, but the individual and his environment are never truly independent.
Parenting techniques and choices clearly affect a child, but they are not one-way
influences; the child's temperament and response to a parent's behavior affects
parenting as well. The child who throws a violent temper tantrum in response
to a serious reprimand is likely to elicit a different reaction from a parent than
the child who responds remorsefully. Furthermore, the behaviors of the parent
and child do not begin as independent; the child with greater physiological
arousal and a tendency to anger easily is more likely to have a parent who
shares that emotionality and has passed it on to the child by both biological
and interpersonal means. This dyad, then, has a conflictual interaction in
which the behavior of each directly affects the behavior of the other, which is
also affected by their shared emotional predispositions. The recognition of
these complex influences on development forms an important foundation for
a thorough understanding of why and how an individual child's maladaptation
occurs within a particular familial and societal context.

The emerging field of epigenetics also supports the concept of transaction.
Epigenetics is the study of the effect of the environment on genetic expression
(Berger, 2012). It adds a third influence to the nature versus nurture debate: the
nature-nurture combination. In this way, we are not entities that are separate
from and merely present in our environments; who we are—even at the level
of genetic influences on development—is dependent upon the environment in
which we live and develop (see Cicchetti, 2008, for a developmental psychopathology application).

Finally, culture is an important aspect of a child's context. Cultural values
and norms as well as the degree of fit between a child's cultural background
and the majority culture of his environment affect both his ability to adapt
easily to environmental demands as well as whether his particular behaviors

are viewed as (mal)adaptive. In addition, children of minority cultural, racial and ethnic groups may face particular environmental challenges in the forms of racism and discrimination (Pachter, Bernstein, Szalacha & García Coll, 2010), which affect mental health and well-being in a variety of ways (García Coll, Lamberty, Jenkins, McAdoo, Crnic, Wasik, & Vasquez García, 1996). Increasingly, research has focused on protective factors, such as having a strong racial or cultural identity, that may ameliorate the effects of prejudice and discrimination on minority youth (Neblett, Rivas-Drake & Umana-Taylor, 2012).

Focus on Pathways

Developmental psychopathology emphasizes the importance of understanding development as occurring along pathways (Cicchetti, 2006). The state of a child's well-being at any given point is the result of the dynamic interaction between that child and her environment over time, and the direction of a developmental pathway at a given point is determined by both individual characteristics and environmental influences. In addition, psychopathology is conceptualized as an outcome of development rather than a disease entity located statically in the individual (Sroufe, 1997). For example, a teenager's depression may develop as the result of the way she cognitively processes the death of a parent that occurred when she was younger. At the time of the death, her cognitive abilities were not developed enough to fully understand the implications of the loss; now that she is older, she is able to think more abstractly, and her new understanding of the meaning of living without both parents, interacting with a genetic vulnerability toward internalizing symptoms, leads to a sense of hopelessness. This hopelessness causes her to withdraw socially and to have difficulty completing her schoolwork, important roles for an adolescent to fulfill and which affect her ongoing social, academic and identity development.

There are a theoretically infinite number of different pathways an individual may follow from conception to a given developmental outcome. Fortunately, we do see certain patterns in the types of factors and experiences that lead to various forms of adaptation and maladaptation. The concepts of equifinality and multifinality (Cicchetti & Rogosch, 1996) provide a framework for thinking about developmental pathways. Equifinality is the idea that individuals may follow different pathways to the same outcome. An adult with borderline personality disorder may have experienced either childhood sexual abuse or an unstable home situation in his youth (or another risk altogether). Both children who are securely attached to their parents and those who experience neglect may mature into adolescents who are able to form healthy relationships with peers. Complementarily, multifinality is observed when individuals who share a developmental "starting point" or experience similar life events diverge in terms of outcome. Monozygotic twins who grow up in the same home with the same parents have about a 50% concordance rate for schizophrenia (Cardno & Gottesman, 2000), indicating significant but far from deterministic heritability. On the other hand, children who experience adversity early in life have a wide variety of outcomes, ranging from very positive to very negative (e.g., Werner & Smith, 1992, 2001). For example, many children whose parents divorce do not display later maladaptation, whereas for others, the experience of parental divorce negatively affects mental health, educational achievement and relationship stability, even into adulthood (Amato & Cheadle, 2005).

In addition, pathways are complicated by the fact that events may influence development not only at the point in time when they occur but well into the future; these continuing influences are known as developmental cascades (Masten & Cicchetti, 2010). In other words, negative or positive influences do not merely influence a child at a given point in development; rather, they actually change the child's developmental course. For example, a young child who is aggressive and oppositional is likely to be rejected by his peers. In turn, he lacks the opportunity to develop social skills and to experience the support of peers during development. As he experiences ongoing rejection, he may develop a negative view of himself. His risk of developing internalizing symptoms such as depression and anxiety in later childhood and adolescence is subsequently higher. In this way, there is a developmental cascade from early externalizing problems to later internalizing symptoms by way of peer difficulties (Van Lier & Koot, 2010).

Developmental cascades can also lead to positive outcomes, as "competence begets competence" (Masten & Cicchetti, 2010, p. 492). A child who develops language early may receive more verbal attention from parents, who reinforce her language skills through their positive attention and direct instruction. When she begins school, her language skills are more advanced than those of her peers, and she learns more in the classroom and reads earlier. Her teachers may respond positively to her academic performance as well as her behavior in the classroom, which is likely to be adaptive due to the positive attention she receives for her intellectual abilities. As her reading skills advance quickly, they form the foundation for continued academic success, and this success is further promoted by a sense of achievement and self-efficacy in the academic arena.

Also important in the discussion of developmental pathways are the concepts of continuity and discontinuity. Often seen as one of the main themes in developmental psychology (Santrock, 2011), the continuity-discontinuity debate revolves around whether development at a given point builds smoothly upon previous development or whether development is better characterized by discrete, step-wise changes over time. Are language milestones such as first gestures and words better understood as discrete changes or as continuities in the underlying process of language learning that just appear to be discontinuous? Whereas developmental psychologists are generally interested in continuity (e.g., What patterns exist in development over time?), clinical psychologists focus on discontinuity (e.g., How do we distinguish disordered from nondisordered? Rutter & Garmezy, 1983). Developmental psychopathology, then, draws from both approaches, suggesting that each of these concepts may characterize functioning in different situations. Rather than merely focusing on rates of psychopathology, developmental psychopathology explores continuities and discontinuities in functioning within an individual across development. This idea underscores the perspective that development does not remain static but rather is fluid and can change across time, which highlights the need for longitudinal research.

The concept of heterotypic continuity helps us understand links among different behaviors over time. Heterotypic continuity occurs when there is continuity in the underlying meaning or function of a behavior over time even when the specific form of that behavior changes (Rutter, 1989). We would conclude that there is consistency in the behavior of a person who hits others as a toddler, swears at his parents as an adolescent, and commits sexual assault as a young adult. Although the specific behaviors change, there is a clear thread of aggression across the development of this individual. Therefore, we must be careful to examine not only obvious continuity in individual behaviors but heterotypic continuity in what a behavior may represent or the purpose it may serve at different points in development.

Risk, Protection and Resilience

The pathways along which an individual develops are not arbitrary or entirely unpredictable; rather, they are influenced by a wide variety of factors that increase the likelihood of either healthy or maladaptive development. Risk factors are influences that increase the probability of a negative outcome by disrupting the process of healthy development (Masten, Best & Garmezy, 1990). Risk factors can be located within an individual, such as in the case of difficult temperament (Mian et al., 2011), neurological deficits (Sasayama, Hayashida, Yamasue, Harada, Kaneko, Kasai, Washizuka & Amano, 2010) or poor coping skills (Carlson & Grant, 2008). They can also occur in the environment or in interactions with others; for example, insecure attachment (Allen, Moore, Kuperminc & Bell, 1998; Cummings & Cicchetti, 1990), parental psychopathology (Murray, Arteche, Fearon, Halligan, Goodyer & Cooper, 2011), association with delinquent peers (Snyder, Schrepferman, McEachern, Barner, Johnson & Provines, 2008), and economic strain (McLoyd, 1998) have all been associated with increased risk for negative behavioral and/or emotional outcomes. In addition, risk factors can be conceptualized as either discrete, highly stressful events (e.g., the death of a parent; Cerel, Fristad, Verducci, Weller & Weller, 2006) or more constant, daily stressors (e.g., family conflict; Holtzman & Roberts, 2012).

It is important to remember that risk factors are dynamic rather than static (Cicchetti, 2006). Most stressors affect individuals in ongoing ways rather than at a single point in time, even in the case of a discrete traumatic event. For example, adolescents who are exposed to violence continue to exhibit physical and emotional symptoms of stress a year later (Peckins, Dockray, Eckenrode, Heaton & Susman, 2012). Violence exposure may have a continuing effect through its impact on the physiological stress response as well as on behavioral and cognitive patterns of functioning. Teenagers who witness or experience violence may find it difficult to trust others and to focus on schoolwork due to heightened physiological arousal as well as persistent thoughts about threat and danger. In this way, community violence does not merely affect an individual at the point of exposure; rather, it influences various aspects of functioning in ongoing ways. Further, the impact of a risk factor will depend on the individual's age and developmental level as well as the presence of other risk factors. A young child's experience of violence and danger may be significantly lessened by the presence of a sensitive caregiver who attends to the child's emotions and responds to her need for verbal comfort and physical proximity; an adolescent, however, may experience a persistent sense of fear and threat—despite appropriate comfort from a caregiver—given her more advanced cognitive functioning and the ability to think more abstractly about the idea of danger and the potential impact of violence on the future. Similarly, the experience of assault may affect the adolescent who lives in a dangerous neighborhood differently than the adolescent who benefits from a general sense of safety and security. One child may be more likely to experience other risk factors—witnessing violence, poverty and family instability—that heighten her sense of threat or danger, whereas another may find a sense of security through protective factors such as her family's economic security.

Perhaps even more important to understand than risk factors are risk mechanisms, or the "how" of the risk's impact on functioning. What is the mechanism or process by which a risk factor alters the course of development toward a more negative outcome? Why does maltreatment, for example, increase a child's risk for emotional and behavior problems? Does it interrupt normal brain development (Teicher, Andersen, Polcari, Anderson, Navalta & Kim, 2003), affect a child's view of others or ability to form healthy relationships (Bowlby, 1969; Cicchetti & Toth, 1995), lead to a chronic sense of fearfulness and danger that leads to self-protective reactions (Davies, Winter & Cicchetti, 2006), or (most likely) a combination of the above? We cannot fully understand a risk factor—or successfully intervene to halt its effects—until we understand *how* and *why* it affects a child.

Risk factors may be either causal in nature or merely markers of the presence of a risk mechanism (Kraemer, Kazdin, Offord, Kessler, Jensen & Kupfer, 1997). Causal risk factors are those variables which in themselves increase the likelihood of a negative outcome. For example, low parental monitoring of adolescents appears to raise a teenager's risk of substance use and delinquent behavior specifically through the lack of parental involvement and awareness of the adolescent's activities and peers (Fulkerson, Pasch, Perry & Komro, 2008). Risk markers, in contrast, are variables which do not in themselves raise risk but which indicate the presence of a related characteristic that does lead to negative outcomes. An example of a risk marker is high school dropout as a predictor of substance use (Cicchetti, 2006). Dropping out of high school in and of itself does not appear to raise an adolescent's risk of drug abuse; rather, the factors that lead to high school dropout—including poverty, school failure and teen pregnancy (Christenson & Thurlow, 2004; Whitman, Bokowski, Keogh & Weed, 2001)—are also causal factors in substance use. In this way, high school dropout merely marks, rather than raises, risk.

It is possible for a given variable to be both a causal risk factor and a risk marker. The link between divorce and childhood behavior problems has long been recognized (Amato & Keith, 1991). Research suggests, however, that it is not divorce that increases problem behavior but the marital conflict that frequently precedes and accompanies divorce (Grych & Fincham, 2001; Najman, Behrens, Andersen, Bor, O'Callaghan & Williams, 1997). In this way, divorce is a risk marker. However, divorce itself often has negative economic consequences for families and children (Amato, 2000), and economic strain has been linked with behavior problems, likely through its effects on parenting and parental well-being (McLoyd, 1998). In this way, then, divorce is also an (indirect) causal risk factor through its impact on family socioeconomic status as well as parents' abilities to remain sensitive to their children in the midst of the stressors and mental health challenges that frequently accompany economic strain.

The relationships among risk factors and outcomes are complex. Adding to the complexity of these relations is the common co-occurrence of risk factors, known as multiple risk. Risk factors often cluster together rather than occurring in isolation (Evans, 2003; Seifer, Sameroff, Baldwin & Baldwin, 1992). For example, a child living in poverty may be more likely to live with a single parent with low occupational attainment who may feel stressed or experience psychopathology and thus discipline harshly. In addition, risk factors are often fairly nonspecific, with a given variable predicting multiple types of maladaptation (e.g., Sameroff, Seifer, Barocas, Zax & Greenspan, 1987). Rather than examining risks individually, cumulative models of risk measurement use the number of risk factors present to predict outcomes (e.g., Rutter, 1979, 1983; Sameroff, Seifer, Baldwin & Baldwin, 1993). Studies of cumulative risk have shown that most children exposed to any one of a number of risk factors do not show maladjustment; however, as the number of risk factors to which children are exposed increases, their levels of behavior problems and psychological distress also increase, whereas positive characteristics such as social competence decrease (Doan, Fuller-Rowell & Evans, 2012; Evans, 2003; Evans & English, 2002; Forehand, Biggar & Kotchick, 1998; Loeber et al., 2005; Seifer et al., 1996; Viana, Gratz & Rabian, 2011).

Fortunately, risks are not the only influences on a child's development. Positive individual and environmental characteristics promote health and even ameliorate the effects of negative influences. Protective factors are characteristics which "protect" a child from harmful outcomes that often accompany risk or adversity (Masten et al., 1990). A wide variety of variables have been found to have this ameliorative effect, including intelligence (Pargas, Brennan, Hammen & Le Brocque, 2010; Masten et al., 1999), problem-solving skills (LeBlanc, Self-Brown, Shepard & Kelley, 2011; Quamma & Greenberg, 1994), good emotion regulation (Kliewer, Reid-Quiñones, Shields & Foutz, 2009; Lengua, 2002), and sensitive parenting (Burchinal, Roberts, Zeisel, Hennon & Hooper, 2006; Haskett, Allaire, Kreig & Hart, 2008). Protective factors may lessen the impact of risk directly or improve an individual's capacity to cope with risk in an adaptive manner.

Some positive influences on development may be best described as protective because their influence is either enhanced or only present when risk is also present. For example, parents' and teachers' educational aspirations for adolescents have a more marked effect on the academic achievement of teenagers from disadvantaged backgrounds than those without economic disadvantage (Schoon, Parsons & Sacker, 2004). Other factors that are commonly called protective are actually better described as promotive factors (Luthar, Cicchetti & Becker, 2000). These characteristics promote competence in all individuals, regardless of the level of risk. For example, high-quality parenting promotes positive development whether or not risk is present (Masten et al., 1999).

Individuals who experience adversity but exhibit health, positive outcomes or competence are known as resilient (Masten & Coatsworth, 1998; Masten, 2001). It is generally agreed that two factors must be present to declare an individual resilient: (1) risk or adversity and (2) positive adaptation or competence (Luthar & Cicchetti, 2000). Such competence may be either broad, such as general positive adaptation to one's environment, or specific, such as success in a particular domain of functioning. Examples of common measures of competence include secure attachment, skill at self-regulation, friendships and social skills, and academic success (Masten & Coatsworth, 1998). Furthermore, an individual who is truly competent or resilient displays positive adaptation in the present as well as the capacity to continue to adapt successfully to future developmental tasks and life demands, thus indicating that the current adaptation is not maladaptive in the long term. Resilience occurs as the result of protective factors and their interaction with risk to reduce its negative effects. People may be resilient at any point in development and in the face of even severe risk, which offers hope for children and families in even the direst of circumstances.

Resilience is a complex concept that can be challenging to assess. Assessment of resilience must be developmentally sensitive, with attention paid to the normative developmental tasks at a given point. For example, a very young child's resilience may be assessed through her secure attachment to her mother despite significant family stressors; however, an adolescent's resilience might better be assessed through his successful identity formation or ability to engage in emotionally intimate relationships with peers despite risk. In addition, an individual may display resilience in some areas of development but not others. If a child whose parents divorce when she is young becomes an adolescent who is socially skilled and has many healthy relationships but drops out of high school, would we consider her resilient? Finally, we must be aware of and sensitive to a child's wider social and cultural context when judging resilience (Masten & Coatsworth, 1998). What is considered healthy, adaptive behavior may vary across settings: upper-class versus impoverished environments, urban versus rural settings, Western versus Eastern cultures.

Prevention and Intervention

Developmental psychopathology emphasizes the application of concepts such as pathways, risk, protection and resilience in the prevention of negative outcomes and the promotion of healthy development (Coie et al., 1993; Coie, Miller-Johnson & Bagwell, 2000). Such concepts allow us to identify not just *what* occurs when a child displays emotional or behavioral symptoms but *why* and *how* these patterns develop. Just as maladaptation is an outcome of development, rather than a disease entity, so health and adaptation are also developmental outcomes. Therefore, the promotion of certain developmental pathways and influences can reduce the occurrence of psychopathology. This is accomplished, broadly, by decreasing the occurrence or influence of risk factors and/or increasing the promotive factors in a child's life. With a focus on both normal and abnormal development, we can recognize developmental deviations and use them in the service of early identification and prevention efforts. Developmental psychopathology offers a distinctly hopeful framework for intervention given its emphasis on understanding these pathways and patterns; if we can identify the specific ways in which psychopathology develops, then we can intervene directly into those processes and disrupt maladaptive development rather than merely treating the outcomes of development. Furthermore, given the common co-occurrence of risk factors and the varied manifestations of protective factors, in any one case, there are generally a number of potential points of intervention. Of course, we humbly recognize that individual differences and the complexity of the interactions between multiple risk and protective factors make this task easier said than done.

There are several different approaches to intervention and prevention from a developmental psychopathology perspective (Masten & Coatsworth, 1998). First, a *risk-focused* approach aims to reduce risk exposure or impact on developmental outcomes. Second, *resource-focused* approaches increase the assets in a child's life in order to provide a type of balance for risk factors that are present. Third, *process-focused* interventions seek to improve a child's ability to cope with and overcome stressors by targeting factors such as parenting or social skills. Current successful intervention and prevention programs suggest that the biggest impact occurs when both positive and negative influences are targeted (Rapp-Paglicci, Dulmas & Wodarski, 2004), and interventions may be most potent when they affect developmental cascades that have long-lasting or snowball affects on development (Masten & Cicchetti, 2010).

When possible, prevention of disorder before it occurs is ideal. The significant cost and difficulty of treating mental health problems once they have surfaced suggests that emphasizing prevention has great pragmatic value (Coie et al., 2000). On a theological level, our responsibility to care for others, particularly those who have less power to care for themselves, such as children, should include the application of prevention knowledge in order to prevent unnecessary suffering and disability. However, given the complexity of children's development and the uniqueness of each circumstance, prevention is not always possible, and disorder develops. In these cases, developmentally informed, individually tailored interventions can prevent further problems and alter the course of development.

In the translation of basic research to intervention and prevention programs, we must be careful to avoid the assumption that psychology students everywhere are warned about: correlation does not equal causation. It can be surprisingly easy to assume that a characteristic that is linked with resilience is a characteristic that leads to resilience or competence. However, the positive characteristics of resilient individuals may be the *result* of competence. For example, resilient children may have high self-esteem due to their success in different domains; if this is the case, then self-esteem is not necessarily a factor that promotes resilience, and interventions to improve self-esteem may not improve outcomes (Masten & Coatsworth, 1998). Just as with risk factors, we must be careful to distinguish *markers* of resilience with *mechanisms* of resilience. Well-designed, accurately interpreted basic research is crucial for the development of effective prevention and intervention programs.

Summary

The key theoretical assumptions and concepts of developmental psychopathology must inform our perspective and foci. As Christian clinicians working within a developmental psychopathology framework, we need to focus on the present reality of at-risk children and presenting problems while also holding on to the future of the children to whom we provide services. We need to value who children are and also who they will become. David Jensen (2005) writes, "Each child who comes into the world is the bearer of a unique personal history—the circumstances of her birth, his cultural heritage, the scarcity or abundance of nourishment in infancy—and as a metaphor of hope for the future" (p. 36). At the same time, our faith can give us hope regarding the role of community, individual strengths and the Holy Spirit's work in children's lives. In fact, *hope* is one thing that we emphasize to our students. As clinicians working with children, we must hold on to the hope that the kingdom is theirs because God loves and embraces them, and we must seek to encourage them and consider their spiritual worth.

Theologian Miller-McLemore (2003) gives a three-point thesis in her book *Let the Children Come* that she proffers as central to both psychology and Christianity: children must be valued as gifts, fully respected as persons and viewed as agents (p. xxiii). These three themes will guide an integrative approach within each chapter of this book.

INTEGRATION THEMES

Valued as gifts

There are several ways in which the nature of children as gifts is portrayed in Scripture. First, Jesus' affirmations of children's worth, and his teachings to welcome, honor and care for children affirm children's designation as spiritual persons and implicates their need for discipleship and positive regard. We must take seriously Jesus' interaction with children, particularly the significance of his "actions of blessing, touching, healing, and lifting up children" (Mercer, 2005, p. 66) for how we approach our own opportunity to serve children. This priority of Jesus is particularly noteworthy in a culture in which children were not highly valued, and it continues to be a priority in a modern society in which children still represent an underserved and overlooked population.

Second, children are frequently promised as the blessings that fulfill God's promises to his people throughout the Old Testament (Gen 15:4-5; 22:15-18; 1 Sam 1:25-27; Lk 1:42-55). The ability to bear children was seen as a sign of God's favor and was often the fulfillment of the covenants God made with his chosen people. Although we are rightfully cautious today to view the inability to bear children as a lack of God's blessing, it is clear that, historically, children have been viewed as gifts of God to his people. Calvin beautifully compared every birth to a visit from God (Miller-McLemore, 2003). This is not merely a sentimental statement but implies that each and every child can be viewed by the practitioner/clinician as a gift from God. That is, every child who comes into treatment should be met with a genuine sense of appreciation and value. They do not have to reach a certain age, developmental level or level of functioning to be considered a gift, because they are created in God's image and are thus reflective of God. With every client, we truly have the opportunity to interact with persons who are loved by God and who have the potential to reflect his love to this world. Finally, we must not forget that the Christ child is the ultimate gift, born as a vulnerable child into vulnerable conditions who gave up his life for us (Jensen, 2005).

Christian clinicians are in a special role to understand and apply the principle of children as gifts through responsible, informed care. As clinicians, we need to provide for children's development, accurately assessing their current state and understanding the developmental trajectories that led them to this point in order to better meet their needs and provide for their healthy adjustment. We are also called to vulnerably open ourselves to the care of these unique and different children and to recognize their worth as gifts from God and be motivated to work with them. Pamela Couture (2000) contends, "Caring with vulnerable children is a means of grace, a vehicle through which God makes God's self known to us and to them" (p. 13). As we are called to submit to one another in Christ, we also are called to engage in a reciprocal relationship with children. We must receive them in their vulnerable status and care for them but at the same time value them in their revelation of God and his love for us (Yust, 2004). We can encounter God in comforting others, which includes vulnerable and *valuable* children. Furthermore, as clinicians working with families, we should strive to encourage parents to value their children as gifts, a task that may feel especially challenging to the parent of an oppositional, hyperactive or angry youngster. Our empathic joining with parents in concert with our modeling of this view of children through our actions and attitudes can be very empowering for parents who are often wearied and frustrated by their children.

Valuing children as gifts should not lead us to a warped or unbalanced view of children as solely innocent and naive; we must balance the view of children as gifts with that of children as agents (see third principle below). As the next generation, they are precious—they are hope and expectation. Yet, at the same time, being in relationship with children and maintaining a view of them as gifts will involve sacrifice and selflessness on the part of caregivers and in our own clinical work. The difficulty of this truth should be fully acknowledged so that we can provide support for adults who are struggling in their interactions with certain children. Mercer (2005) describes the ambivalence we have toward children in religious conversations and circles and within our broader culture: "Society appears to support and affirm children on the one hand . . . while on the other hand ignoring and even doing harm through neglect of their basic needs" (p. 119). She challenges us to see children beyond the simplistic portrayals as "innocents" (and joyful blessings) or "devils" (weak, susceptible to sin and needing discipline), as this can lead to confusing theological understandings and practices. Mercer provocatively reminds us that the children that Jesus welcomed and healed were sick, poor and demon-possessed, and most likely not easy to be around. We must ensure that our valuing of children as gifts does not define children as gifts *only when* adults experience joy and ease of being with children. A truly loving relationship with *all* children, who should be respected as persons in their own right, results in mutual interdependence between adults and children. We must welcome the complexity of children and contend with the complexity of our psychological and theological understandings of their development (Miller-McLemore, 2003). God's redemption of this world and "the least of these" can help us view children as gifts and welcome them while also restoring our relationships with them from hierarchical valuing and perhaps domination to service and mutual respect (Mercer, 2005).

The valuing of children as gifts has implications for broader theological understandings with which we must wrestle as well. We must acknowledge that our theological views will impact our treatment of children. For example, when making the argument that an analysis of childhood can highlight our vulnerability and need for relationships with others and with God, David Jensen

(2005) discusses the doctrine of election and raises some difficult questions that we might ponder in light of our clinical work: Are some children worthy of salvation while others are given up by God? Does this perspective lead us to neglect or dismiss some children, to have hope for some and not others? He asserts that all children are graciously chosen by God to receive his divine love not because of anything they have done or because they possess certain qualities, but simply because *they are*. How might we answer these questions given our particular theological beliefs?

Respected as Persons

Even as we value the vulnerable children in our midst as gifts given by a gracious God, we must also view them as unique persons to be respected. What does it mean to respect children and imbue them with dignity? We proffer that respecting children means to take them seriously, to be attuned to their point of view, to be aware of their feelings and their communications to us, to be able to tolerate their needs and challenges to us, and to be open to learning from them. We must reflect upon our interactions and determine whether we are open to learning spiritual truths from "the least of these." To challenge our thinking, we might reflect on one of our favorite quotes regarding young children's capabilities: "Spiritual aliveness knows no age barriers; the young child and aged philosopher stand on level ground" (Ratcliff & May, 2004, p. 8). Some theologians have reminded us that children are made in the image of God and are intended to participate in his kingdom alongside adults (e.g., Guroian, 2001; 2 Pet 1:4). It is important to note that the image of God includes not just reason, wisdom and power, but also imagination, creativity and joy.

We should be drawn to their unique stories, characteristics and contexts, which developmental psychopathology can emphasize to us. Children are developing individuals with distinct pathways unfolding before them but should also be recognized as fully human and fully created in the image of God. If we do not hold on to this understanding of children as fully human, then we might view childhood as merely a stage we pass through to get to adulthood and thus be less likely to respect children's experience and acknowledge their worth (Anderson & Johnson, 1994). This understanding suggests that children deserve adults' respect and empathy and the same human rights afforded to others (versus causing them to stumble; Mt 18:5-6). Further, respecting the personhood of children acknowledges that they possess God-given capacities for spiritual and moral growth and experience. Respecting children as persons will lead us to look for ways that we can help children know and honor God and be open to the Holy Spirit as well as look for barriers that might interfere with their spiritual formation.

Psychological research supports the idea that respecting children as persons promotes their positive development. For example, families with a "conversation orientation," in which family members are encouraged to share their true feelings and opinions, produce children with higher self-esteem and fewer symptoms of mental health problems (Schrodt, Ledbetter & Ohrt, 2007). It has been suggested that this type of family atmosphere communicates acceptance and a sense of worth or value to children, even when their opinions may not conform to those of other family members. The reverse is true when family expectations inherently demand conformity and individual opinions and experiences are not validated; in such environments, children's outcomes are more negative.

Our understanding of original sin and theological debates regarding sin and accountability may affect our ability to fully respect children, leading us to think simplistically of them along the ends of a continuum: as suffering from natural depravity shown in pride, selfishness and willful rejection of God to being unwitting victims of others' sin and brokenness of community. How *do* we understand sin? When the nature of children and childhood are considered, our understanding of the doctrine of original sin may become complicated, leading some theologians to reinterpret or reject the idea that original sin is inherited (Bunge, 2001a). Further, many theologians have attempted to consider sin in light of childhood, and their views indicate the inherent complexities of the issue. For example, Augustine's view that infants are indeed born sinful but unable to sin given their physical and cognitive reasoning limitations places infants in a state of "non-innocence" until, through maturation, they become increasingly accountable for their sin throughout childhood and adolescence (Stortz, 2001). Likewise, John Calvin is known for his teaching that infants' "whole nature is a seed of sin; thus it cannot be but hateful and abominable to God" (as cited by Pitkin, 2001), but at the same time believing that there is greater accountability for sin with age and, even more striking, that children should be *emulated* by adults in their "natural simplicity" and the lack of knowing malevolence in their sinful actions. Similarly, the teaching of Jonathan Edwards regarding children has been described as presenting a "double image of children" (Brekus, 2001, p. 312); that is, children may be "young vipers" who are completely depraved but also present adults with ideal models of humility and dependence on God with full capacity for strong faith. It is clear that the nature of childhood and development rightfully pose necessary considerations to theologians regarding an understanding of sin.

The idea that sin is a willful act or rebellion against God, and the use of the language of depravity, might lead to particularly harsh views of children's behavioral or emotional difficulties and result in abusive or dismissive actions (e.g., punitive punishment, dismissal from children's ministry activities). Rather, we might understand sin as both natural depravity and personal culpability within a relational framework that highlights the effects of broken relationships with God and between people. This more complex view clearly acknowledges children's dependence on others (within a broken world and sinful relationships) and the transactional influences between them and their environment (Blevins, 2012; Miller-McLemore, 2003; Jensen, 2005; Mercer, 2005). This view might also emphasize the role of God's grace in restoring holy love in relationship to him and others.

How we view psychopathology in relation to sin is no small matter. For example, if we hold the view that children's presenting symptoms are caused by the sins of the adults in their lives, and we attend more to their emotional needs than their sinful nature, in our clinical work we might interact differently with the parents who are "at fault" and miss the influence of children's behavior on their caregivers' parenting. On the other hand, if we can view children as "a complex amalgamation of imperfection and potentiality" (Miller-McLemore, 2003, p. 144), might we hold a more holistic view of the family in front of us, challenging parents to know their children and themselves better and working to promote individual children's growth with accountability? Indeed, Yarhouse, Butman and McRay (2005) assert, "it may well be that an accurate understanding and working through of sin may facilitate greater well-being in the long run than a denial of the reality of sin" (p. 93).

With regard to this issue, David Jensen (2005) again challenges us to seek to understand sin in light of children and childhood. Jensen reviews major theological understandings of sin and notes that, despite their many discrepancies, one commonality is that the view of the child is rarely considered. He asserts that certain doctrinal beliefs assume "that the adult model of the moral agent is the normative lens for understanding sin" or "[pay] less attention to the complexities of human behavior in which we are both actors and acted upon"

(p. 83). If we hold on to the idea that children are agents but also that reciprocal influences exist, particularly as we consider children's vulnerability, then we are better able to approach the doctrine of sin and its relationship with psychopathology in all of its complexity. Overall, the issue of children as sinful must be balanced with their value as full persons, their potential for development and their vulnerable existence in a relational world that should support their needs for love and nurture (Bunge, 2001a). Both theology and child clinical psychology need to be considered to hold the tension here.

Approaching this issue with acknowledgment of the complexity of the doctrine of sin and the complexity of the developmental psychopathology framework could encourage us to encounter children more humbly and compassionately. We might respectfully connect with children as part of a broken world and acknowledge their suffering that is the result of sin in the context of evil and then seek to heal this suffering (Bunge, 2001b; Heitzenrater, 2001; Jensen, 2005). Further, we might seek to respect each individual child for who he or she truly is. This may seem simple, but it is a theological theme with which we do and should wrestle as clinicians. We often challenge our students to think about how they view children who are clearly sinful and where they draw the line regarding the potential for salvation. For example, the film *There Are No Children Here* (based on the book by the same title) follows the lives of several at-risk boys in inner-city Chicago who live in notorious housing projects and navigate gang warfare as they play and travel to school. Are these boys beyond hope? How do we understand the impact of the violent context and the systemic economic and racial inequality into which they were born on their functioning? And how do we flesh out our understanding of sin in relation to this complex, multilevel conceptualization of their current functioning? In a straightforwardly presented Christian explanatory framework, Yarhouse and colleagues (2005) remind us that, as Creator, God declared what he made "good"; that we are made in God's image but that we also are all fallen creatures; that God through his grace has a redemptive plan through Jesus; and that we can have hope through the resurrection of Christ.

Children are influenced by and capable of sin, and yet they are also made in the image of God and capable of growing spiritually and receiving grace. Their adaptive development can benefit from the wisdom, love and guidance of adults who recognize their own sinful nature and its impact on children and who also hold hope for children and extend grace (Miller-McLemore, 2003).

McMinn (2004) makes a beautiful point regarding our work as clinicians: "Good therapy works because it is a place that emulates grace" (p. 37). Regardless of their past and present experiences and functioning, children's trajectories are always capable of moving toward more adaptive outcomes. We must strive to hold the concepts of sin and grace in one hand.

Viewed as Agents

The view of children as moral and spiritual agents contends with the ideas of children's mutuality in relationship with adults and as capable of participating in grace and reconciliation. Children's agency can be understood as their impact on others and their environment and also in their responsibility in their own development and in living in this world. They have the capacity for empathy, for intimacy and for wielding power in ways that improve their world. They are connected to others and benefit from the support of others, which contributes to their resilience; yet this interdependence will inherently entail injuries (such as attachment ruptures) that will need to be repaired and worked through. We can affect children's well-being and their physical, cognitive and socioemotional development, but they also bring their unique characteristics into the world and into their relationships. They are not the passive recipients sometimes assumed by both psychology and Christianity throughout history (Miller-McLemore, 2003). Rather, children's choices and individual characteristics enable them to navigate toward or away from negative outcomes. They can serve as a source of God's revelation and hope to others (e.g., 1 Sam 16; 2 Kings 5:2-4) and as persons in their own right who are experiencing and learning how to be in God's world. For example, Couture (2000) reminds us that our interactions with children can provide us with experiences of God's grace (e.g., a hug from a child for his parent after the parent lost her temper, accepting God's forgiveness when we fail to attend to a child's pain in the moment) and contribute to our own spiritual transformation in the many ways they challenge us that make God more fully known to us. Amazingly, in our care for vulnerable children as clinicians, we may also experience a renewal of our soul, as Couture (2000) beautifully describes: "Resilience, tenacity, and God's grace—seeing children, seeing God, surrounded by a community, we discover a mysterious, remarkable spark, a fight for flourishing life that chastises and energizes tired adults" (p. 17).

The concept of the agency of the child has been identified as one of the main principles of developmental psychopathology (Sroufe & Rutter, 1984; Masten,

2006). In a developmental psychopathology framework, children and adolescents are not passive recipients of environmental influences; rather, children are active shapers of their environment, there is a dynamic interaction between individual and context, and individual perceptions and choices affect the course of development. Eschatological views would lead us to the perspective that children are becoming—they have great potential for learning how to be in this world and are moving forward toward their potential. The theologian Bushnell emphasized the role of parents and social structures as corrupting the potentiality for good in children (Bendroth, 2001); although this view underscores the role of context, it also risks minimizing children's agency. Similarly, John Chrysostom encouraged parents to teach their children (through spiritual disciplines) but also undercut children's agency by describing parents as artists who sculpt their children and whose salvation depends upon their children's outcomes: "One's own virtue is not enough for salvation, but the virtue of those for whom we are responsible is also required" (Guroian, 2001). Yet, in recognizing the agency of children, we affirm that both children and parents stand under the Lord *together*. We should also recognize that adults' and children's agency in this world is surely empowered by the Holy Spirit. We are all called to dependency on God and trust in him, and the presence and knowledge of Christ is available to us all through the Holy Spirit (Mt 21:14-16).

Children's agency is clearly apparent in the idea of reciprocal influences. When we view the influences of the environment on children as unidirectional, we remove the children's role and make them a passive recipient of influence; yet when we recognize the reciprocal nature of the interaction between children and environment, we return agency to the child. Furthermore, we need to be careful as Christians about how we interpret children's behavior in light of the idea of agency. As stated above, we may err at times on the side of viewing children's self-assertion as willful or sinful and focus on the need for discipline; indeed, we need to be careful of how theology informs our views of children and their care so that we do not use theological principles wrongfully. In fact, there is a history of misuse of Scripture in theological thought (Bunge, 2001a; Miller-McLemore, 2003). For example, advice on Christian parenting has sometimes focused on scriptural dictates regarding punishment (Prov 13:24) to the neglect of messages of love, care and warmth toward others that are pervasive in Scripture (e.g., 1 Cor 13; Col 3:21). Especially in moments of frustration with children, we often need to be reminded that a child's behavior is also an adaptation to the environment and may represent an attempt to communicate a need or protect oneself (e.g., crying as an indication of hunger, fear or overstimulation). Such an understanding reflects a true recognition of and respect for the child as an agent in her own development. Respect for the child's agency is not an argument against discipline or correction, as it is clear that such parenting approaches are necessary for healthy development; rather, it highlights the need for discipline and guidance within a context of love (Miller-McLemore, 2003). In fact, research on physical discipline suggests that such techniques are harmful when not embedded in a context of sensitivity and warmth (Alink, Cicchetti, Kim & Rogosch, 2009; Deater-Deckard, Ivy & Petrill, 2006; Larzelere & Kuhn, 2005) and that both care and limits are important components of parenting.

The important role of family, community, educational systems and culture in children's lives is acknowledged in Christian theological circles, albeit most often with regard to their faith development and moral formation (e.g., providing nurture for godliness). Trinitarian teachings help us understand the interdependence of relationships and their optimal foundation in reciprocity and love. Within this view, children should be allotted the same level of influence on their parents as parents have on children (reciprocal influences); in addition, systems are viewed as developmental in nature, with Christ teaching parents and children across time as their context and situations may change and their relationship with God grows. Being in relationship with children inherently changes us (e.g., has the potential to right misplaced priorities or speak truth into our lives); adults must adapt to children's needs, families must respond to changes in homeostasis of the system, and children's very presence calls for our attention to them rather than a "culture of indifference" (Anderson & Johnson, 1994).

This final integrative theme has very real implications for our work with children. How do we understand and hold children accountable for their actions? How do we understand the role of environmental factors? What is our understanding of how children and their environments influence each other over time? Sin and evil should be recognized and taken seriously with regard to intraindividual characteristics and interpersonal and environmental factors. It is not just nature or nurture but rather a bidirectional interplay between these influences. This more complex view holds both children and adults more accountable to each other within their relationships. And we would further argue that this reciprocal responsibility is dependent on grace for ourselves and each other and stems from the Holy Spirit's influence.

As clinicians, we are sometimes in the privileged role of objective observer who can offer an outside perspective infused with grace, hope and love for sometimes difficult dynamics or negative viewpoints. Gundry-Volf (2001) makes a compelling argument that we have explicitly been called by Christ to humbly serve suffering children and that welcoming them is welcoming the suffering Christ (Mk 9:37). Although Jesus' teachings show advocacy for children's social equality under the reign of God, he understood that children are not equal in society (as evidence by commands such as "welcome the least of these"). We have the privilege as clinicians to serve children and not to hinder them, as well as to seek justice for them. If we strive to fully value them as gifts, respect them as persons and view them as agents, our calling to serve children will be strengthened and empowered.

2

Temperament

Amy Mezulis, Kaitlin A. Harding
and Melissa R. Hudson

DEFINITION AND STUDY OF TEMPERAMENT

Temperament is conceptualized as individual personality differences in emotional, behavioral, and attentional reactivity and self-regulation (Rothbart & Bates, 1998). Temperament has aspects of stability which reflect its biological bases, and individual differences in temperament are observed early in infancy and consistently across the lifespan (Caspi, 2000); however, temperament also has dynamic components such that individuals' interactions with their environment may shape their temperament, how it manifests and how it affects functioning. Temperament is the early precursor to adult personality and is comprised of multiple facets across affective, behavioral and self-regulatory domains, which may combine in countless ways; as such, temperament is a key component of what makes each individual unique (McAdams & Olson, 2010; Rothbart, 2011). At the same time, due to its broad influence on affect, behavior and self-regulation, temperament is at the core of many theoretical models of psychopathology. From a developmental psychopathology perspective, understanding how individual differences in temperament may be adaptive in some contexts and maladaptive in others, and identifying the pathways linking infant or childhood temperament to later psychopathology, is central to understanding how and why some individuals deviate from a trajectory of normal development onto a trajectory of emergent psychopathology.

There are several influential and empirically supported conceptualizations of temperament which, despite salient distinctions, share two important features (Buss & Plomin, 1984; Costa & McCrae, 1992; Evans & Rothbart, 2009; Goldberg, 1990; Rothbart & Ahadi, 1994). First, all theories propose that there are numerous distinct facets of temperament. Thomas and Chess (1977), for example, identified nine important dimensions of temperament: activity level, regularity, approach/withdrawal, adaptability, intensity, mood, distractibility, persistence/attention span, and sensitivity. Rothbart and Bates identified as many as fourteen facets of infant temperament (Rothbart, 1981). Second, and more importantly, all major theories of temperament identify broader dimensions of temperament that reflect processes of emotional, behavioral, and attentional reactivity and regulation that tend to cohere within the same individual. Although the similarities and differences among conceptual models of temperament are interesting unto themselves, such a review is beyond the scope and purpose of this chapter. Here we will examine temperament within a developmental psychopathology framework using Rothbart's psychobiological model of temperament, which has been well supported empirically and incorporates important features of most prior conceptual models (Rothbart, Derryberry & Posner, 1994).

Temperament can be viewed as two broad processes of reactivity and regulation. In general, reactivity includes a child's emotional and behavioral arousability to situations (Rothbart, 2004). To illustrate these processes, imagine a child on the first day of school who feels fearful and cries when dropped off at her classroom. This child's tendency to respond fearfully to novel situations reflects the emotional and behavioral reactivity component of temperament. In contrast, another child in the same situation may feel excited and happily part from his parent to join the classroom activity.

Children's ability to recognize, plan for and act to modify their initial reactions reflects the second component of temperament—regulation. For example, our first, fearful child may be able to quickly calm herself and focus on the first classroom activity, demonstrating good self-regulation. By contrast, our second happy and approach-oriented child may be so excited by the new experience that he is unable to sit calmly and focus on his work, demonstrating poor self-regulation. These examples demonstrate not only the key reactivity and regulatory components of temperament but also illustrate several important features of these two components. First, they demonstrate that temperamental reactivity may vary along several dimensions: (1) emotional valence, the extent to which the emotional response includes predominantly negative emotions (e.g., fear, sadness, anger) or positive emotions (e.g., happiness); (2) behavioral instinct, the extent to which the behavioral response is predominantly one of withdrawal/avoidance or activation/approach; and (3) intensity, the magnitude of dominant or typical emotional and behavioral response. Second, they demonstrate that regulation may be considered distinct from reactivity and serve to enhance or impair overall functioning. These facets of reactivity and regulation may then combine in countless ways to contribute to each child's temperament. This combined categorical and dimensional approach to temperament helps explain why each child has a unique temperament at birth and across development that contributes to the infinite number of different pathways an individual may follow.

NORMAL DEVELOPMENT OF TEMPERAMENT

Rothbart (2004) suggests that temperament both emerges and develops over time as manifestations of the joint and reciprocal contributions of genetics and experience. Researchers have suggested that early in infancy, temperament may be best characterized by five dimensions: fearfulness, irritability, positive affect and approach, activity level, and attentional persistence. Over the course of early childhood, these five dimensions consolidate into three broad temperamental dimensions, which include two reactivity dimensions (extraversion/surgency and negative affectivity) and one regulatory dimension (effortful control). Below we describe each of these broad dimensions, the temperamental facets that comprise them, how each is manifest in infancy and childhood, and what characterizes normal development within each dimension.

Extraversion/Surgency

Extraversion/surgency is one of the two reactivity dimensions of temperament. It is characterized emotionally by high levels of positive emotions (e.g., pleasure, joy, happiness) as well as behaviorally by high levels of approach behaviors, high overall activity level, and low prevalence of shy or withdrawal behaviors (Rothbart & Ahadi, 1994). In infancy, extraversion/surgency corresponds to the temperamental constructs of approach or positive affect and activity level, which reflect a tendency toward positive emotions and approach behaviors that anticipate reward or sensory stimulation (Zuckerman, 2008). An infant high in extraversion displays high intensity pleasure through smiling, eye gaze engagement and vocalizations such as cooing as early as two to three months. By six months of age and into the toddler years, these infants display markedly high levels of approach and sociable behaviors, such as seeking interaction with others and an eagerness to explore new items and environments (Rothbart, 2007). High extraversion/surgency infants also tend to display high levels of motor activity, which is manifest as frequent arm and leg movements in infancy and active and intentional crawling, walking and climbing in the toddler months (Gartstein, Putnam & Rothbart, 2012). By six months of age, this temperamental dimension displays strong continuity and stability into childhood. In childhood, extraversion/surgency is manifest as high energy level, frequent and easy smiling, displays of happiness, sociability toward other children, curiosity about the environment, and a willingness and eagerness to explore and engage in new settings. Within the adult personality literature, extraversion/surgency is most related to the adult Big Five personality factor of extraversion (Zuckerman, 1991).

Negative Affectivity

Negative affectivity is the other broad reactivity dimension of temperament. Emotionally, negative affectivity is characterized by high levels of frustration, fear, discomfort and sadness; behaviorally, it is marked by withdrawal from novel or distressing stimuli, low tendency to approach in novel or social situations, and poor soothability (Rothbart, 2007). Fearfulness and irritability are considered early infancy manifestations of negative affectivity. As early as one to two months of age, infants high in negative affectivity display marked distress due to anticipated pain or threat, or startle at novel stimuli, as well as distress over confinement, limitation or goal blocking (Gartstein et al., 2012). Infants high in negative affectivity have often been described as "difficult" (Chess & Thomas, 1986). Similar to extraversion/surgency, by six months of age negative affectivity demonstrates moderate to strong stability into the toddler and childhood years (Lemery, Goldsmith, Klinnert & Mrazek, 1999). For example, a child with high trait negative affectivity may be easily distressed by disruptions in his environment, often respond to change with fear or frustration, have difficulty engaging in novel or distressing situations, have difficulty initiating social interactions, and be difficult to calm after experiencing negative emotions. Within the adult personality literature, negative affectivity is most related to the Big Five personality factor of neuroticism.

Effortful Control

The third component of temperament, effortful control, is considered the regulatory component of temperament. Effortful control develops over the course of infancy, toddlerhood and early childhood (Gartstein & Rothbart, 2003). In infancy, its nascent components are present in a regulatory system that relies heavily on orienting of attention toward and away from objects. Prior to three to four months of age, infants have little orienting control and show difficulty disengaging from objects that catch their attention. Infants can even become distressed by extended orientation on one object. Around four months of age, infants develop some orienting control and are able to disengage attention from one object and intentionally orient toward another object (Gartstein & Rothbart, 2003; Rothbart, Sheese, Rueda & Posner, 2011). According to parent report, even in infancy the capacity to flexibly shift attentional orienting is associated with lower negative emotionality and higher soothability (Johnson, Posner & Rothbart, 1991). Research has found that orienting away from something distressing can act as a temporary distraction. When objects of orientation are subsequently removed, infants return to their distressed state. Therefore, this infancy orienting-based regulatory system is believed to be important for early emotional control (Harman, Rothbart & Posner, 1997).

Orienting appears to serve a regulatory function in early development. When effortful control develops, the reliance on orienting control expands to include executive attention control. Even though orienting ability does not disappear, executive attention control as a regulatory function becomes more dominant later in development. Executive attention control involves detecting errors or discrepancies, as well as inhibiting dominant responses, activating nondominant responses and planning ahead. This more elaborate executive functioning incorporates motivation into a child's regulatory functioning. Therefore, when a child is in a distressing situation, executive attention may involve inhibiting his natural reaction to cry out, replacing it with the response of walking away from the distressing situation and making a plan to talk to someone about the situation later or avoid that situation in the future. Both orienting and executive control collectively contribute to effortful control.

By childhood, then, effortful control has emerged as the internal ability to direct attention, recognize conflicts between situations and reactions, and regulate behavioral and emotional responses (Rothbart, 2007). Typically, effortful control is considered to be comprised of three primary facets: (1) attentional control, or the ability to intentionally direct attention both toward stimuli and away from stimuli; (2) inhibitory control, or the ability to interrupt a dominant or desired response that does not meet situational demands; and (3) activation control, or the ability to instigate behavior in a situation that demands it. Examples may best demonstrate how this temperamental construct is manifest in day-to-day child behavior. Laboratory measures of effortful control often use "delay of gratification" tasks, which require children to recruit attentional and behavioral resources to delay an immediate reward in anticipation of a later, bigger reward. For example, a young child may be told that he may have the one chocolate chip in front of him now or wait five minutes and have ten chocolate chips. The ability to tolerate the five-minute wait requires strong attentional control to both direct attention away from the desired food as well as maintain attention on the later reward. It also requires strong inhibitory control to not reach out and take the available one chocolate chip. Numerous studies of delay of gratification suggest that there are both a normative developmental trajectory of effortful control, such that older children are better able to delay gratification than younger children, and individual differences in this temperamental trait, such that even at the same age some children display better ability to delay gratification than others (see Eisenberg, Smith, Sadovsky & Spinrad, 2004, for a review). There are countless childhood situations in which optimal behavior requires utilization of attentional and inhibitory control. Although less evident, optimal behavior also often requires good activation control. For example, children are often asked or required to engage in activities they do not want to do (e.g., homework, joining an unfamiliar activity) and for which their dominant response would be inaction. Activation control is required to engage in undesired but necessary activities and thus is an important aspect of day-to-day functioning in childhood.

Effortful control develops across infancy and toddlerhood and demonstrates internal consistency and stability around thirty months of age. It continues to develop in preschool and into school years (Kochanska, Murray & Harlan, 2000). It is believed that with the development of effortful control comes attentional flexibility, which is instrumental in the development of empathy and conscience. Effortful control exerts unique predictive effects on childhood psychopathology outcomes and is also important as a moderator of the effects of extraversion/surgency and negative affectivity on these outcomes (Rothbart & Posner, 2006).

Continuity of Childhood Temperament

In support of current research on the continuity of temperament, continuity and discontinuity are specifically indicated in Rothbart's three dimensions of temperament (Rothbart & Bates, 2006). As previously stated, some elements of temperament remain stable over time, whereas other temperamental traits change throughout the course of development. For example, Durbin, Hayden, Klein and Olino (2007) found that positive and negative affectivity are moderately stable from ages three to seven, while the self-regulation of emotion significantly improves as a child develops. Similarly, another study concluded that child temperament demonstrated heterotypic continuity from six months to five and a half years old, with temperamental traits remaining constant while the behavioral manifestations of those traits changed throughout development (Komsi et al., 2008).

Thus there is evidence of heterotypic continuity, which describes age-appropriate manifestations of stable traits, and temperamental change among some youth. According to Kagan's temperament research (Kagan, Snidman & Arcus, 1998), approximately 70% of youth display continuity in their temperament across time, although the manifestations of their temperament may vary in an age-appropriate manner. High negative affectivity in infancy, for example, may be manifest as high displays of negative affect (crying, fussing) to unfamiliar stimuli or persons, while in early childhood high negative affectivity may be more commonly expressed by behavioral withdrawal from the situation. Both displays (crying, behavioral withdrawal) represent age-appropriate responses to what is perceived as a frightening or unfamiliar environment; the infant has no other means with which to express his or her distress other than crying, while the preschooler is able to behaviorally avoid the situation by walking away. However, this same study demonstrated that there was significant discontinuity in temperament as well. Not only did at least 30% of children display marked change in their temperament, but up to 90% displayed more modest change. For example, of the most high negative affectivity infants ("high reactive" in this study), only about 13% remained in the highest group in early childhood—there was significant evidence of regression toward the mean. Thus, since both continuity and discontinuity are normative, explanations for the development of temperament must be able to explain both stability and change. This continuity of temperamental traits is also observed across cultures, although some differences are observed in how extraversion/surgency, negative affectivity and effortful control are interrelated (Ahadi, Rothbart & Ye, 1993). Thus, both stability and change in temperament concurrently exist for every dimension of a child's temperament (Putnam, Rothbart & Gartstein, 2008).

FACTORS THAT AFFECT THE DEVELOPMENT OF TEMPERAMENT

As stated above, child temperament demonstrates both continuity and discontinuity from infancy into adulthood. It is generally accepted that child temperament becomes stable around age three, with underlying trait stability explaining temporal continuity between child temperament and adult personality (Caspi, 2000). Temperament in childhood becomes personality traits in adulthood, with continuity between temperament and personality increasing with age (McAdams & Olson, 2010). Despite substantial evidence of continuity in temperament, however, there is also evidence of discontinuity. The extent to which temperament displays continuity, as well as examination of factors explaining (dis)continuity, provide important insights into the factors which affect the development of temperament. To the extent that temperament demonstrates continuity, it supports more biological theories of temperament. However, to the extent that there is discontinuity, we must consider both how the impact of biological influences on temperament may vary across development as well as the role of other influences, such as psychological, social and environmental factors.

According to a biopsychosocialspiritual perspective, a variety of factors contribute to the development of temperament. These factors are often divided into biological and environmental factors, with biology providing the most observable influences on temperament and often considered to account for stability. Although biological factors account for considerable stability in temperament, biology interacts with environment to ultimately shape temperament. Environmental factors may include other aspects of psychological development as well as key social and environmental experiences which will contribute to the notable change in temperament over time.

Biological Factors

Biological influences on temperament contribute to both the stability and change of traits throughout development. At the genetic level, certain versions of the genes that affect dopamine and serotonin predict variations in infant negative affectivity, as reported by parents over their infant's first year of life (Holmboe, Nemoda, Fearon, Sasvari-Szekely & Johnson, 2011). In particular, possessing two short allele versions of the serotonin 5-HTTLPR gene is linked to the phenotypic expression of high negative affectivity (Auerbach et al., 1999). Certain versions of the DRD4 VNTR dopamine genotype also predict higher levels of negative affectivity among infants and significantly interact with certain versions of the 5-HTTLPR serotonin genotype to predict infants with the highest levels of negative affectivity (Holmboe et al., 2011). Furthermore, other genotypic indicators are associated with individual differences in infant temperament (Ivorra et al., 2011). Hence, genetic endowment seems to be the dominant predictor of temperament, with risky genotypes predicting risky phenotypes.

Brain maturation and physical development also greatly impact the expression of trait tendencies as a child ages (Kagan, 2003). For example, there is evidence that temperament may be influenced by the amygdala's responding to novelty, which is strongly determined by genetics (Schwartz, Wright, Shin, Kagan & Rauch, 2003). Measures of electroencephalography (EEG) asymmetry are also correlated with emotional reactivity in children ages ten to twelve, with right frontal lobe activation associated with high emotional reactivity (McManis, Kagan, Snidman & Woodward, 2002). Just as genetic inheritance predicts temperament, the genetic manifestations of brain maturation and physical development similarly influence the expression of temperament across time. Brain maturation and physical development express the genetic and contextual history of an individual that shapes temperament across time.

Although genetics significantly accounts for the stability of temperament from infancy into adulthood, we know that inherited traits also interact with environmental factors to influence temperament. This interplay between genetics and environment in the expression of temperament is consistent with a developmental psychopathology approach, in which risk factors themselves (in this case, temperament) are elicited by, maintained and expressed in reciprocal interactions with the environment. In a comprehensive study of 3,761 Finnish individuals followed prenatally until adulthood, researchers found that a range of genetic and environmental factors significantly predicted distinct clusters of temperamental traits. Among these factors were early childhood environment and family demographics, physical and neurological development, and adolescent substance use and academic performance (Congdon et al., 2012). The interaction between genetics and environment was also investigated in middle childhood among monozygotic and dizygotic twins, which demonstrated that child negative affectivity and effortful control were predicted equally by genetic inheritance and nonshared environment, although genetic inheritance contributed significantly more than shared environment (Mullineaux, Deater-Deckard, Petrill, Thompson & DeThorne, 2009). At a molecular level, geneticists are also investigating interactions between specific genes that may predict certain temperament patterns (Saudino, 2005). Based on the results of recent investigations of temperament, genetic inheritance in interaction with environmental factors seems to significantly contribute to developmental trajectories for temperament and may be important for understanding why some temperamental traits, while within the normal range in early life, may diverge onto an abnormal trajectory over time, as well as why some more extreme temperamental traits may be pulled back onto a normal trajectory.

Environmental Factors

Environmental factors predominantly include parenting and social interactions as well as stress exposure in childhood. Parenting exerts a large external influence on the development of temperament through many potential mechanisms, including modeling and scaffolding initial emotion regulation, encouraging the development of temperamental characteristics not well represented in the child's initial repertoire, and exacerbating a child's initial behavioral tendencies.

Imagine an infant born high in negative affectivity—a difficult infant, one who cries often with little provocation, who has difficulty soothing himself, and who demonstrates difficulty engaging in play and social interactions. Parenting will play a key role in buffering or exacerbating this infant's predominant temperamental characteristics. For example, parents who similarly model high emotional reactivity and poor soothing will likely exacerbate this display in their child (Calkins & Johnson, 1998). As the child gets older, parenting also sets up consequences for child behavior driven in part by temperament. As the high negative affectivity child has difficulty engaging in social activities or has frequent displays of negative emotions, parents may inadvertently exacerbate these traits by either allowing the child to avoid all emotion-eliciting situations (which reinforces the child's behavior patterns) or punishing or criticizing the child (which reinforces the child's displays of negative affect by modeling continued negative affect). By contrast, parenting that is warm and accepting but also gently encouraging will moderate child displays of the negative affectivity (Chen et al., 1998). Research has suggested that parenting plays a stronger role in shaping the temperaments of children who are high in negative affectivity compared with those low in negative affectivity, suggesting that there is likely a normative regression to the mean for more extreme temperament types (Gallagher, 2002).

Social interactions also provide the situational canvas for temperament development, particularly in the domain of effortful control. In early childhood, when effortful control is developing, children are becoming more self-aware and more socially aware, and the social environment is influencing the standards of behavior they will learn to conform to. By two years of age, children begin to understand standards of behavior in their environment (Kagan, 1989). These standards of behavior interact with their emergent ability to effortfully control their behavior, resulting in increasingly socially appropriate behavior. Thus, the development of effortful control is also believed to contribute to the formation of empathy, guilt and conscience. For example, at eighteen months, children show distress upon viewing or performing a violation of a social standard, an early sign of guilt (Kagan, 1984). Given the long developmental trajectory of the emergence of effortful control, it is no surprise that this aspect of temperament is particularly susceptible to social and environmental influences. Particularly for the subcomponents of activation control and inhibitory control, the role of parental (and later, teacher and peer) feedback regarding appropriate behavior in different environmental contexts will typically scaffold the development of effortful control. For example, the shy child who is gently encouraged and then rewarded for engaging in safe social interactions will develop greater ability to activate that nondominant response while the more active, aggressive child who is consistently redirected or given alternatives to rough play will develop greater ability to inhibit that dominant response.

It is important to note that temperament-environment interactions are reciprocal and bidirectional. That is, in addition to social factors influencing temperament, temperament also influences social situations and social development. The goodness-of-fit model articulates this dynamic relationship between temperament and environmental demands (Thomas & Chess, 1977; Chess & Thomas, 1986). In the model, Thomas and Chess explain that child adjustment depends significantly on the match between temperament and the child's unique social environment, particularly parenting. Certain aspects of the environment may or may not accommodate unique temperament constellations. For example, a shy child may struggle to adjust to a new daycare environment. If a caregiver is not sensitive to this and pushes the child into new activities, the shy child may be frightened by the faster pace and exhibit increases in behaviors such as crying or refusing to attend daycare. Also, children who are highly active and/or highly distractible may struggle in a structured classroom setting. Although there is some flexibility in adjusting for different learning styles, this flexibility may not be sufficient to accommodate high activity and distractibility. Also, temperament influences the interactions an individual has with people and settings, through the child's behavioral style, preferences for social settings, groups and activities, and the degree that temperament impacts the social environment (Scarr & McCartney, 1983; Shiner & Caspi, 2003). For example, children high in positive affectivity will seek highly pleasurable and social activities and are likely to easily interact with peers, whereas children high in negative affectivity may be frightened by such social activities and find it difficult to interact with peers. These natural temperamentally driven preferences will drive a great deal of choices across childhood, including activities and peer groups, which will, in turn, reinforce the child's temperament. In this way, over time environmental expectations change and impact both the goodness of fit as well as the stability of temperament (Bornstein, 1995).

ASPECTS OF DEVELOPMENT AFFECTED BY TEMPERAMENT

Just as biological and environmental factors contribute to the development of temperament, temperament can significantly influence psychological outcomes. Temperamental traits represent both risk and protective factors in the development of various psychological outcomes that may contribute to psychopathology (Shiner & Caspi, 2003). In fact, certain forms of psychopathology may represent extreme levels of continuously distributed temperamental dimensions (Widiger & Clark, 2000). In particular, the affective disorders such as depression and anxiety are characterized substantially by abnormally high frequency, intensity or duration of otherwise normative negative affective states. Though it is still uncertain how childhood temperament may relate to personality disorders in adulthood (Geiger & Crick, 2001), childhood temperament dimensions predict a variety of psychological outcomes from childhood and adolescence into adulthood. An interesting point to consider is that although temperament becomes stable in early childhood, most psychological disorders do not emerge until adolescence and adulthood. As noted above, a developmental psychopathology approach emphasizes that temperament shapes the way that individuals interact with the world, and these interaction patterns may crystalize later in life with concurrent internalizing and externalizing disorders. In this section, we discuss the empirical literature linking temperament with psychopathology as well as critically examine multiple developmental pathways linking temperament with divergent mental health trajectories.

Negative Affectivity as a Risk Factor

Perhaps the temperamental dimension that is most strongly related to adverse psychological outcomes is negative affectivity. Negative affectivity is associated with both internalizing and externalizing symptoms in childhood and adolescence (Rothbart & Bates, 2006). High trait negative affectivity is frequently associated with a difficult temperament, which increases an individual's baseline sensitivity to both positive and negative environmental influences. This high baseline emotional reactivity to environmental stimuli may overwhelm children's regulatory capacities and thus may predispose children to both internalizing and externalizing psychological difficulties (Belsky, 2005). Regarding internalizing disorders, Verstraeten, Bijttebier, Vasey and Raes (2011) found that high trait negative affectivity predicts both depressive and anxiety symptoms among children ages nine to thirteen. Regarding externalizing disorders, high negative affectivity in childhood predicts conduct disorder and severe antisocial behavior from adolescence into adulthood (Sanson & Prior, 1999). As a whole, research demonstrates that high trait negative affectivity is associated with adverse psychological outcomes in childhood and beyond. It is important to note that negative affectivity is a classic example of multifinality—that is, a risk factor associated with a diverse array of mental health outcomes. Thus, temperamentally high negative affectivity may be an early indicator of risk for later psychopathology and thus may be an important focal point for early prevention efforts.

Extraversion/Surgency as a Protective Factor

In contrast to negative affectivity, high extraversion/surgency is shown to provide protective benefits against adverse psychological outcomes, and low levels of this temperamental trait are most often linked with maladaptive psychological outcomes. High levels of extraversion/surgency are associated with strong social support, which in turn predicts positive mental health outcomes (Berkman, Glass, Brissette & Seeman, 2000). Conversely, low extraversion/surgency is indicated as an early vulnerability factor for unipolar depression (Olino et al., 2011), as well as greater adolescent substance use and impulsive behaviors in adolescence and early adulthood, such as unprotected sex and risky driving (Caspi et al., 1997). Whereas low levels of extraversion/surgency may represent a vulnerability to psychopathology, the facets of high activity, agreeableness and affection are shown to confer resiliency to children reared in environments of poverty and high interpersonal stress (Werner & Smith, 1992). Such research suggests that high extraversion/surgency may contribute to beneficial mental health outcomes that become observable starting in childhood.

Effortful Control as a Risk and Protective Factor

As discussed above, effortful control represents the regulatory component of temperament, which includes, in large part, regulating attentional, behavioral and emotional responses to adaptively respond to various situational contexts. As such, effortful control is an important aspect of understanding how individuals remain on or diverge from normal developmental trajectories; effortful control and its effects on child development highlight how complex and dynamic development is. Low effortful control both exerts a unique influence on psychological outcomes as well as exacerbates the effects of high negative affectivity on these outcomes. Within the domain of effortful control is the idea that people self-regulate when they choose to approach or inhibit (Rothbart, 2011). The ability to self-regulate is considered high effortful control whereas failure to self-regulate is considered low effortful control. High effortful control is positively related to use of compliance, empathy and social competence (Eisenberg et al., 2003; Kochanska, 1997) and negatively correlated with internalizing and externalizing problems (Eisenberg, et al., 2000; Lengua, 2003). Conversely, low effortful control is associated with attentional disorders such as ADHD and behavioral disorders such as aggression, substance use and juvenile delinquency (Auerbach et al., 2008).

Low effortful control also moderates the effect of high negative affectivity in predicting psychopathology (Rothbart & Bates, 2006). This moderating effect can be observed for both externalizing and internalizing problems. It is well established that high negative affectivity is associated with externalizing disorders such as behavior problems and aggression. Youth high in negative affectivity may be particularly quick to anger in response to hostile or ambiguous cues in their environment, and a dominant tendency to respond with aggression may be activated. Youth high in effortful control may be able to control this response and suppress their instinct to aggress, but youth low in effortful control may have the greatest difficulties in down-regulating this dominant aggressive response.

Similarly, recent research has shown that low effortful control may exacerbate the effects of high negative affectivity on internalizing disorders, particularly through the effortful control dimension of attentional control. In novel, frightening or stressful situations, high negative affectivity functions in part to direct attention to the feared stimulus (for example, if one is afraid of spiders, that fear response functions to direct attention to both the spider in the room as well as escape routes). Although adaptive in the short term, such emotion-driven attention is maladaptive when it persists beyond the immediate threat. Youth low in effortful control appear to have difficulty redirecting attention away from such emotion-elicited stimuli. Thus, high negative affectivity in combination with low effortful control has been shown to be associated with the tendency to ruminate on negative emotions and situations and in turn predicts both anxiety and depression (see Harvey, Watkins, Mansell & Shafran, 2004; Mezulis, Priess & Hyde, 2011).

Although much research has found that low effortful control is a risk factor in the development of internalizing and externalizing disorders, research has also explored the beneficial aspects of high effortful control. Effortful control may be an important component of resiliency, and has been shown to be associated with better mental health functioning even in the context of exposure to family stress (Lengua & Long, 2002), deviant peer groups (Gardner, Dishion & Connell, 2008), and parental negative emotionality (Valiente et al., 2004). Similarly, effortful control has been found to buffer the effects of poor parenting (Rothbart, 2011) and predict more active coping styles (Lengua & Long, 2002).

In summary, negative affectivity, extraversion/surgency and effortful control represent distinct dimensions of temperament that independently and interactively contribute to psychological outcomes from childhood into adulthood. These components combine in a variety of profiles that, when interacting with environmental factors, contribute to each unique individual's trajectory.

TEMPERAMENT AS A MODERATOR AND MEDIATOR

The strength of the relationship between temperamental dimensions and psychopathology is moderated by an array of influences that interact to express temperament as specific psychological outcomes. In this way, temperamental dimensions function as both risk and protective factors in the development of psychopathology, especially for internalizing and externalizing disorders. Internalizing disorders are characterized by low self-esteem, loneliness, anxiety and depressive symptoms, whereas externalizing disorders are characterized by delinquency, attentional and conduct difficulties, and substance use (Bornstein & Lamb, 2011).

Parenting and temperament may interact to increase risk for psychopathology. For example, parents with depression likely demonstrate and model inability to regulate emotions and may also have difficulty engaging in effective parenting such as monitoring and rule setting. Consistent with this approach, recent research suggests that parental depression may increase child internalizing behaviors, especially if children already exhibit high levels of negative affectivity (Silk et al., 2011). Parental depression is also associated with greater externalizing behaviors among children who already exhibit the behavioral dysregulation that is representative of externalizing disorders (Callender, Olson, Choe & Sameroff, 2012). In addition to parental depression, parenting style may also moderate the temperamental tendency of certain children toward both internalizing and externalizing disorders. For example, Bradley and Corwyn (2008) found that children who were high in negative emotionality, high in reactivity and high in fearfulness constituted a difficult temperament that was more sensitive to parenting style as compared to children who did not exhibit these negative affectivity traits. Interestingly, children with a difficult temperament tend to elicit harsher parenting (Burke, Pardini & Loeber, 2008), which further predisposes them to internalizing and externalizing problems. This study demonstrates that parents and children reciprocally influence each other.

PATHWAYS LINKING TEMPERAMENT WITH PSYCHOPATHOLOGY

Along with factors that moderate and mediate the effects of temperament on psychopathology, the relationship between temperament in predicting psychopathology may be mediated by other processes. That is, certain proximal processes may link temperamental dimensions to internalizing and externalizing outcomes to explain the mechanisms through which temperament influences the development of psychopathology. As discussed next, a variety of cognitive, social and behavioral factors may explain why certain temperamental traits are associated with later psychopathology.

Extensive research has demonstrated that specific cognitive mechanisms may mediate the prospective relationship between temperament and internalizing disorders. This mediational relationship is particularly strong in explaining the association between negative affectivity and internalizing problems. Negative affectivity is associated with strong emotional responses to novel or threatening stimuli, such as stressors or scary images. As discussed earlier, this emotional response is highly adaptive in the short term because strong emotional responses can direct attention toward potential threat so that the individual can be prepared to respond to it. For some individuals, however, the normal fear response to threat or novelty is abnormally high or long, and attention is maintained on the feared object longer than normal. Over time, the tendency to direct attention toward perceived threat and difficulty disengaging attention from threat may become a stable, trait cognitive response to threat or novelty that is itself a risk factor for psychopathology. For example, children high in negative affectivity and low in effortful control often display attentional biases toward threatening stimuli, which in turn mediate the relationship between those temperamental traits and later anxiety symptoms (Lonigan, Vasey, Phillips & Hazen, 2004). Research also supports the mediating role of rumination among children ages eight to thirteen years in the relationship between high negative affectivity and the internalizing symptoms of depression and anxiety (Broeren, Muris, Bouwmeester, van der Heijden & Abee, 2011).

Temperament also influences individuals' characteristic responses to social situations, and thus specific relational factors may also mediate the association between temperament and psychopathology. For example, our affective state tends to influence how we interpret information, particularly in ambiguous and social situations. Children high in extraversion tend to have positive emotional responses to social situations, and this emotional response makes them more likely to interpret others' actions as prosocial, which promotes positive social engagement. This positive developmental cascade helps place and maintain these children on a positive mental health trajectory. By contrast, children high in negative affectivity may have negative emotional responses to ambiguous social situations, and this emotional response may make them more likely to interpret others' actions as hostile or unwelcoming, which promotes social disengagement (Luebbe, Bell, Allwood, Swenson & Early, 2010). Similarly, this negative developmental cascade helps place and maintain these children on a negative mental health trajectory.

Parenting behaviors are also shown to mediate the link between parental temperament—specifically low positive affectivity and high negative affectivity—and child behavior problems (Karazsia & Wildman, 2009), which suggests that temperament influences childhood behaviors intergenerationally. For example, as noted above, high negative affectivity children are often "difficult" to parent and may elicit more negative and hostile parenting, which in turn models a relational style of hostility, negative affectivity and aggression, helping to explain, in part, the link between negative affectivity and externalizing problems.

PRACTICAL SUGGESTIONS

- Assessment of temperament will inform the conceptualization and treatment of children with emotional or behavioral problems. Understanding these individual differences in temperament may help clinicians and parents identify emotional or regulatory deficits that may be appropriate targets of intervention.

- The aspects of temperament most clearly linked with psychopathology are high negative affectivity, low positive affectivity and low effortful control. All three aspects of temperament have been shown to be amenable to change over time, and there are empirically supported interventions that may help modulate high negative affectivity or enhance low positive affectivity or effortful control. For example, emotion regulation skills such as emotion labeling, relaxation and mindfulness skills, distress tolerance, and distraction techniques may all help children cope with intense negative emotions. Cognitive and behavioral interventions encouraging intentional decision making, such as STEPS (Stop, Think, Evaluate, Perform, Self-Praise), may help children develop better behavioral regulation skills. Positive psychology interventions such as gratitude journals or positive events scheduling may help enhance positive affectivity.

- Children develop in contexts, thus we must be mindful of and make use of the relevant developmental contexts in children's lives, such as parenting, school and neighborhood. Extensive research suggests that child development proceeds via a series of bidirectional, reciprocal interactions between a child's temperament and his or her environment. When children present with problems or concerns, evaluating and harnessing the power of these environmental and social influences will be critical to ensuring child success.

INTEGRATIVE THEMES

The introduction to this volume eloquently articulated that Christian Scripture portrays children as gifts from a loving God to his people. It is telling that throughout Scripture children are often portrayed as the fulfillment of God's covenant with us and as signs of divine favor. This call to value children as divine gifts, to respect them as persons and to recognize that they enact agency in their lives, with all of the accompanying responsibilities and challenges of such an approach, is quite evident in the field of temperament and child development, both normal and abnormal.

Valued as Gifts

Any parent or caregiver will tell you that each baby comes into this world with a very strong, unique and identifiable sense of self. While each is precious in his own way, each also brings to the world his own unique temperament, and this temperament will influence how the child engages in and interacts with the world. The broad temperamental domains of negative affectivity, positive affectivity and effortful control may combine in countless ways to make each child unique. But each child was created in God's image, and these differences among us mirror the multiple ways in which God himself is manifest on earth and within us. Each child then requires a unique way of caretaking that will best optimize the child's development. As discussed extensively in this chapter, the relationship between temperament and development is bidirectional, and this mirrors the duality of the image of the child in Scripture. Children are both innocent and naive recipients of their environments and the type of nurturance we impose on them and individual agents with their own wills, points of view and futures.

Respected as Persons

Some children are difficult to parent, and yet Christian Scripture reminds us that even the most difficult child is a gift to be cherished. We should remember that to respect children means to "take them seriously, to be attuned to their point of view, to be aware of their feelings and . . . to be able to tolerate their needs and challenges" (Flanagan & Hall, chapter 1, this volume). Imagine the child high in negative affectivity, low in extraversion and low in effortful control—this child might be quite a challenge to parent effectively and guide through development to a healthy and adaptive adulthood. And yet a Christian worldview honors and respects that child just as much as a child who may be temperamentally "easier." To respect children, then, means to accept and honor these differences and adjust our nurturance of each child to his or her own needs. The high negative affectivity and low effortful control child will struggle in novel and stressful situations and have difficulty controlling her strong negative emotions. This child will benefit most from calm and supportive parenting, good scaffolding and encouragement of emotion regulation skills, and gentle encouragement to take small risks balanced with acceptance of this child's instinctive desires to avoid unknown situations. By contrast, the high positive affectivity and low effortful control child will be a happy-go-lucky and fun child who may have difficulty with situations in which there is a strong social and environmental demand for calm, quiet and focused attention, such as school. This child will benefit most from parenting which scaffolds and encourages behavioral self-regulation in such situations, balanced with appropriate access to high-energy, high-fun activities that naturally appeal to the child. Our ultimate goal as parents, clinicians and members of the Christian community is to nurture each child to a healthy, adaptive and functioning adulthood. As clinicians, we might focus on a child's unique gifts, unique strengths and unique challenges in order to offer a more positive, strengths-based approach to development and psychological outcomes.

Viewed as Agents

The developmental psychopathology approach to child development emphasizes the bidirectional and reciprocal relationship between children and their environments. From this perspective, temperament is one valid influence on children's behavior and development. We must recognize and validate this influence and accept children as key agents in their own development, rather than attempting to mold them to our image of what they should be.

This sense of agency also places responsibility for development at the child's feet as well. Helping children recognize their own predispositions and how these characteristics affect their mood, their choices and their behavior is a key developmental task which will enable children to be productive and adaptive agents of their own development. Individual differences in temperament are not an excuse for poor behavior or the single explanation for an adaptive or maladaptive outcome; rather, these individual differences are a starting point. Thus a child's high negative affectivity or low effortful control is not an excuse for inappropriate behavior, but rather an important component of understanding that behavior and suggesting points of intervention. We should cultivate in children individual self-understanding and self-responsibility so that they can pursue healthy, adaptive adult lives.

3

*For everything God created is good, and nothing is to be
rejected if it is received with thanksgiving, because it is
consecrated by the word of God and prayer.*

1 TIMOTHY 4:4-5

WE ARE CREATED BY GOD, IN HIS IMAGE, including our thoughts,
feelings and capacity for action. Sometimes Christians view emotions as primarily negative and sinful, interfering with our ability to serve God, such as
when we become angry or anxious. However, both Scripture and psychological
research support a view of emotions as having the potential to either enhance
or interfere with healthy development, including spirituality. This chapter will
explore the concept of emotion regulation from a developmental psychopathology framework, covering definitional issues, normative development,
factors that affect and are affected by the development of emotion regulation,
and the three integrative themes explored through this volume.

DEFINITION AND STUDY OF EMOTION REGULATION

Emotion regulation is the process of changing or maintaining the experience
and/or expression of emotion in order to achieve one's goals (Eisenberg &
Spinrad, 2004; Thompson, 1994). Often when we think about individuals who
are affectively well regulated, we think of those who can cope effectively with
sadness or anger. However, emotion regulation is more complex than just the

reduction of negative emotions. It includes reducing, maintaining or enhancing emotions; internal experiences as well as behavioral responses; and both positive and negative emotions (Cole, Michel & Teti, 1994). Emotion regulation occurs in the case of both a child who resists hitting a classmate when he is angry and an adolescent who smiles and congratulates the competitor who has just defeated her in an important athletic event.

How do we define good, skillful or healthy emotion regulation? Several aspects of emotion, behavior and development should be considered. First, skillful emotion regulation is effective. Children (and adults) who are emotionally well regulated are able to both monitor and alter their emotional states effectively (i.e., their attempts to sustain or change emotions are successful). Second, skillful emotion regulation is adaptive. The techniques for emotion regulation—and their outcome—must result in behavior that is appropriate in a given context. A kindergartener whose school anxiety is only alleviated by clinging to his mother is not adapting well to the classroom setting and the need to separate from her. Third, skillful emotion regulation is flexible (Sroufe, 1995). Because different contexts demand different responses, a child must be able to assess the situation and self-regulate in a manner that is contextually appropriate. For example, progressive muscle relaxation might be an appropriate anxiety-reducing strategy when a child is in her bedroom at home but not when she is taking a test at school. In order to support that flexibility, a range of effective regulatory strategies must be available to the individual. Furthermore, different techniques are likely to be effective for regulating different emotions; an adolescent with strong emotion-regulation skills might use self-talk to regulate his anxiety most effectively but find deep breathing more useful when he is extremely angry. Finally, skillful emotion regulation supports the achievement of both short- and long-term developmental goals. Healthy emotional functioning involves the ability to achieve one's goals in the face of emotion and to utilize emotion to facilitate movement toward a goal (cf. functional theories of emotion which state that anger, for example, motivates us to overcome obstacles that block goals; Eisenberg & Spinrad, 2004; Frijda, 1987). In addition, children's emotion regulation abilities are judged according to how they affect movement toward or away from common parental and societal goals for children, such as the ability to form close friendships and to succeed in school and work environments, regardless of whether a child or adolescence shares these goals. In this way, a multisystemic view is necessary to fully assess emotion regulation: in what way do children's emotions and related behavior affect their own sense of well-being *and* their ability to function appropriately in their families, schools and neighborhoods?

As with all other aspects of functioning, a full understanding of emotion regulation requires developmental and cultural sensitivity. Children's emotional experiences and regulatory abilities change over the course of development, and we must be careful to assess regulatory skill in light of appropriate developmental expectations. For example, although we might expect a teenager to be able to regulate anxiety independently, it is developmentally normative for a very young child to depend on a parent—emotionally or physically—for comfort when he is afraid. In addition, we must be sensitive to cultural variations in views of emotions and their roles (Saarni, 1999). Whether emotion and its regulation are adaptive, effective and appropriate depends on the cultural context in which they occur. Cultural variations in understandings of emotion, display rules and the role of the caregiver in emotional instruction affect a child's development of emotion regulation abilities (Cole, Bruschi & Tamang, 2002; Fox & Calkins, 2003; McCarty et al., 1999). For example, despite desiring the same outcomes, children in Thailand are more likely than children in the US to use emotion regulation strategies that minimize the expression of emotion when they are interacting with an adult (McCarty et al., 1999). In addition, cultural emotion practices and beliefs influence significant differences in parental emotion socialization behaviors (Cole, Tamang & Shrestha, 2006; Trommsdorff & Cole, 2011). For example, caste status in Nepal impacts parents' reactions to their children's emotions. Brahman parents ignore children's shame but reason with children about anger, while Tamang parents reason with children when they show shame but scold them when they are angry.

Several methods for studying emotion regulation are present in the literature. Emotion regulation may be studied by focusing on the strategies that individuals may employ. For example, many studies of emotion regulation count the number of times a child uses a strategy such as self-distraction, venting, focusing on a forbidden object or self-talk (Fabes & Eisenberg, 1992; Stansbury & Sigman, 2000); strategies may further be categorized as positive or negative in terms of developmental ideals, often regardless of the ways they are used by specific children in a study. Other research has examined the effectiveness of children's strategies (Buss & Goldsmith, 1998); for example, does self-distraction during a frustrating experience reduce a child's visible distress?

Still other studies have focused not on whether strategies are used but on the overall dynamics of emotion and behavior, including global ratings of the influence of emotionality on the appropriateness of behavior (e.g., using categories such as "on task" and "disruptive"; Hall & Cole, 2007; Hoffman, Crnic & Baker, 2006; Zahn-Waxler, Cole, Richardson, Friedman, Michel & Belouad, 1994), displays of emotional appropriateness within a particular context (Maughan & Cicchetti, 2002; Zalewski, Lengua, Wilson, Trancik & Bazinet, 2011), and observations of the temporal dynamics of emotion (Cole et al., 2011). The temporal dynamics of emotion refer to patterns such as the length of time it takes a child to become emotional or to recover from an emotion and changes in emotion that occur immediately following the use of a regulatory strategy (Thompson, 1994). These dynamic measurements may be a more individualized method for studying the regulation of emotion, though they are complicated and may involve time-intensive research methodologies such as second-by-second coding of emotion and behavior. In addition, emotion regulation may be studied in naturalistic or laboratory settings. While naturalistic study offers the benefits of observing a child in her "real life" settings, the latter is somewhat more common, and there is evidence that lab-based measures of emotion regulation correlate with real-world emotional practices and abilities (Zalewski et al., 2011). In sum, there are a variety of valid methods for studying the complex topic of emotion regulation—ranging from the moment-to-moment dynamics of emotion and behavior to the consideration of the child in her larger context—and the most appropriate choice for a given study depends largely on the aspects of emotion regulation of interest.

NORMAL DEVELOPMENT OF EMOTION REGULATION

We are emotional beings from birth (Bridges, 1931; Fox & Davidson, 1986). Because emotions and their regulation are closely linked, it stands to reason that we are also emotional regulators from birth. Indeed, even young infants employ their limited means of communication and action to regulate arousing experiences; primitive strategies for regulating distress, such as reorientation of gaze, have been observed in infants as young as two months (Moscardino & Axia, 2006). However, parental responsiveness is crucial to young infants' self-regulation; sensitive parents monitor their babies' emotional states and regulate stimulation accordingly in order to provide an optimal level of arousal for the child (Field, 1978, 1994). Infants communicate their emotional needs to caregivers through signs such as crying and turning away from overstimulation and unwanted contact (Kopp, 1989). In this way, even newborns have agency in shaping their own emotional development! Responsive parents are highly effective regulators of their infants' emotions. Infants calm quickly when adults pick them up in response to their cries, and infants as young as one month of age display anticipatory soothing, or a decrease in negative emotion when they are touched in preparation for being picked up (Lamb & Malkin, 1985). Parents also regulate their young children's emotions by selecting their environments so that children are not emotionally overstimulated (Denham, 1998). For example, a sensitive parent would be careful not to expose a young infant to loud, startling noises.

As babies age in supportive developmental contexts, they grow in (1) their ability to communicate their needs to the caregivers who regulate them and (2) their repertoire of techniques for the regulation of their own emotional states. Until three months of age, infants orient toward adults when they are distressed, but between three and seven months, orienting toward adults decreases, while orienting away from adults increases (Lamb & Malkin, 1985); this normative pattern may indicate a decreasing other-reliance for emotion regulation even in the first year of life. By five to six months of age, babies display somewhat more complex regulatory behaviors—including self-soothing, visual distraction, looking to others and avoidance behaviors—during distressing laboratory tasks (Stifter & Spinrad, 2002; Tarabulsy et al., 2003), and the most commonly used strategies appear to change across the first year and beyond (Braungart-Rieker & Stifter, 1996; Mangelsdorf, Shapiro & Marzolf, 1995). Furthermore, there is some indication that emotion becomes less disorganizing as infants age; five-month-olds who are more emotionally reactive to a distressing task show lower levels of regulation, but by ten months, this link between distress and poorer regulation disappears (Braungart-Rieker & Stifter, 1996). Despite some patterns in early development, infants' emerging strategies appear to be strongly affected by situational variables. There is a lack of longitudinal consistency in individual patterns of regulatory behavior during the first year of life (Stifter & Jain, 1996; Braungart-Rieker & Stifter, 1996). Continuity in regulatory behavior may start to increase, however, by the first half of the second year (Stifter & Jain, 1996) as children concurrently begin to talk about their emotions (Bretherton, Fritz, Zahn-Waxler & Ridgeway, 1986). Kovacs, Joormann and Gotlib (2008) characterize the progression of early emotion regulation strategies throughout infancy as moving from primarily body-oriented (e.g., self-soothing) to rudimentarily cognitive (e.g., gaze aversion) to interpersonal (e.g., other-orienting) to behavioral (e.g., self-distraction).

During the first two years of life, children are still largely dependent on the support of responsive parents in order to employ strategies effectively (Sroufe, 1995), and sensitive parents adjust their behavior to meet their developing children's changing needs for emotional support (Grolnick, Kurowski, McMenamy, Rivkin & Bridges, 1998). By the age of two to three years, however, children are purported to be able to regulate their emotions more independently and purposefully (Kopp, 1982, 1989). Indeed, two-year-olds display a wide range of regulatory attempts—such as distraction, self-soothing, comfort-seeking and focusing on a forbidden object—during frustrating lab tasks (Grolnick, Bridges & Connell, 1996). By age three, some strategies are clearly more effective than others (Gilliom, Shaw, Beck, Schonberg & Lukon, 2002). Significant individual variability in both emotionality (Grolnick et al., 1996) and regulation (Hall & Cole, 2007) is still seen at this age. Toddlers frequently use transitional objects, such as blankets and stuffed animals, as sources of comfort, reflecting planful and repeated use of these objects to facilitate emotional self-regulation (Winnicott, 1953; Kopp, 1989). However, at this age, children still normatively rely on caregiver support for emotion regulation, particularly when emotions are strong and potentially disorganizing (Sroufe, 1995). For example, two-year-olds are generally able to distract themselves from a forbidden object by playing with another toy, but they are more likely to engage this strategy in the presence of an adult (Grolnick et al., 1996). During this period of development, children also begin to display evidence of the use of emotions to drive prosocial behavior; one study found that two-year-olds who spilled juice or broke a toy when they were with their mothers tended to display sadness following the mishap and take actions to correct it (Cole, Barrett & Zahn-Waxler, 1992). The emergence of self-conscious emotions during the second year of life enables children to judge their behavior according to social standards and expectations (Lewis, 2007). Indeed, the internalization of behavioral standards that were once entirely external provides motivation to regulate emotions in ways that promote prosocial goals and contextually appropriate behavior (Kochanska, 1993; Sroufe, 1995). In addition, increases in the ability of children to utilize internalized behavioral expectations between the ages of two and four is evident in behavioral appropriateness and compliance even when children are alone (Kochanska, Coy

& Murray, 2001; Kopp, 1989). Improvements in the ability to inhibit automatic responses during this period of development (Wiebe, Sheffield & Espy, 2012) likely support control over emotionality and regulatory attempts.

Children as young as age three display the ability to inhibit socially inappropriate expressions of negative emotions, such as disappointment, in the presence of others (Cole, 1986). Three- and four-year-olds are also able to verbally identify effective emotion regulation strategies, such as self-distraction, though they also view strategies that are typically ineffective, such as venting, as helpful for reducing negative emotions (Dennis & Kelemen, 2009). Children of this age also recognize that different strategies are more effective for regulating different emotions. By the preschool years (around ages 4 to 5), independence in emotion regulation continues to increase, and children begin to show more consistent patterns of emotion regulation strategies and abilities (Sroufe, 1995). While within-person stability becomes more apparent during this period, between-person differences are also observable as some children react emotionally and behaviorally to their surroundings in more adaptive ways than others (Cummings, 1987). Recognition of such early individual differences—in concert with the identification of the risk and protective factors that drive them—is a foundational process for effective intervention and prevention.

In late childhood and early adolescence, self-regulatory independence from caregivers continues to increase (Garber, Braafladt & Weiss, 1995), and various strategies continue to be effective for regulating emotions. Cognitive restructuring, self-distraction and avoidance decrease negative emotions in youth, though maladaptive strategies (e.g., avoidance, rumination) also continue to be used (Tan et al., 2012). Normative decreases in both emotional suppression (generally considered maladaptive) and cognitive reappraisal (generally considered adaptive) have been found during this period of development (Gullone, Hughes, King & Tonge, 2010).

It is important to note that this growth in emotion regulation skill over time is not always steadily upward (Kopp, 1989). Children may experience periods of great growth, periods of slow growth and periods of regression. In addition, certain emotions may be easier to effectively regulate than others. For example, children and young teenagers appear to have more difficulty down-regulating (i.e., decreasing to reduce distress and interference) the experience of anxiety than anger or sadness (Buss & Goldsmith, 1998; Tan et al., 2012).

Both continuity and change can be seen in the development of emotion regulation. In terms of change, improvements in the quantity, quality and effectiveness of children's emotional self-regulatory attempts is normatively seen across development. However, even while change is normative, there is continuity in children's styles of managing emotions from early in life. Children who show better abilities to regulate their attention (e.g., through gaze reorienting) during a distressing tasks at four months are generally more compliant with a parental request to clean up, a manifestation of self-control, at age three (Hill & Braungart-Rieker, 2002). Consistency is seen from the toddler to preschool years in children's styles of responding to emotion-eliciting events (Cummings, 1987), and children's self-regulation at ages four to five predicts their self-regulation four years later (Colman, Hardy, Albert, Raffaelli & Crockett, 2006). However, as with all aspects of children's development, pathways are changeable and outcomes malleable. A young child who is a skillful emotion regulator may experience a trauma that creates dysregulating affect, while another youngster who has trouble regulating emotions early in life may learn effective skills from sensitive adult caregivers and develop into an emotionally healthy adolescent. Therefore, early prevention and intervention are important components of promoting healthy emotion regulation throughout development.

FACTORS THAT AFFECT THE DEVELOPMENT OF EMOTION REGULATION

Throughout development, growth in emotion regulation can deviate from a normal, adaptive course in a number of ways. Among these include the failure to become an independent self-regulator, to gain a repertoire of effective and adaptive regulatory strategies, or to utilize age-appropriate strategies (Kovacs et al., 2008). From a developmental psychopathology perspective, any aspect of behavioral variation between individuals, including differences in emotion regulation skills, is derived from the influences of a combination of developmental process and the demands of the current context (Sroufe, 1995). In this section, the developmental foundations of individual differences in emotion regulation will be discussed. On a broad level, growth in emotion regulation ability is only possible because of concurrent growth in other areas of development, consistent with the developmental psychopathology assumption that development must be studied at multiple levels of functioning. The development of adaptive emotion regulation over time depends on the ability to engage appropriately with one's environment, which is facilitated by the healthy development of motor skills, visuospatial skills, mental representation, memory, sustained attention, executive control, response inhibition, perception of self as an agent and language skill (Cole et al., 1994; Fox & Calkins, 2003; Kopp, 1989; Posner & Rothbart, 2000; Roben, Cole & Armstrong, 2013; Wiebe et al., 2012). Indeed, "emotion regulation is never a purely emotional process" (Calkins, 2010, p. 93). In addition, gender differences in self-regulation abilities and strategies frequently emerge, with girls generally being classified as better emotion regulators at a given age (Cole, 1986; Colman et al., 2006; Fabes & Eisenberg, 1992; Kochanska et al., 2001).

However, there are also specific, individual differences and experiences that may cause a child to veer away from a normal developmental course toward maladaptive emotional management. Indeed, infants' emotional development appears to be fairly stable and continuous *unless* its course is interrupted by factors that undermine a child's emerging emotionality and regulation (Belsky, Fish & Isabella, 1991). Research suggests specific areas of internal and external experience that affect a child's developing emotion regulation skill. A number of these factors are discussed below.

Temperament

Temperament is commonly defined as individual differences in reactivity and regulation (Rothbart & Derryberry, 1981); by this definition, it is an important influence on the development of emotion regulation because it contains elements of both emotionality (reactivity) and self-regulation. Temperament is thought to be innate as well as foundational to adult personality (Rothbart, Ahadi & Evans, 2000), though the reactivity dimension of temperament likely emerges earlier in development than the regulation dimension (Calkins & Hill, 2007). Temperament includes dimensions such as negative affectivity, effortful control, activity level, extroversion and wariness (Rothbart, Ahadi, Hershey & Fisher, 2001; see Mezulis, chapter 2, this volume). Because of its clear conceptual links with emotion regulation, temperament is often characterized as representing a diathesis or disposition toward a particular emotion regulation profile (Calkins, 1994; Saarni, 1999).

Various aspects of temperament have also been empirically linked with childhood emotion regulation. One such temperamental characteristic is effortful control, the ability to inhibit a prepotent (i.e., powerful inherent) response (Posner & Rothbart, 2000). Effortful control generally improves with age, though variations in effortful control have been linked with emotion regulation across childhood. Indeed, children with higher levels of effortful control are better emotion regulators with regard to the appropriate expression of both positive and negative emotions (Carlson & Wang, 2007; Kieras, Tobin, Graziano & Rothbart, 2005; Kochanska, Murray & Harlan, 2000). For example, children who score higher on a measure of effortful control express positive emotion after receiving an undesirable toy as a gift, while children lower in effortful control have more difficulty smiling in this situation, an action that is considered indicative of skillful emotion regulation because it serves a positive relational function (Kieras et al., 2005). In fact, in preschool children, variation in effortful control is a better predictor of emotion regulation skill than age itself (Carlson & Wang, 2007). Because effortful control represents the ability to inhibit an automatic or impulsive reaction, it may underlie skillful emotion regulation by enabling a child to stop an immediate emotional or behavioral response long enough to consider the potential effects of their emotionally driven actions and alter them accordingly (Carlson & Wang, 2007).

Negative affectivity, the tendency to experience high levels of negative emotions (Rothbart et al., 2001), also affects emotion regulation. For example, children who are higher on mother-reported negative affectivity are more likely to respond to frustrating events in maladaptive ways (Santucci et al., 2008). A high level of negative affectivity may overwhelm a young child's ability to regulate his experience and/or expression of negative emotions (Lengua, West & Sandler, 1998). Temperament also interacts with other influences. The link between mother-child affective synchrony in infancy and self-control in the toddler years is stronger for children who are temperamentally fussier, suggesting that maternal support may be particularly important in helping these children learn to self-regulate (Feldman, Greenbaum & Yirmiya, 1999). In addition, negative affectivity has been linked with the later use of less effective emotion regulation strategies for boys whose mothers are harshly controlling toward them but not for those with mothers whose control is warmer (Gilliom et al., 2002).

It is important to note that although a particular temperament profile may predispose a child to certain emotional and regulatory responses, temperament is not deterministic (Saarni, 1999). Within a developmental psychopathology framework, outcomes are the result of the complex interaction of many factors in development; for emotion regulation, this includes temperament and other individual characteristics in concert with interactions with parents, siblings and peers. For example, the effect of early negative emotionality on later self-regulation abilities is moderated by parenting. When parents are more sensitively responsive to their toddlers, negative emotionality is positively correlated with self-regulation; when parents are unresponsive and unconnected with their children, negative emotionality predicts poorer self-regulation (Kim & Kochanska, 2012). Furthermore, in our characterization of children as agents in their own development, we should be careful to resist a deterministic view and instead recognize that children, like adults, have agency to make choices about their emotional behaviors and regulatory strategies, even as we acknowledge the role of environmental and temperamental factors in influencing these choices.

Attachment

Attachment is the trust-based early relationship between a child and her primary caregiver (Berger, 2012). A secure attachment provides the basis for healthy intra- and interpersonal development into later childhood and adulthood (see Seegobin, chapter 4, this volume), including adaptive emotion regulation. Indeed, securely attached children are more skillful emotion regulators across childhood (Bosquet & Egeland, 2006; Brumariu, Kerns & Seibert, 2012; Crugnola et al., 2011; Gilliom et al., 2002; Gresham & Gullone, 2012; Kerns, Abraham, Schlegelmilch & Morgan, 2007; Nachmias, Gunnar, Mangelsdorf, Parritz & Buss, 1996; Panfile & Laible, 2012; Smith, Calkins & Keane, 2006; Zimmermann, 1999). In contrast, attachment insecurity disrupts normal patterns of emotion regulation. For example, twelve- and thirteen-month-olds classified as insecure-avoidant are more likely to display self-reliant regulatory behaviors, such as self-soothing or distraction, than their securely attached peers (Braungart & Stifter, 1991; Diener, Mangelsdorf, McHale & Frosch, 2002). These self-sufficient behaviors are displayed in lieu of normative reliance on caregivers for regulatory support, likely stemming from past interactions in which these infants have learned that their parents are not consistent sources of comfort. In older children, insecure attachment is associated with poorer emotion identification, and insecure-disorganized attachment is linked with the use of fewer active, adaptive strategies to regulate distress (Brumariu et al., 2012).

Secure attachment may promote skillful emotion regulation in a number of ways. To start, the behavior that defines secure attachment in the Strange Situation (Ainsworth, Blehar, Waters & Wall, 1978) may itself be seen as an adaptive emotion regulation strategy, as the child uses proximity to the caregiver and cautious exploration as methods for managing the distress and anxiety evoked by an unfamiliar setting (Esbjorn, Bender, Reinholdt-Dunn, Munck & Ollendick, 2012). In contrast, insecure-avoidant children minimize their expressions of both distress during separation and happiness during reunion (Ainsworth et al., 1978), regulatory behaviors that may be viewed as attempts to distance oneself from a rejecting caregiver (Cassidy, 1994). Children with insecure-ambivalent attachment frequently display heightened distress, which may serve to elicit an attentive response from an inconsistent parent. In both cases, children are practicing regulatory attempts that are adaptive in their contexts; they are using their limited resources to manage their distress and elicit or avoid attention according to their context-specific needs. However, these behaviors are non-optimal because they do not set the child up for long-term healthy functioning (Nolte, Guiney, Fonagy, Mayes & Luyten, 2011). The avoidantly or ambivalently attached youngster who develops the skills to effectively regulate interactions with an insensitive parent may learn to be either under- or overemotional in interactions, growing into an older child who struggles to express emotions toward peers in a normative and socially acceptable manner.

Furthermore, attachment status is linked to child emotionality, which impacts burgeoning regulatory skills. When mother-infant dyads display more of the well-coordinated interactions—in which each individual's behavior is sensitively responsive to the other's—that characterize secure attachment, infants show a decrease in negative emotions and an increase in positive emotions between three and nine months. In contrast, higher levels of insensitive/uncoordinated dyadic interactions predict increases in infant negativity and decreases in positive emotion over time (Belsky et al., 1991). Attachment security in infancy also predicts changes in emotionality into the toddler years; securely attached children become less fearful and angry, even during challenging tasks, while insecurely attached children show increases in these negative emotions and decreases in expressions of joy (Kochanska, 2001). It is thought that sensitive parental responding—and the associated responsiveness that infants learn—both better regulates the infant's negative emotionality and helps him learn to regulate his own distress. On the other hand, some of the maternal behaviors associated with insecure attachment, such as insensitivity to a child's fearfulness, may increase the likelihood that a child's emerging regulatory abilities are overwhelmed by the experience of intense emotion without sensitive adult support (Nachmias et al., 1996). Insecurely attached children also show some abnormalities in their psychophysiological responses to stress (e.g., heightened or dampened cortisol levels; Nachmias et al., 1996; Roque, Veríssimo, Oliveira & Oliveira, 2012), which may undermine regulatory attempts; in contrast, secure attachment predicts faster physiological recovery from a threat in older children (Borelli et al., 2010).

As children age, the parental sensitivity to children's emotional experiences and needs reflected by secure attachment may also affect a child's willingness to express emotions genuinely around caregivers (Cassidy, 1994). This sensitivity in emotional contexts may be experienced by the child as validation of her emotional experiences. Indeed, children who are securely attached are more willing to talk about negative emotions with their mothers than insecurely attached youngsters (Waters et al., 2010).

It is important to note that attachment and emotion regulation exert bidirectional influences on one another (Braungart & Stifter, 1991; Esbjorn et al., 2012). Even as attachment influences emotion regulation, a child's emotion regulation style drives behavior when the child is emotional, including in interaction with parents, which in turn affects the parent-child relationship. In addition, illustrating the complexity of developmental pathways, temperament interacts with other influences, such as parenting, in the prediction of emotion regulation (Tarabulsy et al., 2003).

Parenting

Parent-child interactions are an extremely important influence on the development of emotion regulation (Colman et al., 2006; Tarabulsy et al., 2003). Parents affect children's emerging emotion regulation abilities directly through their interactions with their children as well as through their broader influences on biological functioning (Calkins & Hill, 2007) and schema development (Calkins, 1994). In addition to the manner in which they interact with their children generally, parents impact the development of their children's emotional competence in three specific ways (Eisenberg, Cumberland & Spinrad, 1998).

First, the way in which parents respond to their children's emotions affects emotional development. When parents are unresponsive to children's attempts to engage them during regulatory attempts (e.g., looking at or talking to a parent when upset), children's distress increases (Ekas, Braungart-Rieker, Lickenbrock,

Zentall, & Maxwell, 2011). However, it is important to note that children are able to effectively use other, more independent regulatory strategies, such as playing with a toy, in the presence of an unresponsive parent. When mothers minimize or punish their toddlers' expressions of fear and sadness, children's internalizing symptoms increase over time (Luebbe, Kiel & Buss, 2011). In contrast, maternal validation of children's emotions is linked to children's increased willingness to talk about negative affect (Waters et al., 2010).

Second, parental talk about emotions and discussion of emotions with children affects children's outcomes. For example, research suggests that parents of children with an anxiety disorder spend less time discussing emotion causes and outcomes with their children than parents of non-anxious youth (Suveg et al., 2008), and thus a number of interventions have focused on increasing parental emotion talk.

Third, parental expression of emotion has been linked to child outcomes. Parents who express more positive emotions have children who are better regulated. The findings are more mixed for parental expression of negative emotions, with some studies finding that negative expressivity predicts poorer regulation and others finding that it promotes adaptive self-regulation in children (see Bariola, Gullone & Hughes, 2011, for a review). Social referencing, the process by which young children utilize the emotions and behaviors of trusted adults to guide their own behavior (Berger, 2012), may explain how parental emotion expression affects children's early emotion regulation. For example, socially phobic mothers express more anxiety than nonanxious mothers when their infants are exposed to strangers in a laboratory setting (Murray et al., 2008). The infants of mothers who show more anxiety, in turn, become more fearful and avoidant of unfamiliar adults over time.

Parenting that supports optimal emotion regulation development in children appears to strike a balance between supporting a child and fostering her independence. Both overprotection and intrusiveness interfere with healthy emotional development (Chorpita & Barlow, 1998; Kiel & Buss, 2009). When parents are highly protective, they often shield their children from distressing experiences. Although this behavior is intended to protect children, it actually prevents them from developing the emotional self-regulatory behaviors for which the experience of stress is a prerequisite. Children must experience anxiety or anger in order to learn to regulate these emotions. On the other hand, when parents are intrusive, pushing a child too quickly into an anxiety-provoking situation, children's regulatory abilities may become overwhelmed by intense emotion. In both cases, the parent is taking control away from the child and denying her the opportunity to experience and regulate her emotions at her own pace. Both maternal comfort and encouragement to engage with a frightening stimulus produce high levels of cortisol in toddlers (Nachmias et al., 1996).

Interventions that aim to improve children's emotion regulation skills through the impact of parenting generally focus on parents' interactions with children when children are emotional. One such approach is known as emotion coaching. Gottman and colleagues (1996) have observed parents' interactions with their children in emotional situations and identified five patterns exhibited by what they call emotion-coaching parents. These parents (1) are aware of their own and their children's emotions, (2) validate their children's emotional experiences, (3) approach children's emotions as teaching opportunities, (4) help children to label their emotions, and (5) problem solve with children about handling emotions and emotion-eliciting experiences. Furthermore, these parental behaviors are linked to children's concurrent level of physiological regulation during an emotion as well as later behavioral outcomes and social skills. Fortunately, from an intervention standpoint, these parental behaviors can be promoted; instruction in emotion coaching changes parental behavior and improves children's emotional and behavioral outcomes (Gottman, Katz & Hooven, 1996; Havighurst, Harley & Prior, 2004).

It is important to note that parenting is not an independent influence on a child; rather, the parent and the child interact dynamically. For example, as I have discussed, parental overprotection and intrusiveness have been linked with child anxiety (Hudson & Rapee, 2001, 2005). Conceptually, these behaviors seem to foster anxiety in children by preventing desensitization to anxiety and the normal development of its regulation. However, it is also likely that anxious children are more likely to elicit these behaviors from their parents, who may experience distress themselves at their children's anxiety and avoidance and respond by either facilitating or attempting to eliminate that avoidance.

Parental Psychopathology

Another aspect of parental influence occurs through parental mental health. It has been suggested that the high rates of psychopathology among children of depressed parents might be explained by the effect of parental psychopathology on children's emotion regulation abilities (Silk, Shaw, Skuban, Oland & Kovacs,

2006). Specifically, a significant amount of research has been conducted with depressed mothers and their children, who display higher levels of psychopathology and lower levels of adaptive, active emotion regulation (Feng et al., 2008; Goodman, 2007; Hoffman et al., 2006; Silk, Shaw, Skuban et al., 2006). (Since most research has focused on maternal, rather than paternal, pathology, I focus here on mothers.) There are several pathways through which maternal mental health problems may impact children's emotion regulation. First, there are neurobiological mechanisms of risk. Prenatal maternal depression and high stress exposure predict elevated levels of cortisol in the child (Goodman, 2007), which may increase the likelihood that these young children experience more frequent or intense levels of negative emotions that overwhelm their developing capacity for regulation. Second, depressed mothers may model ineffective or maladaptive patterns of emotion regulation (Garber, Braafladt, & Zeman, 1991; Morris, Silk, Steinberg, Myers & Robinson, 2007). By definition, depression involves either heightened levels of negative emotion or affective blunting that is distressing or interferes with functioning (APA, 2013); such patterns inherently reflect difficulty with emotional regulation, which may be modeled for children.

Finally, maternal psychopathology affects mothers' interactions with their children in a number of ways. Depression and anxiety may interfere with appropriate goals for interactions with children, decrease attention to children's needs, increase negative beliefs about children, and increase negative and decrease positive emotion expression (Dix & Meunier, 2009; Whaley, Pinto & Sigman, 1999). In general, two patterns of interaction with infants are seen within the context of maternal internalizing psychopathology: some anxious or depressed mothers are disengaged and withdrawn from their infants, whereas others are intrusive and overbearing (Cohn, Campbell, Matias & Hopkins, 1990; Field, 1994; Kaitz, Maytal, Devor, Bergman & Mankuta, 2010). Both of these patterns appear to be detrimental for children's development generally and for the development of healthy emotion regulation specifically because they disrupt the normal pattern of parent-child interaction. For example, when mothers are emotionally unavailable to an infant due to psychopathology, children do not receive normative parent-driven regulation of their emotions. In turn, young children's emotionality may overwhelm their rudimentary regulation attempts in the absence of a responsive caregiver, disorganizing their behavior and even their physiological functioning (Field, 1994).

Indeed, maternal depression interferes with the normative use of distress-reducing strategies in infants as young as five months (Manian & Bornstein, 2009). On the other hand, anxious mothers are more controlling of their children's behavior, restricting children's autonomy (e.g., not soliciting children's opinions, not offering explanations); notably, however, this finding is only significant when children are also anxious, highlighting again the transactional nature of influences on children's development (Whaley et al., 1999).

Maternal psychopathology also decreases children's emotional expressions, which may be an indication of over-regulation. When mothers display higher levels of internalizing symptoms, their two-year-olds are less likely to display normative levels of worry and frustration during an upsetting situation, suggesting that these children may be suppressing their emotional reactions to avoid upsetting their mothers (Cole et al., 1992). Even six-month-olds with anxious mothers display less negative affect during a challenge than those with nonanxious mothers (Kaitz et al., 2010). Indeed, depression affects maternal responses to children's emotional expressions; mothers who were depressed as children are less supportive and more rejecting of their children's negative emotions, which in turn predicts higher levels of current and future internalizing symptoms in children (Silk et al., 2011), a link that is mediated by children's emotion regulation abilities (Kam et al., 2011). In addition, depressed mothers are less effective at scaffolding their preschoolers' behaviors and emotions (Hoffman et al., 2006).

Maternal depression appears to interfere with the process of mutual regulation (Beebe et al., 2008). Mutual regulation is thought to be an important part of the healthy parent-infant interaction that promotes positive emotional development (Tronick & Cohn, 1989). The quality of a dyad's mutual regulation is often measured by the degree of dyadic emotional *matching*, being in the same affective state at a given time, and *synchrony*, changing one's emotional expression and behavior to match changes in the other's emotion (Tronick & Cohn, 1989; Weinberg, Beeghly, Olson & Tronick, 2008). Healthy parent-child interactions tend to have a positive affective tone that supports children's emotional development. For example, when mother-child dyads display better affective synchrony in infancy, children display higher levels of self-control during a temptation task, a skill that involves emotional regulation, at age two (Feldman et al., 1999). In contrast, infants with depressed mothers show more negative affect during interactions with their mothers, which may reflect children's matching of the negative expressions of depressed mothers (Cohn et al., 1990). When mothers display more negative emotions, babies match their expressions as they seek to build social bonds and even begin to regulate caregivers' emotions through the process of mirroring. Therefore, when maternal psychopathology interferes with positive emotionality in interactions, infants may not gain optimal experience with positive emotions, particularly in interpersonal situations, and the effects on children's emerging emotional expression and regulation may continue even when maternal symptoms improve (Cohn & Tronick, 1983). Variations in parental behavior toward at-risk children highlight the role of emotional expression; when depressed mothers display higher levels of positive emotion toward their preschoolers, children display more active emotion regulation strategies (Feng et al., 2008). Both maternal involvement and maternal emotion expression affect how well children are able to independently and adaptively regulate their own affect.

Maltreatment

On the extreme end of the spectrum of parental behavior, maltreatment also affects children's emotion regulation abilities. Children who have been maltreated differ from non-maltreated children in their emotion regulation and emotional expression. Maltreated children display poorer emotion regulation abilities, more inappropriate affect, more affective lability and more behavioral disorganization when emotional than their non-maltreated peers (Alink et al., 2009; Kim & Cicchetti, 2010; Maughan & Cicchetti, 2002; Shields & Cicchetti, 1998, 2001). These links are seen in both middle and late childhood, using either questionnaire or observational methodologies, and for multiple types of maltreatment (physical abuse, sexual abuse and neglect). Specific findings include the observation that boys with a history of abuse are more reactive and aggressive when another adult expresses anger toward their mothers (Cummings, Hennessy, Rabideau & Cicchetti, 1994). This behavior may be due to the heightened emotional arousal that some children experience when exposed to conflict; this arousal has been linked to subsequent physical and verbal aggression toward peers (Cummings, 1987). Maltreatment also appears to heighten some forms of sensitivity to emotional cues; maltreated children are quicker to accurately detect anger in others' facial expression than children who have not been maltreated (Pollak & Sinha, 2002). Such sensitivity may be adaptive because it allows children to quickly react in a self-protective way around a potential abuser; however, it also may inhibit recognition of other emotions and/or predispose a child to overreact to low levels of anger (Cicchetti & Toth, 2005).

Children with a history of abuse also show poorer attentional regulation, which mediates the effects of maltreatment on emotion regulation (Shields & Cicchetti, 1998). Abuse appears to disrupt the normal development of attentional processes by simultaneously promoting reduced attention to certain stimuli (e.g., detachment and dissociation as coping mechanisms) and heightening attention to others (e.g., hypervigilance and reactivity to negative stimuli), which in turn increases the likelihood that a child will rely on maladaptive regulatory strategies when emotionally aroused.

The robust links between maltreatment and emotion regulation problems are not surprising given the degree of disruption in the early parent-child relationship represented by abuse. The emotional security hypothesis posits that children's emotional well-being is affected by the sense of safety and consistency shaped by their family environment and early experiences (Cummings et al., 1994; Davies & Cummings, 1994, 1998). Children who are exposed to experiences such as marital conflict and abuse may feel emotionally insecure, and their subsequent behaviors may represent (frequently maladaptive) attempts to regain a sense of safety and security. For example, maltreated children differ in expressions of self-conscious emotions, displaying more shame and less pride than non-maltreated children (Alessandri & Lewis, 1996). These children may down-regulate their expression of negative emotions for self-protection (e.g., to avoid attracting negative parental attention) or because these expressions have been extinguished by a previous lack of response from parents. Alternatively, some children display an increase in externalizing behavior either due to a heightened sensitivity to negative stimuli or in an attempt to intervene in the interadult conflict that may precede abuse (Cummings et al., 1994). Though these responses may be adaptive in the short term by protecting a child from being emotionally overwhelmed or physically harmed, they are problematic because they represent reactions and behaviors that are maladaptive for long-term development and functioning across a variety of contexts (Cummings et al., 1994; Maughan & Cicchetti, 2002).

ASPECTS OF DEVELOPMENT AFFECTED BY EMOTION REGULATION

Emotion and its regulation are central elements in mental health and functioning, including both disorder and its treatment (Cole et al., 1994; Cole,

Dennis, Martin & Hall, 2008; Cole, Hall & Hajal, 2013). Emotional symptoms are key features of most psychological disorders (Cole et al., 2013). The experience of emotion itself is not what comprises maladjustment but rather the *interfering nature of that emotion*. Cole et al. (2013) outline four criteria for emotion dysregulation. First, an emotionally dysregulated individual may be unable to effectively regulate intense or long-lasting emotions. Second, emotion dysregulation may take the form of inappropriate behavior that results from emotionality. In other words, emotions may interfere with a child's ability to behave adaptively given the situation, such as in the case of a child with oppositional defiant disorder who becomes defiant and aggressive when he is angry. Third, dysregulation is reflected in emotional experience or expression that is contextually inappropriate. Examples of context-inappropriate emotions include pleasure derived from another's suffering, a lack of remorse from wrongdoing, fear or anxiety in the absence of actual threat, or emotional numbness (the inability to experience emotions when they would normally be elicited by the context). Fourth, irregularities in the rate of change of emotions may signal dysregulation, including both emotions that change too quickly (e.g., lability or moodiness) and those that are resistant to change (e.g., inability to recover from sadness or anxiety).

There are two elements of emotional dysregulation that are important to note (Cole et al., 1994). First, emotion is never *un*regulated. Even when emotion is strong and interferes with goal-directed behavior, regulation of some kind is still occurring. Second, the regulation of emotion, even when it appears problematic or maladaptive, is an attempt to adapt to the demands of the environment and the situation. As emphasized in a developmental psychopathology framework, we cannot understand an individual's functioning apart from the context. When we take context into consideration, we can often perceive how emotion dysregulation may represent attempts at adaptation. The toddler who throws a temper tantrum may avoid having to clean up his toys; the elementary school child who laughs when he hurts a classmate on the playground feels powerful despite being abused at home; the teenager who self-mutilates when she is upset finds that she is calmed by the pain; the young adult who dissociates during extreme stress may avoid becoming overwhelmed by anxiety with which she cannot otherwise cope.

Internalizing Problems

Children with internalizing disorders are less effective emotion regulators throughout childhood and adolescence (Alink, Cicchetti et al., 2009; Bosquet & Egeland, 2006; Lotze, Ravindran & Myers, 2010; Maughan & Cicchetti, 2002; Neumann, van Lier, Gratz & Koot, 2010; Silk, Steinberg & Morris, 2003), and links between emotion regulatory difficulties and anxiety disorders continue to be seen in adult samples (Cisler, Olatunji, Feldner & Forsyth, 2010). There are a number of specific differences in emotional functioning between children with and without internalizing problems.

First, children with internalizing disorders experience more intense and frequent negative emotions than their peers (Carthy, Horesh, Apter & Gross, 2010; Silk et al., 2003; Suveg & Zeman, 2004). The processes that occur on multiple levels of functioning contribute to this affective pattern. Biologically, youths with anxiety disorders are more likely to experience physiological signs of anxiety during a negative experience (Tan et al., 2012), a link that may be explained by neurological differences (Hannesdotir, Doxie, Bell, Ollendick & Wolfe, 2010). Psychologically, they are more likely to interpret stimuli as threatening, increasing their experience of fear (Carthy et al., 2010). This intense emotionality may quickly overwhelm developing emotion regulation capacities and lead instead to inappropriate, maladaptive behavior. Furthermore, there is evidence that depressed children have poorer emotion understanding (Hughes, Gullone & Watson, 2011), compounding the dysregulating effect of intense emotions.

Second, children with internalizing problems are poorer emotion regulators than asymptomatic children (Suveg & Zeman, 2004), and difficulty with emotion regulation may underlie the link between stress and depression in some children (Hughes et al., 2011; Kovacs et al., 2008). Consistent with a diathesis-stress model, depressive symptoms may manifest when a child predisposed to difficulties regulating negative affect (which may result from a biological predisposition or early environmental experiences) encounters stressors that overwhelm her ability to cope with the affective response that entails. Deficits in the emotion regulatory abilities of children with internalizing disorders have been linked to difficulty utilizing effective regulatory strategies. Some studies have found that these children are able to generate fewer strategies for regulating anger and anxiety than non-anxious children (Suveg et al., 2008), whereas others suggest no difference between anxious and non-anxious youths in the number of strategies they use (Tan et al., 2012). It is clear, however, that youth with internalizing problems have less overall knowledge about emotion regulation strategies, are less likely to use adaptive strategies (such as problem solving and reappraisal) and are more likely to use maladaptive strategies (such as avoidance, denial, rumination and suppression; Carthy et al., 2010; Garber et al., 1995; Hughes et al., 2011; Silk et al., 2003; Southam-Gerow & Kendall, 2000). Strategies such as rumination are likely ineffective because they represent a lack of action to change either the situation or the emotion, and denial and other forms of disengagement may prevent an individual from experiencing the natural decline in negative emotion that comes from desensitization. Furthermore, when anxious youth do use adaptive strategies, they use them less effectively (Carthy et al., 2010; Tan et al., 2012).

Third, internalizing symptoms are linked with lower self-regulatory efficacy. Anxious youth view themselves as ineffective regulators of their negative emotional states (Carthy et al., 2010; Suveg & Zeman, 2004), and older children and adolescents who believe they have less control over their emotional experiences and arousing situations have higher levels of anxiety (Weems, Silverman, Rapee & Pina, 2003). Children with higher levels of depressive symptoms are more likely than their nondepressed peers to rate emotion regulation strategies as ineffective to change negative affect (Garber et al., 1995). If these children view regulatory strategies as ineffective, they may (1) be less likely to attempt to use them, and (2) use them less effectively, in a type of self-fulfilling prophecy.

Does the presence of internalizing symptoms interfere with regulatory attempts, or does poor emotion regulation lead to the development of symptoms? Although it is likely that there is some reciprocal causality, longitudinal research suggests that difficulties with emotion regulation often precede the emergence or worsening of symptoms. Six- to twelve-year-old children who display poorer emotion regulation have higher concurrent levels of internalizing problems, and emotion regulation deficits predict increases in internalizing symptoms over the course of a year (Kim & Cicchetti, 2010). Similarly, emotion regulation difficulties in preschool predict later anxiety symptoms (Bosquet & Egeland, 2006). Finally, certain emotion regulation strategies, such as rumination, have been found to increase symptoms of depression in children (Abela, Brozina & Haigh, 2002). Rumination increases hopelessness and decreases self-esteem, which in turn predicts increases in depressive symptoms over a six-week period.

Externalizing Problems

Problems with emotion regulation have also been linked with externalizing symptoms beginning early in development. Infants with poorer self-regulation abilities at five and ten months of age show more noncompliance and defiance toward their mothers at thirty months (Stifter, Spinrad & Braungart-Rieker, 1999). Links between emotion regulation difficulties and externalizing symptoms, such as aggression, have been found across childhood and adolescence (Alink, Cicchetti et al., 2009; Herts, McLaughlin & Hatzenbuehler, 2012; Neumann et al., 2010; Ramsden & Hubbard, 2002; Silk et al., 2003). Furthermore, research suggests that emotion regulation difficulties may play a causal role in the development of externalizing problems. Poor emotion regulation predicts a trajectory of high levels of externalizing symptoms in girls that differs from the normative decline in these problems across the toddler and preschool years (Hill, Degnan, Calkins & Keane, 2006). In addition, older children who display poorer emotion regulation have higher concurrent levels of externalizing problems, and emotion regulation deficits predict increases in externalizing symptoms over the course of a year (Kim & Cicchetti, 2010).

There are physiological, behavioral and emotional components to the dysregulation seen in children with externalizing problems (Calkins & Dedmon, 2000). Physiologically, these children have lower respiratory sinus arrhythmia (RSA), a measure of physiological adaptability and regulation, during a resting period as well as during a laboratory challenge. Behaviorally, they differ in terms of strategy use. Boys who use less effective emotion regulation strategies at age three have higher levels of teacher-rated externalizing problems at age six (Gilliom et al., 2002). Emotionally, children with higher levels of externalizing problems frequently experience more intense negative emotions (Silk et al., 2003). For example, toddlers who get more upset during a challenging lab task show more aggression and other inappropriate behavior and are less likely to use adaptive regulatory strategies, such as distraction or support seeking (Calkins & Johnson, 1998). Aggressive children may have particular difficulty regulating anger (Sullivan, Helms, Kliewer & Goodman, 2010). However, the emotional dysregulation that leads to later behavior problems is not uniform. Preschoolers who express either high levels of emotion or no emotion during a negative mood induction have more externalizing problems in first grade than moderately expressive children (Cole, Zahn-Waxler, Fox, Usher & Welsh, 1996). In addition, the absence of certain emotions may also reflect dysregulation. Youth offenders who display a lack of remorse and empathy are more likely to engage in multiple types of aggression and to reoffend both violently and nonviolently (Penney & Moretti, 2010).

There are multiple ways in which dysregulated emotions may predispose children to externalizing behaviors (Mullin & Hinshaw, 2007). First, children who experience poorly regulated negative emotions may be more likely to act or react aggressively, as their strong emotions interfere with the ability to inhibit inappropriate behaviors. Second, intense emotions may interfere with cognitive evaluations of social situations, increasing the likelihood that a child will interpret others' words or actions as threatening or antagonistic. Indeed, children who display this hostile attribution bias are more likely to act aggressively toward their peers (Crick & Dodge, 1996).

Social Skills and Peer Relationships

Sroufe (1995) observes that the goal of independent emotion regulation in the toddler years is the ability to return to a form of mutual regulation in the preschool years, this time with peers rather than parents. Indeed, emotional skill is an important aspect of social skill. Halberstadt, Denham and Dunsmore (2001) outline what they call affective social competence, a set of skills that are important for successful social interactions. These skills include emotion awareness, identification, contextualization and regulation. In order to appropriately engage with others in a social context, one must be aware of one's own and others' emotions, be able to judge their appropriateness for the social context, and regulate one's own emotional experience and expression in order to promote the relationship in a way that is also adaptive for oneself.

Many studies support these ideas empirically. Children who are more emotionally well regulated and who use appropriate strategies to regulate their emotions display better social skills (Contreras, Kerns, Weimer, Gentzler & Tomich, 2000; Gottman et al., 1996), engage in more prosocial behavior (Eisenberg et al., 1993; Eisenberg et al., 1995), are more liked by teachers and peers (Spritz, Sandberg, Maher & Zajdel, 2010; Denham et al., 2003), have more friends (Walden, Lemerise & Smith, 1999), and are less likely to be rejected by their peers (Trentacosta & Shaw, 2009). In contrast, children who identify venting as an effective method for reducing negative emotions are rated as less socially skilled by their mothers (Dennis & Kelemen, 2009), and among at-risk preschoolers, those who are more emotionally dysregulated have more conflict with peers (Miller, Gouley, Seifer, Dickstein & Shields, 2004). Emotion regulation skill may contribute to social competence even while it is still developing. Children who are socially competent use more positive emotion regulation strategies than their less socially competent peers, but they are as likely to use maladaptive strategies (e.g., isolation) in response to an interpersonal stressor (Zimmer-Gembeck, Lees & Skinner, 2011).

However, in light of the concept of transaction, it is important to note that social experiences likely also affect emotion regulation (Zimmer-Gembeck et al., 2011). For example, children who are able to positively reappraise a negative peer interaction also report more experiences of peers acting kindly toward them (Goodman & Southam-Gerow, 2010). It may be that children who are well regulated when they are upset act more appropriately toward their peers, facilitating positive peer relationships; however, frequent kind treatment toward peers may enable a child to more easily regulate the negative emotion that occurs during conflict with a peer.

Academic Functioning

Finally, more limited work has linked children's emotion regulation abilities with academic performance and school readiness. At-risk preschoolers with better emotion regulation skills and more emotion knowledge show better classroom adjustment than their poorly regulated peers (Miller et al., 2004; Shields et al., 2001). In addition, emotion regulation predicts kindergarten achievement in reading, math and listening comprehension, even when maternal education and child IQ are controlled for (Howse, Calkins, Anastopoulos, Keane & Shelton, 2003). Children who are poorly regulated may become easily frustrated in the classroom and unable to adaptively regulate their negative emotions, which in turn may interfere with learning (Davis & Levine, 2013).

In conclusion, a large body of research supports the idea that skillful emotion regulation underlies healthy behavioral, emotional and social functioning across childhood and adolescence. However, as emphasized by a developmental psychopathology framework, the impact of self-regulation must be considered in concert with other influences on development in order to capture a truly complex, multilevel and dynamic view of the developmental pathways that lead to both health and maladaptation.

EMOTION REGULATION AS MODERATOR AND MEDIATOR

As developmental psychopathology would suggest, the relationship between emotion regulation and other influences on children's development is complex. The many influences on emotion regulation in combination with the links between emotion regulation and child outcome form the theoretical foundation for the understanding of emotion regulation as a mediator between risk and outcome (Yap, Allen & Sheeber, 2007). Indeed, research supports the idea that emotion regulation is a key part of the mechanism of action of a number of risk factors, a central focus of developmental psychopathologists.

Emotion regulation mediates the link between a number of aspects of parenting and children's outcomes. Children's overall self-regulation abilities mediate the relation between several parental variables and children's cognitive, social and emotional outcomes in rural, African American single-parent families (Brody & Flor, 1998; Brody, Flor, & Gibson, 1999). Emotion regulation mediates the impact of attachment on anxiety (Brumariu et al., 2012), empathy (Panfile & Laible, 2012) and social skills (Contreras et al., 2000). Emotion regulation is also a mediator in the link between maternal depression and children's aggression (Ramsden & Hubbard, 2002) and later popularity with peers (Kam et al., 2011). Children's emotional self-regulation mediates the influence of families' expression of negative emotions and mothers' acceptance of children's emotions on children's aggression (Ramsden & Hubbard, 2002). Parental emotional expressivity of both positive and negative affect predicts better child self-regulation, which in turn predicts higher social competence and lower symptom levels (Eisenberg et al., 2003). Finally, emotion regulation appears to be one of the mechanisms linking overly punitive or abusive parenting with negative outcomes (Chang, Schwartz, Dodge & McBride-Chang, 2003). Emotion regulation mediates the relation between maltreatment and both internalizing and externalizing symptoms (Alink, Cicchetti et al., 2009); however, this link was only present for children who felt insecure in their relationships with their mothers, supporting the emotional security hypothesis as an explanation for the effect of maltreatment on emotion regulation and other outcomes. Another study found that, in a developmental cascade, poor emotion regulation mediates the relation between maltreatment and externalizing symptoms, which in turn predicts later peer rejection (Kim & Cicchetti, 2010). Emotion regulation also mediates the link between maltreatment and both bullying and being bullied by peers (Shields & Cicchetti, 2001).

Children's emotion regulation also mediates the influence of peers and other nonfamilial factors on children's outcomes. Emotion regulation partially mediates the association between victimization by peers and children's aggression, peer rejection, and internalizing symptoms in childhood and adolescence (McLaughlin, Hatzenbuehler & Hilt, 2009; Schwartz & Proctor, 2000). In addition, emotion regulation mediates the impact of exposure to stressful life events and peer victimization of aggression in early adolescence (Herts et al., 2012).

Emotion regulation also serves as a protective factor, moderating the impact of risk on outcome in several at-risk populations. Children's overall self-regulation abilities moderate the effect of multiple risks on children's social and behavioral outcomes (Lengua, 2002). Children and teenagers from very low-income families who are good self-regulators—both in terms of emotion regulation and broader executive functioning—are not at the heightened risk for mental health problems often linked with economic strain (Buckner, Mezzacappa & Beardslee, 2003). More specifically, children's expression of positive emotions during a challenging task is protective against the impact of maternal depression on the development of internalizing problems (Silk, Shaw, Forbes, Lane & Kovacs, 2006). This protective effect occurs on a physiological level as well. For example, for female African American youth with poorer emotion regulation skills, exposure to multiple psychosocial risks factors is linked with higher levels of cortisol, whereas youths with better emotion regulation abilities do not have heightened cortisol levels when exposed to risk (Kliewer et al., 2009). For these youth, the ability to adaptively cope with stressors is protective against the negative physiological effects of stress. Finally, six- to twelve-year-old children of incarcerated mothers who display poorer emotion regulation have higher levels of internalizing symptoms (Lotze et al., 2010). In other words, even among high-risk children, emotion regulation ability distinguishes between children with and without behavior problems.

PRACTICAL SUGGESTIONS

Emotion regulation is an important component of children's development. As such, it is important for clinicians to assess children's regulatory abilities and the factors that may impact them. Below are some practical suggestions for clinicians working with children.

With Children

- Assess children's emotion understanding through the use of drawings, pictures and expressive activities (e.g., making and identifying facial expressions). Ask children to identify situations that elicit specific emotions for them. Accurate understanding of emotions underlies the ability to manage them adaptively.

- Ask children what they do when they are experiencing various emotions in order to get a sense of their knowledge of effective regulatory strategies.

- Observe how children behave when they are experiencing various emotions. Is their behavior appropriate or inappropriate? You might introduce activities designed to elicit low levels of emotions of interest (e.g., worry, frustration) in order to observe children in vivo. Be sure to provide resolutions to these tasks so that negative emotions do not linger after the session.

- Emotion regulation strategies can be taught through the use of both modeling and instruction in therapy. Brainstorm with children ways to appropriately regulate both the experience of emotions and their behavior when they are emotional.

With Adolescents

- Discuss the causes and physiological signs of emotions with adolescents in order to facilitate their emotional awareness and understanding.

- Encourage adolescents to keep an emotion journal to identify their affective reactions to situations as a way to raise self-awareness about regulatory attempts.

- Help adolescents understand the difference between situations that call for problem-focused coping, which aims to change the situation, and those that call for emotion-focused coping, which targets the client's reaction to the situation. The serenity prayer is a nice illustration of this distinction ("Grant me the serenity to accept the things I cannot change, the courage to change the things I can, and the wisdom to know the difference").

- Brainstorm appropriate methods for regulating emotional experience and expression with adolescent clients. Techniques such as cognitive restructuring, deep breathing, relaxation, mindfulness and prayer can be useful tools for regulating emotions.

With Parents

- Encourage parents to be aware of their own emotional reactions and regulatory attempts and the ways in which they are modeling appropriate or inappropriate emotion regulation for children.

- Educate parents about emotion coaching and its benefits so that they can validate children's emotions and support them in their regulatory attempts.

- Communicate with parents the emotion regulation techniques that children and adolescents are learning in therapy so that parents can encourage and reinforce their appropriate use at home.

INTEGRATIVE THEMES

The concept of self-control, a component of emotion regulation, is clearly valued in biblical portrayals and commands (e.g., Prov 25:28; Gal 5:22-23). Furthermore, we see descriptions of even negatively valenced emotions that are righteous (e.g., 2 Cor 7:10). In addition, Jesus, in his sinless humanity, is described as expressing a variety of emotions, including anger (Mk 3:5), sadness (Jn 11:35), happiness (Lk 10:21) and distress (Mk 14:33-34). Finally, certain commands might be taken as guides for emotion regulation, including Ephesians 4:26 ("In your anger do not sin") and Philippians 4:6 ("Do not be anxious about anything, but in every situation, by prayer and petition, with thanksgiving, present your requests to God"). Scripture portrays us as emotional beings with the ability to modulate our emotions, a process that can be done in ways that are righteous or sinful (see Elliott, 2006, for a longer discussion of the topic of emotion in the Bible).

I will focus in this section on how the three integrative themes of this book—children valued as gifts, respected as persons, and viewed as moral and social agents—intersect with and inform our understanding of the development of emotion regulation.

Children as Gifts

It is apparent throughout the risk literature that children are vulnerable. This vulnerability can take many forms—physical, psychological, social, cognitive and emotional. Given the focus of this chapter on emotion regulation, we might especially consider here the emotional vulnerability of children, particularly in light of the vulnerability that occurs as children interact with their environments as developing emotional beings. Emotions and their regulation can be argued to underlie or relate to nearly every aspect of human functioning, including both adaptation and maladaptation. Also, as we have already explored, children's early interactions with close adults are linked with their emotional experiences, expressions, security and regulation. Therefore, the ways in which we instruct, discipline, nurture and otherwise care for children have important implications for their current and future emotional development. Our view of children as gifts should include a practice response that entails purposefully educating ourselves and interacting with them in ways that promote emotional health and adaptive self-regulation. Scripture clearly highlights the role of adults in shaping children's development (e.g., Deut 6:6-9; Prov 22:6; Eph 6:4), and Jesus specifically warns against causing children to sin (Mt 18:6). In light of the research on emotion regulation, it is clear that parents and other adults play an integral role in either helping children handle their emotions in adaptive and appropriate ways or hindering this skill by failing to appropriately support children and give them useful structure, feedback and examples. Therefore, we would be wise to recognize that the charge to prevent youngsters from stumbling includes providing the support and instruction they need to regulate their emotions in a manner that facilitates godly development, including a focus on long-term goals and an understanding of how their emotions and behaviors affect others.

Furthermore, while we are instructed to guide children's discipline and formation, we need to recognize that this is not a uniform process for all children. We must acknowledge that (1) individual differences in children's emotional reactivity and regulatory skill signify that different children need different caregiving approaches, and (2) children will not be equally easy or rewarding to parent around emotional issues. We may be tempted to only recognize as gifts those children who are temperamentally easy and emotionally exuberant and to forget that all children, regardless of their "appeal" to us, are gifts from God (Mercer, 2005). Rather, we must strive to understand the individual children with whom we live and work and seek to care for them in appropriate ways. While one child may only need to be presented with an age-appropriate challenge in order to learn to manage her anxiety fairly independently, another child might require constant reassurance and support as he experiences a new situation with fear and worry.

In addition, the experience of interacting with a young child may increase our understanding of our own emotional and self-regulatory strengths and weaknesses more than any other experience! As Christians, we should consider the ways in which we can learn from our observations of and interactions with children as emotional beings. First, children's emotional responses to us can give us feedback about own our behavior. A child's consistent negative reactions to parental requests or behaviors may indicate that a parent is not being sensitive to the child's needs and may suggest that parental self-evaluation is in order. Even when a child's behavior may clearly be an inappropriate response to parental action (e.g., angrily refusing to turn off the television and come to the dinner table), a truly humble and service-oriented attitude toward a child involves the willingness to admit that there may be a way to respond to a child to help her to behave more positively and to grow (e.g., warning the child about an upcoming mealtime so that she is not caught off guard by the need to transition to a different activity). Again, recognizing that children are gifts includes the acknowledgment that our care has a strong influence on their outcomes; it is likely more important to recognize children's vulnerability to our influence in a given interaction than to seek to justify whether our actions can be defended as reasonable or right.

Second, the normatively reduced regulatory capacity of young children provides us with opportunities to observe more raw expressions of emotion than we may generally experience ourselves or observe in our adult peers. We may learn about both the honesty inherent in fully experiencing and expressing our emotions and the danger of powerful emotions that can dysregulate our behavior. For example, the unbridled joy of a child receiving an undeserved gift can be a model for how we should receive God's grace to us. On the other hand, the self-focused and self-righteous anger of a child who does not get his own way and physically lashes out at his father may be closer to how we sometimes feel in our sinful mindset than we would like to admit. In these ways, children may be seen as gifts not only in the entirety of their being but also in the impact of our interactions with them as emotional beings.

Children as Persons

Early literature on the effects of parenting on attachment, an important influence on emotion regulation, identifies the difference between cooperation and interference (Ainsworth et al., 1978). Mothers who are interfering or intrusive with their infants do not appropriately attend to their babies' signals and act in ways that are insensitive. Intrusive mothers have been observed to restrain or interrupt their babies forcefully and/or frequently and to disregard babies' moods and responses to maternal behavior (Egeland, Pianta & O'Brien, 1993). Such intrusiveness has been linked with insecure attachment (Isabella & Belsky, 1991; Swanson, Beckwith & Howard, 2000). On the other end of the spectrum are mothers who are cooperative, responding sensitively and appropriately to an infant's emotional expressions and expressed needs and desires.

Cooperative mothers foster mutual regulation, discussed above as fundamental for a child's healthy emotional development. At the foundation of cooperative parenting is "respect for the baby as a separate, autonomous person" (Egeland et al., 1993, p. 359). Caregivers who are intrusive are acting on the assumption that their needs are more important than their infant's needs or even that the infant does not have needs and desires that are separate from those of the parent. Theologically, this reflects a lack of respect for the infant as a unique person with needs, rights, and feelings that are as valid as those of an adult. Indeed, given Jesus' emphasis on children as models for certain attitudes and states of being (e.g., humility and vulnerability; Mt 18:3-4), we might view children's approach to the world as even more valid than our own in many ways! As there may be parental variables that constrain a parent's ability to respond sensitively to an infant, such as maternal depression, we should be careful about placing unrestrained blame on parents who struggle with intrusiveness toward their infants. However, recognizing the importance of cooperative interactions with young infants, interventions might do well to focus on changing both the behaviors of at-risk mothers with their infants and the underlying understandings and assumptions these parents hold about their children. Indeed, many interventions designed to improve depressed mothers' interactions with their young children include psychoeducation about children's needs and signals (Bernard et al., 2011; Verduyn, Barrowclough, Roberts, Tarrier & Harrington, 2003), which is inherently an affirmation of their personhood.

Even as children grow older, the parent and child are perhaps best conceptualized as a "team" who work together to facilitate the child's self-regulation (Kopp & Wyer, 1994). This concept is very consistent with the idea of the interconnectedness of the individual members of the body of Christ (e.g., 1 Cor 12). When parents do not grant their developing children appropriate levels of autonomy and freedom, such as in the case of maternal anxiety (Whaley et al., 1999), children do not have the opportunity to fully experience their emotions and experiment with regulatory efforts, leaving them without the necessary basis for the later development of effective, adaptive self-regulation of emotion. Without this early practice, the child is inhibited from developing the skills that will make her into a competent person throughout life.

From a psychoanalytic perspective, individuation must occur, such that the child comes to see herself and her primary caregiver as distinct individuals, in order to meet the developmental demands of the toddler years (Mahler, Pine

& Bergman, 1975). Only once individuation has occurred can the child begin to rely more on herself than on others for emotional regulation. Furthermore, internalization of standards for behavior, which support healthy self-regulation, can only occur once the child recognizes herself as a separate person who can come to adopt behavioral standards that originate in the expectations of external others. Given the role of the parent in facilitating this individuation, a child's ability to separate from the parent is dependent upon the parent's view of the child as a unique other. Kierkegaard (Dru, 1938) discusses the role of the parent in facilitating separation in a wonderful description of a mother who allows her child enough distance and independence to learn to walk but is emotionally and physically available to support him in the process. In other words, she respects her son's autonomy in a way that is also supportive and developmentally sensitive. Without the healthy completion of this separation and individuation process, the child cannot become a competent emotional self-regulator; at the extreme, he may become an adult who is emotionally dependent on his parents for support and regulation, disrupting his ability to function adaptively in contexts such as work and peer and romantic relationships. For this reason, the practical affirmation of a child's unique personhood as valid—not just in our attitudes but in our actions—is an important theological foundation for children's healthy development.

Recognizing that children are full persons entails acknowledging that they possess strengths and weaknesses, arenas of success and struggle, just as adults do. From a theological perspective, the concept of weakness—as distinct from sinfulness—is useful here (Johnson, 1987; Yarhouse et al., 2005). Both are universal human conditions, but while sinfulness is the result of the fall and is unacceptable to God, weakness is our vulnerability to temptation or sin. In his fully human—but also fully divine, and therefore sinless—state, Jesus is said to have been subject to temptation (Heb 4:15). It is also clear that God uses our weakness for his glory, as a showcase of his strength in our need (2 Cor 12:9). Weakness may appear in many forms, including physical, emotional and psychological vulnerabilities. Some children may be said to experience weakness in the form of temperamental predispositions toward intense negative affect or prepotent responses that are difficult to regulate. Rather than either dismissing these individual differences or viewing them merely as an obstacle to be overcome, we should seek to understand them (and help our children and clients to understand them) as aspects of functioning in which God's power and restoration may uniquely shine. For example, a child with an emotional tendency toward anger, if his worldview is based in biblical understandings of right and wrong and justice, might be uniquely gifted to be sensitive toward (angered by) unjust suffering in others. This view does not mean that we do not also seek to ameliorate the detrimental effects of these weaknesses; if anger is more influenced by the sinful nature than the Spirit, it may manifest itself in instances where one feels that circumstances are contrary to one's own desires, rather than to God's will. As parents, clinicians and fellow members in the body of Christ, we play an important role in shaping both a child's views of her own weaknesses and the ways she harnesses them for God's glory. A full recognition of children as persons imbues their weaknesses with both negative and positive possible outcomes, in recognition of the complexity of human nature.

Children as Agents

The emotion regulation literature is quite consistent with the idea of respecting the agency of a child, with particular sensitivity to how this capacity changes during development. The regulation of a newborn's emotions is entirely dependent on the sensitive responsiveness of the parent, due to the limited agency of the young child. Without this early and appropriate parental support, the child is unlikely to be able to regulate his emotions well when he is older. However, the healthy development of this skill is also dependent on the parent's reduction of this regulation "for" the child as the child grows. Parents who remain overly involved in their children's regulatory efforts are not respecting the child's role as an agent in her own emotional life. This unhealthy overinvolvement may take different forms. Some parents may be overprotective of their children, such as in the case of parents who protect their anxious children from any anxiety-provoking experiences. While it may appear that these parents are doing what is best to save their children from suffering, they may actually be hindering their children's emotional development by preventing them from learning to manage their own anxiety, as discussed earlier. Other parents are dismissive or invalidating of their children's emotions; telling a child that he should stop crying or that she shouldn't be afraid of something, particularly when the message is conveyed without empathy, may communicate to a child that his emotions are wrong or invalid. Doing so takes away the child's emotional agency to affectively experience the world in a way that is unique and self-determined.

In contrast, both the concept of the child's agency and the research on emotion coaching indicate that the validation of children's emotional experiences is extremely important in promoting healthy emotional development. Validating a child's emotions involves recognizing the child's feeling and its cause and communicating that it is acceptable to feel this way, rather than dismissing or minimizing the child's emotions (even if these are attempts to help the child feel better; Gottman, 1997). Emotional validation is thought to help a child identify and appropriately regulate her affective states and subsequent behavior. The danger of failing to validate a child's emotions is that the child learns that certain emotions should not be experienced and may lead to attempts to down-regulate certain emotions at any cost. Further, when adults minimize or dismiss children's emotions, they communicate that their interpretation of the situation and of the child's feelings is more accurate—or at least more important—than the child's own assessment, in essence negating the agency of the child to appraise her own experiences. Rather, a sensitive parent works to validate the child's emotional experience as she also helps the child determine an appropriate behavioral response, even if the latter is different from the child's initial response to the emotion. Validating a child's anger at his sister for breaking his toy does not mean validating his choice to throw the pieces at her.

CONCLUSION

In summary, children's emotion regulation abilities are both affected by and affect a variety of other aspects of functioning. The capacity to experience emotions is an integral part of the human experience. We must strive to understand, then, the role that emotion and its expression play in directing developmental pathways across childhood and adolescence. As we seek to understand and to intervene in ways that promote well-being, we should also be careful to ensure that our efforts are theologically informed and that our assumptions and behaviors reflect an understanding of children as gifts, persons and agents.

4

The Parent-Child Relationship

Winston Seegobin

DEFINITION AND STUDY OF PARENT-CHILD RELATIONSHIPS

I was recently tucking our younger son into bed when he indicated that he wanted to talk with me about something. He mentioned that in the past there were knights, American Indian warriors and Samurais who protected people and nations. He wanted to be like Walker, the Texas Ranger, whose reruns we had been watching. He wanted to know why there are not people like these around anymore. I mentioned that the world had changed and we now have armies and soldiers to protect us. At that point, he turned and looked at me and said, "Dad, I would like to become a policeman." As I listened to him, pictures of the dangers and threats of being a police officer came to my mind. What he was saying began to affect me, and my fears got the better of me. I shared with him the safety issues involved with being a police officer, tried to discourage him from this aspiration, and reminded him that he had once said he wanted to be a neurologist and could serve people through this profession. As I left his room, I could sense his disappointment in my response to him. Later that night, as I pondered what he had said to me, I realized that I had completely missed the point of that important conversation. I wept as I realized that I had allowed my fears to influence a powerful conversation with my son about his desire "to protect and serve" with honor. He wanted to be a knight, a warrior, and I could not see beyond my desires and dreams for him. I had missed an opportunity to hear his heart.

Our conversation that night illustrates the importance of the parent-child relationship as well as its reciprocal nature. I was trying to be the good parent and listen to his desires while imparting my wisdom. I was affected by his desires and thoughts that made me fearful as a parent and emotionally moved by how I had missed what he was trying to communicate with me. I had been in the role of the authoritarian parent ("I know what is good for you"), and he helped me to become instead the authoritative, humble and teachable parent ("you share what you think is good for me, we discuss it, and you support me").

The parent-child relationship is one of the most significant relationships that a child will experience; it is also impactful for parents. Its influence goes beyond childhood and affects development into adulthood, including marital relationships (Lamb & Lewis, 2011; Seegobin, Reyes, Hostler, Nissley & Hart, 2007). As such, an understanding of the ways in which both children and parents are affected by this relationship is pertinent. In Scripture, parents are encouraged to not exasperate their children (Eph 6:4), and children are exhorted to be obedient to their parents (Eph 6:1-2). When these two principles are practiced in the parent-child relationship, a more harmonious and healthy relationship develops, resulting in children who behave in ways that honor their parents and parents who treat their children with love and respect. Bunge (2001a) notes that both Luther and Calvin encouraged parents about their responsibility for their children's moral and spiritual formation. She also observes that Schleiermacher "urges parents to build trust in their relationships with children by taking their concerns and interests seriously, by responding empathically to their needs, and by resisting the temptation to live out their dreams and aspirations through their children" (p. 22). We are also encouraged in Scripture to see children as gifts from God and persons in their own right, which influences how we treat them, relate to them and invest in them.

Parenting is a very important concept in the Bible. Parents are instructed to take care, including spiritual care, of their children. Our relationship with God is sometimes seen as a metaphor for the relationship between a parent and a child. In Matthew 7:11, Jesus said that if we know how to give good gifts to our children, how much more will our Father in heaven give good gifts to those who ask him. Here, the Gospel writer is using the principle of good parenting, exemplified through the giving of good gifts to our children, to illustrate God's even greater goodness toward us. The assumption is that good parents are generous and kind toward their children.

The relationship between parents and children has been studied extensively, and there is an abundance of literature on the influence of parents on children.

Many of these studies have examined the impact of parenting styles on child outcomes (Kerr, Stattin & Ozdemir, 2012; Erath, El-Sheikh, Hinnant & Cummings, 2011). Other studies have examined early attachment styles and their impact on child development and security (Prior & Glaser, 2006; Rosen & Rothbaum, 2003). Fewer studies have examined the impact of children on parents (Boyatzis & Janicki, 2003; Kuczynski, 2003). Developmental psychopathology makes important contributions toward better understanding the bidirectional aspects of the relationship (Cicchetti, 2006: Cicchetti & Howes, 1991; Pardini, Fite & Burke, 2008). In this chapter, I will first present models of parent-child relationships. Second, I will look at aspects of normal development. Third, I will examine factors related to the abnormal development of these relationships. Finally, I will discuss integrative themes related to the parent-child relationship. My hope is that the impact of the parent-child relationship on children's development will be clearly and comprehensively understood through the lens of developmental psychopathology, particularly within the context of Christian themes related to relationships.

MODELS OF PARENT-CHILD RELATIONSHIPS

The parent-child relationship plays a crucial role in the development of the child and can result in normal, healthy development or abnormal, unhealthy development. A high-quality relationship between parent and child positively influences the early attachment relationship as well as the emotional health of the child. In contrast, certain parent characteristics may negatively influence child development (Larsson, Viding, Rijsdijk & Plomin, 2008; Pardini et al., 2008), the way children see themselves and how they interact with their world. An extreme example of the detrimental influence of parenting is the impact of child abuse on children's development, resulting in a negative view of self, relationship difficulties and poor emotional self-regulation (Cicchetti, 1987; Cicchetti & Howes, 1991).

There are various models for understanding parent-child relationships (Darling & Steinberg, 1993; Pardini, 2008) that focus on different aspects of the connection between parents and children. The unilateral or unidirectional model emphasizes the influence of parents on children and puts the onus on parents as the main determinant of children's normal and abnormal development. For example, according to this model, parental depression may have a negative impact on the child through the parent's lack of availability to the child, leading to outcomes such as higher rates of emotional and behavioral problems (Weitzman, Rosenthal & Liu, 2011).

The bilateral or bidirectional model emphasizes both the influence of parents on children and the influence of children on parents (Pardini, 2008). In the above example of the depressed parent, this model not only examines the influence of the parent's depression on the child but also how the child may be influencing the depression of the parent (Gross, Shaw & Moilanen, 2008). For instance, the emotional and behavioral problems of the child may cause the parent to believe that she is an ineffective parent, leading to negative emotions and a decreased sense of self-worth. The bidirectional model helps explain why children who share similar parental experiences may have different outcomes (multifinality), and children who share different parental experiences may have similar outcomes (equifinality; Cicchetti & Rogosch, 1996).

A developmental psychopathology perspective emphasizes this bidirectional model, noting that children can influence the parent-child relationship in both positive and negative ways. For instance, the temperament of the child can influence the parent's response to that child. If the child's temperament is positive and warm, parents are more likely to be emotionally warm and communicative, and the relationship healthier. If the child's temperament is difficult (e.g., fussy and demanding), parents may hold back and not form as close a relationship or become frustrated and overwhelmed by the child's needs, which can negatively affect the development of that parent-child relationship (Cummings, Davies & Campbell, 2000). A healthy parent-child relationship includes mutual care and respect as well as open communication.

NORMAL DEVELOPMENT OF THE PARENT-CHILD RELATIONSHIP

According to a developmental psychopathology perspective, the same factors that are involved in the normal development of the parent-child relationship are also involved in abnormal development. Therefore, in order to understand problematic parent-child relationships, we must first understand healthy, normal interactions across development. Normative child development is strongly influenced by parenting. In a healthy parent-child relationship, parents are supportive, warm, sensitive to the psychological states of their children and responsive to their psychosocial needs. They are generally seen as emotionally available and accepting of their children. Such parenting behaviors result in greater sociability, self-regulation, prosocial behavior and constructive play in children (Alessandri, 1992; Darling & Steinberg, 1993; Schofield et al., 2012). Additionally, parental warmth and responsiveness are associated with children who are secure, in control and trusting of their environment. Success in school, better coping strategies and secure attachment in adolescence are also associated with parental warmth (Schofield et al., 2012).

Another characteristic of a healthy parent-child relationship is children's positive contributions to their parents. Children who are caring and respectful and who honor their parents may have parents who are less stressed, more content and happy. In addition, children who are responsible, engaging and helpful create an atmosphere where parents feel appreciated and valued. A third characteristic of a healthy parent-child relationship is stability and consistency even in the face of trauma, difficulties and challenges. Often the relationship gets stronger in these circumstances.

In the following sections, several aspects of the normal development of the parent-child relationship will be considered, including attachment styles, parenting styles, parenting practices and the role of ethnicity/culture.

Attachment Styles

In the course of normal development, attachment plays a significant role in the emotional security of the child and influences personality development (see also chapter 9, this volume). Attachment is defined as the deep emotional connection between infants and their caregivers that begins in the first year (Rosen & Rothbaum, 2003). Children with a close emotional bond with parents have greater respect for their parents and respond more favorably to their directions and discipline (Thompson, 2008). This finding is not surprising given that the emotional bond provides an atmosphere of warmth and acceptance in the home. Cummings et al. (2000) conclude that "the formation and maintenance of emotional bonds between parents and children were a highly desirable state of affairs that predicted positive qualities of children's adjustment" (p. 183). The idea that emotional connections between parents and children significantly influence later development was initially proposed by object relations theorists as well as learning theorists focusing on the notion of dependency (Ainsworth, 1969). As further research occurred, it became clearer that the emotional bond between parents and children was strongly predictive of positive adjustment in children (Bowlby, 1969; Thompson, 2008).

The attachment of the infant to the caregiver determines the quality of the relationship between the parent and the child and the emotional security of the child as he develops (Bowlby, 1969; see chapter 5, this volume). The attachment relationship can lead to a positive relationship with the parent and normal healthy development, or it can result in a strained relationship with the parent and feelings of insecurity resulting in unhealthy relationships and psychopathology (Cummings et al., 2000; Prior & Glaser, 2006). Children who are securely attached see their parents as a secure base because of the warmth and responsiveness of the parent. Examination of parent-child attachment relationships (e.g., the Strange Situation; Ainsworth et al., 1978) shows that securely attached children are upset when the parent leaves the room but easily reestablish contact with the parent and are comforted upon reunion. It is proffered that when the parent is out of sight, these children have an internal representation or cognitive image of the parent that helps them continue to feel secure (Bowlby, 1969); however, their distress upon separation occurs because of the closeness to the parent. Parents are perceived as dependable and trustworthy because of their care for the child and responsiveness to her needs. As a result, these children are able to form close relationships as they develop and have a sense of emotional security (Cummings et al., 2000; Prior & Glaser, 2006; Rosen & Rothbaum, 2003).

The other three attachment styles (avoidant, anxious/resistant and disorganized/disoriented) represent insecure attachment styles and will be discussed in the abnormal development section of the chapter.

Parenting Styles

Along with attachment styles, parenting styles are important determinants of children's outcomes. Cummings et al. (2000) emphasize that "from a developmental psychopathology perspective, it follows that consideration of the effects of parental behavior is an essential component of any model of the effects of families on children" (p. 157). The four parenting styles that have been studied within developmental psychology are authoritative, authoritarian, permissive (Baumrind, 1971) and indifferent/uninvolved (Maccoby & Martin, 1983), all of which vary along dimensions of control and warmth. Baumrind (1996) provides an overview of the parenting styles in this manner: "Authoritative parents are both highly demanding and highly responsive, by contrast with authoritarian parents, who are highly demanding but not responsive, permissive parents, who are responsive but not demanding, and unengaged parents, who are neither demanding nor responsive" (p. 412). The authoritative parenting style will be presented here, and the authoritarian, permissive, and indifferent/ uninvolved parenting styles will be discussed in the abnormal development section of the chapter.

Consistent with the developmental psychopathology concept of dynamic transactions between the child and the environment, it is important to note that parenting styles are flexible within families depending on the child characteristics and the parenting situation (i.e., parents can show different styles in response to different situations or in response to different children). Furthermore, Cummings et al. (2000) underscore the fact that "no optimal parenting style exists for all children of all ages in all situations" (p. 157). They also indicate that parenting occurs within a larger ecological context consisting of the family system, subculture, neighborhood, and developmental period of both the child and the family.

The authoritative parenting style involves both high control and high affection and is often presented as the most effective because children exposed to this style are usually well adjusted. Children are treated with warmth and respect and feel loved and valued. Parents are firm and consistent in their control and make increasing demands of children as they grow older, being sensitive to changing developmental needs and abilities. Additionally, children are invited to participate in the decision-making and problem-solving process, resulting in greater security and confidence. The effectiveness of this approach is its ability to be both strict and loving at the same time. Authoritative parenting has positive influences on children from preschool through adolescence (Cummings et al., 2000; Teyber & McClure, 2011). Baumrind's (1968) description of the prototypic authoritative parent explains the effectiveness of this parenting style:

> She encourages verbal give and take, and shares with the child the reasoning behind her policy. She values both expressive and instrumental attributes, both autonomous self-will and disciplined conformity. Therefore, she exerts firm control at points of parent-child divergence, but does not hem the child in with restrictions. She recognizes her own special rights as an adult, but also the child's individual interests and special ways. The authoritative parent affirms the child's present qualities, but also set standards for future conduct. She uses reason as well as power to achieve her objectives. She does not base her decision on group consensus or the individual child's desires but also does not regard herself as infallible or divinely inspired. (p. 261)

In addition, Spilka, Hood, Hunsberger and Gorsuch (2003) indicate that there is tentative evidence that among adolescents the authoritative parenting style is associated with intrinsic religious orientation, which means that children raised with this parenting style take their religious faith more seriously and seek to live it. This finding suggests that parents who are warm, loving and respectful mirror attributes of God that influence their children to be more authentic in their faith commitment.

Parenting Styles and Parenting Practices

Darling and Steinberg (1993) make a distinction between parenting styles and parenting practices, noting that "parenting style differs from parenting practices in that it describes parent-child interactions across a wide range of situations, whereas parenting practices are by definition domain specific" (p. 493). Parenting practices focus on the specific resources that are available to a child within a specific domain. For example, the parenting practices of attending school functions, ensuring that homework is completed and checking grades affect children's academic achievement. Parenting practices also affect specific behaviors, such as table manners, by having a direct goal attainment or outcome. Interestingly, the reciprocal relationship between parenting practices and the disruptive behavior of children has also been shown to be significant. Unpleasant child behaviors heavily influence parents to discontinue the use of appropriate discipline (Burke, Pardini & Loeber, 2008; Darling & Steinberg, 1993).

The Role of Ethnicity/Culture

The literature indicates that culture plays a significant role in the parent-child relationship. In Western cultures, children are given more influence in the parent-child relationship and participate in decisions that impact the parent-child relationship. In some Eastern countries, children's behaviors are more regimented, and parental influence is stronger, with children being given little say in the relationship. Thus, consistent with a developmental psychopathology emphasis on context, cultural context must be taken into consideration in order to understand whether parenting styles are normative. In some Japanese cultures, parents cater to the needs and influences of the child when he or she is very young, but parental influence strengthens as the child grows older, with children's conformity and compliance to parental desires expected (Kuczynski, 2003; Trommsdorff & Kornadt, 2003).

Authoritarian parenting generally results in negative outcomes for children in European American families but positive outcomes in African American and Asian American families (Deater-Deckard & Dodge, 1997). In both African American and Asian American families, an authoritarian parenting style seems to produce more positive outcomes in children because of the cultural values placed on compliance, rule keeping and the honoring of family traditions. In Baumrind's (1972) study with African American children, she found that families that were high in the authoritarian parenting style had children who were self-assertive and independent.

The cultural context may also determine whether the parent-child relationship is mostly unidirectional or bidirectional. That is, "a culturally informed model of parent-child relationships therefore takes into account the cultural differences and the culture specificities and thus must investigate the relations between bidirectionality and unidirectionality under the specific cultural conditions" (Trommsdorff & Kornadt, 2003, p. 273). In some Asian cultures where collectivism is more prominent, unidirectional aspects of the parent-child relationship are emphasized. For instance, in China, Japan and Korea, where filial piety governs the parent-child relationship, children are expected to obey and honor their parents throughout their life. Parents care for and support their children with the expectation that children will take care of them when they become older. Parents usually do not need to provide explanations for their demands, as they are perceived as authority figures who create the rules. As a result, values such as parental authority and compliance are accepted and honored because of the cultural emphasis on the maintenance of harmony.

These practices stand in contrast to Western culture, where individualism is emphasized, conflicts in the parent-child relationship are expected, and autonomy is celebrated. Children in individualistic cultures have greater influence over their parents when compared with children from collectivistic cultures. The expectation is that they will be involved in negotiations with parents and communicate what they want from parents. However, for both children and parents from collectivistic cultures, following norms and social rules are the expectations and the transmitted value (Trommsdorff & Kornadt, 2003).

The next section focuses on parental pathology and mistreatment's effects on the parent-child relationship.

ASPECTS OF DEVELOPMENT AFFECTED BY THE PARENT-CHILD RELATIONSHIP

There are several ways in which the parent-child relationship may negatively influence children's development. I will focus on aspects of the parent child relationship that affect abnormal development, paying particular attention to the roles of parental mistreatment and parental pathology. I will also discuss the influence of attachment styles and parenting styles on abnormal development, and the parent-child relationship as a moderator and mediator.

Maltreatment

The results of several studies clearly indicate that children who experience a wide variety of maltreatment, including physical and sexual abuse as well as neglect, are at increased risk for the development of psychological disturbances, such as difficulties in relationship with peers, problems with social skills, internalizing symptoms and externalizing behaviors. Additional problems experienced by these children include low self-esteem, difficulties in school and noncompliance (Erath et al., 2011; Hipwell et al., 2008; Larsson et al., 2008).

Several studies describe the development of abnormal behavior as a bidirectional process that further reflects the influence parents and children have on each other even in the process of the development of psychopathology. Providing a key example within the literature, Pardini (2008) describes the bidirectional model of parent-child interactions developed by Patterson and colleagues (Patterson, 1982; Patterson, Dishion & Bank, 1984) as follows:

> The basic premise of the model asserted that children with an irritable and defiant temperament caused unskilled parents to use increasingly harsh discipline techniques in an attempt to gain control of the child's behavior. These harsh parenting practices served to further escalate their child's aversive behaviors rather than eliminate them. As the parent-child conflict intensifies during these aversive exchanges, many parents then withdraw from the interaction as a means of escaping the aversive behaviors of their child. As a result, the child learns that requests can be avoided by increasing the intensity and/or duration of their aversive behaviors, which reinforces an escalation in their conduct problems over time. . . . Importantly, this model has served as the foundation for many successful interventions designed to break the coercive exchanges between parents and children with conduct problems. (p. 629)

Additionally, in a longitudinal study examining the bidirectional relationship between parental negativity and early childhood antisocial behavior, Larsson et al. (2008) found that the association between children's antisocial behavior and parenting was influenced by both parents and children. Parents' negative feelings toward children served as an environmental mediator for antisocial behavior in children, and children's antisocial behavior evoked parental negativity toward children. Another study that assessed the direction of the association between parenting practices and conduct problems in boys found that "the influence of conduct problems on changes in parenting behaviors was as strong as the influence of parenting behaviors on changes in conduct problems across development" (Pardini et al., 2008, p. 647). Other studies have found reciprocal influences between girls' conduct problems and depression and parental punishment and warmth (Hipwell et al., 2008) and between boys' externalizing problems and mothers' depressive symptoms (Gross et al., 2008). Consistent with a developmental psychopathology framework, we can clearly recognize the significance of bidirectional influences of abnormal behaviors in both children and parents.

Attachment Styles

The three insecure attachment styles—avoidant, anxious/resistant and disorganized/disoriented—negatively affect children's development. Children with an avoidant attachment style do not rely on their parents to be present and consistently meet their needs, perceiving them as rejecting, irritable, tense and avoidant of bodily contact. In the Strange Situation, children displaying avoidant attachment show little or no distress when the parent leaves and avoids contact with the parent when she returns; they may even turn away when the parent tries to make contact. These children believe they cannot turn to the parent for assistance in stressful or threatening situations because they are unreliable and untrustworthy; indeed, parents of avoidantly attached children are generally dismissive or rejecting of their infants (Ainsworth et al., 1978; Cummings et al., 2000; Prior & Glaser, 2006; Rosen & Rothbaum, 2003).

In the anxious/resistant attachment style, children display both clingy behavior and anger toward their parents. In the Strange Situation, they cling to the parent and do not show interest in the toys; when she departs, they become very upset. When the parent returns, these children exhibit both anger at the parent and excessive contact with the parent and may vacillate between seeking and resisting the parent. These children are not quickly comforted by the parent's presence, and it takes some time before they feel reassured and can settle down emotionally following the separation. Children may relate to parents in this manner because of parents' inconsistent responses to them and parents' insensitive manner of relating to them (Cummings et al., 2000; Prior & Glaser, 2006, Rosen & Rothbaum, 2003).

Children displaying a disorganized/disoriented attachment style have failed to develop a coherent strategy to respond to stressful situations. These children are stressed when the parent leaves but seem uncertain about how to respond to the parent when he or she returns, exhibiting both avoidant and resistant behaviors. They may appear dazed and disconnected from their surroundings. Disorganized attachment generally results from extreme deficits in parenting, such as in the case of parental psychopathology or maltreatment, in which parents are so insensitive and/or unresponsive that children cannot form a coherent strategy for relating to and depending on them (Cummings et al., 2000; Prior & Glaser, 2006; Rosen & Rothbaum, 2003).

Parenting Styles

There are three parenting styles associated with abnormal development in children: authoritarian, permissive and indifferent/uninvolved. The authoritarian parenting style involves high control and low affection and is common but less effective than authoritative parenting in producing positive outcomes in children. Authoritarian parents demand unquestioned obedience, and consequently, any display of individualistic behavior is punished. Children exposed to this parenting style are less likely to engage in externalizing behaviors such as delinquency, drug use or sexual promiscuity; however, they are more likely to display internalizing symptoms such as low self-efficacy and devaluation of self and to display less autonomy. They also tend to internalize their anger, resulting for some children in angry outbursts (Baumrind, 1968, 1991; Cummings et al., 2000; Darling & Steinberg, 1993; Teyber & McClure, 2011). Teyber and McClure further note that

> without the emotional support and affection so important to the development of a sense of belonging and security, especially during moments of distress, children of authoritarian parents learn to hide any signs of vulnerability from their parents and sadly, eventually from themselves as well. (p. 242)

These children keep people at a distance and their emotions under tight control because they have learned that they cannot depend on their parents for support and closeness.

The permissive parenting style involves low control and high affection. Parents are accepting of most of their children's behaviors, including those that are disruptive or impulsive, and set few rules or constraints (Cummings et al., 2000). Children are unsure of what is expected of them and of the consequences indicating when parental norms are violated. They are unclear about the rules they need to follow and often do not follow the rules because their parents are inconsistent in enforcing them. For instance, they may stay out late with friends because their parents may or may not discipline them for this behavior. As a result, these children do not learn how to live disciplined lives and develop healthy ways of relating to rules and boundaries. They also try to dominate other relationships and become angry when they do not get their way (Teyber & McClure, 2011). Teyber and McClure state that "the balance of power has tipped in permissive families, and children wield too much control in the parent-child relationship" (p. 244). As a result of this parenting style, children may exhibit high self-esteem and self-worth, but they will have difficulties with achievement, maturity, social responsibility and impulse control (Baumrind, 1991). Spilka et al. (2003) report that among adolescents, the permissive parenting style is associated with extrinsic religious orientation, meaning that they tend to use their religion for personal accomplishments rather than have it influence their behavior and lifestyle.

The indifferent-uninvolved parenting style, also referred to as the disengaged parenting style, involves low control and low affection. This parenting style is perceived as very problematic because parents are emotionally uninvolved with their children and engaged only peripherally in their lives. Parents are minimally invested in their role as caretakers, and their disciplinary methods are erratic or inconsistent (Teyber & McClure, 2011). As a result, children have difficulty achieving social and academic competence because they have to negotiate these areas on their own without much parental guidance and support. They are also susceptible to sexual promiscuity, drug use, delinquency and criminal behavior (Cummings et al., 2000). Balswick, Balswick, Piper and Piper (2003) state that these "children often feel unloved, unprotected, and vulnerable. When hopelessness sets in, it leads to depression, apathy, anxiety, and acting-out behavior" (p. 23).

Parent-Child Relationship as Moderator
On the other hand, a positive parent-child relationship can be a protective or promotive factor in children's development. Children who have a close

relationship with their parents have higher self-esteem, exhibit better relationship skills, are more successful in school, and refrain from drug and alcohol abuse (Prior & Glaser, 2006; Rosen & Rothbaum, 2003). When parents are more involved with their children, children are less likely to become involved in problematic behaviors and are emotionally healthier (Schofield et al., 2012).

A close relationship with parents also serves as a protective factor specifically for children who display antisocial behaviors (Masten, 2001). Parents influence and alter their children's behavior by disciplining and providing consistent feedback that helps children behave in ways that are adaptive and socially acceptable. Discipline is particularly effective in promoting positive outcomes for these children when it is carried out in the context of a warm, sensitive relationship between parent and child. It is important to note that these interactions are dynamic. Though parenting influences children, children are not passive recipients of parental influences; rather, they also elicit certain behaviors and responses from parents. Therefore, the links between parenting practices and children's resilience are complex. For example, as infants, resilient children experience higher-quality parenting resources but are also more engaging for parents (Masten, 2001). That is, parental behavior may help children to behave in more prosocial ways, but these children's behaviors and characteristics may also elicit better parenting. It is important to recognize the complexity of the parent-child relationship from both psychological and theological viewpoints.

INTEGRATIVE THEMES IN PARENT-CHILD RELATIONSHIPS

The Role of Religion/Spirituality

Upon first glance, it might seem that religion encourages the unidirectional aspects of the parent-child relationship. In the Bible, greater responsibility is placed on parents for the outcomes of their children. Proverbs 22:6 says, "Start children off on the way they should go, and even when are old they will not turn from it." The onus is on parents to care for, guide and nurture children. Parents are the authority figures in children's lives and are responsible for their physical, emotional, social and spiritual development. The discipline of children is the responsibility of parents. However, children are also given specific charges in their interactions with their parents, including honoring and obeying parents (Ex 20:12; Prov 6:20; Eph 6:1). Although parents may arguably have more responsibility in leading the relationship, children can—and must—play an active role as well.

The parent-child relationship plays a significant role in the Christian faith and is exemplified in several passages in the Bible. In early Jewish tradition, parents played a major role in teaching their children about God and leading them in a spiritual path. The parent-child relationship is often compared to the relationship between God and his children. Additionally, God is often presented in the role of father. In the Old Testament, God is presented as the father of the Israelites (Deut 1:31). He is also presented as a father to the fatherless (Ps 68:5). The fatherhood of God is also present in the New Testament. Romans 8:15-17 says that we have the privilege as God's children to cry out to God as "*Abba*, Father." Perhaps one of the best pictures of God as father is presented in the parable of the prodigal son in Luke 15. In spite of the younger son's belligerence and disobedient behavior, the father continues to love and care for his son. When he returns home, the father is not judgmental or condemning but rather demonstrates deep compassion by restoring to the son what he has lost and celebrating his return home. What an amazing expression of unconditional love and acceptance by a father for his son and a picture of how God, as Father, welcomes and accepts us when we have wandered from him.

Hertel and Donahue (1995) tested the parallels between children's reports of parenting styles and the images of God reported by both children and parents. They found that the more parents viewed God as loving, the more the children viewed the parents as loving and in turn saw God as loving. These findings highlight the significance of the parent-child relationship for children's images of their parents and, in turn, images of God. In another study examining attachment to God and parents, McDonald, Beck, Allison and Norsworthy (2005) found:

> Respondents that reported coming from homes that were emotionally cold or unspiritual exhibited higher levels of avoidance of intimacy in their relationship to God, a trend consistent with a Dismissive attachment style. Overprotective, rigid, or authoritarian homes were associated with higher levels of both avoidance of intimacy and anxiety over lovability in relationship to God, a trend characterized by the Fearful attachment style. (p. 21)

These results indicate that negative parent-child relationships can precipitate both attachment problems and unhealthy or negative relationships with God.

Children as Gifts

Within the context of the family, the Bible clearly describes children as gifts from God to be loved and cherished, valued and protected. How can we value children as divine gifts? One of the primary ways that parents practically value children is through the quality of their relationship, including the effort and time they invest in them. Valuing children means providing a loving and caring atmosphere in the home and having expectations and goals for them that fit with who they are and where they are developmentally. It means providing adequate protection and security for their safety.

Balswick et al. (2003) present a theology of the parent-child relationship consisting of four elements: covenant, grace, empowerment and intimacy. The covenant is the unconditional commitment and love of parents toward their children. Knowing that nothing can separate them from the love of their parents and that they truly are gifts to their families helps in building children's sense of self and self-confidence. Grace, which includes forgiving and accepting forgiveness, develops from the security provided by the covenant love. Empowerment is nurtured in the atmosphere of forgiveness and acceptance created by parents and "comes through equipping, guiding, directing, affirming, encouraging, supporting, in order to help children develop their potential" (p. 37). As children are empowered, they are able to acquire mutual intimacy with their parents, which cycles back to a greater level of commitment to their covenant. Balswick et al. (2003) note that parent-child relationships may initially start with unidirectional love from parent to child but eventually become a bidirectional process, with children also exhibiting love for the parents. In contrast, this relationship can stagnate when we "fixate on contract rather than covenant, law rather than grace, possessive power rather than empowerment, and personal distance rather than intimacy" (p. 38).

Children's views of God are often shaped by their relationship with their parents. This is an awesome responsibility on parents and emphasizes the spiritual significance of parenting styles and practices. In the early psychoanalytic literature, Freud suggested that the "*imago*" of the father influenced children's representation of God (Rizzuto, 1979). Randour and Bondanza (1987) note that for Freud it was during the oedipal period that the child is able to finalize his or her representation of God "through the 'exaltation' and 'sublimation' of instinctual wishes toward the father" (p. 302). Others have suggested that the mother's influence plays a more significant role in the child's God representation because of the early connection between mother and child as the child catches the gaze of the mother (McDargh, 1983; Rizzuto, 1979). Lovinger (1984) contends that the perception of the mother as the good/idealized object serves as a foundation for the child's conception of God. In a study conducted by Seegobin et al. (2007) with college students, results indicated that a positive relationship with parents was correlated with a positive view of God. In fact, the strongest predictor of a positive relationship with God was a positive relationship with mother, which fits well with the attachment literature emphasizing the emotional bond between mother and child. Dickie et al. (1997) also found that when children saw parents as nurturing and powerful, especially when father was seen as nurturing and mother was seen as powerful, they saw God as both nurturing and powerful.

In terms of biblical examples, Abraham saw his son Isaac as a gift from God. When God told him that his children would be as numerous as the sand on the seashore and the stars in the sky, he was emphasizing that Isaac was indeed a significant gift from God (Gen 22:15-18). Hannah also saw Samuel as a gift from God. She was childless and felt despised because of it. She went to the temple and specifically prayed for a child, and when he was born, she recognized him as a gift from God and gave him to God as an act of gratitude (1 Sam 1:11, 27-28).

The shooting of twenty children and six adults at the Sandy Hook Elementary School in Newtown, Connecticut, in December 2012 prompted many parents to see their children as gifts. Through this painful experience and significant loss, one of the lessons learned is that as parents, we need to cherish our children as gifts from God because we do not know when they will be taken from us. The loss of a child is a difficult experience for any parent.

In contrast, one of the most striking areas where children are not seen as gifts of God is when they are aborted. In 2008, 1.21 million abortions were performed in the United States alone (see www.guttmacher.org/pubs/fb_induced_abortion.html). These children were rejected before they were born. Hopefully, as we begin to see children as gifts more clearly, we will stop these negative practices and value each child for their inherent worth.

Children as Persons

In a world where many children are used, abused and neglected, there is a significant need for children to be respected as persons. One of the implicit messages given to many children is that "children should be seen but not heard." Parents can give voice to their children by providing opportunities for them to share their needs, desires and concerns, and by opening the door to mutual communication. We can demonstrate respect for children by providing for their physical, mental, emotional and spiritual needs, a sign that they are real persons with real needs. Another manner is by giving them time and listening to what they have to say. We also respect them when we reason and talk with them at their level of development.

In the Gospels, Jesus demonstrated respect for children by the value he placed on them. He said, "If anyone causes one of these little ones—those who believe in me—to stumble, it would be better for them to have a large millstone hung around their neck and to be drowned in the depths of the sea" (Matthew 18:6). Offenses to children were taken that seriously by Jesus.

Christian parenting styles have been criticized because of the emphasis on the discipline of children and the desire for specific behavioral outcomes. They have also been criticized for using corporal punishment such as spanking. But Christian parents have also exhibited warmth and compassion in their parenting (Spilka et al., 2003). Parents who see their children as gifts from God treat their children with great respect and cherish the relationship with them.

Children as Agents

Of these three integrative themes, viewing children as agents seems to be the most difficult for parents to understand, because it involves recognizing children as moral and spiritual persons who can influence and teach them. Yet, often in the Gospels, Jesus spoke of the significant role of children in the kingdom of God. Gundry-Volf (2001) summarizes it concisely, stating:

> There are five main ways in which the significance of children is underscored in Jesus' teaching and practice. He blesses the children brought to him and teaches that the reign of God belongs to them. He makes children models of entering the reign of God. He also makes children models of greatness in the reign of God. He calls his disciples to welcome little children as he does and turns the service of children into a sign of greatness in the reign of God. He gives the service of children ultimate significance as a way of receiving himself and by implication the One who sent him. (p. 36)

An excellent example of a child as a moral and spiritual agent is the experience of Ruby Bridges. Robert Coles tells of his encounters in the early 1960s with Ruby Bridges, a six-year-old African American girl, which changed his life. On his way to a psychiatric session, he saw Ruby being escorted to school by federal marshals as the result of a federal court order to integrate the school. A mob of white people, many of them waving placards such as "God demands segregation," screamed threats and obscenities and waved their fists at her. Coles was surprised at the reaction of this young girl to her accusers, and it made a lasting impression on him. As Ruby walked through the mob, he noticed that she was moving her lips but could not hear what she said. He later learned that she was praying for God to forgive them for they did not know what they were doing, and that her response was influenced by her parents, church and community (Yancey, 1987). As a child, Ruby was influenced by her parents who took her to church, taught her about God and prayer, and empowered her to stand strong in the face of harsh opposition; she then became an agent of change in her home, school and community.

Christian parenting can play a significant role in furthering the perception of children as moral and spiritual agents. One model of parenting, known as Relationship-Empowerment Parenting, is based on notions of discipleship from the New Testament that encourage parents to help children look outside themselves toward engagement with and service to others (Balswick et al., 2003). The model emphasizes that

> empowerment begins with the recognition that children are uniquely gifted by God to make a significant contribution in the world. Whether the child is able-bodied or developmentally challenged, he or she has a purpose and meaning that can only be achieved by him or her. While affirming the specific strengths, talents, and gifts in each child, we should be careful to move with and not ahead of our children in terms of what we expect of them. In their own way and in their own time, they are able to meet expectations that are within their capacity and time-table. (p. 50)

Seeing children as moral and spiritual agents provides the opportunity for parents to become receptive to children's contribution. Boyatzis and Janicki (2003) examined parent-child communication about religion to determine whether unidirectional or bidirectional patterns were used. They indicate that bidirectional reciprocity occurred when "children and parents are mutually active in their religious communication and both behave in ways that may ultimately influence the other" (p. 254). They encouraged parents in the study to not correct the views of children and to withhold from sharing their own perspectives. They found that the majority of first conversations about religion were initiated by children. Additionally, children were active participants and frequently expressed their ideas about religion, and parents were open to the ideas of their children as they provided the space to express themselves without correcting them.

CONCLUSION

In this chapter, I have examined the parent-child relationship from the developmental psychopathology perspective. I discussed the importance of this relationship for both children and parents, emphasizing bidirectional influences. I also looked at the parent-child relationship through the dimensions of both normal and abnormal development. Finally, integrative themes were presented with a focus on children as divine gifts, respected persons, and moral and spiritual agents.

As I reflect on the bedtime conversation with my younger son presented at the beginning of this chapter, my responses to him in light of what I have covered in this chapter have changed significantly. We continue to have conversations about his desire to be a police officer, which I am careful not to dismiss. I see him even more as a gift from God to be cherished and nurtured, respect his perspective and desires, and with humility accept his role as a moral and spiritual agent in our family. Indeed, God is able to use our children to teach us kingdom principles and practices. Parents have an enormous responsibility for their children, but children also influence parents in significant ways.

PRACTICAL SUGGESTIONS

Clinical work focusing on the parent-child relationship involves assessment and interventions with both children and parents. Depending on the situation or presenting problem, we may see the child, the parent or both in therapy. If we are working primarily on the parent-child relationship, it may be best, if possible, to see both the child and the parent(s). Below are possible assessments or interventions that can be helpful in addressing the parent-child relationship.

Assessment

- Assessment of the parent-child relationship
  - The Parent-Child Relationship Inventory (Coffman, Guerin & Gottfried, 2006, p. 209) is completed by the parent and has five scales: *Satisfaction*

with Parenting: the degree of gratification derived from being a parent; *Involvement:* the level of engagement and familiarity with the child; *Communication:* how capably a parent communicates with his or her child; *Limit Setting:* a parent's perception of the effectiveness of discipline practices utilized; *Autonomy:* the parent's capacity to facilitate his or her child's independence.

- The Parenting Stress Index (Abidin, 1983) is a self-report measure completed by parents and has three domains: stresses related to child characteristics; stresses related to parent characteristics; stresses related to situational and demographic factors.

• Assessment of the nature of the attachment relationship—determines the closeness of the parent-child relationship and the level of security the child experiences.

- The Inventory of Parent and Peer Attachment—Revised for Children (Gullone & Robinson, 2005) is a self-report measure for youth (ages 9-15 years) to assess the quality of attachment to parents and peers. The three aspects of attachment assessed are trust, communication and alienation.

• Assessment of parenting styles—determine which of the four parenting styles is practiced in the home, in response to what types of situations, and the child's response to it.

- The Parenting Style Questionnaire (Robinson, Mandleco, Olsen & Hart, 1995) is a self-report measure completed by parents that identifies three parenting styles: authoritative, authoritarian and permissive.

• Assessment of family constellation with a genogram of the family will be helpful as you assess for the nature of the relationship between family members.

• Assessment of parent-child communication patterns—inquire about the communication patterns that parents use with their children and that children use to communicate with parents.

- Observation of parent-child communication in the session.

• Assessment for parental neglect, abuse or mistreatment

• Assessment of religiosity and spirituality of both parents and children using scales or interviews.

Interventions

Depending on the presenting problems, the following interventions may be helpful.

- Teaching parenting skills. Parenting skills cover a variety of areas, including problem solving, conflict resolution, negotiating and affirmation. A specific program that may be helpful is Child-Parent Relationship Training (VanderGast, Post & Kascsak-Miller, 2010), which assists parents in becoming the primary change agents in their home through the use of child-centered play sessions with their children.

- Teaching parent-child communication skills. These skills can be taught through in-session practice of skills such as listening, empathy and responding, and parents and children can practice at home.

- Facilitating parental acceptance of children and children's acceptance of parents. Emphasize the importance of mutual acceptance in the parent-child relationship, and assist both parents and children in acceptance of each other.

- Doing age-appropriate activities with children to help to build the relationship between parent and child. Having the child choose the activity can be very affirming.

- Addressing parental pathology. If the parent has difficulties that are affecting the parent-child relationship, these can be addressed in the therapy, or the parent can be referred out for therapy.

- Addressing child/adolescent pathology. Therapy sessions can be used to specifically address the difficulties or problems of the child (e.g., attention-deficit/hyperactivity disorder).

- Addressing religiosity or spirituality. Determine what interventions will facilitate the religious or spiritual needs or desires of the parent or child in order to improve their relationship (e.g., a forgiveness intervention).

5

The Marital and Parental Dyad

Mari L. Clements, Tara A. Guarino
and Laura C. Bartos

THE FIRST DOCUMENTED CASE OF MARITAL CONFLICT was the very first marriage, in which Adam blamed Eve for their sin (Gen 3:12). Marital conflict continued throughout the patriarchal narratives, and such marital dysfunction often involved children. For example, Sarah and Abraham clashed over Ishmael (Gen 21:8-11; see also Trible, 1984), and Rebekah conspired with Jacob to deceive Isaac (Gen 27; see also Teugels, 1994).

Within modern society, marital conflict is ubiquitous, as reflected in rates of divorce, domestic violence and distress. Divorce rates in the U.S. have remained stable at approximately 50% since 1980 (U.S. Census Bureau, 2011). Furthermore, 29.5% of households with children ($N = 10.5$ million households) were headed by single parents in 2008 (U.S. Census Bureau, 2011). In addition to divorce, domestic violence is an important concern for marriage. In a meta-analysis of 134 studies, Alhabib, Nur and Jones (2010) documented domestic violence against women in U.S. samples at rates ranging from 2% to 70%, with an overall lifetime prevalence rate in North America exceeding 30%. Furthermore, Halford (2011) reported high rates of relationship distress in married couples. The cumulative effect of these findings is that millions of children are impacted by their parents' conflict each year.

Given the long history and high prevalence of marital conflict, it is not surprising that a great deal of research has addressed the effects of marital conflict on children. Initial research efforts focused on the effects of divorce and father absence, but by the middle of the twentieth century, evidence suggesting the need to look beyond divorce had already begun to accumulate. In a study of 100 randomly selected families of divorce in Switzerland, Haffter (1948) documented multifinality, noting that many of these 210 children had normal and positive outcomes. He further suggested that the difficulties of children who had less positive outcomes could be traced to problematic pre-divorce family functioning.

Subsequent research has implicated exposure to marital conflict as a critical influence on children's functioning. For instance, researchers have found that the functioning of children of conflictual couples resembles that of children of recently divorced parents, and the functioning of both groups is significantly poorer than that of children of happily married parents (Amato, Loomis & Booth, 1995; Hetherington, 1999). Further supporting the role of conflict rather than divorce per se, most children of divorce are resilient, recovering within two to three years after the divorce (Hetherington, 1989).

Economic effects of divorce are arguably longer lasting, but their effects on children's outcomes have received only mixed research support. Noncustodial fathers typically do not experience economic difficulties post-divorce, but custodial mothers frequently do. However, most divorced mothers remarry, which typically returns their income levels to predivorce levels (Furstenberg, 1990). In a meta-analysis of 92 studies, Amato and Keith (1991) documented only weak support for the negative effects of the economic impact of divorce on children. In contrast, they found strong support for the role of conflict in predicting children's functioning. Given the key role of marital conflict in predicting children's outcomes, we have focused on this dimension of marital relations and its role in developmental psychopathology.

In this chapter, we first explore the models of transmission of marital conflict and the subsequent ways that such conflict engenders normal and abnormal development. Within the frame of normal development, we delineate dimensions of conflict and unpack how constructive forms of conflict may serve as protective factors. We then discuss contributions of the marital dyad to normal development and of child characteristics to marital functioning. In doing so, we emphasize the significant effect of context on the association between marital conflict and the development of the child.

We then address abnormal development, focusing on risk factors that leave children increasingly susceptible to negative influences of marital conflict. In addition, we explore protective factors that lead to resilience in the child, the marital dyad and the family unit. We subsequently present aspects of the marital dyad that act as moderators and mediators of other kinds of risks and outcomes. Finally, we address methods of prevention and intervention before concluding with an explication of integrative themes and practical suggestions for clinical work.

Models of Transmission

Various models have been proposed that link marital conflict and child difficulties. The transmission of marital conflict to children is best understood via the developmental psychopathology framework of pathways and mechanisms. Three key models that have received empirical support are the cognitive-contextual framework (Grych & Fincham, 1990), the emotional security theory (Cummings & Davies, 2010; Davies & Cummings, 1994), and the spill-over hypothesis (Erel & Burman, 1995), and researchers have also begun to examine potential genetic pathways of influence.

Cognitive-Contextual Framework

In the cognitive-contextual framework, Grych and Fincham (1990) proposed that children's appraisals of marital conflict serve as important mediators of such conflict and also guide their resulting coping responses. These appraisals are shaped by children's previous experiences of marital conflict, as well as their perspective-taking and causal reasoning skills.

In this model, cognition and affect are interrelated. Children's cognitions about the conflict inform their emotional response to conflict. Appraisals of threat and self-blame are associated with negative emotionality. In turn, children's emotions influence their appraisals of conflict.

Empirical investigations of the cognitive-contextual framework have supported several aspects of the model, including the hypothesized relations between negative emotionality and appraisals of threat and self-blame, and between greater negativity and both intense and child-focused conflicts (Grych & Fincham, 1993). Furthermore, research conducted with both older (i.e., 10- to 14-year-olds; Grych, Fincham, Jouriles & McDonald, 2000) and younger samples (i.e., 7- to 9-year-olds; McDonald & Grych, 2006) support the mediational role of children's appraisals in predicting their response to marital conflict. However, despite the compelling logic of the cognitive-contextual framework and the research support that has accumulated, this model has been the subject of less empirical investigation than the emotional security theory.

Emotional Security Theory

Drawing from both principles of attachment and marital conflict research, Cummings and Davies developed the emotional security theory (Davies & Cummings, 1994; Cummings & Davies, 2010). Cummings (1998) characterized the emotional security theory as building on and complementing the cognitive-contextual framework, while expanding a focus on emotionality in the family.

In this model, children are viewed as active processors of their parents' marital conflict and as motivated to protect and advance their own emotional security. In this framework, marital conflict threatens the stability of the family system, and thus alarms children. Children then seek to reduce their felt insecurity by activation of emotion regulation, internal representations and conflict exposure mechanisms.

Specifically, continuing exposure to marital conflict is thought to induce chronic emotional hyperarousal. Children's internal representations are shaped by their previous experiences with marital conflict and influence their assessments of threat, blame and relevance of marital conflict. Such changes in internal representations are hypothesized to explain why children of conflictual marriages do not habituate to, but rather become sensitized to, marital conflict. Finally, children may respond to felt insecurity by engaging in actions intended to stop, reduce or titrate their parents' marital conflict. Such behaviors range from direct intervention to distraction and, as noted below, tend to vary by age.

Nearly two decades of research on the emotional security theory has accumulated, much of it summarized in Cummings and Davies (2010). Based on this research, Cummings and Davies conclude that there is ample support for the emotional security theory as an explanatory mechanism that links marital conflict with children's outcomes.

Spill-Over Hypothesis

One important pathway by which marital conflict may affect children is through disruptions in the parent-child relationship. In this way, marital conflict is hypothesized to spill over into the parent-child relationship.

The spill-over hypothesis was developed in contrast to a buffering or compensatory hypothesis (see Coiro & Emery, 1998), in which parents in conflictual marriages were theorized to devote extra effort to protecting the parent-child relationship. That is, the parent-child relationship was prioritized, compensating for a marital relationship that was less supportive and satisfying.

Although some early research provided support for a compensatory model, particularly for mothers (e.g., Goldberg & Easterbrooks, 1984), most research has supported the spill-over hypothesis. In an important meta-analysis, Erel and Burman (1995) found strong support for the spill-over hypothesis and little support for a compensatory model. That is, across longitudinal and cross-sectional studies of community, at-risk and clinical samples, with children of varying ages, there was ample support for the idea that marital conflict contaminates parent-child interactions and little support for the idea that parents are able to effectively protect the positivity of the parent-child relationship in the context of a negative marital relationship. Notably, this was true regardless of whether the parents or children were the primary focus of the study. No matter how much parents may wish to buffer their children from negative effects of marital conflict, the data make clear that this is a difficult, if not impossible, task.

Parents engaged in conflict with one another are more likely to parent in an authoritarian rather than authoritative manner, to discipline inconsistently, and to become increasingly insensitive and emotionally unavailable (Zimet & Jacob, 2001). In addition, the spill-over hypothesis may operate through affect contagion, as the emotions of each family member are unconsciously mimicked and synchronized, and through enculturation, as familial values and goals are communicated overtly and subtly through language (Jenkins, Simpson, Dunn, Rasbash & O'Connor, 2005). In this way, spillover can affect children even without direct exposure or modeling of conflict within the family, thus heightening the emotional insecurity of the child and worsening cognitive-contextual factors (Zimet & Jacob, 2001).

Genetic Influences

In addition to models linking marital conflict to child functioning through primarily environmental mechanisms, researchers have begun to examine models including genetic mechanisms. For instance, Horwitz et al. (2011) reported that latent genetic factors accounted for 22% of the variance in overall family conflict, with the strongest links to parental aggressive personality. Similarly, in a study of monozygotic and dizygotic twins, Spotts, Prescott and Kendler (2006) documented heritability of both marital conflict (for both husbands and wives, but stronger for husbands) and warmth (for both spouses, but stronger for wives). Furthermore, Sturge-Apple, Cicchetti, Davies and Suor (2012) found that both oxytocin receptor and serotonin transporter genes were implicated in maternal warmth and sensitivity to the child in conflictual marriages.

These findings are suggestive of genetic risk factors for marital difficulties and family conflict that may be passed from parents to children, but little research has directly addressed genetic pathways linking marital difficulties to concurrent child adjustment problems. In two notable exceptions, Harden et al. (2007) and Schermerhorn et al. (2011) examined the functioning of children of monozygotic and dizygotic twins and the marital functioning of the twins. Harden et al. not only documented genetic contributions to marital conflict but also linked both marital difficulties and children's conduct problems to parental genetic predisposition to antisocial behavior. Using a similar design with a different sample, Schermerhorn et al. documented genetic contributions to marital conflict and children's internalizing and externalizing behaviors.

To be sure, the evidence for genetic transmission is equivocal. For example, Schermerhorn et al. (2011) found evidence for significant genetic influences only when child reports of family conflict were examined, with nonsignificant effects in the model including both parent and child reports. Similarly, using a nationally representative sample of both biological and adoptive families, Amato and Cheadle (2008) concluded that the evidence for a family environmental model (in which the link between children's behavior problems and marital conflict was accounted for by problematic environmental conditions for child socialization) was much stronger than the evidence for either a passive genetic model (in which marital conflict and child behavior problems are accounted for by genetic vulnerabilities) or a child effects model (in which children's behavior problems cause marital conflict). However, Amato and Cheadle also expressly acknowledged equifinality, in that an individual child's outcome may be influenced by family environment, genetic contributions, child characteristics, or a combination of the three.

Normal Development: Marital and Parental Dyad over the Course of Development

As members of a fallen world, all couples experience some degree of marital conflict. If all children, then, live in families in which conflict is unavoidable, what distinguishes the children whose development is significantly impacted by marital conflict from the children whose development progresses more normatively? The developmental psychopathology approach emphasizes the value of understanding normal development in order to shed light on abnormal development; abnormal development can be understood as the inhibition of normal development. Although characteristics of children and families mediate the relationship between marital conflict and child development, dimensions of the conflict itself play a major role in determining the extent to which conflict affects child development. That is, it is the nature of the conflict rather than its occurrence that is critical to understanding its effects on children (Grych & Fincham, 2001).

Dimensions of Conflict

By emphasizing how psychopathology develops through pathways of abnormal development, developmental psychopathology focuses on the significant effects of context at the individual, familial, and societal levels. The critical dimensions of intensity, frequency, content and resolution determine the impact of marital conflict on children (Grych & Fincham, 1990). These dimensions of marital conflict do much to expose the nature of the conflict and the subsequent ways in which conflict is understood by children. Intensity and frequency of conflict often go hand in hand; indeed, chronic exposure to conflict renders children more likely to react to future conflict with distress, disturbance and heightened reactivity (Davies & Cummings, 1994). Both highly intense and frequent conflicts are associated with elevated child internalizing and externalizing behaviors, and this association is particularly pronounced when the conflict involves physical aggression (Parke, 2004). The intensity and frequency of conflict distinguishes the kind of discord that exists as a natural element of the family system from pronounced or persistent antagonism that endangers healthy child development. Accordingly, when conflict remains high, children are more likely to suffer emotional, social and behavioral problems (Zimet & Jacob, 2001).

The content of marital conflict also partially determines the impact that conflict has on the child. Specifically, when children themselves are the subject of the conflict, such as when parents argue over discipline, child activities or other dimensions of child rearing, children exhibit more externalizing and internalizing behavior and experience more shame, self-blame, and a guilty sense of responsibility for the conflict (Jenkins et al., 2005; Zimet & Jacob, 2001).

Resolution. One particularly important positive dimension of marital conflict is its resolution. Cummings and colleagues have repeatedly demonstrated that the resolution of marital conflict abates much of its negative power. Cummings et al. (2000) noted that constructive conflicts that are fully resolved may not cause any distress for children, and that both explanation and resolution significantly reduce children's negative reactions and emotional responses to marital conflict, restoring children's emotional equilibrium and sense of family stability. Furthermore, these positive effects are not all-or-nothing: Conflicts need not be completely resolved nor explanations be of any significant depth in order to benefit the child. When parents partially resolve conflict or communicate that the conflict has been or will be resolved, children also have reduced distress (Cummings et al., 2000), and these results accrue even when explanations are incomplete or resolutions are not directly witnessed (Parke, 2004).

Constructive versus destructive conflict. As noted previously, marital conflict is sufficiently widespread so as to be considered normative; however, all conflict is not equal in its effects on family members. Constructive conflict management has been shown to positively affect children by providing positive models of conflict behaviors. Research indicates that observing conflict behaviors such as support, problem solving and affection between parents is beneficial for children and their development (see Cummings & Davies, 2010), and that even infants can discriminate between constructive and more negative marital conflict (Du Rocher Schudlich, White, Fleischhauer & Fitzgerald, 2011).

Family Factors Facilitating Positive Development

A developmental psychopathology approach also emphasizes the value of protective factors, which can preserve normal development or lead to resilience. A positive marital relationship is foundational for healthy family functioning, forming the basis for successful child emotional and social development, conflict management, and parenting. Marital satisfaction has been associated with family cohesion, secure parent-child attachments and positive coparenting, all of which influence children's development of sense of self and expectations of others (Cummings et al., 2000; Dickstein, Seifer & Albus, 2009).

Family cohesion. Children's emotional security is linked to marital conflict through the ways in which children interpret meaning and consequences of the marital conflict for their own well-being. These interpretations form the basis of internal representations reflecting their evaluation of family functioning, relationships and events. Because children's emotional security is so affected by marital conflict, children regulate their emotional security by controlling their exposure to the conflict. Children in high-conflict homes often manage interparental conflict through over-involvement in or direct efforts to control parental emotions (e.g., Cummings & Davies, 2010). As Thompson and

Calkins (1996) articulated, however, short-term effectiveness at influencing interparental conflict comes at potential long-term cost as children take on the developmentally inappropriate role of their parents' marital therapist.

Attachment. Children are more likely to form secure attachments to their parents when the parents are securely attached to each other. Insecure attachments between parents and children have also been linked to the parents' own insecure attachment histories, but a secure marital attachment appears to buffer the effects of a parent's own insecure attachment history. In turn, insecure marital attachment is associated with more marital conflict. Therefore, parental attachment history and marital attachment is important to children's development and adjustment (Cummings et al., 2000).

Internal working models are based on relationship history, and they inform a person's pattern of social interactions. Research on adult attachment working models has focused on early care-giving relationships and current intimate relationships. Mothers' working models of their early care-giving relationships are strongly linked to the development of the mother-child relationship, and adult working models of marriage influence the extent to which the marital dyad operates from a secure base toward effective parenting, employment and safety in the marital relationship in times of stress (Dickstein et al., 2009). In their review of the literature, Dickstein and colleagues (2009) documented associations between maternal insecure adult attachment and an array of child developmental problems, including toddler sleep disorders, infant failure to thrive, and dysregulated infant-mother attachment and attunement. Furthermore, Dickstein et al. (2009) found that couple and family functioning mediated the relationship between maternal adult attachment security and infant-mother attachment. The development of the mother-child relationship was influenced by the mother's capacity to trust, regulate and maintain perspective, which is informed by the mother's attachment history.

Coparenting. Coparenting can be viewed as lying at the intersection of the marital system and the parent-child system. Specifically, in the context of intact families, coparenting is the dimension of the marital dyad that directly pertains to child rearing, and includes factors such as couple alliance, supporting or undermining the other parent, and division of childcare labor (McHale, Kuersten-Hogan & Rao, 2004).

Morrill, Hines, Mahmood and Córdova (2010) showed that coparenting was more highly related to both marital quality and individual parenting than these two latter constructs were to each other. They found that coparenting mediates the relation between marital quality and parenting, accounting for almost all of the association between these two constructs. They further suggested that the couple alliance dimension of coparenting is particularly important for the quality of both the marriage and parenting. This dimension includes the parents' investment in the child, the valuing of one another's involvement with the child, respect for each other's judgment in child rearing, and the desire to communicate about the child.

The view of coparenting as the mediator between marital quality and parenting has characterized much of the literature. Specifically, marital quality has been argued to impact coparenting, which subsequently impacts parenting. However, Morrill et al. (2010) demonstrated equal support for this model and for a competing model in which coparenting directly and simultaneously impacts both marital quality and parenting. Thus, they concluded that the relationship between marital quality and coparenting is likely reciprocal, with parents' perception of their coparenting affecting marital quality and parenting effectiveness. Coparenting was seen to influence the marital relationship through collaboration, teamwork and family warmth, but also to be influenced by the marital relationship through behaviors such as spousal social support. Finally, they noted that couples with weak coparenting had greater vulnerability to hostility and competition. Such reciprocal pathways are prototypical of the field of developmental psychopathology.

Parent gender and parenting. Research on gender differences in the relation between marital conflict and parenting has been quite mixed. However, it may be more challenging for men to separate the marital and parental subsystems, as there is some suggestion that fathers' parenting is more disrupted by marital difficulties than is mothers' (e.g., Belsky, Youngblade, Rovine & Volling, 1991; Coiro & Emery, 1998; Morrill et al., 2010). One reason for this may be the contexts in which fathers' and mothers' parenting occurs. In infancy and early childhood, when parent-child relationships are emerging, mothers typically spend much more time with their children than do fathers. As a result, mothers' relationships with their children develop in both dyadic and whole family contexts whereas fathers may spend the majority of their time with their children also in the presence of the mother. With such contextual overlap, it may be more difficult for the father-child relationship to develop independently of the marital relationship.

Effects of the Marital and Parental Dyad on Normal Development

There are many stage-salient tasks that children master at particular ages over the course of development; however, handling marital conflict is not among them. Marital conflict is a challenge that children face through every stage of development, but their response to the conflict and their development of psychopathology varies according to an array of mediators and moderators (Cummings et al., 2000).

Age has been argued to moderate the relationship between marital conflict and child outcomes, but assessment of the role of age in this association is complicated by the successive integration of stage-salient tasks, the accumulation of exposure to conflict over time and the transient nature of parental interactions (Cummings & Davies, 2010). Research on child age and marital conflict has been markedly mixed, suggesting both that marital conflict and child maladjustment have a stronger association in younger children than older children (e.g., Mahoney, Jouriles & Scavone, 1997) and that adolescents may be more vulnerable to marital conflict than younger children (e.g., Cummings, Schermerhorn, Davies, Goeke-Morey & Cummings, 2006).

As children develop, they adapt to the stage-salient tasks in succession. A secure marital base supports children's development, whereas marital conflict may interrupt this process and delay the mastery of important emotional and social skills (Cummings & Davies, 2010). Children's problem-solving strategies improve with development as they increase their ability to utilize causal information in each situation (Covell & Miles, 1992). Although children are vulnerable to marital conflict at every age, specific vulnerabilities and expressions of vulnerability may differ with age (Cummings et al., 2000).

Children of different ages exhibit differences in their patterns of responding to marital conflict, and the determination of the effect of accumulated exposure is complicated by the transient nature of parenting. Parents, in addition to their children, experience personal, marital and parental development through the changes and challenges of life. Such changes result in inevitable vicissitudes in the family environment and in the marital conflict to which children are exposed (Cummings & Davies, 2010).

Infancy. Parents interact with young children differently than they do with adolescents, but research has been mixed about whether parents feel comfortable arguing in front of infants or feel the need to shield infants from the conflict (for a review, see Zimet & Jacob, 2001). Infants as young as five months have displayed differentiated emotional and behavioral reactions to constructive versus destructive or depressive marital conflict (Du Rocher Schudlich et al., 2011).

Preschool. Disruptions in the child's relationship with a caretaker subsequent to marital conflict have been shown to lead to emotion dysregulation which in turn may disrupt stage-salient tasks in toddlerhood such as the development of peer relationships (Cummings & Davies, 2010). Preschool children are attuned to marital conflict and respond with self-blame, distress and involvement (Ablow & Measelle, 2010), and they have both low levels of perceived competence in coping and limited emotion regulation abilities and coping skills (Cummings & Davies, 2010).

For these reasons, preschool children become overwhelmed by marital conflict, show high sensitivity to unresolved and chronic conflicts, and respond with behavioral distress to even normative marital conflict (Cummings & Davies, 2010; Cummings et al., 2000). However, these younger children also effectively intervene in their parents' conflicts at higher rates than older children (Covell & Miles, 1992). Note, however, that such regulation and intervention has significant negative long-term consequences (Thompson & Calkins, 1996).

School age. Young children struggle to distinguish between resolved and unresolved conflicts, and they tend to exhibit behavioral problems and react with a greater sense of helplessness than do older children (for reviews, see Cummings et al., 2000; Zimet & Jacob, 2001). In particular, seven- to nine-year-old children seem to have trouble matching their cognitive, social and behavioral skills, and continue to believe that their direct intervention strategies will be effective when, according to parents, they no longer are (Covell & Miles, 1992). These children are at a double disadvantage in that they are ineffective in verbally pleading for their parents to stop fighting and they have greater negative responses to unresolved anger than do either younger (4- to 6-year-old) or older (10- to 12-year-old) children.

Adolescence. Whereas younger children exhibit behavioral problems in association with marital conflict, older children tend to experience affect problems, particularly heightened emotional insecurity (Cummings et al., 2006). Older children have gained social skills, including perspective-taking, which increase their concern for their parents and family functioning. As a result, adolescents feel an obligation to intervene in marital conflict more than any other age group, and may more often become enmeshed in parental conflict (for a review, see Zimet & Jacob, 2001). Despite strong urges to intervene, adolescents (as well as their parents) report that their direct intervention strategies are not effective in alleviating marital conflict. Furthermore, the knowledge that they cannot lessen parental anger can leave preteens and adolescents at a loss in terms of coping with marital conflict (Covell & Miles, 1992).

Marital quality has also been shown to influence adolescents' religious behaviors and development. Working with a large, nationally representative sample, Day et al. (2009) found that adolescents who reported both close relationships with their parents and close marital relationships between their parents had higher levels of religious convictions and church attendance than did adolescents who reported difficulties in either set of relationships. Of course, families' religious commitments may also play a role in their marital and parent-child relationships, so these observed associations may be reciprocal.

Child Factors That Affect the Development of the Marital and Parental Dyad
Clearly the way parents navigate marriage and parenting has dramatic effects on the parent-child relationship, child outcomes and adjustment, but parents are not the sole contributors to this phenomenon. Cummings et al. (2010) argued that children's characteristics and behavior are properly considered to have reciprocal relations with marital and parent-child relationships.

Child behavior. Marital conflict is more likely to end positively and with effective resolution when children show regulated and agentic behavior during marital conflict. Conversely, marital conflict is more likely to end negatively and without resolution when children exhibit negative emotions and dysregulated behavior during interparental conflict (Cummings et al., 2010). Specifically, children's externalizing behaviors as a response to marital conflict can operate in a negative feedback loop by increasing such conflict (Cummings et al., 2010). As a child's externalizing behavior escalates, parents become increasingly likely to argue about the child, a relation that is particularly pronounced in stepfamilies (Jenkins et al., 2005). That is, in the context of interparental conflict, children may engage in externalizing behavior. This behavior may intensify antagonism between the parents and direct the content of the argument toward the child, further heightening the very elements of marital conflict that most directly endanger the healthy adjustment of the child.

Child disabilities. Most research examining marital functioning in families of children with disabilities has focused on the effects of the marriage on either children's adjustment or parents' adjustment. In studies of child adjustment, marital difficulties were associated with poorer sibling relationships in families with a child with autism (Rivers & Stoneman, 2003); more aggression, inhibition and sleep disturbance in children with cleft lip (Starr, 1981); and more severe behavior problems in children with mental retardation or pervasive developmental disorder (Floyd & Zmich, 1991; Siman-Tov & Kaniel, 2011).

In studies of parental adjustment, marital difficulties were associated with lower parental sensitivity for fathers of children with Down syndrome or cleft lip and/or palate (Pelchat, Bisson, Bois & Saucier, 2003), more negative parent-child interactions and lower parenting confidence for mothers and fathers of children with mental retardation (Floyd & Zmich, 1991), and more parenting stress for both mothers and fathers and lower parenting efficacy for mothers of children with developmental disabilities (Kersh, Tedvat, Hauser-Cram & Warfield, 2006).

Research on the effects of child disabilities on marriage has been far more limited, but there is widespread belief that having a child with a major disability such as autism leads to increased risk for divorce (cf. Freedman, Kalb, Zablotsky & Stuart, 2012). However, two recent large, population-based surveys have revealed that children with disabilities are no more likely to reside in single-parent homes than are children without disabilities (Freedman et al., 2012; Hatton, Emerson, Graham, Blacher & Llewellyn, 2010). Similarly, several researchers have found no differences in marital functioning between families with children with a disability and families with typically developing children. For instance, there were no significant group differences in marital hostility (Nixon & Cummings, 1999), family cohesion or adaptability (Tsibidaki & Tsamparli, 2009), or self-reported marital satisfaction (Floyd & Zmich, 1991; Starr, 1981; Tunali & Power, 2002; Wieland & Baker, 2010). These findings were obtained in samples contrasting families with typically developing children to families with children with disorders including autism, mental retardation, cleft lip and cerebral palsy.

On the other hand, Risdal and Singer (2004) reached a somewhat different conclusion in a meta-analysis of thirteen studies involving 6,270 families of children with disabilities and 48,254 families of typically developing children. They documented a small but reliable difference in rates of marital distress, separation and divorce, with all of these more common in families of children with disabilities. Similarly, although there were no differences in their self-reports of marital satisfaction, Floyd and Zmich (1991) found that parents of

mentally retarded children engaged in significantly less positive marital interactions, more marital negative reciprocity, and more aversive parent-child interactions than did parents of typically developing children.

Risdal and Singer (2004) directly commented on the multifinality observed
in marriages of parents of children with disabilities. They noted that some
"families are strengthened and children with disabilities are viewed as contributors to family quality of life," but that "does not, however, negate the finding
that having a child with a disability can . . . be challenging and stressful, placing
a strain on some marriages" (p. 101). Freedman et al. (2012) attributed divergent
findings to sampling differences, with few significant differences arising in
population-based studies, and Hatton et al. (2010) found that socioeconomic
disadvantage accounted for all the variance in marital outcome in a population-
based study of parents of children with cognitive delays and parents of typically
developing children. Freedman and colleagues further identified spousal
support as particularly important for parents of children with disabilities,
serving both as a resource for couples and a constraint to divorce. That is, the
potential loss of one's primary support relationship is a daunting possibility for
parents coping with the stressors of caring for a child with disabilities.

Temperament. Child temperament can have a positive or negative effect on
children's emotional security and related social development. Children with
more difficult temperaments may become more susceptible to particular inse-
curities, as they tend to react strongly to stress, including that caused by marital
conflict. In contrast, children with easier temperaments may be buffered from
conflict and more resilient to marital conflict and hostility. Aggressive temperament places children at particularly heightened risk. School-aged and
toddler boys with aggressive temperaments demonstrated the greatest response
and arousal when exposed to marital conflict (Cummings et al., 2000).

Child temperament has also been shown to influence the coparenting relationship. Particularly from the perspective of mothers, coparenting is less supportive and effective after marital conflict when the child has a difficult temperament (Dush, Kotila & Schoppe-Sullivan, 2011).

Gender. Although the subject of much research, the role of child gender in
response to marital conflict remains unclear. Cummings et al. (2000) noted a
progression of the findings. In early research focusing on externalizing behavior and marital conflict, boys were initially identified as experiencing
greater distress than girls. More recent research has demonstrated that girls

experience comparable distress, albeit manifested in different, and usually more socially acceptable, ways (e.g., anxiety and worry). In fact, girls have been argued to be more affected by marital conflict than are boys, possibly due to girls' greater sensitivity and emotional reactivity to dimensions of conflict, such as resolution, parental conflict history, and discrimination between constructive and destructive conflict. However, other research does not indicate differences in the reactions of boys and girls in the face of conflict, with both genders evidencing aggressive behavioral response patterns.

Parent and child dyads. Cummings and colleagues (2000) reported that the research on the interactive effects of parent and child gender is similarly unclear. Some research indicates that children's perceptions of the father-child relationship are more impacted by marital conflict than are their perceptions of the mother-child relationship. However, in other studies, girls have exhibited more negative emotionality than boys in response to their father's conflict behavior but not to their mother's. Such research suggests a cross-gender dyad phenomenon, in which father-daughter relationships are especially likely to decline with an increase of marital conflict. Similarly, mother-son relationships have also been shown to be more negatively influenced by interparental conflict than mother-daughter or father-son relationships.

Abnormal Development

As noted previously, there are a number of areas of development endangered by severe marital conflict. Children from conflictual homes are at risk for lower academic achievement, particularly when they blame themselves for marital conflict (Harold, Aitken & Shelton, 2007). Marital conflict is also a risk factor for sleep problems in infants, toddlers and school-age children (Keller & El-Sheikh, 2011; Mannering et al., 2011), likely due to negative effects of family stress on children's neurobiological functioning.

The health of the marital dyad affects the capacity of the child to regulate emotions (Parke, 2004). This seems to be a consequence of the way in which marital conflict threatens children's emotional security, rendering them less capable of effectively regulating emotions when they do arise (Davies & Cummings, 1994). Emotion regulation is important in several ways. Poor emotion regulation skills play a significant role in child maladjustment, and poor emotion regulation skills also put children at increased risk of reacting negatively to future marital conflict (Morris et al., 2007).

In response to marital conflict, children with more negative emotionality had more internalizing problems, whereas children with more adaptive emotion regulation responded more positively to such discord (Morris et al., 2007). Thus, emotion regulation capabilities may be conceptualized as both risk and protective factors against the potentially detrimental effects of marital conflict.

Marital conflict and aggression also impact a child's proclivity to bullying. Christie-Mizell (2003) found that interparental discord created a hostile and negative family environment that was internalized by the child, and this internalization had profound effects on the child's developing self-concept. The child's self-concept, then, directly impacted bullying behavior. Whether or not the child was a direct target of parental hostility, the overall aggressive environment led to the child's behavioral disruption.

The Marital and Parental Dyad as Risk Factor

Across research on the effects of the marital dyad on child development, conflict emerges as a critical risk factor for the development of child maladjustment in various areas of functioning. Marital conflict puts children at risk for behavioral, emotional, physiological and relational repercussions across the lifespan (e.g., Cummings & Davies, 2010).

As an example of this rich research literature, Katz and Woodin (2002) identified more nuanced forms and expressions of marital conflict that differentially affect the child's development. Specifically, couples characterized as hostile-detached—those who both attack when speaking and withdraw when listening—created negative family environments that were detrimental to their children. These children showed more maladjustment and peer difficulties than did children of couples who were either solely hostile or solely detached. Children of hostile-detached parents received impoverished models for intimacy, learning instead that families operate via competing assertions of power. The problems of hostile-detached marital dyads in both speaking and listening engendered a family system in which cohesion and play were replaced with parental coerciveness and child externalizing.

Marital aggression. Marital aggression is also particularly detrimental to children. As noted previously, women's lifetime prevalence rate for domestic violence in North America is over 30% (Alhabib et al., 2010). As a result, large numbers of children are exposed to this stressor. Zimet and Jacob (2001) noted that across the literature, children of mothers who are victims of physical violence were almost 20% more likely to evidence clinical levels of maladjustment than were children of mothers who are not abused. In a sample of low-income families, Owen, Thompson, Shaffer, Jackson and Kaslow (2009) documented the negative effects of interparental physical aggression on the cohesion of that family, the mental health of the mother and the extent to which family members are able to relate to one another. Not surprisingly, Owen and colleagues found that these effects were associated with deterioration in the adjustment of the child.

Child characteristics also interact with marital characteristics. For instance, Cummings, El-Sheikh, Kouros and Buckhalt (2009) found that intimate partner aggression was most detrimental to children who had more negative emotional reactivity, lower levels of parasympathetic nervous system activity and dysregulated behavior.

Role reversal. Parental role reversal is an additional mechanism by which conflict in the marital dyad adversely affects child development. In role reversal, the parent-child relationship grows increasingly focused on addressing and fulfilling the needs of the parent rather than the needs of the child. Because the parent's needs are not fulfilled in a conflictual marital relationship, the parent looks outside this relationship for support and affirmation. Macfie, Houts, Pressel and Cox (2008) pinpointed a crossover effect in which conflict directed from the father toward the mother causes the mother to engage in role reversal with the child, and conflict directed from the mother toward the father causes the father to engage in role reversal. Role reversal may negatively affect infants' secure attachment and toddlers' autonomy and self-regulation, because the overly close parent-child relationship can impair emotion regulation.

Coparenting. Marital conflict also takes a toll on coparenting (Katz & Woodin, 2002), but the relationship between conflict and coparenting is mediated by a number of factors. Particularly intriguing research illuminates the kind of coparenting that persists even after a marriage has ended. Dush et al. (2011) found that parents whose relationship was of a higher quality prior to the end of the marriage showed increasingly positive post-divorce coparenting success as time progressed. These parents may build on previous skills in order to effectively coparent their child independent of the marital dissolution. However, Dush and colleagues also found that maternal involvement with a new partner significantly decreased post-divorce coparenting success, with both mothers and fathers reporting decreased supportive coparenting when mothers were involved in new relationships.

The Marital and Parental Dyad as Moderator and/or Mediator

The marital dyad impacts child adjustment not only directly but also through mediated channels. The state of the marital dyad affects how each parent interacts with the child, and these dynamics, in conjunction with the main effects of conflict, often put children of conflictual homes at risk. As marital conflict increases, parents expend less energy and engage in fewer agreeable interactions with their child (Fishman & Meyers, 2000). Mothers in particular showed a sharp distinction between the amounts of time they were able to spend with their child when the marital dyad was healthy versus conflictual. Children with reduced parental attention had higher levels of sadness and conflict with peers.

Parent gender. Children may also respond differentially to parental expressions of conflict based on the gender of the parent responding. Goeke-Morey and Cummings (2007) found that children respond differentially to fathers' and mothers' expressions of emotion during marital conflict. Children experience emotional insecurity most strongly when witnessing their mother's fear and sadness and their father's fear and anger. The father's expressions of general vulnerability put the child at even greater risk for maladjustment than do the mother's. That is, marital conflict enhanced the negative effects of the father's depressed mood on the child. In a like manner, children responded more positively when their father engaged in constructive conflict. Goeke-Morey and Cummings noted that this pattern is consistent with the notion that children rely on the father as a figure of stability and security.

Parental mental health. Parent factors have been shown to mediate the relation between marital conflict and child outcome. Parental mental health is one such important factor. Owen et al. (2009) found that the mental health of the mother as well as the child's conception of the health of the family unit mediated the relationship between intimate partner violence and the effect on the child's adjustment. Similarly, Papp, Goeke-Morey and Cummings (2004) found that mothers' psychological symptomatology interacted with marital functioning to impact child adjustment. On the one hand, children of mothers with psychopathology were most at risk for maladjustment when their mother's disorder was accompanied by marital conflict. On the other hand, a healthy marital dyad served as a protective factor, diminishing the detrimental effects of maternal symptomatology on children's adjustment.

Specifically, marital conflict exacerbates the effect of depression on the child. As mentioned previously, fathers' depressive symptoms remain salient to children, and marital conflict seems to strengthen the link between fathers' depressive symptoms and children's internalizing symptoms, particularly when the conflict involves negativity that is covert on the part of the father and overt on the part of the mother (Keller, Cummings, Peterson & Davies, 2009). Depressed fathers may respond to marital conflict with feelings of helplessness and worthlessness, sentiments that may be catalyzed by the mother's overt threats, defensiveness and similar behaviors. Keller and colleagues (2009) concluded that because the relationship between the father's depressive symptoms, marital discord and child adjustment resulted in internalizing behaviors in the child, there were parallels between fathers' conflict behaviors, their psychological symptoms and their children's responses. It may be that the father's psychological state affects the child most robustly through its concurrent impact on the marital dyad.

Child factors. Child factors also mediate the relation between marital conflict and child adjustment. As specified by both the cognitive-contextual framework (Grych & Fincham, 1990) and the emotional security theory (Cummings & Davies, 2010), a child's cognitions about marital conflict influence coping. For instance, child beliefs that marital conflict is chronic, global or child-focused are associated with higher levels of perceived threat and self-blame (Grych & Fincham, 1993; Grych et al., 2000). In turn, perceptions of threat and self-blame are associated with poorer child adjustment. In this way, child appraisals serve as a powerful mediator of the effects of marital conflict.

In addition, children attempt to reduce their emotional insecurity by adjusting their behavior to impact their parents' marital conflict (Davies & Cummings, 1994). Such coping efforts may target their own emotional response (emotion-focused) or their parents' interactions (problem-focused). In a review of the literature, Zimet and Jacob (2001) concluded that emotion-focused coping in the context of the relatively uncontrollable stressor of marital conflict may function as a protective factor whereas problem-focused coping may increase the child's risk of maladjustment. Even when a child successfully intervenes in interparental conflict, the long-term effects of this sense of control and responsibility are detrimental (Thompson & Calkins, 1996).

Contextual factors including the child's memory of previous interparental conflict, the parents' conflict-induced behaviors and the strength of the child's interpersonal relationships have been argued to moderate the effect of marital conflict as well (Zimet & Jacob, 2001). Specifically, greater child experience with destructive marital conflict has been shown to heighten reactivity to such conflict. Similarly, more negative parental conflict behaviors have been associated with poorer child outcomes, and stronger familial and extrafamilial relationships have been shown to buffer child outcomes (for a review, see Cummings & Davies, 2010).

However, it may be the case that most moderators do not act in a consistent fashion across individuals. In a meta-analysis of sixty-eight studies, Erel and Burman (1995) examined thirteen potential moderators of the relation between marital conflict and parent-child relations, including child factors (e.g., gender, birth order, age), parent factors (e.g., gender, both solely and as contrasted with child gender; clinical, stressed or community sample type), and study factors (e.g., definition of marital quality, definition of parent-child quality, types of ratings, longitudinal vs. cross-sectional nature of study, between-subjects versus within-subjects design, target of observation and type of publication). They found that none of these moderators accounted for significant variability in the relation between marital quality and parenting. They thus concluded that the relation between marital conflict and child maladjustment was quite stable.

Prevention and Intervention

A major focus of the developmental psychopathology approach is the insight provided by prevention and intervention to the understanding of abnormal development. Developmental psychopathology pursues the prevention of abnormal development by addressing risk factors and intervention to encourage normal development by maximizing protective factors.

As applied to marital conflict, the effects of intervention for interparental conflict on children's behaviors shed light on the interrelatedness of family functioning. Such literature is fairly limited, but encouraging. In four separate studies of children with acting-out behaviors, researchers have demonstrated the efficacy of treating marital issues alongside children's behavior problems (Dadds, Schwartz & Sanders, 1987; Sayger, Horne & Glaser, 1993; Snow, 1992; Stedman, 1977).

All four studies demonstrated reductions in child behavior problems, but Dadds et al. (1987) further demonstrated greater maintenance of treatment gains in maritally conflictual families. In the only study of the four in which treatment of the marital dyad was the only intervention, Snow (1992) found that children of parents receiving conjoint marital therapy had lower teacher ratings of child difficulties than did children of parents receiving individual treatment. Taken together, these studies provide evidence that alleviating marital conflict yields significant improvement in children's functioning.

INTEGRATIVE THEMES

Value Children as Divine Gifts

The role of children as divine gifts to parents is repeatedly made clear in Scripture: children are prayed for (1 Sam 1:10-27), schemed for (Gen 19:30-36), rejoiced over (Gen 21:3-8; Jn 16:21), and viewed as blessings (2 Kings 4:13-16; Job 42:12-13). Childless women were seen as objects of reproach (Gen 30:23), scorn (Gen 16:5) or shame (Is 54:1-4), in some cases with the direct implication that childlessness or infant death was judgment for sin (2 Sam 6:20-23; 12:14-18; 1 Kings 14:9-12; Hos 9:11-14). Some women went so far as to use their female servants as surrogates to bear children (Gen 16:1-2; 30:3-6, 9-10).

Given these dynamics, it is not surprising that childbearing conflicts are also documented in Scripture (Gen 16:4-5; 30:1-3; see also Trible, 1984), and that disputes about children remain a significant source of marital conflict (e.g., Stanley, Markman & Whitton, 2002). It is painfully paradoxical that their treasured status may result in contentiousness that deeply harms children.

Respect Children as Persons

Ephesians provides direction for family processes. The caution against exasperating one's children (Eph 6:4) provides explicit acknowledgment of the autonomy of children, and both Ephesians and Proverbs charge parents to provide instruction and training to foster their children's development (e.g., Eph 6:4; Prov 22:6). Finally, the well-known instruction on mutual submission (Eph 5:21) provides a foundation for all respectful family relationships, including parent-child relationships. Children's observation and experience of the mutual respect and concern exhibited by their parents provides a theological framework for relationships as characterized by grace and covenant commitment (Balswick & Balswick, 2007; Cook, Buehler & Blair, 2013).

With regard to marital conflict, it is critical that parents recognize the detrimental effects of poorly managed conflict on their children and their developing sense of self (Christie-Mizell, 2003). Even young children are active processors of their environment (Grych & Fincham, 1990), and respect for children entails recognition of aspects of that environment that may be harmful to them.

Children as Moral and Spiritual Agents

Scripture makes it clear that children bear responsibility for their actions (Prov 20:11). At the same time, children's cognitive and reasoning abilities are expressly not equal to those of adults (Is 10:19; 1 Cor 13:11), and children require protection from and by adults (Ex 22:22; Prov 23:10-11; Mt 18:4-6). As applied to maritally conflictual families, these scriptures convey the need for both parents and children to accept their responsibilities, but the greater weight falls on the adults to provide an appropriate environment that enables children to develop as moral and spiritual agents. That is, children's moral development occurs in the context of the family, and emotional insecurity engendered by marital conflict could easily derail optimal development in this area. Interactions with the parent as a moral agent are fundamental to the child's internalization of moral agency (Kochanska, 2002), and parent-child interactions have been shown to be compromised in frequency and emotional tone by marital conflict (cf. Cummings & Davies, 2010).

CONCLUSION

Both the marital relationship (e.g., Hos 1:2; Eph 5:25; Rev 19:7-9; 21:9, 12) and the parent-child relationship (e.g., Mt 7:11, Eph 5:1, Rom 8:16; 9:8) are used in Scripture as metaphors for God's relationship with his people. It is therefore not surprising that these relationships would also be foundational to human interactions. Several theologians have explicitly noted the central role of the family in the spiritual formation of children (e.g., Bridges, 1985; Bushnell, 1847/1984; Reiff, 1995; Westerhoff, 1976). The daily impact of parents in instructing, caring and disciplining their children necessarily supersedes the less frequent contact with the church. Similarly, parenting extends the covenant between spouses beyond the marriage to also encompass the child (e.g., Browning, 2011; Rubio, 2003). That is, the spousal covenant to love, honor and cherish throughout life is both embodied and extended in the birth of a child.

However, as noted previously, the marriage covenant is frequently broken in U.S. society. A common question within Christian circles is what parents in conflictual, distressed marriages should do. The alternatives typically laid out are (a) divorce to end an unhappy marriage or (b) stay together for the sake of the children. Within these options, the preservation of the marriage is implicitly, and sometimes explicitly, assumed to be the more favorable for the children of dissatisfied partners. Such conclusions are typically grounded in beliefs about parents' responsibility to the marriage, to their children and to God. For instance, drawing from the work of John Chrysostom, Rubio (2003) describes children as the biological manifestation of the spiritual creation of one flesh in marriage. In a review of theological, sociological and psychological literature, she concluded that unless conflict was high and resolution was not possible, couples with children should stay married.

Such dichotomous decisions of *whether* a couple should remain married, however, neglect the dimension of *how* couples should remain in marriage. If marriage is the model of Christ's relationship with the church, and the commands for love and mutual submission in marriage (Eph 5:21-25) are to be taken seriously, remaining in a loveless marriage in which hostile conflict, disinterest and/or mutual withdrawal characterize the relationship between the partners provides children of such marriages with a severely deficient model of marriage and an environment ill suited to their thriving. An additional alternative to divorce or just staying together is clearly necessary, as neither of these options takes seriously the parents' responsibilities to model for their children Christ's love.

Fortunately, dissatisfied couples are not doomed to remain so. Decades of research have demonstrated the effectiveness of various forms of couples therapy, with both behavioral marital therapy (Jacobson & Margolin, 1979) and emotion-focused couples therapy (Johnson, 2004) recognized as evidence-based treatments, and integrative behavioral couples therapy (Jacobson & Christensen, 1998) achieving similar positive results. In their review of the literature, Lebow, Chambers, Christensen and Johnson (2012) concluded that 70% of distressed couples significantly benefit from couples therapy, a percentage that is particularly striking given evidence that marital distress does not typically spontaneously remit.

Despite these documented high rates of improvement, only about one-third of divorcing couples have sought marital therapy (Doss, Carhart, Hsueh & Rahbar, 2010). Divorce is a drastic treatment for marital distress, and given that effective interventions exist, divorcing prior to seeking marital therapy is particularly ill advised: Such behavior is analogous to amputating a broken arm rather than setting the bone and putting the arm in a cast. Stated even more bluntly, distressed couples who stay together for their children owe it to their children to work on their marriages.

PRACTICAL SUGGESTIONS

- Given the ubiquitous nature of marital conflict and the high prevalence of marital aggression, it is critical to assess for the presence of these factors in the families of children presenting for treatment. Because parents are often unaware of the effect of marital conflict on their children, clinicians should assess for the amount, type and content of conflict. Particularly important dimensions to assess are the frequency (are conflicts arising multiple times a week or day?), intensity (how heated do disputes become?), resolution (are couples able to reach a mutually satisfactory conclusion, to agree to disagree or to resolve the dispute in some other way?) and levels of withdrawal (do couples remain engaged or retreat in hostile detachment?).

- Clinicians should also assess for conflict about the child and for conflict that is expressed in physical aggression between parents. Appropriate referrals should be provided to parents, along with clear messages accenting the harm such conflict can do to children and the demonstrated efficacy of marital interventions.

- Clinicians should be alert to the presence of factors that place children at even greater risk for poor outcomes. Assessment of the child should include examination of aggressive temperament, negative emotionality and role reversal, and interventions should be crafted to lessen the negative impact of these risk factors.

- Positive interventions to strengthen the coparenting relationship, family cohesion and parent-child attachment can help buffer children in conflictual families. Clinicians should also work to provide a safe therapeutic space for children in which their concerns and feelings can be processed.

6

Peer Relationships

·······························

Kelly S. Flanagan, Sarah L. Kelly
and Amy Peeler

After a childhood and adolescence of bullying at school, Frank Peretti (2000) recounts his teenage prayer, "Oh, Dear Lord . . . Please . . . I just can't take it anymore. . . . Please, God; please don't do this to me anymore. Don't make me go back there. Have mercy, dear Lord. I haven't fought back, I haven't snitched; I've turned the other cheek. Haven't I suffered enough?" (p. 136).

Interviewer Robert Coles (1991) suggests, "Perhaps children raised in Christian homes are quick to focus on Jesus as a Savior because they know full well their own vulnerability as boys and girls," based on ten-year-old Charlie's reflection: "[Jesus] couldn't forget the way He died. He must remember the way people treated Him. You don't forget, when you're alone. I remember when we moved, and I went to school, and I didn't know anyone at first. Jesus, everyone knew Him—but they didn't like Him, they didn't believe Him, and that's even worse" (p. 212).

THE MANY CHANGING FACETS of social development and peer relationships throughout childhood and adolescence are normative and can be wonderful aspects of development, but they can also be difficult. The complex nature of children's social context requires ongoing growth and navigation, which inherently involves the vulnerability of being in relationships. In his book *Graced Vulnerability: A Theology of Childhood*, David Jensen (2005) avers, "relationality is both the *promise* and *peril* of human existence: opening us to the bedazzling difference of creation itself and the possibility that we may abuse and objectify the others with whom we are called" (p. 32, emphasis added).[1] Further, there are seasons of both wonderful and terrible changes in our life's journey to find purpose and meaning in relationship to God and his creation, including other people (Shults & Sandage, 2006; Eccles 3). Children are not immune to these seasons nor to the promise and peril of human existence; in fact, they are perhaps even more vulnerable than adults within their social relationships because they are in the midst of their "becoming." In reviewing some truths learned from psychology, Miller-McLemore (2003) highlights the assertion that children do not "move from dependence on significant others to independence but rather from immature to more mature connections" (p. xx). That maturation occurs within numerous relationships and social contexts that children must traverse.

This chapter is dedicated to the topic of children's peer relations, which is often overlooked in clinical work despite the fact that peers are integral in childhood and adolescence. A century of research from both developmental and clinical literatures demonstrates the dynamic interplay among peer relations, children's developmental capacities and psychopathology. Peer relations play a crucial role in children's normative development through the egalitarian nature of these relationships; that is, children are able to learn and develop naturally within relationships that are generally more balanced in power— given similar ability and maturity levels—rather than hierarchical (as with adult and sibling relationships; Furman & Buhrmester, 1985; Ladd, 2005). On the other hand, poor peer relations place children at risk for negative outcomes throughout their life. Furthermore, psychopathology places children at risk for the development of poor peer relations, which in turn can inhibit the development of crucial competencies and increase both internalizing and externalizing difficulties. Indeed, the ability to form and maintain healthy relationships is a focus of many interventions, and the inability to do so is implicated in many clinical diagnoses. Thus, an understanding of the literature on peer relations provides an illustration of the intricacies of child development and also begs clinicians to attend to this aspect of children's worlds.

In the first section of this chapter, we will provide an overview of children's

---

[1]Jensen makes the argument that God is a vulnerable God to whom we can relate. He quotes, "To read the biblical narratives is to encounter a God who is, first of all, love (1 John 4:8). Love involves a willingness to put oneself at risk, and God is in fact vulnerable in love, vulnerable even to great suffering" (William Placher, *Narratives of a Vulnerable God* [Louisville, KY: Westminster John Knox Press, 1994], p. xiii).

social development and normative changes in peer relationships and competence across childhood and adolescence (the promise). In the second section,
the multidirectional influences between peer relations and adjustment will be
described, with two examples provided of the negative cycles that ensue for
both internalizing and externalizing trajectories (the peril). Consistent with
the systems perspective of developmental psychopathology, we will discuss
peer relations with the recognition that children's individual characteristics
mutually interact with their peer relations and that family, school and cultural
contexts have effects on the peer context. Finally, as illustrated in the quotes
that opened this chapter, the interaction between children's spirituality and
their peer relations should be considered; thus, we will consider peer relations
in light of the three Christian integrative themes of this volume—children as
valuable gifts, embodied persons and agents in their world.

NORMAL DEVELOPMENT OF PEER RELATIONS

Peer relations provide a crucial and unique context for children and adolescents to grow, explore, learn and adapt. The concept of social competence is
important to this chapter. Broadly, social competence describes how well
children gain and maintain success within peer interactions and relationships.
Thus, the concept includes the cognitive, behavioral and emotional skills that
children possess and utilize in peer interactions (e.g., social initiation and
group entry skills, friendship skills, self-regulation, perspective-taking) as well
as the nature of their peer relationships (e.g., whether they are accepted or rejected by the peer group); that is, social competence includes multiple dimensions that encapsulate children's ability to form and sustain positive peer relationships and avoid negative peer relationships (Ladd, 2005; Rose-Krasnor,
1997; Rose-Krasnor & Denham, 2009). Social competence is an indication of
healthy adjustment and is a foundation for children's adaptation over time. It
is important to keep in mind that just as the skills required for social interactions are multifaceted and complex, so are children's peer relations.

Modern peer relations researchers have emphasized with increasing specificity the incredible variability in risk and resilience pathways in peer relations.
These relationships are influenced by a number of factors that mediate and/or
moderate their links with social competence, including intrapersonal, interpersonal and environmental influences. Furthermore, because a child's ability
to have successful peer relationships develops transactionally with many other

capacities (e.g.. cognition, language, motor development, attachment, executive functioning) and is sensitive to changes in context or environment, it can change drastically over time. Thus, consistent with the tenets of developmental psychopathology, the nature of and processes underlying children's peer relations and social competence are not necessarily linear but demonstrate increasing complexity, flexibility, specificity and differentiation over time.

Influences on Peer Relations

From infancy through adolescence, the relationships children have with parents and caregivers serve as vital first contexts in which social competence develops. Temperament, attachment and emotion regulation serve as critical foundations to these parent-child relationships and later success in peer relations.

From early in a child's life, intraindividual characteristics influence a child's social competence and peer relationships (Brendgen, 2012; Brendgen & Boivin, 2009; Eisenberg, Vaughn & Hofer, 2009). Temperament, as discussed in chapter two of this book, interacts with both genetic and environmental influences to affect how a child self-regulates, reacts and adapts (Gülay, 2012). Temperament has a significant influence on early relationships, affecting factors such a child's reactivity to others, ability to be soothed, and ease of bonding with parent or caregiver (Eisenberg et al., 2009). Temperament remains relatively stable throughout development, and thus it can also later affect how children act in response to others (e.g., parents, teachers, friends) and how they approach peer relationships (Eisenberg et al., 2009; Gülay, 2012). Temperament also has a reciprocal effect on how others respond to the child and the type of support others might provide the child, highlighting the transactional nature of these variables. For example, a fussy child might evoke impatient, unsupportive parenting, which over time leads the child to expect that peers will respond negatively to her.

Although temperament may predispose a child toward a certain developmental pathway, parents and caregivers are formative in a child's early development and influence the effects of temperament on outcome. Relational factors can mediate and moderate intrapersonal and environmental influences on social development, and thus the parent-child attachment relationship is recognized as a basic and necessary aspect of early socialization with substantial and enduring implications for peer relations (Booth-LaForce & Kerns, 2009; Caughy et al., 2012; Ladd, 2005; Maccoby, 1992; see chap. 4 for a more in-depth description of the parent-child relationship). A secure parent-child attachment relationship provides the child with the safety, comfort, sense of worth and confidence needed as foundations for the development of emotion regulation and healthy relationships (Ladd, 2005; Maccoby, 1992). Additionally, it serves as a context for early skill acquisition. Parents model social skills and social competence through the parent-child relationship, interactions within the marital relationship and other family relationships. Additionally, parents promote healthy relationships and social competence by providing opportunities for exposure to peers and facilitating friendships, and by providing direct guidance and instruction, such as helping a child initiate social experiences, manage conflict, utilize healthy coping strategies and learn from negative experiences (Ladd, 2005; Ross & Howe, 2009). Thus, parents are of utmost importance early in a child's life in multiple ways, and barriers to a healthy parent-child relationship, such as disruption in attachment or parental mental illness, are risk factors for later psychopathology and relational problems (e.g., Goodman et al., 2011).

Emotion regulation, as discussed in chapter three, is influenced by genetics, temperament and attachment and is an important intraindividual factor in the development of social competence (Deater-Deckard, 2001). Children who are more skilled at emotion regulation, particularly in response to conflict or frustration, demonstrate higher levels of social competence in their peer interactions and less peer rejection than less regulated peers (Calkins, Gill, Johnson & Smith, 1999; Fabes et al., 1999; Hubbard & Zakriski, 2004). Indeed, emotion regulation—including emotional knowledge, understanding of others' emotions, and ongoing monitoring and modulation of affect in response to social interactions—is necessary for the development of prosocial skills and foundational for the maintenance of relationships (Arsenio, Cooperman & Lover, 2000; Cole et al., 1994; Halberstadt et al., 2001). Additionally, cognitive processes impact emotion (dys)regulation as children interpret peers' social cues, motivations and intentions; manage vague social input; utilize memory and knowledge of previous social situations; and practice perspective-taking (Deater-Deckard, 2001; Lemerise & Arsenio, 2000).

Timing and Course of Development

Social development with peers begins as early as six months of age. An infant demonstrates interest in other infants through babbling and smiling and then proceeds over the next few years to develop capabilities to imitate peers, share activities and objects, and cooperate (Hay, 2005; Ladd, 2005). Individual traits (e.g., temperament, personality) and skills fostered during the first two years of life (e.g., managing joint attention, regulating emotions, inhibiting impulses, understanding cause and effect, and linguistic competence) contribute to social learning (Hay, 2005). Adults and older children model interpersonal interactions as young children observe and practice essential skills. Early play relationships can develop into friendships even in toddlerhood (especially with regular exposure to peers, such as through childcare) (Coplan & Arbeau, 2009).

Parker and colleagues (Parker, Rubin, Erath, Wojslawowicz & Buskirk, 2006) note that "by interacting with playmates in organized play groups and schools, children produce the first in a series of peer cultures in which childhood knowledge and practices are gradually transformed into the knowledge and skills necessary to participate in the adult world" (p. 442). Young children participate in imaginary and pretend play to foster fun, as well as to process their particular context, emotions and experiences. They often coordinate play with others through rituals, routines, scripts and nonverbal behaviors that facilitate reciprocal actions from peers. Increasingly complex sociodramatic play and verbal coordinated play develop between twenty and thirty-two months as cognitive, language, self-regulation and symbolic capacities develop. From toddlerhood through school age, there is a growing shift from object-centered and unstructured or fantasy play toward more structured and rule-based play (e.g., social role playing); further, social relatedness and connectedness become more central as recognition of feelings, intentions, motivations and perspective-taking increases. Physical aggression and "rough and tumble" play is common in toddlers and young children, especially among males, and generally decreases with age as children enter formal schooling and as self-control, cooperativeness, sharing, expression of positive affect, assertiveness, effective communication and prosocial behavior increase (Fabes, Martin & Hanish, 2009; Parker et al., 2006; Underwood, 2004).

Children's interest in peer relations continues to increase, and toward the end of middle childhood and into early adolescence, peers become the primary influence on a child. Youth become increasingly self-aware about social status and peer acceptance or rejection (Ladd, 2005). The social context becomes more complex, and we must understand peer relationships along multiple levels, including both the dyadic level (e.g., individual friendships) and the group level (e.g., cliques, crowds, peer acceptance, popularity), as youth are concerned with their distinct and separate statuses at both levels throughout adolescence (Ladd, Kochenderfer-Ladd, Visconti & Ettekal, 2012).

At the dyadic level, friendships signify mutual recognition of egalitarian relationships that consist of frequent association, affective bonds and certain qualitative features (e.g., intimacy, support, conflict; Ladd, 2009). Bukowski, Motzoi & Meyer (2009) poignantly remark: "Friendship is the relationship that brings the lifespan together" (p. 217). Friendships span our human development, and socialization through friendships provides a primer for adult relationships. Throughout child and adolescent development, these individual friendships provide support for children through (1) self-esteem enhancement and positive self-evaluation, (2) emotional security in new situations, (3) nonfamilial forms of affection, (4) instrumental guidance in new or difficult situations, and (5) companionship (Parker et al., 2006). Additionally, these friendships foster socioemotional skills, including cooperative play skills, language and communication skills, emotional understanding and regulation, aggression control, and social problem-solving (Bierman & Erath, 2004).

Compared to relationships with adults, children may be better able to learn skills in these more symmetrical relationships (e.g., assertiveness), to experiment with different identities and to explore developmental concepts such as sex roles. Within dyadic relationships, children utilize gossip, humor, similarity and shared activities increasingly with age, and these behaviors contribute to the closeness of relationships and children's positive self-image within the larger group context. Friendships also affirm children's view that others are trustworthy and supportive (Buhrmester & Furman, 1987; Ladd & Troop-Gordon, 2003). However, friendships may vary in their degree of mutual affection and knowledge (Berndt & McCandless, 2009). In general, positive friendship qualities include companionship, intimacy, disclosure, support, cooperativeness, understanding and reliable alliance, whereas negative qualities include conflict, criticism, jealousy and rivalry, and dominance attempts.

Although dyadic friendships are incredibly significant, we also know that acceptance by the larger peer group is important to children's well-being and their ability to manage stress. At the group level, cliques and crowds exist in children's social worlds. The distinction between these two groupings is nebulous, though cliques can be considered to have members who direct their interactions toward each other more than toward outsiders, and crowds are usually larger groups denoted by social-behavioral reputations and a shared set of norms (Brown & Dietz, 2009). These groups vary in their size, structure and cohesiveness but are generally thought to provide children with a sense of belonging and shared values.

Several concepts in the research on peer relations help us understand how children relate to one another. The construct of peer acceptance refers to how well liked a child is by his peer group and appears to be mostly stable over time (Newcomb, Bukowski & Pattee, 1993; Parker et al., 2006).[2] Of particular interest to clinicians and peer relations researchers because of its role in mental health outcomes (Bierman, 2005), peer group rejection is "intragroup attitudes or, specifically, the feelings of dislike that peers have toward specific individuals within their peer group" (Ladd, 2009, p. 34). Although disruptions occur in peer relationships, particularly during transitions (e.g., entry to a new middle school), overall status of peer acceptance versus peer rejection appears to be stable over time, for better or for worse (Jiang & Cillessen, 2005). Popularity is considered to be different from peer acceptance and represents the status, visibility and social prominence of particular children (versus being "well liked"). Popularity can include both positive and negative aspects (e.g., popular adolescents may also be aggressive) and is often associated with dominance, power, humor and other valued characteristics within the particular peer group (Cillessen & Mayeux, 2004; LaFontana & Cillessen, 2002; Rodkin, Farmer, Pearl & Van Acker, 2000).

Both individual friendships and larger group memberships cultivate a sense of belonging and connectedness to others, increased confidence, and a context for self-expression (Bukowski et al., 2009; Parker et al., 2006). The benefits of close friendships include opportunities to develop social competencies such as cooperative and competitive problem-solving, buffering of stress, social support, felt sense of attachment (affection, security), reliable alliances and companionship, enhancement of worth, guidance, and nurturance (Bukowski et al., 2009, p. 223). However, the ability to make and maintain friendships, although often associated with positive outcomes, can also be associated with negative outcomes. The "social learning hypothesis"

---

[2]Peer acceptance is often measured through the use of sociometric methods, which entails asking a group of students (e.g., a third-grade class) to provide nominations or ratings of their peers (e.g., "name the kids in your class that you like the most"). These nominations provide scores to each child in that group based on the number of peers who indicate that they like or dislike him or her; the scores are then used to classify children as having a particular sociometric status, including popular (liked by many, disliked by few), rejected (disliked by many, liked by few), neglected (neither liked nor disliked) and controversial (both liked and disliked), that represents the relationship between the child and the larger peer group (Cillessen, 2009; Cillessen & Bukowski, 2000).

asserts that peers are important socializing agents with great influence on each other (Ladd, 2005) across domains of functioning, which can either be to the benefit or the detriment of the child. For example, friendships with negative characteristics can influence and exacerbate oppositional and antisocial behaviors (Bagwell, 2004; Dodge & Pettit, 2003). Thus, it is not the existence of a friendship per se that leads to healthy outcomes but rather the quality of the friendship and whether the friendship encourages positive behaviors, coping and adjustment (Bagwell, 2004). Whether children have or lack friends and whether they experience high- or low-quality friendships exerts a meaningful influence on development.

In general, a child's network of friends tends to increase with age, peaking in middle childhood, after which relationships increase in quality as they decrease in number. This change is thought to allow youth to develop closer and more intimate relationships in adolescence. Indeed, research has shown that youth may need only one good friend to buffer stress and decrease the risks associated with other social difficulties (e.g., peer rejection, peer victimization; Bagwell, 2004; Parker et al., 2006; Woodhouse, Dykas & Cassidy, 2012).

Sex differences in peer relations are important to consider. Research has demonstrated that children demonstrate a preference for same-sex peers starting as early as age three and throughout development (Oberle, Schonert-Reichl & Thomson, 2010; Perry-Parrish & Zeman, 2011; Rose & Smith, 2009). Overall, there are more similarities than differences between female and male same-sex friendships (Parker et al., 2006; Underwood, 2004). For both boys and girls, loyalty, trust and closeness are increasingly emphasized with age in same-sex friendships, and in adolescence, jealousy tends to decrease whereas intimacy and self-disclosure increase (Parker et al., 2006). More social groups begin to include opposite-sex peers in adolescence, increasing teens' exposure to members of the opposite sex and opportunities for romantic experimentation. Although youth continue to favor same-sex friendships, these beginning cross-sex relationships contribute to self-disclosure and closeness among friends and can also serve to bolster a youth's social status or image (Parker et al., 2006). Early romantic relationships, especially in younger adolescents, tend to be extremely sensitive to peer influences, but peer influence lessens with age and as romantic relationships progress beyond early phases.

Contextual factors also need to be considered for a comprehensive understanding of peer relations, including aspects of the family (e.g., family social networks, sibling relationships; e.g., Ross & Howe, 2009), school (e.g., school climate, structure, classroom characteristics, teachers' beliefs and behaviors; e.g., Howes, 2000), neighborhood and community (e.g., socioeconomic status, neighborhood and community violence; e.g., Caughy et al., 2012), and the society or culture (e.g., overarching cultural beliefs and values) with which the child interacts. For example, different cultural "starting points" can lead to different social behaviors, values, judgments and responses that affect how we understand peer relationships and children's social competence (Chen, Chung & Hsiao, 2009). Chen and colleagues (2009) assert that "the nature and quality of children's friendships may depend on complex social, historical, and ecological factors" (p. 442), such as cultural valuing of certain aspects of friendships and social behavior, historical relations between different groups in particular cultural contexts, and economic and social changes within cultures (e.g., increased endorsement of individualistic values). Thus, an accurate understanding of normative peer relations involves a comprehensive recognition of both dyadic relationships and larger group dynamics and the transactions between these relationships and the different ecological levels of influence.

Involving both larger peer group dynamics and dyadic relationships, as well as ecological influences, bullying is defined as frequent, intentional acts of aggression of one or more individuals against a more vulnerable peer in the context of an imbalance of power (Nansel et al., 2001; Olweus, 2010). Bullying/ peer victimization occurs with remarkable prevalence around the world, with reports of 15% of youth being involved in bullying two to three times per month to as many as 75% of youth experiencing bullying *at least once* during their schooling (Jimerson, Swearer & Espelage, 2009). Bullying can take various forms, including direct physical or verbal aggression (e.g., teasing, taunting, hitting, kicking), indirect or relational aggression (e.g., excluding from groups, spreading rumors, manipulation of peer relationships), and cyber/electronic bullying (e.g., using technology to harass or embarrass someone; Smith et al., 2008). Further, frequency, intensity and forms of bullying can shift as children attempt to navigate an increasingly complex social terrain. Many adults may view bullying as a "normative" phenomenon in childhood and adolescence, given the high percentage of children involved as bullies, victims or bystanders; yet, we know from decades of research that bullying has detrimental effects on children's psychosocial adjustment and should be taken seriously.[3] Consistent with a developmental psychopathology framework, bullying interventions can take place on many levels. Specifically, a social-ecological model of bullying calls for us to attend not only to individual variables associated with bullying but also to ecological factors (e.g., adults' attitudes and responses, physical characteristics of the school, race/ethnicity composition of the school, school climate factors) that either encourage or inhibit bullying (Espelage & Swearer, 2004; Swearer, Espelage & Napolitano, 2009).

Relatedly, attention has recently been given to the role of intergroup bias that affects social exclusion (Killen, Rutland & Jampol, 2009). The focus on social exclusion is complementary to the construct of peer group rejection because social exclusion occurs based on specific group membership rather than individual social deficits. With age, children normatively notice and evaluate differences among their peers that deviate from group norms. Killen and colleagues (2009) have demonstrated that children use three domains of knowledge in their social reasoning about whether or not to exclude others: "the moral (fairness, justice, equality, rights), social-conventional (traditions, customs, etiquette, rituals), and psychological (personal, individual discretion, autonomy, theory of mind)" (p. 251). Interestingly, some bullies understand the specific context of normative exclusion and are socially skilled in their use of bullying to fit the context. Contextual factors are again important because the context can either foster or reduce exclusion; for example, a school that has clear prohibitions and sanctions against exclusion and promotes acceptance of diversity and compassion will impede the development of intergroup bias. Thus, the literature suggests that as clinicians, we should be aware of intergroup bias and the particular social-conventional norms within children's contexts as well as how these biases are handled within the context. Further, children's moral, social-conventional and psychological reasoning must be considered in our clinical work.

As noted earlier, the multiple aspects of peer relations at both the dyadic and group levels are distinct phenomena; however, they are not completely independent from each other. For example, friendships are sometimes embedded in groups but can occur outside of groups; yet, a larger social network provides

---

[3]Because a comprehensive treatment of bullying cannot be covered in this chapter, please see Jimerson, Swearer & Espelage (2009) or Vernberg & Biggs (2010) for a thorough review of bullying, its prevention and intervention.

more opportunities for friendships. Further, the same skills that are required for the development of high-quality friendships are also those that impact a child's peer acceptance; thus, children's friendship quality and their status within the peer group may be closely related. Similarly, rejected children are likely to become victimized by their peers and to have low-quality friendships (Bierman, 2005); it may be that children who are not well accepted are easy targets or that their victimization is perceived as justified because of their poor social skills or aggression. These different aspects of peer relations make independent contributions to children's adjustment and represent both risk and protective factors as discussed next.

ABNORMAL DEVELOPMENT

Peer Relations as a Risk Factor

Difficulties with social interactions and impairment of social functioning are diagnostic criteria for numerous childhood disorders (e.g., autism spectrum disorder, oppositional defiant disorder, social phobia, depressive disorders) and are common difficulties associated with other disorders (e.g., attention-deficit/hyperactivity disorder; ADHD). Indeed, the ability to form and maintain healthy relationships is a focus of many interventions. However, the interplay between peer relations and psychopathology is complex, representing various interconnections and processes that highlight the transactional influences and opportunities for either adaptation or increasing difficulties over time (Masten, 2006; van Lier & Koot, 2010). As discussed in the previous section, peer relationships are important for children's normative development. Logically, then, research also indicates that negative peer relations disrupt these important processes and thus are deleterious for children's short- and long-term adjustment (Hymel, Rubin, Rowden & LeMare, 1990; Parker & Asher, 1987).

It is important to note that the links between peer interactions and maladaptive outcomes are dynamic and bidirectional. Psychopathology or other individual risk factors can directly affect peer relations via peers' negative perceptions and thus reactions to symptoms associated with psychopathology or other difficulties (e.g., Swords, Heary & Hennessy, 2011). For example, children with ADHD experience pervasive peer relationship difficulties along multiple levels (e.g., few friendships, greater rejection, social withdrawal and isolation) because other children may be irritated by the negative effects of their hyperactivity, impulsivity, and inattention on their classroom behavior and social interactions (for a review, see Becker, Luebbe & Langberg 2012). Certain risk factors may also inhibit or disrupt social functioning and the formation of healthy peer relations, which can then affect the course of subsequent psychopathology and interpersonal relationships (Becker et al., 2012; Kingery, Erdley, Marshall, Whitaker & Reuter, 2010; Moffitt, 1993). To parse out the dynamic transactions between psychopathology and peer relations, a recent longitudinal study that followed children from kindergarten to grade four provides an illustration of these reciprocal influences over time (van Lier & Koot, 2010). Findings indicated that early externalizing problems negatively influenced peer acceptance, peer victimization and friendlessness. This, in turn, contributed to the perpetuation of externalizing problems and the development of internalizing problems, which appeared to be exacerbated by the decrease in opportunities to experience positive peer relationships and to develop skills in social competence.

Whether particular risk factors contribute to negative peer experiences, or whether the *peril* of the social world confronts children and poses a risk in and of itself, it is clear that the cognitive, emotional and social problems that result from negative peer interactions lead to the development and/or maintenance of psychopathology and other difficulties. Peer relations have the potential to negatively affect children's development in three general areas: view of self and internalizing problems, externalizing problems, and school maladjustment.

Internalizing problems. The quality of peer relationships, including how well we get along with others, how others treat us and how well liked we are, impacts our sense of self. A great deal of research has demonstrated the connection between negative peer experiences (e.g., rejection, victimization, low popularity, low-quality friendships, neglect and alienation) and low self-esteem, loneliness, depressive symptoms, and anxiety (Hawker & Boulton, 2000; Kistner, Balthazor, Risi & Burton, 1999; Ladd & Troop-Gordon, 2003; Prinstein, Rancourt, Guerry & Browne, 2009). In general, there is strong longitudinal evidence that children who experience chronic peer difficulties experience internalizing problems such as anxiety, low self-esteem, and depression and suicidal ideation (Desjardins & Leadbeater, 2011; Ladd & Troop-Gordon, 2003). Demonstrating the complexity of the association between peer relations and other risk factors, though peer rejection is linked to loneliness and isolation, it is most likely the children who are withdrawn *and* experience rejection that are most at risk (Bell-Dolan, Foster & Christopher, 1995). Both peer rejection and victimization contribute to social anxiety, including fear of negative evaluation and social avoidance (Flanagan, Erath & Bierman, 2008; La Greca & Harrison, 2005; Zwierzynska, Wolke & Lereya, 2013). Additionally, victimization, rejection, lack of social support, low levels of popularity and social withdrawal are linked to depression (Allen et al., 2006; Nangle, Erdley, Newman, Mason & Carpenter, 2003; Prinstein & Aikins, 2004). It is proffered that difficulties in peer experiences are a potent trigger for internalizing problems. There are several contributing factors that may explain the role of negative peer relations in the etiology of internalizing problems, including a lack of prosocial skills, distorted social cognitions, disrupted peer attachment relationships, negative peer interaction qualities (e.g., dysfunctional anger, inappropriate dependency) and socialization processes, as discussed in our clinical examples below (Allen et al., 2006; Deater-Deckard, 2001).

Externalizing problems. Negative peer experiences (e.g., rejection by the peer group, lack of close friendships, peer victimization) are associated with increases in externalizing behavior and conduct problems throughout childhood and adolescence and with later delinquency, substance use, physical and social aggression, violence, and poor relationships (Bagwell, Newcomb & Bukowski, 1998; Coie, 2004; Deater-Deckard, 2001; Prinstein et al., 2009). These associations are most likely transactional over time in that negative peer experiences may lead to behavioral problems, and behavioral problems may also elicit negative responses from peers; indeed, the combination of aggression *and* peer rejection is particularly portentous of later externalizing symptoms (Coie, 2004). Delinquent behavior increases as a result of exposure to other delinquent youth and in the context of stable antisocial friendships (Brendgen, Vitaro & Bukowski, 2000; Dishion & Dodge, 2006; Snyder et al., 2005). Although children with behavioral problems tend to have inaccurate perceptions about the level of their acceptance by the peer group and the quality of their friendships (Deater-Deckard, 2001; Sandstrom & Coie, 1999), the strong association between behavioral problems and poor peer relations is well established. Children's lack of prosocial skills and distorted cognitions are also important factors in understanding this association, as discussed in the "Clinical Examples" section of this chapter.

School adjustment. A recently published volume reviewed the extensive literature about the influence of peer relations on school adjustment (Ryan & Ladd, 2012). Peers can influence a child's school engagement, attitudes about school and motivations for learning, and thus academic achievement. Indeed, both peer acceptance and having friends are associated with academic achievement, motivation, academic goals, positive attitudes toward school and school engagement, whereas peer rejection, victimization, friendlessness and low-quality friendships are associated with negative school attitudes, behavioral problems at school, school avoidance, refusal and truancy, and potentially school dropout (Kearney, 2008; Ladd et al., 2012; Wentzel, 2009; Wentzel, Donlan & Morrison, 2012). Peers model, directly communicate and instruct each other with regard to values, goals and behavioral standards that either positively or negatively affect academic achievement (Wentzel et al., 2012). Further, because peer relationships can provide support and felt security that decrease emotional stress, peers might indirectly influence academic functioning by enabling children to effectively engage in school-related activities because they feel confident and secure.

Peer Relationships as a Protective Factor

Peer relations can serve as a protective factor in development as well. Youth who have friends tend to be more self-confident, less lonely and depressed, more involved in school and perform better academically (Bukowski et al., 2009). In contrast to the maladaptive adjustment associated with poor peer relations discussed above, youth with close friendships and greater peer acceptance tend to have more adaptive social cognitions (e.g., positive outcome expectancies and attributions) and fewer internalizing and externalizing problems (Bierman, 2005; Erath, Flanagan & Bierman, 2010; Greco & Morris, 2005). Close, intimate, high-quality friendships that provide emotional support are particularly protective over time and linked to more positive psychological outcomes (e.g., decreases in depressive symptoms). The affection and security of high-quality peer relations may cultivate opportunities to develop relational competencies. Further, positive experiences with peers build skills and prepare the child for later adaptation. Indeed, friendships can serve as a protective factor in the face of adversity and can be a source of support if mental health problems develop (Bolger, Patterson & Kupersmidt, 1998; Erath et al., 2010; Schwartz, Dodge, Pettit & Bates, 2000; Swords, Hennessy & Heary, 2011). In summary, it is obvious that the function of peer relations as either risk or protective factor is dependent on various interacting intrapersonal and contextual factors, clearly illustrating that the promise and peril of the social context are both consistently present throughout childhood and adolescence.

Peer Relations as Moderator and/or Mediator

The interdependence of the various aspects of peer relations and the complex interplay between peer relations and other risk and protective factors over time make it difficult to clearly flesh out the mediating and moderating roles of peer relations. In this section, we will briefly review different ways in which peer relations may represent underlying mediating or moderating processes within children's developmental trajectories.

Longitudinal studies present evidence that as a protective factor, positive peer relations mediate and moderate associations between various risk factors (e.g., low cohesion in the family, marital conflict and harsh discipline) and adjustment (e.g., externalizing problems, social competence, peer victimization; Bolger et al., 1998; Erath et al., 2010; Schwartz et al., 2000). For example, children who experience chronic maltreatment at home but have a high-quality friendship show improvements in self-esteem over time (e.g., Bolger et al., 1998). In contrast, children who experience risk factors in combination with negative peer experiences are at greatest risk for maladjustment (e.g., Flanagan et al., 2008; Valdez, Lambert & Ialongo, 2011). Additionally, maladaptive peer socialization processes mediate the association between early childhood problems and later adjustment. For example, friendship pair similarity (i.e., the degree to which friends possess similar characteristics) between deviant peers mediates the association between family dysfunction and adolescent antisocial behavior (Kim, Hetherington & Reiss, 1999). Maladaptive family dynamics increase the likelihood that adolescents will associate with deviant peers, who in turn model and reward antisocial behavior, as evident in the extreme example of organized gangs.

Different aspects of peer relations may play different roles in mediating/moderating the associations between individual characteristics and maladjustment. For example, a recent longitudinal study demonstrated that popularity mediated the relationship between behavioral inhibition and depressive symptoms, such that increases in inhibition were related to decreases in popularity and heightened levels of depressive symptoms across three years (Buck & Dix, 2012). Furthermore, this study also found that poor friendship quality predicted decreases in popularity and subsequent increases in depressive symptoms, illustrating the complex interaction between individual factors and different aspects of peer relations over time. Similarly, across a six-year period, peer victimization predicted depression, but this association was moderated by peer emotional support (Desjardins & Leadbeater, 2011). Interestingly, peer emotional support was related to increases in depressive symptoms over time. The authors hypothesized that co-rumination processes within friendships or the low quality of this support (e.g., suggesting revenge as a coping strategy) may explain these findings. That is, peers may reinforce depressed or anxious youth's difficulties through the emotionally laden interactions within friendships that lead to dwelling on problems and negative affect (Rose, 2002; Stone, Hankin, Gibb & Abela, 2011) or through encouraging unhelpful responses. Research indicates that socialization processes within friendship groups are particularly potent for increases in depressive symptoms among adolescents, especially for more peripheral group members (i.e., the moderating role of peer group position; Conway, Rancourt, Adelman, Burk & Prinstein, 2011).

Recent research on peer relations that investigates the moderating and/or mediating roles of peer relations, as represented by these studies, demonstrates the complexity of children and adolescents' peer relations and the need to assess multiple aspects of social competence (i.e., social skills as well as social functioning across dyadic and group levels) and the underlying processes that might explain the impact of peer relations (e.g., emotional and social support, socialization processes, reinforcement of [mal]adaptive coping).

Clinical Examples

We will use examples of two distinct developmental trajectories to explicate these dynamic processes and the principles of developmental psychopathology in more depth. Developmental psychopathology provides the framework to integrate intrapersonal, interpersonal and environmental contributors to the developmental trajectories involved in internalizing and externalizing symptomatology. We will look at the peer relations of children with these problems in order to explicate the various ways in which "peer relationship processes operate as part of a complex array of risk and protective factors within the school, neighborhood, and home environments" (Deater-Deckard, 2001, p. 568).

Internalizing. Children normatively experience social fears and evaluative anxiety throughout development, particularly as the importance of peer relationships increases across adolescence. Illustrating the concept of multifinality, some children weather this anxiety well, but some develop clinical levels of social anxiety. In terms of risk factors, Ollendick and Benoit (2012) describe the interaction of child and parental factors that contribute to the onset and maintenance of social anxiety in childhood and adolescence. First, certain temperamental characteristics may place a child at risk for internalizing problems. Specifically, behavioral inhibition, which is characterized by biologically based distress, fear, and reticence to novel or unfamiliar stimuli, is moderately stable and predictive of later shyness, social anxiety and depression (Gladstone & Parker, 2006; Ollendick & Benoit, 2012). However, not all children who are classified as behaviorally inhibited develop internalizing problems, which indicates that other risk factors interact with the child's temperament. Several parental factors have been have been found to increase a child's risk for the development of poor peer relations through their influence on anxiety, including parenting practices (e.g., overprotective, controlling, and critical parenting as well as sensitive and warm parenting that might inadvertently reinforce avoidance and maladaptive cognitions), parental psychopathology and cognitive biases (e.g., heightened anxiety and fear responses and threat perception that are modeled to and reinforced in their children) and attachment processes (e.g., insecure attachment that results in views of others and the world as untrustworthy and unreliable).

The influences of the aforementioned temperamental and parenting factors can lead to a negative pathway of behavioral avoidance and social withdrawal with detrimental implications for social competence and psychopathology (Rubin, Burgess, Kennedy & Stewart, 2003). Socially anxious children often lack motivation to participate in social events, avoid extracurricular activities, and are less likely to initiate social interactions (Beidel, Turner & Morris, 1999; Kingery et al., 2010). By middle childhood and adolescence, peers react negatively to withdrawn individuals due to the non-normative nature of these behaviors within the peer context, leading socially anxious children to be less well liked by their peers than nonanxious youth (Kingery et al., 2010). Unfortunately, in a developmental cascade, the combination of children's avoidance of peers and the resulting peer exclusion of anxious/shy children may lead to fewer opportunities for socially anxious children to develop and practice requisite social skills. Indeed, anxious children tend to have poor social skills in areas such as conversation, cooperation, assertiveness and self-control (Erath, Flanagan & Bierman, 2007; Greco & Morris, 2005; Morgan & Banerjee, 2006; Spence, Donovan & Brechman-Toussaint, 1999). This lack of social skills may invite negative responses from peers (Spence et al., 1999), which contributes to and reinforces avoidance and negative social cognitions over time. Children's distorted or deficient social cognitions that might impede their social engagement include negative/self-defeating attributions, negative outcome expectations, perceptions of lower social support, and low self-efficacy (e.g., Alfano, Beidel & Turner, 2006; Erath et al., 2007).

Anxious children have difficulty establishing many close friendships, although having at least one close friendship may protect children against negative outcomes (Beidel et al., 1999; Chansky & Kendall, 1997; Rubin et al., 2003). However, socially withdrawn children tend to have friends with similar characteristics, including poor social skills and negative peer experiences (Kingery et al., 2010). Additionally, anxious and depressed youth experience more overt and relational victimization and are at risk for difficulty forming healthy romantic relationships (La Greca & Mackey, 2007; Siegel, La Greca & Harrison, 2009; Vujeva & Furman, 2011). Unfortunately, shyness and withdrawn behavior are fairly stable over time and predict increases in both anxiety and depressive symptoms (Beidel & Turner, 2007; Rubin et al., 2003; Stein et al., 2001). As emphasized by developmental psychopathology, developmental timing needs to be considered, as certain developmental periods may increase the role that peer relations play as either a risk or a protective factor. For example, increased stressors within the social realm and decreased social support across adolescence intensify the developmental demands on youth to adjust to intraindividual, interpersonal and environmental changes (e.g., transition to a larger school, changing peer dynamics, decreased structure from adults, and rapid physical and cognitive growth), which may explain the increase in anxiety in early adolescence.

Consistent with a developmental psychopathology perspective, longitudinal designs indicate reciprocal relationships between internalizing problems and peer relations over time (Siegel et al., 2009; Vernberg, Abwender, Ewell & Beery, 1992). Peer victimization negatively affects global self-worth and social self-concept, which are in turn linked to higher levels of anxiety (Grills & Ollendick, 2002; Ladd & Troop-Gordon, 2003). Interestingly, parenting practices that are supportive but encourage anxious children to learn how to cope with their anxiety (versus avoid) and engage socially may moderate the relationship between child temperament and the development of anxiety (Ollendick & Benoit, 2012).

These complex reciprocal interactions among behavioral avoidance, withdrawal, negative social cognitions, negative peer experiences, relational deficits and anxiety are likely to continue without intervention. Understanding this cycle and the possible protective and risk factors that are present allows clinicians to identify multiple points of prevention and intervention to alter a child's trajectory (e.g., parenting training or family therapy, social skills training, cognitive-behavioral therapy to address cognitive biases and behavioral avoidance, interventions that address peer group processes).

Externalizing. As discussed earlier, a great deal of developmental and clinical research has also provided evidence for the reciprocal relationships between children's externalizing problems and multiple aspects of their peer relations. Again, the complex interplay of intrapersonal, interpersonal and environmental influences over time is apparent in the trajectories of externalizing problems. Dodge and Pettit (2003) challenge theorists and researchers of antisocial development "to understand how distal risk factors (such as difficult temperament and socioeconomic disadvantage) relate to life experiences that unfold over time (such as harsh discipline and peer social rejection) to eventuate in proximal processes (such as emotional reactions and cognitive interpretations) that result in violent behaviors" (p. 352). They review a variety of biological predispositions (e.g., impulsivity, attention deficits, difficult temperament), as well as poor parental discipline and monitoring, that represent risk factors that interact with peer relations implicated in the developmental trajectories of conduct problems.

It is well established that early aggressive child behavior is generally met with peer rejection, which predicts increases in future aggressive-disruptive behavior (Coie, 2004; Kupersmidt & Coie, 1990). Similar to the anxiety trajectory described above, rejection by the peer group decreases children's chances for positive peer socialization that promotes social skill development and anger management skills and also increases the likelihood of coercive exchanges between children. Reputational biases may contribute to the continuation of peer rejection and victimization of these children by their peers, such that peers hold hostile biases toward rejected children and display higher rates of aggressive behavior toward these children regardless of the child's (even prosocial) behavior (Bierman, 2005; Prinstein et al., 2009). Aggressive children do have reciprocated friendships, but unfortunately, aggressive children are likely to associate with children similar to themselves (Powers & Bierman, 2013). Friendships with other aggressive youth provide experiences of "deviancy training" or "peer contagion" that serve to model and positively reinforce aggressive behavior and defiance and to promote positive attitudes toward aggression and antisocial activities throughout childhood and adolescence (Dishion & Dodge, 2005, 2006; Dodge, Dishion & Lansford, 2006; Snyder et al., 2005). Indeed, having aggressive friends predicts increases in aggression over time (Powers & Bierman, 2012).

These risk factors and peer relations processes affect the ways externalizing youth process information during social interactions (i.e., social information processing; Crick & Dodge, 1994; Fontaine & Dodge, 2009), which is a crucial component of the developmental trajectories of these youth. Difficulties with social information processing that aggressive youth display include hostile attributional biases for peers' intentions, selective attention to hostile cues, generation of aggressive responses, failure to identify a varied list of possible competent responses to provocative or ambiguous peer interactions, and positive beliefs about the use of aggression to achieve instrumental or relational social goals. Peer rejection and victimization contribute to the maintenance of such maladaptive social cognitions (Dodge et al., 2003; Dodge & Petit, 2003). Over time, aggressive and impulsive children are met with negative experiences within their peer context, which serves to further intensify their maladaptive social cognitions and their propensity for responding in maladaptive and unskilled ways within peer interactions. When peers neglect, actively reject, or isolate their (non-normative) aggressive or hyperactive peers, this group of children may become "bully-victims," or children who both experience peer victimization and also engage in bullying. These children are found to be at the highest risk for referrals for mental health services, suicidal ideation, externalizing problems, school truancy, drop-out and underachievement, and substance abuse.

Further, comorbid difficulties are particularly predictive of negative peer relations and a maladaptive trajectory. For example, aggressive children with a diagnosis of ADHD may be at particular risk given the additional aversive behavioral symptoms of ADHD that are perceived negatively by peers and result in rejection, which contributes to antisocial behavior above and beyond intraindividual characteristics (Coie, 2004). Difficulties with emotion regulation may also represent a comorbid risk factor; for example, aggressive youth whose aggression is more reactive (e.g., demonstrating dysregulated, "hot" angry responses) than proactive (e.g., planned, non-angry aggression) are at greater risk for peer rejection and further aggression (Hubbard, Morrow, Romano & McAuliffe, 2010), demonstrating the interaction among emotion regulation, externalizing problems and peer relations in predicting children's adjustment.

Finally, contextual influences are important in understanding aggressive trajectories. For example, children who are rejected by their peers and also members of aggressive classroom contexts are particularly at risk for deviant peer influence (Powers & Bierman, 2013), representing the moderating influence of classroom ecology. It has also been argued that institutional aggregation of deviant peers (e.g., educational, juvenile justice or community programs) may exacerbate the socialization effects on increased conduct problems (Dishion, McCord & Poulin, 1999; Dodge et al., 2006). Children who spend more unsupervised time with peers after school are also more likely to display externalizing problems (Dodge & Petit, 2003); however, parental knowledge of children's peers and activities moderates the relationship between early risk and the development of later externalizing problems. Further, certain cultural values (e.g., defending one's honor, the importance of self-respect) and socio-cultural factors (e.g., low parental education and socioeconomic status, high rates of community violence) have been identified as significant risk factors for the development of conduct problems (Dodge & Petit, 2003).

Summary. The concepts of both equifinality and multifinality are necessary to consider in understanding children's developmental trajectories. Children with social difficulties who develop internalizing and externalizing problems might have one or several of the discussed risk factors, illustrating equifinality. In addition, children who experience a particular risk factor have different outcomes depending on other intrapersonal and environmental influences; it may be the interaction of risk factors that results in the development of internalizing problems (e.g., no temperament risk factors or harsh parenting but being rejected by the peer group and lacking close friends) or externalizing problems (e.g., having a difficult temperament *and* being rejected by the peer group), representing multifinality.

An understanding of the complex interactions among these multiple factors is necessary in order for clinicians to identify points of intervention. For example, promotion of high-quality peer relations (e.g, peer acceptance, friendship quality) may disrupt the relationship between early family adversity and later child adjustment; similarly, bonding with peers in positive peer activities such as school extracurricular activities may protect youth from the development of conduct problems. It is clear that preventive and intervention efforts must attend to the role of children's peer experiences (in consideration of reciprocal intraindividual, interpersonal and contextual factors) across childhood and adolescence in order to be most effective.

INTEGRATIVE THEMES

Christian theology views all humanity as being interdependent not only with each other but with God and his world.[4] We are bound to one another; we are connected even to others who are different from us and who we inherently feel should care for us as we should care for them (Mt 5:43-48; 7:12). In *Christian Nurture*, Horace Bushnell (1860) writes that "the Scriptures . . . maintain a marked contrast with the extreme individualism of our modern philosophy. They do not always regard the individual as an isolated unit, but they often look upon men as they exist, in families and in races, under organic laws" (p. 39). Although originally written in 1847, these words still ring true. An affirmation of interdependence illuminates the study of child peer relationships so that clinicians can recognize and help restore children's relationships with their peers.

More specifically, the three integrative themes of this book provide such illumination. First, children's inherent value as gifts stems from the fact that they are made in the image of God and as such are created for relationship, including relationship with peers. Second, we respect children as embodied persons because Christ has redeemed humanity through his incarnation. As recorded in the Scriptures, He provides the model and also the power for healthy peer relationships. Finally, we regard children as agents because they too are members of the body of Christ and can influence and be influenced by, in both positive and negative ways, their fellow participants in the kingdom. This interdependence sets the framework for all of us, including children, to become who God intends us to be—beings engaged in morally influential relationships.

Value as Gifts: Made in the Image of God

In the first chapter of Genesis, at the crowning moment of God's creative displays of power and grace, he fashions the human being: "Then God said, 'Let

---

[4]Christian Scripture teaches that humanity is dependent upon God for its existence and sustenance (Gen 1–2; Col 1; Heb 1). Moreover the vision of God's people is communal, not simply individual. The kingdom of God demands a response (Mk 1:14-15), but to do so draws one into a collective people. Interestingly, pronouncements and commands throughout the New Testament are typically addressed to a plural "you" and "us" rather than a singular "you" and "I" (e.g., Mt 3:11; 6:11-13; Mk 10:43-44; Lk 6:24-25; Jn 16; Acts 2:17; Rom 6:11-13). Finally, the redemption of God's people includes within it the restoration of God's creation (Rom 8; Rev 21).

Us make man in Our image, according to Our likeness.' . . . God created man in His own image, in the image of God He created him; male and female He created them" (Gen 1:26-27 NASB). The Judeo-Christian texts affirm at the outset the value of each and every human being. Believers might be so familiar with this idea that it seems commonplace or mundane. Nevertheless, it is worth pondering what the assertion that humans are made in God's image entails.[5] Many different views of the meaning of the *imago Dei* exist, including definitions that are substantive (encompassing physical, psychological, ethical and spiritual characteristics within humans), functional (relating to the purpose and work given to humans in his creation—creativity, energy and authority of our rule of his creation), relational (referring to our capacity for relationship with each other and with God), and teleological (reflecting the future realization of our ultimate objective of existence).

The relational component of humanity as a reflection of the relationality of God is particularly important for this chapter. First, the capacity for relationship begins with a human's relationship to God. The possibility of relationship with God within us translates into relationship with other human beings, which is a definitive mark of what it is to be human *and* to be made in the image of God; indeed, "God's creature is humankind only in community" (Westermann, 1984). Because God is a community of love consisting of three triune persons, human beings designed in the image of God are to be relational as well.

Second, the positive capacities in humanity, including reason, free will, moral responsibility, reciprocity in love, mastery of the passions and exercise of virtue, exist in us because we reflect our creator God. These capacities are possibilities in children's emotional, behavioral, cognitive and moral development, and impact their participation in peer relationships. For example, children who struggle with self-regulation or who do not exert their free will in moral ways tend to struggle with their peer relations. In contrast, children who are able to form and maintain mutually supportive relationships with friends tend to thrive and are able to cope better with stressors. These truths in

---

[5]Gregory of Nyssa, the Cappadocian father from the fourth century, poses a series of questions that remind believers just how radical the *imago Dei* is. "How is the incorporeal likened to a body? How is the temporal like the eternal? That which is mutable by change like to the immutable? That which is subject to passion and corruption to the impassible and incorruptible? That which constantly dwells with evil, and grows up with it, to that which is absolutely free from evil?" (*On the Making of Man* 16:3; in Schaff, 1890–1900, NPNF² 5:404).

the scientific literature reflect children's nature as image-bearers created to be in right relationship with their peers, intimate the potential effects of difficult relationships, and suggest capacities we must attend to in therapy. We agree that "because we are God's image-bearers, our relationship with our fellow image-bearer must be consistent with our relationship with God" (Estep, 2010, p. 11), which also implicates children's spiritual development as a potentially important keystone to their peer relationships.

Third, if affirming that all humans carry the image of God grants value to children as they are, then the youngest humans also offer a way for us to think about what the image of God entails. They cannot survive, have their basic needs met and develop into functioning beings unless they are in relationship. God has designed children in such a way that they clearly demonstrate our dependence on others. David Jensen (2005) states, "A baby is open to any human being who will assuage that gift of otherness" (p. 49). Children also uniquely show us the capacity for delight in relationship that we carry because we are created in God's image. At times God simply delights in his creation; children, primarily in play, particularly with their peers, remind all humans that we have the capacity simply to enjoy life and God's creation *with each other*.

Differences between humans, and in human relationships and social contexts, speak to the difference within God himself, as three trinitarian persons. David Jensen (2005) asserts that the fact that "God creates human persons in the divine image does not impose a mold of conformity that outlines terrestrial life; rather, God creates children who embody the differences that are prerequisites to relationship" (p. 35). Clinicians should recognize that this diversity brings differing types of relational experiences both within the clinical space and within the child's peer context. This diversity necessitates thorough assessment of children's individual characteristics that impact peer relations and the nature of children's existing peer relations. Further, we can value this diversity as a prerequisite to beautifully diverse relationships while also supporting children's social skills in coping with this diversity (e.g., perspective-taking, conflict management, group entry skills) and the sometimes overwhelming social dynamics that result (e.g., clique hierarchies, relational aggression).

Finally, affirming that each child is made in the image of God can become the springboard for the clinician to help the child create and/or maintain healthy peer relationships. If children are picked on by peers or actively isolated from the peer group, then how does that impact their view of self and their view of others as being beautifully created in God's image? As the clinician passes on to the child his vision of the child as the bearer of God's image, she will be able to have the confidence to engage in healthy relationships because she knows her own value. The child must also learn that her peers, too, are images of God and require valuing and moral treatment. Thus, knowing that children are bearers of God's image, planned by God, given by God and declared valuable by God provides a solid foundation for drawing out more clearly children's sense of self-worth and recognition of peers' worth, and the potentiality of their positive contributions to their peer relationships.

Christian theology affirms the relational and embodied *imago Dei* because the image of God in all humanity is patterned off of and exemplified in the person of Christ. Christ's embodiment provides the image for what it means to be human in the way God intended and makes living that intention possible even for fallen humanity.

Respect as Persons: Redeemed by the Incarnation
The Nicene Creed, the words affirmed by thousands of Christians on a regular basis during worship, states, "For us and for our salvation he came down from heaven: by the power of the Holy Spirit he became incarnate from the Virgin Mary and was made man." To become incarnate, literally to be made flesh, implies Jesus is both truly God and truly man. We could observe this baby, this boy, this man, and in so doing relate to his life (Cyril, Catechetical Lectures 12.14; in Schaff, 1890–1900, NPNF[2] 7:75). What better way for the Godhead to reveal himself than by coming in the form with which humanity is most intimately acquainted: humanity itself! Rightly understanding the doctrine of the incarnation provides a wellspring of resources for clinicians of faith in their consideration of children's peer relationships.

Why did he do so? An attempt to catalogue the reasons might be impossible. Athanasius states, "And, in a word, the achievements of the Saviour, resulting from His becoming man, are of such kind and number, that if one should wish to enumerate them, he may be compared to men who gaze at the expanse of the sea and wish to count its waves" (Athanasius, *On the Incarnation* 54; in Schaff, 1890–1900, NPNF[2] 4.65). Nevertheless, church theologians have organized the benefits of his incarnation into two primary categories which have importance for this chapter: knowledge and salvation. Athanasius wrote, "He . . . assumed a body for the salvation of us all, and taught the world concerning his Father," and "He came to heal and to teach those who are suffering" (*On the Incarnation* 32; in Schaff, 1890–1900, NPNF² 4.53; NPNF² 4.59).

By living life among us, he was able to show us the image of his Father (Jn 14:8-9; Heb 1:3), including God's intent for humanity. This was not a one-time didactic lesson but instead a lesson that encompassed a life's worth of lived messages. He shows practical ways to live the abundant life that God desires for his human creation. Jesus shows what it is to be in dependent relationship upon God (Mt 14:15-33; Mk 1:32-39; 6:33-52; Lk 3:21-22; 5:12-26; 9:12-21, 28-29). Out of this relationship comes his ability to relate perfectly with other humans. He demonstrates those characteristics toward which all people, including children, must aspire, such as forgiveness (Mt 6:14-15; Lk 23:34), joy (Jn 2:1-12), compassion (Mt 9:36; 14:14; 20:34; Mk 1:40-41; 8:2), and love (Jn 4:4-26; 19:25-26). He also demonstrates for children the interpersonal qualities that are harder to embrace and incorporate into one's own peer relations, including his willingness to speak the truth with intensity (Mt 23; Mk 7:6-13), to reach out to the unlovely (Mt 8:1-4, Mk 1:40-45; 2:15; Lk 5:12-16; 7:36-39; 17:11-19), to stand up for the oppressed (Jn 8:1-11) and to upset the unhealthy status quo (Mt 21:12-17, 23-27; Mk 11:15-19, 27-33; Lk 19:45-48; 20:1-8; Jn 2:13-16). Practically, he demonstrates both how to be a good friend (part of the *promise*) and how to stand up to the bully (which may bring *peril,* or certain social consequences). The words of Scripture that describe God's intent for all humanity have an interpretive living Word in Jesus, and he invites children into this intention.

Jesus Christ is the example for healthy living, relating well to both God and fellow humans. Yet, he came also to redeem, re-create and restore humanity. In his incarnate body, he defeated the power of death when he died and then rose again (Heb 2:15), and made possible for all humanity the ability to attain again incorruption (Athanasius, *On the Incarnation* 9; in Schaff, 1890–1900, NPNF² 4.41) and eternal corporeal life. Because the incarnation restores the *imago Dei* in humanity, the salvific benefits are not only in the future with ultimate salvation from death in the final resurrection of the body. Instead, the incarnation makes possible transformation during this life (McGrath 2005). A restored human is surely one who can live better with others, but even more explicitly, the incarnation restores not just individuals but relationships. The incarnation is itself a relational act; that is, "the incarnation is not a destructive, aggressive act of invasion in which sinful humanity is battered into submission; it is an act of enticement in which the love of God is shown, and the love of humanity is elicited in response" (McGrath, 2005, p. 20). Those who embrace the restoration he makes possible are empowered to live in healthy relationships that reflect the very being of God. Because he has broken the power of sin, humanity can live morally, including in relationship.[6]

Practically, the Christian doctrine of the incarnation and the belief that Jesus models ideal human life can inform and empower Christian clinicians' work with children. Jesus assumed the entire experience of children—every aspect of their lives, including peer relationships—stands under the redeeming power of the incarnation. As full persons, children are redeemed by Jesus' life as much as adults. No less of an ideal is expected for children than can be expected for adults, namely to have strong dependence upon God, healthy relationships, and consequently, a moral, joyful and compassionate life with peers (1 Tim 4:12).

View as Agents: Interdependence as Members of Body of Christ

As the New Testament authors seek to understand the inclusion of all in the assembly of God's people, they nuance a traditional understanding of the people of God. This new gathering (*ekklesia*) is composed of both Jew and Gentile because God has broken down the walls of separation (Eph 2:14-15; see also Acts 10; Gal 3:28). It is a people who have been filled and empowered by God's own spirit (Acts 2), and who have different gifts but all serve the same Lord (Rom 12:1-8; 1 Cor 12:4-31). If we are to follow the example of Jesus, we must recognize that children are not excluded from this interdependence of humans.

Children must be made aware that they are effective participants not only in the church but in all of their relationships. They can come to understand the power they hold as agents in peer relationships. Children can learn both explicitly and experientially that they are made in the image of God and thus carry the ability and responsibility for relationship with God and others. In fact, in his interactions with children Jesus set them apart as examples (Mt 19:13-15; Mk 10:13-16; Lk 18:15-17); they "qualify as disciples and symbols of the reign of God" (Miller-McLemore, 2003, p. 99). As such, they can be agents for positive change in their peer relationships. Further, because they do affect their peers and social environment (e.g., school climate), then they can positively (or neg-

---

[6]Athanasius claimed that he brings about the unity of people and peace among enemies. (*On the Incarnation* 50; in Schaff, 1890–1900, NPNF[2] 4.64).

atively) influence how a peer treats them in return, though it is obviously the peer's own choice (agency) as to how he or she ultimately treats them. Christian theology of children should optimally empower them to be proactive and confident in their relationships, knowing that they can be positive agents. Christian clinicians can build upon the honored status that children hold biblically to encourage them to serve as examples in peer relations.

Recognizing the *imago Dei* in all of humanity practically includes a transformed attitude toward others, transformed behavior toward others and a greater appreciation for diversity among all of humanity. The beauty of the *imago Dei* reveals the deep relational component at the core of humanity, but the interdependence we have as humans opens children to being hurt and hurting others. Just as children are bearers of the *imago Dei,* they are also sufferers of the relational consequences of sin. As discussed, gossip, exclusion and teasing are often common experiences in childhood, and the more extreme peer difficulty of bullying has reached levels of chronic concern, with the recognition that the bully, the victim and bystanders are damaged in the exchange. Yet children's agency can be defined as "'spiritual freedom,' which is a freedom to choose how we relate to our existence rather than defining what our existence *is* through a system of labels and categories" (Webster, 2005, p. 6). He suggests that children form an identity that is based on their values and the reason for those values; thus, we should challenge children to answer the question "what sort of a person am I to become?" (Webster, 2005, p. 14), so that they choose to relate in a certain (*valued*) way to their environment. As clinicians, we can help children understand that they have the choice to engage (or reengage) their peers, and that with that choice, they also have the right to be treated with love and the responsibility to extend love and appreciate the diversity of their social experiences and context. More importantly, we can help them articulate and act from their values.

Standing on the foundation of the tenets that children are gifts and full persons to be valued and respected, we begin to understand how children can move to mature *inter*dependence with others over the course of their development. Healthy self-love is needed in order to be able to love peers and to be guided by value-oriented behavior. Indeed, peer relationships provide an avenue for moral development (Bukowski et al., 2009). Through peer interactions, children learn about equality, fairness, reciprocity, and acceptance and valuing of others. Children must engage in perspective-taking and provide help, nurturance, loyalty and trust. Peer interactions provide the daily opportunity for children to weigh their own desires and needs with those of their peers. Care of others is central to morality and also to friendship, which highlights the connections between morality and children's social world (see Bukowski & Sippola, 1996). Further, Christian morality should necessarily inform children's agentic interactions with others. For example, the teachings that we are not to curse others created in God's image (Lk 6:28; Rom 12:14; Jas 3:9) but instead reach out to the hurting should inform youth in how to handle such normative peer situations as gossip and reaching out to the isolated kid in class. These moral behaviors contribute to children's growing social competence and can also avert maladaptive trajectories by hindering negative peer interactions that represent risk factors.

The study of spirituality and spiritual development recognizes the reciprocal influences between children's relationships and their spiritual development (Schwartz, Bukowski & Aoki, 2006). Though only a small portion of this research has focused on peer relations (vs. parents, supportive adults/mentors), the extant literature suggests the potential impact of children on one another with regard to spiritual development (e.g., religious participation, experience of God, and religious belief and commitment; King, Furrow & Roth, 2002; Schwartz et al., 2006). Schwartz et al. (2006) note that friendships provide an opportunity for children and adolescents to feel a connection with others and a sense of belonging, and to produce "fruit" (e.g., "goodness") in another's life—in other words, these peer relations underscore interdependence. These authors discuss how religious teachings provide emphasis on qualities and practices that contribute to building healthy friendships, including compassion, self-regulation, humility and prosocial behaviors, among others. Further, children are provided with spiritual rationales for the importance of positive relationships with their peers and romantic partners, and specific practices to maintain these relationships (e.g., Flanagan & Loveall, 2012).

Thus, we have the opportunity to build therapeutic relationships and address clinical goals that truly empower children as agents within their peer relationships. We can model and support responsible decision making and moral development, the practice of altruism and engagement, the development of both a sense of belonging and freedom within peer relationships, and an understanding of free will and responsibility to God's beautiful creation.

As clinicians, we must strive to maintain a hope-filled perspective of children's peer relations. Looking through the lens of the gospel we see that, even though peer relationships can provide opportunity to hurt and be hurt, they can also provide opportunities for personal growth and interpersonal service— *even in the midst of the hurt*. As Paul says, where sin abounds, grace can abound so much more (Rom 5:20). Negative experiences with peers have the potential to encourage personal growth and maturity that contributes to resilience and healthy development long term. Children may realize areas in which they need to change, or they may realize that peers' assessment of them was incorrect and that their personal value lies not in others' opinions but ultimately in their value from God and those closest to them. The Christian tradition does not trivialize suffering and admonish its followers to merely "put on a happy face." Instead, it recognizes that God can use suffering in a positive way to bring about maturity, not because the hardship is ignored but because it is lived through and learned from (Heb 12:5-11; Rom 5:3-5). Interpersonally, when children observe or become involved in conflict with peers, they have the opportunity to be a positive agent within the situation; for instance, they can stand up to a bully on behalf of a victim or relinquish a personal "right" to bring about group consensus or offer kindness to a new child in class. Though children will certainly experience the ramifications of relational aspects of sin in their peer relations, they can mature and learn to follow the most challenging command of all: to treat other children, and even their enemy, as they would hope to be treated (Mt 5:43-48; Lk 6:31).

CLINICAL APPLICATION

A comprehensive understanding of the role that peer relations play in children's developmental trajectories helps us to better intervene. The rationale for addressing peer relations within our clinical work also comes from several applied sources. First, preventive and targeted interventions that include goals for improving social competence and peer relations (e.g., increasing prosocial skills, reducing peer victimization, improving peer acceptance, reducing affiliation with deviant peers) reduce the risk for psychopathological outcomes (Bierman et al., 2002; Greenberg, Domitrovich & Bumbarger, 2001; Vitaro, Brendgen, Pagani, Tremblay & McDuff, 1999). We have learned from intervention research that social skills training, particularly when socially competent peers are included in the interventions, can help children with behavioral and emotional problems (Bierman & Powers, 2009). Further, negative peer relations may impede the success of interventions or have iatrogenic effects, as with the negative influence of deviant peers on other children in interventions (Dodge et al., 2006). Thus, as clinicians, we need to be aware of the potential positive or negative power of peer relations in our clinical work. We close this chapter with practical suggestions to help clinicians to maximize the effectiveness of their work with children and adolescents by attending to peer relations.

PRACTICAL SUGGESTIONS

Assessment

- Observe the child during various peer interactions at school (e.g., group work, unstructured free time).

- Obtain multiple reports (child, parents, teachers) of child's overall functioning, and ask the parent or teacher to compare the child to a "typical" same-age peer. Analyze discrepancies between reporters for clinically useful information.

- Consider child's developmental level, age and grade to determine developmentally appropriate expectations for the following: size and nature of friendship network; qualities of healthy friendships; gender make-up of friends and network (same-sex, opposite sex and romantic relationships).

- Assess developmental history of peer relationships from toddlerhood through adolescence.

- Assess current peer status, likeability and popularity.

- Assess specific social skills and friendship skills (e.g., group entry skills, conversation and interaction skills, empathy, social-cognitive processing, social problem-solving and conflict resolution skills, cooperative play skills, ability to provide emotional and instrumental support, remain loyal and keep confidences).

- Assess quantity and quality of both dyadic friendships and group memberships. Possible questions include: How much time does the child spend outside of school with friends? Who are the child's friends? Describe those friendships. What does the child do with his friends? What groups does the child identify with? What kind of support does the child obtain from his friends? Are there any concerns about the child's friendships? When did the named problems start, and what is their nature?

- Assess how the child perceives herself and her relationships with others.

- Assess the peer norms within the child's specific contexts. Take into account cultural considerations as they relate to families, groups, school environment or community. Assess discrepancies or points of difference that may be causing or could cause points of tension (e.g., family values differ from peer norms, acculturative stress).

- Determine the impact of current cognitive, social, behavioral and academic demands, including any recent or upcoming transitions (e.g., transition to middle school, move to new district), on social competence.

- Determine the reciprocal influences between current social competence and other risk and protective factors, including: language and cognitive ability, emotion understanding and regulation; symptoms of psychopathology; family context (e.g., socioeconomic status, attachment relationships, marital relationship, parental psychopathology, parental monitoring); school climate and access to or association with positive peer influences; community resources and risks (e.g., nature of involvement in any youth groups or clubs, gangs, exposure to community violence); spirituality, spiritual values, or involvement in church or religious activities with peers.

Intervention

Intervene on multiple levels as appropriate for the presenting problem and intraindividual, interpersonal, and contextual characteristics.

- Individual
  - Provide social skills training (e.g., modeling, coaching and role-playing techniques; assertiveness training; conflict resolution skills; giving and interpreting nonverbal communication).
  - Address social cognitive processing.
  - Address symptoms of psychopathology that impact peer relations (e.g., aggression, anxiety, depression, ADHD).

- Family
  - Provide parent training regarding social skills, behavioral and emotional regulation, and coping.
  - Increase parental facilitation and monitoring of peer relations (as age appropriate).

- Improve parent-child relationship and parental modeling of effective social skills.

- Group
  - Determine the setting and composition of group and assess appropriateness for group intervention for targeted problem.
  - Normalize typical peer concerns and clarify developmental expectations.
  - Teach social competence in groups to provide opportunities for peer modeling, a safe environment for practice of new skills and fostering of self-confidence.
  - Harness the power of peer relationships in groups to treat psychopathology (groups provide a chance for peers to challenge each other's cognitive distortions, provide an environment for social exposure, provide opportunities to develop assertiveness and conflict resolution skills, provide opportunity to strengthen affective ties).
  - Focus on perspective-taking and challenge cognitive processing in "real time."

- School
  - Foster teacher, staff, and administration understanding and "buy-in" of interventions targeting peer relations; collaborate and utilize their feedback in development and implementation of interventions.
  - Promote prevention and early intervention of peer problems and victimization (e.g., raise awareness of possible problems and their prevalence; encourage collaboration between school and parents; encourage access to school support staff; equip teachers with external referral information).
  - Promote safety, inclusion and positive school climate that includes valuing of diversity and social emotional learning principles.
  - Promote the inclusion of prosocial peers in treatment of aggressive youth rather than aggregating deviant peers, which exacerbates negative behaviors.
  - Utilize peer leaders in the school to promote positive behaviors and values.

7

Prevention and the Promotion of Thriving

Pamela Ebstyne King and
Casey Erin Clardy

WITHIN THE DEVELOPMENTAL PSYCHOPATHOLOGY literature, scholars and clinicians often agree on what we hope to prevent in children and youth (e.g., depression, addiction, delinquency, promiscuity), but less clarity exists on what society aims to promote. For example, such outcomes as academic achievement, leadership, service, filial piety, athleticism and financial success hold different value among diverse cultures. How, then, as Christian psychologists and educators, do we know what to nurture and promote in children and youth? Additionally, with the increasing traction in the developmental literature of concepts such as thriving, flourishing and resilience, Christians must ask what it means for our youth to thrive and flourish. Are these terms defined by popular culture, science and/or theology?

Theological anthropology is immensely informative on these topics. A trinitarian understanding of the *imago Dei,* or the image of God, suggests that humans are created to be in mutually reciprocating relationships, where people exist as unique, whole individuals in interdependent relationships. From this perspective, it might be said that God's goal for human development is for people to become *reciprocating selves* (see Balswick, King & Reimer, 2005)—to experience simultaneous individual uniqueness and unity with others and God. From this perspective, a *developmental teleology* suggests that as reciprocating selves, people flourish as individuals and simultaneously contribute to families, communities, greater society and the kingdom of God.

This is important to address in a discussion of developmental psychopathology because theological anthropology offers a teleological goal, or *telos*—a vision for what children and youth have the potential to become. Consequently, this chapter addresses not only issues of prevention and resiliency but also promotion and thriving. In order to do so, we turn to theology as a resource to understand what God's goal for human development may be. Specifically, we affirm the importance of a theological understanding of children as gifts, unique persons and agents. We review developmental psychopathology and resilience in light of theological anthropology. Next, we present a relational developmental systems framework to emphasize the importance of the interaction between a young person and the many contexts in which he or she lives, which we place in dialogue with the concepts of thriving, positive youth development and resilience in order to understand optimal development in diverse contexts. We then turn to a practical discussion of the role of prevention and promotion in enabling all young people to thrive.

DEVELOPMENTAL TELEOLOGY

As the Christian tradition developed in dialogue with Western philosophical trends, modern theologians (or theologians under the influence of modernity) came to understand the *imago Dei* passages in the Bible as a means of constructing the *individual* self. During the last century, such understandings of biblical texts have been challenged. With a resurgence in the study of the doctrine of the Trinity and a focus on the "threeness" of the one God, the emphasis on the *individual* self has been questioned and a focus on a *relational* self has emerged. Subsequently, a relational understanding of the Trinity largely informs a current understanding of what it means to reflect God's image as human beings.

The doctrine of the Trinity reveals that God exists as Father, Son and Holy Spirit. The three divine persons of the Godhead live in unity as one, yet remain three distinct persons. The communion of the Godhead does not compromise the distinctiveness of the three. From this perspective, particularity and relatedness co-occur. The relatedness of the three is characterized by perfect reciprocity where the three live with and for each other. To live as beings made in the image of God, to be "image bearers," is to exist as reciprocating selves, as unique individuals living in relationship with others. From this perspective, our developmental teleology—our best understanding of God's goal for human development—is the reciprocating self. To live according to God's design is to glorify God as a distinct human being in communion with God and others in mutually giving and receiving relationships.

Another important consideration that expands the relational interpretation of the *imago Dei* is the relational-functional perspective that acknowledges the "assignment" that God gives Adam and Eve in Genesis—that they are to have dominion over the rest of creation. Philosophical theologian Richard Mouw (2012) points out that this feature of exercising dominion is applied uniquely to human beings among the creatures. Consequently, bearing the image of God is apparent when human beings exercise the authority that God has given to them. Mouw sites Kuitert (1972), who described this relational-functional interpretation of being image bearers as being "covenant partners." This idea of covenant partnership integrates the social and the dominion approaches. "Covenant" emphasizes the importance of relationships, while "partnership" points to the privilege and responsibility of living with God and fellow humans, and exercising dominion over creation.

Coming to an understanding of the image of God is very important. Grenz (2001) contends, "Throughout much of Christian history, the link made in Scripture between humans and the divine image has served as the foundation for the task of constructing a Christian conception of the human person or the self" (p. 183). Interpretation of the *imago Dei* strongly influences our understanding of what it means to be human and has a significant bearing on our understanding of the processes and goals of child and youth development. As we address our understanding of development and the emergence of the self, it is crucial to be clear about our understanding of God's intention for being human.

Consequently, from this perspective we might understand that young people are thriving or flourishing when they are on their way to becoming what God created them to be. From a relational-functional perspective this has to do with being a unique person in reciprocal relationships, where a person contributes to one's own development as well as to the lives of their family and friends, and to society. There is both individual development as well as contribution to the greater good. Thriving is not merely a project of self-development; rather, it involves the increasing of the well-being of the individual and the contexts in which that individual is embedded.

This sense of *telos* emphasizes the developmental process and the idea that human beings are works in process toward the *telos* for which God created them. Such a developmental teleology emphasizes the three themes of integration of this volume. First, children are a divine gift. Each human, no matter what age or stage, is a unique creation of God. It is important to value children, especially the most vulnerable, as a society and as God's people, and to recognize the God-given responsibility of caring for and tending to them in such a way that they have the opportunity to thrive as individuals and become participating members of the larger society. Second, children subsequently are full persons, who are to be loved and treated with respect in order to grow them into secure individuals who have the connections, competencies, confidence, character and compassion to make contributions to the systems in which they live (Lerner, Alberts, Jelicic & Smith, 2006). Development of the whole child is promoted when children are in loving relationships with people who are attuned to their emotions, interests and needs, whether those relationships include parents, pastors, teachers, coaches or youth workers. Lastly, children are agentic beings that live in reciprocity with their families, friends, schools and communities and have an impact on others and their contexts. As Christians, it is important that we have respect for the unique personhood of individual children and seek to empower them to make a contribution out of their personal gifts, talents and interests.

Given the potential of children and youth to influence others and society, it is vital that we intentionally nurture their early moral and spiritual development. As such, we are called to be intentional and take active care of the world's children. We are not called to babysit and make sure they have a good time until their heavenly Father comes home. Instead, we are to be stewards of God's creations and enable them to thrive and grow into the *telos* for which God created them.

Developmental Psychopathology and Resiliency

We affirm a developmental teleology that suggests God's design for optimal human functioning centers around distinct human beings glorifying God through communion with God and others in mutually giving and receiving relationships. This provides a helpful lens for Christian clinicians and scholars to approach the study of developmental psychopathology. Defined as a contextually based discipline that focuses on the interactions among biopsychosocial factors that influence, but do not unilaterally determine, the course of normal or abnormal development (Cicchetti, 2006), developmental psychopathology seeks to examine the relationships between individuals and their environments over time. From a trinitarian theological perspective, the goal of human development is reciprocity of relationship with individuals and others (both God and humans). Therefore, what better developmental yardstick to measure optimal human functioning than striving for a comprehensive assessment of a person's resources, risks and opportunities for growth in *relationship* to the multiple contexts in which that person is embedded?

In relationships, humans are constantly managing a variety of competing demands, needs, resources and challenges. Those who are in relationships that are deemed "healthy" have neither eradicated struggle nor optimized competency but instead have learned to successfully manage these tensions with an "other" over time. For example, a teen who lost her mother in Hurricane Katrina and then her father to cancer was legally adopted by her softball coach. Although the youth continued to struggle with grief and engaged in risk-taking behaviors at times, her adoptive mother and caring coach supported her throughout the ups and downs of her journey, which led to her eventually attending and playing ball at a Division I university.

In the same way, a relational view of development suggests that abnormal, normal and even optimal developmental trajectories are not determined by the degree to which risk is minimized and competence is promoted, but instead the degree to which an individual is able to successfully negotiate and thrive, in the fullest sense of both give and take, in relationship to his or her changing contextual demands over time. That is, youth who engage in mutual, reciprocal relationships with others gain invaluable skills and experience in learning how to negotiate the ongoing processes of ensuring their needs are met while contributing to meeting others' needs. Orienting the study of developmental psychopathology around this mutual give-and-take relational structure of development is not only consistent with developmental systems theory but also offers a distinctly Christian approach, as it mirrors a relational, triune God's loving design for humanity to live in relational reciprocity.

Considering the ever-changing nature of relationships, it is reasonable to assume that human functioning ebbs and flows over time in response to complex, multilayered interactions of person and context. Multiple, bidirectional factors are constantly shaping a child's ability to both respond to and influence his or her environment. These co-occurring processes exist in dynamic relationship to one another, and together contribute to a child's subsequent course of development. Therefore, no particular set of developmental factors can predict a specific set of developmental outcomes (or vice versa). Said another way, children with similar access to developmental resources can end up with vastly different developmental outcomes (*multifinality*), and children with stark contrasts in developmental resources can reach similar developmental outcomes (*equifinality*; Cicchetti & Rogosch, 1996). No developmental trajectory is immune to risk or protection. A child's process of adaptation can flounder or flourish at any point along his or her course of development, forging an entirely different developmental pathway that may lead to alternate developmental outcomes. That said, early development of competence and resources in youth will likely facilitate successful resolution of later developmental tasks and milestones. In the same way, children who do not possess certain resources and abilities early in development may fail to develop subsequent competencies or master certain tasks later in development due to the absence of requisite skills. This notion of *developmental cascades* suggests that the cumulative effects of development accrue over time and will likely "cascade" into other areas of functioning (Masten & Cicchetti, 2010).

Although it is clear that normative development, or even optimal functioning, is not determined by any one set of factors or competencies in youth, how are certain risk factors mitigated in youth who face multiple deficits, chronic stressors and/or extreme adversity? It is important to note that when faced with adversity, the general trend of development is that children tend to respond with *resilience*, also known as the processes by which one "adapts well in the face of adversity, trauma, tragedy, threats, or even significant sources of stress" (APA, 2011). Benard (2004) defines resilience simply as "none other than the process of healthy human development" (p. 9). Again, the importance of context with respect to resilience cannot be overlooked. Brooks (2006) describes resilience as ecological in nature, stating that it "cannot be developed by sheer willpower within the at-risk person; it is developed through interactions within the environment, families, school, neighborhoods, and the larger community" (p. 70).

Resilience can be evidenced in a variety of forms: personal competencies, coping mechanisms and ability to recover from traumatic life events (Masten, 2001). Resilience is not simply an innate quality that children either possess or lack, but instead it is conceptualized as a capacity that changes over time in relation to a child's changing contexts, vulnerabilities, competencies, developmental tasks and environmental influences at any given time. Research has demonstrated that protective factors that promote resilience in children include positive relationships with caregivers, other nurturing adults and friends/peers; strong cognitive and intellectual skills; good self-regulation skills; a positive sense of self-efficacy; healthy relationships with community supports and structures; prosocial cultural values and traditions; realistic goal setting and achievement; and a sense of meaning, purpose and hope for the future (Benard, 2004).

From a Christian perspective, a discussion of resilience would be remiss without acknowledging the role of grace. As Christian clinicians and scholars, we understand that God may work through a variety of mentors, interventions, relationships and experiences at any given point in a child's life to bring healing and wholeness through the power of the Holy Spirit. We also acknowledge that God may work through supervenient powers that are beyond our scientific understanding. (For additional resources on a theology of children and the role of the Holy Spirit, see Marty, 2007; Miller-McLemore, 2003; Nye, 2009.)

Children display not only remarkable resilience but also signs of thriving under less than optimal conditions due to their ability to adapt or cope and the availability of relationships and resources that contribute to resilience under these conditions. Though exposure to certain types of risk factors can serve as vulnerabilities for child populations later in life, at the same time, we must recognize that adversity can serve as a training ground for developing and strengthening the necessary competencies for a youth's survival, and even thriving, across multiple areas of functioning.

DEVELOPMENTAL SYSTEMS THEORIES AND THRIVING

Developmental systems theories (DST) are particularly useful for explaining how development occurs as well as understanding how children and youth may thrive. From this perspective, we discuss resilience and thriving as they relate to prevention and promotion, respectively. Bundick, Yeager, King and Damon (2010) defined thriving as "a dynamic and purposeful process of individual ↔ context interactions over time, through which the person and his/her environment are mutually enhanced" (p. 891).

The significance of the transactions between *person* and *context* is foundational to DST. From this perspective, development occurs through the mutual interactions between individuals and the environments in which they live. The concepts of plasticity and developmental regulation are also central to DST (Lerner, 2006). *Plasticity* refers to the potential for an individual to change systematically in both positive and negative ways (biologically and psychologically) throughout his or her life. As such, plasticity is important in that it legitimates both the optimistic search for characteristics of people and their contexts that promote positive development and thriving as well as the hope for finding strategies and interventions that cultivate thriving.

Developmental regulation refers to changes within the individual and the systems in which the individual is embedded because of the bidirectional interactions between the two. For example, a child may attend and participate in a local congregation. Developmental regulation occurs as various systems within a church (e.g., beliefs, practices, members) influence the child and as the child impacts the congregation. It is the "goodness of fit" between person and environment that is of primary concern in determining different developmental trajectories (see chapter 2, this volume). From this perspective, optimal development occurs when the mutual influences between person and environment maintain or advance the well-being of the individual *and* his or her context. This positive bidirectional relation is referred to as *adaptive developmental regulation*. Continuing our example, a child growing in such areas as her sense of identity, social relationships and faith while simultaneously contributing to the life of the church through leading in singing or bringing joy and delight would be an example of adaptive developmental regulation.

Developmental systems perspectives on plasticity and adaptive developmental regulation contribute to an understanding of human thriving and provide a theoretical framework to understand how thriving may occur. The emphases on the potential for change, the reciprocal transactions between children and their environments, and the mutual advancement of the well-being of individual and society are consistent with our proposed developmental teleology. Developmental systems approaches recognize the significance of the uniqueness of the individual and his or her potential to influence the communities in which that individual is embedded. Acknowledging the importance of context means recognizing how parents, friends, congregations, schools, therapists, and the Holy Spirit may all impact the development of our children. In addition, an understanding of thriving that includes contribution to something greater than oneself directly reflects the functional interpretation of the *imago Dei,* which insists that humans bear God's image when they follow the divine mandate to be stewards and caretakers of God's creation (including fellow humans). Thus, developmental systems theory provides a psychological lens through which to understand how the reciprocating self may be realized and how children are gifts from God, full and unique persons, and active agents in this world.

POSITIVE YOUTH DEVELOPMENT

Although developmental systems approaches provide a theoretical lens through which to view the development of the reciprocating self from infancy to later life, they do not emphasize practical, applied strategies for nurturing children and adolescents into becoming fully reciprocating selves. Positive youth development (PYD) aims to fill this gap. PYD is a broad interdisciplinary movement that includes the study and practice of optimal development in young people. Thriving may be understood, then, as PYD's optimal developmental trajectory. In fact, in the existing literature, the terms "thriving" and "positive youth development" are often used interchangeably. Based on a review of existing literature on PYD and thriving, we offer five concepts foundational to positive youth development: (1) an optimistic view of the child, (2) the importance of context, (3) a developmental and holistic perspective, (4) an emphasis on positive developmental outcomes, and (5) the role of a youth's contribution to others (see Benson, Scales, Hamilton & Sesma, 2006; Bundick et al., 2010; Damon, 2004; Lerner, 2004, 2006).

Optimistic View of Child

PYD emphasizes children and adolescents' potential to grow and to change (Benson & Scales, 2009; Benson et al., 2006; Damon, 2004; Lerner, 2004, 2006). PYD is a strengths-based approach; that is, it is built on the idea that *all* youth have strengths that can be nurtured, and it encourages development through identification and honing of skills, competencies, characters, and interests in a way that helps them reach their full potential. This is especially important when working with children with disabilities or identified risk factors (as discussed in chap. 1). PYD also emphasizes that youth themselves play an active role in their development. Often, youth-engendered development begins with the pursuit of a self-identified passion or spark (Benson & Scales, 2009). PYD approaches help youth identify their spark (e.g., photography, soccer, writing) and nurture and support its development through providing opportunities for training or education. As youth pursue their passion, they continue to refine their abilities to achieve their potential and experience satisfaction. From a PYD perspective, health is not about simply being "problem-free" or competent but rather about developing capacities and pursuing personal interests.

Context

In addition to the potential of the child, understanding the role of context is central to PYD. As previously stated, from a developmental systems perspective, thriving emphasizes that development occurs as a young person interacts with his or her multiple systems. Positive development occurs when these interactions between person and context are mutually beneficial, maintaining healthy and positive functioning of the young person and the systems in which he or she lives. For example, optimal development may be said to be occurring when a child is learning academic and social skills in her classroom setting but also contributing constructively to that environment through her engagement with her teachers and peers. Positive developmental contexts offer youth a place to engage new roles and values through a safe environment. At their best, these contexts provide supports (e.g., relationships, opportunities and resources) so that youth have the tools and abilities necessary for adult life.

Developmental and Holistic

PYD and thriving are developmental concepts that emphasize that the whole child is on a pathway to a hopeful future. Whereas there is no fixed or idealized trajectory toward purposeful, relational and healthy adulthood (Larson, 2000), thriving involves a generally stable upward trajectory across time (Bundick et al., 2010). When youth are adequately supported, obstacles and challenges provide opportunities for increased initiative, flexibility and secure identity (Damon, 2004; Erikson, 1968). Extending Vygotsky's (1978) concept of scaffolding, a PYD approach calls for *developmental scaffolding*, or personalized support around a young person that guides his attitudes and behaviors while he matures in identity and life competencies. For example, a teen might experience turmoil within a peer group at school, causing distress. In response, a parent or mentor might intentionally dialogue with the teen about her experience, offer emotional support, and help steer her toward reconciliation or transitioning into other relationships.

Recognizing the complexity of development and of the whole child, PYD entails thriving in all aspects of life and living with balance. This perspective also acknowledges the reality of adversity, failure and even what might be regarded as decline. From a thriving or PYD perspective, these realities are not necessarily bad. Rather, they may be perceived as opportunities for growth and development. For example, the identity crisis sparked by an adolescent's conflict with her peer group might promote healthy self-examination and the development of an identity not defined by relationships with others. Developmental regulation emphasizes that the individual and the system must adaptively regulate for positive development to occur. Said another way, systems and circumstances always change, and thriving refers to an individual's capacity to grow productively in the face of change. This growth or development is not necessarily linear, but instead occurs over time. A young person adapts in such a way that he or she continues to grow personally and make meaningful contributions to the greater society throughout childhood and adolescence. Consequently, a developmental or long-term perspective allows one to understand how a child or adolescent will ultimately respond to difficult situations or periods of decline across the lifespan.

Positive Outcomes

The standard of health from a PYD perspective is more than the absence of pathology and risk behaviors; it also entails the presence of indicators of positive individual development and social contribution. Consequently, individual outcomes associated with PYD include the absence or reduction of mental illness, violence, delinquency, sexual abuse and substance abuse, as well as the presence or increase of health, life satisfaction, academic achievement, meaning, purpose, identity, altruism and civic engagement. As such, a thriving young person is said to have personal satisfaction and a sense of purpose, as well as the ability to give back to the greater good of society as an agentic being.

One helpful way to conceptualize thriving is the "Six Cs." Lerner and colleagues' (2005) research with the 4-H organization (see www.4-h.org) has yielded a practical and popular approach to conceptualizing positive youth development that is often cited in the literature and has been used in many communities and youth programs. The "Six Cs" (or sometimes referred to as the "Five Cs") of positive youth development deliberately seek to broaden the conceptualization of successful development beyond skills and competencies and include:

- Competence in cognitive, academic, social and vocational areas

- Confidence that encompasses self-esteem, self-concept, self-efficacy, identity and belief in the future
- Connections to family, peers, organizations and community
- Character encompassing areas like positive values, integrity, moral commitments and spirituality
- Caring and compassion

Research has demonstrated that when youth have these five "Cs," they also report having a commitment to service and leadership (Lerner et al., 2005). Consistent with the reciprocating self and our understanding of thriving, the "Six Cs" acknowledge the importance of both the development of the individual as well as the contribution to the greater good.

In addition to promoting success or well-being in children and adolescents, PYD nurtures a commitment to giving back to society (Benson et al., 2006; Bundick et al., 2010; Damon, 2004; Lerner, 2004, 2006; King et al., 2005). This is often reflected in the literature through the domains of civic, moral and spiritual development, and evidenced through civic engagement, volunteerism and various forms of service or caring. This moral emphasis underscores the previously quoted PYD mantra "problem-free is not fully prepared" (Pittman, 1991) and casts a vision for young people who are active agents in their communities. It is important to note that contribution takes on different forms for diverse youth with various abilities, passions and resources, and is always contextually and developmentally appropriate.

Positive youth development contends that children and youth are not "problems to be managed," but rather "resources to be developed." The optimistic perspective of young people and their inherent potential for change, the emphasis on fit between the child and context, the consideration of the complexities of developmental trajectories and the realities of failure and decline, and the emphasis on positive outcomes and contribution provides a vision of youth that is often overlooked in mental health literature. The emphasis is not remedial but developmental. It moves from a deficit model to an asset model (Benson et al., 2006). No doubt, this perspective is idealistic, but it is not unrealistic nor does it deny the adversity and suffering that many children endure. Rather, it provides a hopeful lens through which to view young people—and the families and communities in which they live. Although not faith-based, PYD is a practical approach to parenting or working with children that is consistent with the three main integrative themes of this volume. Central to PYD is the perspective that children are precious gifts, who are to be respected and cared for as unique individuals, and who are to be nurtured to reach their potential, so that they may engage in the world fully equipped and out of their deepest passions, which includes personal spirituality.

SPIRITUAL DEVELOPMENT

An important element of thriving is spirituality. The burgeoning body of literature on thriving and positive youth development increasingly points to the significance of spirituality and religion in the lives of young people (see Benson & Scales, 2009; Lerner, Roeser & Phelps, 2008; King & Benson, 2006; King, Carr & Boitor, 2011; Warren, Lerner & Phelps, 2011). Developmental psychologists point to the significance of young people transcending themselves and growing in their awareness of and commitment to entities beyond themselves, such as family, God, congregations, politics or causes. As Christians, this aspect of development is central to our understanding of being human. The *telos* we have proposed in this chapter explicitly acknowledges that the purpose for which humans were created is to be in relationship with God and others. Recognizing spiritual and religious development as a unique domain of development is vital to understanding young people and the many resources available to them.

Although religion and spirituality are related, it is important to distinguish between them and understand these concepts in light of our theoretical perspectives. We argue that understanding spiritual and religious development to the fullest provides rich resources for interventions and "promotions" for children and adolescents. Frequently in the literature, being spiritual refers to experiencing transcendence, a quest for the sacred, and meaning-making (see Benson, Roehlkepartain & Rude, 2003; King, Ramos & Clardy, 2013; Koenig, McCullough & Larson, 2001; Pargament, 2007; Zinnbauer & Pargament, 2005), whereas religiousness has often referred to adherence to and participation in the beliefs, practices, and rituals of an organized religious tradition (Benson et al., 2003; Koenig et al., 2001; Zinnbauer & Pargament, 2005).

From a developmental systems perspective, spiritual and religious development occur through the interactions of a young person and the many systems in which he or she lives. It is through these interactions, or relationships, that young people experience something of significance beyond the self and gain a growing sense of transcendence. This connection can be to a divine other (e.g., God), it can involve a sense of all of humanity, or it may pertain to a specific religious community, to peers or perhaps even to nature. Such experiences are *spiritual* when they are imbued with meaning to the extent that they inform identity and motivate contribution to the greater good (King et al., 2013; Lerner, Dowling & Anderson, 2003; Lerner et al., 2008). From this perspective, central to spiritual development is the interaction between the self and some generalized or specific other that informs one's beliefs and commitments and propels one to live in a manner mindful of his or her part in a broader web of meaning and connection.

Spiritual development is not simply a quest or meaning-making endeavor but emphasizes the growth that comes from experiencing transcendence and the meaning, identity, and action that stem from this process. Religious development focuses on the changes in an individual's participation in and understanding of an organized system of beliefs, practices, rituals, and symbols that serve to facilitate an individual's closeness to the sacred or a transcendent other (i.e., God, higher power, ultimate truth). It is important to note that although the distinction between the personal and institutional level may be prominent in the literature, to over-emphasize this point and dichotomize these constructs limits an understanding of the complexity of both religion and spirituality, as both have individual, corporate and cultural expressions (see Pargament, Exline, Jones, Mahoney & Shahfranske, 2013).

What do religious or spiritual rituals mean to an adolescent? In a study on global adolescent spiritual exemplars, we found that youth who were nominated for living in their culture with profound spirituality reported the significance of transcendence, fidelity and action in their lives (King, Clardy & Ramos, in press). For example, a Peruvian adolescent girl described her profound experiences of being comforted by God during her parents' divorce, how this shaped her loyalty to and identity in God, and how her allegiance to God motivated her to care for and reach out to others.

From this perspective, religion and spirituality offer many potential ideological, social and transcendent resources for use in promoting positive clinical and developmental outcomes (see King, 2008). The prosocial beliefs, values and morals usually available through religion can enable young people to make sense of the world, provide guidelines for choosing behaviors, and form a constructive identity conducive to thriving. In addition, religious congregations can provide role models and people that exemplify the values and ethics of the faith tradition (Roehlkepartain & Patel, 2006). We should not underestimate the power of these transcendent experiences with God or the broader faith community to inspire and propel young people onto a more positive developmental trajectory.

From a resilience perspective, spirituality and religion provide rich resources for helping youth cope with and overcome adversity. For example, from an ideological perspective, religions generally promote worldviews through which youth can reframe and understand experiences of suffering from an existential perspective. A narrative perspective highlights how youth derive meaning from their overarching understanding of existence, human nature, the creation story and ultimate reality (McAdams, 2006). Meaning is constructed within their particular network of relationships and contexts, including personal experience, family, peers, neighborhood, school, church, society and culture (Quagliana, King, Wagener & Quagliana, 2012). In addition, religious congregations provide opportunities for social support that may provide extra scaffolding in difficulty or when family resources may be challenged. Finally, from a transcendent perspective, experiencing oneself as a beloved child of God or having a prayer answered may sustain young people in difficult times (King et al., 2013; Smith, 2003).

Religion and spirituality are also fertile ground for thriving and positive youth development. The beliefs, values and morals promoted by most religious traditions are prosocial and encourage not only health-oriented behaviors but also acts of compassion, generosity and service (King, 2008; Lerner et al., 2003; 2008). In addition, religious narratives provide opportunities for forming a noble sense of purpose, as children and adolescents discover an understanding of how their personal stories fit within the larger religious narrative (Quagliana et al., 2012). Faith-based programs also often offer adult support outside of the family as well as opportunities for youth to serve and lead in various forms of ministry. Lastly, experiencing oneself as part of something greater can motivate young people to give to others and encourage their efforts to be contributing members of this world.

These are just a few examples of how spiritually oriented interventions can promote both resiliency and thriving in young people and may offer important clinical and developmental resources to children and adolescents (King, 2008; King & Benson, 2006; Quagliana et al., 2012). Next, we turn to a practical discussion of implications for promoting resiliency and thriving in diverse children and adolescents.

IMPLICATIONS FOR PREVENTION AND PROMOTION

Ideally, clinicians should seek to address the prevention needs of communities, families and children instead of only responding to acute and long-term distress with intervention strategies. Specifically, in treating the mental health needs of children, it is particularly important to anticipate their future needs and concerns based on approaching developmental tasks in a proactive versus reactionary stance. Adopting a proactive approach to service delivery is essential to promoting thriving across every stage of development, given that positive youth development can be promoted with each new developmental milestone or interaction with a youth's environment. Traditionally, prevention efforts have emphasized a tiered approach based on level of severity and stage of intervention in a particular population at risk (e.g., primary prevention, or disseminating knowledge to warn and inform; secondary prevention, or reducing risk and intervening with current problems to prevent future crisis or increased distress; and tertiary prevention, or preventing symptom relapse or intensification within existing disease processes; Kerig & Wenar, 2006). (For thorough reviews of youth prevention programs, see CDC, 2007 on youth violence; Lundahl & Nimer, 2006 on child abuse; US DoE, 2009 on dropout.)

However, as Christian ambassadors of holistic health and well-being, we must move beyond the use of narrowly defined preventive efforts in response to the presence of risk factors. Instead we must first begin with understanding how to shift the beliefs and views of the adults in children's families, communities, schools and religious institutions from minimizing risk to encouraging resilience and, ultimately, promoting thriving. Embracing a position of promotion allows those engaged with youth to instill competencies, address deficits, reduce risks and encourage thriving in the lives of all children, their families and their environments.

We believe that emphasizing promotion instead of merely prevention is a more comprehensive, holistic response to the belief that children are gifts, respected persons and agents within the kingdom of God. Designing youth programs to address the promotion of strengths acknowledges the agentic role that children can play in shaping and even transforming their environments, as well as God's ability to work through children as divine gifts and fully human beings who are worthy of respect. Recognizing children as divine gifts, whole persons, and viable agents of moral and spiritual change for themselves as well as their communities is further consistent with a developmental systems framework, as both of these theological and psychological perspectives affirm that a mutually reciprocal relationship exists between children and their environments.

In light of these perspectives, it is our suggestion that adopting a reciprocating view of prevention and promotion strategies may be a helpful framework for Christian scholars and clinicians. In essence, we posit that prevention and promotion strategies should aim to be holistic in nature, seeking to reduce risks, address deficits, bolster competencies, and promote thriving, while striving to be contextually relevant, culturally consistent, developmentally appropriate and spiritually sensitive. It is our view that preventing mental illness and promoting thriving in youth cannot be accomplished without adequate emphasis on the role of relationships in healthy development. As a clinician, this means establishing a solid relationship with the child and his or her many contexts, understanding the impact of the child's formative relationships, and assessing the child's ability to successfully negotiate the relationship between his or her resources and vulnerabilities and environmental demands and opportunities. Further, we acknowledge that such reciprocating strategies affirm children and youth as agentic beings who have the capacity to change, transform and benefit the practitioner/clinician through the mutual give-and-take exchanges available in these types of mentoring relationships.

For prevention and promotion strategies to be contextually relevant, they must act upon both the child and the many systems of which he or she is a part. Perhaps driven by the influence of modernity and individualism, the divorce of prevention programs from children's ecological contexts fails to account for the relationship that exists between child and context. To attempt to exert influence on a child as a separate being apart from her familial, cultural, community, school, social or religious/spiritual contexts is not only limited and ineffectual but also in violation of God's call to be interdependent, mutually reciprocal beings (which includes children).

One example of a contextually driven prevention program is based on the findings of the Mother-Child Interaction Project. The Steps Toward Effective Enjoyable Parenting (STEEP) program was developed to address the prevention needs of impoverished communities by accounting for the specific contextual factors and psychosocial stressors that existed within individual families. In the STEEP program, clinicians provide ongoing home visits and support groups catered to the specific needs, resources, challenges and strengths of individual families from pregnancy through the early years of childhood. This prevention-oriented program provided education, resources and a community of support to these underserved families, which led to higher rates of healthy attachment and positive outcomes (e.g., mother's responsiveness, community life skills, level of organization, etc.) that benefitted these children (for a review, see Egeland & Erickson, 2004). This case demonstrates how promoting a young child's well-being can often be best accomplished by addressing the presenting needs of the parents in order to promote their overall functioning and success as caregivers. Targeting the needs of the child's primary caregivers will not only serve to protect the child from various risk factors but will also help instill positive resources in the parent-child relationship that will aid both parties throughout the course of the child's development.

Another important aspect of designing prevention and promotion programs for success within a child's multi-faceted ecological landscape is seeking to be culturally consistent. Although pursuing cultural consistency often complicates the work of a clinician, we believe that honoring the unique particularities of culture and context is consistent with a Christian worldview, and that affirming diversity is emblematic of the complexity of God as our Creator. Christ came to earth as a human in a specific cultural context. Throughout the Bible, God spoke to specific people at specific times using specific cultural references and symbols. In the same way, we as Christian clinicians and scholars must design programs and therapeutic approaches that are consistent with the cultural values and traditions of the specific population of youth that we aim to serve.

For example, Journeys of the Circle (Marlatt et al., 2003) is an excellent example of a program addressing a particular cultural group's prevention needs by incorporating specific communal values and traditions within the context of treatment. In this preventive program geared toward addressing substance and alcohol use in Native American tribal populations in the Northwest, youth are divided into "canoe families" who commit to intentional activities and mentorship with others who have chosen to abstain from drugs and alcohol for a year. Together with tribal leaders and community elders, these youth learn to work together to construct projects and accomplish tasks in the wilderness and at sea, while learning practical skills (e.g., how to build a canoe), visiting fellow tribes, and participating in traditional rituals and ceremonies. Through the use of "talking circles," youth dialogue with tribal leaders and respected elders in order to solve problems in a proactive manner, which helps communicate long-standing values and traditions such as honor, respect and dignity, as well as providing solutions to help youth cope with conflict and struggle.

Additionally, striving to be developmentally appropriate is critical in developing relevant and effective prevention and promotion strategies for youth. Ascribing to the singular philosophy that a child is a product of his or her environment while failing to consider a child's individual resources and competencies and the child's impact on the environment is insufficient. Therefore, programs that engage in comprehensive assessment of a child's current needs, deficits, competencies, challenges and opportunities can help youth maximize their current developmental context to shape them toward optimal development. Bolstering personal competencies and character, as well as instilling adaptive strategies in youth, equips them with tools for a lifetime of learning. This allows youth to thrive in relationship to their environments across the lifespan, instead of merely addressing deficits at a certain point of contact along their developmental course in order to restore more "normative" functioning at that point.

Although focusing on thriving is a relatively new approach to practice, a handful of programs or frameworks exist. From a holistic and developmental perspective, they emphasize the competencies and character that are necessary for adolescents to transition into prosocial and productive adults. We highlight a few that are consistent with our *telos* of reciprocating selves. For example, Search Institute's 40 Developmental Assets provides a framework for understanding individual and contextual resources that serve as building blocks for positive youth development as well as promote thriving. They acknowledge that all youth need their families, schools and communities to offer various forms and experiences of support, empowerment, boundaries and expectations, and constructive uses of time. They also stress the importance of young people having internal assets such as (1) a commitment to learning, (2) positive values, (3) various social competencies, and (4) a sense of positive identity (see www.search-institute.org/assets).

As mentioned previously, Lerner (2004) indicated that an individual who develops competence, confidence, connection, character and caring over time manifests indicators of positive development. Lerner and colleagues' (2006) research has demonstrated that the first five Cs predict the sixth C, contribution. The extensive studies on the 4-H programs have shown that young people who report higher levels of personal competencies, self-confidence, relationships with others, strong character and a sense of compassion tend to report higher levels of contributions to others beyond themselves. From Lerner and colleagues' (2006) perspective, these youth are said to be thriving because of their capacity to demonstrate positive individual outcomes as well as contribute to the greater good of their surrounding communities.

Building on Search Institute's 40 Developmental Assets and Lerner's (2006) Six Cs, the Thrive Foundation for Youth (see www.thrivefoundation.org) has sought to identify what promotes thriving in young people. The foundation has engaged in extensive collaborative research with scholars and clinicians and has identified indicators of and resources for thriving (see Benson & Scales, 2009; Damon, 2008; King et al., 2005; Lerner et al., 2005) in order to create resources to promote thriving through intentional relationships between adults and youth. They highlight twelve indicators of thriving, or qualities of successful young people, including healthy habits, life skills, love of learning, emotional competence, social skills, positive relationships, spiritual growth, character, caring, confidence, resourcefulness and purpose.

Figure 7.1. Thrive Foundation for Youth's indicators of thriving

In addition, they have developed a clinician and youth-friendly "tool kit" based on recent developmental and educational research that provides the opportunity for a youth and adult to have a structured conversation regarding the processes of thriving in the young person's life (see www.stepitup2thrive.com). The dialogue is comprised of four modules or stages that assist youth in (1) identifying their passion or spark (see Benson, 2008; Benson & Scales, 2009), (2) developing a growth mindset (see Dweck, 2006), (3) reflecting and taking inventory of their indicators of thriving and risk factors that might hinder their growth (Benson & Scales, 2009; Damon, 2004; King et al., 2005; Lerner et al., 2005), and (4) building youths' capacity for goal management (see Gestsdottir & Lerner, 2007). Although cutting-edge research underlies the content, the downloadable materials provide activities and resources that are graphically enticing, approachable and a practical means to engage youth in a manner that intentionally promotes thriving.

A nationwide movement toward implementing prevention-based programs within the school context has included a focus on social and emotional learning (SEL) as a way to target five specific areas of competency (Dusenbury, Zadrazil, Mart & Weissberg, 2011). Instilling self-awareness (recognizing one's emotions and thoughts and their influence on behavior), self-management (regulating one's emotions, thoughts and behaviors effectively in different situations), social awareness (taking the perspective of and empathizing with others), relationship skills (establishing and maintaining healthy and rewarding relationships with diverse individuals and groups), and responsible decision making (making constructive and respectful choices about personal behavior and social interactions) has been demonstrated to promote improvements in overall school climate, students' behavior and academic performance (Durlak, Weissberg, Dymnicki, Taylor & Schellinger, 2011). For example, Lions Quest Social and Emotional Learning program targets increased academic achievement and decreased problem behaviors by focusing on instilling the following prosocial behaviors and socioemotional competencies in youth in kindergarten through grade 12: increasing self-awareness, behavior management, responsible decision making, relationship skills, managing conflict/bullying, service learning and civic engagement. Youth gain the opportunity to learn and practice these skills through group activities with their peers in a school context, as well as through take-home exercises and lessons for use with their family members. By focusing on empowering youth, their families and their educators with the tools, skills, and lessons to promote positive development and success across multiple environments (e.g., academic, social, communal and familial), youth are encouraged to thrive and have demonstrated numerous positive outcomes, including improved attitudes toward and increased knowledge of health-oriented behaviors, decreased risk-taking behaviors, and improved academic performance (Lions Quest, n.d.). (For the latest review of specific outcomes and program details of other SEL-based programs in preschool and elementary school settings, see the CASEL guide, 2013.)

Given the pertinence of spiritual development in both Christian and developmental systems perspectives, it would be remiss not to discuss the importance of being spiritually sensitive in work with children and young people. Not only do religion and spirituality offer many potent resources for fostering resilience and thriving, but also critically engaging with the many existential issues that can arise in clinical work with children and adolescents as it relates to their values, meaning, beliefs, coping and sense of purpose. The spiritual beliefs of children and adolescents can become evident in a psychotherapeutic relationship as young people strive to make sense of their circumstances (Quagliana et al., 2012). As clinicians build relationships with their clients, this relationship can serve as an important context for intentional discussions regarding meaning and purpose and how spiritual and religious values relate to the challenges and opportunities at hand.

In addition, the notions of transcendence and connectedness to others and ideas outside of oneself can be activated in a clinical setting to promote resources for coping or for the formation of compassionate engagement. For instance, a teen who is recovering from child abuse can draw upon his spiritual resources that may include an understanding of and connection to a loving God who forgives him daily to facilitate his journey toward learning to forgive his perpetrator and receive healing support from others. By developing spiritual sensitivity in treatment, clinicians can promote a youth's engagement with the spiritual resources that she may be afforded by the ongoing process of spiritual development. Effective utilization of these resources may enrich the therapeutic process and achievement of particular outcomes in children in a manner that is more culturally consistent and contextually relevant according to their specific faith traditions. (For practical resources to promote spiritual development in children, see Powell & Clark, 2011; Yust, 2004.)

Conclusion

Resilience and thriving are central concepts in the effective application of developmental psychopathology. Maintaining a firm grasp on the tendency toward resilience in children encourages viewing normative and adaptive functioning from a positive youth development perspective. However, incorporating promotion efforts that seek to nurture resilience and thriving moves beyond mere risk reduction to instilling competencies and character and more fully addresses a holistic picture of the complexity of contextual factors at work in child development. This approach emphasizes that children are unique creations and gifts from God, are full persons to be treated with respect, and are to be empowered to realize their full abilities as current and future contributing members of our society as they grow and mature through childhood, adolescence and into adulthood.

Taken together with a Christian worldview, nurturing thriving in youth must include proactive means of promoting their capacity for relationship and spirituality. Viewed this way, optimal development is not merely a reduction of risk factors or even a promotion of competencies. Rather, it is the ability of an individual to successfully negotiate and thrive in a reciprocating relationship to his or her changing contextual demands over time, given the biopsycho-social-spiritual factors in play at a particular point along any given developmental trajectory. From this perspective, adaptability is a core competency necessary for developmental success. Thus, prevention and promotion programs should seek to instill in youth flexibility and the ability to be attuned to one's changing environment in such a way that he or she is enabled to grow as an individual and contribute to the greater world.

As Christian therapists, or therapists who are Christian, we feel a deep conviction to be stewards of the children God has put directly or indirectly (through our students and/or clients) in our paths. Whether it is in our scholarly, clinical or ministerial work, we endeavor to enable God's children to become all that God created them to be. The teleological perspective of the reciprocating self provides a type of lens through which we can view child and adolescent development, intervention, prevention and promotion; understand what is beneficial to development; and evaluate how certain approaches and programs may promote the mutual reciprocity that is inherent to the concept of thriving. Just as development does not occur in a vacuum or in isolation, neither does the implementation of this type of strengths-based, relational reciprocity approach for enabling young people to thrive. We are grateful for the number of committed therapists, educators, youth workers, counselors, caregivers and parents who labor to help children develop more fully into who God has created them to be as contributing members of our world. It is only in working together that we can envision and realize the greatest impact on the life of a child and the many contexts of which he or she is a part. In this way, we partner with God's children as they grow and develop and benefit the greater world.

8

Intervention: Applying a Developmental Psychopathology Framework

Sally Schwer Canning, Kelly S. Flanagan,
Jennifer Hailey and Emely de la O

DEVELOPMENTAL PSYCHOPATHOLOGY HAS BEEN characterized in a variety of ways, as a macroparadigm (Achenbach, 1990), a multi- or interdisciplinary scientific field (Masten, 2006), a subdiscipline (Braet & van Aken, 2006), or an active research domain (Braet & van Aken, 2006). From a practical standpoint, leaders in developmental psychopathology have made explicit that they consider developmental psychopathology neither a singular theory (Masten, 2006) nor a broader framework that necessarily binds adherents to a single theoretical approach (Achenbach, 1990; Toth & Cicchetti, 1999). Rather, it is understood as an *integrative framework* or approach to research and practice (Lambert, 2006; Masten, 2006; Masten & Braswell, 1991). Thus, developmental psychopathology has the potential to be foundational for clinical practice with applicability across the lifespan. The utility for work with children, in particular, is found in this framework's emphasis on understanding the processes underlying normal and abnormal developmental pathways over time and attention to the "child-in-context" in the treatment of childhood disorders (Cummings et al., 2000). The principles of developmental psychopathology provide guidance for both the conceptualization of children's presenting problems and families' functioning as well as their effective treatment.

The emergence of developmental psychopathology in the 1970s was fueled by a complex convergence of developments within multiple disciplines (e.g., developmental and abnormal psychology) and the professional practice of child and adolescent psychiatry and psychology (Lambert, 2006; Masten & Braswell, 1991). Its development both resulted from and provides a unique example of the reciprocity between scientific and theoretical traditions (Masten, 2006). Yet as it emerged as a distinct field of interdisciplinary scholarship, developmental psychopathology focused on generating increasingly complex, comprehensive and robust models of developmental processes. The emphasis was on investigating relationships among individual and contextual risk and protective factors, continuities and discontinuities in developmental pathways, and adaptive and maladaptive child outcomes (see chapter 1, this volume). This emphasis had distinct implications for case formulation, though its direct application for treatment was less clear.

At the same time, expressions of the value of these more robust and comprehensive explanatory models for prevention and treatment were fueled by "a growing recognition of the shortcomings of assessment and intervention methods for children and adolescents" (Masten & Braswell, 1991, p. 35). Continued improvements in research methods and greater investment in longitudinal studies have enabled scholars to investigate phenomena over longer periods of time, and across a spectrum of ages and ranges of both normal and abnormal development (Masten, 2006). By the 1990s, research findings from developmental psychopathology were more widely touted as relevant to clinical practice (Toth & Cicchetti, 1999), even viewed as "the starting point for the design of interventions" (Shirk, Talmi & Olds, 2000, p. 835). Leaders in the field articulated the contributions of *both* clinicians and researchers in the ongoing evolution of developmental psychopathology, viewing transactions between the two traditions as having the potential to improve both theory and intervention (Masten & Braswell, 1991). Importantly, developmental psychopathology has been characterized as ultimately "grounded in a practical mission, to prevent or ameliorate behavioral problems and disorders and to promote positive development" (Masten, 2006, p. 47).

Significant applications to clinical practice have indeed resulted from the contributions of the developmental psychopathology framework. Meaningful applications for clinical work with children and adolescents derived from this framework include: (1) *assessment* approaches that inform a comprehensive *case formulation,* (2) *general principles* aimed at guiding the design and implementation of interventions informed by developmental psychopathology, (3) *evidence-based practices,* often in the form of structured protocols targeting specific clinical problems, that are based on ongoing assessment and case conceptualization and guided by the general principles, and (4) the integration of developmental psychopathology for *intervention practices* of major systems of child treatment (e.g., psychodynamic, behavioral, cognitive-behavioral and family systems).

In this chapter, we focus on the first three applications of developmental psychopathology for clinical work. We first review the ways in which the developmental psychopathology approach can inform assessment practices and case formulation. Second, we briefly review developmental psychopathology literature as it pertains to clinical work to distill the predominant general principles for practitioners to guide their treatment of childhood disorders. Third, we discuss the connections between developmental psychopathology and the current focus in psychology on evidence-based practices. Fourth, we highlight some continuing challenges in the direct application of developmental psychopathology for clinical practice. Finally, we look at the practice of child therapy through the lens of the three integrative themes of this volume. The remaining section of this volume (chapters 9–12) contains extended discussions of the fourth application and demonstrates how clinicians approach clinical work with children and adolescents from four major theoretical orientations within the integrative framework of developmental psychopathology.

APPLYING DEVELOPMENTAL PSYCHOPATHOLOGY TO CHILD CLINICAL WORK: CONTRIBUTIONS TO ASSESSMENT AND CASE FORMULATION

The treatment of children and adolescents is necessarily preceded by formulation of the child's functioning. A comprehensive discussion of the implications of a developmental psychopathology approach on assessment and case formulation deserves its own chapter. However, important observations, as well as a few conceptualization "tools," will be provided in this section in order to guide practitioners in applying the developmental psychopathology framework to their clinical practice.

First, developmental psychopathology provides a body of knowledge and a set of lenses through which to determine whether psychopathology exists and, if so, at what level of severity. Perhaps the most fundamental task prior to intervention is to determine whether a particular behavior or cluster of "symptoms" is actually a "disorder" requiring "treatment." In order to conduct valid assessments and derive valid diagnoses that avoid under- and over-diagnosis

(Holmbeck & Kendall, 1991), assessment strategies must be capable of capturing adaptive as well as maladaptive functioning (Masten & Braswell, 1991), and interpretation of findings must consider normative expectations at various developmental periods. Certain responses in children (e.g., fear of thunderstorms that results in distress and comfort-seeking from a parent, anxiety about the start of school) may be expected at particular ages (preschool to early school years) but not others (late adolescence). At the same time, normative responses might reach a level of intensity that is not developmentally normative (e.g., the preschooler who cannot go outside if there is a threat of clouds in the sky, or the child who screams and clings to her mother in the fourth month of the school year) and which warrants intervention. Other childhood problems may not rise to the level of psychopathology because they represent time-limited adaptations to stressful circumstances, such as the developmental regression of the previously "dry" six-year-old who begins to wet the bed after moving to a new home and the eight-year-old who becomes clingy and reverts to baby talk at times during her mother's extensive hospitalization following a car accident. A developmental history of these two children may reveal no concerns up to this point, and monitoring the behavior over time might reveal a return to previous levels of functioning with appropriate support from the children's environment. An assessment that places the presenting problem in the context of developmental norms, in the context of the child's individual development and seeks to understand the *function* of the problem will result in a more accurate determination of whether the child should receive treatment.

Likewise, viewing functioning from a developmental psychopathology perspective can also reveal when a child may still be functioning within developmental expectations but showing signs of strain from exposure to risk factors that increase the *potential* for developing psychopathology. In such cases, the task for clinicians may not be treatment so much as clarification and normalization of developmental expectations and assistance for those who are caring for the child. It might include advising a "wait and see" attitude or lead the practitioner to provide assistance or support in navigating developmental tasks in ways that are likely to harness protective factors and foster adaptation. In other instances, consideration of the long-term consequences of withholding treatment may be judged too risky. The holism that characterizes developmental psychopathology leads adherents to view child functioning as greater than the sum of its parts and to pay attention to the ways in which problems in one area of development affect and are affected by others. The mood features of bereavement, for example, might be expected to resolve within a specific time period. However, consideration of the impacts of sad mood, difficulty attending to class material when upset, and impaired ability to express positive affect with peers on social functioning and school adjustment over time might lead the practitioner to recommend interventions designed to mitigate longer term, negative developmental outcomes.

Second, assessment strategies consistent with a developmental psychopathology framework will be developmentally sensitive in a variety of ways (Ollendick, Grills & King, 2001). Assumptions underlying particular methods should be examined for their developmental relevance, and selection of techniques should take into consideration the cognitive, social and emotional capacities of the child being assessed (for extended and excellent discussions see Frick, Barry & Kamphaus, 2009; Mash & Hunsley, 2007; Sattler, 2006; Whitcomb & Merrell, 2013). Clinicians interviewing children, for example, must consider developmentally relevant abilities in domains such as memory, expressive and receptive language, and cognition (e.g., perspective-taking, self-reflection) and modify communication strategies in order to capitalize on the child's competencies at a particular age. Subsequently, interpretation of findings should be informed by normative expectations for functioning and differences in the expected expression of behavior problems at varying ages and across contexts, as well as expectations that child functioning displays both stability and change across time and context (Dirks, De Los Reyes, Briggs-Gowan, Cella & Wakschlag, 2012; Masten & Braswell, 1991). For example, teacher reports of children's executive functioning for various academic tasks may hold more weight than parents' report given teachers' interactions with children in the school setting, but the expectations for children's capacity for organization, task initiation and time management will change across the school years.

Third, assessment strategies informed by developmental psychopathology will aim to identify pathways leading up to the child's current functioning as well as to illuminate the underlying mechanisms that explain both adaptive and maladaptive functioning. It is this characteristic of a developmental psychopathology–informed assessment that can perhaps be most challenging for the clinician to apply. Limitations in access, time and resources for investigating and piecing together pathways extending over many years complicate the assessment process for the practitioner who is entering the life of a child or adolescent and his family at a *particular* moment in their lives and for typically a short period of time. Yet, the sketch of even the broad outlines of a child's developmental trajectory is integral for guiding our assessment of underlying processes that contribute to current functioning that then guides the development of the most effective treatment plan. Developmental psychopathology principles of *equifinality* and *multifinality* illustrate the importance of going beyond a cross-sectional, descriptive approach to assessment. These principles sensitize the clinician to the fact that although two children present in the clinic with the same disorder or exposure to risk factors, the pathways to those disorders or in response to the risk factors may look very different. Let us take, for instance, the following description of two children (Cummings et al., 2000):

> At 1 year of age, Nicole and Lisa, childhood friends, were each securely attached to their parents and came from homes in which the parents were happily married. In third grade, Lisa's mother died and she suffered from feelings of depression and sadness in response to her loss and did poorly in school that year. By contrast, Nicole's family situation remained stable and well-functioning. That year, Nicole and Lisa were assessed by school counselors and had very different psychological profiles, with Lisa diagnosed with an affective disorder. By seventh grade, Nicole had developed difficulties in school and peer relationships following a move to another state, and Lisa continued to have problems after her dad remarried. However, by early adulthood, with sensitive and responsive care from their parents and other adults in their lives, and despite the various forms of adversity, both were again well adjusted. (p. 95)

It is possible to "map" these two developmental trajectories in order to represent the different pathways by which Nicole and Lisa reached similar levels of adjustment in early adulthood (see figure 8.1). We can then seek to identify protective/risk factors and to understand the underlying processes that might have fueled these trajectories. For example, Lisa's attachment to her father was said to be secure, but how did the process of grieving, its effects on parenting and parent-child communication, and the support for emotion regulation impact Lisa's functioning after her mother's death? How did Nicole's social functioning and the characteristics of the new school context affect the nature of her peer relations following her family's move? An appreciation for principles of developmental psychopathology not only helps the clinician understand how the problem developed (case formulation) but also informs prognosis and decision about treatment.

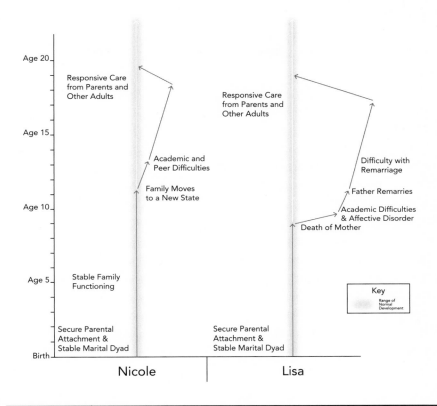

Figure 8.1. Developmental trajectory maps

Fourth, the parameters of assessment and the process of case formulation will reflect the complementary principles within developmental psychopathology of *contextualism* and the view of the *child as an active agent*. Traditional diagnostic classification systems give limited attention to contextual considerations (Dishion & Stormshak, 2007; Mash & Hunsley, 2007; Masten & Braswell, 1991). Sensitivity to both intraindividual and contextual considerations in assessment requires flexibility and comprehensiveness. This sensitivity should result in assessment approaches that go beyond simple categorization of a disorder and are multidimensional and vary according to child characteristics, interpersonal relationships, and the contexts in which problems are manifested. Assessment strategies consistent with the developmental psychopathology approach will likely include multiple informants (e.g., child, parent, teacher, childcare provider) and methods (e.g., report forms, interviews, observations) that gather information from both the child and the child's relevant contexts (i.e., a multimethod, multisource and multisetting assessment; Dirks et al., 2012). Child, parent and teacher reports about a child's internal experiences, for example, may yield discrepancies that reflect important information. Instead of questioning whose view is correct, the clinician should view this discrepancy as potentially revealing and seek to understand why it exists (Dirks et al., 2012). In other words, the child clinician will seek to thoughtfully integrate the information across informants, settings and methods to best understand the child's current functioning. For example, greater validity may be provided to children's self-report of internalizing problems (e.g., depression, anxiety) than to their externalizing problems (e.g., impulsivity, aggression), particularly when they have good insight and communication skills. Similarly, if parent report but not teacher report indicates significant levels of behavior problems, we might inquire about the differences in the home versus school context (e.g., structure, behavioral expectations) or about the reliability of the reporter (e.g., adult perspectives of normative child behavior).

Furthermore, single theory approaches have historically overemphasized the influence of parents on children. Developmental psychopathology has certainly contributed to a greater understanding of the processes underlying parents' influence on child development, such as the link between limitations in emotional availability and parental psychopathology (e.g., depression). At the same time, in its emphasis on a transactional view of development, the developmental psychopathology approach assumes not only that caregivers and others in the environment shape child development but also that children's behavior shapes caregivers' and other adults' behaviors and perceptions. The practitioner who observes harsh, critical comments from the parent in the first session will explore how characteristics of the child (e.g., behavior, temperament) have helped to shape that response over time in addition to exploring the inverse (e.g., how the parent's individual characteristics or parenting has contributed to the child's behavior).

It should be acknowledged that practitioners enter the lives of children and caregivers at a particular moment in time. We have astonishingly limited access to the pathways leading up to that moment, let alone the numerous relationships and contexts that influence and are influenced by our child clients. Some clinical settings and situations in particular severely constrain the amount of time and resources that may be feasibly and reasonably spent on discovering continuity and discontinuity in developmental pathways, and the risk and protective factors that dynamically operate between the child and her important contexts. The clinician who wants to apply the developmental psychopathology framework to assessment and treatment must understand enough about (ab) normal development, pathways, contexts, risk and protective factors, and individual differences to select and apply an effective assessment approach that can lead to a comprehensive case formulation and effective treatment plan, but must also work within the confines and demands of their specific setting (Weisz, Ugueto, Cheron & Herren, 2013).

Fifth, the relationship between assessment and treatment is intended to be one in which there is a high degree of continuity (Lochman, 2006; Mash, 2006). Explanatory models of the problem being targeted should be tightly tied to treatment, which underscores the need for case formulation to be informed by a comprehensive and ongoing assessment process (Kazdin, 2005a; Mash & Hunsley, 2007). Case formulation within this framework can be complex given the developmental, holistic focus on the child within her context and the identification of underlying processes that impact child functioning. Thus, a case formulation worksheet for the practitioner to use is provided in appendix A of this book in order to provide some structure for this task. A clinical example will clarify the way in which case formulation might flow out of a developmental psychopathology approach to assessment. Let's refer back to Lisa from the previous brief example.

A case formulation worksheet example has been completed at the end of this chapter with relevant information obtained through a multi-informant (i.e., Lisa, her father, her current seventh-grade homeroom teacher and her school social worker), multi-method (i.e., interviews, objective measures, observations) and multi-setting (i.e., home, school, church) assessment. Lisa was referred for therapy by her school social worker toward the end of her seventh-grade school year due to increasing concerns about her inability to attend to class work, low levels of motivation and reported emotional distress that have worsened in the last six months prior to the intake session. Lisa's father and step-mother expressed concern about Lisa's temperamental outbursts at home and her increasing negative self-statements and withdrawal from family activities. Lisa stated that she wanted help for "all [her] worries and depression" and frequent mood swings.

A developmental psychopathology framework helps to guide the clinician

in both the solicitation of information and the interpretation of that information so that informed diagnostic conclusions and treatment recommendations can be made. In completing the case formulation worksheet, the clinician
will first review the collected information from the assessment (stage 1). The
clinician will organize assessment data by recording specific information about
various domains of the child's current functioning. Yet, in order to be consistent with a developmental psychopathology perspective, the clinician should
reflect on the information gathered in a way that goes beyond an additive, or
"check list," approach to combining the data. The goal is to consider the *reciprocal transactions* between contexts, risk and protective factors, and domains
of child functioning, and how they influence each other *over time*. Identification of transactions over time can yield working hypotheses useful for for-
mulating a comprehensive, explanatory conceptualization of the child's current
functioning that is consistent with a developmental psychopathology
framework. This complex process for the clinician can be broken down into
smaller steps within the subsequent stages of case formulation.

In stage 2, important transactions between the domains of child functioning
as reviewed in stage 1 are noted in recognition of the child's nature as a holistic
organism. At a relatively simple level in our example, transactions between two
aspects of Lisa's functioning can be identified. For example, her ruminative,
anxious, distracted cognitive style places greater demands on her emotion
regulation abilities; conversely, Lisa's under-developed emotion regulation
abilities may provide inadequate resources for coping with a ruminative,
anxious cognitive style. At a more complex level, child transactions across multiple domains of child functioning may be uncovered. As one illustration provided in the sample worksheet, Lisa's early maturation in puberty (physical
domain) likely exposed her to older age mates (social), with subsequently
earlier exposure and access to high-risk behaviors such as smoking, going
"AWOL" and cutting (behavioral) that she learned to use to soothe her anxiety
in place of more adaptive approaches to regulation (emotional).

The clinician will next want to consider the child's holistic functioning in
light of important contexts. In other words, processes in which intraindividual,
interpersonal and environmental influences interact can be fleshed out. In our
example, Lisa's physical (early maturation), cognitive (rumination), emotional
(dysregulation, anxiety and depression) and behavioral (smoking, going out,
cutting) functioning may be considered in light of important contexts. A ca-

lamitous event in her family context (the death of her mother during third grade) threw Lisa unexpectedly into a bereavement process that likely overwhelmed both her own resources and that of her remaining parent, who was also grieving while needing to continue working to support the family and thus had difficulty providing optimal emotional and practical support to Lisa. Additional contexts that would be important to consider at this point in Lisa's development would be her school, congregation and community. For example, information provided about the school ("few resources") might indicate that some of Lisa's academic and social problems in this context could reflect limitations in this environment's resources as well as a difficulty meeting Lisa's current needs in that setting. Conversely, her congregation ("family regularly attends a church, Lisa attends weekly youth group . . . prays to God") is a source of Lisa feeling "heard" and potentially provides her with some emotionally supportive, socially adaptive interactions. Both of these contexts should be considered in their impact on Lisa's current functioning and in the identification of feasible and effective treatment recommendations. Case information should also be considered with attention to risk and protective factors. Identification of specific risk and protective factors may indicate potential points of intervention, strengths to draw upon for treatment, and mark particular mediating/moderating processes to be addressed in treatment (e.g., emotion regulation strategies and cognitive problem solving [child], inconsistent parenting and poor parental monitoring in the evenings and on weekends [family], socialization processes among friends at school and in youth group [peers]). Finally, the child's specific developmental trajectory can be considered with a focus on continuities and discontinuities over time.

In stage 3, the clinician generates a set of differential diagnoses that appear relevant for consideration in light of the referral question(s) and the hypotheses and pathways arrived at through the earlier steps of this process. Specifically, these diagnoses should take into consideration the concerns identified in the referral and at the intake, be considered in light of knowledge of both normal development and abnormal psychology, and provide accurate descriptions of the child's current functioning. Diagnostic conclusions reached from the comprehensive review of the assessment data and diagnostic criteria should then be recorded. The process of selecting the most reasonable diagnosis or diagnoses is not antithetical to a developmental psychopathology–informed process of conceptualization. Rather, the two can be mutually informative.

At this point, a fairly complex set of hypotheses about the relationships among child domains of functioning, contexts, and risk and protective factors has been generated. In stage 4, the clinician may now reflect upon these hypotheses and set this information into a developmental context in order to identify the specific multidimensional, transactional influences and processes over time that help to explain the child's current functioning. Here it may be helpful to first pictorially represent the child's functioning across the lifespan by generating a "map" such as the one presented earlier (see figure 8.1 on Nicole and Lisa). In order to be consistent with the perspective that psychopathology is best understood as process (versus category), the clinician attempts to re-create a pathway to the child's current functioning, and shows how this development is influenced by the presence or absence of important risk and protective factors (appendix B at the end of the book provides a blank, reproducible worksheet for this purpose).

After arriving at diagnostic conclusions, and upon reflection of the child's developmental pathway, a case formulation is ready to be written (stage 5). We identify desirable characteristics of a case formulation through the acronym ECCIII: Explanatory, Comprehensive, Conclusive, (Selectively) Inclusive, Illustrative and Informative for treatment. The acronym can serve as a reminder that useful case conceptualizations will (E) explain the child's functioning (adaptive and maladaptive) within a consistent framework, not simply describe it; (C) comprehensively tie together information across various domains of functioning, contexts and periods of development; (C) be as conclusive in both tone and content as is possible and professionally prudent; (I) include as much available information about child functioning, contexts, risk and protective factors as is relevant given the particular case and clinical formulation; (I) clearly illustrate the suitability of explanations, diagnoses and other conclusions within the formulation through linkages to information particular to the case; and (I) inform the nature, direction and emphases for treatment going forward.

Finally, the clinician will want to assess the written case formulation for the degree to which it reflects a developmental psychopathology framework as well as the individual child/family/context. Both are essential to generating a working explanation for presenting problems that will be helpful to children, families, teachers and other professionals who are the beneficiaries of our formulations and recommendations. Formulations that are thick with developmental psychopathology concepts but thin in their communication of how those concepts reflect the individual child in question are to be avoided. For example, the statement "risk factors in John's important contexts increased his vulnerability to psychopathology, resulting in discontinuity in his development across multiple domains" is certainly consistent with a developmental psychopathology perspective; however, it is a statement that could be applied to virtually anyone in a clinical context. It neither synthesizes particular case information into an explanatory whole, nor demonstrates how presenting problems arose or were maintained in a way that is meaningful or can be informative for treatment.

In contrast, but also to be avoided, are case conceptualizations in which constructs within the developmental framework are absent or so implicit as to be nearly invisible. These are "formulations" in name only, remaining at a relatively descriptive level as restatements of the presenting problems more than explanations. The goal instead is to articulate how the particular child, in his particular contexts, has arrived over time at his current level of functioning in ways that enable professionals, children and the important adults in their lives to arrive at shared understandings of the challenges they face and to map a course of treatment together; that is, the case formulation should provide clients, referral sources and clinicians a clear understanding for individualized treatment recommendations and interventions. Further evidence that the case formulation is informed by a developmental psychopathology perspective includes the following: (1) emphasis on developmental concerns, (2) a description of the child's functioning in multiple domains, (3) a portrayal of the child as an active, holistic organism, (4) representation and consideration of important contexts, (5) communication of transactional influences between the child and important contexts, (6) consideration of relevant risk and protective factors, (7) characterization of normal and abnormal development as processes, (8) evidence of a developmental pathway, and (9) communication of continuity and/ or discontinuity. Although demanding for the clinician, the result has the potential to significantly inform treatment.

The sample case formulation at the end of this chapter, written for the current clinical example of Lisa, illustrates how treatment can and should be informed by the conceptualization. For example, the following statement is included: "Lisa is a bright, insightful early adolescent who understands her emotions, all of which represent significant strengths that can be utilized in the school setting and in treatment. However, when she becomes distressed or overwhelmed, she resorts to maladaptive regulation strategies." Similar information throughout the case formulation is useful to the clinician, Lisa and her family, and the referral source (school) as they consider and select appropriate treatments. First, particular cognitive and emotional strengths and resources are identified (bright, insightful, creative, well liked), as illustrated by competencies she currently displays (ability to identify emotions, ability to make and maintain friends) along with the contexts in which they have been observed (school and clinic). These observations allow the clinician to have some confidence in Lisa's capacity to meet the significant cognitive demands of evidence-based interventions for depression that could be options for her, such as cognitive-behavioral or interpersonal therapy for depression. Second, a specific developmental domain (emotion regulation) is identified that can and should be intentionally targeted in treatment, given its prominence in the formulation. Additionally, the domain is linked to the conditions under which she needs to successfully deploy developmentally expected competencies (e.g., "when she becomes distressed or overwhelmed") as well as the important contexts (e.g., parent-child relationship at home) in which these competencies must be expressed.

From a comprehensive case formulation, appropriate and effective recommendations and treatment plan can be developed (Finch, Lochman, Nelson & Roberts, 2012). A clear example of the close relationship between an explanatory model of pathology and corresponding interventions are parent training approaches to child oppositional problems (e.g., the manual *Defiant Children* by Russell Barkley, 2013). This type of treatment flows out of Gerald Patterson's (1982) extensive observational studies of family interactions involving child defiance. A pattern of mutually reinforcing parent-child transactions was empirically identified as a basis for explaining childhood defiance from a social learning perspective. Family context variables (e.g., divorce, poverty, parental psychopathology, criminality) were also identified as risk factors at the macrosystem level that impact family management (e.g., parenting practices, monitoring, involvement) and which could be addressed with interventions (Dishion & Patterson, 1999). Based on the identification of this explanatory model, parent training interventions seek to disrupt the predictable, mutually reinforcing interactions between parent and child, build more effective family management, and strengthen relationships (e.g., Kazdin, 2005b; McMahon & Forehand, 2003; Webster-Stratton, 2011). Such interventions aimed at decreasing child defiance and improving parenting effectiveness are highly consistent with an explanatory model of observable relational patterns between parents and children. The clinician using these parent training approaches would have, ideally, assessed and identified not only the child behavior problem as one of defiance but also identified and observed a pattern of parent-child interactions similar to Patterson's model that would be subsequently addressed and modified through this intervention. Furthermore, the clinician would also have assessed risk and protective factors within the family and cultural context that might need to be addressed with a comprehensive and integrated treatment (e.g., Multisystemic Therapy; Henggeler, Schoenwald, Borduin, Rowland & Cunningham, 2009). In other words, clinicians seeking to implement treatments that are informed by developmental psychopathology should first assess and conceptualize clinical material from within the developmental psychopathology framework.

GENERAL PRINCIPLES TO GUIDE INTERVENTIONS

From a case formulation, clinicians proceed to the development of a treatment plan. The identification of effective treatments with children and adolescents should also be explicitly guided by developmental psychopathology principles. With knowledge about both normal and abnormal development, developmental psychopathology scholars have highlighted what they see as flawed assumptions underlying interventions with children that consequently erode the effectiveness of treatment (Holmbeck, Devine, Wasserman, Schellinger & Tuminello, 2012; Shirk & Russell, 1996). The "developmental level uniformity myth" (Kendall, 1985), or the tendency for clinicians to overemphasize the similarities children and adolescents share regardless of their age, is viewed as devaluing developmental considerations in the application of treatments to particular clients at particular levels of development. Similarly, the "developmental continuity myth" (Shirk, 1999) is viewed as leading clinicians to apply assessments and treatments originally developed for adults to children without sufficient consideration of how developmental differences should impact this downward extension of intervention concepts and strategies (Ollendick & King, 1991).

Developmental psychopathologists have thus sought to counter these myths that often led to ineffective treatment of children and have called for greater consideration of the implications of developmental differences between children and adults in the design, implementation and evaluation of child treatments (e.g., Cicchetti & Toth, 1992; Cicchetti & Cohen, 1995;

Shirk, 1988). One form these corrective efforts have taken is the articulation of how the specific principles of developmental psychopathology (see chapter 1, this volume) are relevant for assessment and treatment. The intent is to identify general guidelines for the *practical application* of developmental psychopathology for child and adolescent treatment approaches with developmental understandings at the forefront. Multiple sets of practical applications of developmental psychopathology principles have been published (e.g., Masten & Braswell, 1991; Ollendick et al., 2001). Although the scope and content vary, we offer a compilation of some of the more widely represented guidelines below as descriptions for pre-treatment, treatment and post-treatment.

Practical Suggestions for Applying Developmental Psychopathology Principles

Pre-treatment

- Conduct comprehensive and multidimensional assessment of children and their contexts (i.e., multiple informants, methods and contexts) from a systems perspective and with attention to processes and pathways to adaptive and maladaptive functioning (Shirk et al., 2000; Sauter, Heyne & Westenberg, 2009; Toth & Cicchetti, 1999).

- Determine whether and when treatment is needed based upon an understanding of assessment data in light of comparative developmental norms and transitions regarding various dimensions (e.g., cognitive, emotional, behavioral, social functioning, and gender, socioeconomic status, race, culture, etc.) and by making accurate diagnostic judgments to avoid under- or over-diagnosis (Holmbeck & Kendall, 1991; Masten & Braswell, 1991; Ollendick et al., 2001; Toth & Cicchetti, 1999).

- In order to make effective recommendations for treatment, consider the best context(s) for treatment for specific constellations of problems and with sensitivity to individual differences (Holmbeck et al., 2012; Masten & Braswell, 1991; Ollendick et al., 2001; Toth & Cicchetti, 1999).

- Select developmentally appropriate treatment techniques, goals and targets (Holmbeck et al., 2012; Holmbeck & Kendall, 1991; Masten & Braswell, 1991; Ollendick et al., 2001; Sauter et al., 2009; Toth & Cicchetti, 1999) that are derived from a comprehensive assessment and case formulation and that address relevant risk and protective factors and the underlying mechanisms/processes (Mash, 2006; Shirk et al., 2000; Toth & Cicchetti, 1999).

Treatment

- Select, tailor (e.g., language, materials, activities) and sequence the selected treatments for developmental and cultural fit (Toth & Cicchetti, 1999; Sauter et al., 2009; Holmbeck et al., 2012).

- "Match" and engage the child or adolescent's cognitive, emotional, and social abilities and motivations with specific treatments and tasks (Ollendick et al., 2001; Sauter et al., 2009).

- Foster a therapeutic perspective that change (within limits) is always possible given individuals' active, self-organizing orientation toward adaptation in the face of new experiences and reorganizations (Toth & Cicchetti, 1999).

- Focus on developmentally salient tasks and milestones, taking advantage of opportune transitions that provide increased susceptibility to developmental reorganization (Holmbeck et al., 2012; Toth & Cicchetti, 1999).[1]

- Engage significant others in the child's environment (e.g., parent, peers) and enhance their developmental sensitivity to the child (Holmbeck et al., 2012; Sauter et al., 2009).

- Target multiple biological and psychosocial dimensions of child functioning and influences on adaptive outcomes (Shirk et al., 2000).

- Anticipate and discuss future difficulties, developmental tasks and milestones, along with possible and expected trajectories of adjustment with prevention planning and promotion of resilience in mind (Holmbeck et al., 2012).

Post-treatment

- Monitor for divergence from expected developmental trajectories, providing reevaluation or assistance as needed (Toth & Cicchetti, 1999).

---

[1]For example, interpersonal psychotherapy has been adapted for use with depressed adolescents whose symptoms can be associated with problems in relationships. Both the focus and the mode of treatment takes advantage of the salience of peer and romantic relationships for individuals in this developmental period.

EVIDENCE-BASED PRACTICES AND
DEVELOPMENTAL PSYCHOPATHOLOGY

In addition to the articulation of developmental psychopathology principles for treatment, developmental psychopathologists have also recognized the need for empirical evidence examining the efficacy of child- or adolescent-focused treatments, in large part due to the focus on the scientific basis of knowledge within this field. This focus corresponds with the focus in clinical research and application in general on evidence-based practice (EBP). A multitude of EBPs for children and adolescents have been developed over the past half a century (Weisz et al., 2013). Numerous books have been published on EBP with children and adolescents (APA, 2006; e.g., Barrett & Ollendick, 2004; Christophersen & VanScoyoc, 2013; Weisz & Kazdin, 2010; Spirito & Kazak, 2006). The increasing use of technology and the Internet has also facilitated the creation of several searchable online databases specifically designed to highlight evidence-based practice with children and adolescents (e.g., www.effective childtherapy.com; www.whatworks.ed.gov; www.nrepp.samhsa.gov).

What is evidence-based practice? The 2005 Presidential Task Force on Evidence-Based Practice of the American Psychological Association defined EBP as the "integration of the best available research with clinical expertise in the context of patient characteristics, culture, and preferences" (p. 273). The purpose of EBP is twofold: (1) to promote effective psychological practice and (2) to enhance public health through the use of "empirically supported principles of psychological assessment, case formulation, therapeutic relationship, and intervention" (APA Presidential Task Force on Evidence-Based Practice, 2006, p. 273). Intervention and prevention programs are generally considered empirically supported if treatment manuals are available, at least two randomized trials demonstrate efficacy, and treatment effects have been replicated, preferably by more than one investigator (Chorpita et al., 2011; Kazdin, 2003). In general, EBP includes an approach to knowledge that is objective and scientifically based, and a focus on performance outcomes (Ollendick & King, 2004). The specific need to demonstrate the effectiveness of EBPs for youth in the "real world" of everyday practice has also been argued (APA Task Force on Evidence-Based Practice for Children and Adolescents, 2008; Weisz et al., 2013). More specific recommendations have been outlined by the APA Task Force on Evidence-Based Practice with Children and Adolescents (2008), including the need to consider developmental, cultural, familial and other contextual factors in the development of EBPs for children, adolescents and their families, emphases that are consistent with a developmental psychopathology framework.

Evidence-based interventions that have been developed specifically for children and adolescents target a range of specific psychopathologies and populations. To illustrate the breadth of currently available treatments, we have compiled and described a number of well-supported interventions in appendix C. Targeted childhood disorders and high-risk behaviors include anger/aggression, anxiety, attention-deficit/hyperactivity disorder (ADHD), autism, conduct disorder, depression, disruptive behavior disorder, eating disorders, elimination problems, foster care placement, grief, juvenile offenders, obsessive-compulsive disorder, oppositional defiant disorder, posttraumatic stress disorder (PTSD), substance and alcohol use, suicide, and trauma-related stress (Chorpita et al., 2011; Chorpita & Daleiden, 2009; Gruttadaro, Burns, Duckworth & Crudo, 2007; Kazdin, 2003).

The scope of targeted problems is matched by the widening age range of children and youth for whom EBPs are now available. Some interventions specifically target children in early and/or middle childhood (e.g., Homework Success for Children with ADHD; The Incredible Years). Others are designed specifically for adolescents (e.g., Adolescents Coping with Depression; Multidimensional Family Therapy for Adolescent Drug Abuse). Still others span wide age ranges, with versions of the intervention available for both children and adolescents (e.g., Defiant Children/Teens; FRIENDS for Life; Multisystemic Therapy for Antisocial Behavior in Children and Adolescents).

These interventions also vary in their characteristics (e.g., their structure, formats, settings and facilitators), which indicates consideration of research regarding childhood disorders and associated risk and protective factors and underlying processes. Although many interventions may be structured into weekly sessions over the course of ten to twelve weeks with booster sessions a few weeks or months post-treatment, an increasing number of interventions vary significantly from this common structure. For example, Teen Intervene is a brief, three-session intervention for adolescents displaying early stages of alcohol or substance use that is delivered over the course of ten days. Multisystemic Therapy is typically delivered over the course of three to five months; however, intervention is available twenty hours a day, seven days a week, for a total of at least sixty hours of direct intervention. Conversely, other interventions extend over longer periods of time, such as the Coping Power program, which treats aggressive and disruptive behavior over the course of thirty-four weeks, and Family-Based Treatment of Anorexia Nervosa with Adolescents, which is a one-year intervention. Furthermore, intervention delivery ranges from individual formats, child-only groups, parent-child dyads, child-only groups with parent components, adolescent-only groups, parent groups with child components, and individual family to multifamily formats. Likewise, interventions have been developed for or can be adapted to outpatient and inpatient settings, homes, hospitals, schools and community settings.

How do evidence-based practices relate to developmental psychopathology principles? From the perspective of developmental psychopathology, the empirical findings from the field should necessarily impact the development and nature of interventions with children and adolescents. Whether designed to prevent or treat psychopathology, many evidence-based interventions that have arisen reflect at least some of the guiding principles identified by developmental psychopathology scholars. For example, it has been recommended that EBPs for youth should be applied "within a developmentally driven and culturally responsive contextual model," reflecting a meta-systems perspective that considers individual differences and developmental trajectories, as well as sociocultural context and environmental influences on children's adaptation and development (Kazak et al., 2010), which clearly mirrors major tenets of developmental psychopathology. In reviewing the practical application of developmental psychopathology, Masten (2006) states, "As the developmental patterning and timing of specific problems and disorders is increasingly well known, particularly in relation to risks, protections, cascades, and progressions, it becomes possible to intervene with increasingly strategic timing and targets" (p. 51).

Indeed, developmental psychopathology–informed EBPs should be designed to address the mechanisms that are assumed to be at play in the development of particular psychopathologies, outlining treatment protocols built upon the foundations of explanatory models generated through research. In addition to the developmental considerations that are often built into child interventions, EBPs should be designed with risk and protective factors in mind (Kazak et al., 2010). In other words, variables that have been identified as moderators and mediators in pathways toward particular forms of psychopathology should be targeted within interventions (e.g., Dishion & Patterson, 1999), and protective factors (strengths) should be considered and built upon.

Successful treatment and prevention programs growing out of developmental psychopathology have been characterized as bearing "a tight link between developmental epidemiology and intervention design" (Shirk et al., 2000, p. 836), specifically emphasizing the connection between risk and protective factors that can be modified to positively impact developmental outcomes.

Similar to the nature of developmental psychopathology as an integrative framework, available EBPs for children and adolescents derive from a variety of underlying theoretical orientations and approaches, including behavioral, cognitive-behavioral, interpersonal, multisystemic and family systems. In keeping with the meta-paradigmatic nature of developmental psychopathology, the diversity of underlying frameworks reflects the emphasis on scientific methods and developmental approaches to understanding the mechanisms and processes that underlie both normal and abnormal development, rather than being confined by a fundamental or rigid commitment to one particular theoretical framework (Ollendick et al., 2001). In appendix C, we provide brief descriptions of some of the underlying frameworks reflected in the included EBPs.

Still, manualized treatments that have arisen appear "cross-sectional" in nature, and in this sense are not as easily recognizable as flowing out of the process-oriented, pathways-focused developmental psychopathology approach. As they are articulated in manuals, interventions may include strategies with limited age ranges of application, and with relatively limited direction provided to the clinician about how to consider and modify intervention components in response to recipients' ages, developmental capabilities and comorbid difficulties, and the treatment setting; thus, the role of the clinician is to approach case formation and treatment planning with developmental principles in mind (e.g., Garland, Hawley, Brookman-Frazee & Hurlburt, 2008; Sauter et al., 2009). As used in clinical practice, EBPs address a particular problem at a particular point in a child or adolescent's development (e.g., depression in a 13-year-old girl); yet, these treatment approaches can be designed and utilized with the principles and knowledge base of developmental psychopathology research and consideration of the treatment context.

SUMMARY

As discussed, developmental psychopathology research has contributed to the three aspects of child clinical work that have been described thus far (i.e., assessment and case formulation, the articulation of principles to guide the development of interventions, and evidence-based treatments). Yet, communities of psychological scholars and clinicians, even those who share a common concern for and commitment to children, tend to be largely separated from one another by differing perspectives, functions, language, methods, objectives, contexts and resources (Weisz et al., 2013). Certainly, contributions of this interdisciplinary theoretical framework to our understanding of child psychopathology and treatment have broadly influenced the training and practice of clinicians who treat children and adolescents and their families. For example, the specialty within professional psychology of clinical child psychology emphasizes the need for clinicians to have a thorough background in normal child and family development, developmental psychopathology and contextual influences on children, all predicated on a strong evidence base for assessments and interventions (Finch et al., 2012). Indeed, as an "interdisciplinary science," the *multilevel principle* of developmental psychopathology maintains that only with an understanding of processes involved along multiple levels of functioning (as understood from multiple disciplines) can a comprehensive understanding of a presenting problem be understood (Masten, 2006; Toth & Cicchetti, 1999). Practically speaking, the goal of this field is to provide a framework for integrating information across various disciplines in order to understand and promote change with well-informed prevention and intervention (Masten, 2006).

As a meta-paradigm that can guide practice, developmental psychopathology continues to be hampered by the all-too-persistent chasm in the discipline of psychology as a whole between research and practice, between the contributions and perspectives of the therapist and scholar. Translation of the knowledge base of developmental psychopathology has been described as a "bidirectional bridge across the divide of theory and practice" (Masten, 2006, p. 51). Truly, prevention and intervention have become more complex as the identification of risk and protective factors, mediating and moderating factors, and (dis)continuity has become more nuanced. For example, longitudinal research conducted with ecological systems and individual differences in mind necessarily leads to a more complex model for psychopathology and thus intervention (e.g., Dishion & Peterson, 1999). At the same time, prevention and intervention studies provide us with tests of etiology, mediating and moderating factors, and models of risk and resilience that inform our understanding of both normal and abnormal development (Cicchetti & Hinshaw, 2002). Applied research optimally contributes to theory building and a more nuanced understanding of development.

In short, child interventions are increasingly theory-based, informed by solid developmental and clinical research, and multidisciplinary, which requires a broad knowledge base and a coordination of treatment (Mash, 2006). We hope that the tools of this chapter assist the child clinician in thinking through and organizing the application of the developmental psychopathology framework for practice. Christian clinicians' understanding and enactment of their role in the treatment of children are also influenced by a theological understanding of children and treatment.

CHRISTIAN UNDERSTANDINGS OF DEVELOPMENTAL PSYCHOPATHOLOGY–INFORMED TREATMENT

One of the core aspects of treatment from a developmental psychopathology perspective is the notion that pathology is a process rather than an entity. This perspective posits that "deviance and resilience do not reside exclusively in the child but reflect the conditions that maintain or redirect individual developmental trajectories" (Shirk et al., 2000, p. 837). In many ways, Christian theology supports both a categorical view of what is wrong (i.e., we are sinners who either accept or reject the grace offered to us through Christ) and a process view (i.e., sanctification, fruit-bearing). A Christian understanding of the unfolding nature of sanctification provides a framework for appreciating the notion of development in general. More specifically, the child clinician may particularly remember the Christian anticipation that aspects of the human heart (along with the rest of creation) that have gone awry may, over time, be brought back into alignment, and things that are damaged or broken may be restored or transformed.

There is optimism or even hopefulness built into the developmental psychopathology approach in general and into the application of treatment specifically that flows from the process perspective identified above. In other words, our observations about multifinality and equifinality suggest that the development of pathology in individuals is not deterministic, nor is it a foregone conclusion. Neither is psychopathology something that is easily explainable by "main effects" models or single pathogenic theories. Rather, the emergence of psychopathology is explained from a developmental psychopathology perspective by the complex interplay of risk and protective factors in a variety of dynamic systems transacting over time. Thus, it is also considered possible that psycho-pathology can be headed off or treated; we can fend off or change some of these risk and protective influences in order to preserve or foster well-being (pre-vention/promotion) and/or restore individuals to a more normal develop-mental trajectory (treatment). As such, we have hope for change, and we base our efforts as clinicians on this hope. We draw our hope not only on the prin-ciples of this theoretical framework but also on our Christian faith and our view of children as gifts, as full persons, and as agents in their own development and in the world.

Valued as Gifts

The notion of children as gifts has extremely important implications for the fundamental perspectives and roles of parents, clinicians, and communities in relationship with children. Children are unearned gifts from God. At the same time, they require responsible action on the part of those to whom they are given. This conception of gift as necessitating task is reflective of the funda-mental tenet of salvation in orthodox Christian theology. Indeed, God's gift of personal salvation is freely given yet also calls for responsible action on the part of believers in the way of worship, care for others and stewardship of God's creation (Olson, 2002). Miller-McLemore (2003) describes "the dialectic be-tween gift and the need to care for the gift" as "rich" (p. 93), and she explains that "children as gift demand responsible action on the part of adults" (p. 104). Thus, the focus on our responsibility to children flows out of the more central idea of the child as a gift. This view has relevance not just for parents but for the clinician as well. In what ways might the children who "come through our doors" be gifts?

Children are inherently gifts because they are persons created and loved by God and entrusted by him into the hands of adults. To best accept and care for children as gifts, it is important for child clinicians to first understand the complexities inherent in the nature of the gifts themselves. As described in the first chapter of this book, clinicians must strive to view children as neither solely innocent and joyful nor primarily weak and prone to sin. Certainly, the children that Jesus welcomes and cherishes as an essential and vital part of God's kingdom are often poor, sick and possessed by demons (Mercer, 2005). In the Old Testament, children are typically portrayed as a divine gift and a sign of God's blessing; yet, they are not romanticized (Gundry-Volf, 2001). With a nuanced and complex understanding of children as full persons and agents (as described in the subsequent sections), clinicians are better equipped to conceptualize and treat children as they are, with a focus on both strengths and risk factors. To focus on one aspect of the gift at the expense of another is to fail to recognize the inherent worth of the child and to risk overlooking salient components of the child's treatment.

Understanding this complex perspective of children as neither idealized nor devalued gifts is critical for maintaining the ability to engage in clinical work with children and their families throughout one's career. When children are brought to therapy, they often provide a clear illustration that childhood is not simply "a time of ease, enjoyment, and emotional blessing" (Mercer, 2005, p. 66). There is danger in simplistically basing the child's status as a blessing from God on the "joy or ease adults may experience being around a child" or in thinking of childhood as an enchanting time of amazement and delight (Mercer, 2005, p. 66). Certainly, clinicians who work with children with significant disruptive behaviors, developmental delays and mood difficulties know that children do not always elicit easy feelings of wonder, delight and enjoyment. In any given session, assessment and treatment with child clients may involve waiting out loud tantrums, curbing displays of physical aggression, facing lack of motivation to engage in carefully planned activities, and hearing difficult, emotional content about their struggles and risk-laden environments. What is it, then, that sustains clinicians on these days when work with our child clients provokes feelings of frustration, anger, sadness and exhaustion rather than happiness, joy and awe?

We first advise clinicians to reflect on children's inherent value as gifts with great purpose in this world. Perhaps, as Mercer (2005) postulates, "children and childhood are gifts from God not because they are carefree, but because God has a purpose for children" (p. 66). The opportunity to provide clinical services for children is a blessing because it is both an opportunity to simply be in relationship with children, who are gifts in and of themselves, as well as to influence the development of young human beings for which God has a kingdom purpose. When clinicians help children to develop emotion regulation abilities, understand the cognitive processes that underlie learning difficulties, acquire skills for relating to peers or develop the ability to be in trusting relationships with others, they are ultimately helping these young persons to live out God's purposes for their lives with as few impediments as possible. The deep conviction that God has a purpose for children and that we, as clinicians, are entrusted with the care of specific aspects of these precious lives may impel us to a higher standard of work with children and sustain us in our service-oriented roles.

Second, the notion of children as gifts that bring responsibilities to those who receive them is an especially important one for the child clinician. According to Miller-McLemore (2003), it is precisely when adults recognize children as gifts that "they are emboldened to care for them properly" (p. 103). This perspective has the potential to shape our approach to the children with whom we work. What might it mean to think of and carry out our tasks of assessment, intervention and prevention if we view children as gifts that deserve and require responsible action on the part of adults? Certainly as clinicians it is not difficult to identify with the responsibility we take upon ourselves in our clinical work. Although we may differ widely in orientation and technique, professionals share a common awareness of the ethical and clinical responsibilities we assume when we work with a client or patient. This awareness may be especially acute, and the responsibility particularly weighty, for child clinicians. In contrast with adults, children and adolescents typically come into clinical contexts at the behest of others, and most are too young to legally consent to treatment. The perspectives and agendas of adults (e.g., parents, teachers, physicians, therapists) typically initiate and determine the nature, intensity, goals, and process of assessment and treatment. Due to this vulnerability inherent in the child's role in treatment, the child clinician has an especially important role in upholding and protecting the child as gift in clinical contexts.

In part, the view of the child as a "responsibility" fits well with a professional, vocational view of therapy. Children and families come with concerns that need to be addressed and are characterized as "cases" that are "diagnosed" and "treated" as we monitor "outcomes." This language is certainly compatible with our sense of responsibility to help foster children's healthy development. However, child clinicians are called to a higher interaction with their clients that involves embracing a responsible clinical stance that regards them as gifts. As we seek to fully know children and their families, to be aware of our reactions to children, to be focused on their development and maintain hope for their future, and to be well prepared for participation in treatment, we engage in responsible action that flows from our acceptance of children as gifts. We also strive to help others in the child's environment (e.g., parents, teachers) to view them as gifts and to responsibly care for these gifts.

Third, in addition to the gift of children, including the opportunity to help children develop and live out God's purpose for their life, it is also important for clinicians to recognize and receive the more immediate gifts that working with children provide. This stance reflects the coming of God's kingdom from the dialectical perspective of "already but not yet" (Olson, 2002). Even as the historical Christian consensus teaches that the fullness of God's reign is eschatological, Christians also "believe that the kingdom of God is already real. It is not an exclusively future reality; it is also a present reality" (Olson, 2002, p. 332). Thus, we do not have to wait until the fullness of a child's developmental trajectory is made known in order to rejoice in the gift of children. Whenever we conduct an assessment of a child's cognitive, academic, social and emotional functioning, we are reminded of the greatness of God's gift in all of his or her unique complexities. Though we utilize a specific psychological approach (e.g., Parent-Child Interaction Therapy) to strengthen relationships between parents and children, we are able to directly witness God's work of reconciliation on earth. As we watch a child with developmental delays speak words for the first time as a result of a carefully designed motivation-based intervention such as Pivotal Response Treatment, we have the opportunity to see the power of the language capacities that God has given to humans. These experiences serve as potent reminders that we are privileged to play a role in the development of the children whom God has created in his image and given to this world as gifts.

Respected as Persons
Understanding children as full persons is another vital component of the clinician's capacity to work with children from a developmental psychopathology perspective. Miller-McLemore (2003) asserts that, "as created in God's image, children merit the immense respect and empathy all too often unjustly and wrongly denied them" (p. 140). In the clinical context, it is not uncommon to witness the maladaptive effects that ensue when a child's personhood is undervalued. With an anthropological understanding of the goodness of children as persons created in God's image, the child clinician is in a unique position to advocate for the dignity of children's personhood to be upheld in their intrapersonal, interpersonal and environmental contexts.

Though children, like adults, are entirely dependent on God for their every breath, thought, feeling and movement, the Creator has also given them free will and a spirit of "power, love and self-discipline" (2 Tim 1:7). The depiction of God's creation of man in Genesis illustrates the paradox that humans are simultaneously "creatures" and "persons" (Hoekema, 1986). In Genesis 2:7, the author explains that "the LORD God formed a man from the dust of the ground and breathed into his nostrils the breath of life, and the man became a living being." Here, the fact that man was formed from the dust of the ground is symbolic of the notion that man is meaningless and lifeless without God; at the same time, the action of God breathing into man the breath of life (unlike he did with any of his other creation) is symbolic of the power that humans (including children) have been given by God. In Psalm 8:4, David beautifully articulates this paradox as he wonders at the majesty, power, and glory of God and his creation that makes man pale in comparison, humbly asking, "What is mankind that you are mindful of them, human beings that you care for them?" At the same time, however, David recognizes that God has given humans great authority and responsibility, and he tells God, "You made [humans] rulers over the works of your hands; you put everything under their feet" (Ps 8:6). Certainly, the fact that children, as full human persons, are both "creatures" dependent on God and willful, efficacious "persons" with a role here on earth has important implications for the clinical treatment of child psychopathology.

In our attempts to prevent, assess and intervene, we must be mindful of the reality that children "are neither entirely virtuous nor entirely depraved" (Miller-McLemore, 2003, p. 144). When the concepts of sin and grace, as well as agency and dependency, are held in tension, clinicians are in a better position to help promote children's growth through respecting their full personhood. First, this work occurs through clinicians' interactions with their young clients as well as through relationships with family members, teachers, physicians and other environmental influences. For example, there are times when setting limits and enforcing consequences are most helpful for a child's adaptation to a specific context, and there are other instances when the child needs explicit expressions of forgiveness and warm emotionality from the adults in his life. When we listen carefully to children, take them seriously, attend to their feelings and communication, accept the challenges they present to us, and allow ourselves to learn from and be changed by them, we communicate a fundamental respect for our young clients and a valuing of their full personhood. Regardless of the child's presenting concerns, the clinician's loving, compassionate response toward the child and her family, with an appreciation for the child's capacity to receive grace and grow spiritually, nurtures respect for the child's personhood.

Second, we must recognize that as full persons created in God's image, children are imbued by God with structural, functional and relational capacities (McMinn & Campbell, 2007). These capacities include children's developing physical bodies and organs, their abilities to use their minds and bodies to exert influence on their environments, and their inclinations toward relating to the people in their lives. The developmental psychopathology perspective, with its conceptualization and treatment emphasis on understanding the complex interplay of intrapersonal, interpersonal and environmental factors, implicitly suggests an appreciation of the structural, functional and relational aspects of children's personhood. By extension, when clinicians acknowledge the complexities inherent in these facets of children's development from infancy to adulthood, and then respond to children's physical, emotional and social needs with sensitivity and compassion, we help to affirm young people's dignity. Striving to understand children and conceptualize their strengths and concerns in the contexts of their holistic development includes (but is not limited to) appreciating and intervening in issues related to their gender, ethnicity, cultural and familial influences as well as other individual and environmental differences across emotional, physical, cognitive, behavioral, social and spiritual domains of development.

Third, along with recognizing children's unique attributes, it is important to understand that children's capacities are still developing; in a sense, these capacities reflect the eschatological tension of "already but not yet." Children, as a "complex amalgamation of imperfection and potentiality," are "full persons trying to learn how to wield power appropriately and how to have a real say in their lives" (Miller-McLemore, 2003, p. 144). Clues from Scripture indicate that children are "*already* expressive of the purposes of God. Childhood is thus a time of vocation, a time of being called to purposive participation in the divine action in the world" (Mercer, 2005, p. 67). Clearly, childhood is not merely a stage for children to pass through so that their life purposes can be realized in adulthood; rather, childhood is a time that allows young people simultaneously to live out their current purposes as they *are* as children and to prepare for their future roles as adults. We would do well to remember that even as adults we are continuing to change and develop, and our life purposes have likewise not yet been fully revealed to us. When we acknowledge that we too are "complex amalgamations," complete in our personhood yet still developing, imbued with great purpose yet still progressing toward the full revelation of that purpose, we can model to children the acceptance and grace that God gives us throughout our developmental processes as his children.

Viewed as Agents

It is imperative that clinicians respect and value children's agency, which is the third theological perspective that should influence our clinical work with children and their families. Children impact their environments, and they affect others when in relationship with them. Although adults play a strong role in influencing children's development across all domains, children also exercise power and responsibility in their own lives. Through their choices and individual characteristics, they play active roles in navigating toward or away from specific developmental outcomes. As clinicians, we must recognize that children, as agentic beings, can take active roles in their treatment.

When engaged in clinical work with children, the clinician maintains many responsibilities, such as conceptualizing the child's needs, selecting appropriate interventions for implementation and eliciting the child's engagement in the treatment process. However, the child as agent must also take an active role in his or her treatment. Consistent with the principles of the developmental psychopathology approach, the manner in which children are expected to participate in their treatment varies substantially, depending on factors such as age, cognitive ability, emotional development and presenting concerns. For example, in order for a thirteen-year-old boy with internalizing symptoms of anxiety and depression to experience success in his cognitive-behavioral therapy, he must actively engage in activities such as identifying the connections between his thoughts, feelings and behaviors, learning to replace maladaptive thoughts with more helpful thoughts, and selecting effective coping skills to use at appropriate times. Though it is important for the clinician to guide, teach and assist the child in this process, the treatment will be effective only if the clinician respects and engages the child as an agent in his treatment.

Although it may be easier to imagine older children as dynamic participants in the therapeutic process, very young children are also actively incorporated into treatment; this involvement can occur either through the children's tangible participation or through a recognition of the children's agency in work with caregivers. For instance, in order to address the concerns of a two-year-old girl presenting with disruptive behavior difficulties, a clinician may choose to implement the Parent-Child Interaction Therapy (PCIT) protocol (Hembree-Kigin & McNeil, 1995) with the patient and her caregiver(s). Within this intervention, the child's responsibilities include actively engaging with her parents during child-directed play, listening to her parents' instructions during parent-directed interactions, remembering directions and family rules, and complying with these directions. Even when the child does not choose to respond appropriately to parental directives, she must act as an agent in her own time-out procedure as she is required to sit on a chair, regulate complex emotions such as anger, frustration and sadness without others' attention, and then actively comply with her parents' instructions so that she can return to a more desirable activity. In many interventions, the responsibilities placed on the child are both explicit and implicit. By recognizing both the explicit and implicit responsibilities placed on the child in treatment, and by understanding that the child's response to these expectations will vary according to individual characteristics and experiences (such as expressive and receptive language skills and previous adult responses to her behaviors), the clinician is in a stronger position to help set appropriate expectations for the child's behavior and thus honor her inherent agency and individuality.

To actively incorporate children's expressions of agency in the treatment process, it is necessary that clinicians and caregivers fundamentally respect children's abilities to gradually assume responsibility. Miller-McLemore (2003) asserts that "society has infantilized children as fundamentally incapable of constructive thought and action. This has led people to mistake shaping children into socially acceptable adults as the chief task of parenting. Instead, at the center should stand the gradual transfer of appropriate responsibility" (p. 143). That is, by respecting children where they are and recognizing their agency but also their still developing capacities, adults can move with children, helping them along their developmental trajectory toward their unique purpose. Miller-McLemore (2003) uses the phrase "transitional hierarchy" to describe the concept of "a temporary inequity between persons—whether of power, authority, expertise, responsibility, or maturity—that is moving toward but has not yet arrived at genuine mutuality" (p. 130). Rather than viewing all imbalances of authority between persons as bad or harmful, this understanding of transitional hierarchy has developmental considerations at its core. Because of differences in developmental levels, the relationship between parents and children, as well as between clinicians and children, is characterized as dynamically moving toward mutuality as opposed to having already arrived there. Therefore, it is appropriate for the balance of authority in these relationships to be temporarily shifted toward the adult and then gradually transferred to the child as he or she progresses in development. Even so, it is important to recognize that it is children's capacity for mutuality in relationships, and *not* their agency, that increases with their capabilities. Children might become increasingly self-regulated and more aware of their agency as they grow, but they are nevertheless agentic beings even at young ages.

Certainly, there is a complex interplay between the agency of children and that of adults, and the distinction between child choice and adult behavioral control is often delicate. As a simple illustration of this "fine line," Christine Gudorf (1994) explains that children should not "be made to eat when they are not hungry, but neither should they be allowed to consistently substitute nonnutritious snacks for meals. Children should not be made to adopt a parent's dress choices, but neither should they be allowed to wear shorts in the snow" (p. 203). At the same time that the needs of children deserve deep respect from adults, children do not always know what they need or how to best meet these needs (Miller-McLemore, 2003). Many evidence-based treatments for children and adolescents implicitly recognize the tension embedded in the concept of transitional hierarchy and offer to clinicians and parents practical guidelines for navigating within a framework that respects the knowledge and authority of caregivers as well as the decision-making capacities and rights of children. For example, the protocol of The Incredible Years (Webster-Stratton, 2011) recommends that in many daily decisions, parents should allow their children the freedom to choose between several options that are provided by adults. Thus, caregivers maintain control in their ability to provide acceptable options of clothes, food, toys and so on, and their children are simultaneously permitted to exert independence in their ability to select desired option(s). In Pivotal Response Treatment (PRT; Koegel, Koegel, Frea & Fredeen, 2001; Koegel, Koegel, Harrower & Carter, 1999), typically used for teaching children with autism fundamental skills that are necessary for the acquisition of a wide variety of additional skills, this principle is called "shared control." In shared control, both the adult and the child have some influence on the therapeutic activity. Whereas the adult may scaffold the majority of the interactions at the beginning stages of learning, the child is encouraged to take an increasing amount of control as he or she becomes more familiar with the social routines and expectations (Vismara, 2009). The empirically supported intervention of social stories (Gray, 2010; Gray & Garand, 1993) also illustrates the notion of respecting children's agency in a developmentally appropriate manner. When writing social stories, adults are encouraged to take the perspective of a child and explain concepts in a simplified way that the child can understand according to his or her developmental level. Because concepts that may appear to be "self-evident" to an adult might be confusing to a child (e.g., giving hugs, exchanging gifts, following all the steps for using the restroom, understanding appropriate and inappropriate touching), social stories attempt to break down and elucidate the essential components of these concepts in concrete and simplified language. Although these simplified explanations may seem trivial to adults, offering them expresses a fundamental respect of children's unique bodies, minds, and means of relating to their environments and their agency.

Implicit in all of these treatment approaches is the understanding that as children advance in their developmental capabilities, they should be provided with more options and/or increased flexibility in choosing. These views respect children as agents who "are worthy of rights and capable of taking responsibility commensurate with their development" (Cooey, 1996, p. 103), and who interact with their environments in dynamic ways as they move along their developmental trajectories. Children impact their environments in diverse ways as they develop, and thus they elicit and deserve flexible responses from those around them. When adults sensitively consider the evolving skills and needs of children, and allow ourselves to be changed in the process of flexibly responding and relating to children, we convey esteem for children's status as full agents capable of acting within and upon their spheres of influence.

As clinicians we must also remain open to the likelihood that our interactions with agentic children will result in changes to the implementation of our treatment plans and, perhaps more dauntingly, changes within ourselves. If we view children merely as static "sponges," we might expect them to "absorb" what we want to teach them. However, "if we view them as pilgrims, we will help children enter into the story and interact with it in any number of ways" (May, Posterski, Stonehouse & Cannell, 2005, p. 7). From the developmental psychopathology perspective, we understand that children can change course on their developmental pathways. When we come alongside children and interact with their "stories" in the clinical context, we should continuously assess and adapt to their responses to interventions. When one motivational "tool" is not effective for engaging a child in treatment, we try another; when one assessment measure shows the need for additional testing, we schedule follow-up appointments; when we discover that a grandparent's or teacher's input is needed to ameliorate a concern, we make an extra phone call. We work hard for and with our child clients who evoke "unique obligations, intimacies, and transformations because, unlike any other work, they are subjects in themselves capable of their own work, love, gifts, and contributions" (Miller-McLemore, 2003, p. 124). Indeed, our clinical work with children can rightly be characterized as a "labor of love" (Miller-McLemore, 2003, p. 124).

As we engage in this labor of love, we inevitably experience changes within ourselves as a response to their agency in our lives. In order to establish strong therapeutic alliances and empathize with children, we must by necessity let them enter into parts of our emotions and our psyches. When we hear their stories, we are affected in ways that naturally result in modifications to our thoughts, emotions and behaviors. As we seek to truly know these young people as gifts, persons and agents, we cannot help but be changed in the process. Miller-McLemore (2003) avows that "attending to children in such a way that one is altered is precisely a key ingredient of good parenting" (p. 154). We contend that this is a key ingredient of good clinical work as well.

Although we understand our work with children to be marked by love, we are careful to recognize that "mutual love seldom begins mutually. . . . Love is a process. Sometimes one's gifts are greater and one's needs lesser in the beginning of relationships, but the balance often shifts. Sometimes time runs out before the balance shifts. But the intention is always that it shall" (Gudorf, 1985, pp. 189-90). As clinicians who engage in the labor of love with children, we usually enter into children's lives for short periods of time when the "balance" is shifted toward the needs of the children. However, we maintain optimism that our work will contribute to our clients' eventual capacities for mature mutuality and interdependence in their relationships outside of therapy. Our perspective on mutuality is also rooted in community; that is, we hope that our work with children will help them to develop into persons who are ultimately healthy and productive members of society, able to give to their families and communities (see chapter 8, this volume). This perspective, like the foundation for all of our work with children, is anchored in an eschatological hope; it is a step toward ensuring that the kingdom is made a reality in the present while our hope for the full revelation of God's kingdom lies in the future.

LOOKING AHEAD: APPLICATION FROM THEORETICAL ORIENTATIONS

Clinical psychologists interested in having their treatment of children and adolescents informed by developmental psychopathology research are working from a historical context that prizes theoretical frameworks as the foundation for practice. In practice, many clinicians who treat children and adolescents have been trained in and work out of the major theoretical schools (e.g., cognitive-behavioral, psychodynamic). Although the predominance of particular theories has evolved over the years (and varies globally), the priority for a theoretical framework as the starting point of practice has remained preeminent. In the next section of this volume, authors will explore how the principles of developmental psychopathology can inform clinical practice from four major theoretical orientations for working with children and adolescents. Specifically, the following four chapters will explore how an understanding of developmental psychopathology can contribute to effective treatment from psychodynamic, behavioral, cognitive-behavioral, and family systems approaches in working with youth and their families.

Case Formulation Worksheet Example

Name: Lisa Young Lady

Assessment Information: Interviews with Lisa, father, teacher and school social worker; parent, teacher, and self-reports of BASC; CDI; Sentence Completion Task

D.O.B.: March 13

Age: 13 years, 1 month

Date: April 20; April 27

STAGE 1: Review case information and record information relevant to a developmental psychopathology framework.

Current Functioning:

Cognitive   Lisa is a bright, young girl who is reportedly "academically capable when she applies herself," though she often seems disengaged and distracted. She understands abstract concepts and displays high level of insight and perspective-taking. Creative and expresses herself artistically. She tends to ruminate on her family relationships, interpersonal hurts and her desire for things to be different. She expresses worries about her abilities, what others think of her, her school work, her father's health, her family members' safety and her future.

Emotional   For the past 6 months, Lisa has often been dysregulated at home, displaying irritability and quick changes between anger, sadness, silliness, and contentment. She does not often appear happy or joyful at home. Not interested in activities she used to enjoy alone and with her family. She cries often and described both appropriate ways she soothes herself (e.g., music, journaling, talking to her friends) as well as inappropriate strategies (e.g., smoking, cutting her arm with a safety pin).

Physiological   Lisa matured early for her age, having experienced her first menstruation at the beginning of 4th grade. She expressed discomfort with her maturing body and a lack of knowledge about what to expect. She thinks she is unattractive and does not like the attention she receives from boys for her physical appearance. Difficulty falling to sleep and waking early, little appetite.

Behavioral   Lisa obeys rules at school and is respectful of teachers and peers. She has become increasingly inattentive at school, having trouble focusing on and completing tasks. She fights frequently and intensely with her father and stepmother (talking back, yelling, slamming doors, throwing objects in her room). She is often disrespectful of her parents. She takes care of her younger siblings (cooks dinner, helps with homework) but has started to withdraw emotionally from them. She started smoking cigarettes "to calm down," though she is not permitted. Her parents do not know where she is at times in late evening and on the weekends; Lisa often goes to her friends' houses or retreats to her bedroom.

Social   Lisa has a few older, close friends she hangs out with regularly after school and confides in. She tends to "float" between different groups at school and seems to be well liked by everyone, though these relationships are not deep, trustworthy ones. She often is shy and inhibited in large-group settings. Lisa has had a few movie dates with boys but is wary of their attention. She has not been sexually active.

Child Characteristics (e.g., age, developmental level, gender, ethnicity, temperament):
Lisa was a fussy baby but could be easily soothed by her parents. Developmental transitions and new situations (e.g., toilet training, school entry, starting a sport) were difficult for Lisa, who became tearful and clingy. With assurances she was able to navigate transitions and novel situations. Lisa is concerned about her appearance and frequently diets and does not eat during the school day. Her family has low SES with both parents working overtime to provide for the family's financial needs. Lisa is Caucasian but attends an ethnically diverse school in an urban setting where she is in the minority. Few resources at school, but teachers and social worker want to help her. Her friends are diverse in ethnic backgrounds.

STAGE 2: Ask yourself questions to help you to understand the case from a developmental psychopathology framework (i.e., consider the child as holistic/multidimensional, the transactions between child and important contexts, risk and resilience factors, developmental pathways including continuities/discontinuities). Record relevant information.

Child as Holistic Organism (preliminary observations about important transactions between child characteristics):

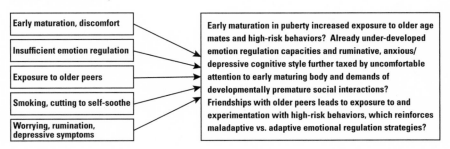

Early maturation, discomfort	Early maturation in puberty increased exposure to older age mates and high-risk behaviors? Already under-developed emotion regulation capacities and ruminative, anxious/depressive cognitive style further taxed by uncomfortable attention to early maturing body and demands of developmentally premature social interactions? Friendships with older peers leads to exposure to and experimentation with high-risk behaviors, which reinforces maladaptive vs. adaptive emotional regulation strategies?
Insufficient emotion regulation	
Exposure to older peers	
Smoking, cutting to self-soothe	
Worrying, rumination, depressive symptoms	

Contextual Characteristics (e.g., parent-child, parental psychopathology, marital relationship, sibling relationships, family characteristics, peer relations, teacher, school context, neighborhood, cultural context):
Lisa lives with her father, stepmother and siblings. Her biological mother died when she was 9 years old. Lisa has two younger biological siblings and was described to have a good relationship with them; she "takes care" of them after school and in evening. She used to talk

about her biological mother but stopped when her father started dating her stepmother two years ago. Her stepmother's parenting was described as more rigid and demanding; her father is permissive and disengaged because he "works so much." Father lost his job just before his remarriage and has since taken a low-paying job with inflexible hours. Her parents expressed feeling that Lisa keeps many things from them. Lisa and her father were described as "mutually supportive" until his remarriage last year. Family regularly attends a church, and Lisa attends weekly youth group. She daily prays to God and her mother for help; she feels "heard but lonely here without them with me."

Contextual Transactions (preliminary observations about important transactions between Contexts):

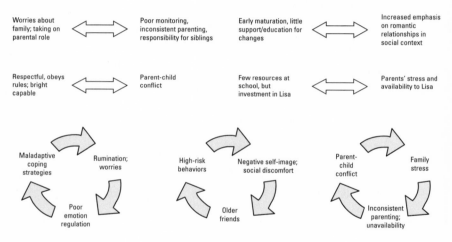

Vulnerability and Risk Factors (proximal & distal)	Resilience and Protective Factors (proximal & distal)
Anxious temperament Emotionally dysregulated Inconsistent parenting (permissive & demanding) Few resources at school Little monitoring outside of school Disrupted attachment relationship Change in relationship with father Low SES/few resources Early physical maturation	High intelligence, creative and artistic Cognitive abilities (insight, perspective-taking) Ability to make and maintain friends Caring adults at school and home Early strong attachment relationships Caring parents who want to help Lisa & improve their relationship Supports at church Spirituality—sense of God's love

Developmental Pathways (Continuities and Discontinuities):

Early dysregulation and anxiety → Secure attachment relationships and support for regulation from parents → Loss of mother → Relationship with father supportive though perhaps enmeshed → Father dating and remarriage → Increased anxiety and depression in age-normative areas (e.g., school, social context/relationships, future orientation)

STAGE 3 (Differential Diagnosis): Consider all relevant *DSM* diagnoses, rule out diagnoses, come to a conclusion.

Relevant Rule Outs
ADHD—distractibility, inattention at times, but most likely due to anxious thoughts and depressive symptoms Depression (MDD, persistent depressive disorder) ODD/Conduct Disorder Anxiety disorders (Social phobia, GAD)
Diagnostic Conclusions:
MDD GAD

STAGE 4 (Reflections & Trajectory Map): Review your notes from the case. Reflect on the material in order to identify the specific multidimensional, transactional influences and developmental pathways that help to explain current functioning. Based on your reflections about the presented case material, you may want to draw out a complete developmental pathway depicting the child/adolescent's functioning on the Developmental Trajectory Map worksheet.

STAGE 5 (Case Formulation):

Complete a written formulation of the case, identifying and explaining the concluding diagnosis(es). Your formulation should be *ECCIII*: Explanatory, Comprehensive, Conclusive, (Selectively) Inclusive, Illustrative and Informative for treatment. It should clearly show evidence of working from a developmental psychopathology framework (see Reflection on Case Conceptualization checklist). Assess your formulation for the degree to which it reflects a developmental psychopathology framework as well as the individual child/family/context in order to be useful. **Revise as needed.**

Case Formulation Example

Note: The sample case formulation is longer than what would typically be written as part of an intake or assessment report in order to illustrate how the developmental psychopathology framework informs the case formulation.

Lisa is a thirteen-year-old female who has been struggling with depressive symptoms for at least the past six months. She cries frequently, is often irritable, is seldom happy and is disengaged from her parents. She has experienced a loss of pleasure in activities that she previously enjoyed. She frequently makes negative self-statements and is highly critical of herself. Further, she expresses low self-esteem and pessimism about the future. She also displays sleep and eating difficulties. Lisa currently meets criteria for *major depressive disorder*.

Lisa is also currently displaying severe anxiety symptoms that impair her functioning across multiple domains and settings. She experiences excessive worry on a daily basis about multiple things. She worries about harm to significant others, her abilities and performance, and her future. Lisa spends a great deal of time anticipating problems that might occur and has difficulty controlling her intense worry. Her anxiety leaves her feeling restless and irritable. She has difficulty concentrating and experiences anxious rumination. Therefore, Lisa currently meets the criteria for *generalized anxiety disorder*. Her difficulty completing tasks and concentrating at school and home is most likely a result of her anxiety and depressive symptoms and is not likely due to symptoms of ADHD. She has a solid history of academic success and no previous problems with inattention. However, her recent concentration and academic problems only contribute further to her low self-esteem and anxiety.

Lisa's difficulties have most likely developed due to the transaction of multiple individual, interpersonal and environmental factors, which contribute to the maintenance of problematic areas of functioning. Her development was within normal limits until the death of her mother at age nine. Early emotional and cognitive functioning, however, reveals significant vulnerability to internalizing problems within a context of protective environmental resources until being overtaxed by the multiple, significant impacts of the loss of Lisa's mother. Specifically, Lisa's vulnerability to depression and anxiety reaches back to the anxious temperament she displayed as an infant and can be seen in her history of reacting to new or challenging situations, distressing stimuli, and transitions with high levels of emotional intensity, fearfulness and negative cognitions.

Lisa was able to successfully navigate early developmental transitions and regulate her emotions through the support of others. Her reported ability to be easily soothed by her parents and her tendency to seek support from caregivers when under stress indicate that she likely drew upon the resources of stable attachments to her primary caregivers. The death of her mother was a significant developmental disruption that resulted in negative emotional, cognitive and social discontinuities related to bereavement and a rupture in emotional security. Lisa continued to have her relationship with her father as a resource. However, the family's subsequent financial stress and low socioeconomic status coupled with Lisa's father's own bereavement process, resulted in parental stress and decreased physical and emotional availability to support Lisa's grieving. In fact, Lisa took on additional responsibilities within the family at that time, as evidenced by her caregiving role for her younger siblings. Thus, expectations for Lisa exceeded that which would be developmentally reasonable for a girl her age in general, and for Lisa's emotional needs in particular.

Furthermore, an early history of behavioral inhibition, along with more recent evidence of "shyness," social withdrawal from siblings and relatively superficial peer relationships in middle school, may indicate a more enduring, inhibited social style. This inhibition, in combination with depressive cognitions, would increase her vulnerability to anxiety, especially in social situations. Her current worries about the safety of her family and her father's health are understandable focal points for anxiety. It is likely that the loss of her mother overwhelmed Lisa's emotional and cognitive resources, so that previously subclinical levels of anxiety became so emotionally intense and cognitively distracting as to begin disrupting her functioning at school (e.g., disengagement and distraction) and home (e.g., increased isolation and parent-child conflict). Overall, Lisa is a bright, insightful early adolescent who understands her emotions, which is a significant strength that can be utilized in the school setting and in treatment. However, when she becomes distressed or overwhelmed, she resorts to maladaptive regulation strategies.

The likelihood of Lisa developing internalizing problems in early adolescence was increased by the loss of her mother and the resultant risk processes. Transitions during this time included a change from elementary to middle school, which disrupted social relationships and increased academic and social demands. Lisa's history of difficulties with transitions made it likely that these transitions would have already been challenging for her; however, unlike earlier transitions, fewer resources were available for Lisa. Because many girls are prepared by their mothers for the physical and emotional changes involved in puberty, it is likely that Lisa was inadequately equipped for these changes, which resulted in her increasingly negative emotions and sense of self. Lisa's father's own grief process and heavy work demands, potentially along with his perception of his paternal role at this stage of her development, would have made it less likely that he would be adequately attuned to Lisa's experience and able to respond with the support she needed to adaptively navigate this normal developmental transition. Lisa's dissatisfaction with her body, dieting behavior and discomfort around boys appear linked to this less than adaptive transition to puberty. Although she does not appear to be exhibiting an eating disorder at this time, these symptoms in the context of depression and family conflict may increase her risk for developing one in the future.

Lisa has also begun to exhibit some conduct problems, though not to a degree that would warrant a diagnosis at this time. Her externalizing problems appear to have arisen out of the earlier development of depressive and anxious symptoms. Lisa's early physical maturation and entry into middle school exposed her to older age mates and high-risk behaviors. Lisa's difficulty regulating emotion (already overstressed by bereavement and the demands of adolescent transitions), along with the tendency for adolescents to experiment with risky behaviors, set the stage for her to experiment with maladaptive coping strategies, such as smoking and cutting. Lisa's experience of a short-term reduction in emotional distress after employing these strategies increased the likelihood that she would continue their use. Adaptively, Lisa also finds some solace and support in her few close friends and is spending more time with them, which is consistent with the increased importance of peer relationships as a source of emotional support and identity development in early adolescence. Yet, the degree to which Lisa's friendships are prosocial in nature is unclear. Additionally, Lisa may be using time with peers to avoid family relationships and conflict. The latter may be adaptive to some degree, but could also reinforce an avoidant, unproductive interpersonal style. Unfortunately, Lisa's increasing distress and engagement in maladaptive coping strategies went unnoticed in the context of a school with "few resources" and a family with parents working overtime and young siblings for whom Lisa has caregiving responsibilities. Although she does not currently meet criteria for an externalizing disorder, without significant changes in her functioning and that of her family, these conduct problems may worsen.

Lisa is also experiencing significant levels of conflict and disconnection from her father and stepmother. The frequency and intensity of fighting with her parents is greater than would be expected developmentally. Further, the family's ongoing stressors at the time of her father's remarriage may have resulted in little attention given to helping Lisa navigate this transition. This conflict occurs in the context of an increasingly limited reserve of positive interactions and relationship quality from which to draw. By all reports, there is poor parental monitoring of Lisa's activities coupled with high expectations for her responsible behavior for herself and her siblings. Lisa's ruminations about "family relationships, interpersonal hurts and desire for things to be different" suggest that the parent-child conflict in the home is likely related to Lisa's feelings of hurt, sadness, disappointment and/or anger about her relationship with her father, the new family constellation, and ongoing grief over the loss of her mother. Lisa's underdeveloped emotion regulation makes it more likely that she will internalize negative emotions and also avoid conflict with her parents by withdrawing, but then erupt in anger through disrespect and fighting. These responses increase her parents' level of stress and make it difficult for them to better understand her perspective, provide support and engage her in more positive ways. Lisa's well-developed cognitive abilities are protective resources, as she has the capacity to understand and empathize with the perspectives of her family members; however, these abilities coupled with her negative self-view may lead her to feel culpable in conflict situations and result in her direction of guilt, anger and sadness toward herself (e.g., through nonsuicidal self-injury by cutting) or outward (e.g., slamming doors and throwing things in her room). Her parents' work schedule and financial stress likely complicates their ability to interpret and respond to Lisa's behaviors with empathy, warmth and appropriate limits, or to help her to express and manage her strong emotions. The marital subsystem appears stable, and Lisa's parents acknowledge their inconsistent parenting, which can provide a basis for effective co-parenting. However, at this time, the quality of the parent-child subsystem is not optimal as the family struggles to renegotiate roles, rules and expectations as necessitated by the family's structural and developmental changes.

Finally, Lisa's ruminative cognitive style, negative emotions and increasing distress over family relationships most likely make it more difficult to concentrate on academic tasks. Her somewhat restricted access to social support at school likely makes it more difficult for Lisa to counteract emotional and cognitive distress. Should present levels of distraction and disengagement continue or worsen, it is likely her school performance will be further affected, threatening an important and previously stable source of positive academic and social feedback and self-esteem. Given Lisa's proneness to negative self-evaluation, internalization of distress, and social inhibition, she is unlikely to seek adequate levels of support or engage in optimally adaptive coping in this context, which already has few resources. However, Lisa's positive interactions with teachers suggest that there may be one or more adults who could serve in a supportive role. It is likely that Lisa would respond positively to this kind of support and increase her engagement during school. Decreasing depressive and anxious symptoms, along with improving parent-child and peer relationships, would make it even more likely that her school performance would return to previously successful levels.

9

Psychodynamic and Attachment-Based Approaches to Treatment

Jana D. Pressley and Kristin K. Vanden Hoek

PSYCHODYNAMIC APPROACHES TO CHILD and adolescent treatment have been built on a rich and complex history of theory, spanning from the era of Freud to contemporary dynamic models of treatment. Broadly considered, psychodynamic theories and treatment models are consistent in their conception of psychopathology as "the result of developmental, dynamic, intrapsychic, and relational disruptions that can best be ameliorated through a relationship with a helping professional whose focus is the individual child" (Hughes & Baker, 1990, p. 89). For most psychodynamically oriented clinicians, the central feature of therapy is the development of the therapeutic alliance between the child and the clinician. The child must come to feel safe and trusting enough with the therapist to reveal her thoughts, feelings, and behaviors without fear of rejection or abandonment. Historically, traditional psychoanalytic theory has advocated for long-term, individual treatment of the child. This approach allows a child the time and opportunity to develop a secure attachment to the clinician in order to reveal and work through unconscious wishes, fears and conflicts. There are many examples of this work, often accomplished through the practice of play therapy, beginning with the work of Anna Freud (1966–1980) and Melanie Klein (1975a, 1975b).

Although there are still many competent child clinicians who operate in this modality of long-term individual child therapy, with the emergence of psycho-logical and neurobiological research related to the caregiver's critical role in the development of emotion regulation skills and co-regulation of affect (Hall, chapter 3, this volume), many contemporary models of child and adolescent treatment involve caregivers as an essential component of the healing process (Bromfield, 2007; Hughes, 2007; Lieberman & van Horn, 2005; Schore, 2003; Siegel & Hartzell, 2004; Siegel & Bryson, 2011). This chapter will consider the overarching theoretical assumptions of psychodynamic theory, with a focus on object relations theory and attachment theory. Additionally, we will consider contemporary psychodynamic practice with children and families in light of developmental psychopathology and the integration of faith and theory.

Although Sigmund Freud is the theorist recognized for the birth of psycho-analytic theory, he wrote minimally about direct work with children. Much of the early writing related to child-focused treatment was born out of the work of Anna Freud and Melanie Klein, who both expanded Freud's model and preserved the integrity of the original drive theory model. Although Freud retained many loyal followers, psychoanalytic thinkers began to break off in groups based on various conceptual models. One of the predominant models became known as object relations theory.

OBJECT RELATIONS THEORY

"Object relations" refers to our interpersonal relationships and how they have shaped our view of self and others over time. "Object relations theory explores the process whereby people come to experience themselves as separate and independent from others, while at the same time needing profound attachment to others" (Berzoff, Flanagan & Hertz, 1996, p. 127). In this theory, *object* suggests that the "inner residues of past relationships" shape an individual's current manner of interaction (St. Clair, 2000, p. 1). Although Freud originally used the term *object* with a focus on biological and instinctual drives in the infant-caregiver relationship, some of his psychoanalytic successors shifted the focus of human desire to be relational. Melanie Klein was a pioneer in the shift toward a more relational emphasis; however, she remained loyal enough to Freud to maintain a significant focus on biological drives. One of the groups that broke conceptually from Freud's original drive theory is known as the British Object Relations School. We focus below on the work of three leading theorists—W. R. D. Fairbairn, D. W. Winnicott and John Bowlby—who came out of this school of thought and profoundly shaped the theories of contemporary relational psychodynamic theory and therapy, particularly as they relate to children.

From Freud to Fairbairn

W. R. D. Fairbairn (1889–1964) is considered one of the most influential theorists in object relations theory because of his role in crafting a model of psychoanalytic theory that intentionally deemphasized biological drive theory and set out to be more purely psychological (Scharff & Birtles, 1994). Fairbairn continued to use the term *libido,* although he clarified that he rejected Freud's instinct-focused drive theory. Whereas Freud focused on human drives as located in the id—motivated by seeking pleasure and reducing tension in a primal and physical way—Fairbairn understood human motivation as the ego striving for a relationship with a meaningful other (the object). In this model of human development, libido (drive) is *object-seeking,* as opposed to Freud's model of libidinal *pleasure-seeking.* Fairbairn explained, "The real libidinal aim is the establishment of satisfactory relationships with objects; and it is, accordingly, the object that constitutes the true libidinal goal" (Scharff & Birtles, 1994, p. 113). In other words, our fundamental human motivation is not sexual gratification and tension reduction but *connections with others* as an end in itself. As in any theory of human functioning, object relations theory has a set of assumptions related to healthy development, psychopathology and the conditions needed for therapeutic change. Object relations theory assumes that relationships in early life leave a lasting impression within the psyche of the individual, and treatment explores how these inner representations manifest in our current relationships.

Object Relations Theory and Development

When considering the roots of relational development, Fairbairn focused largely on the early relationship between the infant and the primary caregiver, which during his time was almost exclusively the mother. Early in life, a child bonds to her primary caregiver through whatever form of contact the caregiver provides, and this style of connection becomes the blueprint for a lifelong pattern of attachment and future relationship to others. Fairbairn believed that healthy parenting would produce individuals who would seek connections with others and be outwardly oriented; likewise, if caregivers provide painful connections, the child will come to expect and seek out (albeit unconsciously) painful connection in the future.

D. W. Winnicott (1896–1971), another member of the British Object Relations School, also contributed significantly to contemporary relational psychodynamic theory. Winnicott defined the quality of an infant's relational experience during the early months of life as crucial for the emergence of personhood, or what he referred to as the *true self*. For Winnicott, the true self is at the core of personality, involving our uniqueness, individuality, distinct talents, likes and dislikes. By contrast, the false self seeks to suppress individuality and molds itself to meet the need of others in order to preserve attachments. A child (or adult) who operates as a false self feels unsafe being genuine in relationships and often experiences a sense of feeling empty or fragmented (Mitchell & Black, 1995; St. Clair, 2000). Winnicott, consistent with Fairbairn's writings, asserted that healthy child development is the result of consistent emotional/relational responsiveness of the caregiver to an infant's needs. He referred to this necessary condition as the *facilitating environment*, in which the mother is constantly adapting to the child's changing developmental needs. Winnicott described healthy caregiving in his famous coining of the term *good-enough mother*. The good-enough mother is one who is attuned to the needs and affect of the child and shapes her responsive behaviors according to the changing needs of the child. Winnicott also described this critical developmental time as the *holding environment*—both a physical and a psychological space in which the infant is cared for and protected. Gradually throughout development, the child's dependency needs decrease, and the primary caregivers continue to adapt accordingly. Winnicott was deeply convinced of the inextricable link between healthy child development and maternal care, famously stating, "There is no value whatever in describing babies in the earliest stages except in relation to the mother's functioning" (Winnicott, 1965, p. 57).

As a physician, Winnicott also acknowledged the presence of biologically based, inherited traits and potential, stating: "Infants come into *being* differently according to whether the conditions are favourable or unfavourable. At the same time, conditions do not determine the infant's potential. This is inherited, and it is legitimate to study this inherited potential of the individual as a separate issue, provided always that it is accepted that the inherited potential of an infant cannot become an infant unless linked to maternal care" (Winnicott, 1965, p. 43). This "inherited potential," as stated by Winnicott, overlaps conceptually with the construct of temperament (chapter 2, this volume), as does the idea that there is a bidirectional relationship between the temperament of the child and the caregiver(s). Additionally, Winnicott acknowledged the need for a culture that supports healthy caregiving in stating, "It should be noted that mothers who have it in them to provide good-enough care can be enabled to do better by being cared for themselves in a way that acknowledges the essential nature of their task" (Winnicott, 1965, p. 49). In an era when mothers were often blamed for many forms of child psychopathology, Winnicott's acknowledgment of the mother's need for care and support was an important notation. In contemporary writing on attachment theory and co-regulation of emotion, Schore and Schore (2008) reinforce this need for the larger environment to support healthy caregiving, stating: "Individual development arises out of relationship between brain/mind/body of both infant and caregiver held within a culture and environment that supports or threatens it" (p. 10). This statement reflects the contextual values of developmental psychopathology as well as the influence that developmental theories have had on shaping contemporary revisions of psychodynamic theory to considering both the internal and external world of the individual child.

Object Relations Theory and Pathology
In an object relations theory conceptualization of pathology, psychological symptoms and relational difficulties develop due to the child engaging in relational and behavioral patterns of self-protection and interpersonal adaptation. Fairbairn, along with other psychoanalytic theorists, conceptualized children as coping with emotionally unavailable, frustrating or harmful caregivers by "mentally splitting the object into good and bad aspects and then taking in or internalizing the bad aspect" (St. Clair, 2000, p. 50). In other words, the child takes into herself the "bad aspect" in order to survive and preserve her attachment to her caregivers. This splitting allows the child to separate the negative from her caregivers, preserving a sense of safety and control. For the short term, this can serve as an effective and adaptive solution, as the child does not have the insight or emotional maturity to understand and survive in a world where her caregivers are actually behaving in ways that are harmful. This view of psychopathology is consistent with the premise in developmental psychopathology that adaptive functioning can become maladaptive in the long term (Flanagan & Hall, chapter 1, this volume). As summarized by Blaustein and Kinniburgh (2010), "Human behavior is not random: our behavior and actions are largely functional, or else arose to serve some function and continue because no more effective or sophisticated adaptation yet exists. Even the most seemingly 'patho-

logical' of children's behaviors may make sense, when understood in light of the purpose they serve for the child" (p. 25). However, the cost to the child is often high. That which is internalized negatively can ultimately manifest as a variety of symptoms and psychological disorders, such as depression, anxiety, behavioral disorders, eating disorders, substance abuse, self-harm, and interpersonal difficulties with peers and adults alike. The types of symptoms developed are shaped by the nature and intensity of the original painful experiences, the developmental stage during which the conflicts occurred, and the types of defenses the child attempted in order to protect himself from psychic pain. Additionally, the internalization of bad objects can lead to ways of viewing self and others that are fairly rigid and resistant to change, if not addressed. The resistance to change stems from the fear of releasing bad objects, because with this would come the realization of the sad world "peopled with devils which are too terrifying for him to face" (Fairbairn, 1954, p. 69). Herein lies a conundrum for any wounded person: continue to internalize the "badness" and rely on defenses, or face the painful realities of an unsafe, unjust world. When individuals do not have the chance to acknowledge and therapeutically work through childhood wounds, they are at risk to struggle as adults with shame, insecurity, unhealthy relational patterns or a variety of psychological symptoms in later life.

In Winnicott's theory, a child is considered to be at risk for pathology or symptom development when he does not have a safe enough holding environment in which to grow. Winnicott used the term *impingement* to describe when a child is prematurely psychologically forced into coming to terms with and adapting to the scary world, due to a lack of developmentally appropriate physical and emotional protection and attunement. Similar to Fairbairn's ideas of survival-based splitting, Winnicott believed that chronic caregiver failure to provide necessary safety and nurturance leads to "the radical split within the self between the genuine wellsprings of desire and meaning (the true self) and a compliant self (the false self)" (Mitchell & Black, 1995, p. 131). For children who sense that they need to conform to a certain way of being in order to earn parental love and approval, the subtle and subconscious development of a compliant, false self can provide alternatives to feared rejection and abandonment.

ATTACHMENT THEORY

John Bowlby (1907–1990) is also often linked to the original British Object Relations group, and his theory of healthy and unhealthy relational development comes to very similar conclusions as those of Fairbairn and Winnicott. However, Bowlby was one of the first to discuss attachment as an absolute necessity for survival of the human species, and he defined attachment theory from the beginning as an ecological model (Bowlby, 1969). Infants and their mothers are *biologically programmed* for a close connection, and the infant and mother both exhibit behaviors and characteristics that keep the mother close in proximity and increase infant's chance of survival (Bowlby, 1988). Before Bowlby's writings, it was widely assumed that physical needs, such as food and shelter, were the primary survival needs. For Bowlby and his successors, however, attachment behaviors are largely conceived to be related to emotional and relational needs. Bowlby describes the social interactions between a mother and an infant as a process in which the mother is attuning her focus, affect and level of intensity very carefully to that of the child—modulating the volume of her voice or the pace of her movements to match the child's signals. He states, "On the one hand is the mother's intuitive readiness to allow her interventions to be paced by her infant. On the other is the readiness with which the infant's rhythms gradually shift to take account of the timing of his mother's interventions. In a happily developing partnership each is adapting to the other" (Bowlby, 1988, p. 8). In a relational synchronicity that has often been described as a dance, caregivers have the opportunity to guide their infant in the ability to relationally engage and disengage as needed and to develop the building blocks needed for later emotional regulation (see Hall, chapter 3, this volume). It is through the healthy or unhealthy interplay of this daily interaction that the foundation of secure, insecure or disorganized attachment develops.

Although much of attachment theory is based on the quality of the interactions during the initial year of life, Bowlby writes extensively about attachment needs throughout childhood, adolescence and adulthood. He describes how, during the second year of life and after a child has obtained some minimal level of self-soothing, attachment behavior becomes activated and deactivated based on environmental conditions. Bowlby (1988) states, "A child's attachment behavior is activated especially by pain, fatigue, and anything frightening, and also by the mother being or appearing to be inaccessible" (p. 3). He describes the level of soothing that the child needs from the primary caregiver as corresponding to the intensity of the arousal. When it comes to older childhood and adolescence, Bowlby continues to address the central role of parents functioning as a secure base from which the child or teen explores and develops a sense of competence. He describes the central feature of his concept of parenting as creating a home where the child or adolescent feels safe to journey into the outside world and live out new experiences, "knowing for sure that he will be welcomed when he gets there, nourished physically and emotionally, comforted if distressed, reassured if frightened. In essence this role is one of being available, ready to respond when called upon to encourage and perhaps assist, but to intervene actively only when clearly necessary" (Bowlby, 1988, p. 11).

In Bowlby's conceptualization of secure attachment and personality development, attachment security enables a child to venture out and explore her world, knowing that she can continue to return to the *secure base* of her caregiver. Attachment theory suggests that this consistent model of nurturing over time imprints upon a child the belief that others can be trusted and relied upon, and that the world is generally a safe place. This pattern also presumably leads to a healthy internal working model—the blueprint by which we conceptualize our future adult relationships. In a healthy internal working model, the child comes to view herself as loved and valued, which supports the development of the requisite skills for future healthy relationships. When attachment relationships are not safe, stable or healthy during critical developmental periods, however, the inverse is true (see Seegobin, chapter 4, this volume). When children experience relationships as rejecting, unsafe or tumultuous, attachment theorists hypothesize that children develop insecure or disorganized attachment styles. These rejecting or neglectful relational experiences often translate into long-term negative beliefs about self and others and impaired patterns of relating, such as a sense of self as unworthy or unable to depend on others for help, and a sense of others as unreliable, frightening or intrusive (see Clements, Guarino & Bartos, chapter 5, this volume).

Psychodynamic Practice: Assessment and Treatment

In order to facilitate the necessary conditions for emotional healing and behavioral change, the therapist has to provide a secure and safe enough environment for a client (child or adult) to release internalized "bad objects" from the unconscious. Object relations theorists argue that people will not likely give up the powerful ties to old, internalized objects unless they can come to believe in new, healthier patterns of relatedness; the interpersonal risks are simply too high, and the protective defenses have often served their adaptive purpose well. Psychodynamic therapists believe that clients must experience directly that there is another way to relate to others in which they will feel seen, cared for and understood. Winnicott discussed the therapeutic environment utilizing the same term he used for the mother-infant relationship: the holding environment. A therapist creates a "holding environment" in treatment where a client can explore past and present experience of self without fear of rejection, abandonment or criticism. The safe therapeutic environment is one that allows enough emotional safety for true self to emerge. Similarly, Bowlby described the therapist's role as creating a "secure base" in which clients could feel safe enough to form a healthy attachment relationship, facilitating the ability for trust and authentic disclosure of painful affect.

In treatment with young children, there is a common assumption that play is a natural therapeutic holding environment through which children can communicate information about their experience, affect and inner world. The language of play gives a child an opportunity to project meaning, emotion and conflicts in a nonthreatening (or at least less threatening) and symbolic manner. The expression of strong emotions such as fear or hostility can feel extremely risky for a child, with the danger (perceived or actual) of rejection from caregivers. Play gives children the opportunity to express emotions that would be otherwise threatening to their defenses and sense of safety. Play therapy will be further discussed in a later section of this chapter as one example of psychodynamic theory in practice.

Whether it is through play therapy with young children or talk therapy with older children and adolescents, contemporary psychodynamic models of treatment begin with common therapeutic goals that are similar to the goals of many other theoretical models. For the psychodynamic child therapist, it is critical to thoroughly assess the child in context in order to understand the child's needs, losses and resulting emotional/behavioral symptoms that have brought the child to therapy. This focus on the need for thorough contextual understanding is consistent with the underlying premises of developmental psychopathology as summarized by Flanagan and Hall (chapter 1, this volume) when they stated, "We cannot determine whether a behavior is adaptive or normative outside of its context" (p. 21). Delgado (2008) describes how a good psychodynamic assessment emerges from a solid psychodynamic conceptual framework: "As is commonly said, a picture speaks louder than words, and what better picture than the one that emerges from interacting with a child to evaluate his temperament, attachment style, and ego functions according to his or her developmental stage" (p. 69). It is critical to provide the child with an environment and therapeutic attachment where she feels safe to play or talk freely. This sense of safety will enable effective assessment and therapy. Developmentally sensitive assessment will also respect the defense mechanisms that children employ to protect their fears and fragile sense of self. It is unhelpful, in the spirit of developing a safe therapeutic environment, to confront a young child's denial or projection, unless those defenses are severely interfering with positive coping. At the same time, the therapist does not need to feel the pressure to collude with the child when she is using denial or other defense mechanisms to cope. Hughes and Baker (1990) state, "Often an empathic statement that conveys to the child both respect for the child's struggle to cope and acceptance of the child's feelings will shore up self-esteem and lead the way to more open communication" (p. 56). Delgado (2008) describes the ideal context of the initial sessions by explaining, "To allow the picture of the child's internal world to emerge in the office, we need to create a psychological space to observe the content and encourage the process to develop. This task is enhanced if we astutely 'watch, wait, and wonder' during our interview" (p. 69).

Psychodynamic treatment would view the holding environment and the therapeutic relationship as key components of allowing the child to begin to achieve the goals of (1) expressing emotions without fear and (2) developing a deeper awareness of self. A child who begins to experience healthy emotional expression in therapy will ideally begin to decrease in fear of her own emotions and/or fear of others' reactions to her emotions. A child who begins to develop a deeper sense of self may also begin to understand and accept her own desires, wishes, hopes or losses. In the treatment guideline for evidence-based psychodynamic therapy for child trauma, Foa and colleagues (2009) summarized the common element of psychodynamic treatment succinctly: "A core aspect of psychodynamic psychotherapies is that the ultimate goal is to promote personality coherence and healthy development rather than to alleviate symptom severity alone" (p. 586).

In addition to the relational interventions of therapy, psychodynamic treatment places a high value on the importance of the *frame* of therapy. Psychodynamic therapists emphasize the meaning that can come from providing safe and consistent boundaries and limits in the actual routines of therapy: (1) the physical space of the treatment room, which contributes to the safety of the holding environment; (2) consistent timing of therapy—this includes beginning and ending on time and keeping a predicable schedule, which assists the client in experiencing a sense of control and constancy; (3) understanding how confidentiality is managed, in order to develop trust and minimize a sense of betrayal; and (4) limit setting, which assists children in experiencing healthy limits in the context of a nonjudgmental and accepting relationship (Bromfield, 2007).

In his practical guide to psychodynamically oriented child and adolescent therapy, Bromfield (2007) identifies therapy as including the following components: making a safe place, holding a child's stories and emotions, intervening (through empathic reflections, encouragement, confrontation and acknowledgment of empathic failures), bringing about insight, helping the child view himself more honestly (even when it is painful), providing hope and future orientation, supporting healthy coping, and utilizing practical interventions, including psychoeducation, modeling, and problem solving when appropriate. Above all, the empathic attunement of the therapist to the child is believed to be the most powerful tool for intervention. Empathy guides our interventions in a way that both respects a child's defenses and recognizes her readiness to be challenged toward growth. Bromfield states,

> It is our empathy that enables us to gauge where children are in terms of tension and affect so that we intervene at the proper time and to the right degree. We seek to push them to deal with as much as they adaptively can. To overwhelm a child's resources is counterproductive and can set them back; to underwhelm them supports the status quo, inviting regression and complacency. By titrating how much we emotionally confront children—ever striving to provide the optimal amount of intervention—we psychically stretch them. (p. 39)

INCLUDING CAREGIVERS: DYADIC AND FAMILY MODELS OF PSYCHODYNAMIC TREATMENT

Many of the contemporary models of psychodynamic therapy with children have been heavily informed by the foundations of attachment theory, with increasing focus on the inclusion of caregivers in treatment. When reflecting on the critical role of the connection between child and caregiver, and the emotional health of the caregiver, clinicians and researchers have begun to recognize the need for treatment models that educate and support parents alongside their children. Although there is certainly still a place for individual child treatment, many presenting issues—if viewed through the lens of object

relations and attachment theories—would benefit from bringing caregiver inclusion into the "frame" of therapy. Psychodynamic therapy is often referred to
as insight oriented, in that treatment seeks to assist clients in understanding
the meaning of underlying behavior in order to promote deep change. This
stance could be used to support the importance of assisting caregivers in understanding their children's emotions, behaviors, and interpersonal style in
order to impact long-term change. More specifically, some of the goals of caregiver inclusion in psychodynamic treatment of children include rebuilding (or
building for the first time) a secure, connected attachment relationship, increasing caregiver self-reflective abilities, increasing caregiver recognition and
management of his or her own emotions, coaching caregivers on skills related
to co-regulation of affect, and support/generalization of the caregiver's ability
to teach and model affect regulation skills to his or her child (Hughes, 2007;
Siegel & Hartzell, 2003; Siegel & Bryson, 2011).

Over the past several years, the specific issue of emotion regulation has
benefitted from a wealth of neurobiological research, pointing toward the
critical role of caregivers in co-regulation of affect (Siegel, 2001; Siegel &
Hartzell, 2003; Siegel & Bryson, 2011; Schore, 2003; Schore & Schore, 2008).
The resulting field of interpersonal neurobiology has made a significant impact
on attachment-focused psychodynamic clinicians, emphasizing the need for
caregivers to also possess affect regulation skills, including the ability to identify,
modulate and express emotions. When the caregiver is struggling with depression, anxiety or relational disturbance, for example, parenting can be negatively impacted, and the ability to be an effective co-regulator of affect for one's
child can be significantly influenced. For caregivers with their own chaotic and/
or traumatic histories, affect may be chronically dysregulated, often leading to
disrupted attachment relationships and cyclical conflictual patterns between
children and parents (Blaustein & Kinniburgh, 2007; Siegel & Hartzell, 2003).
Therefore, models of dyadic psychotherapy with caregivers and young children
(e.g., Child-Parent Psychotherapy; Lieberman & van Horn, 2005) and models
of attachment-focused family treatment (Attachment-Based Family Therapy;
Diamond, Siqueland & Diamond, 2003; Attachment-Focused Family Therapy;
Hughes, 2007) have shown great promise in the contemporary psychodynamic
child treatment literature.

In addition to compelling theoretical arguments in support of psychodynamic treatment, treatment outcome research has found psychodynamic

therapy to be effective (Shedler, 2010), particularly with children who are struggling with internalizing symptoms or disorders (Fonagy & Target, 1996; Midgley & Kennedy, 2011). Psychodyamic treatment models have found research support most consistently for children and adolescents dealing with trauma (Foa et al., 2009; Lieberman & van Horn, 2005; Midgley & Kennedy, 2011) and depression (Diamond et al., 2003; Midgley & Kennedy, 2011; Target & Fonagy, 1994).

THEORETICAL AND PRACTICAL IMPLICATIONS OF DEVELOPMENTAL PSYCHOPATHOLOGY FOR PSYCHODYNAMIC APPROACHES

Developmental psychopathology is a broad framework from which to conceptualize the intricacies of child and adolescent development as they relate to outcomes. As described in this book, the aim of this field of study is to "achiev[e] a science that can unravel the dynamic-process relations underlying pathways of normal development and the development of psychopathology" (Cummings et al., 2000, p. 17). These dynamic processes are understood through a multifaceted and reciprocal mix of positive and negative influences that foster change on the continuum of adaption to maladaptation. A clear understanding of these etiological influences then allows the therapist to intervene through a wide variety of avenues.

Within a developmental pathology framework, psychodynamic approaches to case formulation and treatment represent one model that can help clinicians understand and address deviations from expected stage-salient issues and objectives. Based on the heavy relational emphasis that underlies object relations theory, psychodynamic formulations focus largely on the individual impact of the dyadic relationship between child and caregiver. However, as emphasized by a developmental psychopathology framework, psychodynamic approaches extend to a wide range of relational influences and contextual dynamics that impact social functioning and identity development. This requires a highly individualized conceptualization and incorporates layers of relationships within a context with varying levels of influence over time. From a developmental pathology perspective, each child is embedded in multiple systems. One perspective from which to consider context is Bronfenbrenner's ecological systems model, which incorporates influences ranging from microsystems—such as the child's neighborhood, school, family and peer group—to macrosystems that include attitudes and ideologies of the child's cultural context

(Bronfenbrenner, 1994; Kerig, & Wenar, 2005; Masten, 2006). The task, then, is for the clinician working within this framework to understand and consider the complexity of the social context of each child, while also working with accessible systems and relationships, most commonly the therapeutic and family relationships, to restore the child to a healthy developmental trajectory.

A developmental psychopathology view of pathology appreciates the complex influences and transactional nature of etiology. This perspective broadens a traditional psychodynamic conceptualization that focuses primarily on how impingements by the caregiver influence the development of pathology in the child. Therefore, when a clinician works from a developmental psychopathology framework with a psychodynamic approach to therapy, any deviation from the expected trajectory is conceptualized as resulting from the interaction among the child's inherent capacities, relational influences of others, and environmental demands and limitations. As described earlier in this chapter, contemporary attachment-focused authors acknowledge the role of an environmental and cultural context that either "supports or threatens" the child-caregiver relationship and child development overall (Schore & Schore, 2008, p. 10). This thinking reflects the contextual values of developmental psychopathology, which emphasizes that individual characteristics, interpersonal dynamics, and the context reciprocally interact and influence one another.

Developmental psychopathology provides a rich understanding of the agency and influence of the child within interpersonal relationships as well as protective and risk dynamics inherent in the child's environment. Furthermore, developmental psychopathology is concerned with how pathology results from the child's interaction with these influences over time (Cummings et al., 2000). This perspective continues to expand traditional psychodynamic approaches, which appreciate how internal representations of others persist over time but not specifically how they evolve over time based on subsequent experiences. In some cases, coping that was once adaptive can develop into maladaptive behavior as the contextual expectations of the child change. Consider the following example: Luke spent the first eight years of his life in a chaotic and violent home, with a father who was emotionally and physically abusive to him and his mother. During those years, Luke's father demonstrated that "being a tough guy" was the way for Luke to earn his respect, and he belittled Luke for any display of sadness, fear or relational need.

Luke learned to relate to others, including peers at school, through intimidation and aggression. He had internalized the sense of self developed within his early relationships and learned to survive in ways that made sense within those relationships, though they were maladaptive in other contexts. To further complicate matters, Luke's school system was overwhelmed by need and lacked resources; therefore, Luke's view of self and resulting actions were further reinforced by his teachers' negative reactions to him (as one of the "problem kids") and by acceptance into a peer group of other aggressive children. When later removed from his biological parents and placed in a foster home with patient and loving caregivers, Luke's view of himself and his "tough guy" behavior continued, much to the confusion of his new caregivers. It took two years of consistent intervention and acceptance by his new community for Luke to begin to demonstrate new patterns of behavior and relational engagement, and for several years he continued to struggle with an internalized view of himself as "weak" when displaying vulnerability. Although many treatment perspectives, including traditional psychodynamic approaches, focus on pathology within the individual, a developmental psychopathology approach allows for the possibility that pathology develops in the interaction between the child and influences such as family, school or community. Thus, from this perspective the complexity of pathology is readily acknowledged, and intrapersonal, interpersonal and systemic factors are all examined and considered as sources of influence.

An example of two intrapersonal influences that lie within each child are temperament and emotion regulation. As discussed in previous chapters (chapters 2 and 3), these internal dynamics involve an interplay of biological and interpersonal influences, which can serve as both risk and protective factors in response to stress, trauma or other deviations from an expected developmental trajectory. Psychodynamic approaches may examine the relationship to the primary attachment figure in order to understand these influences. Specifically, the therapist may assess the match between the caregiver's ability to soothe the child and attune to the child's temperamental needs and abilities (i.e., goodness of fit between caregiver and child). The same child may elicit varied reactions based on the abilities and temperament of the caregiver as the two reciprocally influence one another. For example, an energetic and active child may feel overwhelming to one parent, whereas the same child could seem vivacious and spirited to another parent; these two parents might respond differently to the child and, accordingly, meet the child's needs to a greater or lesser extent.

A psychodynamic approach regards the parent-child attachment as foundational for the development of the child's basic sense of self-awareness, self-regulation, mastery and self-worth. This foundation is created not only through the internalization of the parent-child attachment but also through the emotional and behavioral security of the environment (see chapter 5, this volume) as the child experiences the emotional protection and stability of the parent-child relationship and within the marital dyad. This framework with a psychodynamic approach gives equal emphasis to the aversive aspects of parenting as well as resilient influences of a caring and nurturing figure in the child's life (Cummings et al., 2000). When a parent-child relationship is strained by an insecure attachment that may stem from a lack of parental sensitivity and responsiveness, mismatched temperaments between the child and parent, or inconsistency in parenting practices, a developmental psychopathology–informed intervention may not focus only on the parent-child relationship in isolation. Rather, given the child's embeddedness in multiple systems, the goal may be to increase the child's connection and support with the parent as well as with other resources available at school, in the community and through religious programs. Such supports would help facilitate the return to a normal trajectory not only through directly targeting maladaptive parent-child relational patterns but also by providing nurturing role models, reinforcing the development of problem-solving and social skills, and providing a venue for skill acquisition and a sense of efficacy to flourish (Masten, Best & Garmezy, 1990).

At times the use of psychodynamic-based treatments within a developmental psychopathology framework may address the relational wounds created by inattentive or unresponsive caregivers and will facilitate the amelioration of some of these experiences through the therapeutic relationship. Specifically, treatment might focus on assisting the child in developing a stable and secure selfhood by creating opportunities for the development of trust and healthy relational experiences with the therapist and other important figures in the child's life. For many children, a more adaptive developmental trajectory might be obtained if the child's immediate context is strengthened by involving the parent in the therapeutic space and thus addressing the attachment relationship directly (Kerig & Wenar, 2005). Attachment disruptions then can be addressed through treatment approaches such as attachment-focused family therapy (Hughes, 2007) and child-parent psychotherapy (Lieberman & van Horn, 2005).

Given the complex nature of the parent-child relationship, a psychodynamic approach within a developmental psychopathology framework considers the impact of attachment over time and how other salient relationships are likely to influence and be influenced by a child's emerging working models of self and others. Specifically, as discussed in chapters five and six, the parental dyad and peer relationships each have a profound impact throughout childhood and adolescence on the child's identity, connection and sense of safety in the world. These relationships have their own trajectories and are in a constant state of flux due to multiple systemic influences, which may directly or indirectly affect the child. For example, a child's experiences of parental support may be highly influenced by the stability and emotional support in the marital relationship, which also draws from each parent's finite emotional resources. Further, in therapy this approach often considers retrospectively how attachment and emotional security with caregivers now influences their relationships with salient individuals such as peers and siblings. Thus, a developmental psychopathology–informed psychodynamic approach both acknowledges the influences of these current relationships and incorporates early relational experiences into the holistic conceptualization of the child's rich relational world.

In summary, psychodynamic treatments complement and flow easily from the developmental psychopathology framework. This perspective examines relational pathways and processes over time on a continuum from adaptive to maladaptive. The primary relational focus is often between the caregiver and child (e.g., attachment, goodness of fit) but also incorporates and considers other salient relationships in the child's context (e.g., peers) who are highly influential to the child's identity, connectedness and sense of safety. The etiological conceptualization of this perspective is transactional and complex by nature, with intrapersonal (e.g., temperament, emotion regulation), interpersonal and systematic reciprocal influences. Given the complexity of these influences, therapy can intervene on a number of relational levels. It may involve a corrective relational experience with the therapist, an attachment-focused approach to increase the connection and support between caregiver and child, a focus on connecting the child with healthy and supportive institutions (e.g., school, clubs) and community members, or a combination of these approaches.

PRACTICAL SUGGESTIONS

- The therapist should be attuned to the distinct attachment needs and relational patterns of the child or adolescent client, with recognition that the therapeutic relationship serves as a primary change component in the treatment process.

- The therapist should prioritize creating a "holding environment" and developing the therapeutic relationship as key components in order to allow the child to begin to achieve the goals of (1) expressing emotions without fear and (2) developing a deeper awareness of self.

- Given the importance of relational experiences in children's developmental trajectories, a thorough assessment should consider the multiple relational systems in which the child is embedded, including the family, peer group, school, community and larger social/cultural context.

- Case conceptualization and treatment should be informed by an assessment of the child-caregiver relationship (current and historical) and the goodness-of-fit of child and caregiver.

- Case conceptualization and treatment should also be guided by an assessment of the emotional regulation abilities and patterns of both the child and the primary caregivers, with attention also given to the caregivers' emotional vulnerabilities that might be triggered by particular child behaviors. When appropriate, therapy for caregivers addressing relational wounds and trauma in their own history can be a crucial component in the process of helping the caregiver regulate her own and her child's emotional responses.

- The therapist should be attuned to the defense mechanisms that the child or adolescent may be employing in order to maintain a cohesive sense of self. The empathically attuned therapist will respect the role that defenses have played in protection of the child and gradually confront defenses at a pace that neither overwhelms the child's developmental capacities nor colludes with the defenses.

- The therapist will identify the ways in which the child or adolescent's internal working model and resulting relational needs are expressed, and will work to facilitate healthy expression of relational needs though age-appropriate interventions. Those interventions will vary by age and developmental level, with a focus on play therapy and caregiver-child models for younger children and more insight-oriented individual psychotherapy for older children and adolescents.

SPECIFIC TREATMENT MODELS

To further delineate the theoretical underpinnings of psychodynamic approaches, as informed by developmental psychopathology, we will explore three psychodynamic models of treatment. In particular, we will examine how play therapy, relational psychotherapy, and attachment-focused family therapy conceptualize and address the central components of developmental psychopathology. Although unique in presentation, client population and techniques, these treatment approaches are united by a rich appreciation of the role of early attachment experiences and the role relationships play in the life of a child.

Play Therapy

Play therapy is a common treatment approach with children that utilizes play as the primary means of expression and communication. As a child-directed process, play allows the child to naturally act out salient issues (Semrund-Clikeman, 1995). The term *play* encompasses a wide array of activities and can refer to almost any activity that is developmentally appropriate for the child. Materials can include a variety of manipulatives and toys, such as dolls, puppets, clay, games, sand trays and dollhouses, with techniques such as drawing, role playing and storytelling. Children are naturally creative, so many objects can be used in a play therapy session; they are especially helpful if they draw on the child's imagination rather than skills (Kerig & Wenar, 2005). Given children's developmentally normative imagination and relative lack of inhibition, play represents a natural way to access a child's inner world.

Based on the needs and history of the child, play can assist the child through a variety of avenues. Play, both within and outside of therapy, allows for meaning making and processing of a child's experiences. The nature of play distances the child from traumatic experiences or overwhelming emotions and allows the child to explore and share at a comfort level that feels safe (Kerig & Wenar, 2005). This safety is created through the projection of unconscious emotions, thoughts and experiences onto benign objects. For example, a child feeling self-conscious about school refusal due to social anxiety may feel more comfortable talking through a puppet.

Play also allows for the therapist to note these protective responses and provides a means for children to safely face these defenses. Similar to adult treatment, exploration of defense occurs through the careful use of interpretations to increase the client's awareness of her behavior so she can learn to make healthier decisions (Kerig & Wenar, 2005). This can be done through drawing attention to what the child is not aware of or by pointing out discrepancies between the child's play and what she reports (Bromfield, 2003). For example, a child may say she hates her mother in therapy and yet display themes of significant fear of separation when playing with figures representing a child and mother. Once a safe therapeutic relationship has been established, the therapist can "wonder about" the themes reflected in the play and how those themes might be connected to the child's experience. Play therapy also allows for the use of metaphors to discuss an injury at a distance. For example, a therapist may say to a child going through her parents' divorce, "I noticed this princess doll keeps looking back at her dad's castle when she is in her mom's castle. I wonder what she is feeling and if she misses her dad when she is not at his castle?" In this example, the therapist notices the girl projecting her experience onto the princess and helps the child begin to explore some of her non-verbally communicated ambivalence and sadness.

Another essential objective of play therapy is to support the development of self-integration. A child who may disown feelings such as anger and sadness may be able to acknowledge and express these feelings through play (Wachtel, 2004). Therapists can facilitate this growth through deferring to the child about what a puppet would say or what kind of a face should be drawn on a stick figure. The therapist can also model for the child through good-natured play that disowned feelings are not threatening. For example, the therapist might have a child in the doll house family say to the new baby, "You wake up from your nap when I want to spend time with mom. That makes me so mad I want to send you back to the hospital where mom got you!" Thus, play is a unique technique that can serve many purposes, including meaning making, exploring experiences at a safe distance, and developing self-integration and personal awareness.

The role of the therapist is the facilitation of these processes through observation of themes that emerge in play and through creating an empathic and respectful environment (Kerig & Wenar, 2005). This requires the therapist to be present, observant and, at times, childlike and playful as he or she joins with the child in order to be an attentive witness of the child's experience through empathic listening and reflection (Bromfield, 2003). Through empathy the therapist is able to connect with and "contain" the child's overwhelming emotions until the child is slowly able to withstand them (Altman, Briggs, Frankel, Gensler & Pantone, 2002). Further, the therapeutic alliance serves to meet previously unsatisfied relational needs for a safe, consistent and attuned caregiver. Without such a therapeutic environment, the authentic expressions, vulnerability and risk taking necessary for growth are unlikely to occur.

As this relationship is established, *themes* in the child's play develop. Themes refer to speculations about important, concealed emotional and psychological issues observed by the therapist (Ryan & Edge, 2012). Given that themes are based on recurring verbal and nonverbal expressions toward the materials in play and/or the therapist, the development of themes is a continual process that can be supported or overturned by future experiences with the child. Ryan and Edge (2012) proposed that themes serve three purposes. First, reflection on themes increase the therapist's emotional connection and help the therapist respond appropriately in order to develop and strengthen attunement to the child's emotional state. Second, themes maintain the child's confidentiality by guarding specific sensitive information when discussing treatment with caretakers and other professionals. And third, themes serve as markers of progress. For example, Wilson and Ryan (2005) noted that themes typically progress from indiscriminate emotional demonstrations to expressions that are more positive in nature and involve exploration of developmentally appropriate issues. For example, the play of a seven-year-old boy struggling with the birth of a sibling may initially express aggressive behaviors and violent themes and then transition over time to themes of mild and almost humorous sibling rivalry, which is developmentally expected for a boy his age.

The method of theme development occurs through close observation of the child, especially in terms of repetition and disruption (Kerig &Wenar, 2005). Themes tend to become more readily apparent over time as they are repeated across diverse or multiple play experiences. They may be associated with increased expressed affect, regression to more infantile patterns of play and interaction, decreased self-control during the play (e.g., throwing or smashing play objects), or minimization of conflict, such as ending an intense story with "they lived happily ever after."

The process of play therapy described above is consistent with a developmental psychopathology framework in several respects. First, this approach takes into account the developmental ability and communication styles of children and uses their preferred means of communication to explore their inner experiences. Second, psychodynamic play therapists understand the emotional intensity of therapeutic content and respond by providing the necessary safety and distance in order to make the discussion manageable yet stretching, much like a developmental therapist would. Third, this approach emphasizes the developmental importance of modeling and provides scaffolding for children to experiment with emerging capacities. Finally, play therapy draws on developmental psychology during ongoing evaluation and observation throughout the treatment so that behavior might be understood in light of developmentally expected coping and capacities.

Relational Psychotherapy

Relational psychotherapy is an approach to treatment that focuses on interpersonal relationships and the internal working models of these relationships as motivational and transformational processes. The aim of this treatment is to rework previous ways of living through the interpersonal experience of therapy. Thus, in many respects the traditional one-person approach to psychoanalysis in children becomes a two-person psychology in which the relationship between the child and therapist becomes the focal point for exploration and transformation.

This two-person psychology, similar to the transaction process of developmental theorists, relies on a working therapeutic alliance and careful observations of what responses the child elicits from the therapist as well as what reactions the therapist draws out of the child. For example, a child who is resistant to any form of interaction with the therapist (e.g., parallel or interactive play, talking, eye contact) out of fear and anxiety impacts the therapist differently than a child who is resistant to suggestions of the therapist out of oppositional tendencies. As a reciprocal process, therapy is conceptualized as "an intermingling of two subjective worlds, and of internal and external realms, in a way that makes it impossible to draw sharp lines of distinction between who's who, and what was preexisting in the patient's internal object world and what was evoked by the analyst" (Altman et al., 2002, p. 9). Thus, much like Winnicott's understanding of the involved mother-child relationship, in therapy the world is constructed based on the interplay of two subjective realities. In this relationship, a sort of relational dance is created in which both participants are continually eliciting a reply from the other and responding to the other (Masten, 2006). Inside this dance of intertwined subjective reality, social development occurs, offering an opportunity for the child to ponder, reflect and ascribe new meaning to the self. It is from this exploration in a safe and accepting environment that the true self can be understood and false selves can be relinquished. For instance, a common theme in working with adolescents in therapy is the exploration and reflection on different aspects of their personhood that may have shifted or changed in response to a traumatic experience. For example, a seventeen-year-old adolescent female who is grieving the loss of a parent may also be facing increased responsibility at home as a caretaker for younger siblings as well as increased autonomy to make personal decisions due to the decreased supervision and availability of her surviving parent. At school and at home she feels the pressure to "keep it together" and "be strong," as she knows others are depending on her. This creates a "false self" that externally portrays a strength that she does not experience internally as a part of her "true self." These contextual and relational changes will likely impact her identity and self-expectations and may result in difficulties such as maladaptive self-criticism and identify confusion. This adolescent could use therapy as a safe environment in which to remove the veneer of her false self in order to process the premature changes to her identity as well as to receive support and comfort for her own mourning process that her caregiver may be unable to provide due to his or her own grief.

In order to understand a child's process of developing a sense of self, a clear understanding of her attachment and interpersonal experiences is necessary. Formative relationships contain the potential to foster growth and nurture autonomy through provision of a secure emotional base or to damage and derail an expected developmental trajectory. Relational therapy in particular draws on the work of Daniel Stern's Field Theory, which describes how a child takes on parental roles and images the parent places on the child (Altman et al., 2002). The child learns through the response of the parents which aspects of self are enjoyed and accepted by caregivers and which should be disavowed due to the contempt or anxiety they elicit. For example, if a parent acknowledges and encourages the energetic temperament of her son, then this aspect of the child can be internalized as a valued part of himself and may be conceptualized as a potential factor of resilience. Over time, it is this attunement and responsiveness between the child's experiences and the feedback from caregivers that fosters a sense of personal identity.

Although early experiences with caregivers are formative influences in a child's development of self, relational theory also holds that a child is a co-creator of his own self-image and can alter it unconsciously or consciously through insight and experience. To hold to this model the therapist must have a high regard for the agency of the child to contribute to his own development and the therapeutic process (Masten, 2006). As this agency and selfhood increase over the course of childhood, the child has increased independence on how to apply ego-strengthening insights and make choices that will increasingly impact his own experiences and circumstances and assist him in meeting challenges at each stage of development. For example, a therapist may facilitate a problem-solving process with the child about the choices he made in a given situation, while exploring what internal experience might have contributed to his choices. From this perspective, the primary role of the therapist is to facilitate exploration of self and relationships in order to create insight and autonomy in an age-appropriate manner.

Given the nature of the painful experiences that necessitate therapy for many children, this exploration may require the therapist to contain and witness the emotional experience of the child as these experiences are uncovered to support individuation and an emerging sense of self. In this way the therapist provides a holding environment that offers emotional security for the child. This exploration can occur frequently through examination of transference and what internal objects the child projects onto the therapist or other safe objects. For example, if a therapist is talking with a child about her frequent lying behavior, the therapist may begin the discussion by asking, 'Why do you think other children lie?' as a way to let the child potentially project her own motives onto other children. As the discussion progresses the child reveals that she lies because she feels like she is "bad" and that her mom hates her when she gets several time-outs. The therapist's role is then to hold this information and, at the appropriate time, reflect insight back to the child or adolescent in a more manageable form. Through this reworking of internalized objects and emotions, therapy becomes a process to challenge the distorted internal representations and deconstruct false selves to foster a realistic and balanced view of self.

The process of relational psychotherapy is complementary to developmental psychopathology, as a developmental perspective informs and alters these relational interventions in many respects. First, there is an emphasis on the transformative influence of relational contexts as a source of an emotionally secure attachment from which an emerging sense of self develops or as a potential source of harm through inconsistency, lack of responsiveness and insensitivity. Through a developmental perspective, the relational context of the child broadens to include a wider array of relationships (e.g., peers, siblings, school personnel, community members) with adaptive and maladaptive influences on the child's developing personhood. Second, both perspectives appreciate the rich complexity of each child's inner life, which is influenced through a variety of intrapersonal, interpersonal and contextual dynamics that deserve consideration throughout treatment. Developmental psychopathology then provides a framework from which to incorporate these transactional dynamics and understand how they contribute to the developmental pathway of the child over time. For example, how children relate to and depend on their father will most likely be expressed differently based on the environment of the child (e.g., park versus school), the chronological and developmental age of the child, and the temperament of the child. Third, this perspective offers a nuanced view of relationships as varying within the dynamic developmental pathways of risk, protection and resilience that have the potential to prevent negative outcomes and promote healthy development. Overall, relational psychotherapy within the developmental psychopathology framework provides a unique and individualized approach to attend to the relational and identity needs of children and adolescents, as it appreciates the complexity of development over time and the transformative impact of relationships.

Attachment-Focused Family Therapy

The third and final treatment example is attachment-focused family therapy (AFFT; Hughes, 2007), a model that is based on the work of various attachment and/or developmentally informed authors (Becker-Weidman & Shell, 2005; Fosha, 2000; 2003; Schore, 2003; Siegel, 2001; Siegel & Hartzell, 2003). AFFT is steeped in attachment and intersubjectivity theory, focusing on the inclusion of the family in child treatment. The term *intersubjectivity* refers to "those moments when the parent and child are in synch: when they are affectively and cognitively present to each other; when the vitality of their affective states are matched . . . and their intentions are congruent" (Hughes, 2007, p. 14). In light of this attachment and intersubjectivity focus, Hughes describes the overall intentions of psychotherapy as "to create experiences in the present that will influence experiences from the past and generate hope for more healing and integrative experiences in the future" (p. 46).

Although AFFT highly values the therapeutic relationship with the child, equal value is placed on the development of a secure relationship with the parents/family or the healing of the relationship between the child and the parents. This emphasis on both child and caregiver(s) is informed by a bidirectional, transactional view of relationships, similar to that which is represented in a developmental psychopathology perspective. Intersubjectivity is believed to be equally impactful for children and parents. Hughes (2007) states, "During those moments of the attuned dance between parent and child, both are being impacted deeply at the core of their sense of self" (p. 30). In families seeking treatment, past missteps in the "dance" of attunement have often led to painful decline in child-parent relationships, and treatment may be less successful without the opportunity to empathize with and empower parents to reconnect with their children, and vice versa. Due to the importance of caregiver emotional health in the process of developing secure attachment, co-regulation of affect, and experiencing relational satisfaction, therapists place a high priority on the caregiver needs and experience in therapy. At the beginning of therapy, and during critical periods throughout the treatment process, the therapist will typically meet individually with parents to learn about parents' own relational histories, strengths, areas of vulnerability and insecurity, triggers, and beliefs/feelings about parenting (Hughes, 2007). Although this is a contemporary relational approach, AFFT remains strikingly consistent with the views of Winnicott (1965) that children fundamentally become who they are in relationship to caregivers and that caregivers are best equipped to shape healthy internal working models when also feeling supported and cared for in their environment.

One of the central goals of AFFT is to enable children and their parents to engage in an affective/reflective dialogue with the therapist and with each other. This model is informed by five essential developmental themes:

1. *Safety and exploration.* When children feel safe and accepted in relationship with secure caregivers, they are able to experience themselves as worthy of relationship and grow in their sense of agency to take risks toward mastering new experiences.

2. *The continuity of breaks and repairs in relationship.* In secure attachment, caregivers communicate through verbal and nonverbal behavior that they will always be there for the child, that separations will lead to reunification, and that when the child and parent get out of step in the relational "dance," there is space for repair.

3. *Coregulation of affect.* When parents are emotionally attuned to an infant's affective state, parent-child joint attention and affective matching (or soothing) bring order and meaning to the child's inner experience. As children grow

older, parents strive to stay attuned during negative emotional experiences, with the goal of enabling children to express affect in healthy ways and to learn to recover from dysregulated states.

4. *Co-creation of meaning.* In secure parent-child relationships, children identify with caregivers in the process of interpreting and understanding experiences, beliefs, feelings, and thoughts. As children grow older, they begin to develop autonomous meaning-making experiences while remaining respectful (and feeling respected) in the midst of divergent views from parents.

5. *The development of a coherent sense of self.* This construct is viewed as the healthy, integrated outcome of the attachment security that comes from the first four themes. When relationships have been primarily safe and continuous, contributing to regulated affect and ability to engage in meaning making, an individual is most likely to experience the self in a positive manner.

AFFT assumes that the above themes, when achieved positively, lead to optimal development. In contrast, insecure parent-child relationships that lack continuity and opportunities for co-regulation of affect and meaning place children and families at risk for emotional, behavioral, cognitive and relational disturbance.

Treatment from the AFFT perspective begins with the assumption that a solid therapeutic relationship—with child and caregivers—is the essential healing component. The therapeutic stance considered most conducive to success involves playfulness, acceptance, curiosity and empathy (PACE). Through the expression of these four ways of being with children and their caregivers, the therapist fosters an environment that allows children and their parents to engage, or re-engage, in helpful affective/reflective dialogue. The affective/reflective dialogue is the "substance" of therapy—the verbal exchanges facilitated by the therapist in which family members learn to listen and explore one another's experiences nonjudgmentally. The hope of the therapist is that the family members will also begin to reflect the PACE qualities in interactions with one another and particularly that parents can hear and respond to the child's concerns with increased playfulness, acceptance, curiosity and empathy. The cycle of the affective/reflective dialogue will happen repeatedly throughout treatment and includes a sequence with the following components: (1) an event is described by the client (often related to a struggle that has occurred in recent life); (2) the therapist guides the client(s) in separating the event from the experience of the event; (3) the therapist explores the motive the client has attributed to self and/or others surrounding the event; (4) the therapist is gaining a deep enough empathic experience of the client's experience that she can begin to engage in a process of co-creating new meaning of the event; (5) through the therapist's expression of empathic acceptance and reflective curiosity, the shame and fear originally experienced related to the event begin to lessen, leading to the possibility of greater understanding of self and others; (6) the therapist encourages (and assists when needed) the child in communicating new meaning and understanding of the event to the parents; and (7) the therapist guides the parent(s) in expressing understanding and empathy for the child's experience and meaning of the event. At this stage, parents are coached to refrain from correcting thoughts or explaining behavior until a later time, after the child's experience has been heard and validated (Hughes, 2007). Through this repeated process of the affective/reflective dialogue over time, the family is learning and experiencing co-regulation of affect and co-creation of meaning, which ultimately serves as the basis for treatment gains.

When working within the AFFT model, there are many aspects of intervention that are informed and enhanced by a developmental psychopathology framework. The individual temperament of children and caregivers is believed to have an impact on the relational patterns and subsequent feelings of security versus shame in the relationship. Additionally, child emotional regulation is viewed in AFFT as inextricably connected to the co-regulation of affect in the attachment relationship. The health of the parent-child relationship and the marital relationship (or caregiver support system in general) are seen as highly integral in allowing for optimal support for the child and family. Although peer and larger systems relationships are not an explicit focus in AFFT, there is a general belief that peace with one's inner self and supportive caregivers will lead to increased ability to enter into healthy and fulfilling peer relationships. Finally, the focus on intervening with the family system in AFFT flows from the theoretical position that relationships are bidirectional and dynamic and that mutual understanding between child and caregivers can produce lasting relational healing.

CASE STUDY

The following is a discussion of a child treatment case from the therapeutic perspective of attachment-focused family therapy. Additionally, this case discussion will integrate the psychodynamically oriented treatment with a developmental psychopathology perspective and a Christian worldview.

The Peterson family initially sought treatment for their son Matthew. Matthew is a ten-year old, Caucasian boy, the oldest of two sons. Matthew lives with his mother, stepfather and eighteen-month-old half-brother, Brandon. Matthew was referred for treatment due to symptoms of anxiety and depression, initially noted by his fourth-grade teacher and acknowledged by his mother and stepfather. The Peterson family was referred to the therapist through their state-funded Medicaid program. Due to their financial limitations and the limited number of Medicaid providers for psychotherapy in their area, the Peterson family has to commute forty-five minutes from home to access therapy. They live in a rural, small town, and although both parents work full time, they fall in a low-income bracket of family earnings. Mrs. Peterson works as a housekeeper, and Mr. Peterson is self-employed as a local truck driver.

During his early childhood, Matthew's mother and biological father were married, and his biological father was reportedly physically abusive to his mother. Mrs. Peterson denied any direct physical abuse of Matthew but admitted that her ex-husband would often "threaten to hurt Matthew just to scare and control me." Matthew's biological father left the family when Matthew was three, and Mrs. Peterson stated that he has only sporadically acknowledged Matthew on occasional holidays and a few birthdays since that time. Matthew is aware that his biological father is remarried to "a new family" and becomes visibly uncomfortable when the topic of his father comes up in session.

When asked about her relationship with Matthew during those difficult years, Mrs. Peterson explained that she had always found Matthew to be "an easy child to parent because he is so much like me." She described the early weeks and months of Matthew's life as an "emotional rollercoaster," however, with peaceful days at home with Matthew fluctuating with tense moments when her ex-husband would be home at night. Mrs. Peterson admitted that she always just "hoped and prayed that Matthew wouldn't remember the past," as she tearfully recalled the sound of him screaming alone in his crib while she and his biological father were fighting. She stated, "I knew he was safer in there alone, but hearing him cry and knowing he needed me to hold him was even more painful than the beatings from my husband."

Mrs. Peterson described Matthew as her "rock" after the divorce. Although the family had always struggled financially, it wasn't until her first husband left that she had to go to work full time, in addition to relying on financial-assistance programs for survival. Although there was some limited family social support, Mrs. Peterson did not consider much of her own family of origin as a resource, given several family members' struggle with substance abuse. She described Matthew as a young child who would seemingly work hard to please her at home but who would also become easily overwhelmed and tearful when he could not accomplish a task. For example, as a young child Matthew enjoyed building blocks but would begin to cry uncontrollably when his building fell down. Mrs. Peterson described this dynamic as one that continued into increasingly complex tasks, such as learning to tie his shoes and learning to read. When trying to calm him down, Mrs. Peterson reported that Matthew would always become shaky and nervous and make statements about his fear of her leaving him. The older Matthew became, the more he reportedly began to take on the "man of the house" role, which Mrs. Peterson described proudly. Matthew agreed that he was happy to be his mother's "little man" and to "keep her from feeling sad and lonely."

When Matthew was seven, his mother met Chuck Peterson, the man who would become Matthew's stepfather. Mrs. Peterson described her relationship with him as "whirlwind," but also described him as a "role model" that she had wanted for Matthew. Chuck was described by his wife as "strict and tough, but always loving," and this is a description that Matthew seemed to reiterate. Mrs. Peterson married Chuck six months after they began dating, and they were expecting a baby within the first year of their marriage. When Brandon was born, it was quickly apparent to Mrs. Peterson that he was not as "easy to parent" as she had experienced Matthew to be. She described Brandon as fussy, a terrible sleeper and often colicky during the first six to eight months of life. She described Matthew during this phase as getting even more "responsible" around the house with chores but also simultaneously more nervous and crying more easily. Mr. Peterson, although described as a good father, has always struggled with Matthew's "sensitivity" and wishes that he could just "act like a man" now that their whole family is intact. To complicate matters further, soon after Matthew turned nine, his family lost their home to a fire. They had recently moved into Mr. Peterson's trailer after Brandon was born, and one day when they were all away for work and school, the home burned due to an electrical failure. Matthew described this as a time that "felt like a bad dream," and he spoke sadly about the lost toys and treasured belongings that were in the fire. Over the past year since the fire, Mrs. Peterson has noticed that Matthew has seemed even more "sensitive" and "quick to explode" than usual. When asked to describe his explosions, Mrs. Peterson explained that "flashes of anger" will occur—particularly toward his baby brother—but that he will quickly apologize and then dissolve in tears and hide in his room for hours. She further described him as trying to make up for his behavior the next day by making gifts for everyone in the family. The family pursued therapy at the urging of Matthew's teacher, who was expressing growing concern about his self-deprecating comments and withdrawal in the classroom. Additionally, Mrs. Peterson stated that Matthew's stepfather had become increasingly frustrated with and confused by Matthew's behavior and his inability to control his emotions.

After the initial intake session, the therapist met with the Peterson family to describe her approach using attachment-focused family therapy and created a plan for initial sessions that would be conducted alone with the parents and alone with Matthew. When meeting with Mr. and Mrs. Peterson alone, the therapist used this time to get to know more about the individual histories of each adult in addition to their life together in the present day. As an important focus in AFFT, the therapist explored the relational histories and parenting beliefs, joys, struggles, and triggers of both Mr. and Mrs. Peterson. Mrs. Peterson was willing to authentically engage in discussions about her own shame related to "not protecting Matthew" during the first three years of his life and the fear that she had permanently damaged him. She admitted to years of feeling helpless and demoralized as a parent when he would become sad and anxious, experiencing herself as a "bad mother" for having stayed in an abusive relationship, in addition to shame for the financial condition of her family. Mr. Peterson responded with surprise to his wife's story, admitting he had never been aware of this aspect of her inner experience. Although he was personally more reserved in the pace of his disclosure, Mr. Peterson did admit to struggling with Matthew's anxiety and "neediness." He stated that such emotional expression was never tolerated in his own family of origin, and that he wanted to live up to his wife's expectations of a role model for Matthew by "toughening him up for the real world." Both Mr. and Mrs. Peterson were open, albeit mildly skeptical, to the process of AFFT, which would encourage Matthew and his parents to engage in honest discussions about each other's thoughts, feelings and experiences. In the context of a solidly developed rapport with the therapist, they agreed that they would be willing to try anything that might help shift Matthew's behaviors at home and prevent any further decline at school.

In his own initial individual sessions, Matthew presented as friendly, agreeable and compliant with the therapist. Matthew's compliance, however, was playfully acknowledged early in the therapeutic relationship as something that may be challenged as a result of therapy. Although Matthew was able to admit to anxiety about the therapist's stated (and only partially joking) goal that he become a "less productive member of society," Matthew agreed that he would pay attention if his therapist wanted to encourage him to speak up for his own feelings and thoughts. The therapist utilized some sessions to hear more of Matthew's story from his perspective and prepare him for family sessions in which he would be asked to begin to express some of his experience in dialogue with his mother and stepfather.

In the family sessions to follow, the Peterson family demonstrated the ability to slow down their reactivity and anxious responses to one another in order to listen and reflect. Matthew demonstrated great courage, as was named by the therapist, in taking risks to verbalize some of his frustrations of "events" (things that had happened during the previous week), and his parents gradually learned to listen fully and quietly, without lecturing or invalidating his experience. As this cycle progressed over a few sessions and Matthew's abandonment fears began to decrease, Mr. and Mrs. Peterson reported a reduction of anxious outbursts at home and school. Additionally, Matthew was able to gradually move into processing some of the historically significant and painful events, including the house fire, the rapid changes in the family when his mother remarried and had a baby, and the ongoing grief and rejection related to the loss of his biological father. During this phase of treatment, Mrs. Peterson needed additional support from the therapist (by way of individual sessions) in order to process some of her own shame and fear in a way that allowed her experience to be acknowledged without silencing Matthew. For many years, Matthew's and Mrs. Peterson's individual fears and shame had led to reciprocally unhealthy patterns (Matthew caretaking but becoming overwhelmed, Mrs. Peterson becoming paralyzed by shame when Matthew exploded, Matthew further caretaking). Allowing both Matthew and Mrs. Peterson to experience and process these feelings (separately and together in appropriate ways) led them both down a path of developing increased self-empathy and self-understanding. At the end of treatment, Matthew's anxious explosions had nearly disappeared, and when he did relapse into dysregulated behavior, the family reported an increased ability to assist him in regulating affect and coping more effectively.

As is true for many clients, Matthew's history was filled with a complex combination of risk and protective factors. At the time of referral, he had a loving mother and stepfather who were seeking treatment, and a concerned teacher who had expressed concerns. Additionally, Matthew possessed many intrapersonal qualities that made him likable and engaging, even for his overwhelmed parents. However, all members of the Peterson family also came with past struggles (domestic violence, loss of home, poverty, limited social support) and shameful/fearful beliefs about themselves that were keeping them stuck in unproductive relational cycles. Mr. and Mrs. Peterson did not know how to assist Matthew in affect regulation skills in a way that honored his experience. Matthew did not know how to communicate his feelings without being overcome by his fears of abandonment. From both a psychodynamic and developmental psychopathology perspective, the members of the Peterson family were having a negative bi-directional impact on one another. Attachment-focused family therapy, informed by the tenets of developmental psychopathology, was able to lead them to a place of reconnection and attunement as a family.

Psychodynamic therapy and, more specifically in this case, attachment-focused family therapy, can find much common ground with the Christian integration values outlined by Miller-McLemore (2003) and described earlier in this text: valuing children as divine gifts, respecting children as persons, and viewing children as moral and spiritual agents. In a passage reinforcing children as divine gifts, Miller-McLemore states, "Children require unearned 'gifting,' without which they will not survive, demanded simply because of what children are in and of themselves. A genuine gift creates an ongoing relationship because a gift leaves a disequilibrium that suggests the hope that sharing gifts will continue ad infinitum" (p. 102). This "gifting" required by children is consistent with the psychodynamic perspective of attachment-based needs for optimal development; likewise, the sharing of ongoing gifting is also reflected in the mutual satisfaction that results from a truly attuned parent-child relationship. Hughes (2007) captures the mutual benefits of valuing the child in stating: "when the parent maintains attunement during positive experiences, children are enabled to experience joy and delight. . . . Children can elicit delight in their parents' eyes—they can cause their parents to experience happiness. The child's parents are discovering and responding to a positive quality that involves who the child is" (p. 27). A psychodynamic approach to treatment emphasizes the therapeutic relationship and aspires to assist children in connecting to an increased sense of self-worth and value. AFFT specifically reinforces this important theme by assisting caregivers in identifying times and ways in which they struggle to experience attunement and working toward a more attuned caregiver-child relationship.

When considering the spiritual value of respecting children as persons, AFFT as a particular model is also a positive example of how this value can intersect with psychodynamic theory. With the goal of attunement and intersubjectivity, parents are guided toward responding to their children with the characteristics of playfulness, acceptance, curiosity and empathy. These core values assist the child in experiencing her uniqueness and feeling accepted for who she truly is. At the same time, the parent "experiences a deeper and broader sense of self through the intersubjective presence of her child within her own subjective narrative" (p. 21). There is potential for a deep sense of satisfaction with such parenting, but AFFT would suggest that it is not without the same type of intentionality that Miller-McLemore (2003) described as a "labor of love" (p. 105).

Finally, there are points of intersection between psychodynamic treatment and the idea of children as moral and spiritual agents. Miller-McLemore advocates for the moral guidance of children in terms that are consistent with the developmental and attachment theory-friendly construct of scaffolding, by describing that children need "a gradual transfer of power that involves receiving responsibility for progressively greater choices within a range appropriate to their age and situation" (p. 143). Miller-McLemore's nuanced conceptualizing of a child's moral and spiritual agency warns against naively viewing children as completely innocent, while also reminding us that "the depth and extent of their corrupt behavior is usually in direct proportion to the actions of the adults in their midst" (p. 158).

This perspective is interesting in light of Winnicott's early writings on the moral education of children. In an essay on this topic, Winnicott (1965) argues for the importance of a foundation of secure relational connection in order to impart cultural and spiritual values. Although he openly disagreed with the idea of original sin, Winnicott was a proponent of providing children with exposure to cultural and religious values so that they will have specific customs with which to identify. However, in the discussion of how much and when to externally implant morality, Winnicott stated, "There is more to be gained from love than from education. Love here means the totality of infant and child care, that which facilitates maturational processes. . . . Education means sanctions and the implantation of parental or social values *apart from* the child's inner growth or maturation" (p. 100). Believing fervently in the critical formative importance of the parent-child relationship, Winnicott further stated, "The child who is not having good enough experiences in the early stages cannot be given the idea of a personal God as a substitute for infant-care. . . . Moral education is no substitute for love" (p. 97).

For the therapist integrating these concepts of psychodynamic theory with the process of scaffolding a sense of moral and spiritual agency in children, there are key components of therapeutic work that can be identified. Insight-oriented work with caregivers about how their own relational histories and emotional triggers influence parenting can assist in preventing the separation of education and love that Winnicott warns about above. When focusing on the development or repair of attachment safety in the family, a secure base is developing from which children will ideally be able to learn—through trial and error, rupture and repair—how to live out the shared values of a family and community. Working with caregivers on how to impart spiritual values that are embedded within an attuned and safe relationship will maximize the potential that children will develop an authentic set of values (as opposed to learning to follow a rote set of rules).

CONCLUSION

A psychodynamic approach to child and adolescent therapy, embedded within the larger framework of developmental psychopathology, encourages therapeutic attention to individual child characteristics, emotional regulation skills (of both child and caregiver), relational themes between the child and caregivers, and the larger emotional (and physical) context in which the child is developing. There is a natural point of connection between psychodynamic theory and developmental psychopathology, which honors the adaptive nature of behaviors while simultaneous seeking to understand how and why previously adaptive functioning has become maladaptive. Finally, themes of Christian faith integration can be found in the value of fostering healing connections in the relational world of the child.

10

Behavioral Approaches to Treatment

Amanda M. Blackburn, Christine Weisgerber
and Michelle Shelley

BEHAVIORAL THERAPY IS ONE METHOD utilized to better understand and predict human behavior. With its emphasis on external, observable behaviors, behavioral therapy has attempted to move the social sciences in a more objective and scientific direction. The following chapter begins with an overview of behavioral therapy's history, fundamental assumptions, interventions and specific evidence-based therapy models. Theoretical and clinical implications of behavioral therapy are discussed and then illustrated with a case example.

HISTORY OF BEHAVIORAL THERAPY

Behavioral therapy was recognized as a formal school of psychology around the 1950s. As psychology had primarily embraced psychoanalysis as its method of understanding persons, psychologists were ready for a more empirical, modernist approach to understanding human behavior. Historically, there are three "waves" of behavioral therapies: behavioral, cognitive-behavioral (CBT), and acceptance-based behavioral (Antony & Roemer, 2011). This chapter is dedicated to understanding the first—a purely behavioral orientation to treating children and adolescents—as CBT approaches will be discussed in another chapter.

Prior to the emergence of behavioral therapy as a school of psychology, researchers were already beginning to study animal and human behavior. Ivan Pavlov (1927) first introduced the concept of classical conditioning when he discovered that dogs could be trained to salivate to a previously neutral stimulus (e.g., a ring tone or a light) when the neutral stimulus was paired with a more meaningful stimulus (e.g., food). John Watson later applied Pavlov's classical conditioning to human behavior with the famous and controversial Little Albert experiments. Watson and Raynor (1920) discovered that baby Albert could be "taught" to fear a rat simply by pairing a scary noise with the presence of the rat. Watson (1913) published what has been called the "Behaviorist Manifesto," which outlined the foundational propositions of *behaviorism*, the new school of psychology. Other researchers experimented with classical conditioning principles and developed early behavioral intervention strategies like modeling, in vivo exposure, and the "bell and pad" method for stopping bedwetting (Jones, 1924; Mowrer & Mowrer, 1938). Thorndike and Skinner studied operant conditioning principles in order to better understand how reinforcement and punishment can change the frequency of a behavior (Skinner, 1938; Thorndike, 1911). Their research was most influential on the rise of behaviorism in the United States (Antony & Roemer, 2011).

Later behaviorists developed *applied behavior analysis*, which utilized operant conditioning principles to systematically alter problematic behaviors. Research students of B. F. Skinner, Ayllon and Azrin (1965) used reinforcement-based strategies for persons struggling with substance addictions to develop a token economy system to change problematic behaviors in populations with chronic and severe mental disorders. Albert Bandura's (1969) contribution of social learning theory demonstrated to behaviorists that learning of adaptive and problematic behaviors can also occur through modeling and observation. Behavioral therapies eventually expanded to include cognitive and acceptance-based strategies. Albert Ellis (2001) and other cognitive-behavioral therapists incorporated behaviorally based techniques, including desensitization, psychoeducation and in vivo homework assignments, for helping clients reduce irrational beliefs, while Marsha Linehan (1993) and others began to combine mindfulness and acceptance-based interventions with common behavioral strategies.

Behavioral therapy is the most researched therapy. In fact, a majority of the evidence-based treatments recommended by the American Psychological Association are classified as behavioral therapy models (Antony & Roemer, 2011), and over twenty scientific journals publish research primarily on behavioral therapies. Throughout the past century, behavioral therapies here transitioned from a new and unfamiliar treatment approach to a commonly utilized approach (Antony & Roemer, 2011).

OVERVIEW OF BEHAVIORAL THERAPY

As previously stated, behavioral therapy guides us in understanding human behavior and provides a "road map" to helping people develop functional, adaptable behavior that fits their context and meets desired goals (Drossel, Rummel & Fisher, 2009). Early behavior therapies focused primarily on behavior manipulation and symptom reduction, while current behavioral therapies now focus more heavily on developing flexible behaviors that promote health. Since clinical symptoms are often the presentation of a narrow range of behavioral responses to a certain context or situation, the clinician's goal is generally to increase the repertoire of adaptable responses, as having experience and openness to respond in new and adaptable ways is essential given that context and environment often change.

There are several common assumptions that form the theoretical foundation of behavioral therapy and help to separate it from other therapies (Antony & Roemer, 2011). Behavior therapy's primary focus includes decreasing the frequency of undesired behaviors, increasing the frequency of desired behaviors and enhancing the range of flexible, adaptable behaviors. *Behaviors* include specific thoughts, emotions, obvious and hidden behaviors, or internal, physiological responses to events (Antony & Roemer, 2011). Behavior therapy is an active process that focuses more on the present and less on past events. By focusing on current and specific behaviors, the therapist determines operationalized, measurable goals and monitors progress and treatment outcomes.

Behavioral therapy is empirical in nature. Therapists evaluate treatment outcomes and use evidence-based treatment modalities in an effort to provide clients with current, relevant and effective services. Due to the empirical nature of behavioral interventions, therapy usually occurs in a brief, time-limited format. Therapists develop hypotheses about problematic behaviors and their antecedents and consequences and then work with clients to test whether their hypotheses are accurate and target specific behaviors. This approach to reducing problem behaviors empowers clients to learn and develop new, more adaptable behaviors instead of blaming clients for problems. Therapists also teach clients that their "behavior makes sense," or that our behaviors serve a specific function that is logically linked to biology, experiences, context and our desired consequences (Antony & Roemer, 2011).

How Behaviors Are Learned

Behavioral therapy assumes that all behavior is learned. Behavioral therapists hold that individuals learn behavior and habitual responses through several commonly understood and researched processes. First is the assumption that learning occurs through association, as described earlier. Humans learn to associate external or internal stimuli and events that occur together, or are *paired*. There are two types of associative learning: classical conditioning and operant conditioning. Classical conditioning strengthens an existing association, while operant conditioning uses reinforcement to alter or develop a new association. In classical conditioning, a seemingly neutral stimulus is paired with either an aversive or attractive response, and over time, responses may be generalized to a broader range of situations, such as in Pavlov's classic experiments with salivating dogs. Although much of associative learning research demonstrates learned association of behaviors to external stimuli, internal stimuli (e.g., physiological arousal or internal sensations and thoughts) are also often paired with behavioral responses. An example of such an internal association might be a child who, after becoming nauseous and vomiting following consumption of a large amount of cotton candy at the county fair, learns to associate nausea and feeling "sick" with cotton candy, a previously neutral (or even positive!) stimulus. As a result, she may develop a distaste for the treat in the future.

In operant conditioning, learning through association becomes meaningful as we experience the pleasant or unpleasant consequences that follow our actions. Reinforcements are consequences that are likely to increase the rate of our behaviors, while punishments are consequences that result in a decrease in frequency of behaviors. More specifically, *positive reinforcement* is the presentation of a consequence following a specific behavior that increases the likelihood of that behavior occurring again. For example, a child who becomes paralyzed by anxiety in anticipation of social events feels tempted to avoid stressful social situations in order to reduce his anxiety. However, a positive social interaction with friends at his first party (i.e., positive reinforcement) increases the likelihood of his attendance at future parties. *Negative reinforcement* increases the likelihood of a behavior occurring again as the result of the removal of something aversive following the specific behavior. The same child is also likely to attend future parties due to the absence (or removal) of his uncomfortable, paralyzing anxiety following his first party as he realizes it was not as bad as he had anticipated. *Punishment* is the presentation of an aversive consequence or removal of pleasant consequence that decreases the frequency of a specific behavior. *Natural or social reinforcers*, such as attention or verbal praise, are especially powerful reinforcement strategies with long-term impact since they occur innately within our context. These types of re-inforcers lead to behaviors that are more likely to generalize beyond a therapy context (Spiegler & Guevremont, 2010). Research demonstrates that re-inforcement is preferable to punishment, as punishment is often associated with negative emotional responses, has the potential to create more narrow, rigid behavioral responses, and does not produce healthy, adaptable ways of responding to situations (Antony & Roemer, 2011; Drossel et al., 2009).

Reinforcement schedules, or the frequency with which behaviors are rein-forced, are also significant to behavioral therapy. The type of reinforcement schedule employed often influences which specific behavioral responses occur and how difficult they may be to change later. When a new behavior is being learned, immediate and continuous reinforcement is most successful in establishing the new behavior and, conversely, the frequency of the be-havior is more easily reduced through elimination of such reinforcement (Doughty & Lattal, 2003). For example, the immediate reinforcement present for certain behaviors, such as the altered state of consciousness and physio-logical response that follows substance use, is more powerful than deferred or delayed reinforcement (Antony & Roemer, 2011).After a new behavior is established, it can best be maintained by only reinforcing the behavior some of the time on an intermittent reinforcement schedule; this schedule also makes a behavior more difficult to extinguish. The principles and patterns of operant conditioning explain many of the problematic behaviors commonly encountered by clinicians.

Other problematic behaviors or symptoms that present in clinical situations may be the result of negative reinforcement in the form of *experiential avoidance* (Antony & Roemer, 2011; Hayes, Wilson, Gifford, Follette & Strosahl, 1996). Reduction of internalized anxiety immediately following an avoidant behavior reinforces the avoidance and also interferes with other learning processes, such as extinction. When we continue to avoid situations that may not actually be threatening, there is no opportunity for the situation to become unlinked with the negative consequence we fear. Hence, behaviors related to fear or perceived threat that are immediately reinforced are usually the most difficult to reduce or eliminate, as the immediate reinforcer of reduced anxiety is much more powerful than the deferred or delayed reinforcement of recognizing that one's perception was not reality-based. Such is the case with school refusal; the child who avoids attending school in order to avoid feeling anxious is negatively reinforced by the reduction of her anxiety as a result of avoiding school.

One's perception of "dangerous" situations is usually based on environmental cues. A *cue* is a discriminant stimulus, or a "stimulus in the presence of which a particular response will be reinforced" (Malott, 2007). As they are associated with a certain behavior and resulting reinforcement or punishment, cues prime us to behave in certain ways in the future and help us to distinguish among contexts. Cues associated with threatening or fearful situations are quickly noticed in the environment in order to avoid potentially dangerous situations. Normatively, this response helps keep us safe from harm. However, when we do not learn to accurately distinguish between threatening and neutral stimuli, we may respond to every cue in the same fearful way, and clinical symptoms may develop (Antony & Roemer, 2011).

Though behavioral therapists originally believed that behavior was only learned through association and direct intervention, later research by Bandura (1977) indicated that behavior can also be learned vicariously, or through observation. For example, a new kindergarten student who observes his peer get in trouble for speaking out of turn may vicariously learn to sit quietly. In "rule-governed learning," or verbal instruction, we can also learn about associations and consequences through hearing them described to us by someone we respect and trust (Antony & Roemer, 2011). This type of behavioral instruction can promote either adaptive or maladaptive outcomes, depending on the type of behavior being taught.

Behavioral Therapy Process

Behavioral therapy typically follows a standard process that involves thorough behavioral assessment and subsequent use of evidenced-based behavioral interventions (Antony & Roemer, 2011). The goal of behavioral assessment is to understand the client's problematic behavior, the symptom(s) caused by the behavior, possible antecedents and/or consequences (e.g., reinforcements) of the behavior, treatment options that best fit the problematic behavior, and necessary methods to measure the treatment outcomes. A behavioral therapist assumes that (1) behaviors are related to one's development and environment and may vary across time, and (2) behavior occurs at the individual level (i.e., each individual's behavior is unique). Clinicians seek to understand a client's unique behavior over time and within her specific context and to both explain and better understand an individual's variability across contexts (Antony & Roemer, 2011).

Behavioral assessment usually begins with an attempt to understand the *function* (purpose or reasoning) behind a client's behaviors. A functional behavioral assessment includes recognizing factors that sustain the behavior, the environment or context in which the behavior occurs, and how the behavior is either reinforced or punished (Antony & Roemer, 2011). More specifically, functional assessment includes three parts: (1) identifying problematic behaviors, antecedents (i.e., events that come before the problematic behavior) and consequences (i.e., events that follow the problematic behavior), (2) performing a functional analysis (i.e., a case formulation from a behavioral perspective in which the environment is manipulated and problematic behaviors are assessed), and (3) implementing a treatment plan designed based on the functional analysis (Kenny, Alvarez, Donohue & Winick, 2008). The process of functional analysis is further illustrated in the case study at the end of this chapter.

First, problematic behaviors are described in concrete, operational terms that include their appearance, frequency, duration and intensity. *Target behaviors* are identified as problematic behaviors that interfere with normal functioning. As the assessment is ongoing, behavioral therapists obtain information before, during and after the intervention. Standard methods of behavioral assessment include clinical interviews, self-monitoring, self-report scales, behavioral observation and psychophysiological assessment (Antony & Roemer, 2011).

Second, a functional analysis aims to describe the complex, causal relationships among problematic behaviors, antecedents and consequences. Behavioral therapy is based on the assumption that problematic behaviors are the direct result of the environment in which the behavior occurs, in contrast, for example, to personality theories that posit that problematic behaviors are due to long-term personality traits (Antony & Roemer, 2011). Behavioral therapists carefully examine how behaviors vary over time and development and across situations, paying special attention to the idiosyncratic ways the behavior is manifested.

Finally, data from the functional analysis is used to design a treatment plan that targets the problematic behaviors (Antony & Roemer, 2011). Once the type of problematic behavior is identified and goals are set, the behavioral therapist can select appropriate treatment strategies. Common strategies with children and adolescents include psychoeducation, exposure-based strategies, response prevention, parent training, biofeedback and social skills training.

BEHAVIORALLY BASED THERAPIES WITH CHILDREN AND ADOLESCENTS

Behavioral therapies with children and adolescents have existed for almost half a century. They were first utilized in educational settings, with the main application involving the operant conditioning of severely problematic student populations who had not responded to traditional psychoanalytic approaches (Hersen & Van Hasselt, 1987). Several common behavioral strategies have emerged as effective with multiple problematic behaviors and/or diagnoses.

Psychoeducation is a common strategy that may include instructions on completing forms, discussions within the therapy session or books assigned as homework (i.e., bibliotherapy). As previously stated, behavioral therapy is highly transparent, and psychoeducation begins when the clinician explains the rationale and steps of the treatment process at the onset of therapy. For example, a clinician working with an anxious child may explain the nature of anxiety, the helpful, adaptive function of anxiety (e.g., survival and avoidance of dangerous situations) and the process through which anxiety often becomes maladaptive (e.g., experiential avoidance) to help the child develop a better understanding of her anxiety. Psychoeducation is utilized with almost every type of problematic behavior, and research supports psychoeducation as an effective stand-alone intervention for some problem behaviors (Lincoln, Wilhelm & Nestoriuc, 2007). Modeling often accompanies psychoeducation; a client may learn a new behavior through observation by watching another person (such as the therapist) perform the behavior. Modeling is usually utilized in conjunction with other behavioral strategies like self-monitoring or social skills training (Antony & Roemer, 2011; Morrison & Blackburn, 2008).

Many exposure-based strategies use recurrent, methodical exposure to a feared stimulus to reduce the fear reaction (Moscovitch, Antony & Swinson, 2009). This approach is most often used with anxiety disorders and phobias. Current literature identifies three main types of exposure: in vivo exposure (exposure to stimuli in everyday life), imaginal exposure (exposure in thoughts, memories or imagination), and interoceptive exposure or flooding (intentionally experiencing feared physiological sensations until they no longer produce a fear response; Antony & Roemer, 2011). A child with a phobia of dogs may first think about dogs in the therapy office, then look at pictures of dogs, then observe a real dog in a cage and, finally, visit a friendly dog—all the while practicing self-soothing and anxiety-reducing skills in each situation. Similar to exposure-based strategies, response (or ritual) prevention strategies help eliminate the association between a stimulus and a response by exposing a client to an anxiety-provoking situation and preventing the previously learned behavioral response (Nock, 2005). The client can be physically prevented from practicing the learned response or positively reinforced for choosing to not engage in the learned behavioral response. For example, a child who compulsively blinks his eyes may be asked to close his eyes for specific amount of time in order to prevent the compulsive blinking behavior that follows the urge to blink. While exposure-based strategies are used to treat a variety of anxiety disorders, response prevention is most often used to treat compulsive behaviors usually related to obsessive-compulsive disorder (Antony & Roemer, 2011).

Reinforcement- or punishment-based behavioral strategies directly manipulate elements of the client's environment in order to reduce the recurrence of problematic behaviors. Differential reinforcement rewards a client for not engaging in the problematic behavior or for choosing to engage in a more adaptable behavior (Antony & Roemer, 2011). Examples of differential reinforcement include token economies, in which youth are rewarded with symbolic tokens for desired behavior, and contingency management, in which the environment is manipulated to prevent reinforcement for problematic behaviors. Such interventions are often utilized with difficult-to-manage acting-out behaviors in school and home contexts, such as tantrums, hitting, name-calling and foul language. Social reinforcements, or naturally occurring reinforcements within relationships, focus on interpersonal positive reinforcements. For example, children on the autism spectrum may be naturally rewarded (e.g., a smiling peer who invites them to play) when they act in socially appropriate ways. Finally, aversive conditioning is a punishment-based strategy that subjects a client to an undesirable consequence following the problematic behavior. Although this strategy is not often employed with children, it is occasionally used with such undesirable behaviors as thumb-sucking (e.g., by application of a distasteful, unpleasant substance on the child's thumb to decrease the likelihood that the child will suck his thumb).

Social and communication skills training promotes social competence by teaching clients how to communicate and interact more effectively with others (Antony & Roemer, 2011), and includes a wide spectrum of skills, from basic (e.g., making eye contact) to more advanced (e.g., assertiveness). Teaching social skills often involves other behavioral strategies, including modeling, psychoeducation and behavioral rehearsal. Appropriately demonstrated social skills are then positively reinforced in order to increase and generalize the frequency of these desired interpersonal behaviors (Morrison & Blackburn, 2008). Another common behavioral skill, relaxation, teaches clients strategies to relax their bodies and minds in order to reduce problematic behavioral responses. One of the most commonly used relaxation approaches is progressive muscle relaxation (PMR), in which clients are taught in session how to release muscle tension and instructed to apply the relaxation technique as they detect anxiety-producing cues throughout the day (Bernstein, Borkovec & Hazlett-Stevens, 2000).

Parent training involves teaching parents to respond to their children in ways that promote positive behavior. It usually involves helping parents understand and adjust the antecedents and consequences surrounding a child's problematic behavior. Often parents utilize contingency management or contingency contracting with children to reduce the frequency of problematic behaviors in the home (Twardosz & Nordquist, 1987). Some behavioral strategies, such as those taught in Parent-Child Interaction Therapy, enhance the attachment bond between parent and child by using behavioral strategies to teach parents how to build a secure relationship with their child through individual behavioral interactions (Foote, Eyberg & Schuhmann, 1998).

Acceptance-based mindfulness and emotion regulation strategies have been combined with more recently developed and researched behavioral strategies. *Acceptance* involves simultaneously "allowing, tolerating, embracing, experiencing, or making contact with a source of stimulation that previously provoked escape, avoidance, or aggression" (Cordova, 2001, p. 215). This type of behavioral acceptance is empirically validated in the form of acceptance and commitment therapy (ACT; Hayes, Strosahl & Wilson, 1999) and dialectical behavior therapy (DBT; Linehan, 1993). Acceptance is also a fundamental component of the exposure-based behavioral strategies mentioned previously. *Mindfulness*, briefly, involves increasing a client's focus on the present moment and is utilized to assist clients in facilitating a stance of acceptance, rather than avoidance, of distressing emotions (Antony & Roemer, 2011). Specifically, mindfulness skills training is included in one of the components in the Attachment, Self-Regulation, and Competency (ARC) treatment framework (Blaustein & Kinniburgh, 2010). ARC is a components-based model that focuses on helping both child and caregiver work together to develop "building blocks" of attachment, self-regulation and competency to assist with the impact of developmental trauma. The self-regulation components of ARC incorporate a number of behavioral skills, such as deep breathing, progressive muscle relaxation and mindfulness, and other skills to help the child increase her "awareness and understanding of internal experience, ability to modulate that experience, and ability to share that experience with others" (p. 38). Both acceptance and mindfulness are also often components of *emotion regulation skills training*, which helps clients learn to identify, understand and more adaptively respond to distressing emotions. This training requires clients to monitor their triggers, emotional responses and consequences in order to promote healthier emotional responding. The inclusion of acceptance, mindfulness and emotional regulation enhances more traditional behavioral strategies as clients are encouraged to consider the healthier perspective of releasing some control of needing to change their behavior or environment (Antony & Roemer, 2011; Linehan, 1993).

SPECIFIC EVIDENCE-BASED BEHAVIORAL THERAPIES FOR YOUTH

Though behavioral theory is a relatively unified method of understanding human behavior, educators, psychologists and researchers have developed many different manualized, evidence-based behavioral techniques based on different behavioral treatment models. We will review three therapy modalities, including Parent Management Training (PMT; Barkley, 1997), Parent Child Interaction Therapy (PCIT; Bell & Eyberg, 2002) and applied behavioral analysis (ABA; Koegel et al., 1999; Steege, Mace, Perry & Longenecker, 2007), as examples of evidence-based interventions that utilize behavioral strategies to reduce problematic behaviors with children and adolescents.

Parent Management Training

Parent Management Training (PMT) is an adjunct to traditional behavioral therapy, in which therapists coach parents to change a child's problematic behaviors at home using principles from behavior modification and social learning theories (Kazdin, 1997). Both theories emphasize the environmental and interpersonal contingencies that reinforce child conduct problems. The PMT model assumes that problematic behaviors are maintained through a "coercive family process," in which children's conduct problems are inadvertently established and maintained by their interactions with their parents (Patterson, 1982; Patterson, Reid & Dishion, 1992). The coercive family process, or unhelpful, "overlearned" reciprocal behavioral reinforcement, occurs between parent and child within the home (Hagen, Ogden & Bjørnebekk, 2011; Patterson et al., 1992). This idea posits that family members are caught in a power struggle with one another, each trying to change the other's behaviors through negative, coercive tactics. For instance, when a parent gives a command and the child is noncompliant, the parent might respond aggressively in an attempt to gain the child's obedience. Parents often unknowingly contribute to the maintenance of children's poor behavior through positive reinforcement of problematic behavior (e.g., "giving in" to the child's tantrum), confuse children by frequently misusing punishment, and fail to reinforce positive, adaptive behaviors. PMT increases adaptive behaviors and decreases maladaptive behaviors through a focus on proper use of reinforcement. PMT assumes that as parents change their behaviors in the home, the child will also improve (Nix, Bierman & McMahon, 2009).

PMT's primary goal is to teach parents the skills to better manage their children's behavior. The model has several core characteristics. First, parents are taught the skills of basic functional analysis, learning to observe and identify the antecedents, behaviors and consequences (e.g., punishment/reinforcement) of problematic behaviors (Kazdin, 1997). Second, the therapist teaches the parent behavior modification strategies based on operant conditioning principles for use with the child at home, including positive reinforcement (e.g., providing praise, privileges or desired objects), punishment (e.g., time out) and behavior contingency contracts (Kazdin, 1997). Third, PMT primarily involves therapeutic contact with parents with limited interaction between the therapist and the child or adolescent (Kazdin, 1997). Therapists use these sessions to educate parents about basic intervention skills, practice and role-play implementation of the skills, and evaluate how parents are utilizing the skills at home. Parents can then begin to evaluate their own parenting skills (through self-monitoring and self-evaluation) and whether their behavior modification strategies are successful. Once the parents become confident in their skill acquisition and observe consistent behavior change in the child, the therapist works with the parent to promote changes in behavior in other contexts (e.g., school).

Much research has demonstrated the effectiveness of PMT with externalizing behaviors in children from preschool through adolescence (Eyberg, Nelson & Boggs, 2008; Hautman et al., 2009; Kazdin, 1997; Ostberg & Rydell, 2012). More specifically, PMT is commonly used to decrease the conduct problems commonly associated with attention-deficit/hyperactivity disorder, oppositional defiant disorder and conduct disorder (Hagen et al., 2011; Kazdin, 1997; 2005b; 2010; Nix et al., 2009; Ostberg & Rydell, 2012). PMT has also been adapted and effectively utilized to improve parenting skills and reduce conduct problems in children in the difficult and unique setting of urban foster homes (Leathers, Spielfogel, McMeel & Atkins, 2011). PMT's effectiveness and success in both mental health and community settings fits well with a developmental psychopathology approach, as it incorporates a variety of interpersonal influences (i.e., family and community systems) and acknowledges varying developmental pathways that promote both risk and resilience. One specific PMT model, Parent Management Training—the Oregon Model (PMTO), suggests that consistent, effective parenting and discipline, alongside a warm parenting style and family cohesion, mediates the relation between improvements in family cohesion and observed prosocial alterations in children's behavior (Biederman, Mick, Faraone & Burback, 2001; Hagen et al., 2011; Patterson, 2005; Prevatt, 2003).

Parent-Child Interaction Therapy

Developed by Sheila Eyberg, Parent-Child Interaction Therapy (PCIT) is an effective treatment for increasing appropriate behaviors and decreasing problem behaviors in preschool age and young children with conduct problems or within high-risk families (Bell & Eyberg, 2002; Brinkmeyer & Eyberg, 2003; Chaffin et al., 2004; Eyberg et al., 2001; McNeil & Hembree-Kigin, 2010; Thomas & Zimmer-Gembeck, 2011; Timmer, Urquiza, Zebell & McGrath, 2005). The PCIT model is based on principles of operant conditioning, attachment theory and social learning theory (Foote et al., 1998). Building upon the behavioral principles of PMT, PCIT emphasizes developing and strengthening secure and nurturing (attachment) relationships between parents and children in order to increase appropriate behaviors and decrease negative behaviors in children (Bowlby, 1988). Furthermore, as previously stated, Patterson's (1982) coercive family process model suggests that children's conduct problems are inadvertently established and maintained by their interactions with parents. In essence, the parent's aggressive behavior has been positively reinforced by the child's compliance.

PCIT begins with a thorough assessment of a child's presenting problems. A semi-structured interview with the caregiver(s) provides an opportunity to outline the treatment structure of PCIT and allows the therapist to gain valuable information regarding reinforcers that may be maintaining the presenting problem (i.e., developmental, social, medical and educational history, and previously used forms of discipline and their effectiveness). Various behavior rating scales and other assessments are used throughout treatment in order to better inform the therapist about problem behavior frequency and intensity and caregiver psychological health and to help determine when behavioral problems have decreased to acceptable levels, indicating completion of treatment (Querido, Bearss & Eyberg, 2002). Often, negative behaviors are observed in a variety of other contexts, such as school. Teachers may also complete a classroom behavior assessment. The final assessment component involves a live observation of a parent and child interacting in a play situation in an effort to gain insight into the patterns of interaction that may need to be modified. The Dyadic Parent-Child Interaction Coding System II (DPICS-II) is used to code certain aspects of parent-child interactions, including the level of positive parenting skills, the use of critical statements by parents, the use of parental commands and the rate of child compliance (Eyberg, Bessmer, Newcomb, Edwards & Robinson, 1994). DPICS-II enables the therapist to create a baseline measure and can be used to measure the parent's acquisition of skills in later sessions. Throughout the assessment and treatment process, therapists provide psychoeducation to parents about developmentally appropriate expectations for children and how unhealthy parent-child interactions may negatively impact their child (Querido et al., 2002).

After assessment, parents and children participate in weekly, sixty-minute PCIT sessions. The initial stage of therapy, Child Directed Interaction (CDI), focuses on developing parental skills meant to enhance healthy attachment. This phase of therapy helps parents learn to allow the child to lead the play and also to learn and apply PRIDE skills. PRIDE skills include *praising* the child's appropriate behavior, *reflecting* appropriate talk, *imitating* appropriate play, *describing* appropriate behavior, and being *enthusiastic* in play (Querido et al., 2002). Any inappropriate, attention-seeking behaviors are ignored to avoid positively reinforcing undesired behaviors, providing a form of behavior management. Parents practice during a weekly therapy (coaching) session and are also asked to conduct a daily, five-minute play time at home in order to practice the skills and continue the process of parent-child relationship enhancement. Coaching sessions continue until parents have mastered these skills. Each phase of therapy begins with a teaching session as the therapist uses modeling and role-play to teach the skills to the parent without the child present. Meetings following the teaching sessions alternate between the therapist coaching (i.e., modeling and assisting parents to apply new skills) and observing the parent actively using their newly acquired skills with the child (Querido et al., 2002).

The second phase of therapy, Parent Directed Interaction (PDI), emphasizes giving effective commands and implementing discipline techniques. PDI builds on the skills of CDI and emphasizes decreasing inappropriate behaviors that are too risky to be ignored, reinforced by something other than parental attention or difficult to extinguish. Positive reinforcement for appropriate behaviors and ignoring of inappropriate behaviors are still utilized; however, parents now also use commands and discipline in order to direct the child's behaviors and apply consequences when necessary. First, in the absence of the child, parents are taught effective commands as well as specific steps to follow in the case of compliance or noncompliance. If a child obeys a command, a *labeled praise* is given. If the child is noncompliant, the parent is taught to proceed with the *time-out sequence* (Querido et al., 2002). The time-out procedure starts with a warning and can lead to the time-out chair or the time-out room. Utilizing a time-out (punishment) will remove any positive reinforcement (parental attention, toys) and thus will decrease the likelihood that the child will be noncompliant in the future. The use of the time-out room as a next level of punishment is used sparingly, and its utilization should gradually decrease as PCIT progresses (Querido et al., 2002).

In the final stage of treatment, coaching sessions focus on the child's specific problem behavior as reported by the parent. Parents gradually work toward giving commands and following through with the time-out procedure without therapist assistance. Parents should gradually generalize the time-out sequence to other settings, such as in public. It is recommended that parents schedule a booster session following program completion to maintain progress made in treatment (Querido et al., 2002).

PCIT is a well-established behavioral intervention for decreasing conduct problems in young children (Chaffin et al., 2004; Dishion & Patterson, 1992; Ruma, Burke & Thompson, 1996; Strain, Young & Horowitz, 1981; Thomas & Zimmer-Gembeck, 2011; Timmer et al., 2005). The importance of targeting these behaviors is highlighted by research linking early behavior problems with later psychological disorders, such as delinquency, criminal behavior, peer rejection, academic problems, depression and school dropout (Campbell, 1995; Fischer, Rolf, Hasazi & Cummings, 1984; Kellam, Werthamer-Larsson, Dolan & Brown, 1991; McNeil & Hembree-Kigin, 2010; Webster-Stratton, Reid & Stoolmiller, 2008).

Naturalistic Applied Behavior Analysis

Applied behavioral analysis (ABA) is another evidenced-based behavioral treatment modality. ABA involves the examination and targeting of socially significant behavioral responses through modifying context or environment (Koegel et al., 1999). This evidenced-based behavioral method is used with children and adolescents to teach new skills, maintain already acquired skills, generalize skills to broader contexts or restrict conditions in which behaviors are maintained (Steege et al., 2007). ABA incorporates direct observation, measurement, and functional analysis of the relationship between environment and behavior (including the behavior's antecedent, stimuli and consequences) to produce practical changes in socially relevant behavior (Moran & Mallott, 2004). Behavior modification techniques of ABA include self-monitoring (i.e., keeping track or monitoring one's own behavior), chaining (i.e., successive reinforcement of successive behaviors, each behavior providing a cue for the next behavior) and shaping (i.e., reinforcements of successive approximations of a desired behavior) to change problematic behaviors and increase desired prosocial behaviors. ABA interventions include a broad continuum of single, narrowly focused strategies within educational contexts. Although frequently mistaken as a rigid, one-on-one coaching technique like discrete trial training (DTT), ABA is actually a flexible behavioral strategy often used to implement social skills programs in naturalistic, general settings (Morrison & Blackburn, 2008; Sasso, Garrison-Harrell, McMahon & Peck, 1998; Strain & Odom, 1986).

Naturalistic ABA, or naturalistic teaching, involves teaching skills in the actual environment in which the child would need to use the skill (Kohler, Anthony, Steighner & Hoyson, 2001; Simpson et al., 2005). Loosely structured sessions, indirect teaching methods (e.g., modeling), everyday or commonplace situations, child initiation, naturally occurring reinforcement, and peer inclusion are critical components of naturalistic ABA (Delprato, 2001). Peer inclusion incorporates two important behavioral principles: modeling and positive reinforcement. Typical peers model appropriate interpersonal behaviors and provide natural positive reinforcements for children with autism spectrum disorders. The use of peer inclusion in naturalistic interventions may produce longer-term maintenance and skill generalization than more simplistic, one-on-one treatments (Delprato, 2001; Kohler et al., 2001; Kohler, Strain, Hoyson & Jamieson, 1997). In fact, research has shown naturalistic ABA to be an effective tool for improving social competence and peer interactions for youth with autism spectrum disorders (Jones & Schwartz, 2004; Reichow & Volkmar, 2010; Strain & Schwartz, 2001).

The base of research evaluating naturalistic interventions and peer inclusion programs in education and social settings is growing. Whereas many studies have evaluated the efficacy of early intervention, such as in the preschool years (Boulware, Schwartz, Sandall & McBride, 2006; Lewis, Trushell & Woods, 2005; Odom et al., 2003; Simpson et al., 2005), there are fewer studies examining the effects of inclusion with older children and adolescents (Eskow & Fisher, 2004; Morrison & Blackburn, 2008). One such study evaluated a full-inclusion social skills summer program for adolescents with Asperger's syndrome in which instructors helped participants build social skills and social competence by teaching self-monitoring skills and community building. Both qualitative and quantitative outcome data suggested significant behavioral changes and generalized social skills in adolescents who participated in the program (Blackburn, 2008).

Behavioral Interventions and a Christian Worldview

Numerous behavioral interventions are used to treat children and adolescents; however, many of these are behaviorally based models that incorporate Christian principles as a supplement, as opposed to fully integrating both faith and behavioral components into a single, comprehensive model. Also, many of the techniques that include a faith component specifically target adult populations, utilize psychoeducation as the preferred intervention method, and have been used in the treatment of addiction, self-esteem, grief and post-divorce adjustment (Collins, Whiters & Braithwaite, 2007; Nedderman, Underwood & Hardy, 2010; Priester et al., 2009). One adult program that integrates a Christian worldview into a primarily behavioral model is Celebrate Recovery. This program is similar to the 12-Steps for Freedom from Addictive Behaviors approach to alcohol and drug abuse (www.12step.org). Celebrate Recovery was developed to assist individuals struggling with multiple issues, including alcohol and drug addiction, sexual addiction, eating disorders and other addictions. The eight recovery principles are based on the Beatitudes found in the Sermon on the Mount. This program has been adapted for use with children (Celebration Station; www.celebraterecovery.com/and-more/celebration-station) and adolescents (The Landing; www.saddlebackresources.com/The-Landing-Celebrate-Recovery-for-Students-1-Kit-P7708.aspx).

No behavioral models for children and adolescents found in the literature appear to fully integrate a Christian worldview; however, at least one program addresses the needs of youth through a combination of behavioral and Christian principles. DivorceCare For Kids, a thirteen-week program designed specifically for children five to twelve years old whose parents are divorcing, takes an inherently integrative approach. The program uses behavioral techniques such as relaxation and coping skills, music and singing, expression of feelings through art and journaling, and Scripture reading (www.dc4k.org/about/topics, 2012). This approach reflects the view that children are valued as gifts, respected as persons and viewed as agents (Miller-McLemore, 2003). DivorceCare for Kids allows adults to come alongside children while they experience varying emotions. Each child is able to express his feelings, points of view and needs through the framework of the program. In addition, children witnessing relational upset within their family are empowered to be agents of change and active shapers of their environment, as children and parents have a reciprocal impact on one another's behavior.

In summary, there is a dearth of programs designed for children and adolescents that fully integrate a Christian worldview with behavioral interventions. Therefore, an opportunity for growth exists in the creation of these types of programs for youth.

THEORETICAL AND CLINICAL IMPLICATIONS OF DEVELOPMENTAL PSYCHOPATHOLOGY FOR BEHAVIORAL APPROACHES

Behavioral orientations tend to assume a linear etiology of problematic behaviors. As previously stated, functional analysis helps behavioral therapists to understand how problematic behaviors are learned and reinforced and to suggest that causal factors are typically found in one's environment and context (i.e., reinforcements). Although historically behavioral therapies have incorporated contributions from other empirical disciplines (Hersen & Van Hasselt, 1987), a glaring limitation of a behavioral orientation is the tendency to ignore the complex interplay and integration of potential factors involved in determining the "why" of problematic behaviors.

Although behavioral therapy and developmental psychopathology both emphasize factors such as genetic predisposition, economic status, traumatic experiences and organic factors in the development of specific problematic behaviors, developmental psychopathology introduces pathways and the principles of equifinality and multifinality. Equifinality signifies that there are many diverse origins or "starting points" for persons demonstrating similar maladaptive behaviors, or "subgroups of individuals manifesting similar problems [having] arrived at them from different beginnings" (Cicchetti, 2006, p. 13). Multifinality means that "development is neither a static process nor predetermined by early events or characteristics. Quite the contrary, development is dynamic, involving a constant transaction between the family and other events, and children's own characteristics" (Cummings et al., 2000, p. 39). Developmental psychopathology informs a behavioral orientation as it suggests the inherent "interplay between normality and pathology" (Cicchetti, 2006, p. 1) results from the ongoing, ever-evolving relationship between the individual's intrapsychic and biological processes and the interpersonal context and environment.

Biological

Behavioral therapy and developmental psychopathology both focus on the ways that organic or biological systems may contribute to the development and maintenance of a variety of psychological disorders. Modern behavioral therapies recognize that our internal processes reinforce certain behaviors. For example, consider the child who is anxious about making new friends. By not initiating interactions with new people, she does not have to experience "butterflies in her stomach," headaches and other symptoms associated with anxiety. Through avoiding anxiety and arousal (i.e., negative reinforcement), she is rewarded with a decrease in her level of distress; however, this avoidance results in conditions such as social anxiety disorder (Antony & Roemer, 2011). Whereas modern behavioral therapy recognizes the contribution of biological factors, developmental psychopathology broadens this focus to include an understanding of how biological predispositions (i.e., genetics and organic disorders) and internal processes may interact with other factors to influence behavior (Cummings et al., 2000). Although a behaviorist might understand a socially anxious child's withdrawal and her anxious parent's unintentional rewarding of her withdrawal in simple terms of reinforcement or social learning constructs, developmental psychopathology recognizes the family's genetic predisposition toward anxiety and the mother's support in helping the child avoid uncomfortable situations as a cyclical and interactive process reaching beyond simple reinforcement. This approach helps those working from a behavioral perspective to more fully understand how behaviors are not only the result of responses to external cues but also involve "the quality of integrations across multiple behavioral and biological systems within the child, [including] . . . specific patterns of responding to stresses and other events at specific points in time" (Cummings et al., p. 40).

Behavioral clinicians working from a developmental psychopathology framework will take a client's biology and neurobiology into account when conceptualizing cases, considering factors such as a client's medical history and previous organic diagnoses. Present organic disorders may significantly influence which behavioral treatment strategies are most appropriate. Physical maladies can also cause certain children to learn very specific adaptive behaviors; however, once the organic issue is resolved the child may still engage in the now maladaptive behavior and require behavioral intervention. For example, young children who have undiagnosed vision problems, such as myopia or hyperopia, may squint while looking at the chalkboard in a classroom or reading. When a child is prescribed glasses to correct his vision, he may continue to squint, a behavior that was previously adaptive but is now unnecessary, as the problem has been addressed. Moreover, medications can alter biology or certain physiological responses that can supplement behavioral strategies. In these situations, a referral to a psychiatrist to prescribe medication that can assist in the reduction of internal reinforcement may be necessary for some children and adolescents. Although biological components are important contributing factors, other components must also be considered in determining why problematic behaviors develop.

Practical suggestions.

- Prior to treatment or intervention, recommend a complete medical evaluation to assess for any presenting organic issues that may contribute to the problematic behaviors.

- Obtain a thorough family medical history during the assessment phase in order to account for any organic or psychological parent pathology that may contribute to the child's biological predispositions.

- Specific attention should be given to a child's internal and/or physiological responses surrounding problematic behaviors, as these "symptoms" may be unobservable in a simple functional analysis.

Psychological

Developmental psychopathology also highlights the role of significant intra-psychic processes that contribute to the development of problematic behaviors. Historically, behavioral therapies do not address most, if any, of the psychological components of persons in determining behavior. With a focus on identifying the function of and changing behavior, this model traditionally targets only learned, observable behaviors and does not account for meaningful underlying psychological concerns. However, when combined with developmental psychopathology, therapists working from a behavioral therapy perspective may be better able to address the psychological dimensions that contribute to health or pathology.

Intrapsychic factors that may play a role in psychopathology and related problematic behaviors include, but are not be limited to, temperament, attachment style, developmental level, developmental delays, cognitive functioning, birth order, psychological sequelae of experiencing trauma and/or abuse, parental psychopathology, learning styles, and learning disabilities. Whereas some of these may be causal risk factors, for many individuals these factors are actually risk markers, or elements that denote the presence of other risk factors but are not causally related to negative outcomes (Cicchetti, 2006). Even when such variables are not directly linked to problematic behaviors or psychopathology, therapists are able to create a more robust treatment plan by considering factors such as temperament, attachment style, and other internal processes in the development, reinforcement or cessation of certain behaviors (both desired and problematic). This increases the likelihood that specific techniques used throughout therapy will be appropriately selected to address not only the targeted behaviors but also the root causes of the behaviors, considering possible targets for intervention and barriers to progress throughout therapy. For example, a behavioral therapist utilizing naturalistic ABA with a child on the autism spectrum will include an analysis of the child's environment, considering reinforcers and functional analysis of interactions in the environment. Though this approach alone may be effective for many children, a more robust treatment plan might also include intrapsychic considerations. The therapist might consider how the developmental age of the child compared to his peers contributes to problematic or desired behaviors or to the child's individual learning style in order to identify effective positive reinforcers. Taking the child's individual learning style into consideration may increase the likelihood that he is able to comprehend the material, which may reinforce the his behavior (paying attention) in a classroom setting, thus increasing the likelihood of this desired behavior. By considering such factors, adults involved in the child's therapy (therapist, teachers, caregivers) can work together to place the child in an age-appropriate peer environment and avoid simplifying previously triggering contexts and social situations.

Developmental psychopathology also emphasizes the importance of understanding normative development in order to gain a better picture of psychopathology and/or maladaptive behaviors (Cicchetti, 2006). By better understanding normative development across different stages of life, therapists can address an individual's current behaviors, concerns, adaptations and so on from a broader perspective. In combination with a behavioral therapy model, we can identify what behaviors are normative and expected. In addition, this understanding helps clinicians and families identify normative responses to the stressors associated with moving through different developmental stages. For example, a clinician working with a mother who complains about her four-year-old son's frequent insistence on telling others (including his parents and older sibling) what to do during play and mealtime might educate her about appropriate developmental expectations and stages. This educational piece fits nicely with most behavioral therapy models and also incorporates an understanding of normative development, as intervention moves beyond addressing problem behaviors directly to also helping the mother cope with her stress by normalizing (and not improperly pathologizing) certain behaviors in childhood. By using the framework of developmental psychology and its consideration of psychological risk factors and normative development, therapists can increase the possibility of lasting change for both the child and the family.

Practical suggestions.

- Assessment of risk factors (both causal and risk markers) should include both a functional analysis of problematic behaviors as well as consideration of temperament, attachment style and other internal factors in order to promote lasting change in the individual and family.

- Include a focus on normative development when working from a behavioral therapy perspective in order to help families develop a better understanding of what is normal and expected, as well as ways to resolve stressors related to normal developmental stages.

Social and Contextual

The identification of contextual factors as a key component in the development of problematic behaviors is important in working from a behavioral approach integrated with a developmental psychopathology framework. A child's family and friendships, school, home, and community environment can significantly impact her intrapsychic, interpersonal and neurobiological development. As a result, these contexts often influence the growth and maintenance of problematic behaviors. Behavioral therapies have long since recognized how environmental factors (e.g., consequences or reinforcements) play a primary role in whether a problematic behavior becomes learned or extinguished. For example, a toddler who throws a temper tantrum in the grocery store candy aisle will likely repeat this behavior on the next grocery trip if the parent relents and reinforces the tantrum behavior by purchasing desired candy in order to stop the screaming and resulting embarrassment (i.e., positive reinforcement). The reverse is also true: the parent becomes more likely to purchase candy for the child next time he screams in a public place since the child has reinforced this parental behavior by stopping the tantrum and no longer embarrassing the parent (i.e., negative reinforcement). Both the child's and parent's behaviors are intrinsically linked to the reinforcements provided within the environment.

However, behavioral therapy's more limited acknowledgment of context does not account for the complexities of environmental factors, such as parental psychopathology or bullies, which interact with behavioral reinforcements to produce additional problematic behaviors. For example, a parent suffering from severe depression may either have less patience with the tantrum behavior or no energy to address the tantrum at all. The child who throws tantrums unceasingly in the grocery store and receives no explicit reinforcement from his mother (e.g., no candy and no attention) may eventually stop but may develop difficulties regulating his emotions and trusting caretakers to meet his needs. As a result, he may withdraw from additional interactions with his mother, which may produce increased feelings of inadequacy in his mother and cyclically impact her depression.

Developmental psychopathology implores clinicians to acknowledge the multiple levels of relational, environmental and cultural influences that can produce and maintain problematic behaviors in children and adolescents. Sroufe and Rutter (1984) originally suggested that developmental psychopathology was the "study of the origins and course of individual patterns of *behavior maladaptation*" (p. 18). Researchers today assert that the interplay between context and development is critical for a thorough understanding of symptoms and treatment of problematic behaviors (Cummings et al., 2000). Risk and protective factors, as well as subjective cultural interpretations of adaptive versus maladaptive behaviors, also contribute to the development and identification of problem behaviors. Moreover, cultural experiences may actually produce risk and protective factors, as specific cultural beliefs, norms and values influence definitions of normal development and the ideal self (Cicchetti, 2006). Both cultural interpretations and the subjective experience of the environmental context influence the development of maladaptive behaviors.

From a developmental psychopathology perspective, the behavioral therapist should understand that we live within reciprocal relationships—with other people, the environment and the community as a whole—and recognize that maladaptive behavioral responses develop as the results of the interplay among neurobiology, interpersonal interactions and intrapsychic experiences (i.e., brain development influences behavior, which influences social and psychological experiences in unique and varying contexts across development; Cicchetti, 2006). Moreover, context becomes the defining factor in the determination of whether a behavior is normative or adaptive. For instance, a history of complex trauma, or childhood maltreatment, may result in an "environmentally induced complex developmental disorder" (De Bellis, 2001, p. 540) as a child "learns" that an expressive, assertive emotional response is punished by her abusive father. In turn, she learns to respond to stress with muted, passive emotions and relies on acting-out behaviors in order to cope. She develops into a teenager who struggles to effectively regulate her emotions and/or behaviors. De Bellis (2001) suggests that a "dysfunctional and traumatized interpersonal relationship" (p. 540) with people and environment creates an overwhelming interaction of stressors, which often results in restricted emotional and behavioral responses to stress. More specifically, a series of adaptive behaviors that allow a client to "survive" as a child create significant difficulties in her interpersonal relationships as an adult. These responses are the result of compromised neurological pathways that may make these clients more difficult to treat in a therapy setting. Clinicians must recognize the complex developmental pathways that have led to the current maladaptive behavior.

Practical suggestions.

- Assessment should include an evaluation of the history of significant social relationships and contexts to assess for complex trauma or difficult interpersonal relationships and/or environments that may have contributed to the development of maladaptive behavioral responses.

- Assessment should include an inquiry about whether the problematic behavior was/is somehow adaptive within the child's past/current context.

- Functional analysis of problematic behaviors should include more than a simplistic, A-B-C assessment of antecedent, behavior and consequence. A functional analysis informed by a developmental psychopathological approach should also include additional information about the context, environment and relationships associated with the maladaptive behaviors.

CONCLUSION

A developmental psychopathology approach to understanding maladaptive behaviors informs a behavioral orientation by recognizing the complex interplay among biological predispositions, intrapsychic processes and personality, and the environment in the development of problematic behaviors, instead of merely examining behavioral outcomes (Cicchetti, 2006). The concepts of multifinality and equifinality also inform behavioral therapies by highlighting that there are many pathways to the same resulting symptoms and that symptoms are not always the direct outcome of a specific biology, personality or context. Developmental psychopathology also highlights the importance of understanding normal, adaptive behavior versus abnormal, maladaptive behaviors across developmental contexts and adjusting expectations of behavior as a result. In addition, a behavioral approach is informed by developmental psychopathology's focus on resilience in children and adolescents, as resilience provides a unique sense of hope for children, adolescents and families who struggle.

CASE STUDY

Janie is an eleven-year-old Caucasian female living in the rural southeastern United States who was referred for counseling services by her school counselor due to recent trouble fighting with other students, being disrespectful toward her teachers and not following directions in the classroom. Janie has received in-school suspension four times over the past two months and has also been given out-of-school suspension for getting into a fistfight with a classmate. She is failing four out of her six classes this semester and has a history of academic struggles. The school counselor reports that Janie's problematic behaviors began at the start of the school year and that Janie's records show that she has attended five different schools in five years.

The school counselor has had multiple conferences with Janie and her mother, Ms. Stern, about Janie's problematic behavior. Janie's mother frequently complains that Janie needs to "shape up her behavior" and "get better grades." She reports that Janie has been "causing a ton of trouble lately"—acting disrespectfully, "talking back," not following directions and getting into arguments with her older brothers at home. During these tense meetings, Janie usually sits quietly with her arms crossed and looks down, but sometimes she gets into arguments with her mother, to which the school counselor responds by sending Janie back to class. The school counselor states that the school desires to see Janie demonstrate more respectful behaviors in the classroom and learn better ways to resolve her problems with peers.

Janie's mother reports that she and Mr. Stern have experienced significant relational difficulties over the past few years and have recently divorced. Ms. and Mr. Stern were married at age sixteen, after Ms. Stern became pregnant with her oldest daughter, Robin (age 24), who is now out of the home. She reports that their family seemed to function "fine" until Mr. Stern lost his job five years ago. Since then, the family has moved to five different towns across two states. These family transitions have created significant marital distress, as evidenced by an increase in arguing and a decrease in family activities. Prior to their recent divorce, Ms. Stern discovered that Mr. Stern was having an affair and asked her husband to leave their home. Since then, Ms. Stern has attempted to raise Janie and her two older brothers, who are still in the home, while simultaneously seeking consistent full-time employment for herself. Although she has held two different jobs within the past year, Ms. Stern is currently unemployed. Mr. Stern has had minimal contact with Janie and her brothers. Ms. Stern reports that Janie often requests to live with her father when Ms. Stern upsets her.

Ms. Stern states that she is overwhelmed by Janie's behaviors and has "given up" trying to manage Janie's behavior at home. She reports that she has tried numerous ways of getting Janie to "do the right things," including rewarding her, giving her consequences (such as taking things away), yelling at her, even using corporal punishment, but "nothing ever works." She has experienced similar disappointing outcomes with Janie's older sister Robin's history of conduct problems and her brothers' current problematic behaviors at home. Ms. Stern states that the "only thing that will get Janie to do her chores" is if Ms. Stern promises to do an activity with Janie (e.g., go out for ice cream, have a movie night). When promised a shared activity, Janie will usually follow through with Ms. Stern's behavior request. However, Ms. Stern reports that consistent participation in shared activities is difficult, as she often does not have the energy to do something with Janie. Ms. Stern is moderately open to counseling for Janie but expresses reservations that counseling will help resolve Janie's behavior problems.

Janie reports that she would not have these problems if "everyone would just stop making [her] mad and leave [her] alone." She explains that the girls at school make fun of her or call her names, so the only way she can "get them to shut up" is to fight with them. She also states that she "hates" that her dad left the family and expresses specific anger about Mr. Stern spending so much time with his girlfriend, Lily. Janie reports feeling frustrated that her mother "lays around on the couch all day and doesn't do anything" with her anymore.

Assessment: How Did These Behaviors Develop?

Janie's mother and school (e.g., teachers and school counselor) are willing to be involved in her counseling process. Parental involvement in treatment is crucial, particularly in using specific behavior modification techniques, such as parent training and contingency contracting. School involvement will help Janie generalize learned skills and allow for consistent implementation of behavioral techniques across contexts. In many situations, involvement of all systems is not a possibility or is very difficult; however, optimally for this case, all systems would be involved.

For the Christian therapist, the principle of children valued as gifts (Miller-McLemore, 2003) is incorporated into the initial stages of therapy through a thorough assessment that aims to outline the developmental trajectories, behavioral adaptations and interpersonal cycles that have contributed to Janie's current behaviors, rather than seeing Janie herself as the inherent problem; thus, this valuing ensures that treatment is conducted in a responsible, informed manner.

In these initial stages, being attuned to Janie's point of view when collecting initial information will reflect the therapist's respect for Janie's personhood and will ideally increase Janie's ability to recognize her own agency throughout the therapeutic process. Additionally, developing rapport with and engaging in a relationship with both child and parent together will instill a sense of hope by acknowledging Janie as a gift to the family (even in the midst of difficulties), the family's ability to change maladaptive patterns, and Janie's agency to choose to navigate away from (as opposed to toward) negative behaviors. Throughout the rapport-building process, demonstrating respect for Janie's personhood to both Janie and her mother, as well as her agency to effect change in her own life, will be crucial to building a safe, empathic environment that will support behavioral interventions.

However, therapists must also remember that the initial stages of therapy can be the most challenging, specifically when encountering "difficult" children (i.e., those who are angry, opposed to therapy or have little sense of hope in their own ability to change). When encountering these children, we must remember that, in the role of therapist, we are called to work even with those whom others may perceive as "difficult" because they too deserve to be valued as gifts. Further, we need to recognize that all clients have the agency to effect change in their own lives and the lives of others with whom they are in relationship. In working with Janie, the therapist can facilitate this initial rapport-building process by also focusing on the therapeutic relationship with Ms. Stern. By empathically joining with Ms. Stern, in tandem with modeling respect for Janie's personhood, valuing her as a gift and recognizing her agency throughout the therapeutic process, the therapist may empower Ms. Stern to implement these principles into her daily interactions with Janie and her other children.

An assessment that incorporates the principle of children as valued gifts and that is informed by both a behavioral orientation and a developmental psychopathology perspective first involves a functional analysis identifying risk and protective factors to ensure that treatment is conducted in a thoroughly informed manner. By conducting interviews with Janie, the school counselor and Ms. Stern, the therapist can conduct a functional analysis that considers all points of view while also emphasizing Janie's point of view, her understanding of her behaviors and how her adaptations to her circumstances have helped her cope with a variety of different situations. This process also considers the reciprocal interaction of Janie and Ms. Stern's behaviors within the context of a relationship impacted by sin; Janie and Ms. Stern's brokenness influences their relationship with one another, their behavioral adaptations and the presence of other risk factors.

Key behavioral concerns in two contexts are identified: school (getting into fights, being disrespectful toward teachers and not following directions in the classroom) and home (being disrespectful toward her mother, talking back, not following directions and getting into arguments with her older siblings). Behavioral therapy's functional analysis focuses on the antecedents and consequences related to the target behavior. As an illustration, we will identify these components of one target behavior: Janie getting into fights at school. Based on reports from Janie and the school counselor, Janie often fights with other students (target behavior) when they "bug" her (antecedent; i.e., make fun of her, act in ways that trigger anger or frustration). In response to the anger that she feels when "bugged," Janie fights with other students and then receives consequences (punishments) for her behaviors (e.g., suspensions). However, Janie continues to display these problematic behaviors, which may indicate that either this punishment is not effective (behavioral perspective) or that Janie's behavior is in some way adaptive (developmental psychopathology perspective) and that the adaptation results in a benefit which overshadows the negative consequence for Janie. Essential to this analysis is the understanding that Janie's behaviors are not an inherent part of herself but rather functional adaptations to stressful or problematic situations and events in her life that have now become maladaptive in new contexts. By valuing Janie in this way (and avoiding pathologizing her), the therapist is able to focus on Janie's behaviors. Additionally, the understanding that Janie has been able to adapt to her circumstances in the past allows the therapist to emphasize Janie's ability to effect change now, in a healthier, more adaptive manner. In assessing Janie's history and presentation, we also identify risk factors that may have led to the development or maintenance of problematic behaviors. Exposure to maladaptive coping techniques, parental conflict and divorce, her father's affair, and her siblings' histories of modeling negative behaviors are common risk factors for developing maladaptive behaviors. As a result, Janie has developed poor coping and conflict resolution skills.

The next component of assessment involves identifying ways that Janie's problematic behavior may be adaptive within her cultural, familial and relational contexts. In other words, which behaviors labeled problematic at home and school has Janie developed as a way to adapt to process, or survive, her experiences? This process also takes into consideration that Janie is to be valued as a person in her own counseling by listening to her perspective regarding how she has developed behaviors to cope more effectively with situations she views as being problematic in her life. Given this, Janie's behaviors can be considered adaptive in two ways. First, Janie's behavior is a response to her experiences of loss and serves as a protective measure to prevent her from additional emotional harm as a result of people "getting too close and then leaving." By being angry and disruptive at school, Janie creates safety for herself in relationships and avoids the possibility of additional interpersonal loss and increased emotional distress, which reinforces this cycle of anger and negative behavior. However, although this behavior is adaptive, it is also problematic or maladaptive, as it prevents her from forming meaningful, developmentally appropriate relationships, improving her social skills and succeeding in school. A second way Janie's behavior could be adaptive relates to her desire for attention. Janie has experienced a decrease in the amount of attention from both parents as a result of their divorce and has discovered that misbehaving is one "solution" that always results in attention. When she acts out at home, her mother gives her the attention she desires, regardless of the quality of the attention (negative or positive), and Janie's need is therefore satisfied and her negative behavior reinforced. Further, Janie may also desire attention in her school context and choose to apply the same principle in this environment as well. However, her behaviors are not as adaptive in the school context and have resulted in increased discipline and interpersonal consequences there.

Despite these risk factors, protective factors are also present in Janie's life that might offset the effects of negative life experiences and possibly facilitate healthier development (Cicchetti, 2006). Janie possesses both external and internal protective factors. First, Janie's mother seems to have an understanding of appropriate parenting skills, even though her own depressive symptoms currently seem to be preventing effective implementation of them. We notice specifically that she has found that giving Janie attention (or "spending time together") is a good reinforcement for Janie to do her chores. Also, the family seems to have support from the school system and appears open to this support. This community support may have served a protective function in keeping Janie's symptoms from getting too extreme, and it will also be a helpful resource during therapy. Janie also possesses a number of internal protective factors. She appears to be determined and passionate, evidenced by her consistent attempts to get attention from others through externalizing behaviors (this externalizing suggests that Janie is attempting to communicate her needs to others). Additionally, per her mother, Janie historically has had many friends and been a social child, often getting along with others. Ms. Stern describes that, although this has changed with their multiple moves, Janie still occasionally expresses a desire to have friends over and/or to go to friends' houses to play. These factors are reminders to both clinician and parent that Janie has the ability to effect change in her own life, and this agency should be respected within the therapeutic process.

Finally, assessment must also consider the ways in which context, family factors and biological predispositions may have contributed to the development of Janie's behaviors. First, we notice that Janie's behaviors have developed in the context of chaotic transitions, new and unfamiliar environments, and a tense home life. As discussed above, it is possible that many of her behaviors are reactions or adaptations to the changing characteristics of these environments, but we also need to consider the developmental timing of the transitions—what developmental tasks was she traversing at this time and what skills was she (un)able to develop? Additionally, family factors, such as parental divorce (and subsequent family structure changes) as well as her mother's unemployment, may have resulted in a need for Janie to adjust her role or function in the family system. Last, we notice that Janie's mother seems to be struggling with depressive symptoms, and her siblings have a long history of behavior and substance abuse problems. It will also be important to pay attention to possible organic roots for some of Janie's behaviors. Despite all of these psychological, biological and social factors, to move into treatment the therapist must keep in mind that Janie is not just a passive recipient of these influences but an active participant in shaping her behaviors and choices who has the ability to learn how to channel her potential to more adaptive ways of living in her environment.

TREATMENT: WHAT DOES INTEGRATIVE, CHRISTIAN TREATMENT FROM A BEHAVIORAL, DEVELOPMENTAL PSYCHOPATHOLOGY PERSPECTIVE LOOK LIKE?

In order to proceed effectively with treatment, it is important to operationally define the target behaviors, taking into consideration the information gathered in assessment. Two objectively defined goals for Janie might be that she will (1) demonstrate an increase in the frequency of compliant behaviors (i.e., following directions when asked) from once per week to once daily over the next six months and (2) demonstrate a decrease in the number of physical altercations (e.g., fist fights, pulling hair, kicking) with other students from once per week to zero in the next six months. These goals, once objectively defined, can be addressed in relevant contexts (school, home and relationships), utilizing the relational context (between Janie and Ms. Stern, as well as between Janie and her peers) to provide both accountability and support for Janie's process of behavior change.

Further, in the initial stages of treatment, there are both clinician and parent considerations to keep in mind when incorporating the principle of children are respected as persons. For the clinician, keeping this perspective in work with Janie will involve respecting and taking seriously Janie's opinions, perspectives and emotions (both in response to her environment and to treatment interventions) while also modeling this approach for Ms. Stern. For example, by having Ms. Stern participate in joint sessions with Janie, the therapist can model ways for her to ask about and understand Janie's story. This approach emphasizes the reciprocal influence within Janie and Ms. Stern's relationship versus demanding conformity and invalidating Janie's opinion. Additionally, during both the assessment and treatment process, through valuing Janie's personhood, the therapist should be open to learning from Janie—developing a better understanding of her environment, the function and adaptation of her behavior, and what Janie's needs are for her to be successful in her environment. For Ms. Stern, this perspective may be somewhat more difficult for her to incorporate. However, the therapeutic process will ideally encourage Ms. Stern to get to know and understand her daughter better (*Note: Ms. Stern is already doing this at times, specifically when using "time together" as a reinforcer for Janie's positive behaviors*), thus helping her recognize Janie's potential as well as her "imperfections" and helping the pair work together toward developing each other in the reciprocal relationship recognized by the developmental psychopathology framework. The therapist can help Ms. Stern learn how to do this more effectively through modeling this respect for Janie in conjoint family sessions as well as utilizing psychoeducational techniques to teach Ms. Stern specific ways to communicate this respect to Janie. For example, on rides home from school, Ms. Stern might be encouraged to ask Janie how her day was and to use reflective listening techniques (such as "it sounds like you really enjoyed going to art class today" if Janie tells a particularly exciting story about an activity from her art class) to help emphasize Ms. Stern's awareness of and respect for Janie and her views.

Further, it is imperative to identify specific positive behaviors that the family and school are already demonstrating. As already mentioned, Ms. Stern seems to have a basic understanding of positive reinforcement: by giving Janie something she desires (spending time with her mother) as a reward for performing a desired behavior (doing her chores), Ms. Stern has seen an increase in Janie's compliance. Additionally, Ms. Stern is actively seeking employment and participating in the counseling process. By verbally praising Ms. Stern, the therapist can reinforce what Ms. Stern is already doing well and provide a basis for continuing therapy within the framework of seeing Janie as a valued gift and respecting her as a person (Miller-McLemore, 2003). This framework prompts Ms. Stern to focus on implementing parenting skills (such as reflective listening, developing appropriate reinforcements and consequences, and modeling appropriate behavior) that respect Janie as an individual and view her responsibility as a parent as that of steward without abusing her power within the family system. This approach also encourages Ms. Stern to consider Janie's opinion and needs in her approach to parenting. For example, when considering positive reinforcers for Janie's positive behaviors, Ms. Stern will want to consider input from Janie. Not only does this increase the likelihood that Janie will engage in the desired behavior (as the reward will be more salient), it also demonstrates that Janie is valued as a gift and respected as a person by honoring her input in this process.

A primary method of behavioral modification with children and adolescents is parent training. Ms. Stern can learn to communicate to Janie in a clear, detailed way what behaviors she would like from her (Shapiro, Friedberg & Bardenstein, 2006). As noted in the case presentation, historically Ms. Stern's parenting has reflected a tense, aggravated approach due to feeling overwhelmed at times. However, if we encourage Ms. Stern to approach her new parenting skills through the view that Janie has the ability to effect change on her environment and future (i.e., viewing her as an agent), we can cause a significant shift in this approach. For Janie and Ms. Stern, the focus will be on developing appropriate reinforcements and consequences in the home through contingency contracting in order to increase the frequency of desired behaviors and decrease the frequency of undesired behaviors. Contingency contracting involves working with Ms. Stern and Janie to develop a chart in which Janie receives a "mark" for each desired behavior, with each goal preferably worded in a positive manner (e.g., Janie will complete her [specific] daily chore, get along with brothers instead of getting into arguments or fighting most of the time, taking prescribed medication, etc.). At the end of each week, Janie can then receive larger, more desired rewards based on the number of "marks" she receives. Two components are key in contingency contracting: reinforcement must be consistent, and desired behavior should be rewarded with a reinforcement (whether social, symbolic, or tangible) that is desirable for the child, otherwise the reinforcement will demonstrate low effectiveness (Shapiro et al., 2006). As mentioned previously, by involving Janie in the process of defining specific rewards (e.g., time spent with her mother, getting to go to the movies with friends), we work under the theme that Janie is to be respected as a person and seek to increase the saliency of the reinforcer. Additionally, contingency contracting is rooted in the principle that Janie, as an agent, is able to make choices that will effect change in her own relationships, environment and (eventually) future. This perspective decreases the likelihood that contingency contracting will be a power struggle and increases the possibility that Janie and Ms. Stern will work together in this part of the therapeutic process. Further, in order to generalize this means of reinforcement and behavior modification, the family may choose to add school-related goals to the behavior chart in conjunction with the school counselor and increase the likelihood that Janie will continue to engage in desired behaviors. Throughout this process, the therapist must take caution to not reduce Janie to the sum of her behaviors. Despite the focus on her behaviors in the use of contingency contracting, it will be essential for Ms. Stern and the therapist to care as much about Janie as a person as they do about her behavior, avoiding defining "normative" behavior as Janie being happy and cooperative. Instead, progress may look more like Janie exercising her agency to effect change in her environment and relationships as well as developing a strong sense of self.

Another focus of parent training might be on how Ms. Stern can appropriately model desired behaviors for her daughter. Currently, Ms. Stern is demonstrating depressive symptoms and frustration with Janie's behavior and has a history of resolving conflict through arguing. By adjusting her own behavior, Ms. Stern may be able to model desired behavior for Janie. For example, instead of yelling at Janie when she is feeling frustrated with Janie's behavior, Ms. Stern could model taking a time out to calm down before discussing the problem with Janie. By not responding immediately in anger, but instead modeling appropriate tone, timing and communication skills, Janie's mother might help her be able to develop these communication skills for herself. In this process, due to the reciprocal nature of relationships and Janie's agency in the parent-child relationship, Ms. Stern may also find that as she is modeling desired behaviors for Janie, she can learn ways of coping and adapting from Janie as well.

Behavioral therapy and developmental psychopathology also address modifying behaviors on an individual level through recognizing the interplay between internal processes and external behaviors. This focus also falls within the understanding of children as persons and as agents who can effect change. To determine what areas to target, developmental psychopathology provides us with the perspective that we can look at what behaviors are normative for a child Janie's age (both chronologically and developmentally). By taking into consideration what Janie has and has not learned in context of normal development, we can have a better understanding of what these behaviors are and how they may or may not have developed given her environment, experiences, genetic predispositions and so on. Key areas that Janie may need to focus on in therapy include emotion regulation, problem-solving and social skills training (specifically, assertiveness and communication skills to assist her in appropriately communicating her feelings, needs and concerns to others). Janie's frequent outbursts and fighting suggest difficulty managing her emotions. Working from a behavioral perspective, these difficulties may be able to be addressed through mindfulness techniques, using body feedback and skills often used within dialectical behavior therapy (DBT). By helping Janie to tune into the feedback from her body (e.g., when she feels angry, her stomach gets tight, her hearts beats quickly and her breathing becomes more rapid), she can break down these cues into smaller components and begin to learn how to manage her emotions through skills like deep breathing or progressive muscle relaxation. These body-based calming and coping skills will help Janie activate her sympathetic nervous system to respond to increased stress and thus decrease hyperarousal, increasing the possibility that she can respond calmly. Once she is able to learn the calming skills, Janie will be more able to learn and implement problem-solving and communication skills, as these skills require more cognitive functioning that is not accessible when children experience heightened arousal (Blaustein & Kinniburgh, 2010). Social skills training involves explaining, modeling, skills practice and feedback (Shapiro et al., 2006). Explaining the rationale for social skills training as well as the function of each specific skill, modeling the skill, encouraging Janie to practice the skill, and then providing feedback for her through constructive comments about strengths and areas for improvement will help Janie cognitively understand and behaviorally experience the skill.

Overall, the therapy process should emphasize the dynamic interaction between different systems. For example, during behavioral rehearsal of communication skills, the therapist can remain cued into behaviors or signals that indicate increased anger for Janie and encourage previously learned relaxation skills to help calm these emotions and increase the effectiveness of her communication skills, which reflects respect for Janie as a person. Parent training can also reinforce the development of skills as Ms. Stern models positive communication in the home. Throughout each stage of treatment, Janie's learned skills will be reinforced in multiple contexts—home and school.

CONCLUSION

Since its emergence as a formal school of psychology in the 1950s, behavioral therapy has provided a basis for many empirically based approaches to understanding human behavior and for clinical work. From early to more modern models, the focus of behavioral therapy has been on helping individuals to develop adaptive patterns of behaviors. This goal is accomplished primarily by helping individuals decrease the frequency of undesired behaviors and increase the frequency of desired behaviors, while boosting the range of flexible, adaptive behaviors, all through using positive and negative reinforcements and punishments.

Psychoeducation, exposure-based strategies, reinforcement- and punishment-based strategies, relaxation-based strategies, social and communication skills training, parent training, mindfulness, emotion regulation, and acceptance-based strategies are some common behavioral approaches with children and adolescents. Parent-Child Interaction Therapy (Bell & Eyberg,

2002), Parent Management Training (Kazdin, 1997), and naturalistic applied behavioral analysis (Koegel et al., 1999) are specific behavioral therapies designed for therapists working with youth and their caregivers. From a Christian integrative perspective, a review of the literature yields concern: few models attempt to fully integrate behavioral therapy techniques with a Christian worldview and work with youth populations. At best, there are behavioral models used in the context of churches and other community settings that put a "Christian spin" on behavioral interventions. Considering children as gifts, persons and agents can help us overlay a Christian theological perspective on traditional behavioral interventions.

Finally, a behavioral orientation's strength is its focus on functional analysis: defining a problem, identifying the origins of that problem and developing a treatment plan. However, its limitation is a tendency to overlook the diverse origins for maladaptive behaviors and dynamic interplay across the lifespan between biological predispositions, temperament, personality and environment in the development of problematic behaviors. A behavioral orientation under the developmental psychopathology framework can foster a more robust understanding of maladaptive behaviors and consider the function of "normal" development within a treatment context.

11

Cognitive-Behavioral
Approaches to Treatment

....

Donald F. Walker, Katherine J. Partridge,
Anastasia Whitesell, Brittany Montes
and Sarah E. Hall

IN THIS CHAPTER WE CONSIDER cognitive-behavioral therapies (CBT) for children and adolescents from an integrative perspective, drawing on both a developmental psychopathology framework and Christian theology. We begin by reviewing basic principles of some of the major cognitive-behavioral therapies that have contributed to the historical development of the movement. Next, we review cognitive-behavioral treatments developed specifically for use with children and adolescents. In this portion of our review, we discuss some spiritually based cognitive-behavioral therapy interventions and adaptations. Third, we discuss the implications of developmental psychopathology for cognitive-behavioral work with youth. Finally, we conclude by presenting a case study and integrating theological considerations in treating children from a cognitive-behavioral orientation.

Cognitive-behavioral therapies came in three "waves" over the course of the twentieth century (Antony & Roemer, 2011). The first wave consists of therapies traditionally associated with behaviorism. The second wave, associated with Aaron Beck and Albert Ellis, consists of approaches focused on identifying and altering maladaptive thoughts, and the third wave involves mindfulness-based approaches to therapies. Because behavioral approaches are covered elsewhere in this book, we focus here on the second and third waves of cognitive-behavioral therapies, which form much of the underpinning for contemporary cognitive-behavioral therapies for children.

HISTORY OF COGNITIVE-BEHAVIORAL THERAPY

Along with behavioral theories, cognitive-behavioral thinking, developed largely in the 1950s and 1960s, denoted a drastic departure from psychoanalytic conceptualizations and techniques. Aaron Beck and Albert Ellis, pioneers of cognitive therapy (CT) and rational-emotive behavioral therapy (REBT), respectively, voiced discontent with Freudian analysis. Ellis received extensive training in psychoanalysis and even underwent analysis himself, yet after significant questioning and his own work in private practice, he began to view maladaptive thoughts and behaviors as a more accurate explanation of psychological problems. Similarly, Beck was originally trained as a psychoanalyst yet came to the belief that Freud's conceptualization of depression as anger turned inward was misguided. By Beck's account, negative attributions and cognitive distortions were more relevant to the formation and maintenance of depressive symptomatology over time. Based on these new understandings, Ellis and Beck developed their respective cognitively based approaches to understanding disorder and treatment (see Ellis, 1962; Beck, 1967a). According to these CBT approaches, the crux of human functioning lies in an individual's interpretation of the events in his life and the patterns of thought that develop and impact emotions and behaviors. The following sections will provide an overview of the theoretical and applied principles of cognitive-behavioral therapy.

Rational Emotive Behavior Therapy

Throughout his career, Ellis viewed humans as fallible beings who are continually subject to a complex interplay of thoughts, feelings and behaviors. Most importantly, according to Ellis, every person has the capacity for both *rational* and *irrational thought*. Rational thought is logical and accurate; irrational thought is inaccurate and not based in reality. Ellis believed that rational thinking can lead to a healthy style of living and an unconditional regard for and acceptance of self and others. By contrast, irrational thinking often leads one to develop self-defeating and dysfunctional thought and behavioral patterns. Irrational beliefs are viewed as the root of the negative emotions, which lead to pathology. Ellis proposed twelve basic irrational beliefs that can be subsumed under three core irrational beliefs revolving around oneself, others and the world: (1) "I must do well and win approval of others or else I am no good," (2) "Other people must do 'the right thing' or they are no good and deserve to be punished," and (3) "Life must be easy, without discomfort or inconvenience." These beliefs—and their ingrained nature—lead to cognitive distortions in the interpretation of one's experiences. A child who holds Ellis's third core irrational belief may become angry when she fails a test, reflecting her irrational belief that schoolwork should not be difficult, while a child for whom the first core belief is central might become very sad in the same situation, interpreting her test results as a failure to please others that indicates her unworthiness. Ellis posited that the longer one holds to these patterns of irrational thinking, the more embedded they become, highlighting the importance of intervening in childhood to promote ongoing mental health.

The formation of rational or irrational patterns of thought occurs through *philosophical conditioning*, the process by which individuals make sense of the world and develop a unique belief system. This process of cognitive interpretation is believed to occur on both conscious and unconscious levels and is responsible for the development self-defeating and dysfunctional thinking and behaviors. For example, an adolescent may interpret a classmate's decision not to sit with her at lunch in multiple ways, including (1) "she wants to talk with her other friends today," (2) "she doesn't want to be my friend," or (3) "I am unlikable." While we cannot truly judge the rationality of the teen's thoughts without knowing more about the situation, it is likely that the third interpretation is irrational or disconnected from reality. REBT practitioners believe that patterns of thinking begin to form in childhood and are influenced by many factors, including genetic make-up, societal influences, parenting practices and family dynamics. The adolescent in the lunchroom may be more likely to believe that her friend's behavior reflects that she is unlikable if she has already begun to develop this belief as the result of abuse in childhood. While belief systems are developed early, subsequent developmental events affect the course of cognitive patterns, which can, in turn, be altered by therapeutic intervention.

REBT uses an alphabet acrostic for detailing the cognitive process. First, an activating event (A) occurs, and a belief (B), which may be either rational or irrational, is formed during the interpretation of the event. This belief results in consequential (C) feelings and behaviors. If irrational beliefs occur in step B, negative feelings and maladaptive behaviors result. As events continue to occur, and beliefs recur, a specific, ingrained belief system, or *schema*, develops. For example, a child may develop the fearful patterns of thinking that characterize a specific phobia as the result of repeated interactions with large barking dogs (A) that he views as dangerous and threatening (B), resulting in anxiety and avoidance (C). Once a cognitive structure has developed, it becomes the default operating system through which thoughts and experiences are filtered. Unless the child's beliefs about dogs are examined, he will continue to process information in an irrational manner. Fortunately, schemata can be changed through therapeutic intervention, resulting in alterations to problematic patterns of feeling and behavior following changed thought patterns.

Once A (activating event), B (beliefs) and C (consequences) have been identified, the process of creating a rationally based belief system begins with the work of disputing (D), or challenging, the irrational belief. Disputing can be accomplished using a variety of methods. One strategy involves viewing cognitive reactions as theories rather than absolute facts. This allows the cognition to be challenged even before it is internalized. Another strategy is Socratic questioning, in which the therapist asks the client leading but open questions that allow the client to identify beliefs as irrational. This dialogue can be used to discuss situations in which negative emotional reactions occurred and to examine past experiences in order to identify irrational schema. Three basic questions can be used to guide this practice: (1) What is the evidence for and against that belief? (2) What are alternative interpretations of the event or situation? (3) What are the real implications if the belief is correct? As clients answer these questions, they begin to examine the rationality of their thought patterns.

Sometimes it is not prudent to ask these basic questions when a belief involves inferences and assumptions of others, as it may not be possible to accurately flesh out and dispute inferences. For example, if an adolescent's irrational thoughts are based on assumptions about a stranger's motivations, the client and therapist may not have enough information about the stranger to challenge the accuracy of the client's thoughts. In this case, it may be more beneficial to use questions that address the *meaning* of the clients' inferences. This process can be accomplished using the downward arrow technique, in which inferences are met with questions, and each answer produces another question (e.g., What if X is true? And what about X bothers you?). This line of questioning can clarify inferences in a way that leads a client to identify an irrational belief that can be then be disputed. For example, an adolescent athlete who believes that peers in the weight room are making fun of him for being weak might be asked, "What if they are making fun of you for being weak? And what about being made fun of for being weak bothers you?" This line of questioning might uncover the client's irrational belief that he must be physically strong in order to be liked by others, which the therapist and the client can then work to dispute, regardless of whether the onlookers are truly making fun of him.

Finally, once irrational thoughts have been identified and challenged, they must be replaced with rational inferences. In the last step of Ellis's framework, the client and the therapist work together to develop a new effective response (E). Based on the evidence uncovered as irrational thoughts are disputed, clients can formulate rational thoughts to replace the irrational ones that have been proven false. In order to facilitate this process, REBT therapists may give children or adolescents homework in the form of keeping a thought record, in which they record their thoughts during activating events throughout the week, to provide fodder for therapeutic discussion as well as opportunities for clients to become more aware of and dispute their own irrational thoughts. Once an effective response has been formulated and the client's schemata have become more rational, her emotional and behavioral reactions to events in her life, as the result of rational interpretations of her experiences, will become healthier and more adaptive. Ultimately, the goal of the process of REBT is not only to identify and dispute current irrational beliefs but also to give the child the tools to continue to do this independently in order to prevent the development of future problems.

Cognitive Therapy

Beck, like Ellis, proposes that the key to understanding emotional disturbance is to understand the cognitions associated with upsetting events or lines of thought. Cognitive theorists believe that thoughts, feelings and behaviors are interconnected and that the root of both psychological health and abnormality lies in thought patterns; in the case of disorder, thought patterns are inaccurate and unhelpful, leading to negative emotions and maladaptive behaviors. Beck posits that negative patterns of thinking, once established, become ingrained, or *automatic*. When we experience events, then, these negative *cognitive distortions* are activated and impact our affective and behavioral reactions.

The foundational piece of Beck's theory relates to what he terms the *cognitive triad* (Beck, 1967b; Beck, Rush, Shaw & Emery, 1979). This triad involves negative beliefs about oneself, the world and the future. Psychological problems lie in a person's tendency to blame himself for failures and negative events (oneself), to focus on the negative aspects of his life and experiences (the world), and to believe that difficulties will resist change, continuing indefinitely (future). These thoughts ultimately lead to symptoms such as hopelessness, a depressed mood and excessive anxiety.

Beck & Weishaar (2008) outline several patterns of cognitive distortions commonly seen in people with mental health problems. Individuals may make *arbitrary inferences*, or conclusions that lack sufficient evidence. This is also known as catastrophizing. For example, a child whose mother has not arrived on time to pick him up from school might jump to the conclusion that she must have been injured in a car accident. *Overgeneralization* occurs when people apply beliefs formed in specific experiences to broader situations in which they may not apply. This pattern is demonstrated by the adolescent who receives one college rejection letter and thinks to herself that she will not get into any schools. In *personalization*, an individual erroneously attributes an external event to personal causal factors; for example, a child may believe that if she had been more well-behaved and obedient, her mother would not have developed cancer. Finally, *dichotomous thought*, also known as black-and-white thinking, occurs when a client sees himself and his experiences in terms of extremes, failing to recognize the nuances that characterize most situations. Statements that include extreme terms such as *always, never, everyone* and *no one* often highlight dichotomous thinking (e.g., "No one likes me," "Everyone is a better student than I am," "I will never be successful"). Because of their developing cognitive abilities, children and adolescents may be more naturally prone than adults to black-and-white thought.

Beck and Beck (2011) also distinguish among several different levels of beliefs involving cognitive distortions. Cognitive distortions can be differentiated as consisting of (1) automatic thoughts, (2) attitudes, rules and assumptions, and (3) core beliefs. Within this framework, automatic thoughts are conceptualized as being the most superficial level of beliefs and are often situation-specific. Automatic thoughts are generally spontaneous, rapid and brief, as opposed to resulting from deliberation or reasoning. Therapists can identify them by attending to shifts in affect, behavior and/or physiology. "I am going to play poorly in my soccer game" is an example of an automatic thought.

In contrast, *attitudes, rules and assumptions* compose an intermediate class of beliefs that are often unarticulated but relate to deeper core beliefs. Consider the following examples of attitudes, rules and assumptions related to failure. The automatic thought about the soccer game might reflect an attitude related to failure that "It's terrible to fail when your teammates are depending on you." A related rule could be, "Give up if a challenge seems too great." Finally, a corresponding assumption might be: "If I try to do something difficult, I'll fail. If I avoid doing it, I'll be okay."

Finally, *core beliefs* are the most fundamental level of cognition. These are beliefs that are global, rigid and overgeneralized. A core belief of the client described above might be, "I'm going to perform poorly in my soccer game because I'm a failure." Core beliefs are at the root of automatic thoughts and intermediate beliefs. Cognitive theorists posit that core beliefs and intermediate beliefs arise from early developmental attempts to make sense of one's environment in the form of interactions with the world and with others. For example, the child who believes that it is unacceptable to fail or that he is a failure might have developed this thought pattern in a household in which he was rarely praised and frequently scolded for misbehavior but often observed his siblings being praised for their accomplishments.

The goal of cognitive therapy is to help a client unlearn these dysfunctional beliefs and replace them with more reality-based and useful new beliefs through the process of *cognitive restructuring*. Therapists help clients identify and challenge automatic thoughts through techniques such as asking specific questions, Socratic questioning, guided discovery, cognitive restructuring and behavioral experiments (Beck & Beck, 2011). An example of a specific question is, "What is going through your mind right now?" Specific questions are useful for identifying clients' thoughts when they are describing a distressing situation, negative emotion or dysfunctional behavior. Similar to REBT, Socratic questioning and guided discovery can be used to more indirectly facilitate the client's own discovery of his cognitive distortions. Beck and Beck (2011) suggest the following questions as facilitators of guided discovery:

1. What is the evidence that your thought is true? What is the evidence on the other side?

2. What is an alternative way of viewing this situation?

3. What is the worst that could happen, and how could you cope if it did? What's the best that could happen? What's the most realistic outcome of this situation?

4. What is the effect of believing your automatic thought, and what could be the effect of changing your thinking?

5. If your friend or family member were in this situation and had the same automatic thought, what advice would you give him or her?

6. What should you do?

These prompts are designed to help the client look at her thoughts in a more objective, scientific way, testing their accuracy and usefulness in light of the objective evidence. They may also provide a gateway to the process of cognitive restructuring. For example, a child exhibiting school refusal may believe that the teacher is going to embarrass her when she gives the wrong answer in class. The therapist might ask her to describe the evidence for and against this idea, to think about times when she has given the wrong answer as well as times she has given the correct answer. The therapist may also ask the child questions to help her identify alternative outcomes to the situation (e.g., if she gets the answer wrong, the teacher might embarrass her, or the teacher might correct her nicely). As the child becomes less certain that the feared outcome will occur, her cognitive distortions are reduced. In addition, the therapist may help her develop self-talk as a method of cognitive restructuring. When she begins to notice the anxious automatic thought that she is going to be embarrassed, she can replace that thought with positive self-talk, such as "I often get the answer right—there is a good chance I will get it right this time," or "The teacher is usually nice when kids get the answer wrong, so I don't think she will embarrass me."

Finally, behavioral experiments allow clients to practically test the utility of their cognitions, including both old (distorted) cognitions and new (restructured) thoughts. A therapist might encourage an adolescent wrestling with the distortion that nobody wants to be friends with him to approach one new person each day to engage in conversation. The adolescent is likely to find that at least some of these people are friendly and want to talk with him, challenging his automatic thought and helping reinforce alternative, restructured thoughts (e.g., "People want to be friends with me, and I can make new friends by talking to people I don't know").

In the process of therapy, Beck and Beck (2011) suggest placing initial emphasis on identifying and modifying automatic thoughts that occur in direct reaction to clients' experiences and working over time toward identifying the deeper beliefs that these thoughts reflect. Because of the centrality of intermediate and core beliefs to a client's sense of meaning and reality, therapists are in danger of losing credibility and threatening the therapeutic alliance if the validity of these beliefs is addressed too early.

Principles of Dialectical Behavior Therapy (DBT)

Marsha Linehan developed dialectical behavior therapy (DBT) in an effort to provide a therapy modality that would effectively treat individuals suffering from borderline personality disorder, who are thought to have a core problem in emotion dysregulation that results in impulsive behavior and interferes with the development of healthy relationships (Linehan, 1993). DBT has also been found to be effective with individuals experiencing overwhelming emotionality and severe emotional dysregulation more broadly (McKay, Wood & Brantley, 2007). DBT-A is an adaptation designed for use with suicidal adolescents, who may struggle with these difficulties (Miller, Rathus & Linehan, 2007; Miller, Rathus, Linehan, Wetzler & Leigh, 1997). As a third-wave approach, DBT combines traditional CBT understandings with elements such as mindfulness and acceptance of thoughts and emotions.

DBT rests upon four essential skills or treatment modules that are designed to teach individuals how to better manage their overwhelming emotional states (Linehan, 1993). These four skills are distress tolerance, mindfulness, emotion regulation and interpersonal effectiveness. First, *distress tolerance* aims to help clients tolerate the experience of negative emotions so they can better cope with painful events and situations without reacting impulsively or maladaptively. Individuals with borderline personality traits or suicidal or parasuicidal behavior are often very dysregulated by the experience of negative emotions and take drastic measures, such as cutting, to reduce them; therefore, increased tolerance of such affect is likely to reduce problematic behavior. The goal of distress tolerance is to accept oneself and one's current situation in a nonjudgmental fashion. Distress tolerance also involves *radical acceptance*, or choosing to accept one's reality as it is rather than attempting to change it.

Second, the goal of *mindfulness* is to assist the individual to "experience more fully the present moment while focusing less on painful experiences from the past or frightening possibilities in the future" (McKay et al., 2007, p. 2). The core aspect of mindfulness involves learning how to be in control of rather than controlled by one's mind. DBT posits that there are three states of the mind. The reasonable mind focuses on rational and logical thinking. The emotional mind involves the state in which one's emotions direct behavior. The wise mind integrates the emotional mind with the reasonable mind. The wise mind uses both rational and emotional thought to inform reactions and decisions rather than rejecting emotionality altogether or allowing it to guide one's behavior without the influence of rational, non-emotional thought. The goal of mindfulness is for the individual to achieve the "wise mind" state of functioning. Three basic techniques—observation, description and participation—are used therapeutically to improve the client's mindfulness. When the individual is observing his or her experiences, she is instructed to notice various aspects without getting "caught up" in the experience; the goal of observation is merely to notice, rather than to judge, one's experiences, thoughts and feelings. It is often helpful to have individuals observe their surroundings through their senses, focusing on what they see, hear, smell and feel through touch. Next, individuals describe their experience, which facilitates both awareness and the ability to be fully present, helping the client reduce the need to ruminate or judge thoughts or feelings. To practice mindfulness, a client might be encouraged to engage in a pleasant activity, such as taking a walk outside, and to describe the sensory experiences she notices. Thoughts or emotions that she experiences should be nonjudgmentally observed and acknowledged, then released, rather than becoming the focus of attention or efforts to change. The individual should not evaluate the "goodness" or the "badness" of the experience; the focus is solely on the objective experience. Once a client has mastered the basic techniques of mindfulness, she is encouraged to apply them to more emotionally charged situations.

While distress tolerance and mindfulness are necessary components of healthy functioning from a DBT perspective, there are times when strong emotions do need to be actively managed so that they do not lead to problematic behavioral responses. The third component, *emotion regulation skills,* is designed to help the individual recognize and manage her feelings in adaptive ways. Through emotion regulation activities, it is hoped that clients will better understand the emotions they experience, especially as they learn to observe and describe their emotional states. It is also hoped that individuals will reduce their emotional vulnerability through physical self-care, such as developing healthy eating and sleeping habits and exercising regularly. Clients are also encouraged to engage in activities that they find pleasurable and from which they derive a sense of mastery or accomplishment; such activities generally produce positive emotional experiences. Finally, emotion regulation strives to decrease emotional suffering by helping the individual let go of (i.e., not dwell on) painful emotions through mindfulness while simultaneously changing these emotions through opposite action. Opposite action occurs when a client behaves in a manner that is incongruent with his emotional state. For example, an adolescent who is feeling upset may want to withdraw from others; opposite action would entail instead going over to a friend's house or talking to a parent. Opposite action not only creates more adaptive behavioral responses but can also change the emotion itself, serving as an emotion regulation strategy.

Finally, *interpersonal effectiveness skills* provide the individual with the ability to express beliefs and needs, set boundaries, and problem solve while carefully guarding relationships (McKay et al., 2007). Individuals with borderline traits or emotional dysregulation often struggle to maintain healthy relationships because they have only learned how to engage with others in a highly emotional manner. To improve their interpersonal interactions, clients must learn both how to manage their own strong emotions and how to relate to others in positive, adaptive ways. Through individual and group work, the client builds skills in relational areas such as balancing priorities, saying no, being assertive, negotiating, validating others, and being fair and honest. Clients are also educated about factors such as certain emotional reactions and thought patterns that can interfere with healthy relationships.

DBT has a wide variety of applications and has been successful in a variety of settings (Linehan, 1993). DBT-A applications commonly include individual, group and family components, and it has been found to reduce suicidality, parasuicidal behavior, and both internalizing and externalizing symptoms in at-risk adolescents (Fleischhaker et al., 2011; Katz, Cox, Gunasekara & Miller, 2004).

COGNITIVE-BEHAVIORAL THERAPIES FOR CHILDHOOD DISORDERS

Cognitive-behavioral work with children generally combines cognitively focused interventions, based on the principles discussed above, with behavioral principles for treatment (Blackburn et al., chapter 10, this volume). In this section, we review specific the applications of various forms of cognitive-behavioral therapies for specific childhood disorders, including anxiety, trauma, depression and eating disorders. When present in the literature, we discuss Christian adaptations for these treatments as well as spiritually focused interventions.

Anxiety

Given the nature of anxiety, which includes physiological, cognitive and behavioral components, the treatment of choice is commonly CBT, given its capacity to address multiple aspects of the experience and impact of problematic anxiety. Kendall's (1990) Coping Cat is an empirically supported program for the treatment of childhood anxiety disorders. It is effective for the treatment of both generalized anxiety and more specific anxiety disorders, including social phobia and separation anxiety disorder (see Kendall, Furr & Podell, 2010, for a review). The Coping Cat is a manualized treatment that was originally developed for use with children ages seven to thirteen, though a parallel version, the CAT, has been adapted for use with adolescents (Kendall, Choudhury, Hudson & Webb, 2002).

The *Coping Cat* manual is divided into skill-building and practice components. The treatment is structured around the FEAR Plan, an acronym that represents the process of understanding and changing anxious responses. The first component, "Feeling Frightened?" focuses on helping children identify the physiological manifestations of anxiety as well as their own anxiety triggers. Emotion identification is considered a necessary prerequisite for its effective management. In the second step, "Expecting Bad Things to Happen?" the clinician and the child work together to identify the child's cognitive distortions around anxiety. In step three, "Attitudes and Actions That May Help," anxiety management skills, such as cognitive restructuring, problem solving and relaxation, are introduced. Finally, the fourth component, "Results and Rewards," includes the concepts of self-evaluation and rewarding oneself for successful anxiety management. Initially, children are asked to help a feline character (the "Coping Cat") navigate ambiguous and anxiety-provoking situations through the use of activities such as identifying the Coping Cat's self-talk using cartoon thought bubbles. Using the workbook, children are shown different thoughts that the Coping Cat might have. Then, they are taught to modify the Coping Cat's self-talk so that it is more accurate and adaptive, resulting in the reduction of anxiety. Later in treatment, children are taught to apply the same principles to their own experiences.

In addition, children apply the FEAR plan in a graduated-exposure model involving an anxiety hierarchy. For example, a child who is socially anxious might identify (1) talking to a close friend, (2) asking a teacher for help, (3) talking in front of a class that is not his own, and (4) talking in front of his class as anxiety-provoking situations that progress from least to most stressful. In the graduated-exposure model, the client would first imagine himself in each situation, using the therapist's verbal description, while concurrently practicing relaxation techniques such as deep breathing. Later, after the child has progressed through the hierarchy in his imagination, he would be encouraged to experience each of the anxiety-provoking situations in vivo, again moving from least to most threatening using relaxation and self-talk to manage his anxiety.

Pediatric Obsessive-Compulsive Disorder

Treatment for pediatric obsessive-compulsive disorder (OCD) typically involves a combination of exposure and response prevention (ERP) and selective serotonin reuptake inhibitors (SSRIs; Franklin, Freeman & March, 2010). While ERP is traditionally considered a behavioral intervention, adaptations of this approach for children have included explicitly cognitive components. March and Mulle's (1998) ERP treatment manual begins with assessment of the nature of past and current OCD symptoms and resulting impairment. Treatment is strength-based, and client strengths are assessed early in treatment. In addition, the treatment is designed to include parents in psychoeducation as well as in assisting their children with the application of anxiety-management strategies at home. Parents should be warned that progress is not immediate, as this is a common expectation.

The treatment protocol consists of fourteen sessions over twelve weeks, including modules covering (1) psychoeducation, (2) cognitive retraining (restructuring), (3) "mapping" OCD, (4) exposure and ritual prevention, and (5) relapse prevention and generalization training. Module one, *psychoeducation*, includes information for children and parents about anxiety in general and OCD specifically. *Cognitive retraining*, the second component, involves teaching clients to use adaptive self-talk to manage the feelings, behaviors and impulses experienced with OCD. Children are taught to use adaptive self-talk to replace thoughts about their inability to manage their OCD with positive, encouraging self-statements. For example, a child with obsessions around contamination may use self-talk to help her touch a door handle at school, saying to herself, "I know how to manage my anxiety—even if this is hard, I can do it." Adaptive self-talk also encompasses the child's conversation with OCD itself, known as "talking back to OCD." For example, a child might be encouraged to say "Go away, OCD. I will decide what I want to do" or "Not this time, OCD—you can't make me wash my hands again." This form of self-talk has the effect of externalizing OCD while simultaneously increasing the child's motivation to engage in exposure and response prevention. Cognitive retraining also entails helping children reduce their attachment to obsessions, allowing them to come and go on their own accord rather than trying to control them (Franklin et al., 2010). This module is designed to build children's skills in the cognitive management of anxiety as well as to increase their self-efficacy around symptom reduction.

The third component, *mapping OCD*, focuses on outlining the child's obsessions and compulsions, triggers, and consequent thoughts and feelings. As the child's unique experience of OCD is laid out, the cognitive techniques learned earlier continue to be applied to her specific obsessions and compulsions. Module four, *exposure and ritual prevention*, reflects the "first wave" of cognitive therapies that is behavioral in nature. Following exposure to feared situations, children's anxiety, expressed in the form of obsessive thoughts or compulsive behaviors, is expected to diminish as children become desensitized to anxiety itself and are prevented from responding to it in the maladaptive ways to which they have become accustomed. When a child is exposed to an anxiety-provoking stimulus (triggering obsessions) and prevented from engaging the compulsion used to manage her anxiety, she learns that (1) her anxiety will naturally decrease with time, and (2) the compulsion is not necessary for anxiety management. Finally, *relapse prevention and generalization training* aims to equip children and parents to use the skills they have learned to manage similar or different symptoms that may emerge in the future.

Childhood Trauma

Trauma-focused cognitive-behavior therapy (TF-CBT) has become one of the most commonly used empirically supported treatments for anxiety and trauma resulting from childhood physical and sexual abuse (Cohen, Mannarino, Deblinger & Berliner, 2009; Cohen, Mannarino & Deblinger, 2010). The underlying mechanism of change within TF-CBT is exposure to past traumatic events through the development a trauma narrative. This places part of TF-CBT within the "first wave" of cognitive-behavioral treatments, as trauma-related symptoms are expected to diminish over time following imagined exposure through remembering of past traumatic events. TF-CBT also draws on interventions that are more squarely rooted in Beck's cognitive therapy. These interventions involve identifying and correcting trauma-related cognitive distortions. For example, some children blame themselves for abuse when it occurs. Boys in particular sometimes feel that they should have been stronger or able to prevent the abuse from happening. A common challenge to this kind of distortion is to refer to the policy of police officers to travel in pairs whenever they confront dangerous situations. This reminds children that even strong, trained law enforcement officials do not expect to be able to manage dangerous situations by themselves.

TF-CBT typically takes place over twelve to fourteen sessions, though the manual itself is flexible and intended to be tailored to individual children and adolescents. TF-CBT takes a multifaceted approach to treatment, summarized using the PRACTICE acronym (Deblinger, Cohen & Mannarino, 2012). The modules, which are presented in order, are as follows:

- *Psychoeducation.* Information is presented to the client and family about trauma and its effects as well as the treatment protocol.

- *Parenting skills training.* The clinician works with the parents to build parental skills around the establishment of a safe and secure environment through routine and structure; improvement in the parent-child relationship through communication skill and the use of praise; and reduction of parental reinforcement of problematic child behavior.

- *Relaxation training.* Children are taught to manage the physiological experience of anxiety through the use of relaxation techniques such as deep breathing, progressive muscle relaxation and guided imagery. Mindfulness techniques may also be introduced.

- *Affective expression and modulation.* Clinicians work with children and families to facilitate emotion identification and awareness, effective communication and listening skills around emotional expression, and adaptive management of negative emotions.

- *Cognitive coping skills.* Cognitive distortions and links among thoughts, feelings and behaviors are identified. Clients are taught to identify and challenge distortions through self-monitoring and cognitive restructuring.

- *Trauma narrative development and processing.* The focus of treatment shifts to the traumatic experience itself, and the client is encouraged to process the trauma through the creation of a "trauma narrative." A trauma narrative is the client's telling of the story of the trauma, including his subjective experience; with children, this is frequently laid out in the form of a book that may involve pictures as well as words, depending on the client's developmental level. The trauma narrative offers opportunities for exposure and desensitization as well as the identification and challenging of cognitive distortions.

- *In-vivo exposure.* Clinicians and parents work with clients to help them face anxiety-provoking stimuli related to the trauma to increase desensitization and reduce avoidance.

- *Conjoint parent-child sessions.* Depending on the needs of the individual client, parent-child sessions may focus on psychoeducation, implementation of parenting skills, parental modeling of adaptive emotion modulation, facilitation of effective communication, and/or the child's sharing the trauma narrative with the parents.

- *Enhancing safety and future development.* The final TF-CBT module focuses on building the client's safety-enhancing skills (e.g., awareness of danger, assertiveness, problem solving, and communication between parents and child about risk and safety) in order to prevent future trauma. It is emphasized that these topics must be approached cautiously and only after treatment has had a positive impact so as to avoid increasing a child's fearfulness or self-blame.

We have developed a spiritually oriented or Christian accommodative version of TF-CBT with children (Walker, Reese, Hughes & Troskie, 2010; Walker, Quagliana, Wilkinson & Frederick, 2013). This treatment manual incorporates prayer, Scripture and religious imagery with traditional TF-CBT treatment components. First, we have found that prayer is an effective adjunct to secular forms of relaxation training, particularly during deep breathing for relaxation. Prayer is also an effective means of coping with the inherent stress of discussing past abuse. We tend to focus on "simple prayer" (i.e., talking to God spontaneously and from the heart rather than in a scripted manner) as an effective means of working through spiritual struggles related to abuse during clients' telling of their trauma narratives. We also recommend prayer as a tool for coping with anxiety-provoking situations in the in vivo module and the safety planning and future development modules. Prayer can be utilized to ask God for strength and courage while experiencing anxiety as well as to reinforce truths that may help children counter distortions.

During progressive muscle relaxation religious imagery can help children and adolescents achieve a deeper level of relaxation, as described below. It may also be used in conjunction with references to Scripture during the affective expression and modulation module to assist clients with the replacement of distressing thoughts with more pleasant cognitions. It is important to remember that although we highlight spiritual interventions separately here, these interventions are presented in the context of the TF-CBT modules in actual practice. This makes their presentation more seamless and natural rather than broken into distinct "secular" and "Christian" components.

Depression

Several treatments have been found to be effective in the treatment of child and adolescent depression, including some CBT interventions. Indeed, a significant number of treatments for child and adolescent depression that are considered well established or probably efficacious are cognitive-behavioral in nature (www.effectivechildtherapy.com). Effective CBT treatment for youth can take place in either group or individual therapeutic formats and generally includes (1) psychoeducation about depression and the links among thoughts, feelings and behaviors; (2) identification of cognitive distortions and automatic thought triggers; (3) challenging distortions through cognitive restructuring; and (4) increasing involvement in enjoyable activities, particularly those that are active and/or social. CBT interventions for depression frequently include self-monitoring homework for clients in the form of a thought diary, in which a record of thoughts, feelings and behaviors throughout the week is kept to assist in the identification of cognitive distortions.

An example of a CBT treatment for childhood depression is Stark and colleagues' group intervention (Stark, Streusand, Krumholz & Patel, 2010). The program was developed for children ages nine to thirteen and assumes that depression is due to multiple causes, including neurochemical imbalances, maladaptive behavioral patterns, family stressors and cognitive distortions. In considering these multiple factors related to depression, the therapy inherently operates from a developmental psychopathology framework. The treatment itself involves teaching children a combination of coping skills, problem-solving skills and techniques for challenging cognitive distortions. Cognitive disputation is achieved via techniques such as Socratic questioning and asking children to evaluate the evidence for various beliefs related to depression. While the process of challenging cognitive distortions is similar to that used in treatments for anxiety disorders, the distortions displayed in depression are likely to reflect a negative view of oneself rather than false beliefs about external threats. Examples of common cognitive distortions among depressed individuals include black-and-white thinking ("No one likes me; I am terrible at everything"), selective abstraction ("A friend wouldn't go out on a date with me—I must be unlovable"), and focusing on the negative aspects of a situation ("I missed that one problem on the test; I am so stupid"). In addition, behavioral activation is utilized, as children keep a daily log of activities and then are encouraged to spend more time engaging in activities that they find to be mood-enhancing. Recent research has focused on the application of the model in treating depression among girls, but the manual itself can be used with boys as well.

Another example of an empirically based treatment for depression is the approach used in the Treatment for Adolescents with Depression Study (TADS Team, 2007). This multisite study examined the effectiveness of CBT and antidepressant medication alone and in combination for the treatment of depression in adolescents. The CBT treatment included individual, parent and family sessions and typical components such as psychoeducation, behavioral activation and cognitive restructuring. Adolescents treated with a combination of CBT and an antidepressant showed the greatest reduction in depressive symptoms and suicidality.

When cognitive-behavioral therapies are used to treat childhood mood disorders such as depression and anxiety, disputation of irrational beliefs, cognitive restructuring and replacing dysfunctional self-talk are core interventions. In explicitly Christian child and adolescent psychotherapy, reference to Scripture is typically used for both purposes. As others have pointed out (Tan & Johnson, 2005; Walker et al., 2012), reference to Scripture to dispute irrational beliefs can occur at several levels. Indirect reference to Scripture involves referencing biblical truths without specifically citing chapter or verse. For example, broadly speaking, a depressed Christian teenager who expresses the belief that she is unlovable could be reminded that God loves her without citing a specific Bible verse. The idea that God loves the client is consistent with truth from Scripture, but in this case, no specific Scriptures are provided.

Cognitive disputations can also be done with specific references to biblical passages. A clinician might remind the adolescent discussed above that God promises that he "will never leave you nor forsake you" (Deut 31:6) as a way to help her replace automatic thoughts that God will abandon her because of her unworthiness. A child who is socially anxious might practice reciting Isaiah 41:10 ("So do not fear, for I am with you; do not be dismayed, for I am your God. I will strengthen you and help you; I will uphold you with my righteous right hand") when he notices his distortions around fears of failure. Clinicians may choose to explicitly include the chapter and verse of the passage for the client to further familiarize him with Scripture and begin to equip him to use it on his own as a tool in cognitive restructuring.

Christian cognitive-behavior therapy for depression or anxiety may also involve guided imagery involving biblically based ideas about God and his interactions with us. As an example, a child struggling with anxiety could practice imagining Jesus holding him while doing guided imagery for relaxation training. An adolescent struggling with depression might picture Jesus walking next to her (Mt 28:20) to counter distortions about abandonment and aloneness, or picture God literally rejoicing over her (Zeph 3:17) or pouring out his love on her (Rom 5:5) when she experiences distortions about being unlovable or unworthy.

Eating Disorders

Robin and Le Grange (2010) describe behavioral family systems therapy (BFST) as the treatment of choice for teens with anorexia nervosa. BFST teaches adolescents to challenge cognitive distortions and to restructure family relationships following the restoration of weight. These interventions are implemented in the context of a multimodal treatment package that begins by teaching parents to implement an at-home behavioral weight program. Therapy then shifts to a focus on individuation from the family once the adolescent has achieved her target weight gain and is beginning to gain control over her eating habits. BFST occurs in three separate phases—assessment, weight gain and weight maintenance—that typically take place over approximately nine to sixteen months. Cognitive restructuring techniques address cognitive distortions associated with the disorder. For example, Robin and LeGrange (2010) cite the example of a teenager diagnosed with anorexia believing that "my stomach is fat and sticks out" as a cognitive distortion that occurred as she moved toward a healthy weight. The therapist working with the teenager prescribed an experiment in which the teen identified four people she trusted, then showed each person a picture of herself at various stages before and during therapy. The therapist then asked the teenager to review the various photos and

select the one that represented a "healthy" range. Three of the four people selected the current photo of the teenager as healthiest, and none of them believed that her stomach stuck out. An exercise such as this is designed to create
evidence for the adolescent that her distortions are false, equipping her to use
more accurate and helpful self-talk.

Although writing about both adolescents and adults, Richards, Hardman
and Berrett (2007) describe several spiritual problems that females with eating
disorders commonly experience. First, they suggest that eating disorders are
inherently rooted in the loss of one's spiritual identity, as attempts to control
one's weight and body image take over one's identity. In a related vein, since
eating disorders frequently involve attempts to increase control, they also note
that women and girls with eating disorders may have difficulty with the aspect
of religious faith that requires surrender on their part. Finally, they note that
many clients with eating disorders view themselves as defective and unworthy
of the love of God or other people. In addressing these problems, they recommend spiritually integrative CBT, in which Scripture is used to challenge
cognitive distortions related to these problems. For example, a teenage girl who
is struggling to view herself as lovable might challenge this cognitive distortion
by reminding herself of Romans 5:8, which states that "God shows his love for
us in that while we were still sinners, Christ died for us" (ESV).

THEORETICAL AND CLINICAL IMPLICATIONS OF DEVELOPMENTAL
PSYCHOPATHOLOGY FOR COGNITIVE-BEHAVIORAL APPROACHES

Cummings et al. (2000) suggest that developmental psychopathology provides
new frameworks for understanding and studying developmental pathways and
directing prevention and intervention programs toward resolving developmental processes underlying the onset of disorder. Furthermore, as a macroparadigm, developmental psychopathology attempts to understand the combination of intrapsychic, interpersonal and ecological influences on adjustment
over time. In this section, we discuss how some of the central elements of developmental psychopathology might inform treatment from a cognitive-behavioral perspective.

Contextualism

Contextualism is the recognition that a child is embedded in multiple layers of
context, which affect behavior and inform the understanding of functioning.
In particular, Bronfenbrenner's (1979) ecological theory considers the devel-

oping child to be embedded in a series of nested, interconnected wholes, or networks of activity, at multiple levels of analysis, including the intraindividual (e.g., interplay among biology, cognition and affect), interpersonal (e.g., family or peer relationship quality), and ecological (e.g., community, subculture, culture) subsystems. Development results from the interactions among multiple factors, events and processes at several levels that unfold over time (Cummings et al., 2000).

Contextualism can inform cognitive-behavioral therapy with children in several ways. First, children develop beliefs about themselves, others and the world through interactions with other people—including parents, siblings, teachers and peers—in multiple systems. Context is a crucial influence on the development of cognitive distortions. For example, the child who grows up in a hostile, high-conflict home and is teased and bullied by peers may be more likely to develop a negative pattern of thinking about his worth and abilities than the child who is explicitly praised, valued and cared for by others. Second, most psychotherapy with children involving CBT interventions either implicitly or explicitly addresses family systems and/or community systems factors. Implicitly, this occurs when cognitive-behavioral treatment packages include parents either by referring them to their own therapy or by asking them to reinforce treatment concepts at home. More explicitly, a number of cognitive-behavioral theorists (the authors of this chapter included) consider the importance of family therapy in treatment planning and make appropriate referrals for family therapy as warranted while simultaneously working with children individually in treatment. Because of the significant influence of the child's context on her functioning and development, including her cognitive patterns, treatment must address the influence of various systems within her environment in order for intervention to have a meaningful and lasting impact.

Risk and Protective Factors

Within their contexts, children are influenced by both risk and protective factors. In the context of cognitive-behavior therapy, clinicians must recognize that maladaptation results from the interaction of a child's biological predispositions with environmental stressors (cf. a diathesis-stress model). For example, a child with a neurochemical imbalance that places her at risk for depression is substantially more likely to be depressed when her parents are divorcing and she lives in an impoverished neighborhood. Therefore, even as they focus on addressing cognitive patterns of dysfunction, CBT clinicians may also need to address other influences on a child's functioning, including biological factors (e.g., through the use of medication) and environmental factors (e.g., through parenting skills training). Fortunately, many CBT approaches, such as TF-CBT, incorporate multifaceted approaches to treatment that address a variety of risk and causal factors.

Cicchetti (2006) suggests that in light of developmental psychopathology, clinicians must consider the impact of risk factors for a particular disorder in the context of protective factors that a child may also experience. He notes, for example, that the negative effects of maternal drug abuse may be reduced for children who are placed in adoptive homes that provide structure, active engagement, warmth and closeness. Given this pattern, cognitive-behavioral therapists should seek to identify not only the contextual risk factors that may negatively impact a child's developing thought patterns but also how these variables interact with protective factors. A child whose mother experiences severe depression that causes her to be withdrawn and unresponsive to him is at a heightened risk for depression because of the way he may attribute her behavior to causes endemic to who he is; however, if he has a warm, open relationship with his father, the ability to discuss his negative thoughts and feelings throughout his development may protect him from depression as his father challenges these distortions through his words (e.g., telling his son that his mother's depression is not his fault) and his actions (e.g., communicating his care for his son by spending time with him).

Resilience

Cicchetti (2006) defines resilience as a person's ability to successfully adapt and function competently despite experiencing chronic adversity or prolonged and severe trauma, such as childhood abuse. Studying resilience involves understanding the mechanisms and processes that lead to successful adaptation in the presence of adversity. Cognitive-behavioral therapists may be specifically interested in children's cognitive resilience. That is, how likely is a given child to be able to resist developing distorted thought patterns following exposure to risk? After being bullied repeatedly by peers, one (nonresilient) child may develop school refusal based on the belief that all children at school will be mean to him, while another (resilient) child recognizes that a few children's cruelty does not mean that his classmates will all be aggressive. It is likely that the latter child in this example possesses protective qualities such as high self-esteem, a positive relationships with parents, high intelligence and good problem-solving skills that prevent his thought patterns from becoming distorted as the result of one (or even several) negative experiences. Identifying the internal and external factors that contribute to cognitive resilience—the ability to sustain helpful, accurate, and adaptive thoughts about and perceptions of oneself and the world—will help us better intervene with children who are negatively affected by risk.

Developmental Pathways

Cummings et al. (2000) describe development as an interplay between a changing child and a changing world. As a result, there are multiple pathways to adaptive as well as maladaptive outcomes. While traditional CBT with adults is generally more individually focused, many recent applications with children and adolescents utilize cognitive-behavioral interventions within a family systems and community systems context in order to promote development in a positive direction. Children's patterns of thinking and behavior are shaped not only by their proximal experiences but also by the collection of events and interactions that have occurred in previous stages of development. As CBT clinicians, we must go beyond the surface of understanding how children's thoughts and behaviors affect their functioning and may be maladaptive and seek to recognize how they may represent the outcome of developmental processes that have led to this point. How might a child's previous interactions with family members or peers contribute to particular cognitive distortions? How might past perceived successes or failures in different domains (social, academic, athletic, artistic) predispose an adolescent to react to current experiences with particular automatic attributions about himself and his abilities? In addition, as development pathways continue, children's current patterns of functioning will affect their future mental health and well-being. How might we help a child think about and conceptualize her parents' divorce in a way that will prepare her to view her future relationships (including relationship failures) in an accurate and healthy manner? What are likely to be the ongoing behavioral outcomes for the child who exhibits unreasonable fearfulness of attending school? As CBT clinicians, we must understand a child's functioning in light of the concept of pathways.

Further, we recognize that positive cognitive and behavioral outcomes can occur as the result of many different developmental experiences and that these influences of outcomes *interact*. We cannot assess single risk factors as if they were occurring alone; rather, we must attend to risk and protective factors in each domain of a child's context in order to understand their collective and dynamic impact on behavior, cognition, and overall functioning across the course of development. For example, a child with poor critical thinking skills may be more likely to jump to an inaccurate conclusion about a peer's behavior and to react to a perceived slight with aggression; however, if this child receives emotion regulation guidance from a sensitive parent, he may learn over time to modulate his anger in a way that allows him to slow down and think about the consequences of his actions. As he grows, he is able to regulate his emotional reactions in novel social situations and cognitively process his experiences in ways that facilitate adaptive, prosocial behaviors. We cannot understand his functioning without looking at multiple influences on his development *over time*. Therefore, as clinicians, our assessment and intervention must be tailored to each child, given his unique strengths, vulnerabilities, context, and risk and protective factors, with an eye toward understanding how these influences interact to affect functioning over the course of development.

Practical Suggestions

- While many of the basic methods of traditional CBT are useful with children, they will likely need to be adapted in order to be developmentally sensitive. Be sure that children understand the terminology you use. For example, a young child may not understand the terms "cognitive distortions" or "self-talk"; instead, you could explain these concepts to the child as "thought bubbles" or "things we tell ourselves in our heads." Children may also have difficulty with abstract concepts, such as cognitive restructuring, and be aided by concrete examples or images. For example, you might use the cartoon-based image of an angel and a devil on the child's shoulders talking to him in contrasting ways to illustrate cognitive distortions (the devil) versus helpful self-talk (the angel).

- Thoroughly assess risk and protective factors *as well as* the specific ways in which they contribute to a child's thought patterns. If a child has experienced the death of a parent, how does she think about and understand that event? What does she believe caused it? What does it mean for how she views herself, other people and the world? Accurately understanding the impact of such experiences on the child's functioning will allow you to address her thoughts and behaviors directly, through CBT techniques as well as by ameliorating the negative effects of risk factors.

- Seek to understand the child's thoughts and behaviors in his context. In what ways is the child's functioning helping him *adapt* to the demands of his surroundings? For example, a child who has experienced repeated peer rejection might be socially withdrawn and state, "No one likes me—I'm never going to have any friends again." While these thoughts and behaviors are likely to interfere with healthy functioning and development, they may also serve the function of protecting the child from experiencing further rejection in interactions with peers. Understanding the adaptive nature and function of a child's thoughts and behaviors will help us replace them with patterns that meet the child's needs while helping him to adapt more appropriately to the demands of the environment.

- Given the multifaceted nature of development and functioning, treatment is best approached from multiple angles. While individual, traditional CBT work with the child may be useful, it is likely to be enhanced by work with other family members. The nature of this work will vary depending upon the presenting problem but may include psychoeducation about the nature of cognitive distortions, training with parents to reward positive behavior and ignore/punish negative behavior, and work with family members to help them identify the patterns of thinking they are modeling for the client.

CASE STUDY

Consider the following case study, amalgamated from similar clients seen by the first author in clinical practice over the years.

Dion, a sullen nine-year-old African American boy, is literally dragged into the office by his aunt and legal guardian, Ms. Jones. Close behind her is his six-year-old brother. Before the therapist can even explain the limits of confidentiality to Ms. Jones and the client, the client's younger brother notices the toys in the therapist's room and blurts out his intention to play with them. His aunt interrupts him and informs him that he needs to be quiet. Dion and his brother play together in the corner of the therapy room throughout the interview, but it is apparent that Dion is listening closely to the conversation between the therapist and his aunt.

Later in the interview, the therapist learns from Ms. Jones that Dion has been diagnosed with attention-deficit/hyperactivity disorder (ADHD) and oppositional defiant disorder (ODD). Dion displays hyperactivity and inattention at both home and school. His teacher reports that he is frequently disruptive in the classroom but that he responds positively to praise and attention; one of the most effective rewards for good behavior that she has found is allowing Dion to sit and talk with her during lunch. Dion has also recently been exhibiting school refusal; two to three mornings a week, he tells his aunt that his stomach hurts and he does not want to go to school. Some days, Ms. Jones allows him to stay home when he has a stomachache. She reports that he usually feels better by mid-morning and spends much of the day either watching television with her or following her around the house as she does chores. The therapist also learns that Dion was repeatedly physically and sexually abused before being removed from his biological parents' care by the state. Dion's father is currently in prison for assaulting another man during a drug deal, but his biological mother is seeking custody, which there is a possibility she could earn back in the next eighteen months. During the interview, the therapist notices that whenever his aunt mentions either of his parents, Dion becomes quiet and still, ceasing his play and watching the adults cautiously.

Ms. Jones frequently works afternoons and evenings at the local supermarket, so Dion and his brother are generally by themselves for a few hours after school. Dion's grandmother frequently comes over and stays with the children in the evening, making them dinner and putting them to bed. Ms. Jones states that Dion's behavior has become difficult for his grandmother to manage and wonders if she can continue to care for him while Ms. Jones is at work. Before concluding the interview, Ms. Jones states that she has been taking Dion to church in an effort to "raise him the right way." She reports that Dion enjoys interacting with the youth pastor but that he has been in frequent fights with other children at church. She ends by expressing her hope that she will get help in "raising him up in the Lord" and in controlling his behavior.

When the therapist attempts to interview Dion, Dion is willing to talk about basic topics, such as his friends and the activities he enjoys. However, when the therapist asks his about his feelings about school or his family, Dion frequently says "I don't know" or tries to change the subject. He gravitates from one toy to another in the therapy office with boundless energy and is enthralled by the contents of the therapy room. When the therapist informs him that it is time to clean up so that he can leave, Dion throws a substantial tantrum, raising his voice defiantly and pouting, resulting in his aunt threatening to give him "a whooping." Through defiant huffs, he angrily puts the toys away, refusing to acknowledge the therapist's presence on the way out the door.

In future sessions with Dion, as he begins to trust the therapist, he shares his thoughts and feelings more openly. As the therapist comes to recognize that significant portion of Dion's joys and worries revolve around the reactions of the adults in his life, he focuses on exploring these relationships in more depth with Dion. Dion reports that he often thinks about his parents and wonders what they are doing and whether they think about and miss him. He appears sad and makes little eye contact when discussing the thoughts. Dion says that he loves his aunt but that he wonders when she will become tired of taking care of him and whether he will be taken away from her too. He reports that he does not like going to school because he would rather be at home with her; the times that he is happiest is when he and his aunt spend time alone together (which generally only occurs while his brother is at school). When talking about his teacher and his youth pastor, Dion's mood brightens as he describes the conversations he enjoys having with his teacher and the way his youth pastor jokes with him and pats him on the back. However, the change in Dion's behavior is apparent when he mentions that he might not be allowed to go to youth group anymore because he keeps getting into fights with other kids. Dion notes that he really tries to get along with his peers, but he gets angry when the youth pastor pays more attention to other kids and chooses them instead of him to participate in activities and role-plays during youth group. Dion says gloomily, "I'll never be good enough for him to like me best."

This case presents a conglomerate of factors that are important to consider in working with children and teens from a developmental psychopathology perspective. In considering Dion's case, the effect of his family and his interactions with them on his developmental pathways via his thought patterns is important to consider. For example, how does Dion make sense of his family relationships based on his interactions with his parents and other caregivers over the years? How does he subsequently see and understand his world, its events and the people in it? Related, how do we as clinicians understand the developmental timing of key events in his life (e.g., his past physical and sexual abuse, his separation from his biological mother, and his subsequent change in living situation), with particular regard to how he processed these events cognitively at each age? What are some potential risk factors (e.g., lack of adult supervision, uncertain living situation, frequent school absences) that might be addressed in order to change Dion's likely outcomes? What protective factors (e.g., family religiosity, positive relationships with adults outside the family) could be recognized and sustained in order to ameliorate the impact of risk? Furthermore, how do Dion's individual characteristics (e.g., temperament, emotional regulation abilities, cognitive development, impulsivity) interact with the demands of his context? How might his gender and race have influenced previous therapists' diagnoses and treatment of him? His aunt appears to be heavily invested in his care, yet she also demonstrated a willingness to engage in physical coercion to gain his compliance. How might this parenting style on her part affect his behavior as well as his views of himself and expectations about adults, especially given his history of physical abuse? Might her parenting style be modified to better fit Dion's temperament? Finally, Ms. Jones said that she has actively engaged Dion in the church and wants help from her congregation in raising him. How well are the church generally and his youth pastor specifically equipped understand Dion's developmental trajectory and to help her shape his behavior? Finally, how do his diagnosed ADHD and past history of abuse affect his ability to experience a personal relationship with God? In what ways may his beliefs about fathers, as shaped by his relationship with his biological father as well as other adult males, shape his view of God's character, understood also in light of the normative cognitive abilities of a child his age? In this section, we apply first a developmental psychopathology framework and then a theological framework to conceptualize Dion's case.

CASE CONCEPTUALIZATION FROM A DEVELOPMENTAL PSYCHOPATHOLOGY PERSPECTIVE

Contextualism

In our view, the effects of several different levels of systems operating on Dion should be considered in his case conceptualization. Although they are not currently part of his life, Dion was initially raised by his biological parents and abused by them. The effects of their abuse on his behavior and thought patterns should be assessed and addressed with TF-CBT if necessary. In addition, the role of his current family system in contributing to or reducing his ADHD and ODD symptoms should also be considered. That is, his aunt's coercive parenting may function to gain compliance in the short run, but it may not be effective in the long term. Given Dion's history of past abuse, threats from his aunt may trigger traumatic reminders of previous physical abuse, potentially increasing his post-traumatic reactions, which may include irritability and anger. They may also affect his underlying views of himself and of adults in negative ways, inherently communicating that adults always represent a danger to his safety and well-being.

Given a contextual view of development, we believe that Dion's presenting issues warrant a combination of individual and family therapy. This is common in child cases and consistent with a developmental psychopathology framework. Individual therapy was recommended to help Dion process his past abuse, identify and challenge distorted cognitions, and help him learn to regulate his anger appropriately. Family therapy was recommended to provide support to his aunt and grandmother and to improve relational boundaries within the family. In addition, based on Dion's significant externalizing symptoms, parent management training was recommended, in which Dion's aunt and grandmother worked with a clinician to implement effective strategies for managing his behavior using consistent, appropriate consequences. Addressing Dion's symptoms at multiple levels is more likely to produce an effective and lasting impact on his development, changing the way he engages with his contexts rather than merely changing his behavior as an individual entity.

Risk and Protective Factors

The potential risk factors stemming from Dion's relationship with his parents should not be ignored, particularly as he may be placed with his mother in the future. Dion was abused in his parents' home, and his father was arrested for assault. These experiences are likely to have affected Dion's sense of safety and security in addition to having modeled aggressiveness and violence. Further, these experiences have likely affected Dion's view of himself as lovable and may underlie his drive for relationships with adults and his fearful thoughts that they are likely to abandon him. The degree to which Dion's neighborhood and surrounding community contain additional risk or protective factors should be assessed. In particular, peer groups that may serve to move him toward or away from delinquency should be considered.

In addition, the potential role of his diagnosed ADHD and his past abuse as risk factors related to his religious and spiritual functioning should be considered. His aunt expressed a desire to help him grow in his relationship with God but may have difficulty engaging him in religious socialization and instruction as a result of his ADHD symptoms. It may be helpful to educate her as well as the youth ministry staff at Dion's church about the ways Dion's individual characteristics (e.g., impulsivity, hyperactivity, aggression, trauma history) may affect his engagement with God and with peers and adults in the church. Due to his past history of abuse, Dion may have difficulty trusting God or deriving meaning from church participation. His therapist should explicitly explore whether Dion experiences any spiritual struggles stemming from his abuse and, if necessary, process them in a trauma-focused form of therapy.

Religion and spirituality may also serve a protective function for Dion. His aunt's religious commitment is evident in the initial interview. A community of Christians can provide Dion with relational support for his struggles, models for righteous behavior and a peer group dedicated to prosocial behaviors. While his relationship with God may be negatively affected by his past interactions with his parents and other adults, it may also provide an attachment base to help Dion cope with his symptoms and make meaning out of his history and experiences.

CASE CONCEPTUALIZATION FROM A THEOLOGICAL PERSPECTIVE

Although we concur with the position that children should be *valued as gifts* from God, in Dion's case, it was initially difficult for the clinician to view him in this way in their initial interactions. Early in treatment, Dion was often controlling in the therapy office and difficult for both the therapist and his aunt to view as a gift. However, the therapist worked with Dion's aunt to identify his strengths and reframe some of their thoughts about him, seeking purposefully to view Dion not as a "problem child" but as "a child who is having problems but who also has the potential for change and good behavior." As CBT clinicians, we might do well to recognize how our own thoughts about a child can become distorted if we view their behavior as representing a pattern that is difficult to break and lose hope for change. We can seek to recognize how our own views of a child interfere with our ability to work effectively with him.

When we truly value our young clients as gifts, we will take seriously Jesus' charge to welcome them and not cause them to stumble (Mt 18:5-6). As CBT clinicians, we recognize in particular the role of cognitive distortions in causing children and adults to behave in maladaptive, problematic ways, including engaging in sinful actions. If a person erroneously believes, for example, that God's love for her is based on her actions and her success in life (e.g., financially, academically, occupationally), she will live with a constant fear of never being good enough and may behave in ways that seek to maximize success, regardless of its impact on her relationships and her spiritual well-being. In the same way, if

Dion believes, based on his previous experiences, that adults are untrustworthy and likely to harm him, he may believe that this is also true of God and have difficulty believing the promises laid out in Scripture. Therefore, in recognizing the importance of cognitive patterns for a child's present and future functioning, including spiritual health, we may see cognitive restructuring as a practice with spiritual as well as psychological value. By helping a child or an adolescent to challenge the accuracy or helpfulness of distorted thoughts, particularly in light of biblical truth, we are helping her to know God more and to "demolish arguments and every pretension that sets itself up against the knowledge of God, and . . . take captive every thought to make it obedient to Christ" (2 Cor 10:5). On the contrary, if we recognize that a child is experiencing untrue ways of thinking about herself, others and the world and fail to help her change her thinking, we might be said to be causing a child to stumble. The divinely appointed responsibility to children that accompanies their gift status includes the shaping of their thoughts and behaviors, which we are in a unique role to do as clinicians.

We are also called to *respect children as persons*. This charge entails the recognition that like adults, children are fully human because they are endowed with the *imago Dei*. As fully human individuals, children are capable of experiencing a full range of emotions, thoughts and behaviors, which become more complex as development progresses. CBT clinicians who work with children recognize each of these aspects of children's functioning as valid. Furthermore, respecting children as persons means recognizing that their cognitive patterns, as discussed earlier, will impact their emotions and behavior throughout development. Children who hold strong cognitive distortions are likely to become adults who hold strong cognitive distortions. Because there is continuity in both development and personhood, we respect the adult that the child will become by setting him up for future healthy functioning, which includes addressing cognitive distortions and maladaptive behavior. In addition, along with valuing children as gifts, recognizing their creation in the image of God gives us hope for positive change. Even in Dion's case, given the presence of multiple risk factors and his highly disruptive behavior, we must remember that God has created Dion in his image. Because Dion possesses the *imago Dei*, he has the capacity to think and behave in ways that are healthy and glorifying to God and which fulfill God's purposes for him. Dion's distortions and disruptive behavior can be changed because of God's ongoing work in his life. Reminding Dion of his worth as a child of God, whom God has endowed with his image, can also serve to empower Dion and challenge his distortions of unworthiness in the eyes of others.

Finally, children are to be *viewed as agents.* This can be a challenging charge in work with children who exhibit high levels of externalizing behavior. Once, knowing he would be expected to discuss a recent episode of misbehavior at school in a therapy session, Dion engaged in a substantial temper tantrum in the waiting room of the clinic. He threw toys and refused to clean them up, proudly and loudly announcing his defiance. Consultation with a colleague helped the therapist reframe Dion's control in therapy as functional, representing his desire to be a leader rather than a follower. This reframe helped the therapist to remember to view Dion as an agent in his own development rather than to become distant in response to Dion's behavior. Dion was acting in a manner that gave him an increased sense of control over his environment and helped him adapt to a sense of lacking control, given his history of abuse and changing family settings. Dion's beliefs about his inability to hold the attention of adults in his life in adaptive ways (as this had not proven effective previously) have spurred him to act disruptively and defiantly in order to receive the attention he craves. When we view Dion as an agent, we can better understand the links among his thoughts, feelings and behaviors. In addition, we can empower Dion to change others' responses to him by changing his thoughts and behaviors. As we help Dion to identify and challenge his distorted beliefs about himself and other people, he is able to (1) correct his false beliefs and (2) change his behavior to match his new beliefs, acting in a more adaptive manner that is likely to change his developmental course.

After reframing Dion's early attempts at control in therapy, the therapist was eventually able to better empathize with Dion, helping in the formulation of a working alliance. Therapy proceeded slowly, as Dion was distrustful of the therapist's motives. In time, Dion was able to verbalize his fears of returning to his biological mother's care as well as his fear that he would not be able to live up to his aunt's strict standards for behavior. Dion was also eventually able to express his worries that he would be abused at his aunt's house or in his neighborhood. As a result, the therapist utilized the safety skills and planning module from the TF-CBT manual. Developing a sense of competency in his personal safety skills gave Dion a sense of agency that made him less vigilant and overreactive at home. In addition, the therapist worked with Dion to create a trauma narrative about his experience of abuse. During his telling of the trauma narrative, Dion was able to express his anger at God that God had not protected him from his father's abuse. Although it did not occur immediately, before he left treatment, his aunt commented that Dion had asked to go to church and that he was actively participating in youth activities there. However, Dion continued to fear that he would be returned to his biological mother. The therapist helped coach Dion on how to discuss this fear with his Department of Child and Family Services caseworker. Although the caseworker was not able to guarantee Dion his future placement, the experience of expressing himself assertively was effective in reducing Dion's anger because it helped challenged his belief that he could only gain adults' attention through misbehavior and explosive anger.

The therapist also engaged Dion's aunt and grandmother in individual sessions. Dion's aunt was initially interested in learning techniques for managing Dion's behavior; however, she had difficulty attending sessions regularly due to her work schedule. With Ms. Jones' permission, Dion's therapist began working with his grandmother on parent training. It soon became apparent that she lacked the energy to consistently monitor and discipline Dion and that she was concerned about a possible physical altercation if he became too upset. Therefore, the therapist helped Dion's grandmother consider and evaluate potential options for addressing Dion's behavior effectively. She eventually decided to enroll Dion in an after-school program at her church for several hours immediately after school and to enlist the help of a male friend from church in watching Dion at home in the evenings. With the support of her friend, Dion's grandmother was able to apply consistent consequences for Dion's behavior. Although Dion's misbehavior spiked immediately afterward in response, his compliance was eventually gained after she modified material presented to her in parent training. In her case, she applied the first author's suggestion to allow Dion to experience the law of natural consequences described in Galatians by asking her male friend from church to take several of Dion's prized possessions (including his video game system and accompanying games) and put them up in storage until he could behave at home. The friend did, and it took approximately a month, but Dion became more compliant over time to the point where she no longer felt concerned.

After approximately ten months of treatment, the Department of Child and Family Services determined that Dion's biological mother had failed to complete the conditions of her required program to regain custody of him. This fact was processed in both individual therapy with Dion and family therapy with Dion, his aunt and his grandmother. Prior to terminating treatment, Dion was legally adopted by his aunt—an act that was celebrated with cake in a family session. Through individual work with the therapist and the establishment of a stable home environment in which consequences were predictable and stable, Dion was able to reframe his distortions about himself and others and to behave in more appropriate ways that were undergirded by his new way of thinking about the world.

CONCLUSION

Clinicians who work with children and adolescents have a complex but sacred responsibility. Work that is cognitive-behavioral in nature focuses on the problematic impact of irrational, inaccurate and unhelpful thought patterns on children's emotions, behaviors and functioning. However, from a developmental psychopathology perspective, concepts such as developmental pathways, risk and protective factors, and contextual influences must be considered in concert with cognitive processes. As a result, treatment commonly entails collaboration with psychiatrists, teachers and school personnel, youth pastors, and other professionals from various community agencies with whom clients have contact in order to fully understand the child's environment and adaptation. Even in light of the complexity of our work as child and adolescent clinicians, we believe deeply in its inherent value. We view integrative Christian psychotherapy as an opportunity to look inside the hearts of our child and teenage clients, to see them the way that God sees them, and to help them become the people God created them to be.

12

Family Systems Approaches to Treatment

Sandra Y. Rueger and David van Dyke

And he passed in front of Moses, proclaiming, "The LORD, *the* LORD,
the compassionate and gracious God, slow to anger, abounding in love
and faithfulness, maintaining love to thousands, and forgiving wickedness,
rebellion and sin. Yet he does not leave the guilty unpunished; he
punishes the children and their children for the sin of the
parents to the third and fourth generation.

EXODUS 34:6-7

There is no doubt that it is around the family and the home
that all the greatest virtues, the most dominating
virtues of human society, are created,
strengthened and maintained.

WINSTON CHURCHILL

Resilience does not come from rare and special qualities,
but from the everyday magic of ordinary, normative human resources
in the minds, brains, and bodies of children, in their families
and relationships, and in their communities.

ANN MASTEN

HOW ARE FAMILIES INVOLVED in the healthy development of children? How do children affect family interactions? The writer of Exodus speaks to the reality of both joy and pain experienced in families and the ways in which we pass on legacies of functioning, whether blessings or curses, to our children and even beyond to subsequent generations. Consistent with this view, Winston Churchill recognized the importance of the family in the healthy development of both children and, ultimately, our society. The quote by developmental psychopathologist Ann Masten echoes the first two quotes, highlighting the important role that families and family relationships play in the adaptational systems from which children and adolescents draw strength and healthy development in the face of adversity (Masten, 2001).

The idea that our society's well-being, not just the well-being of the child, hinges on the health of relationships in the family underscores (1) the importance of focusing on family functioning as context for the treatment of children and adolescents and (2) the value in understanding a systems approach to working with families. These foci are consistent with scriptural notions of the family as the context in which children experience the love and grace that God intends to empower them to healthy maturity and deeper levels of intimacy in relationships (Balswick & Balswick, 2007). However, because we live in a fallen world, all families fall short in the provision of the love, grace and adaptational resources that were intended by God and, worse yet, can contribute to the challenges and adversity with which youth must contend during development. Thus, working effectively with children and adolescents to help them overcome risk trajectories involves an intentional focus on families in order to strengthen or restore their protective role in the lives of youth.

As such, the goal of this chapter is to provide an integrative approach for more effective work with children and their families within a developmental psychopathology framework grounded in a Christian belief system. The field of developmental psychopathology acknowledges the importance of understanding the ways in which adaptive systems across multiple levels (e.g., biological, psychological and social-contextual) impact and are impacted by development and how these systems either support or hinder a child or adolescent's developmental trajectory. It is our belief that a better understanding of family systems theories can inform the assessment and treatment of youth from a developmental psychopathology approach and increase understanding of the ways in which child or adolescent behavior serves a function in a family context.

A clear understanding of the theoretical background of family systems approaches and the fundamental concepts from which current systemic interventions are drawn is important to facilitating an integration of systemic family therapy with this broader developmental psychopathology framework. Thus, we will provide a general overview of family systems theories and current treatment models and trends in the field of family therapy. We will also review concepts from developmental psychopathology that are particularly relevant to working from a family systems approach. Further, as clinicians and developmental psychopathologists who are Christian, we recognize the value and importance that God places on children and their role in families and in society as a whole. This integrative family therapy/developmental psychopathology framework will be placed within the context of an explicitly Christian perspective. We will draw from the three main themes regarding children woven throughout this book—children as valued, respected persons with moral and spiritual agency (Miller-McLemore, 2003). We will end with a case example that demonstrates one way in which this integration can look in clinical practice.

It should be noted that as clinicians, we follow the ethical principle of respecting our clients' dignity and rights and work with the utmost respect for cultural, individual and role differences, including those based on religion. Thus, the overall goal of this chapter is to provide a Christian integrative perspective on family therapy based in a developmental psychopathology framework that can be useful to a clinician whether working with a family who is actively engaged in their Christian faith and spiritual life and is seeking treatment from a Christian perspective, or with a family who has little interest in bringing issues of faith or spirituality into the therapy room. As such, the case example will also highlight ways in which the treatment approach could be modified based on the values and faith background of the presenting family.

A FAMILY SYSTEMS APPROACH TO TREATMENT

Basic Assumptions

Although family systems theories each have their own unique theoretical emphasis and clinical focus for intervention, there are basic assumptions common across all family systems theories: family as unit of analysis, circular causality, family homeostasis and feedback loops. A central tenant of family systems theory is that the loci of pathology are primarily within relationships, not within an individual person (Smith & Hamon, 2012). When the focus of treatment is on *the family as the unit of analysis*, then the goal is to understand the nature and workings of relationships in the family to change patterns of relationships to allow new possibilities. However, systemic therapists can work clinically with an individual (e.g., child, adolescent, adult) as well as with dyads (e.g., couples, parent-child) or families.

Circular causality is another basic assumption that focuses on how influence in a family is reciprocal (e.g., individuals are affecting others and affected by others) and maintained through interacting loops of repeating cycles between family members (Smith & Hamon, 2012; Nichols, 2010). Models that are founded on linear explanations of mental illness and psychopathology (e.g., individual therapy and medical models) treat emotional and psychological problems as symptoms of internal dysfunction with historical, static causes. Linear explanations often focus on *content* (e.g., why an event/emotion is happening). However, circular and reciprocal explanations focus on *process and context* (e.g., what or how an event/emotion is happening) and take into account mutual influences and mutual interactions among persons *and* context. This reciprocity necessitates the treatment of distress in one family member because that person's distress will affect various family processes, such as patterns of communication, family structures and behavioral sequences.

It is not uncommon for families to come to therapy thinking of their problems in linear terms. For example, parents may bring a "surly and irresponsible" twelve-year-old to therapy with concerns that there is something wrong with the young adolescent that requires "fixing." Although there may be causal factors that are typically conceptualized as unilateral influences (e.g., personal traits related to difficulties with emotion regulation, low levels of serotonin, lack of appropriate parenting skills), assumptions about unilateral causal factors can lead to blaming and finger pointing and, ironically, to feelings of helplessness in a situation. Helping families to see the circularity in problem formation and maintenance, which is a primary goal across all family systems models, can help family members move beyond looking at problematic situations in terms of victims and villains and empower them to reconsider aspects of the problem that they can influence. It may be that the twelve-year-old boy has been quietly sad since the death of his grandmother two years ago and his surly behavior distracts the family from the pain each member is feeling about this significant loss. The parents can be helped to recognize that their son only became the focus of concern and attention when he began withdrawing and not completing his chores in the last three months, and that his irritability is often in response to his parents' badgering and scolding him for being "irresponsible." Further complicating the situation is the father's grief over the loss of his own mother; as a result he has less emotional energy and fewer resources to provide the support his son needs to deal with this significant loss.

Negative and positive feedback loops from cybernetic theory as applied to family functioning are also central to family systems theories (Smith & Hamon, 2012; Nichols, 2010). Cybernetic theory focuses on feedback mechanisms in self-regulating systems and the ways in which a system maintains homeostatic balance by using information about its performance as feedback. Homeostasis refers to a process of self-regulation within a system with a goal of maintaining stability in that system. When applied to family systems, *family homeostasis* helps to explain the tendency of families to resist change and maintain a certain balance of functioning. A *negative feedback loop* provides error-correcting information and directs a system back to its original state. For example, an eleven-year-old child stays out past 10:00 p.m. (behavior moving away from the family expectation to obey a curfew rule) and responds to her parents' yelling (feedback) with feelings of guilt and remorse by coming home on time the next weekend (feedback reduces change to restore homeostasis = negative feedback loop). A *positive feedback loop* provides information that amplifies a process of change. For instance, a fifteen-year-old stays out past his curfew, but he responds to his parents' yelling (feedback) with anger and resentment and comes home past curfew the following week (feedback encourages change away from homeostasis = positive feedback loop). It is important to recognize that negative feedback loops provide information that maintains stability, whether this state of homeostasis is adaptive or maladaptive, and positive feedback loops provide information that facilitates changes, whether the new end state is adaptive or maladaptive. Understanding the processes of feedback loops and underlying family homeostasis can clarify mechanisms that maintain either a healthy sense of stability or resistance to needed change. In addition to these fundamental concepts common across systemic family therapy models, there are also systemic concepts relevant to integration with developmental psychopathology that are uniquely tied to specific models.

Theoretical Models

Classic systemic models. The role of anxiety and tensions between equally important but opposing needs for connectedness and individuality as precipitants to unhealthy family dynamics is emphasized in *Bowenian family systems theory* (Kerr & Bowen, 1988). Bowen believes that healthy individuals have high levels of *self-differentiation*, which is the ability to be intentional in balancing internal tensions and interpersonal boundaries. Those with lower levels of self-differentiation are prone to handle internal anxiety with unhealthy family processes, such as *triangulation,* or the avoidance of anxiety that exists between two people by pulling in a third person or object (e.g., alcohol, work, affairs, sporting teams). Triangles are considered the smallest stable unit and can provide a sense of stability to the original dyad (e.g., a three-legged stool provides stability). For example, a husband and wife who have low levels of self-differentiation are more likely to experience conflicts as overly anxiety-producing, so they manage their anxiety and seek stability by focusing on a third "party," such as problems with a child. As long as the child misbehaves (third leg of the stool), the couple can join together to deal with the situation and ease (i.e., distract from) the anxiety they experience in their relationship. However, the cost of triangulation is unresolved conflict for the couple and stunted emotional growth for the child, which leads to low levels of self-differentiation in the child (Kerr & Bowen, 1988; Nichols, 2010). This child will then be vulnerable as an adult to marrying another person with similar levels of self-differentiation and detouring marital conflicts by overly focusing on their child. This process, by which unhealthy patterns of functioning are passed down through the generations via interlocking relational triangles, is called *multigenerational transmission.* A key assessment and intervention tool in Bowenian therapy for tracking patterns across the generations is the *genogram*, a visual representation of at least three generations in the family (McGoldrick, Gerson & Petry, 2008). Through the use of a genogram, information about family structure, relationships, and important facts and patterns is gathered to inform assessment of family functioning and intervention decisions. Ultimately, the goal of Bowenian therapy is to help families change unhealthy patterns by strengthening the capacity for at least one family member to choose actions purposefully, even in the face of stress and family conflict (McGoldrick & Carter, 2001).

Another important concept in Bowenian theory is the idea that family development parallels the developmental stages of individual family members, and that family stress is greatest during transitions in the *family life cycle* (Mc-Goldrick, Carter & Garcia-Preto, 2011). Family life cycle theory posits that the family progresses through different stages of life, including young adults separating from parents, marriage and the coming together of two families, the birth of a baby and adjusting to children, changes during adolescence, launching children and dealing with empty nesting, growing older, and dealing with losses through death. Family life cycles include different stages for families who have experienced divorce and remarriage or families with parents who have never married and will vary depending on the cultural background of the family. Common to all life cycle stages is the notion that transitions are particularly stressful, and family problems are often precipitated in part by the stress of the transition.

Structural family systems theory stresses the importance of an appropriate *family hierarchy,* with parents in healthy caretaking and authority roles over the children, and clear *boundaries* for healthy family functioning (Minuchin, 1974; Nichols, 2010). Parental failure to provide guidance and nurture in a family are seen as indications of inappropriate hierarchical structure and poor family boundaries, whether too diffuse (leading to *enmeshed* relationships) or too rigid (leading to *disengaged* relationships), as sources of individual problems. Unhealthy *coalitions* and *scapegoating* processes among family members play a key role in conflict avoidance. Coalitions involve an alliance between two members of a family against a third; a cross-generational coalition is of most concern, as this involves an inappropriate alliance between a parent and child against the other parent or another member of the family. This concept is very similar to the concept of triangulation from Bowenian theory.

Among the many techniques unique to structural family therapy, *joining* and *restructuring* are central. Joining a family, or entering into the family system in a way that fosters trust and rapport, allows the therapist to intervene and alter family structure (e.g., creating a more appropriate family hierarchy or more appropriate boundaries between family members or between the family and other larger systems). *Enactments*, or opportunities to observe a family or purposeful elicitation of typical family interactions surrounding the presenting problem, can be used to assess family functioning or intervene to produce a therapist-directed, in-session change in behavior (Minuchin & Fishman, 1981). For example, a therapist may ask the parents and their six-year-old daughter to show him what happens when the mother tries to get the child to finish her dinner and what the father is doing when this is happening. Alternatively, the therapist could ask the family of an adolescent who is presenting with depression to enact a conversation in which both parents are able to listen to the ways in which the teen has felt unimportant without trying to defend themselves or provide answers.

Postmodern models. *Narrative therapy* and *solution-focused therapy* are based on a postmodern constructivist philosophy, which posits that we construct our own realities and that there is no truth other than what we create (Nichols, 2010). Narrative therapy emphasizes the power of story and focuses on the family's dominant narrative. Families make sense of their shared experience but also maintain their reality through the continual retelling of these primary stories (or dominant discourses). The family of a nine-year-old girl who is constantly disagreeing with her parents might construct stories such as: she is naughty and disrespectful; she is defiant; she is passionate about her beliefs; she is trying to be helpful to the best of her ability. Each of these stories creates a certain reality about the girl and her relationship with her parents. The first two stories (naughty/defiant) may be seen as negative, oppressive stories that lead to narrow and self-defeating attitudes and behaviors perhaps rooted in cultural themes and messages from society (e.g., good girls keep quiet). The other two stories (passionate/helpful) construct a different reality of the girl, her relationships and her intent.

One focus of narrative approaches with children is on the *externalization of the problem*, which can help a family and child start to separate the person from the problem, create new meanings of the presenting problem through the stories they tell and ultimately find new ways to empower change (Freeman, Epston & Lobovits, 1997). For example, the therapist can begin to talk with a family of a child with ADHD about hyperactivity as its own entity, and the family could even be encouraged to provide a name for the hyperactivity: "So, Billy was having a fairly good day until 'Joey' (the hyperactivity) came out again and kept him from being able to finish his homework without the constant reminders and yelling. I wonder, have there been times that Billy was able to get his homework done, even when Joey was around? Billy, what could you do differently next time Joey comes out during homework time? Mom and Dad, what could you do to help Billy tell Joey to go sit down in the corner until he is done with his math?" A focus on *sparkling events* or *unique outcomes* (i.e., times when a client was not affected by the problem) is key to changing a problem-saturated story to one that is more adaptive (Freedman & Combs, 1996; Nichols, 2010).

Solution-focused therapy also emphasizes the importance of shifting perceptions in fostering change, but focuses on past solutions from the family's repertoire. It is a strengths-based approach; the underlying belief is that the family already has access to the solutions but is prevented from utilizing them because of their problem-focused perspective (De Shazer, 1985; 2005). Thus, an important aim in therapy is helping family members shift their thinking from trying to understand the presenting problem to remembering times when the family or individual did not have the problem and fostering a change process that involves intentionally implementing past solutions.

The hallmark intervention of solution-focused therapy is *the miracle question*: "Suppose one night while you were asleep, a miracle occurred and your problem was solved. When you wake up, how would you know that this miracle had occurred? What would be different?" The miracle question helps to guide goal setting by helping the client focus on what life could look like if change occurred, as well as to facilitate change from a problem-focused mindset to one focused on solutions. The scaling question also facilitates a focus on solutions: "On a scale from 0 to 10, with 0 being the worst depression you have ever felt and 10 being the best you have felt, like after the miracle happens, how do you feel now?" If the client says 3, then the therapist asks, "What would it take for you to feel like a 4? What would have to be different?" A focus on exceptions (very similar to a focus on unique outcomes in narrative therapy) as well as questions about how the family and/or family member has managed to cope thus far can also make the problem feel more controllable and foster hope for change (De Shazer, 1988; Miller & Berg, 1995; Nichols, 2010).

Integrative approaches and common factors. These classic and postmodern family therapy models, along with others not summarized in this chapter (e.g., strategic: Haley, 1987; cognitive-behavioral: Dattillo, 2010; experiential: Satir, 1983; object relations family therapy: Scharff & Scharff, 1987) guided the way to a family focus in child and adolescent treatment beginning in the late 1960s and early 1970s. The current movement in family therapy is toward integration of model-based treatment approaches (e.g., Breunlin, Pinsof, Russell & Lebow, 2011; Gouze & Wendel, 2008; Lebow, 2005; Pinsof, Breunlin, Russell & Lebow, 2011). These integrative approaches are consistent with the biopsychosocial emphasis of developmental psychopathology and include a consideration for individual therapy and medication management as needed as well as interventions in extra-familial systems (Hoagwood, Burns, Kiser, Ringeisen & Schoenwald, 2001).

Integrative module-based family therapy (IMBFT; Gouze & Wendel, 2008) is a framework that guides clinicians through a diagnostic assessment and evaluation of nine psychosocial domains of functioning for systemic case conceptualization. In addition to consideration of psychiatric/related medical conditions, psychosocial domains of functioning include attachment/relationship quality, family structure, family communication, developmental issues, affect regulation, behavior regulation, cognitive/narrative concerns, mastery and community. Assessment of these domains includes a rating of stability of symptoms and consideration for both strengths and weaknesses in the family to guide case conceptualization and treatment planning using evidence-based treatments and best practice standards. IMBFT was developed for use in a multidisciplinary setting, but this approach can be used by clinicians in any setting to guide assessment and treatment planning for family therapy that is consistent with developmental psychopathology. Wendel and Gouze (2010) have developed a module-based assessment with sample questions for each domain to guide the diagnostic interview.

The newest integrative framework is the integrative problem-centered metaframeworks model (IPCM; Breunlin et al., 2011; Pinsof et al., 2011). IPCM is a multisystemic perspective for working with families, couples and individuals that combines two previously established integrative models: integrative problem-centered therapy (Pinsof, 1996) and the metaframeworks model (Breunlin, Schwartz & MacKune-Karrer, 1992). IPCM therapy is guided by a "blueprint" for organizing and integrating various models of family therapy, which includes hypothesizing, planning, conversing and feedback. More specifically, this model guides therapists in developing (1) hypotheses about constraints in the client's life that prevent problem resolution and (2) a treatment plan based on these hypotheses. The IPCM framework integrates specific family therapy models within "planning metaframeworks" (Pinsof et al., 2011) and emphasizes the use of "common factor" strategies and techniques that cut across models (Sprenkle, Davis & Lebow, 2009).[1] Treatment planning is fo-

---

[1]Consistent with IPCM, the family therapy literature has been increasingly influenced by a consideration of general therapeutic factors that drive effective therapy, often referred to as "common factors"

cused on the client's presenting problem so that all interventions are linked to the presenting concern in some way, and regular communication and evaluation of results with the client guides decisions to modify the formulation and intervene again with a different empirically validated treatment if intervention is not initially successful (Breunlin et al., 2011).

Empirical Basis of Family Systems Concepts and Processes

The empirical study of family process and interactional sequences can be a challenge because of the complexities of studying the recursive family processes central to family systems theories. However, there is growing support in the literature for the relationship between systemic family concepts and processes and child psychopathology. For example, a wide range of children's behavior and psychological problems—such as depression, anxiety and attention-deficit/hyperactivity disorder—has been associated with structural family therapy concepts of hierarchical structure (Shaw, Criss, Schonberg & Beck, 2004) and enmeshed or diffuse boundaries in marital, co-parental, and parent-child relationships (Davies, Cummings & Winter, 2004; Jacobvitz, Hazen, Curran & Hitchens, 2004). For example, kindergarteners in enmeshed and disengaged families show greater internalizing and externalizing symptoms, both concurrently and one year later, and development of these individual symptoms are mediated by insecurity in the interparental relationship (Davies et al., 2004). In addition, less appropriate family hierarchies (via maternal report of parenting behaviors and observational coding of intergenerational boundaries assessed when youth were ten years old) are associated with more antisocial behaviors in youth one year later (Shaw et al., 2004). There is also evidence for the mediating role of parent-child conflict in relation to the impact of marital conflict on child outcomes (El-Sheikh & Elmore-Station, 2004; Grych, Raynor & Fosco, 2004; Lindahl, Malik, Kaczynski & Simons, 2004), which supports the concept of triangulation from Bowenian and structural theories. In addition, a review of twenty different meta-analyses of various marriage and family therapy (MFT) interventions demonstrated that MFT interventions were comparable to or better than alternative treatments, including

(Sprenkle et al., 2009). Four common factors unique to systemic family therapy include relational conceptualization of the problem (keeping the whole family system in mind in case conceptualization), expanded direct treatment system (making efforts to include more than the identified patient), expanded therapeutic alliance (effectively joining with each family member, family subsystems and the family as a whole) and disruption of dysfunctional relational patterns (Sprenkle & Blow, 2004; Sprenkle et al., 2009).

traditional individual and medical treatments (Shadish & Baldwin, 2009).

The use of empirically supported treatments (ESTs) has been emphasized in clinical psychology and psychiatry, with the randomized clinical trial as the gold standard for evaluation of clinical interventions (Chambless & Hollon, 1998). There are now several family-based interventions that incorporate systemic concepts and processes that are considered ESTs for treatment of child and adolescent psychopathology (see Lebow, 2005, for a review). For example, multidimensional family therapy (Liddle, Rodriguez, Dakof, Kanzki & Marvel, 2005), multisystemic family therapy (Henggeler, Clingempeel, Brondino & Pickrel, 2002), functional family therapy (Sexton & Alexander, 2005) and brief strategic family therapy (Szapocznik, Hervis & Schwartz, 2003) are considered ESTs for treatment of a broad range of externalizing disorders, including conduct disorder, substance abuse and delinquency, and attachment-based family therapy (ABFT; Diamond, 2005) is considered an EST for adolescent depression. The following is a brief overview of selected family-based ESTs that can be used for two common presenting childhood problems: depression and externalizing disorders.

Depression. Attachment-based family therapy (Diamond, 2005) is a family-based EST developed to address adolescent depression. The underlying assumption of ABFT, based on attachment theory, is that problems in the parent-child relationship have led to poor attachment bonds, which interfere with healthy family functioning and lead to depression in the adolescent. ABFT utilizes interventions from emotion-focused therapy (Greenberg and Johnson, 1988) and structural family therapy (Minuchin, 1974) to address problems contributing to adolescent depression, such as parental criticism, adolescent motivation, parental stress and ineffective parenting, family disengagement and conflict, affect constriction, and adolescent negative self-concept. Reframing and enactments from structural theory are primary intervention strategies. Reframing helps the family to shift from the identified patient as the problem to the family as the cure. Use of enactments help to focus sessions on content and affect in need of repair (i.e., family dynamics that led to attachment problems and vulnerable emotions). Alliance building with both the adolescent and the parents is a central clinical task. Ultimately, the goal is to facilitate rebuilding of trust and intimacy in the parent-teen relationship as the adolescent discloses his concerns and parents respond with sensitivity and empathy. A more positive relationship with parents is then used as a new, secure base from which the adolescent can explore his autonomy and competencies and rebuild his life at school with peers.

Externalizing problems. Empirically supported family-based treatments for externalizing problems in childhood, such as oppositional defiant disorder (ODD), focus on building more effective parenting skills (e.g., Parent Management Training; Barkley, 1997). These behaviorally based interventions focus on the parent-child relationship and aim to change parenting behaviors to break the coercive family process of mutually reinforcing negative behaviors between parent and child (Patterson, 1982). These interventions have been described in more detail in a previous chapter (Blackburn et al., chapter 10, this volume). In addition to these interventions, brief strategic therapy (BST; Szapocznik et al., 2003) is a family-based EST that focuses on behavior problems in adolescence, including ODD, conduct disorder, delinquency, and substance abuse and dependence.

The theoretical foundation of BST is systemic in that members of a family are considered interdependent and interrelated. Thus, the behavior of the adolescent is evaluated and treated within the larger context of the family. BST aims to change maladaptive interactional patterns in three broad stages: joining, assessment and restructuring. The first stage of BST involves the therapist joining a family in their current pattern of functioning by validating each family member and the family as a whole. Joining serves several important functions in BST, including building rapport, establishing positive regard and trust, and facilitating assessment of family functioning. The second stage involves assessing the family and developing a clinical formulation to guide treatment decisions. Enactments are used to assess family interactions and formulate a picture of their function along five dimensions: organization (family hierarchy, organization of subsystems and family communication), resonance (family boundaries and the degree to which family members are sensitive to each others' needs and emotionally connected to one another), developmental stage (family's awareness of the appropriate tasks and roles of its life stage and barriers to managing the transition), identified patienthood (the degree to which the family places blame on one person for all the family problems), and conflict resolution (the degree to which conflicts are overt and allowed to emerge, and barriers to effectively resolving conflicts, such as denial, avoidance or diffusion). The final stage is focused on restructuring the family in order to facilitate change in maladaptive interactional patterns. The four restructuring techniques used in BST are focusing on process over content, reframing negative aspects of functioning to shift family perceptions of the problem (e.g., anger as pain or loss; conflicted relationships as close and passionate), restructuring boundaries and alliances to be more adaptive, and use of in-session and out-of-session tasks geared toward changing maladaptive interaction patterns (Szapocznik et al., 2003).

Summary of Family Systems Approaches

The evolution of family therapy began with the development of distinct family systems theories as a response to the individual focus of psychology and development in the mid-twentieth century and focused attention on pathology residing not in individuals but in relational systems. Integrative approaches have guided family therapy to consider a wider range of factors influencing the development of child psychopathology, including individual and contextual factors (Breunlin et al., 2011; Gouze & Wendel, 2008; Pinsof et al., 2011). The current emphasis in the broader field of clinical psychology on the use of ESTs has also impacted the field of family therapy. Several family-based ESTs include elements of systemic interventions, such as reframing to facilitate engagement and motivation (Liddle et al., 2005) and enactment to change problematic parent-adolescent interactions (Sexton & Alexander, 2005). Some of these ESTs rely more heavily on systemic models, notably structural/strategic (Szapocznik et al., 2003) and emotion-focused family therapy (Diamond, 2005; Efron, 2004; Johnson & Lee, 2000), and include a focus on process versus content, joining, reframing, and working with boundaries and alliances.

In a parallel process, individually focused disciplines, such as clinical psychology, psychiatry and developmental psychology, have broadened their focus to include larger family and contextual factors (e.g., Stiles-Shields, Hoste, Doyle & Le Grange, 2012: Wells, 2005; Young & Fristad, 2007). Although this chapter focuses on family systems theoretical models and systemic elements of family-based interventions, it is important to note the vital role of families in the treatment of child and adolescent problems in the mental health community. For example, family-based treatment of anorexia nervosa includes family participation to support renourishment, establish independence around weight management, and facilitate a healthy relationship between parent and adolescent (Le Grange, Crosby, Rathouz & Leventhal, 2007; Lock, Le Grange, Agras, Moye, Bryson & Jo, 2010). Family-focused treatment of bipolar disorder (FFT; Miklowitz et al., 2004) includes psychoeducation on the disorder, communication skills training and problem-solving skills training. Currently, there is tremendous overlap in these disciplines as all recognize the importance of a range of factors for child problems (biological, psychological, family and larger contextual factors), which is consistent with developmental psychopathology.

THEORETICAL AND PRACTICAL IMPLICATIONS OF DEVELOPMENTAL PSYCHOPATHOLOGY FOR FAMILY SYSTEMS APPROACHES

As described throughout this book, developmental psychopathology is a multidisciplinary approach that applies principles from the study of development to the understanding of maladaptation as well as healthy adaptation. The aim of developmental psychopathology is to integrate knowledge across disciplines to create a unique, multisystemic perspective for understanding child functioning (Cicchetti, 2006). There are several concepts integral to understanding child and adolescent development from a developmental psychopathology framework, including normalcy/abnormality, risk and protective factors, trajectories of development, and equifinality and multifinality (Flanagan & Hall, this volume). There is considerable overlap in core developmental psychopathology concepts and family systems theory. A closer consideration of the similarities in each perspective can be useful for informing clinical practice from an integrative family systems/developmental psychopathology approach in order to expand and broaden the scope and effectiveness of interventions within families.

Key Overlapping Concepts

Normalcy and abnormality. In developmental psychopathology, a consideration of normalcy and abnormality in functioning is based on the belief that understanding both normal and abnormal development is vital to efforts to intervene with childhood disorders. Normalcy from a family systems perspective can be viewed as a function of cohesion in relationships (how the family balances emotional bonding and togetherness with individuality and separateness) and adaptability of roles and rules (how flexible the family is with regard to changing roles, relationships and rules in times of stress; Olson & Gorall, 2003). Healthy family functioning is viewed on a continuum (from enmeshed to diffuse cohesion, and from rigid to chaotic adaptability) rather than discrete categories of "functional" or "dysfunctional." In addition to balance and flexibility of family functioning, normalcy is defined in relation to culture and societal norms. Thus, family functioning is considered adaptive at different points along the continuum on cohesion, adaptability and communication depending on the cultural and contextual factors impacting a family. For example, families from a collectivist culture that highly values interdependence among family members could function in a manner that looks to be more on the enmeshed end of the cohesion dimension but still be considered healthy and normal within their cultural context. Families living in poverty and high crime areas may need to function with higher levels of rigidity in roles in order to offer protection and guidance to children. However, the more extreme ranges of functioning along these dimensions, even within cultural contexts, are considered unbalanced and present risk for maladaptive responses to stress.

In defining abnormality, family systems theories focus on the "stuck" system and mutually influencing, relational trajectories rather than defining abnormality in terms of the individual diagnostic categories found in the *DSM*. This view is consistent with criticisms of the use of *DSM* diagnostic system in the developmental psychopathology approach (Flanagan & Hall, chapter 1, this volume). The core systemic understanding from a family systems perspective is that individual functioning cannot be understood apart from the context of relationships. More specifically, the use of an individual diagnosis implies a linear explanation that the maladaptation related to a presenting symptom lies solely with one family member. Thus, both fields find the current *DSM*-based diagnostic system to be potentially misleading, as symptoms are identified and considered often without taking into account the larger context. The diagnosis of oppositional defiant disorder (ODD) is a prime example in that a child can be given this diagnosis if she manifests four of eight symptoms, without regard for the capacity of parents to provide the structure and family environment needed for healthy child development. The use of such a diagnosis, from a family systems perspective, only serves to blame one family member for a dysfunctional system and enforces a linear explanation for these behavior problems.

Risk and protective factors. Risk factors are negative influences that can disrupt the process of healthy development and increase the likelihood of a negative outcome (Masten et al., 1990). Risk factors associated with maladaptive family processes include regular experience of triangulation in family relationships (El-Sheikh & Elmore-Station, 2004; Grych et al., 2004; Lindahl et al., 2004), inappropriate boundaries (whether enmeshed or rigid) between family members (Davies et al., 2004; Jacobvitz, et al., 2004), or hostile family interactions and expressed emotions (Miklowitz, 2004). Protective factors are positive influences and characteristics that support the process of healthy development or buffer individuals or families from experiences of risk or adversity, increasing the likelihood of a positive outcome. Family processes that offer protection include a combination of warmth and appropriate hierarchical structure in the parent-child relationship (authoritative parenting; Baumrind, 1966; 1991; Lamborn, Mounts, Steinberg & Dornbusch, 1991; Maccoby & Martin, 1983), perceptions of available parental support (Rueger, Malecki & Demaray, 2010), and clear, healthy communication patterns (Gutman, Eccles, Peck & Malanchuk, 2011).

Both developmental psychopathology and family systems approaches emphasize reducing risk and increasing protective factors to shore up a family's resources (Masten & Coatsworth, 1998). For example, reducing negativity in communication, restructuring family boundaries to be less rigid or enmeshed (e.g., facilitating more appropriate closeness in family relationships), or guiding parents to provide appropriate nurture and guidance in a family (e.g., helping parents set and enforce boundaries for appropriate behavior) reduces risk for the development of problems in individual family members (Belsky & Fearon, 2004; Rogosch, Cicchetti & Toth, 2004; Shaw et al., 2004). Helping families discern and build on areas of family strengths can enhance the protective functions of the family.

For children and families from minority cultures, there are unique risk factors, such as racism and discrimination, and unique protective factors, such as a strong racial or cultural identity, that both developmental psychopathology and family systems theory would deem crucial to consider. Narrative family therapy, in particular, incorporates the role of cultural stereotypes in problem formation in a child, as family members unwittingly endorse the narrow perspective inherent in stereotypes and weave aspects of these stereotypes into the family narratives by which they are viewing their problems. For example, the stereotype of African Americans as prone to deviant behavior and crime can set the context for observers to attribute internal causal factors, such as temperament, to problem behaviors of an African American child and even predispose the family to more readily internalize the cause of problem behavior themselves. Helping families deconstruct such a destructive and narrow narrative and reconstruct a narrative that allows for consideration of contextual factors playing a role in the child's misbehavior (e.g., hostile attributions about misbehavior create a context in which the child is treated with disrespect, which fuels more anger and behavioral acting out) can free the child and family to live out their lives authoring a different story.

Trajectories of development. Systemic thinking considers the many inter-related forces at work that provide a growth-promoting trajectory for children. In family systems theories, the family life cycle adds an important context for potential deviations from a growth-promoting trajectory to one that is con-sidered at risk. Just as there are normal developmental stages in an individual's life, there are normal developmental stages through which a family traverses over time, with tasks that need to be resolved for healthy adaptation within that family life cycle stage. When healthy adaptation and adjustment to the needs inherent in the particular life stage are not negotiated, family members are conceptualized as being at risk, not only for problems in that particular life stage but also for continued challenges in managing subsequent family life cycle stages. For example, difficulty navigating the changes in a family with the birth of a new child could create stress for a family and negative behavior in a preschool-aged sibling. This is a commonly occurring adjustment difficulty that can be resolved, especially in the presence of other protective factors, such as a strong, unified couple who are able to provide parental nurture and as-surance to the older sibling balanced with gentle limit setting.

However, in a family with additional risk factors, such as a difficult child temperament and parents whose marital conflict interferes with their sensi-tivity to the emotional and behavioral needs of the preschooler, the situation is ripe for the development of a coercive cycle of escalating aggression. In such a situation, the parents will be more likely to inadvertently reinforce negative behavior by offering attention only through attempts to control negative be-havior (Patterson, 1982). In this way, failure to negotiate a life cycle transition may put a family on a risk-promoting trajectory. If this negative cycle leads to continued misbehavior that impacts academic functioning and peer social in-teractions, the child will be at continued risk for problems not directly related to the birth of a new sibling. The initial family-based problem handling a nor-mative life cycle transition has led to a change in this child's developmental course through negative developmental cascades (Masten & Cicchetti, 2010). In this way, risk factors within families beget more risk factors and set the stage for potential maladaptive functioning in a child's life.

Similar processes lead to developmental cascades that enhance adaptive functioning/well-being (i.e., protective factors within families beget more protective factors). In particular, prevention efforts in the family to help parents and young adolescents manage life cycle transitions can place youth on a positive, adaptive developmental trajectory. For example, by increasing flexibility of boundaries to accommodate an adolescent's developmentally appropriate movement in and out of the family system, the family is able to support the adolescent's changing needs, leading to better decision making and continued academic success. In addition, healthy family relationships are more likely to support the development of healthy adolescent peer relationships. Success in academics and peer relationships leads to stronger self-esteem and optimism about the world and provides a strong foundation for the transition to young adulthood. It should be noted that a systemic emphasis in this life stage would also consider the abilities of parents to effectively manage their own developmental issues, such as mid-life issues or the stress of caring for aging parents. In emphasizing the needs of parents as individuals, clinicians help to empower the parent in a way that supports the adolescent's changing needs.

Equifinality and multifinality. Equifinality and multifinality are concepts from developmental psychopathology emphasizing that various pathways confer risk and protection to children and adolescents at various stages of development. These concepts also apply to family processes. Equifinality is evidenced in the development of similar symptoms within families with different adaptive and maladaptive elements. For example, two teens develop a tendency to overeat emotionally and are on a trajectory toward developing binge eating disorder; one has experienced sexual abuse that plays a significant role in the maintenance of the symptoms, whereas the other has not been abused but has experienced unrealistically high expectations and perfectionism in her family. Both binge eat to manage negative emotions, but their negative emotions are different in type and are triggered by different circumstances.

An example of multifinality can be seen in the study of authoritarian parents, who are characterized by high levels of control and low levels of warmth (Baumrind, 1966; 1991; Maccoby & Martin, 1983). Authoritarian parenting is typically associated with negative outcomes in children (Steinberg, 2001), but this strict form of discipline has been found to be associated with higher levels of adaptation in African American families (Gonzales, Cauce & Mason, 1996; Lamborn et al., 1991). It is possible that an authoritarian parenting style may have protective effects depending on contextual factors, such as living in a high-risk neighborhood. In addition, children in some cultures may interpret an authoritarian approach as a sign that parents care for them (Ballenger, 1992). However, cultural variants of authoritarian parenting may have different meanings. One example is the emphasis on training in the context of harmonious family relationships in Chinese families (Chao, 2001). These research findings on cultural differences in the effects of parenting underscore the importance of a comprehensive assessment of family functioning within a family's cultural context for appropriate case conceptualization and treatment planning.

PRACTICAL SUGGESTIONS

In our integration of family systems therapy and developmental psychopathology, we offer the following practical suggestions to further enhance understanding of the role of systemic family processes in the development of psychopathology in children and adolescents and to foster new pathways to healthy development for children and interventions in the family.

- Be mindful of the *theoretical basis* of your interventions. The benefits of an integrative model of treatment are greater flexibility in treatment and the capacity to tailor an intervention to the unique needs of each presenting family. However, the potential for a shallow understanding of the mechanism by which an intervention works and subsequent loss of clinical flexibility is greater for those who are not aware of the theoretical underpinnings of the various interventions in an integrative model. Stated another way, the use of *integrative approaches*, and even *empirically supported treatments*, is strengthened by a deeper understanding of the specific intervention's theoretical roots. It has been said that you must know the rules well in order to break them properly; the value in understanding the theory behind the intervention is the flexibility to modify it for different needs in different families.

- Be mindful of developing skills in the areas of *common factors* of treatment effectiveness, especially those unique to systemic family therapy (Sprenkle et al., 2009). Intentionally learning how to best develop a therapeutic alliance with each family member and to effectively join the family system contributes significantly to a clinician's effectiveness with a family. For example, in family therapy, effective joining involves finding a way to support individuals on both sides of a conflict (e.g., parent and teen, or two conflictual parents). It is also vital to consider the family system in case conceptualization and treatment planning and to take an active role in disrupting dysfunctional relational patterns. Finally, maintaining hope for change as a family therapist and instilling that hope to each family member, such as by casting a vision for how the family's unique strengths can be the foundation for positive change, will be essential for effective family work.

- Be mindful of the *unit of analysis* you are considering. We encourage considering both smaller units (e.g., individual person level) as well as contextual units larger than the family (e.g., cultural context) in assessment and treatment planning. Although family systems approaches have historically underemphasized, even eschewed, a focus on individual functioning in assessment, such as with the use of *DSM* diagnostic categories, family-based treatments are increasingly attending to biological and individual risk factors. As family-based interventions are increasingly utilized in a wide variety of settings, including psychiatric and mental health settings, a working diagnosis can provide a common language among multidisciplinary service providers. As important as a focus on individual functioning is a consideration of contextual factors beyond the family, including culture and societal norms and messages. The old African proverb "It takes a village to raise a child" is no less true in the United States than in a small African village. Family rules that are inconsistent with societal norms, even when family rules are healthy and societal norms are unhealthy, are more challenging to enforce and can be an added stressor. Encouraging families to be a part of a larger community that embraces their values and can commit to walking with that family on life's journey can be one of the most significant "interventions" that a family therapist can utilize.

- Be mindful of the *systemic understanding* of problem behavior as embedded in a larger context. The functional view of individual problems (i.e., that pathology may serve a purpose or function in the family system) is central to some family systems theories (e.g., structural family therapy); other family systems theories (e.g., narrative family therapy) recognize that the individual family member's problem may be an expression of dysfunction on a larger societal or cultural level. Even if interventions begin with an assumption that this functional view is not operative, it is advisable to consider the role that symptoms may be playing in cases that are resistant to interventions.

- Be mindful of the various *contexts* that are contributing to and constraining new possibilities for the child and family. The systemic and developmental literature focuses on the trajectories created by the recursion between our choices and the contexts in which we are embedded. Individual and contextual forces mutually influence each other, creating a goodness-of-fit for the current behavior and the trajectory that is being maintained. Addressing both the context and the individual can increase the probability of changing a behavioral trajectory.

CASE STUDY

The following case study is an example of a family systems approach integrated with a developmental psychopathology framework and grounded in a Christ-centered perspective. We take a structural/brief strategic approach to case conceptualization and treatment planning (Szapocznik et al., 2003) to address the needs of a family adjusting to significant life stressors associated with divorce that are complicating their life cycle transition into the "families with adolescents" stage. We draw from structural and solution-focused approaches to shift family perceptions of the identified patient as the "problem child" and build on individual and family strengths to change problematic patterns in family interactions. Finally, we consider ways in which our faith-based presuppositions about children as divine gifts, respected persons, and agents of moral and spiritual action (Miller-McLemore, 2003) guide our case conceptualization and treatment planning.

Presenting Problem

The identified patient, Ryan Smith, is an eleven-year-old Caucasian male who lives with his mother, Susan, and fourteen-year-old sister, Sarah. Ryan's mother called for a therapy appointment because he had been showing oppositional behavior and angry outbursts at home during the past year. She also noted during the telephone interview that his problem behavior at home has been escalating into fits of rage in the last four months. She further commented that his behavior has become "uncontrollable" in the last few weeks, and that his teacher even contacted her with concerns over his declining academic functioning and negative attitude toward school.

Initial Sessions

In the initial intake session, both Ryan and Sarah presented as quiet and polite and readily engaged in discussions about their friends, interests and school. Ryan reported playing soccer since he was in kindergarten but stated that he stopped playing last year because "it wasn't fun anymore." He had reportedly been a good student but stated that school has been "boring" this year. He also joked that "recess" was his favorite subject in school.

When asked about the reason for coming to therapy at this time, Ms. Smith reported that Ryan had recently become so belligerent and agitated that he threw a plate at her. The family recounted the incident through an enactment and described how Ryan had ignored his mother's first two requests to clear the dinner table. After Ryan responded with defiance to his mom's third angry reminder, she turned off the TV, which infuriated Ryan. He started clearing the table in a reckless manner, which Mom promptly criticized. It was at that point that Ryan threw the plate at his mother, telling her to clean up the kitchen herself. Ms. Smith reported feeling exasperated and overwhelmed with these escalations and did the only thing that came to mind: she sent Ryan to his room where he continued his rage-filled outburst, throwing his belongings around his room. When asked how he was able to calm himself down, Ryan responded that he did not know. Although he began the session with an attitude of blame on his mother, he looked remorseful when talking about his outbursts and said he wanted to be able to control his anger.

Assessment of family structure and relational patterns, as well as significant events that could be related to the presenting problem, revealed important details about family context. Ryan's parents had been married for fourteen years and then separated for twelve months before divorcing four months ago. At the time of the separation, Mr. Smith moved into an apartment about an hour away, while the rest of the family stayed in their home. Mr. and Ms. Smith currently share joint custody, with Ms. Smith as the custodial parent and Mr. Smith having visitation with the children every other weekend. The separation came as a surprise to the children, as the parents had not fought openly in front of them, and Ryan became tearful discussing the changes that ensued after the separation and divorce, such as his father's unavailability to help with homework and attend his soccer games. The divorce was also distressing to Ms. Smith's extended family because it was "against their Catholic religion." The family reported that both children had received their First Communion (a religious sacrament in their faith) in second grade but that the family has not otherwise been actively involved in the church (e.g., attending mass regularly or participating in youth group).

In preparation to end the intake session, the therapist shifted the focus from assessment of the presenting problem to setting initial goals and casting a positive vision for change by asking the miracle question (as previously described). When the family responded with a focus on Ryan not arguing and fighting with Mom, they were asked to consider what would be different in their family once that happened. Ryan said that the family would watch TV together after dinner if they weren't fighting. Sarah mentioned that she and her mother would go shopping together more. Mom said that she would like both of those things to happen. When asked how things might be different with their father, Sarah said that she would be able to talk to her mother about what she does on the weekends when she visits her father, and Ryan said that he would spend more time with his father. The therapist ended the session by affirming these desires, commenting on how admirable it was that the teenagers want to spend time with the family and expressing hope that the family's commitment to come to therapy together would help them make changes to be able to spend more time together as a family and be involved in each other's lives in meaningful ways.

In the second session, the therapist inquired about family patterns and family history regarding the expression of negative emotions, such as anger and sadness, and conflict management. Ms. Smith reported that negative emotions, especially anger, were not "allowed" in her family and that Ryan has always been emotional like his father. Further inquiry about Mr. Smith and his relationship with both children led to the disclosure that their father has lived with a girlfriend since the separation and that he and his girlfriend were expecting the birth of a new baby. The children reported that they had recently been asked to help their father and his girlfriend prepare the nursery during their weekend visits, including shopping for nursery furniture with them, which Sarah has been willing to do. Ryan has not been interested in helping with preparations, so has mainly played video games during his visits. Ms. Smith was unaware until recently of the pregnancy and the children's involvement in the preparation for the new baby. She learned this fact after Mr. Smith cancelled a weekend visitation, and Ryan commented that he was probably busy getting ready for their new baby. Ms. Smith reported that she was shocked and "did not handle the news well" when she learned about the pregnancy and the children's level of involvement in preparations. However, she and her children had not subsequently talked about the new baby.

Discussion of the parents' marital history and details surrounding the divorce continued in an individual appointment with Ms. Smith. During this interview, Ms. Smith revealed that she had initiated the separation (i.e., "kicked him out of the house") after discovering her husband's involvement in an extramarital relationship. However, he later initiated the divorce, which was painful for her because she had hoped that they could reconcile. Ms. Smith also recounted that her own relationship with Mr. Smith involved a pregnancy before marriage. They had decided to marry quickly because of her religious convictions, but she subsequently miscarried the baby. She stated that they were both deeply saddened by this loss but that Mr. Smith seemed to move on more quickly than she did. She became pregnant with Sarah within the year, but she still felt a deep sense of loss and pain over the miscarriage. Ms. Smith reported that she currently spends most evenings in her room away from the children because she feels depressed and hopeless about her life circumstances and overwhelmed with parenting alone. The therapist normalized her feelings in light of her many losses and life changes and the difficulty of parenting her children without the cooperation of her ex-husband. They explored together the potential for Mr. Smith to join the family in treatment. Ms. Smith was initially reluctant but was willing to invite him. She later reported that he was not willing to come to therapy, stating that he was not having problems with the children at his house.

The Smith family was seen for nine more weekly sessions. A solution-focused approach helped the family work toward change by highlighting times that Ms. Smith was effectively enforcing family rules with clarity and consistency, Ryan was cooperative and nondefensive, and family members were spending time with each other in meaningful ways. In addition, the family was also able to hear each other's experience of the separation and divorce and the unique perceived losses in the adjustment. The majority of sessions were conducted as conjoint family sessions, but several sessions were split among the three family members (i.e., mini sessions for each individual family member) or with individuals and subsystems (e.g., individual time with Ms. Smith and joint time with Ryan/Sarah; individual time with Ryan and joint time with Ms. Smith/Sarah) in order to provide support to Ms. Smith in her role as parent while further assessing individual needs of each child.

Over the course of treatment, as Ms. Smith's parenting efforts became less reactive and emotional and family connections were strengthened, Ryan's oppositional behavior and irritability decreased. Toward the end of treatment,

Sarah opened up in an individual session and disclosed her own feelings of loneliness and mild depression since the divorce. She described a growing and enjoyable relationship with her father's girlfriend but felt guilty that she was betraying her mother. Helping her to resolve her loyalty conflict involved coaching her to share her feelings with her mother. To prepare Ms. Smith to be open and receptive to this new information in a joint session, the therapist broached the subject of the relationships between her children and Mr. Smith's girlfriend in an individual session. This was challenging for Ms. Smith, but she was able to process these issues in individual sessions enough to begin to accept the idea of this new relationship between Sarah and the girlfriend and to give Sarah permission to establish this relationship without a sense of guilt.

Case Formulation and Treatment Plan

Ryan is an eleven-year-old boy who has been experiencing problems with oppositional, argumentative behavior, angry outbursts, irritability and defensiveness primarily at home for the past year, with escalations in symptoms and problems with friendships and academics developing over the past three to four months. Information gathered about the timing of the parents' divorce and the upcoming birth of the father's new baby offered a broader context for understanding Ryan's externalizing problems. The initial onset of problems coincided with the separation and divorce, and recent escalation in symptoms coincided with the news of the baby. Ms. Smith also described her own personal difficulties in adjusting to life as a single mother and admitted that life stressors are interfering with her ability to effectively parent. In addition to significant stressors associated with the divorce, the lack of communication between family members was exacerbating the stress of the family life cycle changes.

In the case of the Smith family, the stress of the divorce impacted vulnerabilities in the family structure. Family report of functioning before the divorce highlighted rigid boundaries between Mr. and Mrs. Smith (i.e., lack of connectedness and intimacy), which were taken to an extreme as Ms. Smith dealt with the pain of her divorce by cutting off lines of communication over parenting issues with Mr. Smith. Consequently, the parental subsystem was not functioning effectively after the divorce. For example, they were not communicating about important details that affect the children, and the children were trying to adapt to significant family events without the awareness and support of their mother. In addition, Ms. Smith was no longer functioning effectively as an authority in the family, and with growing enmeshment in their relationship, she was arguing with Ryan as a peer. Further, Mr. Smith became more emotionally distanced from his children after the divorce and was not actively involved in their school and extracurricular activities due to the distance between homes. He was becoming increasingly disengaged from his children during visitations with the anticipated arrival of the new baby. Mr. Smith's refusal to participate in family therapy was an additional challenge to Ms. Smith, but she readily accepted the importance of working toward more open communication between them because of the need to continue in their roles as parents.

Significant strengths in each family member, and in their relationships, are noteworthy as protective factors. First, a healthy level of attachment was evidenced by nonverbal behaviors among family members while discussing the presenting problem (e.g., good eye contact, ease of interaction, spontaneous laughter and joking). In general, they seemed to feel comfortable in the same room together, were able to talk about challenges in their life with humor and verbalized a desire for more time together. Second, the family evidenced flexibility in their family narrative. The family (including Ryan) came with a narrative of Ryan as the problem child, but all were amenable to a focus on the larger family context. Consequently, success is anticipated in efforts to deconstruct the notion that there is something wrong with Ryan and reconstruct a narrative focused on the impact of family losses and stressors as well as strengths within Ryan, the family and larger community.

Further, since our working hypothesis is that Ryan's maladaptive response is actually a healthy response to an unhealthy situation, one of the goals for assessment is to consider ways in which the unhealthy situation is creating risk for other family members. For example, after gathering family history and learning of the separation, divorce and new baby, the therapist made efforts to connect the growing difficulties with Ryan to these significant life stressors that impact the whole family. The therapist commented on the significant number of changes in the last four months and the stress these changes create for each family member, speculating that much of the conflict between Ryan and his mother might be connected to these life changes. The therapist also wondered out loud if the stress might be impacting Sarah as well, even though she is not showing the same kind of angry outbursts as Ryan.

Inquiring about the perspective of each family member regarding the presenting problem is a standard systemic assessment procedure that provides a comprehensive view of family functioning surrounding the presenting problem. In the Smith family, the process of discussing the presenting problem as a family was empowering for both Ryan and Sarah, as the lack of communication in the family fostered a sense of isolation that was previously only broken by Ryan's oppositional behavior and outbursts. Fostering opportunities for all family members to share their perspectives was an important first step to opening new channels of communication in the family.

In addition, using structural interventions of tracking structure/boundaries and enactments in the assessment of parent-child problems can provide the therapist with a wealth of information about the parents' capacity to balance respectful provision of appropriate boundaries with firm and consistent consequences. In the case of the Smith family, the initial enactment demonstrated a lack of respect between Ryan and his mother in the discipline process, on both sides of the interaction. Developmentally, the family is entering the "family with adolescents" stage, in which the task is facilitating growing independence and expansion of the social world. Letting go of adolescents in age-appropriate ways to allow them more independence is likely challenging for Ms. Smith at this time, as she is also dealing with the loss of her marriage. Relatedly, affect regulation appeared to be a problem for both Ms. Smith and Ryan, and Ryan's behavioral dysregulation appeared to be part of a coercive, bidirectional process fueled by ineffective parenting and his lack of emotion regulation skills. This focus on individual work with both Ryan and his mother is a more comprehensive treatment consistent with working within the developmental psychopathology framework. Ms. Smith is in need of guidance and support in her parenting so that she can provide both care and authority in this time of stress. She would benefit from interventions focused on maintaining a respectful stance while being clear and firm with discipline. In addition, Ryan needs assistance learning to label and manage negative emotions.

Based on the case conceptualization developed after the initial three assessment sessions, the following treatment goals were established to guide the subsequent sessions with the Smith family. The first goal was to restructure the family hierarchy and boundaries to facilitate more effective limit setting, with individual sessions for Ms. Smith to provide extra support in her role as parent (Minuchin & Fishman, 1981; BST: Szapocznik et al., 2003). The second goal was to shift family perceptions of the problem from anger to pain and loss, and to support all family members in managing the transitions related to divorce and subsequent life changes (Szapocznik et al., 2003). The third goal was to highlight and build on family relational strengths by reframing conflicted relationships as close and passionate and to use a solution-focused approach to increasing positive interactions (De Shazer, 2005). The family was also in need of improving communication, which was the fourth goal. The therapist addressed this need by loosening rigid boundaries and encouraging expression of thoughts and feelings, first in session and then out of session (BST; Szapocznik et al., 2003). Finally, a focus on building emotion recognition and emotion regulation skills (e.g., Gottman et al., 1996) in family members as the fifth goal supported and complemented the systemic interventions.

INTEGRATION WITH CHRISTIAN FAITH

As clinicians who are Christian, we begin our work with the presupposition that children are created wholly and completely in the image of God. However, acknowledging that life on earth is no longer as God intended due to the presence of sin, we recognize that children will struggle between healthy and maladaptive trajectories across their lifespan. In spite of this, we have hope as we affirm the truth of the gospel message and God's promises that he is daily transforming us, children included, closer to the relational beings he intended. Although we may not recognize the wholeness that God sees from his eternal perspective, we can trust that he is working to make "everything new" (Rev 21:5) and that he will not stop working in our lives until his good work is complete (Phil 1:6).

Building on these presuppositional beliefs, we acknowledge that we are called to *value children as divine gifts*, as Jesus affirmed the value of children and the call to be like children in his own ministry (Mt 19:13-15; Mk 10:13-16; Lk 18:15-17). Second, we believe we are called to *respect children as persons*, as they are created in God's image and invited into a personal relationship with their Creator. Third, we recognize that *children are moral and spiritual agents* and that they are actively engaged in bidirectional relationships with adults, capable of participating in God's grace and reconciliation and used by God as a source of his revelation and hope to others. Thus, as we work with the Smith family and other clients, we aim to restore children and adolescents to a more health-promoting developmental trajectory by helping each family member—parents and children—understand these spiritual realities. In addition, we aim to foster parents' awareness of their role in supporting children's needs within the family context so that they might live out these realities as God intended.

In family therapy it is essential to model the valuing of children and promote an appreciation for children as divine gifts. As early as the initial intake appointment, we can assess the worth and value placed on a child by parents and family. Does the child have a clear sense of being loved and valued? What are the ways that "I love you" is conveyed from parent to child? What are the ways that efforts to communicate love get lost in the translation of daily life and discipline, and how can we foster clearer communication of value and love from parent to child? In the case of the Smith family, although there was significant conflict between Ryan and his mother in their current relationship, there was evidence that the children have felt valued and loved in the family's positive nonverbal behaviors and each member's stated desires for more time together as a family. The ways in which Ms. Smith made heroic efforts to modify her parenting in spite of the personal challenges she was facing spoke volumes of her love for her children as well.

Families with significant child-related problems often focus on the child as anything but a gift. Helping families to reframe the meaning of a child's problem behavior may provide space for a family's appreciation of that child as a gift, with good intentions and positive qualities. Constructing new family patterns that allow the family to embrace this spiritual truth can facilitate hope for change and direct families onto a positive trajectory of change. This allows opportunities for family members to see ways in which the identified patient is helping the family to honestly focus on important family issues that have been overlooked. Structural interventions using enactments and reframing were effective in shifting everyone's perspective from Ryan as the family problem to the family hero. In this recently divorced family, it was clear that Ms. Smith was still struggling with the pain of her husband's affair and subsequent abandonment. By reframing the child as caring for the well-being of the family, the therapist normalized the ways in which children take on blame for a failed marriage and reframed Ryan's behavior as a heroic attempt to keep mom focused on something other than the grief brought on with the divorce. Because the Smith family was currently minimally involved in their Catholic faith tradition, there was no intentional focus on the role that God may be playing in efforts to change the family narrative about Ryan as the problem child. However, for some Christian families, it can be helpful to directly point out how God is using the identified patient to bring the family to a healthier level of functioning, closer to what God intends for them. This is consistent with the ways in which "God works for the good of those who love him" (Rom 8:28).

Because other children in the family can often be overlooked when the family's focus and energy are directed at the identified patient, including all family members in therapy sessions presents opportunities to highlight the ways in which all the children in the family are divine gifts and the ways in which the family communicates love and care to all members. For this reason it was important in working with the Smith family to include Sarah in the sessions, even from the first intake session. Sarah also needed to be affirmed in her value and worth in the family, directly by facilitating affirming family enactments in session and indirectly by inviting her to be a significant part of the family solution.

We are also called to respect children as persons, which spurs us to assess whether a child is respected as his own person in the family. Are there good, clear boundaries in the family that allow the child to develop as an individual within the context of a close, loving family? Do parents allow age-appropriate choices and opportunities for individuation by distinguishing between rules and parental preferences? Are children seen as capable of making their own decisions? When, if ever, is it okay to disagree with parents? Do parents teach their children to disagree with respect but still obey when they are dealing with a "rule" or when parental authority is needed?

Respecting children as persons underlies the family assessment process based on the assumption that each family member has something valuable to share in providing a full understanding of the presenting problem. Thus, including Ryan and Sarah in this process and asking for their unique perspectives on the situation aimed to communicate respect for them as persons who have a valuable place in the family and to model for their mother a respect for the identified patient and his sibling. Respecting children as persons is also an inherent component of both Bowenian and structural family therapy. The individuality of each person in the family is an important aspect of health from these two models, whether conceptualized as high levels of differentiation (in Bowenian theory) or clear personal boundaries (in structural theory). Children need to be raised in families that respect this individuality and yet provide the nurture and support needed by all human beings. From a family systems perspective, fostering a combination of emotional connectedness and nurture with developmentally appropriate autonomy is key to the healthy development of children. Both Bowenian and structural theories speak to ways in which parents are hindered in their ability to provide this healthy balance by their own personal challenges in these areas. Not unlike the instructions during a flight for parents to put on the oxygen mask first before helping children with theirs, family therapists often encourage parents to work on some of their own issues that seem to be impeding their ability to follow through with effective parenting techniques. Consequently, treatment considerations when working with the Smith family included helping Ms. Smith shift her attention to some of her own challenges that were limiting her parenting abilities and encouraging her to focus on important changes in her own life.

Lessons for parents about proper discipline in love are often cited in the Bible (e.g., Prov 22:6; Col 3:21), but equally helpful is the lesson modeled by Jesus himself at age twelve (Lk 2:41-52). Jesus did not follow his parents on their family journey but stayed behind to talk to priests at the temple. This caused great concern on the part of his parents, who had to retrace their steps to find him. Upon finding Jesus, his parents scolded him, perhaps out of fear or anger. In response, Jesus asserted that he stayed behind because of his mission and highlighted the importance of his reason, yet he also obeyed his parents and returned home with them, growing "in wisdom and in stature and in favor with God and all the people" (Lk 2:52 NLT) while he waited for God's perfect timing for the continuation of his ministry. Thus, in the midst of a family life cycle transition to adolescence, during which children are assuming increasing autonomy and his parents are adjusting to these changes, Jesus as a preteen modeled a God-given capacity for spiritual and moral growth in his humanness. Respecting children as persons involves seeing them with the same capacities. This could involve intentionally asking about family values related to faith development and the ways in which parents are (or are not) intentional about the spiritual development of the child. In the case of Ryan and Sarah, out of respect for the family's minimal commitment to organized religion, the focus of conversation in this area initially centered on issues of moral values rather than spiritual values (e.g., the family's values and ideas about treating others with love and compassion). However, conversations focused on the spiritual aspects of healthy child development unfolded naturally in the context of considering ways to establish and expand networks of support, such as returning to greater involvement in their church.

Acknowledging that children have moral and spiritual agency, effective work with families involves helping parents treat children in such a way as to foster the development of their moral and spiritual decision making. Questions to consider in assessing the health of the family include: Do parents recognize that children were created by God to håve free will and that God works through the practice of their agency? How can parents best hold children accountable for their actions so that they can learn through the natural or logical consequences of sinful choices and allow God to use even sinful choices for good (i.e., his transforming work in the lives of our children)? Do parents provide the scaffolding needed to facilitate godly choices (those that God has designed for us)—providing spiritual nurture and care, teaching and modeling God's Word, and providing spiritual education through a local church in order to help foster the child's personal relationship with God as the context for making godly moral and spiritual decisions? How can parents foster opportunities for children to learn through giving and receiving grace within the context of the family, and thereby learn the spiritual realities of grace, forgiveness and reconciliation in relation to God? When working with families who do not espouse a Christian faith, similar questions can be asked of their own faith background to facilitate deeper consideration of ways that they can embrace and live more congruently with values that are important to them.

The Smiths' commitment to the children attending religious education in first grade in preparation for making their First Holy Communion in second grade was evidence of the parents' desire and efforts to provide for the children's spiritual development. In addition, building on Ms. Smith's commitment to her Catholic faith and desire for her children to live in ways that are consistent with the moral teachings of the church, the family was encouraged to consider ways in which the church community might provide support and resources for the children as well as the family as a unit. This discussion led to their commitment to explore involvement in the youth group and other ministries of the church. Although the family made the decision to to re-engage with their church more for the social resources and support found in this community than resources for their spiritual faith development, a commitment to a larger community that can walk alongside the family can be an important first step.

CONCLUSIONS

It is our hope that after reading this chapter you have a better understanding of the ways children's problems can be treated from a family therapy perspective that is informed by developmental psychopathology, and of how a Christian worldview can inform conceptualization and interventions. Just as Moses pointed out in Exodus 34, what we learn from relationships in our families travels with us for generations. Family relationships provide the default mode from which we conceptualize what it means to be a person. This framework exists until we have new experiences or are able to see our relationships from a new perspective. We tend to be bound by the patterns of relating learned in childhood and hold views about what it means to be a child that are established based on our early experiences. It is in this cauldron of the family that our views are formed and maintained. These views tend to place us on trajectories of behaviors, emotions and thoughts which prove either adaptive or maladaptive in our subsequent contexts. The task of changing these pathways may seem daunting; however, we must remember that there is a great deal of plasticity in our trajectories. Our early family experiences and trajectories are not deterministic. Rather, there is hope—hope that we can intentionally attend to how we view and treat children, how we relate to one another, and how we respond to the love that God has shown us in Christ through the generations.

Developmental psychopathology and family systems provide frameworks for attending to and changing our relationship trajectories. Both approaches emphasize the importance of context and timing. As Christians, we believe that we are created in the image of God to be in relationship with him and others. This image is manifest in the person of the child in the form of relational abilities, creativity and the ability to be intentional (agency). Family systems approaches offer various ideas on how to intentionally, through relationships, foster our children's abilities to create and impact the world. We rejoice that through Christ's life, death and resurrection, God has interceded in our sinful trajectories away from him and provided the possibility of a growth-promoting trajectory toward relationship with him. This is the beginning of new possibilities in relationships, and although negative influences on our development and relationships still exist, we trust that this trajectory provides opportunities for adaptation and growth until we are made complete again and can live in this newness of life even now.

Appendix A

Case Formulation Worksheet

Name _____   **D.O.B.** _____

Assessment Information: _____   **Age:** _____

_____   **Date:** _____

_____

STAGE 1: Review case information and record information relevant to a developmental psychopathology framework.

Current Functioning:

Cognitive

Emotional

Physiological

Behavioral

Social

Child Characteristics (e.g., age, developmental level, gender, ethnicity, temperament):

STAGE 2: Ask yourself questions to help you to understand the case from a developmental psychopathology framework (i.e., consider the child as holistic/multidimensional, the transactions between child and important contexts, risk and resilience factors, developmental pathways, including continuities/discontinuities). Record relevant information.

Child as Holistic Organism (preliminary observations about important transactions between child characteristics):

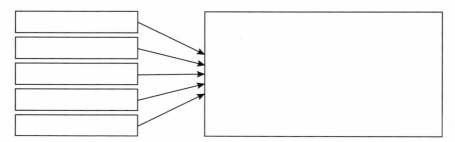

Contextual Characteristics (e.g., parent-child, parental psychopathology, marital relationship, sibling relationships, family characteristics, peer relations, teacher, school context, neighborhood, cultural context):

Contextual Transactions (observations about important transactions between child and context characteristics):

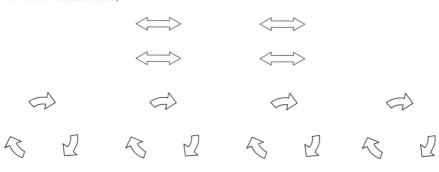

Vulnerability and Risk Factors (proximal & distal)　　**Resilience and Protective Factors** (proximal & distal)

Vulnerability and Risk Factors (proximal & distal)	Resilience and Protective Factors (proximal & distal)

Developmental Pathways: Continuities and Discontinuities (use Developmental Trajectory Map if helpful)

STAGE 3 (Differential Diagnosis): Consider all relevant *DSM* diagnoses, rule out diagnoses, come to a conclusion.

Relevant Rule Outs
Diagnostic Conclusions:

STAGE 4 (Reflections and Trajectory Map): Review your notes from the case. Reflect on the material in order to identify the specific multidimensional, transactional influences and developmental pathways that help to explain current functioning. Based on your reflections about the presented case material, you may want to draw out a complete developmental pathway depicting the child/adolescent's functioning on the Developmental Trajectory Map Worksheet.

STAGE 5 (Case Formulation):
Complete a written formulation of the case, identifying and explaining the concluding diagnosis(es). Your formulation should be **ECCIII**: *E*xplanatory, *C*omprehensive, *C*onclusive, (Selectively) *I*nclusive, *I*llustrative and *I*nformative for treatment. It should clearly show evidence of working from a developmental psychopathology framework (see Reflection on Case Conceptualization checklist). Assess your formulation for the degree to which it reflects a developmental psychopathology framework as well as the individual child/family/context in order to be useful. **Revise as needed.**

Appendix B

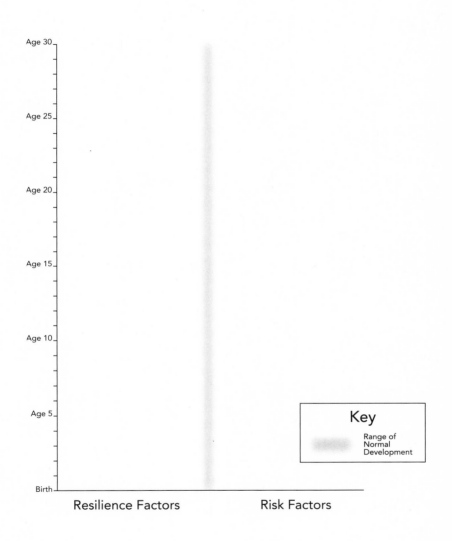

Age 30

Age 25

Age 20

Age 15

Age 10

Age 5

Birth

Resilience Factors   Risk Factors

Key

Range of
Normal
Development

Appendix B. Developmental Trajectory Map

Appendix C

Select Examples of Evidence-Based Treatments

Target Problem	Intervention Name Source	Purpose of Intervention	Underlying Frameworks	Intended Recipients	Intervention Format Certification[1] Media[2]	Structure of Intervention
Anxiety	Kendall, P. C., & Hedtke, K. A. (2006). *Coping cat workbook* (2nd ed.). Purchasing information available at www.workbookpublishing.com	Skills training and exposure sessions through cognitive-behavioral therapy for separation anxiety disorder, generalized anxiety disorder or social phobia	Physiological, cognitive and behavioral conceptualization of anxiety	Children and adolescents ages 7–13 with SAD, GAD or social phobia; youth with other anxiety disorders may also benefit from treatment	Individual sessions, with two parent-only sessions DVD	16 weekly sessions • Sessions 1–8: skills building • Sessions 10–16: practice and exposure • Sessions 4 and 9: parent-only sessions
Attention deficit/ hyperactivity disorder	Robin, A. L. (1998). *ADHD in adolescents: Diagnosis and treatment.* Purchasing information available at www.guilford.com	Provides adolescents and families with strategies for managing ADHD at home and school	Cognitive restructuring, behavior management, problem-solving and communication training, and psycho-pharma-cology	Adolescents with attention deficit/ hyperactivity disorder and their parents	Individual and family format	20 sessions: • sessions 1–15: intervention sessions • sessions 16–20: follow-up sessions
	Power, T. J., Karusti, J. L., & Habboushe, D. F. (2001). *Homework success for children with ADHD: A family-school intervention program.* Purchasing information available at www.guilford.com	Provides homework and behavioral modification strategies, facilitates home-school collaboration and addresses parent-child relationships	Behavioral within an ecological framework	Children in 1st through 6th grade with attention deficit/hyperactivity disorder and their parents; may be adapted for children and adolescents with homework challenges without a diagnosis	Family groups or individual family sessions; components may also be supplemental to individual or family therapy or brief consultations	16 sessions: • 2 pretreatment sessions; one with parents and one parent-teacher conference • 7 parent sessions • 7 child sessions
Conduct and Social Problems	Lochman, J. E., Wells, K. C., & Lenhart, L. A. (2008). *Coping power.* Program and purchasing information available at www.copingpower.com	Targets social cognitive skills and contextual factors in children and adolescents with antisocial behavior	Social information processing	Children in late elementary to early middle school with externalizing or aggressive behaviors and their parents	Parent and child group format DVD	34 child sessions and 16 parent sessions over a period of 15 months

Target Problem	Intervention Name Source	Purpose of Intervention	Underlying Frameworks	Intended Recipients	Intervention Format Certification[1] Media[2]	Structure of Intervention
Conduct and Social Problems (continued)	Barkley, R. A. (2013). *Defiant children: A clinician's manual for assessment and parent training* (3rd ed.). Purchasing information available at www.guilford.com	Evaluates child defiance and behavior problems and includes parent behavior-management training	Social learning theory, behavior modification and management	Children ages 2–12 with defiant, oppositional or noncompliant behavior and their parents	Individual family or group format with 6–10 families. DVD	10 sessions; 1 booster session
	Barkley, R. A., Edwards, G. H., & Robin, A. L. (1999). *Defiant teens: A clinician's manual for assessment and family intervention.* Purchasing information available at www.guilford.com	Behavior management and family relationship improvement training for parents and adolescents	Family systems theory, behavior modification and management	Adolescents ages 13–18 with externalizing behaviors (oppositional defiant disorder, conduct disorder, ADHD) and their parents	Individual family or group format	18 sessions; 1 booster session if needed
	Larson, J., & Lochman, J. E. (2010). *Helping schoolchildren cope with anger* (2nd ed.) (Anger Coping Program). Purchasing information available at www.guilford.com	Targets reduction of aggressive and disruptive behavior and improvement in teacher-parent collaboration	Social cognitive model, social information processing	Children in grades 3–6	Group format (5–7 children); can also be utilized in individual format. DVD	18 sessions, 60–90 minutes
	Webster-Stratton, C. (2011). *The incredible years: Parents, teachers, and children's training series.* Program (including sample video clips), purchasing and training information available at www. incredibleyears.com	Treatment and prevention of aggressive behavior, conduct problems and ADHD for children, parents and teachers	Cognitive social learning theory, Patterson's coercion hypothesis of negative reinforcement, Bandura's theory of modeling and self-efficacy, Piaget's developmental interactive learning methods	Children ages 0–13 with behavior and conduct problems and their parents; teachers, depending on series	Group format. CR DVD	• Parent series: 8–20 sessions depending on child's age • Teacher series: 6 days or 42 hours • Child series: 22 sessions

Target Problem	Intervention Name Source	Purpose of Intervention	Underlying Frameworks	Intended Recipients	Intervention Format[1] Certification[2] Media[2]	Structure of Intervention
Conduct and Social Problems (continued)	Henggeler, S. W., Schoenwald, S. K., Borduin, C. M., Rowland, M. D., & Cunningham, P. B. (2009). *Multisystemic therapy for antisocial behavior in children and adolescents* (2nd ed.). Program (including sample video clips), purchasing and training information available at http://mstservices.com and www.guilford.com	Intensive multi-context treatment of antisocial behavior in youth with their families	Bronfenbrenner's social ecological model	Adolescents with antisocial behavior; also appropriate for youth with substance abuse disorders or sexual behavior problems	Family and home-based. CR	Session structure is intense and fluid: 60+ hours of direct contact over a period of 3–5 months.
	Eyberg, S., & Funderbunk, B. (2011). *Parent-child interaction therapy protocol 2011.* Program (including sample video clips), purchasing and training information available at www.pcit.org	Treatment of disruptive behavior disorders in young children by focusing on improving parent-child interactions	Attachment theory, social learning theory, Baumrind's parenting styles, Patterson's coercion theory	Children ages 3–6 and their parents.	Parent or caregiver and child; has also been adapted into group format CR	12 sessions, including pre- and post-assessment • 4–5 sessions focused on CDI • 5–7 sessions on PDI • booster sessions as needed
	Kazdin, A. E. (2005). *Parent management training: Treatment for oppositional, aggressive, and antisocial behavior in children and adolescents.* Purchasing information and program materials available at www.oup.com/us/pmt	Parent training for parents of children or adolescents with conduct or oppositional defiant disorders, or with oppositional, aggressive and antisocial behaviors; PMT can be used in conjunction with problem-solving skills training for children above 7 years of age	Social learning theory, behavior theory	Parents of children ages 5–14 with oppositional, aggressive and antisocial behaviors	Individual parent format, with two family sessions and a therapist-teacher consultation	12 sessions

Target Problem	Intervention Name Source	Purpose of Intervention	Underlying Frameworks	Intended Recipients	Intervention Format[1] Certification[2] Media	Structure of Intervention
Conduct and Social Problems (continued)	Sanders, M. R., Markie-Dadds, C., & Turner, K. M. (2001). *Triple P System (Positive Parenting Program).* Program, purchasing and training information available at www. triplep.net	Multi-level parent training and family support for the prevention and early intervention of behavioral, emotional and developmental problems in children and adolescents	Social learning theory, cognitive-behavioral theory, developmental theory	Parents of children and adolescents ages 0–16	Format includes individual and group consultations/ seminars according to level of intervention CR DVD	Sessions range from consultations/ seminars to 10 self-directed, phone, individual or group sessions according to level of intervention
Depression	Stark, K. D., Simpson, J., Schnoebelen, S., Hargrave, J., Molnar, J., & Glen, R. (2007). *Action workbook: Cognitive-behavioral therapy for treating depressed girls.* Purchasing information available at www.workbookpublishing.com/index.php	Treatment of unipolar depression in girls, in conjunction with their parents	Cognitive-behavioral theory, developmental pathways in cognitive, neurochemical, behavioral and family domains	Girls ages 9–13	Group format	20 group sessions and 2 individual sessions over 11 weeks; 10 parent training sessions over 11 weeks
	Clarke, G., Lewinsohn, P., & Hops, H. (2000). *Adolescents coping with depression.* Manuals available for download at www.kpchr.org/acwd/acwd.html	Treatment of unipolar depression in adolescents	Social learning model, cognitive-behavioral theory	Adolescents ages 13–18; exclusionary criteria: active psychotic disorders, bipolar disorder, imminent suicide risk	Group format with 4–8 adolescents; individual format available	16 2-hour sessions
	Mufson, L., Dorta, K. P., Moreau, D., & Weissman, M. M. (2011). *Interpersonal psychotherapy for depressed adolescents* (2nd ed.). Program and purchasing information available at http://interpersonalpsychotherapy.org/ipt-for-adolescents and www.guilford.com	Prevention and treatment for adolescents with mild to moderate depression related to interpersonal relationship patterns	Interpersonal theory of depression, attachment theory	Adolescents ages 12–18; exclusionary criteria: active suicidality, active substance abuse, bipolar disorder, mental retardation, psychotic symptoms	Individual format; parent involvement is encouraged CR	12 sessions

Target Problem	Intervention Name Source	Purpose of Intervention	Underlying Frameworks	Intended Recipients	Intervention Format[1] Certification[1] Media[2]	Structure of Intervention
Developmental Disorders	Koegel, R. L., & Koegel, L. K. (2006). *Pivotal response treatment for autism.* Purchasing information available at www.koegelautism.com	Treatment of autism spectrum disorders in children	Pivotal response therapy and applied behavior analysis	Children ages 2–16 and their parents	Parent and child dyad	Intensive sessions, varied hours per week, varied treatment length
	Lovaas, O. I. (2003). *Teaching individuals with developmental delays.* (ABA) Purchasing information available at www.lovaas.com/approach-method .php	Treatment for children with autism	Behavior theory—applied behavior analysis	Children ages 2–8	Individual sessions, with parent participation CR DVD	Typically 40 hours per week for 3 years
Eating Disorders	Lock, J., & Le Grange, D. (2012). *Treatment manual for anorexia nervosa: A family-based approach* (2nd ed.). Purchasing information available at www.guilford.com	Maudsley family-based treatment of anorexia nervosa in adolescents, with parents placed in charge of the adolescent's eating	Family systems theory and developmental considerations	Adolescents with anorexia nervosa	Family sessions over three phases	Up to 22 sessions over 6–12 months at variable weekly intervals
Elimination Problems	Schroeder, C. S., & Gordon, B. N. (2002). Toileting: Training, enuresis, and encopresis. In Assessment and treatment of childhood problems (2nd ed.) Purchasing information available at www.guilford.com	Treatment of encopresis in children over age 4, varying according to type of encopresis	Incorporates medical, physiological, emotional, learning, family and contextual factors	Children over age 4 and their parents	Requires physician consult prior to treatment; initial interview with child and parents. Subsequent therapist-family communication by phone and written contact.	Varies according to type of encopresis; contact with therapist is encouraged for up to one year

Target Problem	Intervention Name Source	Purpose of Intervention	Underlying Frameworks	Intended Recipients	Intervention Format Certification[1] Media[2]	Structure of Intervention
	Schroeder, C. S., & Gordon, B. N. (2002). Toileting: Training, enuresis, and encopresis. In *Assessment and treatment of childhood problems* (2nd ed.)	Treatment of nocturnal enuresis in children over age 5, with the use of a urine alarm	Targets underlying physiological mechanisms through conditioning or operant intervention	Children over age 5 and their parents	Initial interview with child and parents; after initial session, parent and family communicate with therapist via phone and written contact	Treatment duration may be up to 3 months and is considered successful after 30 dry nights
Loss, Grief and Trauma	Jaycox, L. H. (2003). *Cognitive behavioral interventions for trauma in schools.* Program, online training, and purchasing information available at http://cbitsprogram.org	School-based treatment of students with PTSD, depression, and behavioral problems resulting from exposure to traumatic life events	Cognitive-behavioral theory, social learning theory	Students in 6th–9th grade	Group format (6–8 children in each group), with 1–3 individual sessions; also includes 2 parent psychoeducational and 1 teacher educational session CR DVD	10 sessions
	Deblinger, E., & Heflin, A. H. (1996). *Treating sexually abused children and their nonoffending parents: A cognitive behavioral approach.* Purchasing information available at www.sagepub.com	Treatment of children who have been sexually abused and their nonoffending parents.	Cognitive-behavioral theory	Children ages 3–13 and their nonoffending parents	Individual sessions initially; parent component, gradually moving to family sessions	12–40 sessions
	Cohen, J. A., Mannarino, A. P., & Deblinger, E. (2006). *Treating trauma and traumatic grief in children and adolescents.* (TF-CBT). Purchasing information available at www.guilford.com; additional information and training on TF-CBT available at www.musc.edu/tfcbt	Treatment for problems specifically associated with traumatic events experienced or witnessed by children or adolescents	Cognitive-behavioral theory; includes attachment, family, humanistic and psychodynamic principles	Children and adolescents ages 3–18 with primary trauma symptoms	Parallel individual child and parent sessions, as well as conjoint child-parent sessions CR	8–20 sessions, 60–90 minutes in length

Target Problem	Intervention Name Source	Purpose of Intervention	Underlying Frameworks	Intended Recipients	Intervention Format Certification[1] Media[2]	Structure of Intervention
Obsessive-Compulsive Disorder	Exposure-based cognitive-behavioral therapy (Franklin, Foa & March, 2003; Freeman, Garcia, Coyne, Ale, Przeworski, Himle & Leonard, 2008; Pediatric OCD Treatment Study Team, 2004)	Treatment for children and adolescents with obsessive-compulsive disorder	Cognitive-behavioral theory, including exposure and ritual prevention	Children and adolescents ages 7–17 with obsessive-compulsive disorder	Individual sessions with parent participation in 5 sessions	14 sessions; 1 between-visit 10-minute telephone conversation during sessions 5–12
Substance Abuse	Liddle, H. A. (2009). *Multidimensional family therapy for adolescent drug abuse.* Manual available for download at http://kap.samhsa.gov/products/manuals/cyt/pdfs/cyt5.pdf	Individual and family treatment to eliminate or reduce substance use (and other problem behavior) in adolescents	Family and developmental psychology, risk and protective factors	Adolescents ages 11–18	Individual or family sessions CR	12–16 weekly or biweekly sessions about 60–90 minutes
Suicide and Self-Injury	Miller, A. L., Rathus, J. H., & Linehan, M. M. (2006). *Dialectical behavior therapy with suicidal adolescents.* Program and purchasing information available at http://behavioraltech.org/ and www.guilford.com	Treatment for adolescents at high risk for suicide and self-injurious behavior	Cognitive-behavioral theory, client-centered, interpersonal theories	Adolescents ages 14–18	Individual, group and family format	12–16 weeks of weekly individual and family sessions

[1] = CR: Certification required

[2] =DVD: DVD materials available for training or for treatment

References

Abela, J. R. Z., Brozina, K., & Haigh, E. P. (2002). An examination of the response styles theory of depression in third- and seventh-grade children: A short-term longitudinal study. *Journal of Abnormal Child Psychology, 30*, 515-27.

Abidin, R. R. (1983). *Parenting Stress Index: Manual, administration booklet, and research update*. Charlottesville, VA: Pediatric Psychology Press.

Ablow, J. C., & Measelle, J. R. (2010). Capturing young children's perceptions of marital conflict. In M. S. Schultz, M. K. Pruett, P. K. Kerig & R. D. Parke (Eds.), *Strengthening couple relationships for optimal child development: Lessons from research and intervention* (pp. 41-57). Washington, DC: American Psychological Association.

Achenbach, T. M. (1990). Conceptualizations of developmental psychopathology. In A. J. Sameroff, M. L. Lewis & S. M. Miller (Eds.), *Handbook of developmental psychopathology* (pp. 3-14). New York: Plenum.

Achenbach, T. M. (2000). Assessment of psychopathology. In A. J. Sameroff, M. Lewis & S. M. Miller (Eds.), *Handbook of developmental psychopathology* (2nd ed., pp. 23-56). New York: Kluwer Academic/Plenum.

Ahadi, S. A., Rothbart, M. K., & Ye, R. (1993). Children's temperament in the US and China: Similarities and differences. *European Journal of Personality, 7*(5), 359-77.

Ainsworth, M. D. S. (1969). Object relations, dependency, and attachment: A theoretical review of the infant-mother attachment relationship. *Child Development, 40*, 969-1025.

Ainsworth, M. D. S., Blehar, M. C., Waters, E., & Wall. S. (1978). *Patterns of attachment: A psychological study of the Strange Situation*. Hillsdale, NJ: Erlbaum.

Alessandri, S. M. (1992). Mother-child interactional correlates of maltreated and normal-treated children's play behavior. *Development and Psychopathology, 4*, 257-70.

Alessandri, S. M., & Lewis, M. (1996). Differences in pride and shame in maltreated and nonmaltreated preschoolers. *Child Development, 67*, 1857-69.

Alfano, C. A., & Beidel, D. C. (2011). *Social anxiety in adolescents and young adults: Translating developmental science into practice*. Washington, DC: American Psychological Association.

Alfano, C. A., Beidel, D. C., & Turner, S. M. (2006). Cognitive correlates of social phobia among children and adolescents. *Journal of Abnormal Child Psychology, 34,* 189-201.

Alhabib, S., Nur, U., & Jones, R. (2010). Domestic violence against women: Systematic review of prevalence studies. *Journal of Family Violence, 25,* 369-82.

Alink, L. A., Cicchetti, D., Kim, J., & Rogosch, F. A. (2009). Mediating and moderating processes in the relation between maltreatment and psychopathology: Mother-child relationship quality and emotion regulation. *Journal of Abnormal Child Psychology, 37,* 831-43.

Alink, L. R. A., Mesman, J., van Zeijl, J., Stolk, M. N., Juffer, F., Bakermans-Kranenburg, M. J., van IJzendoorn, M. H., & Koot, H. M. (2009). Maternal sensitivity moderates the relation between negative discipline and aggression in early childhood. *Social Development, 18,* 99-120.

Allen, J. P., Insabella, G., Porter, M. R., Smith, F. D., Land, D., & Phillips, N. (2006). A social-interactional model of the development of depressive symptoms in adolescence. *Journal of Consulting and Clinical Psychology, 74*(1), 55-65.

Allen, J. P., Moore, C., Kuperminc, G., & Bell, K. (1998). Attachment and adolescent psychosocial functioning. *Child Development, 69*(5), 1406-19.

Altman, N., Briggs, R., Frankel, J., Gensler, D., & Pantone, P. (2002). *Relational child psychotherapy.* New York: Other Press.

Amato, P. R. (2000). The consequences of divorce for adults and children. *Journal of Marriage and the Family, 62*(4), 1269-87.

Amato, P. R., & Cheadle, J. (2005). The long reach of divorce: Divorce and child well-being across three generations. *Journal of Marriage and Family, 67,* 191-206.

Amato, P. R., & Cheadle, J. E. (2008). Parental divorce, marital conflict and children's behavior problems: A comparison of adopted and biological children. *Social Forces, 86,* 1139-61.

Amato, P. R., & Keith, B. (1991). Parental divorce and the well-being of children: A meta-analysis. *Psychological Bulletin, 110,* 26-46.

Amato, P. R., Loomis, L. S., & Booth, A. (1995). Parental divorce, marital conflict, and offspring well-being during early adulthood. *Social Forces, 73,* 895-915.

American Psychological Association. (2011). *The road to resilience.* The Help Center. Retrieved from www.apa.org/helpcenter/road-resilience.aspx#.

American Psychological Association. (2013). *Diagnostic and statistical manual of mental disorders* (5th ed.). Arlington, VA: American Psychiatric Publishing.

American Psychological Association Presidential Task Force on Evidence-Based Practice. (2006). Evidence-based practice in psychology. *American Psychologist, 61*(4), 271-85.

American Psychological Association Task Force on Evidence-Based Practice for Children and Adolescents. (2008). *Disseminating evidence-based practice for children and adolescents: A systems approach to enhancing care.* Washington, DC: American Psychological Association.

Anderson, H., & Johnson, S. B. W. (1994). *Regarding children: A new respect for childhood and families.* Louisville, KY: Westminster John Knox Press.

Antony, M. M., & Roemer, L. (2011). *Behavior therapy.* Washington DC: American Psychological Association.

Arsenio, W. F., Cooperman, S., & Lover, A. (2000). Affective predictors of preschoolers' aggression and peer acceptance: Direct and indirect effects. *Developmental Psychology, 36*(4), 438-48.

Asher, S. R., & Coie, J. D. (1990). *Peer rejection in childhood.* Cambridge, MA: Cambridge University Press.

Auerbach, J. G., Berger, A., Atzaba-Poria, N., Arbelle, S., Cypin, N., Friedman, A., & Landau, R. (2008). Temperament at 7, 12, and 25 months in children at familial risk for ADHD. *Infant and Child Development, 17*(4), 321-38.

Auerbach, J., Geller, V., Lezer, S., Shinwell, E., Belmaker, R. H., Levine, J., & Ebstein, R. P. (1999). Dopamine D4 receptor (D4DR) and serotonin transporter promoter (5-HTTLPR) polymorphisms in the determination of temperament in 2-month-old infants. *Molecular Psychiatry, 4*(4), 369-73.

Ayllon, T., & Azrin, N. H. (1965). The measurement and reinforcement of behavior of psychotics. *Journal of Experimental Analysis of Behavior, 8,* 357-83.

Bagwell, C. L. (2004). Friendships, peer networks, and antisocial behavior. In J. B. Kupersmidt & K. Dodge (Eds.), *Children's peer relations: From development to intervention* (pp. 37-57). Washington, DC: American Psychological Association.

Bagwell, C. L., Newcomb, A. F., & Bukowski, W. M. (1998). Preadolescent friendship and peer rejection as predictors of adult adjustment. *Child Development, 69*(1), 140-53.

Ballenger, C. (1992). Because you like us: The language of control. *Harvard Educational Review, 62*(2), 199-208.

Balswick, J., Balswick, J., Piper, B., & Piper, D. (2003). *Relationship-empowerment parenting: Building formative and fulfilling relationships with your children.* Grand Rapids, MI: Baker Books.

Balswick, J. O., & Balswick, J. K. (1999). *The family* (2nd ed.). Grand Rapids, MI: Baker Academic.

Balswick, J. O., & Balswick, J. K. (2007). *The family: A Christian perspective on the contemporary home* (3rd ed.). Grand Rapids, MI: Baker Academic.

Balswick, J. O., King, P. E., & Reimer, K. S. (2005). *The reciprocating self: Human development in theological perspective.* Downers Grove, IL: InterVarsity Press.

Bandura, A. (1969). *Principles of behavior modification.* New York: Holt, Rinehart, & Winston.

Bandura, A. (1977). *Social learning theory.* Englewood Cliffs, NJ: Prentice Hall.

Bandura, A. (1986). *Social foundations of thought and action: A social cognitive theory.* Englewood Cliffs, NJ: Prentice Hall.

Bariola, E., Gullone, E., & Hughes, E. K. (2011). Child and adolescent emotion regulation: The role of parental emotion regulation and expression. *Clinical Child and Family Psychology Review, 14,* 198-212.

Barkley, R. A. (1997). *Defiant children: A clinician's manual for assessment and parent training* (2nd ed.). New York: Guilford.

Barkley, R. A. (2013). *Defiant children: A clinician's manual for assessment and parent training* (3rd ed.). New York: Guilford.

Barkley, R. A., Edwards, G. H., & Robin, A. L. (1999). *Defiant teens: A clinician's manual for assessment and family intervention.* New York: Guilford.

Barrett, P. (2004). *Friends for life: Workbook for children* (4th ed.). Queensland, Australia: Australian Academic Press.

Barrett, P. M., & Ollendick, T. H. (Eds.). (2004). *Handbook of interventions that work with children and adolescents: Prevention and treatment.* Hoboken, NJ: Wiley.

Barrett, P., Turner, C., & Webster-Lowry, H. (2006). *Friends for life: Workbook for youth.* Queensland, Australia: Australian Academic Press.

Barth, K. (2009). *Church dogmatics.* 4 vols. Edinburgh: T & T Clark, 1956-1975.

Barton, S. C. (Ed.). (1996). *The family in theological perspective.* Edinburgh: T & T Clark.

Baumrind, D. (1966). Effects of authoritative parental control on child behavior. *Child Development, 37*(4), 887-907.

Baumrind, D. (1967). Child care practices anteceding three patterns of preschool behavior. *Genetic Psychology Monographs, 75,* 43-88.

Baumrind, D. (1968). Authoritarian v. authoritative parental control. *Adolescence, 3,* 255-72.

Baumrind, D. (1971). Current patterns of parental authority. *Developmental Psychology Monograph, 4* (1, pt. 2), 1-103.

Baumrind, D. (1972). An exploratory study of socialization effects on black children: Some black-white comparisons. *Child Development, 43,* 261-67.

Baumrind, D. (1991). The influence of parenting style on adolescent competence and substance use. *Journal of Early Adolescence, 11,* 56-95.

Baumrind, D. (1996). The discipline controversy revisited. *Family Relations, 45,* 405-11.

Beasly-Murray, G. (1965-1966). Church and child in the New Testament, *Baptist Quarterly, 21,* 195-205.

Beck, A. T. (1967a). *The diagnosis and management of depression.* Philadelphia: University of Pennsylvania Press.

Beck, A. T. (1967b). *Depression: Clinical, experimental, and theoretical aspects.* New York: Hoeber.

Beck, J. S., & Beck, A. T. (2011). *Cognitive behavior therapy: Basics and beyond* (2nd ed). New York: Guilford.

Beck, A. T., Rush, A. J., Shaw, B. F., & Emery, G. (1979). *Cognitive therapy of depression.* New York: Guilford.

Beck, A. T., & Weishaar, M. E. (2008). Cognitive therapy. In R. J. Corsini & D. Wedding (Eds.), *Current psychotherapies* (8th ed., pp. 263-94). Belmont, CA: Brooks/Cole.

Becker, S. P., Luebbe, A. M., & Langberg, J. M. (2012). Co-occurring mental health problems and peer functioning among youth with attention-deficit/hyperactivity disorder: A review and recommendations for future research. *Clinical Child and Family Psychology Review, 15,* 279-302.

Becker-Weidman, A., & Shell, D. (Eds.). (2005). *Creating capacity for attachment.* Oklahoma City, OK: Wood 'N' Barnes.

Beebe, B., Jaffe, J., Buck, K., Chen, H., Cohen, P., Feldstein, S., & Andrews, H. (2008). Six-week postpartum maternal depressive symptoms and 4-month mother-infant self- and interactive contingency. *Infant Mental Health Journal, 29,* 442-71.

Beidel, D. C., & Turner, S. M. (2007). *Shy children, phobic adults: Nature and treatment of social phobia.* Washington, DC: American Psychological Association.

Beidel, D. C., Turner, S. M., & Morris, T. L. (1999). Psychopathology of childhood social phobia. *Journal of the American Academy of Child and Adolescent Psychiatry, 38*(6), 643-50.

Bell, S., & Eyberg, S. M. (2002). Parent-child interaction therapy. In L. VandeCreek, S. Knapp & T. L. Jackson (Eds.), *Innovations in clinical practice: A source book* (Vol. 20, pp. 57-74). Sarasota, FL: Professional Resource Press.

Bell-Dolan, D. J., Foster, S. L., & Christopher, J. (1995). Girls' peer relations and internalizing problems: Are socially neglected, rejected, and withdrawn girls at risk? *Journal of Clinical Child Psychology, 24*(4), 463-73.

Belsky, J. (2005). Differential susceptibility to rearing influences: An evolutionary hypothesis and some evidence. In B. Ellis & D. Bjorklund (Eds.), *Origins of the social mind: Evolutionary psychology and child development* (pp. 139-63). New York: Guilford.

Belsky, J., & Fearon, R. M. P. (2004). Exploring marriage-parenting typologies and their contextual antecedents and developmental sequelae. *Development and Psychopathology, 16,* 501-23.

Belsky, J., Fish, M., & Isabella, R. (1991). Continuity and discontinuity in infant negative and positive emotionality: Family antecedents and attachment consequences. *Developmental Psychology, 27,* 421-31.

Belsky, J., Youngblade, L., Rovine, M., & Volling, B. (1991). Patterns of marital change and parent-child interaction. *Journal of Marriage and the Family, 53,* 487-98.

Benard, B. (1991). *Fostering resiliency in kids: Protective factors in the family, school, and community.* Portland, OR: Northwest Regional Educational Laboratory.

Benard, B. (2004). *Resiliency: What we have learned.* San Francisco: WestEd.

Bendroth, M. (2001). Horace Bushnell's Christian nurture. In M. Bunge (Ed.), *The child in Christian thought* (pp. 350-64). Grand Rapids, MI: Eerdmans.

Benson, P. L. (2008). *Sparks.* San Francisco: Jossey-Bass.

Benson, P. L., Roehlkepartain, E. C., & Rude, S. P. (2003). Spiritual development in childhood and adolescence: Toward a field of inquiry. *Applied Developmental Science, 7,* 204-12.

Benson, P. L., & Scales, P. C. (2009). The definition and preliminary measurement of thriving in adolescence. *The Journal of Positive Psychology, 4,* 85-104.

Benson, P. L., Scales, P. C., Hamilton, S. F., & Sesma, A., Jr. (2006). Positive youth development: Theory, research and applications. In W. Damon & R. M. Lerner (Eds.), *Handbook of child psychology: Theoretical models of human development* (6th ed., Vol. 1, pp. 894-941). New York: Wiley.

Berger, K. S. (2012). *The developing person through the life span* (8th ed.). New York: Worth Publishers.

Berkman, L. F., Glass, T., Brissette, I., & Seeman, T. E. (2000). From social integration to health: Durkheim in the new millennium. *Social Science & Medicine, 51*(6), 843-57.

Bernard, R. S., Williams, S. E., Storfer-Isser, A., Rhine, W., Horwitz, S., Koopman, C., & Shaw, R. J. (2011). Brief cognitive-behavioral intervention for maternal depression and trauma in the neonatal intensive care unit: A pilot study. *Journal of Traumatic Stress, 24,* 230-34.

Berndt, T. J., & McCandless, M. A. (2009). Methods for investigating children's relationships with friends. In K. H. Rubin, W. M. Bukowski & B. Laursen (Eds.), *Handbook of peer interactions, relationships, and groups* (pp. 63-81). New York: Guilford.

Bernstein, D. A., Borkovec, T. D., & Hazlett-Stevens, H. (2000). *New directions in progressive relaxation training: A guidebook for helping professionals.* Westport, CT: Praeger.

Berzoff, J., Flanagan, L. M., & Hertz, P. (1996). *Inside out and outside in: Psychodynamic clinical theory and practice in contemporary multicultural contexts.* Northvale, NJ: Jason Aronson.

Biederman, J., Mick, E., Faraone, S. V., & Burback, M. (2001). Patterns of remission and symptom decline in conduct disorder: A four-year prospective study of an ADHD sample. *Journal of the American Academy of Child and Adolescent Psychiatry, 40,* 290-98.

Bierman, K. L. (2005). *Peer rejection: Developmental processes and intervention strategies.* New York: Guilford.

Bierman, K. L., Coie, J. D., Dodge, K. A., Greenberg, M. T., Lochman, J. E., McMahon, R. J., & Pinderhughes, E. E. (2002). Using the Fast Track randomized prevention trial to test the early-starter model of the development of serious conduct problems. *Development and Psychopathology, 14,* 925-43.

Bierman, K. L., & Erath, S. A. (2004). Prevention and intervention programs promoting positive peer relations in early childhood. In R. E. Tremblay, R. G. Barr & R. DeV. Peters (Eds.), *Encyclopedia on Early Childhood Development* [online]. Montreal: Centre of Excellence for Early Childhood Development (1-5). www.child-encyclo pedia.com/documents/Bierman-ErathANGxp.pdf

Bierman, K. L., & Powers, C. J. (2009). Social skills training to improve peer relations. In K. H. Rubin, W. Bukowski & B. Laursen (Eds.), *Handbook of peer interactions, relationships, and groups* (pp. 603-21). New York: Guilford.

Blackburn, A. M. (2008). *Take the challenge: Adolescents with Asperger's syndrome developing social competence within community.* (Unpublished doctoral dissertation). Wheaton College: Wheaton, IL.

Blakeney, R. F., & Blakeney, C. D. (2006). Delinquency: A quest for moral and spiritual integrity? In E. C. Roehlkepartain, P. E. King, L. Wagener & P. L. Benson (Eds.), *The handbook of spiritual development in childhood and adolescence* (pp. 371-83). Thousand Oaks, CA: Sage.

Blaustein, M. E., & Kinniburgh, K. M. (2007). Intervention beyond the child: The intertwining nature of attachment and trauma. *British Psychological Society, Briefing Paper 26,* 48-53.

Blaustein, M. E., & Kinniburgh, K. M. (2010). *Treating traumatic stress in children and adolescents: How to foster resilience through attachment, self-regulation, and competency.* New York: Guilford.

Blevins, D. G. (2012). What "has" happened to sin? Reconceptualizing childhood depravity. In K. E Lawson (Ed.), *Understanding children's spirituality: Theology, research, and practice* (pp. 60-83). Eugene, OR: Cascade Books.

Bodiford McNeil, C., & Hembree-Kigin, T. L. (2010). *Parent-child interaction therapy* (2nd ed.). New York: Springer Verlag.

Bolger, K. E., Patterson, C. J., & Kupersmidt, J. B. (1998). Peer relationships and self-esteem among children who have been maltreated. *Child Development, 69*(4), 1171-97.

Booth-LaForce, C., & Kerns, K. A. (2009). Child-parent attachment relationships, peer relationships, and peer-group functioning. In K. H. Rubin, W. M. Bukowski & B. Laursen (Eds.), *Handbook of peer interactions, relationships, and groups* (pp. 490-507). New York: Guilford.

Borelli, J. L., Crowley, M. J., David, D. H., Sbarra, D. A., Anderson, G. M., & Mayes, L. C. (2010). Attachment and emotion in school-aged children. *Emotion, 10,* 475-85.

Bornstein, M. H. (1995). Form and function: Implications for studies of culture and human development. *Culture and Psychology, 1*(1), 123-37.

Bornstein, M. H., & Lamb, M. E. (2011). *Developmental science: An advanced textbook* (6th ed.). Mahwah, NJ: Erlbaum.

Bosquet, M., & Egeland, B. (2006). The development and maintenance of anxiety symptoms from infancy through adolescence in a longitudinal sample. *Development and Psychopathology, 18,* 517-50.

Boulware, G., Schwartz, I. S., Sandall, S. R., & McBride, B. J. (2006). Project DATA for toddlers: An inclusive approach to very young children with autism spectrum disorder. *Topics in Early Childhood Special Education, 26*(2), 94-105.

Bowlby, J. (1969). *Attachment and loss* (Vol. 1). London: Hogarth Press.

Bowlby, J. (1988). *A secure base: Parent-child attachment and healthy human development.* New York: Basic Books.

Boyatzis, C. J., & Janicki, D. L. (2003). Parent-child communication about religion: Survey and diary data on unilateral transmission and bi-directional reciprocity styles. *Review of Religious Research, 44,* 252-70.

Bradley, R. H., & Corwyn, R. F. (2008). Infant temperament, parenting, and externalizing behavior in first grade: A test of the differential susceptibility hypothesis. *Journal of Child Psychology and Psychiatry, 49*(2), 124-31.

Braet, C., & van Aken, M. (2006). Developmental psychopathology: Substantive, methodological and policy issues. *International Journal of Behavioral Development, 30*(1), 2-4.

Braungart, J. M., & Stifter, C. A. (1991). Regulation of negative reactivity during the Strange Situation: Temperament and attachment in 12-month-olds. *Infant Behavior and Development, 14,* 349-64.

Braungart-Rieker, J. M., & Stifter, C. A. (1996). Infants' responses to frustrating situations: Continuity and change in reactivity and regulation. *Child Development, 67,* 1767-77.

Brekus, C. A. (2001). Children of wrath, children of grace: Jonathan Edwards and the Puritan culture of child rearing. In M. Bunge (Ed.), *The child in Christian thought* (pp. 300-328). Grand Rapids, MI: Eerdmans.

Brendgen, M. (2012). Genetics and peer relations: A review. *Journal of Research on Adolescence, 22*(3), 419-37.

Brendgen, M., & Boivin, M. (2009). Genetic factors in children's peer relations. In K. H. Rubin, W. M. Bukowski & B. Laursen (Eds.), *Handbook of peer interactions, relationships, and groups* (pp. 455-72). New York: Guilford.

Brendgen, M., Vitaro, F., & Bukowski, W. M. (2000). Stability and variability of adolescents' affiliation with delinquent friends: Predictors and consequences. *Social Development, (9)*2, 205-25.

Bretherton, I., Fritz, J., Zahn-Waxler, C., & Ridgeway, D. (1986). Learning to talk about emotions: A functionalist perspective. *Child Development, 57,* 529-48.

Breunlin, D., Pinsof, W., Russell, W., & Lebow, J. (2011). Integrative problem-centered metaframeworks therapy I: Core concepts and hypothesizing. *Family Process, 50*(3), 293-313.

Breunlin, D., Schwartz, R., & MacKune-Karrer, B. (1992). *Metaframeworks: Transcending the models of family therapy.* San Francisco: Jossey-Bass.

Bridges, J. C. (1985). Major life shapers: Marriage and family. *Perspectives in Religious Studies, 12*(4), 49-66.

Bridges, K. M. B. (1931). *The social and emotional development of the pre-school child.* Oxford, England: Kegan Paul.

Brinkmeyer, M., & Eyberg, S. M. (2003). Parent-child interaction therapy for oppositional children. In A. E. Kazdin & J. R. Weisz (Eds.), *Evidence-based psychotherapies for children and adolescents* (pp. 204-23). New York: Guilford.

Brody, G. H., & Flor, D. L. (1998). Maternal resources, parenting practices, and child competence in rural, single-parent African American families. *Child Development, 69,* 803-16.

Brody, G. H., Flor, D. L., & Gibson, N. M. (1999). Linking maternal efficacy beliefs, developmental goals, parenting practices, and child competence in rural single-parent African American families. *Child Development, 70,* 1197-1208.

Broeren, S., Muris, P., Bouwmeester, S., van der Heijden, K. B., & Abee, A. (2011). The role of repetitive negative thoughts in the vulnerability for emotional problems in non-clinical children. *Journal of Child and Family Studies, 20*(2), 135-48.

Bromfield, R. N. (2003). Psychoanalytic play therapy. In C. E. Schaefer (Ed.), *Foundations of play therapy* (pp. 1-13). Hoboken, NJ: John Wiley & Sons.

Bromfield, R. N. (2007). *Doing child and adolescent psychotherapy: Adapting psychodynamic treatment to contemporary practice* (2nd ed.). Hoboken, NJ: John Wiley & Sons.

Bronfenbrenner, U. (1979). *The ecology of human development: Experiments by nature and design.* Cambridge, MA: Harvard University Press.

Bronfenbrenner, U. (1986). Ecology of the family as a context for human development: Research perspectives. *Developmental Psychology, 22,* 723-42.

Bronfenbrenner, U. (1994). Ecological model of human development. *International Encyclopedia of Education, 3* (2nd ed.) Oxford, England: Elsevier.

Brooks, J. E. (2006). Strengthening resilience in children and youths: Maximizing opportunities through the schools. *Children and Schools, 28,* 69-76.

Brown, B. B., & Dietz, E. L. (2009). Informal peer groups in middle childhood and adolescence. In K. H. Rubin, W. M. Bukowski & B. Laursen (Eds.), *Handbook of peer interactions, relationships, and groups* (pp. 361-76). New York: Guilford.

Browning, D. S. (2011). The best love of the child? An integrational view. In T. P. Jackson (Ed.), *The best love of the child: Being loved and being taught to love as the first human right* (pp. 347-72). Grand Rapids, MI: Eerdmans.

Brumariu, L. E., Kerns, K. A., & Seibert, A. (2012). Mother-child attachment, emotion regulation, and anxiety symptoms in middle childhood. *Personal Relationships, 19,* 569-85.

Buck, K. A., & Dix, T. (2012). Can developmental changes in inhibition and peer relationships explain why depressive symptoms increase in early adolescence? *Journal of Youth and Adolescence, 41*(4), 403-13.

Buckner, J. C., Mezzacappa, E., & Beardslee, W. R. (2003). Characteristics of resilient youths living in poverty: The role of self-regulatory processes. *Development and Psychopathology, 15,* 139-62.

Buhrmester, D., & Furman, W. (1987). The development of companionship and intimacy. *Child Development, 58*(4), 1101-13.

Bukowski, W. M., Motzoi, C., & Meyer, F. (2009). Friendship as process, function, and outcome. In K. H. Rubin, W. M. Bukowski & B. Laursen (Eds.), *Handbook of peer interactions, relationships, and groups* (pp. 217-31). New York: Guilford.

Bukowski, W. M., & Sippola, L. K. (1996). Friendship and morality. In W. M. Bukowski, A. F. Newcomb & W. W. Hartup (Eds.), *The company they keep: Friendship during childhood and adolescence* (pp. 238-61). New York: Cambridge University Press.

Bundick, M. J., Yeager, D. S., King, P. E., & Damon, W. (2010). Thriving across the lifespan. In R. M. Lerner, M. E. Lamb & A. M. Freund (Eds.), *The handbook of life-span development* (pp. 882-923). Hoboken, NJ: Wiley.

Bunge, M. J. (2001a). Introduction. In M. Bunge (Ed.), *The child in Christian thought* (pp. 1-28). Grand Rapids, MI: Eerdmans.

Bunge, M. J. (2001b). Education and the child in eighteenth-century German Pietism: Perspectives from the work of A. H. Francke. In M. Bunge (Ed.), *The child in Christian thought* (pp. 247-78). Grand Rapids, MI: Eerdmans.

Bunge, M. J. (2008). Introduction. In M. Bunge, T. Fretheim & B. Gaventa, (Eds.), *The child in the Bible* (pp. xiv-xxvi). Grand Rapids, MI: Eerdmans.

Burchinal, M., Roberts, J. E., Zeisel, S. A., Hennon, E. A., & Hooper, S. (2006). Social risk and protective child, parenting, and child care factors in early elementary school years. *Parenting: Science and Practice, 6,* 79-113.

Burke, J. D., Pardini, D. A., & Loeber, R. (2008). Reciprocal relationships between parenting behavior and disruptive psychopathology from childhood through adolescence. *Journal of Abnormal Child Psychology, 36*(5), 679-92.

Bushnell, H. (1860). *Christian nurture.* New York: Charles Scribner.

Bushnell, H. (1984). Discourses on Christian nurture. In D. L. Smith (Ed.), *Horace Bushnell: Selected writings on language, religion, and American culture* (pp. 107-11). Chico, CA: Scholars Press. (Reprinted from *Views of Christian Nurture,* pp. 6, 14-22, by H. Bushnell, 1847, Hartford, CT: Edwin Hunt)

Buss, A. H., & Plomin, R. (1984). *Temperament: Early developing personality traits.* Hillsdale, NJ: Erlbaum.

Buss, K. A., & Goldsmith, H. H. (1998). Fear and anger regulation in infancy: Effects on the temporal dynamics of affective expression. *Child Development, 69,* 359-74.

Calkins, S. D. (1994). Origins and outcomes of individual differences in emotion regulation. In N. A. Fox (Ed.), *The development of emotion regulation: Biological and behavioral considerations. Monographs of the Society for Research in Child Development, 59*(2-3, Serial No. 240), 53-72.

Calkins, S. D. (2010). Commentary: Conceptual and methodological challenges to the study of emotion regulation and psychopathology. *Journal of Psychopathology and Behavioral Assessment, 32,* 92-95.

Calkins, S. D., & Dedmon, S. E. (2000). Physiological and behavioral regulation in two-year-old children with aggressive/destructive behavior problems. *Journal of Abnormal Child Psychology, 28,* 103-18.

Calkins, S. D., Gill, K. L., Johnson, M. C., & Smith, C. L. (1999). Emotional reactivity and emotional regulation strategies as predictors of social behavior with peers during toddlerhood. *Social Development, 8,* 310-34.

Calkins, S. D., & Hill, A. (2007). Caregiver influences on emerging emotion regulation: Biological and environmental transactions in early development. In J. J. Gross (Ed.), *Handbook of emotion regulation* (pp. 229-48). New York: Guilford.

Calkins, S. D., & Johnson, M. C. (1998). Toddler regulation of distress to frustrating events: Temperamental and maternal correlates. *Infant Behavior and Development, 21,* 379-95.

Callender, K. A., Olson, S. L., Choe, D. E., & Sameroff, A. J. (2012). The effects of pa-

rental depressive symptoms, appraisals, and physical punishment on later child externalizing behavior. *Journal of Abnormal Child Psychology, 40*(3), 471-83.

Campbell, S. B. (1995). Behavior problems in preschool children: A review of recent
research. *Journal of Child Psychology and Psychiatry, 36,* 113-49.

Canning, S. S., Case, P. W., & Kruse, S. J. (2001). Contemporary Christian psychological
scholarship and "The least of these": An empirical review. *Journal of Psychology and
Christianity, 20,* 205-23.

Cardno, A. G., & Gottesman, I. I. (2000). Twin studies of schizophrenia: From bow-
and-arrow concordances to Star Wars Mx and functional genomics. *American
Journal of Medical Genetics, 97,* 12-17.

Carlson, G. A., & Grant, K. E. (2008). The roles of stress and coping in explaining
gender differences in risk for psychopathology among African American urban
adolescents. *Journal of Early Adolescence, 28*(3), 375-404.

Carlson, S. M., & Wang, T. S. (2007). Inhibitory control and emotion regulation in
preschool children. *Cognitive Development, 22,* 489-510.

Carthy, T., Horesh, N., Apter, A., & Gross, J. J. (2010). Patterns of emotional reactivity
and regulation in children with anxiety disorders. *Journal of Psychopathology and
Behavioral Assessment, 32,* 23-36.

Caspi, A. (2000). The child is father of the man: Personality continuities from childhood
to adulthood. *Journal of Personality and Social Psychology, 78*(1), 158-72.

Caspi, A., Begg, D., Dickson, N., Harrington, H., Langley, J., Moffitt, T. E., & Silva, P. A.
(1997). Personality differences predict health-risk behaviors in young adulthood:
Evidence from a longitudinal study. *Journal of Personality and Social Psychology,
73*(5), 1052-63.

Caspi, A., Harrington, H., Milne, B., Amell, J. W., Theodore, R. F., & Moffitt, T. E. (2003).
Children's behavioral styles at age 3 are linked to their adult personality traits at age
26. *Journal of Personality, 71*(4), 495-513.

Caspi, A., Henry, B., McGee, R. O., Moffitt, T. E., & Silva, P. A. (1995). Temperamental
origins of child and adolescent behavior problems: From age three to age fifteen.
Child Development, 66, 55-68.

Caspi, A., & Silva, P. A. (1995). Temperamental qualities at age three predict personality
traits in young adulthood: Longitudinal evidence from a birth cohort. *Child Development, 66*(2), 486-98.

Cassidy, J. (1994). Emotion regulation: Influences of attachment relationships. In N. A.
Fox (Ed.), *The development of emotion regulation: Biological and behavioral consid-
erations. Monographs of the Society for Research in Child Development, 59*(2-3, Serial
No. 240), 228-49.

Caughy, M., Franzini, L., Windle, M., Dittus, P., Cuccaro, P., Elliott, M. N., & Schuster, M. A. (2012). Social competence in late elementary school: Relationships to parenting and neighborhood context. *Journal of Youth and Adolescence, 41*(12), 1613-27.

Centers for Disease Control and Prevention. (2007). The effectiveness of universal school-based programs for the prevention of violent and aggressive behavior: A report on recommendations of the Task Force on Community Preventive Services. *Morbidity and Mortality Weekly Report, 56*(7), 1-12.

Cerel, J., Fristad, M. A., Verducci, J., Weller, R. A., & Weller, E. B. (2006). Childhood bereavement: Psychopathology in the 2 years postparental death. *Journal of the American Academy of Child and Adolescent Psychiatry, 45*(6), 681-90.

Chaffin, M., Silovsky, J. F., Funderburk, B., Valle, L. A., Brestan, E. V., Balachova, T., . . . Bonner, B. L. (2004). *Journal of Consulting and Clinical Psychology, 72*(3), 500-510.

Chambless, D. L., & Hollon, S. (1998). Defining empirically supported therapies. *Journal of Consulting and Clinical Psychology, 66*, 7-18.

Chang, L., Schwartz, D., Dodge, K. A., & McBride-Chang, C. (2003). Harsh parenting in relation to child emotion regulation and aggression. *Journal of Family Psychology, 17*, 589-606.

Chansky, T., & Kendall, P. C. (1997). Social expectancies and self-perceptions in anxiety-disordered children. *Journal of Anxiety Disorders, 11*(4), 347-63.

Chao R. (2001). Extending research on the consequences of parenting style for Chinese Americans and European Americans. *Child Development, 72*, 1832-43.

Chen, X., Chung, J., & Hsiao, C. (2009). Peer interactions and relationships from a cross-cultural perspective. In K. H. Rubin, W. M. Bukowski & B. Laursen (Eds.), *Handbook of peer interactions, relationships, and groups* (pp. 432-54). New York: Guilford.

Chen, X., Hastings, P. D., Rubin, K. H., Chen, H., Cen, G., & Stewart, S. L. (1998). Child-rearing attitudes and behavioral inhibition in Chinese and Canadian toddlers: A cross-cultural study. *Developmental Psychology, 34*(4), 677-86.

Chess, S., & Thomas, A. (1986). *Temperament in clinical practice.* New York: Guilford.

Chorpita, B. F., & Barlow, D. H. (1998). The development of anxiety: The role of control in the early environment. *Psychological Bulletin, 124*, 3-21.

Chorpita, B. F., & Daleiden, E. L. (2009). Mapping evidence-based treatments for children and adolescents: Application of the distillation and matching model to 615 treatments from 322 randomized trials. *Journal of Consulting and Clinical Psychology, 77*(3), 566-79.

Chorpita, B. F., Daleiden, E. L., Ebesutani, C., Young, J., Becker, K. D., Nakamura, B. J., . . . Starace, N. (2011). Evidence-based treatments for children and adolescents: An updated review of indicators of efficacy and effectiveness. *Clinical Psychology: Science and Practice, 18*(2), 154-72.

Christenson, S. L., & Thurlow, M. L. (2004). School dropouts: Prevention considerations, interventions, and challenges. *Current Directions in Psychological Science, 13*(1), 36-39.

Christie-Mizell, C. A. (2003). Bullying: The consequences of interparental discord on child's self-concept. *Family Process, 42,* 237-51.

Christophersen, E. R., & VanScoyoc, S. M. (2013). *Treatments that work with children: Empirically supported strategies for managing childhood problems* (2nd ed.). Washington, DC: American Psychological Association.

Cicchetti, D. (1987). Developmental psychopathology infancy: Illustrations from the study of maltreated youngsters. *Journal of Consulting and Clinical Psychology, 55,* 837-45.

Cicchetti, D. (1989). Developmental psychopathology: Past, present, and future. In D. Cicchetti (Ed.), *The emergence of a discipline: Rochester symposium on developmental psychopathology* (Vol. 1, pp. 1-12). Hillsdale, NJ: Lawrence Erlbaum.

Cicchetti, D. (2006). Development and psychopathology. In D. Cicchetti & D. J. Cohen (Eds.), *Developmental psychopathology* (2nd ed., Vol. 1, pp. 1-23). Hoboken, NJ: Wiley & Sons.

Cicchetti, D. (2008). A multiple-levels-of-analysis perspective on research in development and psychopathology. In T. P. Beauchaine & S. P. Hinshaw (Eds.), *Child and adolescent psychopathology* (pp. 27-57). Hoboken, NJ: Wiley & Sons.

Cicchetti, D., & Aber, J. L. (Eds.). (1998). Contextualism and developmental psychopathology [Special issue]. *Development and Psychopathology, 10,* 137-426.

Cicchetti, D., & Cohen, D. J. (1995). Perspectives on developmental psychopathology. In D. Cicchetti & D. J. Cohen (Eds.), *Developmental psychopathology, Vol. 1: Theory and methods* (pp. 3-20). Oxford, England: John Wiley & Sons.

Cicchetti, D., & Hinshaw, S. P. (2002). Prevention and intervention science: Contributions to developmental theory [Editorial]. *Development and Psychopathology, 14*(4), 667-71.

Cicchetti, D., & Howes, P. W. (1991). Developmental psychopathology in the context of the family: Illustrations from the study of child maltreatment. *Canadian Journal of Behavioral Science, 23,* 257-81.

Cicchetti, D., & Rogosch, F. A. (1996). Equifinality and multifinality in developmental psychopathology. *Development and Psychopathology, 8*(4), 597-600.

Cicchetti, D., & Toth, S. L. (1992). The role of developmental theory in prevention and intervention. *Development and Psychopathology, 4,* 489-93.

Cicchetti, D., & Toth, S. L. (1995). A developmental psychopathology perspective on child abuse and neglect. *Journal of the American Academy of Child and Adolescent Psychiatry, 34*(5), 541-65.

Cicchetti, D., & Toth, S. L. (2005). Child maltreatment. *Annual Review of Clinical Psychology, 1*, 409-38.

Cillessen, A. H. N. (2009). Sociometric methods. In K. H. Rubin, W. M. Bukowski & B. Laursen (Eds.), *Handbook of peer interactions, relationships, and groups* (pp. 82-99). New York: Guilford.

Cillessen, A. H. N., & Bukowski, W. M. (2000). *Recent advances in the measurement of acceptance and rejection in the peer system.* San Francisco: Jossey-Bass.

Cillessen, A. N., & Mayeux, L. (2004). Sociometric status and peer group behavior: Previous findings and current directions. In J. B. Kupersmidt & K. A. Dodge (Eds.), *Children's peer relations: From development to intervention* (pp. 3-20). Washington, DC: American Psychological Association.

Cisler, J. M., Olatunji, B. O., Feldner, M. T., & Forsyth, J. P. (2010). Emotion regulation and the anxiety disorders: A review. *Journal of Psychology and Behavioral Assessment, 32*, 68-82.

Clarke, G., Lewinsohn, P., & Hops, H. (2000). *Leader's manual for adolescent group: Adolescents coping with depression course.* Retrieved from www.kpchr.org/acwd/acwd.html.

Coffman, J. K., Guerin, D. W., & Gottfried, A. W. (2006). Reliability and validity of the Parent-Child Relationship Inventory (PCRI): Evidence from a longitudinal cross-informant investigation. *Psychological Assessment, 18*, 209-14.

Cohen, J. A., Mannarino, A. P., & Deblinger, E. (2006). *Treating trauma and traumatic grief in children and adolescents.* New York: Guilford.

Cohen, J. A., Mannarino, A. P., & Deblinger, E. (2010). Trauma-focused cognitive behavioral therapy for traumatized children. In J. R. Weisz & A. E. Kazdin (Eds.), *Evidence-based psychotherapies for children and adolescents* (2nd ed., pp. 295-311). New York: Guilford.

Cohen, J. A., Mannarino, A. P., Deblinger, E., & Berliner, L. (2009). Cognitive-behavioral therapy for children and adolescents. In E. B. Foa, T. M. Keane, M. J. Friedman & J. A. Cohen (Eds.), *Effective treatments for PTSD: Practice guidelines from the International Society for Traumatic Stress Studies* (pp. 223-44). New York: Guilford.

Cohn, J. F., Campbell, S. B., Matias, R., & Hopkins, J. (1990). Face-to-face interactions of postpartum depressed and nondepressed mother-infant pairs at 2 months. *Developmental Psychology, 26*, 15-23.

Cohn, J. F., & Tronick, E. Z. (1983). Three-month-old infants' reaction to simulated maternal depression. *Child Development, 54,* 185-93.

Coie, J. D. (2004). The impact of negative social experiences on the development of antisocial behavior. In J. B. Kupersmidt & K. A. Dodge (Eds.), *Children's peer relations: From development to intervention* (pp. 243-67). Washington, DC: American Psychological Association.

Coie, J. D., Miller-Johnson, S., & Bagwell, C. (2000). Prevention science. In A. J. Sameroff, M. Lewis & S. M. Miller (Eds.), *Handbook of developmental psychopathology* (2nd ed., pp. 23-56). New York: Kluwer Academic/Plenum.

Coie, J. D., Watt, N. F., West, S. G., Hawkins, J., Asarnow, J. R., Markman, H. J., . . . Long, B. (1993). The science of prevention: A conceptual framework and some directions for a national research program. *American Psychologist, 48*(10), 1013-22.

Coiro, M. J., & Emery, R. E. (1998). Do marriage problems affect fathering more than mothering? A quantitative and qualitative review. *Clinical Child and Family Psychology Review, 1,* 23-40. doi:10.1023/A:1021896231471

Cole, P. M. (1986). Children's spontaneous control of facial expression. *Child Development, 57,* 1309-21.

Cole, P. M., Barrett, K. C., & Zahn-Waxler, C. (1992). Emotion displays in two-year-olds during mishaps. *Child Development, 63,* 314-24.

Cole, P. M., Bruschi, C. J., & Tamang, B. L. (2002). Cultural differences in children's emotional reactions to difficult situations. *Child Development, 73,* 983-96.

Cole, P. M., Dennis, T. A., Martin, S. E., & Hall, S. E. (2008). Emotion regulation and the early development of psychopathology. In M. Vandekerckhove, C. von Scheve, S. Ismer, S. Jung & S. Kronast (Eds.), *Regulating emotions: Culture, social necessity, and biological inheritance* (pp. 171-88). Malden, MA: Blackwell.

Cole, P. M., Hall, S. E., & Hajal, N. (2013). Emotion dysregulation as a risk factor for psychopathology. In T. Beauchaine & S. Hinshaw (Eds.), *Child and adolescent psychopathology* (2nd ed., pp. 341-73). Hoboken, NJ: Wiley.

Cole, P. M., Michel, M. K., & Teti, L. O. (1994). The development of emotion regulation and dysregulation: A clinical perspective. In N. A. Fox (Ed.), *The development of emotion regulation: Biological and behavioral considerations. Monographs of the Society for Research in Child Development, 59*(2-3, Serial No. 240), 73-100.

Cole, P. M., Tamang, B. L., & Shrestha, S. (2006). Cultural variations in the socialization of young children's anger and shame. *Child Development, 77,* 1237-51.

Cole, P. M., Tan, P. Z., Hall, S. E., Zhang, Y., Crnic, K. A., Blair, C. B., & Li, R. (2011). Developmental changes in anger expression and attention focus during a delay: Learning to wait. *Developmental Psychology, 47,* 1078-89.

Cole, P. M., Zahn-Waxler, C., Fox, N. A., Usher, B. A., & Welsh, J. D. (1996). Individual differences in emotion regulation and behavior problems in preschool children. *Journal of Abnormal Psychology, 105*, 518-29.

Coles, R. (1991). *The spiritual life of children.* New York: Mariner Books.

Collaborative for Academic, Social, and Emotional Learning (CASEL). (2013). *2013 CASEL guide: Effective social and emotional learning (SEL) programs—preschool and elementary school edition.* Chicago: Author.

Collins, C. E., Whiters, D. L., & Braithwaite, R. (2007). *The saved sista project: A faith-based HIV prevention program for black women in addictions recovery, 22*(2), 76-82.

Colman, R. A., Hardy, S. A., Albert, M., Raffaelli, M., & Crockett, L. (2006). Early predictors of self-regulation in middle childhood. *Infant and Child Development, 15*, 421-37.

Compas, B. E. (1987). Coping with stress during childhood and adolescence. *Psychological Bulletin, 101*, 393-403.

Congdon, E., Service, S., Wessman, J., Seppänen, J. K., Schönauer, S., Miettunen, J., . . . Freimer, N. B. (2012). Early environment and neurobehavioral development predict adult temperament clusters. *Plos ONE, 7*(7), e38065.

Contreras, J. M., Kerns, K. A., Weimer, B. L., Gentzler, A. L., & Tomich, P. L. (2000). Emotion regulation as a mediator of associations between mother-child attachment and peer relationships in middle childhood. *Journal of Family Psychology, 14*, 111-24.

Conway, C. C., Rancourt, D., Adelman, C. B., Burk, W. J., & Prinstein, M. J. (2011). Depression socialization within friendship groups at the transition to adolescence: The roles of gender and group centrality as moderators of peer influence. *Journal of Abnormal Psychology, 120*, 857-67.

Cooey, P. M. (1996). *Family, freedom, and faith: Building community today.* Louisville, KY: Westminster John Knox Press.

Cook, E. C., Buehler, C., & Blair, B. L. (2013). Adolescents' emotional reactivity across relationship contexts. *Developmental Psychology, 49*, 341-52.

Coplan, R. J., & Arbeau, K. A. (2009). Peer interactions and play in early childhood. In K. H. Rubin, W. M. Bukowski & B. Laursen (Eds.), *Handbook of peer interactions, relationships, and groups* (pp. 143-61). New York: Guilford.

Cordova, J. V. (2001). Acceptance in behavior therapy: Understanding the process of change. *Behavior Analyst, 24*, 213-26.

Costa, P. T., & McCrae, R. R. (1992). *Revised NEO Personality Inventory (NEO-PI-R) and NEO Five-Factor Inventory (NEO-FFI) professional manual.* Odessa, FL: Psychological Assessment Resources.

Couture, P. (2000). *Seeing children, seeing God: A practical theology of children and poverty.* Nashville: Abingdon Press.

Couture, P. (2007). *Child poverty: Love, justice, and social responsibility.* Danvers, MA: Chalice Press.

Covell, K., & Miles, B. (1992). Children's beliefs about strategies to reduce parental anger. *Child Development, 63,* 381-90.

Crick, N. R., & Dodge, K. A. (1994). A review and reformulation of social information-processing mechanisms in children's social adjustment. *Psychological Bulletin, 115*(1), 74-101.

Crick, N. R., & Dodge, K. A. (1996). Social information-processing mechanisms in reactive and proactive aggression. *Child Development, 67,* 993-1002.

Crugnola, C., Tambelli, R., Spinelli, M., Gazzotti, S., Caprin, C., & Albizzati, A. (2011). Attachment patterns and emotion regulation strategies in the second year. *Infant Behavior and Development, 34,* 136-51.

Cummings, E. M. (1987). Coping with background anger in early childhood. *Child Development, 58,* 976-84.

Cummings, E. M. (1998). Children exposed to marital conflict and violence: Conceptual and theoretical directions. In G. W. Holden, R. Geffner & E. N. Jouriles (Eds.), *Children exposed to marital violence: Theory, research, and applied issues* (pp. 55-93). Washington, DC: American Psychological Association.

Cummings, E. M., & Cicchetti, D. (1990). Toward a transactional model of relations between attachment and depression. In M. T. Greenberg, D. Cicchetti & E. M. Cummings (Eds.), *Attachment in the preschool years: Theory, research, and intervention* (pp. 339-72). Chicago: University of Chicago Press.

Cummings, E. M., & Davies, P. T. (2010). *Marital conflict and children: An emotional security perspective.* New York: Guilford.

Cummings, E. M., Davies, P. T., & Campbell, S. B. (2000). *Developmental psychopathology and family process: Theory, research, and clinical implications.* New York: Guilford.

Cummings, E. M., El-Sheikh, M., Kouros, C., & Buckhalt, J. (2009). Children and violence: The role of children's regulation in the marital aggression–child adjustment link. *Clinical Child & Family Psychology Review, 12,* 3-15.

Cummings, E. M., Hennessy, K. D., Rabideau, G. J., & Cicchetti, D. (1994). Responses of physically abused boys to interadult anger involving their mothers. *Development and Psychopathology, 6,* 31-41.

Cummings, E. M., Schermerhorn, A. C., Davies, P. T., Goeke-Morey, M. C., & Cummings, J. S. (2006). Interparental discord and child adjustment: Prospective investigations of emotional security as an explanatory mechanism. *Child Development, 77,* 132-52.

Dadds, M. R., Schwartz, S., & Sanders, M. R. (1987). Marital discord and treatment outcome in behavioral treatment of child conduct disorders. *Journal of Consulting and Clinical Psychology, 55,* 396-403.

Damon, W. (2004). What is positive youth development? *The Annals of the American Academy of Political and Social Science, 59, 13-24.*

Damon, W. (2008). *The path to purpose: How young people find their calling in life.* New York: Free Press.

Darling, N., & Steinberg, L. (1993). Parenting style as context: An integrative model. *Psychological Bulletin, 113,* 487-96.

Dattillo, F. (2010). *Cognitive-behavioral therapy with couples and families.* New York: Guilford.

Davies, P. T., & Cummings, E. (1994). Marital conflict and child adjustment: An emotional security hypothesis. *Psychological Bulletin, 116,* 387-411.

Davies, P. T., & Cummings, E. (1998). Exploring children's emotional security as a mediator of the link between marital relations and child adjustment. *Child Development, 69,* 124-39.

Davies, P. T., Cummings, E. M., & Winter, M. A. (2004). Pathways between profiles of family functioning, child security in the interparental subsystem, and child psychological problems. *Development and Psychopathology, 16,* 525-50.

Davies, P. T., Winter, M. A., & Cicchetti, D. (2006). The implications of emotional security theory for understanding and treating childhood psychopathology. *Development and Psychopathology, 18*(3), 707-35.

Davis, E. L., & Levine, L. J. (2013). Emotion regulation strategies that promote learning: Reappraisal enhances children's memories or educational information. *Child Development, 84,* 361-74.

Day, R. D., Jones-Sanpei, H., Price, J. L. S., Orthner, D. K., Hair, E. C., Moore, K. A., & Kaye, K. (2009). Family processes and adolescent religiosity and religious practice: View from the NLSY97. *Marriage and Family Review, 45,* 289-309.

De Bellis, M. D. (2001). Developmental traumatology: The psychobiological development of maltreated children and its implication for research, treatment, and policy. *Development and Psychopathology, 13,* 539-64.

De Shazer, S. (1985). *Keys to solution in brief therapy.* New York: W. W. Norton.

De Shazer, S. (1988). *Investigating solutions in brief therapy.* New York: W. W. Norton.

De Shazer, S. (2005). *More than miracles: The state of the art of solution-focused therapy.* Binghamton, NY: Haworth Press.

Deater-Deckard, K. (2001). Annotation: Recent research examining the role of peer relationships in the development of psychopathology. *Journal of Child Psychology and Psychiatry, 42*(5), 565-79.

Deater-Deckard, K., & Dodge, K. A. (1997). Externalizing behavior problems and discipline revisited: Nonlinear effects and variation by culture, context, and gender. *Psychological Inquiry, 8,* 161-75.

Deater-Deckard, K., Ivy, L., & Petrill, S. A. (2006). Maternal warmth moderates the link between physical punishment and child externalizing problems: A parent-offspring behavior genetic analysis. *Parenting: Science and Practice, 6,* 59-78.

Deblinger, E., Cohen, J. A., & Mannarino, A. P. (2012). Introduction. In J. A. Cohen, A. P. Mannarino & E. Deblinger (Eds.), *Trauma-focused CBT for children and adolescents* (pp. 1-26). New York: Guilford.

Deblinger, E., & Heflin, A. H. (1996). *Treating sexually abused children and their nonoffending parents: A cognitive behavioral approach.* Newbury Park, CA: Sage.

Delgado, S.V. (2008, May). Psychodynamic psychotherapy for children and adolescents: An old friend revisited. *Psychiatry, 5,* 67-72.

Delprato, D. J. (2001). Comparisons of discrete-trial and normalized behavioral language intervention for young children with autism. *Journal of Autism and Developmental Disorders, 31*(3), 315-25.

Denham, S. A. (1998). *Emotional development in young children.* New York: Guilford.

Denham, S. A., Bassett, H., Mincic, M., Kalb, S., Way, E., Wyatt, T., & Segal, Y. (2012). Social-emotional learning profiles of preschoolers' early school success: A person-centered approach. *Learning and Individual Differences, 22,* 178-89.

Denham, S. A., Blair, K. A., DeMulder, E., Levitas, J., Sawyer, K., Auerbach-Major, A., & Queenan, P. (2003). Preschool emotional competence: Pathway to social competence? *Child Development, 74,* 238-56.

Dennis, T. A., & Kelemen, D. A. (2009). Preschool children's views on emotion regulation: Functional associations and implications for social-emotional adjustment. *International Journal of Behavior Development, 33,* 243-52.

Desjardins, T. L., & Leadbeater, B. J. (2011). Relational victimization and depressive symptoms in adolescence: Moderating effects of mother, father, and peer emotional support. *Journal of Youth and Adolescence, 40,* 531-44.

Diamond, G. S. (2005). Attachment-based family therapy for depressed and anxious adolescents. In J. L. Lebow (Ed.), *Handbook of clinical family therapy* (pp.17-41). New York: Wiley.

Diamond, G., Siqueland, L., & Diamond, G. M. (2003). Attachment-based family therapy for depressed adolescents: Programmatic treatment development. *Clinical Child and Family Psychology Review, 6*(2), 107-27.

Dickie, J. R., Eshleman, A. K., Merasco, D. M., Shepard, A., Vander Wilt, M., & Johnson, M. (1997). Parent-child relationships and children's images of God. *Journal for the Scientific Study of Religion, 36,* 25-43.

Dickstein, S., Seifer, R., & Albus, K. E. (2009). Maternal adult attachment representations across relationship domains and infant outcomes: The importance of family and couple functioning. *Attachment & Human Development, 11,* 5-27.

Diener, M. L., Mangelsdorf, S. C., McHale, J. L., & Frosch, C. A. (2002). Infants' behavioral strategies for emotion regulation with fathers and mothers: Associations with emotional expressions and attachment quality. *Infancy, 3,* 153-74.

Dirks, M. A., De Los Reyes, A., Briggs-Gowan, M., Cella, D., & Wakschlag, L. S. (2012). Annual research review: Embracing not erasing contextual variability in children's behavior—theory and utility in the selection and use of methods and informants in developmental psychopathology. *Journal of Child Psychology and Psychiatry, 53,* 558-74.

Dishion, T. J., & Dodge, K. A. (2005). Peer contagion in interventions for children and adolescents: Moving towards an understanding of the ecology and dynamics of change. *Journal of Abnormal Child Psychology, 33*(3), 395-400.

Dishion, T. J., & Dodge, K. A. (2006). Deviant peer contagion in interventions and programs: An ecological framework for understanding influence mechanisms. In K. A. Dodge, T. J. Dishion & J. E. Lansford (Eds.), *Deviant peer influences in programs for youth: Problems and solutions* (pp. 14-43). New York: Guilford.

Dishion, T. J., McCord, J., & Poulin, F. (1999). When interventions harm: Peer groups and problem behavior. *American Psychologist, 54*(9), 755-64.

Dishion, T. J., & Patterson, G. R. (1992). Age effects in parent training outcome. *Behavior Therapy, 23*(4), 719-29.

Dishion, T. J., & Patterson, G. R. (1999). Model building in developmental psychopathology: A pragmatic approach to understanding and intervention. *Journal of Clinical Child Psychology, 28,* 508-12.

Dishion, T. J., & Stormshak, E. A. (2007). *Ethical and professional standards in child and family interventions.* Washington, DC: American Psychological Association.

Dix, T., & Meunier, L. N. (2009). Depressive symptoms and parenting competence: An analysis of 13 regulatory processes. *Developmental Review, 29,* 45-68.

Doan, S. N., Fuller-Rowell, T. E., & Evans, G. W. (2012). Cumulative risk and adolescent's internalizing and externalizing problems: The mediating roles of maternal responsiveness and self-regulation. *Developmental Psychology, 48*(6), 1529-39.

Dodge, K. A., Dishion, T. J., & Lansford, J. E. (2006). *Deviant peer influences in programs for youth: Problems and solutions.* New York: Guilford.

Dodge, K. A., Lansford, J. E., Burks, V. S., Bates, J. E., Pettit, G. S., Fontaine, R., & Price, J. M. (2003). Peer rejection and social information-processing factors in the development of aggressive behavior problems in children. *Child Development, 74,* 374-93.

Dodge, K. A., & Pettit, G. S. (2003). A biopsychosocial model of the development of chronic conduct problems in adolescence. *Developmental Psychology, 39,* 349-71.

Doss, B. D., Carhart, K., Hsueh, A. C., & Rahbar, K. P. (2010). Serving rather than recruiting couples: Thoughts on the delivery of current and future couple interventions. In K. Hahlweg, M. Grawe-Gerber & D. H. Baucom (Eds.), *Enhancing couples: The shape of couple therapy to come* (pp. 201-15). Cambridge, MA: Hogrefe Publishing.

Doughty, A. H., & Lattal, K. A. (2003). Response persistence under variable-time schedules following immediate and unsignalled delayed reinforcement. *Quarterly Journal of Experimental Psychology: Section B, 56*(3), 267.

Dowling, E. M., Gestsdottir, S., Anderson, P. A., von Eye, A., & Lerner, R. M. (2003). Spirituality, religiosity, and thriving among adolescents: Identification and confirmation of factor structures. *Applied Developmental Science, 7,* 253-60.

Drossel, C., Rummel, C., & Fisher, J. E. (2009). Assessment and cognitive behavior therapy: Functional analysis as key process. In W.T. O'Donohue & J. E. Fisher (Eds.), *General principles and empirically supported techniques of cognitive behavior therapy* (pp. 15-41). Hoboken, NJ: Wiley.

Dru, A. (1938). *The journals of Søren Kierkegaard.* Oxford: Oxford University Press.

Du Rocher Schudlich, T. D., White, C. R., Fleishhauer, E. A., & Fitzgerald, K. A. (2011). Observed infant reactions during live interparental conflict. *Journal of Marriage and Family, 73,* 221-35.

Durbin, C., Hayden, E. P., Klein, D. N., & Olino, T. M. (2007). Stability of laboratory-assessed temperamental emotionality traits from ages 3 to 7. *Emotion, 7*(2), 388-99.

Durlak, J. A., Weissberg, R. P., Dymnicki, A. B., Taylor, R. D., & Schellinger, K. B. (2011). The impact of enhancing students' social and emotional learning: A meta-analysis of school-based universal interventions. *Child Development, 82,* 405-32.

Dusenbury, L., Zadrazil, J., Mart, A., & Weissberg, R. P. (2011). *State learning standards to advance social and emotional learning.* Chicago: Collaborative for Academic, Social, and Emotional Learning (CASEL).

Dush, C. M. K., Kotila, L. E., & Schoppe-Sullivan, S. J. (2011). Predictors of supportive coparenting after relationship dissolution among at-risk parents. *Journal of Family Psychology, 25,* 356-65.

Dweck, C. (2006). *Mindset: The new psychology of success.* New York: Ballantine Books.

Efron, D. (2004). The use of emotionally focused family therapy in a children's mental health center. *Journal of Systemic Therapies, 23,* 78-90.

Egeland, B., & Erickson, M. F. (2004). *Treating parent-infant relationship problems: Strategies for intervention.* New York: Guilford.

Egeland, B., Pianta, R., & O'Brien, M. A. (1993). Maternal intrusiveness in infancy and child maladaptation in early school years. *Development and Psychopathology, 5,* 359-70.

Ehrenreich, J. T., Goldstein, C. R., Wright, L. R., & Barlow, D. H. (2009). Development of a unified protocol for the treatment of emotional disorders in youth. *Child and Family Behavior Therapy, 31,* 20-37.

Eisenberg, N., Cumberland, A., & Spinrad, T. L. (1998). Parental socialization of emotion. *Psychological Inquiry, 9,* 241-73.

Eisenberg, N., Fabes, R. A., Bernzweig, J., Karbon, M., Poulin, R., & Hanish, L. (1993). The relations of emotionality and regulation to preschoolers' social skills and sociometric status. *Child Development, 64,* 1418-38.

Eisenberg, N., Fabes, R. A., Murphy, B., Maszk, P., Smith, M., & Karbon, M. (1995). The role of emotionality and regulation in children's social functioning: A longitudinal study. *Child Development, 66,* 1360-84.

Eisenberg, N., Guthrie, I. K., Fabes, R. A., Shepard, S., Losoya, S., Murphy, B. C., . . . Reiser, M. (2000). Prediction of elementary school children's externalizing problem behaviors from attention and behavioral regulation and negative emotionality. *Child Development, 71*(5), 1367-82.

Eisenberg, N., & Spinrad, T. L. (2004). Emotion-related regulation: Sharpening the definition. *Child Development, 75,* 334-39.

Eisenberg, N., Smith, C. L., Sadovsky, A., & Spinrad, T. L. (2004). Effortful control: Relations with emotion regulation, adjustment, and socialization in childhood. In R. F. Baumeister & K. D. Vohs (Eds.), *Handbook of self-regulation: Research, theory, and applications* (pp. 259-82). New York: Guilford.

Eisenberg, N., Valiente, C., Morris, A., Fabes, R. A., Cumberland, A., Reiser, M., . . . Losoya, S. (2003). Longitudinal relations among parental emotional expressivity, children's regulation, and quality of socioemotional functioning. *Developmental Psychology, 39,* 3-19.

Eisenberg, N., Vaughan, J., & Hofer, C. (2009). Temperament, self-regulation, and peer social competence. In K. H. Rubin, W. M. Bukowski & B. Laursen (Eds.), *Handbook of peer interactions, relationships, and groups* (pp. 473-89). New York: Guilford.

Eisenberg, N., Zhou, Q., Losoya, S. H., Fabes, R. A., Shepard, S. A., Murphy, B. C., . . . Cumberland, A. (2003). The relations of parenting, effortful control, and ego control to children's emotional expressivity. *Child Development, 74*(3), 875-95.

Ekas, N. V., Braungart-Rieker, J. M., Lickenbrock, D. M., Zentall, S. R., & Maxwell, S. M. (2011). Toddler emotion regulation with mothers and fathers: Temporal associations between negative affect and behavioral strategies. *Infancy, 16,* 266-94.

Ekman, P., Friesen, W. V., & Hager, J. C. (2002). *Facial Action Coding System: The manual on CD-ROM*. Salt Lake City: A Human Face.

Elliott, M. A. (2006). *Faithful feelings: Rethinking emotion in the New Testament*. Grand Rapids, MI: Kregel.

Ellis, A. (1962). *Reason and emotion in psychotherapy*. New York: Lyle Stuart.

Ellis, A. (2001). The rise of cognitive behavior therapy. In W. T. O'Donohue, D. A. Henderson, S. C. Hayes, J. E. Fisher & L. J. Hayes (Eds.), *A history of the behavioral therapies: Founders' personal histories* (pp. 183-94). Reno, NV: Context Press.

El-Sheikh, M., & Elmore-Station, L. (2004). The link between marital conflict and child adjustment: Parent-child conflict and perceived attachments as mediators, potentiators, and mitigators of risk. *Development and Psychopathology, 16*, 631-48.

Erath, S. A., El-Sheikh, M., Hinnant, J. B., & Cummings, E. M. (2011). Skin conductance level reactivity moderates the association between harsh parenting and growth in child externalizing behavior. *Developmental Psychology, 47*, 693-706.

Erath, S. A., Flanagan, K. S., & Bierman, K. L. (2007). Social anxiety and peer relations in early adolescence: Behavioral and cognitive factors. *Journal of Abnormal Child Psychology, 25*(3), 405-16.

Erath, S. A., Flanagan, K. S., & Bierman, K. L. (2010). Friendships moderate psychosocial maladjustment in socially anxious early adolescents. *Journal of Applied Developmental Psychology, 31*(1), 15-26.

Erel, O., & Burman, B. (1995). Interrelatedness of marital relations and parent-child relations: A meta-analytic review. *Psychological Bulletin, 118*, 108-32.

Erikson, E. H. (1968). *Identity: Youth and crisis*. New York: Norton.

Esbjorn, B. H., Bender, P. K., Reinholdt-Dunn, M. L., Munck, L. A., & Ollendick, T. H. (2012). The development of anxiety disorders: Considering the contributions of attachment and emotion regulation. *Clinical Child and Family Psychology Review, 15*, 129-43.

Eskow, K., & Fisher, S. (2004). Getting together in college. *Teaching Exceptional Children, 36*, 26-32.

Espelage, D. L., & Swearer, S. M. (2004). *Bullying in American schools: A social-ecological perspective on prevention and intervention*. Mahwah, NJ: Lawrence Erlbaum Associates.

Estep, J. R. (2010). Christian anthropology: Humanity as the *imago Dei*. In J. R. Estep, J. H. Kim, T. I. P. Jones & M. S. Wilder (Eds.), *Christian formation: Integrating theology and human development* (pp. 9-35). Nashville: B & H Academic.

Estep, J. R., & Kim, J. H. (2010). *Christian formation: Integrating theology and human Development*. Nashville: B & H Academic.

Evans, D. E., & Rothbart, M. K. (2009). A two-factor model of temperament. *Personality and Individual Differences, 47*(6), 565-70.

Evans, G. W. (2003). A multimethodological analysis of cumulative risk and allostatic load among rural children. *Developmental Psychology, 39,* 924-33.

Evans, G. W., & English, K. (2002). The environment of poverty: Multiple stressor exposure, psychophysiological stress, and socioemotional adjustment. *Child Development, 73*(4), 1238-48.

Eyberg, S. M., Bessmer, J., Newcomb, K., Edwards, D., & Robinson, E. (1994). *Dyadic parent-child interaction coding system: II. A manual.* Social and Behavioral Sciences Documents (Ms. No. 2897). San Rafael, CA: Select Press.

Eyberg, S. M., & Bussing, R. (in press). Parent-child interaction therapy. In M. Murrihy, A. Kidman & T. Ollendick (Eds.), *Clinical handbook of assessing and treating conduct problems in youth.* New York: Springer.

Eyberg, S., & Funderburk, B. (2011). *Parent-child interaction therapy protocol 2011.* Gainesville, FL: PCIT International.

Eyberg, S. M., Funderburk, B. W., Hembree-Kigin, T. L., McNeil, C. B., Querido, J. G., & Hood, K. K. (2001). Parent-child interaction therapy with behavior problem children: One and two year maintenance of treatment effects in the family. *Child & Family Behavior Therapy, 23*(4), 1-20.

Eyberg, S. M., Nelson, M. M., & Boggs, S. R. (2008). Evidence-based psychosocial treatments for children and adolescents with disruptive behavior. *Journal of Clinical Child and Adolescent Psychology, 37,* 215-37.

Fabes, R. A., & Eisenberg, N. (1992). Young children's coping with interpersonal anger. *Child Development, 63,* 116-28.

Fabes, R. A., Eisenberg, N., Jones, S., Smith, M., Guthrie, I., Poulin, R., . . . Friedman, J. (1999). Regulation, emotionality, and preschoolers' socially competent peer interactions. *Child Development, 70*(2), 432-42.

Fabes, R. A., Martin, C., & Hanish, L. D. (2009). Children's behaviors and interactions with peers. In K. H. Rubin, W. M. Bukowski & B. Laursen (Eds.), *Handbook of peer interactions, relationships, and groups* (pp. 45-62). New York: Guilford.

Fairbairn, W. R. D. (1952). *Psycho-analytic studies of the personality.* London: Tavistock Publications.

Fairbairn, W. R. D. (1954). The repression and the return of bad objects. In *An object-relations theory of the personality* (p. 59-81). New York: Basic Books. (Original work published 1943)

Fairbairn, W. R. D. (1994). In defence of object relations theory. In D. E. Scharff & E. F. Birtles (Eds.), *From instinct to self: Selected papers of W. R. D. Fairbairn, Vol 1: Clinical and Theoretical Papers*, (p. 111-28). London: Jason Aronson.

Feldman, R., Greenbaum, C. W., & Yirmiya, N. (1999). Mother-infant affect synchrony as an antecedent of the emergence of self-control. *Developmental Psychology, 35,* 223-31.

Feng, X., Shaw, D. S., Kovacs, M., Lane, T., O'Rourke, F. E., & Alarcon, J. H. (2008). Emotion regulation in preschoolers: The roles of behavioral inhibition, maternal affective behavior, and maternal depression. *Journal of Child Psychology and Psychiatry, 49,* 132-41.

Field, T. (1978). The three Rs of infant-adult interactions: Rhythms, repertoires, and responsivity. *Journal of Pediatric Psychology, 3,* 131-36.

Field, T. (1994). The effects of mother's physical and emotional unavailability on emotion regulation. In N. A. Fox (Ed.), *The development of emotion regulation: Biological and behavioral considerations. Monographs of the Society for Research in Child Development, 59*(2-3, Serial No. 240), 208-27.

Finch, A. J., Lochman, J. E., Nelson, W. M., & Roberts, M. C. (2012) *Specialty competencies in clinical child and adolescent psychology.* New York: Oxford University Press.

Fischer, M., Rolf, J. E., Hasazi, J. E., & Cummings, L. (1984). Follow-up of a preschool epidemiological sample: Cross-age continuities and predictions of later adjustment with internalizing and externalizing dimensions of behavior. *Child Development, 55,* 137-50.

Fishman, E. A., & Meyers, S. A. (2000). Marital satisfaction and child adjustment: Direct and mediated pathways. *Contemporary Family Therapy, 22,* 437-52.

Flanagan, K. S., Erath, S. A., & Bierman, K. L. (2008). Unique associations between peer relations and social anxiety in early adolescence. *Journal of Clinical Child and Adolescent Psychology, 37*(4), 759-69.

Flanagan, K. S., & Loveall, R. (2012). Forgiveness, peer relations, and children's spirituality. In K. E. Lawson (Vol. Ed.), *Children's spirituality: Theology, research, and practice* (pp. 373-98). Eugene, OR: Wipf & Stock.

Fleischhaker, C., Böhme, R., Sixt, B., Brück, C., Schneider, C., & Schulz, E. (2011). Dialectical Behavioral Therapy for Adolescents (DBT-A): A clinical trial for patients with suicidal and self-injurious behavior and borderline symptoms with a one-year follow-up. *Child and Adolescent Psychiatry and Mental Health, 5*(3).

Floyd, F. J., & Zmich, D. E. (1991). Marriage and the parenting partnership: Perceptions and interactions of parents with mentally retarded and typically developing children. *Child Development, 62,* 1434-48.

Foa, E. B., Keane, T. M., Friedman, M. J., & Cohen, J. A. (Eds.). (2009). *Effective treatments for PTSD: Practice guidelines from the International Society for Traumatic Stress Studies* (2nd ed.). New York: Guilford.

Folkman, S., & Lazarus, R. S. (1980). An analysis of coping in a middle-aged community sample. *Journal of Health and Social Behavior, 21,* 219-39.

Fonagy, P., & Target, M. (1996). Predictors of outcome in child psychoanalysis: A retrospective study of 793 cases at the Anna Freud Centre. *Journal of the American Psychoanalytic Association, 44*(1), 27-77.

Fontaine, R., & Dodge, K. A. (2009). Social information processing and aggressive behavior: A transactional perspective. In A. Sameroff (Ed.), *The transactional model of development: How children and contexts shape each other* (pp. 117-35). Washington, DC: American Psychological Association.

Foote, R., Eyberg, S., & Schuhmann, E., (1998). Parent-child interaction approaches to the treatment of child behavior problems. *Advances in Clinical Child Psychology, 20,* 125-51.

Forehand, R., Biggar, H., & Kotchick, B. A. (1998). Cumulative risk across family stressors: Short- and long-term effects for adolescents. *Journal of Abnormal Child Psychology, 26*(2), 119-28.

Fosha, D. (2000). *The transforming power of affect.* New York: Basic Books.

Fosha, D. (2003). Dyadic regulation and experiential work with emotion and relatedness in trauma and disorganized attachment. In M. F. Solomon & D. J. Siegel (Eds.), *Healing trauma: Attachment, mind, body, and brain* (pp. 221-81). New York: W. W. Norton.

Fox, N. A., & Calkins, S. D. (2003). The development of self-control in emotion: Intrinsic & extrinsic influences. *Motivation & Emotion, 27,* 7-25.

Fox, N. A., & Davidson, R. J. (1986). Taste-elicited changes in facial signs of emotion and the asymmetry of brain electrical activity in human newborns. *Neuropsychologia, 24,* 417-22.

Franklin, M. E., Foa, E. B., & March, J. S. (2003). The pediatric OCD treatment study (POTS): Rationale, design and methods. *Journal of Child and Adolescent Psychopharmacology, 13*(Suppl. 1), 39-52.

Franklin, M. E., Freeman, J., & March, J. S. (2010). Treating pediatric obsessive-compulsive disorder using exposure-based cognitive behavioral therapy. In J. Weisz & A. Kazdin (Eds.), *Evidence-based psychotherapies for children and adolescents* (pp. 80-92). New York: Guilford.

Freedman, B. H., Kalb, L. G., Zablotsky, B., & Stuart, E. A. (2012). Relationship status among parents of children with autism spectrum disorders: A population-based study. *Journal of Autism and Developmental Disorders, 42,* 539-48.

Freedman, J., & Combs, G. (1996). *Narrative therapy: The social construction of preferred realities.* New York: W. W. Norton.

Freeman, J. B., Garcia, A. M., Coyne, L., Ale, C., Przeworski, A., Himle, M., & Leonard, H. L. (2008). Early childhood OCD: Preliminary findings from a family-based cognitive-behavioral approach. *Journal of the American Academy of Child & Adolescent Psychiatry, 47*(5), 593-602.

Freeman, J., Epston, D., & Lobovits, D. (1997). Playful approaches to serious problems: Narrative therapy with children and their families. New York: W. W. Norton.

Freud, A. (1966–1980). *The writings of Anna Freud: 8 Volumes*. New York: International Universities Press.

Frick, P. J., Barry, C. T., & Kamphaus, R. W. (2009). *Clinical assessment of child and adolescent personality and behavior*. New York: Springer.

Frijda, N. H. (1987). *The emotions*. Cambridge, England: Cambridge University Press.

Fulkerson, J. A., Pasch, K. E., Perry, C. L., & Komro, K. (2008). Relationships between alcohol-related informal social control, parental monitoring and adolescent problem behaviors among racially diverse urban youth. *Journal of Community Health, 33*(6), 425-33.

Furman, W., & Buhrmester, D. (1985). Children's perceptions of the personal relationships in their social networks. *Developmental Psychology, 21*(6), 1016-24.

Furstenberg, F. F., Jr. (1990). Divorce and the American family. *Annual Review of Sociology, 16*, 379-403.

Gallagher, K. (2002). Does child temperament moderate the influence of parenting on adjustment?. *Developmental Review, 22*(4), 623-43.

Garber, J., Braafladt, N., & Weiss, B. (1995). Affect regulation in depressed and nondepressed children and young adolescents. *Development and Psychopathology, 7,* 93-115.

Garber, J., Braafladt, N., & Zeman, J. (1991). The regulation of sad affect: An information-processing perspective. In J. Garber & K. A. Dodge (Eds.), *The development of emotion regulation and dysregulation* (pp. 208-40). New York: Cambridge University Press.

García Coll, C., Lamberty, G., Jenkins, R., McAdoo, H. P., Crnic, K., Wasik, B. H., & Vasquez García, H. (1996). An integrative model for the study of developmental competencies in minority children. *Child Development, 67*(5), 1891-914.

Gardner, T. W., Dishion, T. J., & Connell, A. M. (2008). Adolescent self-regulation as resilience: Resistance to antisocial behavior within the deviant peer context. *Journal of Abnormal Child Psychology, 36*(2), 273-84.

Garland, A. F., Hawley, K. M., Brookman-Frazee, L., & Hurlburt, M. S. (2008). Identifying common elements of evidence-based psychosocial treatments for children's disruptive behavior problems. *Journal of the American Academy of Child And Adolescent Psychiatry, 47,* 505-14.

Gartstein, M. A., Putnam, S. P., & Rothbart, M. K. (2012). Etiology of preschool behavior problems: Contributions of temperament attributes in early childhood. *Infant Mental Health Journal, 33*(2), 197-211.

Gartstein, M. A., & Rothbart, M. K. (2003). Studying infant temperament via the revised infant behavior questionnaire. *Infant Behavior and Development, 26*(1), 64-86.

Geiger, T. C., & Crick, N. R. (2001). A developmental psychopathology perspective on vulnerability to personality disorders. In R. E. Ingram & J. M. Price (Eds.), *Vulnerability to psychopathology: Risk across the lifespan* (pp. 57-102). New York: Guilford.

Gestsdottir, S., & Lerner, R. M. (2007). Intentional self-regulation and positive youth development in early adolescence: Findings from the 4-H Study of Positive Youth Development. *Developmental Psychology, 43*, 508-21.

Gilliom, M., Shaw, D. S., Beck, J. E., Schonberg, M. A., & Lukon, J. L. (2002). Anger regulation in disadvantaged preschool boys: Strategies, antecedents, and the development of self-control. *Developmental Psychology, 34*, 222-35.

Gilmore, D. (1990). *Manhood in the making: Cultural conceptions of masculinity*. New Haven, CT: Yale University Press.

Gladstone G. L., & Parker, G. B. (2006). Is behavioral inhibition a risk factor for depression? *Journal of Affective Disorders, 95*, 85-94.

Goeke-Morey, M. C., & Cummings, E. M. (2007). Impact of father involvement: A closer look at indirect effects models involving marriage and child adjustment. *Applied Developmental Science, 11*, 221-25.

Goldberg, L. R. (1990). An alternative 'description of personality': The Big-Five factor structure. *Journal of Personality and Social Psychology, 59*(6), 1216-29.

Goldberg, W. A., & Easterbrooks, M. A. (1984). Role of marital quality in toddler development. *Developmental Psychology, 20*, 504-14.

Gonzales, N. A., Cauce, A. M., & Mason, C. A. (1996). Interobserver agreement in the assessment of parental behavior and parent-adolescent conflict: African American mothers, daughters, and independent observers. *Child Development, 67*, 1483-97.

Goodman, K. L., & Southam-Gerow, M. A. (2010). The regulating role of negative emotions in children's coping with peer rejection. *Child Psychiatry and Human Development, 41*, 515-34.

Goodman, S. H. (2007). Depression in mothers. *Annual Review of Clinical Psychology, 3*, 107-35.

Goodman, S. H., Rouse, M. H., Connell, A. M., Broth, M. R., Hall, C. M., & Heyward, D. (2011). Maternal depression and child psychopathology: A meta-analytic review. *Clinical Child Family Psychology Review, 14*, 1-27.

Gorsuch, R. L. (2002). *Integrating psychology and spirituality?* Westport, CT: Praeger.

Gottman, J. (1997). *Raising an emotionally intelligent child.* New York: Simon & Schuster.

Gottman, J. M., Katz, L. F., & Hooven, C. (1996). Parental meta-emotion philosophy and the emotional life of families: Theoretical models and preliminary data. *Journal of Family Psychology, 10,* 243-68.

Gouze, K. R., & Wendel, R. (2008). Integrative module-based family therapy: Application and training. *Journal of Marital and Family Therapy, 34*(3), 269-86.

Gray, C. A. (2010). *The new social story book.* Arlington, TX: Future Horizons.

Gray, C. A., & Garand, J. D. (1993). Social stories: Improving responses of students with autism with accurate social information. *Focus on Autistic Behavior, 8*(1), 1-10.

Greco, L. A., & Morris, T. L. (2005). Factors including the link between social anxiety and peer acceptance: Contributions of social skills and close friendships during middle childhood. *Behavior Therapy, 36,* 197-205.

Greenberg, L. S., & Johnson, S. M. (1988). *Emotionally focused therapy for couples.* New York: Guilford.

Greenberg, M. T., Domitrovich, C., & Bumbarger, B. (2001). The prevention of mental disorders in school-aged children: Current state of the field. *Prevention & Treatment, 4*(1).

Greenberg, M. T., Kusche, C. A., Cook, E. T., & Quamma, J. P. (1995). Promoting emotional competence in school-aged children: The effects of the PATHS curriculum. *Development and Psychopathology, 7,* 117-36.

Grenz, S. J. (2001). *The social God and the relational self: A trinitarian theology of the imago Dei.* Louisville, KY: Westminster John Knox Press.

Gresham, D., & Gullone, E. (2012). Emotion regulation strategy use in children and adolescents: The explanatory roles of personality and attachment. *Personality and Individual Differences, 52,* 616-21.

Grills, A. E., & Ollendick, T. H. (2002). Peer victimization, global self-worth, and anxiety in middle school children. *Journal of Clinical Child and Adolescent Psychology, 31,* 59-68.

Grolnick, W. S., Bridges, L. J., & Connell, J. O. (1996). Emotion regulation in two-year-olds: Strategies and emotional expression in four contexts. *Child Development, 67,* 928-41.

Grolnick, W. S., Kurowski, C. O., McMenamy, J. M., Rivkin, I., & Bridges, L. J. (1998). Mothers' strategies for regulating their toddlers' distress. *Infant Behavior and Development, 21,* 437-50.

Gross, H. E., Shaw, D. S., & Moilanen, K. L. (2008). Reciprocal associations between boys' externalizing problems and mothers' depressive symptoms. *Journal of Abnormal Child Psychology, 36,* 693-709.

Gross, J. J., & John, O. P. (2003). Individual differences in two emotion regulation processes: Implications for affect, relationships, and well-being. *Journal of Personality and Social Psychology, 85,* 348-62.

Gruttadaro, D., Burns, B., Duckworth, K., & Crudo D. (2007). *Choosing the right treatment: What families need to know about evidence-based practices.* Arlington, VA: National Alliance on Mental Illness.

Grych, J. H., & Fincham, F. D. (1990). Marital conflict and children's adjustment: A cognitive-contextual framework. *Psychological Bulletin, 108,* 267-90.

Grych, J. H., & Fincham, F. D. (1993). Children's appraisals of marital conflict: Initial investigations of the cognitive-contextual framework. *Child Development, 64,* 215-30.

Grych, J. H., & Fincham, F. D. (2001). *Interparental conflict and child development: Theory, research, and applications.* Cambridge, England: Cambridge University Press.

Grych, J. H., Fincham, F. D., Jouriles, E. N., & McDonald, R. (2000). Interparental conflict and child adjustment: Testing the mediational role of appraisals in the cognitive-contextual framework. *Child Development, 71,* 1648-61.

Grych, J. H., Raynor, S. R., & Fosco, G. M. (2004). Family processes that shape the impact of interpersonal conflict on adolescents. *Development and Psychopathology, 16,* 649-65.

Gudorf, C. E. (1985). Parenting, mutual love, and sacrifice. In B. H. Andolsen, C. E. Gudorf & M. D. Pellauer (Eds.), *Women's consciousness and women's conscience: A reader in feminist ethics* (pp. 175-91). San Francisco: Harper & Row.

Gudorf, C. E. (1994). *Body, sex, and pleasure: Reconstructing Christian sexual ethics.* Cleveland: Pilgrim Press.

Gülay, H. (2012). Temperament and peer relations: Investigating the effect the temperament of 5-6-year-olds has on their peer relations. *Early Child Development and Care, 182*(10), 1383-97.

Gullone, E., Hughes, E. K., King, N. J., & Tonge, B. (2010). The normative development of emotion regulation strategy use in children and adolescents: A 2-year follow-up study. *Journal of Child Psychology and Psychiatry, 51,* 567-74.

Gullone, E., & Robinson, K. (2005). The Inventory of Parent and Peer Attachment—Revised (IPPA-R) for Children: A psychometric investigation. *Clinical Psychology and Psychotherapy, 12,* 67-79.

Gundry-Volf, J. M. (2001). The least and the greatest: Children in the New Testament. In M. Bunge (Ed.), *The child in Christian thought* (pp. 29-60). Grand Rapids, MI: Eerdmans.

Guroian, V. (2001). The ecclesial family: John Chrystostom on parenthood and children. In M. Bunge (Ed.), *The child in Christian thought* (pp. 61-77). Grand Rapids, MI: Eerdmans.

Gutman, L. M., Eccles, J. S., Peck, S., & Malanchuk, O. (2011). The influence of family relations on trajectories of cigarette and alcohol use from early to late adolescence. *Journal of Adolescence, 34,* 119-28.

Haffter, C. (1948). *Kinder aus geschiedenen Ehen* [Children from broken homes]. Oxford, England: Hans Huber. English abstract retrieved from PsycINFO database. (Accession No. 1950-00120-000)

Hagen, K.A., Ogden, T., & Bjørnebekk, G. (2011). Treatment outcomes and mediators of parent management training: A one-year follow-up of children with conduct problems. *Journal of Clinical Child and Adolescent Psychology, 40*(2), 165-78.

Halberstadt, A. G., Denham, S. A., & Dunsmore, J. C. (2001). Affective social competence. *Social Development, 10,* 79-119.

Haley, J. (1987). *Problem-solving therapy* (2nd ed.). San Francisco: Jossey-Bass.

Halford, W. K. (2011). *Marriage and relationship education: What works and how to provide it.* New York: Guilford.

Hall, S. E., & Cole, P. M. (2007). Toddlers' emotional self-regulation: Stability and change across time. Poster presented at the biennial meeting of the Society for Research in Child Development.

Hannesdottir, D., & Ollendick, T. H. (2007). The role of emotion regulation in the treatment of child anxiety disorders. *Clinical Child and Family Psychology Review, 10,* 275-93.

Hannesdotir, D. K., Doxie, J., Bell, M. A., Ollendick, T. H., & Wolfe, C. D. (2010). A longitudinal study of emotion regulation and anxiety in middle childhood: Associations with frontal EEG asymmetry in early childhood. *Developmental Psychobiology, 52,* 197-204.

Harden, K. P., Turkheimer, E., Emery, R. E., D'Onofrio, B. M., Slutske, W. S., Heath, A. C., & Martin, N. G. (2007). Marital conflict and conduct problems in children of twins. *Child Development, 78,* 1-18.

Harman, C., Rothbart, M. K., & Posner, M. I. (1997). Distress and attention interactions in early infancy. *Motivation and Emotion, 21*(1), 27-43.

Harold, G. T., Aitken, J. J., & Shelton, K. H. (2007). Inter-parental conflict and children's academic attainment: A longitudinal analysis. *Journal of Child Psychology and Psychiatry, 48,* 1223-32.

Harvey, A., Watkins, E., Mansell, W., & Shafran, R. (2004). *Cognitive behavioural processes across psychological disorders.* Oxford, England: Oxford University Press.

Haskett, M. E., Allaire, J. C., Kreig, S., & Hart, K. C. (2008). Protective and vulnerability factors for physically abused children: Effects of ethnicity and parenting context. *Child Abuse and Neglect, 32*(5), 567-76.

Hathaway, W. (2003). Integration in clinical child psychology: Introduction to the special issue. *Journal of Psychology and Christianity, 22,* 99-100.

Hathaway, W. L., & Barkley, R. A. (2003). Self-regulation, ADHD, and child religiousness. *Journal of Psychology and Christianity, 22,*101-14.

Hathaway, W. L., & Childers, J. (in press). Clinical child assessment of religious/spiritual issues. In D. F. Walker & W. L. Hathaway (Eds.), *Spiritual interventions in child and adolescent psychotherapy.* Washington, DC: American Psychological Association.

Hathaway, W. L., & Tan, E. (2009). Religiously oriented mindfulness-based cognitive therapy. *Journal of Clinical Psychology, 65,* 158-71.

Hatton, C., Emerson, E., Graham, H., Blacher, J., & Llewellyn, G. (2010). Changes in family composition and marital status in families with a young child with cognitive delay. *Journal of Applied Research in Intellectual Disabilities, 23,* 14-26.

Hautman, C., Stein, P., Hanisch, C., Eichelberger, I., Pluck, J., Walter, D., & Dopfner, M. (2009). Does parent management training for children with externalizing problem behavior in routine care result in clinically significant changes? *Psychotherapy Research, 19*(2), 224-33.

Havighurst, S. S., Harley, A., & Prior, M. (2004). Building preschool children's emotional competence: A parenting program. *Early Education & Development, 15,* 423-45.

Hawker, D. J., & Boulton, M. J. (2000). Twenty years' research on peer victimization and psychosocial maladjustment: A meta-analytic review of cross-sectional studies. *Journal of Child Psychology and Psychiatry, 41,* 441-55.

Hay, D. F. (2005). Early peer relations and their impact on children's development. In R. E. Tremblay, R. G. Barr & R. DeV. Peters (Eds.), *Encyclopedia on Early Childhood Development* [online]. Montreal, Canada: Centre of Excellence for Early Childhood Development (1-6): www.child-encyclopedia.com/documents/HayANGxp-Peers.pdf.

Hayes, S. C., Strosahl, K. D., & Wilson, K. G. (1999). *Acceptance and commitment therapy: An experiential approach to behavior change.* New York: Guilford.

Hayes, S. C., Wilson, K. G., Gifford, E. V., Follette, V. M., & Strosahl, K. D. (1996). Experiential avoidance and behavioral disorders: A functional dimensional approach to diagnosis and treatment. *Journal of Consulting and Clinical Psychology, 64,* 1152-68.

Heitzenrater R. P. (2001). John Wesley and children. In M. Bunge (Ed.), *The child in Christian thought* (pp. 279-99). Grand Rapids, MI: Eerdmans.

Hembree-Kigin, T. L., & McNeil, C. B. (1995). *Parent-child interaction therapy.* New York: Springer.

Henggeler, S. W., Clingempeel, W. G., Brondino, M. J., & Pickrel, S. G. (2002). Four-year follow-up of multisystemic therapy with substance abusing and dependent juvenile offenders. *Journal of the American Academy of Child and Adolescent Psychiatry, 41,* 868-74.

Henggeler, S. W., & Schaeffer, C. (2010). Treating serious antisocial behavior using multisystemic therapy. In J. Weisz and A. Kazdin (Eds.), *Evidence-based psychotherapies for children and adolescents* (pp. 259-76). New York: Guilford.

Henggeler, S. W., Schoenwald, S. K., Borduin, C. M., Rowland, M. D., & Cunningham, P. B. (2009). *Multisystemic therapy for antisocial behavior in children and adolescents* (2nd ed.). New York: Guilford.

Hersen, M., & Van Hasselt, V. B. (1987). Developments and emerging trends. In M. Hersen & V. B. Van Hasselt (Eds.), *Behavior therapy with children and adolescents: A clinical approach* (pp. 3-28). New York: Wiley and Sons.

Hertel, B. R., & Donahue, M. J. (1995). Parental influences on God images among children: Testing Durkheim's metaphoric parallelism. *Journal for the Scientific Study of Religion, 34,* 186-99.

Herts, K. L., McLaughlin, K. A., & Hatzenbuehler, M. L. (2012). Emotion dysregulation as a mechanism linking stress exposure to adolescent aggressive behavior. *Journal of Abnormal Child Psychology, 40,* 1111-22.

Hetherington, E. M. (1989). Coping with family transitions: Winners, losers, and survivors. *Child Development, 60,* 1-14.

Hetherington, E. M. (1999). Should we stay together for the sake of the children? In E. M. Hetherington (Ed.), *Coping with divorce, single parenting, and remarriage: A risk and resiliency perspective* (pp. 93-116). Mahwah, NJ: Erlbaum.

Hill, A. L., & Braungart-Rieker, J. M. (2002). Four-month attentional regulation and its prediction of three-year compliance. *Infancy, 3,* 261-73.

Hill, A. L., Degnan, K. A., Calkins, S. D., & Keane, S. P. (2006). Profiles of externalizing behavior problems for boys and girls across preschool: The roles of emotion regulation and inattention. *Developmental Psychology, 42,* 913-28.

Hipwell, A., Keenan, K., Kasza, D., Loeber, R., Stouthamer-Loeber, M., & Bean, T. (2008). Reciprocal influences between girls' conduct problems and depression, and parental punishment and warmth: A six year prospective analysis. *Journal of Abnormal Child Psychology, 36,* 663-77.

Hoagwood, K., Burns, B., Kiser, L., Ringeisen, H., & Schoenwald, S. (2001). Evidence-based practice in child and adolescent mental health services. *Psychiatric Services, 52*(9), 1179-89.

Hoekema, A. A. (1986). *Created in God's image.* Grand Rapids, MI: Eerdmans.

Hoffman, C., Crnic, K. A., & Baker, J. K. (2006). Maternal depression and parenting: Implications for children's emergent emotion regulation and behavioral functioning. *Parenting: Science and Practice, 6,* 271-95.

Holmbeck, G. N., Devine, K.A., Wasserman, R., Schellinger, K., & Tuminello, E. (2012).

Working with adolescents: Guides from developmental psychology. In P. Kendall (Ed.), *Child & adolescent therapy: Cognitive-behavioral procedures* (4th ed., pp. 429-70). New York: Guilford.

Holmbeck, G. N., & Kendall, P. C. (1991). Clinical-childhood-developmental interface: Implications for treatment. In P. Martin (Ed.), *Handbook of behavior therapy and psychological science: An integrative approach* (pp. 413-34). Oxford, England: Pergamon Press.

Holmboe, K. K., Nemoda, Z. Z., Fearon, R. P., Sasvari-Szekely, M. M., & Johnson, M. H. (2011). Dopamine D4 receptor and serotonin transporter gene effects on the longitudinal development of infant temperament. *Genes, Brain and Behavior, 10*(5), 513-22.

Holtzman, R. J., & Roberts, M. C. (2012). The role of family conflict in the relation between exposure to community violence and depressive symptoms. *Journal of Community Psychology, 40*(2), 264-75.

Horn, A. B., Pössel, P., & Hautzinger, M. (2011). Promoting adaptive emotion regulation and coping in adolescence: A school-based programme. *Journal of Health Psychology, 16,* 258-73.

Horwitz, B. N., Ganiban, J. M., Spotts, E. L., Lichtenstein, P., Reiss, D., & Neiderhiser, J. M. (2011). The role of aggressive personality and family relationships in explaining family conflict. *Journal of Family Psychology, 25,* 174-83.

Howes, C. (2000). Social-emotional classroom climate in child care, child-teacher relationships and children's second grade peer relations. *Social Development, 9*(2), 191-204.

Howse, R. B., Calkins, S. D., Anastopoulos, A. D., Keane, S., & Shelton, T. L. (2003). Regulatory contributors to children's kindergarten achievement. *Early Education and Development, 14,* 101-19.

Hubbard, J. A., Morrow, M. T., Romano, L. J., & McAuliffe, M. D. (2010). The role of anger in children's reactive versus proactive aggression: Review of findings, issues of measurement, and implications for intervention. In W. Arsenio & E. Lemerise (Eds.), *Emotions, aggression, and morality in children: Bridging development and psychopathology* (pp. 201-17). Washington, DC: American Psychological Association.

Hubbard, J. A., & Zakriski, A. L. (2004). Children's understanding and regulation of emotion in the context of their peer relations. In J. B. Kupersmidt & K. Dodge (Eds.), *Children's peer relations: From development to intervention* (pp. 81-99). Washington, DC: American Psychological Association.

Hudson, J. L., & Rapee, R. M. (2001). Parent-child interactions and anxiety disorders: An observational study. *Behaviour Research and Therapy, 39,* 1411-27.

Hudson, J. L., & Rapee, R. M. (2005). Parental perceptions of overprotection: Specific to anxious children or shared between siblings? *Behaviour Change, 22,* 185-94.

Hughes, D. A. (2007). *Attachment-focused family therapy*. New York: W. W. Norton.

Hughes, E. K., Gullone, E., & Watson, S. D. (2011). Emotional functioning in children and adolescents with elevated depressive symptoms. *Journal of Psychopathology and Behavior Assessment, 33*, 335-45.

Hughes, J. N., & Baker, D. B. (1990). *The clinical child interview*. New York: Guilford.

Hymel, S., Rubin, K. H., Rowden, L., & LeMare, L. (1990). Children's peer relationships: Longitudinal prediction of internalizing and externalizing problems from middle to late childhood. *Child Development, 61*(6), 2004-21.

Isabella, R. A., & Belsky, J. (1991). Interactional synchrony and the origins of infant-mother attachment: A replication study. *Child Development, 62*, 373-84.

Ivorra, J. L., D'Souza, U. M., Jover, M. M., Arranz, M. J., Williams, B. P., Henry, S. E., Sanjuan, J., & Molto, M. D. (2011). Association between neonatal temperament, SLC6A4, DRD4 and a functional polymorphism located in TFAP2B. *Genes, Brain and Behavior, 10*(5), 570-78.

Izard, C. E., King, K. A., Trentacosta, C. J., Morgan, J. K., Laurenceau, J., Krauthamer-Ewing, E., & Finlon, K. J. (2008). Accelerating the development of emotion competence in Head Start children: Effects on adaptive and maladaptive behavior. *Development and Psychopathology, 20*, 369-97.

Izard, C. E., Trentacosta, C. J., King, K. A., & Mostow, A. J. (2004). An emotion-based prevention program for Head Start children. *Early Education and Development, 15*, 407-22.

Jacobson, N. S., & Christensen, A. (1998). *Acceptance and change in couple therapy: A therapist's guide to transforming relationships*. New York: Norton.

Jacobson, N. S., Christensen, A., Prince, S. E., Cordova, J. V., & Elderidge, K. (2000). Integrative behavioral couples therapy: An acceptance-based, promising new treatment for marital discord. *Journal of Consulting and Clinical Psychology, 68*, 351-55.

Jacobson, N. S., & Margolin, G. (1979). *Marital therapy: Strategies based on social learning and behavior exchange*. New York: Brunner/Mazel.

Jacobvitz, D., Hazen, N., Curran, M., & Hitchens, K. (2004). Observations of early triadic family interactions: Boundary disturbances in the family predict symptoms of depression, anxiety, and attention-deficit/hyperactivity disorder in middle childhood. *Development and Psychopathology, 16*, 577-92.

Jaycox, L. H. (2003). *Cognitive behavioral interventions for trauma in schools*. Longmont, CO: Sopris Press.

Jenkins, J., Simpson, A., Dunn, J., Rasbash, J., & O'Connor, T. G. (2005). Mutual influence of marital conflict and children's behavior problems: Shared and nonshared family risks. *Child Development, 76*, 24-39.

Jensen, D. H. (2005). *Graced vulnerability: A theology of childhood*. Cleveland, OH: Pilgrim Press.

Jiang, X., & Cillessen, A. H. N. (2005). Stability of continuous measures of sociometric status: A meta-analysis. *Developmental Review, 25*(1), 1-25.

Jimerson, S. R., Swearer, S. M., & Espelage, D. L. (2009). *Handbook of bullying in schools: An international perspective*. New York: Routledge.

Johnson, B. R., Jang, S. J., Li, S. D., & Larson, D. B. (2000). The invisible institution and black youth crime: The church as an agency of local social control. *Journal of Youth and Adolescence, 29,* 479-98.

Johnson, E. L. (1987). Sin, weakness, and psychopathology. *Journal of Psychology and Theology, 15,* 218-26.

Johnson, M. H., Posner, M. I., & Rothbart, M. K. (1991). Components of visual orienting in early infancy: Contingency learning, anticipatory looking, and disengaging. *Journal of Cognitive Neuroscience, 3*(4), 335-44.

Johnson, S. M. (2004). *Creating connection: The practice of emotionally focused marital therapy* (2nd ed.). New York: Brunner/Routledge.

Johnson, S. M., & Lee, A. (2000). Emotionally focused family therapy: Restructuring attachment. In E. Bailey (Ed.), *Working with children in family therapy*. New York: Brunner/Mazel.

Jones, C. D., & Schwartz, I. A. (2004). Siblings, peers, and adults: Differential effects of models for children with autism. *Topics in Early Childhood Special Education, 24*(4), 187-98.

Jones, M. C. (1924). A laboratory study of fear: The case of Peter. *Journal of General Psychology, 31,* 308-15.

Jones, S. L., & Butman, R. E. (2011). *Modern psychotherapies: A comprehensive Christian appraisal* (2nd ed.). Downers Grove, IL: InterVarsity Press.

Kagan, J. (1984). *The nature of the child*. New York: Basic Books.

Kagan, J. (1989). Temperamental contributions to social behavior. *American Psychologist, 44*(4), 668-74.

Kagan, J. (2003). Biology, context and developmental inquiry. *Annual Review of Psychology,* 541-23.

Kagan, J., Snidman, N., & Arcus, D. (1998). Childhood derivatives of high and low reactivity in infancy. *Child Development, 69*(6), 1483-93.

Kagan, J., Snidman, N., Kahn, V., & Towsley, S. (2007). The preservation of two infant temperaments into adolescence: I. Introduction. *Monographs of the Society for Research in Child Development, 72*(2), 1-9.

Kaitz, M., Maytal, H. R., Devor, N., Bergman, L., & Mankuta, D. (2010). Maternal anxiety, mother-infant interactions, and infants' response to challenge. *Infant Behavior & Development, 33,* 136-48.

Kam, C., Greenberg, M. T., Bierman, K. L., Coie, J. D., Dodge, K. A., Foster, M. E., . . . Pinderhughes, E. E. (2011). Maternal depressive symptoms and child social preference during the early school years: Mediation by maternal warmth and child emotion regulation. *Journal of Abnormal Child Psychology, 39,* 365-77.

Karazsia, B. T., & Wildman, B. G. (2009). The mediating effects of parenting behaviors on maternal affect and reports of children's behavior. *Journal of Child and Family Studies, 18*(3), 342-49.

Katz, L. F., & Woodin, E. M. (2002). Hostility, hostile detachment, and conflict engagement in marriages: Effects on child and family functioning. *Child Development, 73,* 636-51.

Katz, L. Y., Cox, B. J., Gunasekara, S., & Miller, A. L. (2004). Feasibility of dialectical behavior therapy for suicidal adolescent inpatients. *Journal of the American Academy of Child & Adolescent Psychiatry, 43,* 276-82.

Kazak, A. E., Hoagwood, K., Weisz, J. R., Hood, K., Kratochwill, T. R., Vargas, L. A., & Banez, G. A. (2010). A meta-systems approach to evidence-based practice for children and adolescents. *American Psychologist, 65,* 85-97.

Kazdin, A. E. (1997). Practitioner review: Psychosocial treatments for conduct disorder in children. *Journal of Child Psychology and Psychiatry, 38*(2), 161-78.

Kazdin, A. E. (2003). Psychotherapy for children and adolescents. *Annual Review of Psychology, 54,* 253-76.

Kazdin, A. E. (2005a). Evidence-based assessment for children and adolescents: Issues in measurement development and clinical application. *Journal of Clinical Child and Adolescent Psychology, 34,* 548-58.

Kazdin, A. E. (2005b). *Parent management training: Treatment for oppositional, aggressive, and antisocial behavior in children and adolescents.* New York: Oxford University Press.

Kazdin, A. E. (2010). Problem-solving skills training and parent management training for oppositional defiant disorder and conduct disorder. In J. Weisz and A. Kazdin (Eds.), *Evidence-based psychotherapies for children and adolescents* (pp. 211-27). New York: Guilford.

Kearney, C. A. (2008). School absenteeism and school refusal behavior in youth: A contemporary review. *Clinical Psychology Review, 28*(3), 451-71.

Kellam, S. G., Werthamer-Larsson, L., Dolan, L. J., & Brown, C. H. (1991). Developmental epidemiologically based preventative trials: Baseline modeling of early target behaviors and depressive symptoms. *American Journal of Community Psychology, 19*(4), 563-84.

Keller, P. S., Cummings, E. M., Peterson, K. M., & Davies, P. T. (2009). Marital conflict in the context of parental depressive symptoms: Implications for the development of children's adjustment problems. *Social Development, 18,* 536-55.

Keller, P., & El-Sheikh, M. (2011). Children's emotional security and sleep: Longitudinal relations and directions of effects. *Journal of Child Psychology and Psychiatry, 52,* 64-71.

Kendall, P. C. (1985). Toward a cognitive-behavioral model of child psychopathology and a critique of related interventions. *Journal of Abnormal Child Psychology, 13,* 357-72.

Kendall, P. C. (1990). *Coping cat workbook.* Ardmore, PA: Workbook Publishing.

Kendall, P. C., Choudhury, M., Hudson, J., & Webb, A. (2002). The CAT project manual. Ardmore, PA: Workbook Publishing.

Kendall, P. C., Furr, J. M., & Podell, J. L. (2010). Child-focused treatment of anxiety. In J. Weisz & A. Kazdin (Eds.), *Evidence-based psychotherapies for children and adolescents* (pp. 45-61). New York: Guilford.

Kendall, P. C., & Hedtke, K. A. (2006). *Coping cat workbook* (2nd ed.). Ardmore, PA: Workbook Publishing.

Kenny, W. C., Alvarez, K., Donohue, B. C., & Winick, C. B. (2008). Overview of behavioral assessment with adults. In M. Hersen & J. Rosqvist (Eds.), *Handbook of psychological assessment, case conceptualization, and treatment: Vol. 1. Adults* (pp. 3-25). Hoboken, NJ: Wiley.

Kerig, P. K., & Wenar, C. (2005). *Developmental psychopathology: From infancy through adolescence* (5th ed). Boston: McGraw Hill.

Kerns, K. A., Abraham, M. M., Schlegelmilch, A., & Morgan, T. A. (2007). Mother-child attachment in later middle childhood: Assessment approaches and associations with mood and emotion regulation. *Attachment and Human Development, 9,* 33-53.

Kerr, M., & Bowen, M. (1988). *Family evaluation.* New York: Norton.

Kerr, M., Stattin, H., & Ozdemir, M. (2012). Perceived parenting style and adolescent adjustment: Revisiting directions of effects and the role of parental knowledge. *Developmental Psychology, 48,* 1540-53.

Kersh, J., Tedvat, T. T., Hauser-Cram, P., & Warfield, M. E. (2006). The contribution of marital quality to the well-being of parents of children with developmental disabilities. *Journal of Intellectual Disability Research, 50,* 883-93.

Kiel, E. J., & Buss, K. A. (2009). Maternal accuracy and behavior in anticipating children's responses to novelty: Relations to fearful temperament and implications for anxiety development. *Social Development, 19,* 304-25.

Kieras, J. E., Tobin, R. M., Graziano, W. G., & Rothbart, M. K. (2005). You can't always get what you want: Effortful control and children's responses to undesirable gifts. *Psychological Science, 16,* 391-96.

Killen, M., Rutland, A., & Jampol, N. S. (2009). Social exclusion in childhood and adolescence. In K. H. Rubin, W. M. Bukowski & B. Laursen (Eds.), *Handbook of peer interactions, relationships, and groups* (pp. 490-507). New York: Guilford.

Kim, J., & Cicchetti, D. (2010). Longitudinal pathways linking child maltreatment, emotion regulation, peer relations, and psychopathology. *Journal of Child Psychology and Psychiatry, 51,* 706-16.

Kim, J. E., Hetherington, E., & Reiss, D. (1999). Associations among family relationships, antisocial peer, and adolescents' externalizing behaviors: Gender and family type differences. *Child Development, 70*(5), 1209-30.

Kim, S., & Kochanska, G. (2012). Child temperament moderates effects of parent-child mutuality on self-regulation: A relationship-based path for emotionally negative infants. *Child Development, 83,* 1275-89.

King, P. E. (2008). Spirituality as fertile ground for positive youth development. In R. M. Lerner, R. Roeser & E. Phelps (Eds.), *Positive youth development and spirituality: From theory to research* (pp. 55-73). West Conshohocken, PA: Templeton Foundation Press.

King, P. E., & Benson, P. L. (2006). Spiritual development and adolescent well-being and thriving. In E. C. Roehlkepartain, P. E. King, L. Wagener & P. L. Benson (Eds.), *The handbook of spiritual development in childhood and adolescence* (pp. 384-98). Thousand Oaks, CA: Sage.

King, P. E., Carr, A., & Boitor, C. (2011). Spirituality, religiosity, and youth thriving. In R. M. Lerner, J. V. Lerner & J. B. Benson (Eds.), *Advances in child development and behavior* (Vol 1., pp. 161-95). Amsterdam: Elsevier Press.

King, P. E., Clardy, C. E., & Ramos, J. R. (in press). Adolescent spiritual exemplars: Exploring adolescent spirituality among diverse youth. *Journal of Adolescent Research.*

King, P. E., Dowling, E. M., Mueller, R. A., White, K., Schultz, W., Osborn, P., . . . Scales, P. C. (2005). Thriving in adolescence: The voices of youth-serving practitioners, parents, and early and late adolescents. *Journal of Early Adolescence, 25,* 94-112.

King, P. E., Furrow, J. L., & Roth, N. (2002). The influence of families and peers on adolescent religiousness. *Journal of Psychology and Christianity, 21,* 109-20.

King, P. E., Ramos, J. S., & Clardy, C. E. (2013). Searching for the sacred: Religion, spirituality and adolescent development. In K. I. Pargament, J. J. Exline & J. W. Jones (Eds.), *APA handbook of psychology, religion, and spirituality: Vol. 1: Context, theory, and research* (pp. 513-28). Washington, DC: American Psychological Association.

Kingery, J., Erdley, C. A., Marshall, K. C., Whitaker, K. G., & Reuter, T. R. (2010). Peer experiences of anxious and socially withdrawn youth: An integrative review of the developmental and clinical literature. *Clinical Child and Family Psychology Review, 13*(1), 91-128.

Kistner, J., Balthazor, M., Risi, S., & Burton, C. (1999). Predicting dysphoria in adolescence from actual and perceived peer acceptance in childhood. *Journal of Clinical Child Psychology, 28*(1), 94-104.

Klein, M. (1975a). *Envy and gratitude and other works, 1946-1963.* New York: Delta. (Original work published 1957)

Klein, M. (1975b). *The psychoanalysis of children* (Vol. 2). New York: Delacorte Press.

Kley, H., Heinrichs, N., Bender, C., & Tuschen-Caffier, B. (2012). Predictors of outcome in a cognitive-behavioral group program for children and adolescents with social anxiety disorder. *Journal of Anxiety Disorders, 26,* 79-87.

Kliewer, W., Reid-Quiñones, K., Shields, B. J., & Foutz, L. (2009). Multiple risks, emotion regulation skill, and cortisol in low-income African American youth: A prospective study. *Journal of Black Psychology, 35,* 24-43.

Kochanska, G. (1993). Toward a synthesis of parental socialization and child temperament in early development of conscience. *Child Development, 64,* 325-47.

Kochanska, G. (1997). Multiple pathways to conscience for children with different temperaments: From toddlerhood to age 5. *Developmental Psychology, 33*(2), 228-40.

Kochanska, G. (2001). Emotional development in children with different attachment histories: The first three years. *Child Development, 72,* 474-90.

Kochanska, G. (2002). Committed compliance, moral self, and internalization: A mediational model. *Developmental Psychology, 38*(3), 339-51.

Kochanska, G., Coy, K. C., & Murray, K. T. (2001). The development of self-regulation in the first four years of life. *Child Development, 72,* 1091-11.

Kochanska, G., Murray, K. T., & Harlan, E. T. (2000). Effortful control in early childhood: Continuity and change, antecedents, and implications for social development. *Developmental Psychology, 36*(2), 220-32.

Koegel, L. K., Koegel, R. L., Frea, W. D., & Fredeen, R. M. (2001). Identifying early intervention targets for children with autism in inclusive school settings. *Behavior Modification, 25,* 745-61.

Koegel, L. K., Koegel, R. L., Harrower, J. K., & Carter, C. M. (1999). Pivotal response intervention I: Overview of approach. *Journal of the Association for Persons with Severe Handicaps, 24*(3), 174-85.

Koegel, R. L., & Koegel, L. K. (2006). *Pivotal response treatment for autism: Communication, social, and academic development.* Baltimore, MD: Paul H. Brookes Publishing.

Koegel, R. L., Koegel, L. K., Vernon, T. W., & Brookman-Frazee, L. I. (2010). Empirically supported pivotal response treatment for children with autism spectrum disorders. In J. R. Weisz & A. E. Kazdin (Eds.), *Evidence-based psychotherapies for children and adolescents* (2nd ed., pp. 327-44). New York: Guilford.

Koenig, H. G, McCullough, M. E., & Larson, D. B. (2001) *Handbook of religion and health.* New York: Oxford University Press.

Kohler, F. W., Anthony, L. J., Steighner, S. A., & Hoyson, M. (2001). Teaching social interaction skills in the integrated preschool: An examination of naturalistic tactics. *Topics in Early Childhood Special Education, 21*(2), 93-104.

Kohler, F. W., Strain, P. S., Hoyson, M., & Jamieson, B. (1997). Merging naturalistic teaching and peer-based strategies to address the IEP objectives of preschoolers with autism: An examination of structural and child behavior outcomes. *Focus on Autism and Other Developmental Disabilities, 12*(4), 196-206.

Komsi, N., Räikkönen, K., Heinonen, K., Pesonen, A., Keskivaara, P., Järvenpää, A., & Strandberg, T. E. (2008). Transactional development of parent personality and child temperament. *European Journal of Personality, 22*(6), 553-73.

Kopp, C. B. (1982). Antecedents of self-regulation: A developmental perspective. *Developmental Psychology, 18,* 199-214.

Kopp, C. B. (1989). Regulation of distress and negative emotions. *Developmental Psychology, 25,* 343-54.

Kopp, C. B., & Wyer, N. (1994). Self-regulation in normal and atypical development. In D. Cicchetti & S. L. Toth (Eds.), *Rochester symposium on developmental psychopathology, volume 5: Disorders and dysfunctions of the self* (pp. 31-56). Rochester, NY: University of Rochester Press.

Kovacs, M., Joormann, J., & Gotlib, I. H. (2008). Emotion (dys)regulation and links to depressive disorders. *Child Development Perspectives, 2,* 149-55.

Kovacs, M., & Lopez-Duran, N. L. (2012). Contextual emotion regulation therapy: A developmentally based intervention for pediatric depression. *Child and Adolescent Psychiatric Clinics of North America, 21,* 327-43.

Kovacs, M., Sherrill, J., George, C. J., Pollock, M., Tumuluru, R. V., & Ho, V. (2006). Contextual emotion-regulation therapy for childhood depression: Description and pilot testing of a new intervention. *Journal of the American Academy of Child & Adolescent Psychiatry, 45,* 892-903.

Kraemer, H., Kazdin, A. E., Offord, D. R., Kessler, R. C., Jensen, P. S., & Kupfer, D. J. (1997). Coming to terms with the terms of risk. *Archives of General Psychiatry, 54*(4), 337-43.

Kuczynski, L. (2003). Beyond bidirectionality: Bilateral conceptual frameworks for understanding dynamics in parent-child relationships. In L. Kuczynski (Ed.), *Handbook of dynamics in parent-child relations.* Thousand Oaks, CA: Sage.

Kuitert, H. (1972). *Signals from the Bible*. Grand Rapids, MI: Eerdmans.

Kupersmidt, J. B., & Coie, J. D. (1990). Preadolescent peer status, aggression, and school adjustment as predictors of externalizing problems in adolescence. *Child Development, 61*(5), 1350-62.

La Greca, A., & Mackey, E. (2007). Adolescents' anxiety in dating situations: The potential role of friends and romantic partners. *Journal of Clinical Child and Adolescent Psychology, 36*(4), 522-33.

La Greca, A. M., & Harrison, H. M. (2005). Adolescent peer relations, friendships, and romantic relationships: Do they predict social anxiety and depression? *Journal of Clinical Child and Adolescent Psychology, 34*(1), 49-61.

Ladd, G. W. (2005). *Children's peer relations and social competence*. New Haven, CT: Yale University Press.

Ladd, G. W. (2006). Peer rejection, aggressive or withdrawn behavior, and psychological adjustment from ages 5 to 12: An examination of four predictive models. *Child Development, 77*, 822-46.

Ladd, G. W. (2009). Trends, travails, and turning points in early research on children's peer relationships: Legacies and lessons for our time? In K. H. Rubin, W. M. Bukowski & B. Laursen (Eds.), *Handbook of peer interactions, relationships, and groups* (pp. 20-41). New York: Guilford.

Ladd, G. W., Kochenderfer-Ladd, B., Visconti, K., & Ettekal, I. (2012). Classroom peer relations and children's social and scholastic development: Risk factors and resources. In A. M. Ryan & G. W. Ladd (Eds.), *Peer relationships and adjustment at school* (pp. 11-49). Charlotte, NC: Information Age Publishing.

Ladd, G. W., & Troop-Gordon, W. (2003). The role of chronic peer difficulties in the development of children's psychological adjustment problems. *Child Development, 74*(5), 1344-67.

LaFontana, K. M., & Cillessen, A. H. N. (2002). Children's perceptions of popular and unpopular peers: A multi-method assessment. *Developmental Psychology, 38*, 635-47.

Lamb, M. E., & Lewis, C. (2011). The role of parent-child relationships in child development. In M. H. Bornstein & M. E. Lamb (Eds.), *Developmental science: An advanced textbook* (6th ed.). New York: Psychology Press.

Lamb, M. E., & Malkin, C. M. (1985). The development of social expectations in distress-relief sequences: A longitudinal study. *International Journal of Behavioral Development, 9*, 235-49.

Lambert, M. C. (2006). Normal and abnormal development: What the child clinician should know. In C. Essau (Ed.), *Child and adolescent psychopathology: Theoretical and clinical implications.* (pp. 1-25). London: Routledge.

Lamborn, S. D., Mounts, N. S., Steinberg, L., & Dornbusch, S. M. (1991). Patterns of competence and adjustment among adolescents from authoritative, authoritarian, indulgent, and neglectful families. *Child Development, 62,* 1049-65.

Landreth, G. (2002). *Play therapy: The art of the relationship* (2nd ed.). New York: Routledge.

Larson, J., & Cochman, J. E. (2010). *Helping schoolchildren cope with anger* (2nd ed.). New York: Guilford.

Larson, R. W. (2000). Toward a psychology of positive youth development. *American Psychologist, 55,* 170-83.

Larsson, H., Viding, E., Rijsdijk, F., & Plomin, R. (2008). Relationships between parental negativity and childhood antisocial behavior over time: A bidirectional effects model in a longitudinal genetically informative design. *Journal of Abnormal Child Psychology, 36,* 633-45.

Larzelere, R. E., & Kuhn, B. R. (2005). Comparing child outcomes of physical punishment and alternative disciplinary tactics: A meta-analysis. *Clinical Child and Family Psychology Review, 8*(1), 1-37.

Le Grange, D., Crosby, R. D., Rathouz, P. J., & Leventhal, B. L. (2007). A randomized controlled comparison of family-based treatment and supportive psychotherapy for adolescent bulimia nervosa. *Archives of General Psychiatry, 64,* 1049-56.

Leathers, S. J., Spielfogel, J. E., McMeel, L. S., & Atkins, M. S. (2011). Use of a parent management training intervention with urban foster parents: A pilot study. *Child and Youth Services Review, 33*(7), 1270-79.

LeBlanc, M., Self-Brown, S., Shepard, D., & Kelley, M. (2011). Buffering the effects of violence: Communication and problem-solving skills as protective factors for adolescents exposed to violence. *Journal of Community Psychology, 39*(3), 353-67.

Lebow, J. (2005). Family therapy at the beginning of the 21st century. In J. Lebow (Ed.), *Handbook of clinical family therapy* (pp. 1-14). Hoboken, NJ: John Wiley & Sons.

Lebow, J. L., Chambers, A. L., Christensen, A., & Johnson, S. M. (2012). Research on the treatment of couple distress. *Journal of Marital and Family Therapy, 38,* 145-68.

Lemerise, E. A., & Arsenio, W. F. (2000). An integrated model of emotion processes and cognition in social information processing. *Child Development, 71*(1), 107-18.

Lemery, K. S., Goldsmith, H., Klinnert, M. D., & Mrazek, D. A. (1999). Developmental models of infant and childhood temperament. *Developmental Psychology, 35*(1), 189-204.

Lengua, L. J. (2002). The contribution of emotionality and self-regulation to the understanding of children's response to multiple risk. *Child Development, 73,* 144-61.

Lengua, L. J. (2003). Associations among emotionality, self-regulation, adjustment problems, and positive adjustment in middle childhood. *Journal of Applied Developmental Psychology, 24*(5), 595-618.

Lengua, L. J., & Long, A. C. (2002). The role of emotionality and self-regulation in the appraisal-coping process: Tests of direct and moderating effects. *Journal of Applied Developmental Psychology, 23*(4), 471-93.

Lengua, L. J., West, S. G., & Sandler, I. N. (1998). Temperament as a predictor of symptomatology in children: Addressing contamination of measures. *Child Development, 69,* 164-81.

Lenze, S. N., Pautsch, J., & Luby, J. (2011). Parent-child interaction therapy emotion development: A novel treatment for depression in preschool children. *Depression and Anxiety, 28,* 153-59.

Lerner, R. M. (2002). *Concepts and theories of human development* (3rd ed.). Mahwah, NJ: Lawrence Erlbaum Associates.

Lerner, R. M. (2004). *Liberty: Thriving and civic engagement among American youth.* Thousand Oaks, CA: Sage.

Lerner, R. M. (2006). Developmental science, developmental systems, and contemporary theories of human development. In W. Damon & R. M. Lerner (Eds.), *Handbook of child psychology* (6th ed., Vol. 1, pp. 1-17). Hoboken, NJ: Wiley.

Lerner, R. M., Alberts, A. E., Jelicic, H., & Smith, L. M. (2006). Young people are resources to be developed: Promoting positive youth development through adult-youth relations and community assets. In E. Clary & J. E. Rhodes (Eds.), *Mobilizing adults for positive youth development: Strategies for closing the gap between beliefs and behaviors* (pp. 19-39). New York: Springer.

Lerner, R. M., Dowling, E. M., & Anderson, P. M. (2003). Positive youth development: Thriving as the basis of personhood and civil society. *Applied Developmental Sciences, 7*(3), 171-79.

Lerner, R. M., Lerner, J. V., Almerigi, J., Theokas, C., Phelps, E., Gestsdottir, S., . . . von Eye, A. (2005). Positive youth development, participation in community youth development programs, and community contributions of fifth-grade adolescents: Findings from the first wave of the 4-H Study of Positive Youth Development. *Journal of Early Adolescence, 25,* 17-71.

Lerner, R. M., Roeser, R. W., & Phelps, E. (Eds.). (2008). *Positive youth development and spirituality: From theory to research.* West Conshohocken, PA: Templeton Foundation Press.

Lewis, L., Trushell, J., & Woods, P. (2005). Effects of ICT group work on interactions and social acceptance of a primary pupil with Asperger's Syndrome. *British Journal of Educational Technology, 36*(5), 739-55.

Lewis, M. (2007). Early emotional development. In A. Slater & M. Lewis (Eds.), *Introduction to infant development* (2nd ed., pp. 216-32). Malden, MA: Blackwell.

Liddle, H. A. (2009). *Multidimensional family therapy for adolescent drug abuse: Clinician's manual.* Center City, MN: Hazelden.

Liddle, H. A., Rodriguez, R. A., Dakof, G. A., Kanzki, E., & Marvel, F. A. (2005). Multidimensional family therapy: A science-based treatment for adolescent drug abuse. In J. L. Lebow (Ed.), *Handbook of clinical family therapy* (pp. 128-63). New York: Wiley.

Lieberman, A. F., & van Horn, P. (2005). Don't hit my mommy: A manual for child-parent psychotherapy with young witnesses of family violence. Washington, DC: Zero-to-Three Press.

Lincoln, T. M., Wilhelm, K., & Nestoriuc, Y. (2007). Effectiveness of psychoeducation for relapse, symptoms, knowledge, adherence, and functioning in psychotic disorders: A meta-analysis. *Schizophrenia Research, 96,* 232-45. doi:10.1016/j.schres.2007.07.022

Lindahl, K. M., Malik, N. M., Kaczynski, K., & Simons, J. S. (2004). Couple power dynamics, systemic family functioning, and child adjustment: A test of a meditational model in a multiethnic sample. *Development and Psychopathology, 16,* 609-30.

Linehan, M. (1993). *Cognitive-behavioral treatment for borderline personality disorder.* New York: Guilford.

Lions Quest (n.d.). Enhancing Youth Development through Home-School-Community Collaboration: Evaluation Report. Retrieved from www.lions-quest.org/pdfs/EvaluationResultsShortReport.pdf on February 20, 2013.

Lochman, J. E. (2006). Translation of research into interventions. *International Journal of Behavioral Development, 30*(1), 31-38.

Lochman, J. E., Wells, K. C., & Lenhart, L. A. (2008). *Coping power: Child group facilitator's guide.* New York: Oxford University Press.

Lock, J., & Le Grange, D. (2012). *Treatment manual for anorexia nervosa: A family-based approach* (2nd ed.). New York: Guilford.

Lock, J., Le Grange, D., Agras, W. S., Moye, A., Bryson, S. W., & Jo, B. (2010). Randomized clinical trial comparing family-based treatment with adolescent-focused individual therapy for adolescents with anorexia nervosa. *Archives of General Psychiatry, 67*(10), 1025-32.

Loeber, R., Pardini, D., Homish, D. L., Wei, E. H., Crawford, A. M., Farrington, D. P., . . . Rosenfeld R. (2005). The prediction of violence and homicide in young men. *Journal of Consulting and Clinical Psychology, 73,* 1074-88.

Lonigan, C. J., Vasey, M. W., Phillips, B. M., & Hazen, R. A. (2004). Temperament, anxiety, and the processing of threat-relevant stimuli. *Journal of Clinical Child and Adolescent Psychology, 33*(1), 8-20.

Lotze, G. M., Ravindran, N., & Myers, B. J. (2010). Moral emotions, emotion self-regulation, callous-unemotional traits, and problem behavior in children of incarcerated mothers. *Journal of Child and Family Studies, 19*, 702-13.

Lovaas, O. I. (2003). *Teaching individuals with developmental delays: Basic intervention techniques.* Austin, TX: PRO-ED.

Lovinger, R. J. (1984). *Working with religious issues in therapy.* New York: Jason Aronson.

Luebbe, A. M., Bell, D. J., Allwood, M. A., Swenson, L. P., & Early, M. C. (2010). Social information processing in children: Specific relations to anxiety, depression, and affect. *Journal of Clinical Child and Adolescent Psychology, 39*(3), 386-99. doi:10.1080/15374411003691685

Luebbe, A. M., Kiel, E. J., & Buss, K. A. (2011). Toddlers' context-varying emotions, maternal responses to emotions, and internalizing behaviors. *Emotion, 11*, 697-703.

Lundahl, B. W., & Nimer J. (2006). Preventing child abuse: A meta-analysis of parent training programs. *Research on Social Work Practice, 16*(3), 251-62.

Luthar, S. S., & Cicchetti, D. (2000). The construct of resilience: Implications for interventions and social policies. *Development and Psychopathology, 12*(4), 857-85.

Luthar, S. S., Cicchetti, D., & Becker, B. (2000). The construct of resilience: A critical evaluation and guidelines for future work. *Child Development, 71*(3), 543-62.

Maccoby, E. E. (1992). The role of parents in the socialization of children: An historical overview. *Developmental Psychology, 28*(6), 1006-17.

Maccoby, E. E., & Martin, J. A. (1983). Socialization in the context of the family: Parent-child interaction. In P. H. Mussen and E. M. Hetherington (Eds.), *Handbook of child psychology, Vol. 4: Socialization, Personality, and Social Development* (4th ed., pp. 1-101). New York: Wiley.

Macfie, J., Houts, R. M., Pressel, A. S., & Cox, M. J. (2008). Pathways from infant exposure to marital conflict to parent-toddler role reversal. *Infant Mental Health Journal, 29*, 297-319.

Maedgen, J., & Carlson, C. L. (2000). Social functioning and emotional regulation in the attention deficit hyperactivity disorder. *Journal of Clinical Child Psychology, 29*, 30-42.

Mahler, M., Pine, F., & Bergman, A. (1975). *The psychological birth of the human infant.* New York: Basic Books.

Mahoney, A., Jouriles, E. N., & Scavone, J. (1997). Marital adjustment, marital discord over childrearing, and child behavior problems: Moderating effects of child age. *Journal of Child Clinical Psychology, 26*, 415-23.

Malott, R. (2007). *Principles of behavior.* Upper Saddle River, NJ: Pearson Prentice Hall.

Mangelsdorf, S. C., Shapiro, J. R., & Marzolf, D. (1995). Developmental and temperamental differences in emotion regulation in infancy. *Child Development, 66*, 1817-28.

Manian, N., & Bornstein, M. H. (2009). Dynamics of emotion regulation in infants of clinically depressed and nondepressed mothers. *Journal of Child Psychology and Psychiatry, 50,* 1410-18.

Mannering, A. M., Harold, G. T., Leve, L. D., Shelton, K. H., Shaw, D. S., Conger, R. D., . . . Reiss, D. (2011). Longitudinal associations between marital instability and child sleep problems across infancy and toddlerhood in adoptive families. *Child Development, 82,* 1252-66.

March, J. S., & Mulle, K. (1998). *OCD in children and adolescents: A cognitive behavioral treatment manual.* New York: Guilford.

Marker, C., Weeks, M., & Kraegel, I. (2007). Integrating faith and treatment for children with high functioning autism spectrum disorders. *Journal of Psychology and Christianity, 26,* 112-21.

Marlatt, G. A., Larimer, M. E., Mail, P. D., Hawkins, E. H., Cummins, L. H., Blume, A. W., . . . Gallion, S. (2003). Journeys of the circle: A culturally congruent life skills intervention for adolescent Indian drinking. *Alcoholism: Clinical and Experimental Research, 27*(8), 1327-29.

Marty, M. E. (2007). *The mystery of the child.* Grand Rapids, MI: Eerdmans.

Mash, E. J. (2006). Treatment of child and family disturbance: A cognitive-behavioral systems perspective. In E. J. Mash & R. A. Barkley (Eds.), *Treatment of childhood disorders* (3rd ed., pp. 3-62). New York: Guilford.

Mash, E. J., & Barkley, R. A. (2006). *Treatment of childhood disorders* (3rd ed.). New York: Guilford.

Mash, E. J., & Hunsley, J. (2007). Assessment of child and family disturbance: A developmental-systems approach. In E. J. Mash & R. A. Barkley (Eds.), *Assessment of childhood disorders* (4th ed., pp. 3-50). New York: Guilford.

Masten, A. S. (2001). Ordinary magic: Resilience processes in development. *American Psychologist, 56*(3), 227-38.

Masten, A. S. (2006). Developmental psychopathology: Pathways to the future. *International Journal of Behavioral Development, 30,* 47-54.

Masten, A. S., Best, K. M., & Garmezy, N. (1990). Resilience and development: Contributions from the study of children who overcome adversity. *Development and Psychopathology, 2*(4), 425-44.

Masten, A. S., & Braswell, L. (1991). Developmental psychopathology: An integrative framework. In P. R. Martin (Ed.), *Handbook of behavior therapy and psychological science: An integrative approach* (pp. 35-56). Elmsford, NY: Pergamon Press.

Masten, A. S., & Cicchetti, D. (2010). Developmental cascades. *Development and Psychopathology, 22*(3), 491-95.

Masten, A. S., & Coatsworth, J. (1998). The development of competence in favorable and unfavorable environments: Lessons from research on successful children. *American Psychologist, 53*(2), 205-20.

Masten, A. S., Hubbard, J. J., Gest, S. D., Tellegen, A., Garmezy, N., & Ramirez, M. (1999). Competence in the context of adversity: Pathways to resilience and maladaptation from childhood to late adolescence. *Development and Psychopathology, 11,* 143-69.

Maughan, A., & Cicchetti, D. (2002). Impact of child maltreatment and interadult violence on children's emotion regulation abilities and socioemotional adjustment. *Child Development, 73,* 1525-42.

Maughan, A., Cicchetti, D., Toth, S. L., & Rogosch, F. A. (2007). Early-occurring maternal depression and maternal negativity in predicting young children's emotion regulation and socioemotional difficulties. *Journal of Abnormal Child Psychology, 35,* 685-703.

May, S., Posterski, B., Stonehouse, C., & Cannell, L. (2005). *Children matter: Celebrating their place in the church, family, and community.* Grand Rapids, MI: Eerdmans.

McAdams, D. P. (2006). *The redemptive self: Stories Americans live by.* New York: Oxford University Press.

McAdams, D. P., & Olson, B. D. (2010). Personality development: Continuity and change over the life course. *Annual Review of Psychology, 61,* 517-42.

McCarty, C. A., Weisz, J. R., Wanitromanee, K., Eastman, K. L., Suwanlert, S., Chaiyasit, W., & Band, E. B. (1999). Culture, coping, and context: Primary and secondary control among Thai and American youth. *Journal of Child Psychology and Psychiatry, 40,* 809-18.

McDargh, J. (1983). *Psychoanalysis object relations theory and the study of religion: On faith and the imaging of God.* Lanham, MD: University Press of America.

McDonald, A., Beck, R., Allison, S., & Norsworthy, L. (2005). Attachment to God and parents: Testing the correspondence vs. compensation hypotheses. *Journal of Psychology and Christianity, 24,* 21-28.

McDonald, R., & Grych, J. H. (2006). Young children's appraisals of interparental conflict: Measurement and links with adjustment problems. *Journal of Family Psychology, 20,* 88-99.

McGoldrick, M., & Carter, B. C. (2001). Advances in coaching: Family therapy with one person. *Journal of Marital and Family Therapy, 27,* 281-300.

McGoldrick, M., Carter, B., & Garcia-Preto, N. (2011). *The expanded family life cycle: Individual, family, and social perspectives.* Boston: Pearson Education.

McGoldrick, M., Gerson, R., & Petry, S. (2008). *Genograms: Assessment and intervention.* New York: W. W. Norton.

McGrath, A. E. (2005). *Incarnation*. Minneapolis: Fortress.

McHale, J. P., Kuersten-Hogan, R., & Rao, N. (2004). Growing points for coparenting theory and research. *Journal of Adult Development, 11,* 221-34.

McKay, M., Wood, J. C., & Brantley, J. (2007). *The Dialectical Behavior Therapy Skills Workbook: Practical DBT exercises for learning mindfulness, interpersonal effectiveness, emotional regulation, and distress tolerance.* Oakland, CA: New Harbinger Publications.

McLaughlin, K. A., Hatzenbuehler, M. L., & Hilt, L. M. (2009). Emotion dysregulation as a mechanism linking peer victimization to internalizing symptoms in adolescents. *Journal of Consulting and Clinical Psychology, 77,* 894-904.

McLoyd, V. C. (1998). Socioeconomic disadvantage and child development. *American Psychologist, 53*(2), 185-204.

McMahon, R. J., & Forehand, R. L. (2003). *Helping the noncompliant child: Family-based treatment for oppositional behavior* (2nd ed.). New York: Guilford.

McManis, M. H., Kagan, J., Snidman, N. C., & Woodward, S. A. (2002). EEG asymmetry, power, and temperament in children. *Developmental Psychobiology, 41*(2), 169-77.

McMinn, M. R. (2004). *Why sin matters: The surprising relationship between our sin and God's grace.* Wheaton, IL: Tyndale House.

McMinn, M. R., & Campbell, C. D. (2007). Integrative psychotherapy: Toward a comprehensive Christian approach. Downers Grove, IL: InterVarsity Press.

McNeil, C. B., & Hembree-Kigin, T. L. (2010). *Parent-child interaction therapy.* New York: Springer.

Meilander, G. (1990). What are families for? *First Things, 6,* 34-41.

Mercer, J. A. (2005). *Welcoming children: A practical theology of childhood.* St. Louis, MO: Chalice Press.

Mezulis, A., Priess, H., & Hyde, J. S. (2011). Rumination mediates the relationship between infant temperament and adolescent depressive symptoms. *Depression Research and Treatment.* http://dx.doi.org/10.1155/2011/487873.

Mian, N. D., Wainwright, L., Briggs-Gowan, M. J., & Carter, A. S. (2011). An ecological risk model for early childhood anxiety: The importance of early child symptoms and temperament. *Journal of Abnormal Child Psychology, 39*(4), 501-12.

Midgley, N., & Kennedy, E. (2011). Psychodynamic psychotherapy for children and adolescents: A critical review of the evidence base. *Journal of Child Psychotherapy, 37*(3), 232-60.

Miklowitz, D. J. (2004). The role of family systems in severe and recurrent psychiatric disorders: A developmental psychopathology view. *Development and Psychopathology, 16,* 667-88.

Miklowitz, D. J., George, E. L., Axelson, D. A., Kim, E. Y., Birmaher, B., Schneck, C., . . . Brent, D. A. (2004). Family-focused treatment for adolescents with bipolar disorder. *Journal of Affective Disorders, 82*(suppl. 1), 113-28.

Miller, A. L., Gouley, K., Seifer, R., Dickstein, S., & Shields, A. (2004). Emotions and behaviors in the Head Start classroom: Associations among observed dysregulation, social competence, and preschool adjustment. *Early Education and Development, 15,* 147-65.

Miller, A. L., Rathus, J. H., & Linehan, M. M. (2006). *Dialectical behavior therapy with suicidal adolescents.* New York: Guilford.

Miller, A., Rathus, J., Linehan, M., Wetzler, S., & Leigh, E. (1997). Dialectical behavior therapy adapted for suicidal adolescents. *Journal of Practical Psychiatry and Behavioral Health, 3,* 78-86.

Miller, S., & Berg, I. K. (1995). *Miracle method: a radically new approach to problem drinking.* New York: W. W. Norton.

Miller-McLemore, B. J. (2003). *Let the children come: Reimagining childhood from a Christian perspective.* San Francisco: Jossey-Bass.

Miller-McLemore, B. J. (2007). *In the midst of chaos: Care of children as spiritual practice.* San Francisco: Jossey-Bass.

Minuchin, S. (1974). *Families and family therapy.* Cambridge, MA: Harvard University Press.

Minuchin, S., & Fishman, H. C. (1981). *Family therapy techniques.* Cambridge, MA: Harvard University Press.

Mitchell, S. A., & Black, M. J. (1995). *Freud and beyond: A history of modern psychoanalytic thought.* New York: Basic Books.

Moffitt, T. E. (1993). Adolescence-limited and life-course-persistent antisocial behavior: A developmental taxonomy. *Psychological Review, 100*(4), 674-701.

Moltmann, J. (2000). Child and childhood as metaphors of hope. *Theology Today, 56*(4), 592-603.

Moran, D. J., & Malott, R. W. (2004). *Evidence-based educational methods.* San Diego: Elsevier Academic Press.

Morgan, J., & Banerjee, R. (2006). Social anxiety and self-evaluation of social performance in a nonclinical sample of children. *Journal of Clinical Child and Adolescent Psychology, 35*(2), 292-301.

Moriarty, G. L. (2010). *Integrating faith and psychology: Twelve psychologists tell their stories.* Downers Grove, IL: InterVarsity Press.

Morrill, M. I., Hines, D. A., Mahmood, S., & Córdova, J. V. (2010). Pathways between marriage and parenting for wives and husbands: The role of coparenting. *Family Process, 49,* 59-73.

Morris, A., Silk, J. S., Steinberg, L., Myers, S. S., & Robinson, L. (2007). The role of the family context in the development of emotion regulation. *Social Development, 16,* 361-88.

Morrison, R. S., & Blackburn, A. M. (2008). Take the challenge: Building social competency in adolescents with Asperger's syndrome. *TEACHING Exceptional Children Plus, 5*(2) Article 5. Retrieved 7-2-2012 from http://escholarship.bc.edu/education/tecplus/vol5/iss2/art5

Moscardino, U., & Axia, G. (2006). Infants' responses to arm restraint at 2 and 6 months: A longitudinal study. *Infant Behavior and Development, 29,* 59-69.

Moscovitch, D. A., Antony, M. M., & Swinson, R. P. (2009). Exposure-based treatments for anxiety disorders: Theory and process. In M. M. Antony & M. B. Stein (Eds.), *Oxford handbook of anxiety and related disorders* (pp. 461-75). New York: Oxford University Press.

Mouw, R. J. (2012). The *imago Dei* and philosophical anthropology. *Christian Scholar's Review, 41,* 253-66.

Mowrer, O. H., & Mowrer, W. M. (1938). Enuresis: A method for its study and treatment. *American Journal of Orthopsychiatry, 8,* 436-59.

Mufson, L., Dorta, K. P., Moreau, D., & Weissman, M. M. (2011). *Interpersonal psychotherapy for depressed adolescents* (2nd ed.). New York: Guilford.

Mullin, B. C., & Hinshaw, S. P. (2007). Emotion regulation and externalizing disorders in children and adolescents. In J. J. Gross (Ed.), *Handbook of emotion regulation* (pp. 523-41). New York: Guilford.

Mullineaux, P. Y., Deater-Deckard, K., Petrill, S. A., Thompson, L. A., & DeThorne, L. S. (2009). Temperament in middle childhood: A behavioral genetic analysis of fathers' and mothers' reports. *Journal of Research in Personality, 43*(5), 737-46.

Muratori, F., Picchi, L., Bruni, G., Patarnello, M., & Romagnoli, G. (2003). A two-year follow-up of psychodynamic psychotherapy for internalizing disorders in children. *Journal of the American Academy of Child and Adolescent Psychiatry, 42*(3), 331-39.

Murray, L., Arteche, A., Fearon, P., Halligan, S., Goodyer, I., & Cooper, P. (2011). Maternal postnatal depression and the development of depression in offspring up to 16 years of age. *Journal of the American Academy of Child and Adolescent Psychiatry, 50*(5), 460-70.

Murray, L., de Rosnay, M., Pearson, J., Bergeron, C., Schofield, E., Royal-Lawson, M., & Cooper, P. J. (2008). Intergenerational transmission of social anxiety: The role of social referencing processes in infancy. *Child Development, 79,* 1049-64.

Nachmias, M., Gunnar, M., Mangelsdorf, S., Parritz, R. H., & Buss, K. (1996). Behavioral inhibition and stress reactivity: The moderating role of attachment security. *Child Development, 67,* 508-22.

Najman, J. M., Behrens, B. C., Andersen, M., Bor, W., O'Callaghan, M., & Williams, G. M. (1997). Impact of family types and family quality on child behavior problems: A longitudinal study. *Journal of the American Academy of Child and Adolescent Psychiatry, 36*(10), 1357-65.

Nangle, D. W., Erdley, C. A., Newman, J. E., Mason, C. A., & Carpenter, E. M. (2003). Popularity, friendship quantity, and friendship quality: Interactive influences on children's loneliness and depression. *Journal of Clinical Child and Adolescent Psychology, 32*(4), 546-55.

Nansel, T. R., Overpeck, M., Pilla, R. S., Ruan, W. J., Simons-Morton, B., & Scheidt, P. (2001). Bullying behaviors among US youth: Prevalence and association with psychosocial adjustment. *Journal of the American Medical Association, 285,* 2094-2100.

Neblett, E. W., Rivas-Drake, D., & Umana-Taylor, A. J. (2012). The promise of racial and ethnic protective factors in promoting ethnic minority positive development. *Child Development Perspectives, 6*(3), 295-303.

Nedderman, A. B., Underwood, L. A., & Hardy, V. L. (2010). Spirituality group with female prisoners: Impacting hope. *Journal of Correctional Health Care, 16*(2), 117-32.

Neumann, A., van Lier, P. A. C., Gratz, K. L., & Koot, H. M. (2010). Multidimensional assessment of emotion regulation difficulties using the Difficulties in Emotion Regulation Scale. *Assessment, 17,* 138-49.

Newcomb, A. F., Bukowski, W. M., & Pattee, L. (1993). Children's peer relations: A meta-analytic review of popular, rejected, neglected, controversial, and average sociometric status. *Psychological Bulletin, 113*(1), 99-128.

Newman, D. L., Caspi, A., Moffitt, T. E., & Silva, P. A. (1997). Antecedents of adult interpersonal functioning: Effects of individual differences in age 3 temperament. *Developmental Psychology, 33*(2), 206-17.

Nichols, M. P. (2010). *Family therapy: Concepts and methods.* Boston: Pearson Education.

Nix, R. L., Bierman, K. L., & McMahon, R. J. (2009). How attendance and quality of participation affect treatment response to Parent Management Training. *Journal of Consulting and Clinical Psychology, 77*(3), 429-38.

Nixon, C. L., & Cummings, E. M. (1999). Sibling disability and children's reactivity to conflicts involving family members. *Journal of Family Psychology, 13,* 274-85.

Nock, M. K. (2005). Response prevention. In M. Hersen & J. Rosqvist (Eds.), *Encyclopedia of behavior modification and cognitive behavior therapy, Vol. 1: Adult clinical applications* (pp. 489-93). Thousand Oaks, CA: Sage.

Nolte, T., Guiney, J., Fonagy, P., Mayes, L. C., & Luyten, P. (2011). Interpersonal stress regulation and the development of anxiety disorders: An attachment-based developmental framework. *Frontiers in Behavioral Neuroscience, 5,* 1-21.

Nye, R. (2009). *Children's spirituality: What it is and why it matters.* London: Church House Publishing.

Oberle, E., Schonert-Reichl, K. A., & Thomson, K. C. (2010). Understanding the link between social and emotional well-being and peer relations in early adolescence: Gender-specific predictors of peer acceptance. *Journal of Youth and Adolescence, 39*(11), 1330-42.

Odom, S. L., Brown, W. H., Frey, T., Karasu, N., Smith-Canter, L. L., & Strain, P. S. (2003). Evidence-based practices for young children with autism: Contributions for single-subject design research. *Focus on Autism and Other Developmental Disabilities, 18,* 166-75.

Olino, T. M., Lopez-Duran, N. L., Kovacs, M., George, C. J., Gentzler, A. L., & Shaw, D. S. (2011). Developmental trajectories of positive and negative affect in children at high and low familial risk for depressive disorder. *Journal of Child Psychology and Psychiatry, 52,* 792-99.

Ollendick, T. H., & Benoit, K. E. (2012). A parent-child interactional model of social anxiety disorder in youth. *Clinical Child and Family Psychology Review, 15,* 81-91.

Ollendick, T. H., Grills, A. E., & King, N. J. (2001). Applying developmental theory to the assessment and treatment of childhood disorders: Does it make a difference? *Clinical Psychology & Psychotherapy, 8,* 304-14.

Ollendick, T. H., & King N. J. (1991). Developmental factors in child behavioral assessment. In P. R. Martin (Ed.), *Handbook of behavior therapy and psychological science: An integrative approach* (pp. 57-72). New York: Pergamon Press.

Ollendick, T. H., & King, N. J. (2004). Empirically supported treatments for children and adolescents: Advances toward evidence-based practice. In P. M. Barrett & T. H. Ollendick (Eds.), *Handbook of interventions that work with children and adolescents: Prevention and treatment* (pp. 3-25). New York: John Wiley & Sons.

Olson, D. H., & Gorall, D. M. (2003). Circumplex model of marital and family systems. In F. Walsh (Ed.), *Normal family processes* (3rd ed., pp. 514-47). New York: Guilford.

Olson, R. E. (2002). *The mosaic of Christian belief: Twenty centuries of unity and diversity.* Downers Grove, IL: InterVarsity Press.

Olweus, D. (2010). Understanding and researching bullying: Some critical issues. In S. R. Jimerson, S. M. Swearer & D. L. Espelage (Eds.), *Handbook of bullying in schools: An international perspective* (pp. 9-34). New York: Routledge.

Ostberg, M., & Rydell, A-M. (2012). An efficacy study of combined parent and teacher management training programme for children with ADHD. *Nordic Journal of Psychiatry, 66,* 123-30.

Owen, A., Thompson, M., Shaffer, A., Jackson, E., & Kaslow, N. (2009). Family variables that mediate the relation between intimate partner violence (IPV) and child adjustment. *Journal of Family Violence, 24,* 433-45.

Pachter, L. M., Bernstein, B. A., Szalacha, L. A., & Coll, C. (2010). Perceived racism and discrimination in children and youths: An exploratory study. *Health and Social Work, 35,* 61-69.

Panfile, T. M., & Laible, D. J. (2012). Attachment security and child's empathy: The mediating role of emotion regulation. *Merrill-Palmer Quarterly, 58,* 1-21.

Papp, L. M., Goeke-Morey, M. C., & Cummings, E. M. (2004). Mothers' and fathers' psychological symptoms and marital functioning: Examination of direct and interactive links with child adjustment. *Journal of Child & Family Studies, 13,* 469-82.

Pardini, D. A. (2008). Novel insights into longstanding theories of bidirectional parent-child influences: Introduction to the special section. *Journal of Child Psychology, 36,* 627-31.

Pardini, D. A., Fite, P. J., & Burke, J. D. (2008). Bidirectional associations between parenting practices and conduct problems in boys from childhood to adolescence: The moderating effect of age and African-American ethnicity. *Journal of Abnormal Child Psychology, 36,* 647-62.

Pargament, K. I. (2007). *Spiritually integrated psychotherapy: Understanding and addressing the sacred.* New York: Guilford.

Pargament, K., Exline, J., Jones, J., Mahoney, A., & Shafranske, E. (Eds.). (2013). *APA handbooks in psychology: APA handbook of psychology, religion, and spirituality.* Washington, DC: American Psychological Association.

Pargas, R., Brennan, P. A., Hammen, C., & Le Brocque, R. (2010). Resilience to maternal depression in young adulthood. *Developmental Psychology, 46*(4), 805-16.

Parke, R. D. (2004). Development in the family. *Annual Review of Psychology, 55,* 365-99.

Parker, J. G., & Asher, S. R. (1987). Peer relations and social adjustment: Are low-accepted children "at risk"? *Psychological Bulletin, 102,* 357-89.

Parker, J. G., Rubin, K. H., Erath, S. A., Wojslawowicz, J. C., & Buskirk, A. A. (2006). Peer relationships, child development, and adjustment: A developmental psychopathology perspective. In D. Cicchetti & D. J. Cohen (Eds.), *Developmental psychopathology, Vol 1: Theory and method* (2nd ed., pp. 419-93). Hoboken, NJ: John Wiley & Sons.

Patterson, G. R. (1982). *A social learning approach to family interventions: III. Coercive family process.* Eugene, OR: Castalia.

Patterson, G. R. (2005). The next generation of PMTO models. *The Behavior Therapist, 35,* 27-33.

Patterson, G. R., Dishion, T. J., & Bank, L. (1984). Family interaction: A process model of deviancy training. *Aggressive Behavior, 10,* 253-67.

Patterson, G. R., Reid, J. B., & Dishion, T. J. (1992). *Antisocial boys*. Eugene, OR: Castalia.

Pavlov, I. (1927). *Conditioned reflexes: An investigation of the physiological activity of the cerebral cortex*. London, England: Oxford University Press.

Pearce, M. J., Jones, S. M., Schwab-Stone, M. E., & Ruchkin, V. (2003). The protective effects of religiousness and parent involvement on the development of conduct problems among youth exposed to violence. *Child Development, 74*, 1682-96.

Peckins, M. K., Dockray, S. D., Eckenrode, J. L., Heaton, J., & Susman, E. J. (2012). The longitudinal impact of exposure to violence on cortisol reactivity in adolescents. *Journal of Adolescent Health, 51*(4), 366-72.

Pediatric OCD Treatment Study Team. (2004). Cognitive-behavior therapy, Sertraline, and their combination for children and adolescents with obsessive-compulsive disorder: The pediatric OCD treatment study (POTS) randomized controlled trial. *Journal of the American Medical Association, 292*(16), 1969-76.

Pelchat, D., Bisson, J., Bois, C., & Saucier, J-F. (2003). The effects of early relational antecedents and other factors on the parental sensitivity of mothers and fathers. *Infant and Child Development, 12*, 27-51.

Penney, S. R., & Moretti, M. M. (2010). The roles of affect dysregulation and deficient affect in youth violence. *Criminal Justice and Behavior, 37*, 709-31.

Peretti, F. E. (2000). *The wounded spirit*. Nashville: Thomas Nelson.

Perry-Parrish, C., & Zeman, J. (2011). Relations among sadness regulation, peer acceptance, and social functioning in early adolescence: The role of gender. *Social Development, 20*(1), 135-53.

Pfiffner, L. A., Barkley, R. A., & DuPaul, G. J. (2006). Treatment of ADHD in school settings. In R. A. Barkley (Ed.), *Attention-deficit/hyperactivity disorder: A handbook for diagnosis and treatment* (3rd ed., pp. 547-89). New York: Guilford.

Pinsof, W. M. (1996). *Integrative problem-centered therapy*. New York: Basic Books.

Pinsof, W., Breunlin, D., Russell, W., & Lebow, J. (2011). Integrative problem-centered metaframeworks therapy II: Planning, conversing, and reading feedback. *Family Process, 50*(3), 314-36.

Pitkin, M. B. (2001). "The heritage of the Lord": Children in the theology of John Calvin. In M. Bunge (Ed.), *The child in Christian thought* (pp. 160-93). Grand Rapids, MI: Eerdmans.

Pittman, K. J. (1991). *Promoting youth development: Strengthening the role of youth-serving and community organizations*. Report prepared for the US Department of Agriculture Extension Service National Initiative Task Force on Youth at Risk. Washington, DC: Center for Youth Development and Policy Research.

Pollak, S. D., & Sinha, P. (2002). Effects of early experience on children's recognition of facial displays of emotion. *Developmental Psychology, 38,* 784-91.

Posner, M. I., & Rothbart, M. K. (2000). Developing mechanisms of self-regulation. *Development and Psychopathology, 12,* 427-41.

Powell, K. E., & Clark, C. (2011). *Sticky faith: Everyday ideas to build lasting faith in your kids.* Grand Rapids, MI: Zondervan.

Power, T. J., Karusti, J. L., & Habboushe, D. F. (2001). *Homework success for children with ADHD: A family-school intervention program.* New York: Guilford.

Powers, C. J., & Bierman, K. L. (2013). The multifaceted impact of peer relations on aggressive-disruptive behavior in early elementary school. *Developmental Psychology, 49*(6), 1174-86.

Prevatt, F. (2003). The contribution of parenting style in a risk and resiliency model of children's adjustment. *The British Journal of Developmental Psychology, 21,* 469-80.

Priester, P. E., Scherer, J., Steinfeldt, J. A., Jana-Masari, A., Jashinsky, T., Jones, J. E., & Vang, C. (2009). The frequency of prayer: Meditation and holistic interventions in addictions treatment: A national survey. *Pastoral Psychology, 58,* 315-22.

Prinstein, M. J., & Aikins, J. W. (2004). Cognitive moderators of the longitudinal association between peer rejection and adolescent depressive symptoms. *Journal of Abnormal Child Psychology, 32,* 147-58.

Prinstein, M. J., Rancourt, D., Guerry, J. D., & Browne, C. B. (2009). Peer reputations and psychological adjustment. In K. H. Rubin, W. M. Bukowski & B. Laursen (Eds.), *Handbook of peer interactions, relationships, and groups* (pp. 548-67). New York: Guilford.

Prior, V., and Glaser, D. (2006). *Understanding attachment and attachment disorders: Theory, evidence and practice.* London, England: Jessica Kingsley Publishers.

Putnam, S. P., Rothbart, M. K., & Gartstein, M. A. (2008). Homotypic and heterotypic continuity of fine-grained temperament during infancy, toddlerhood, and early childhood. *Infant and Child Development, 17*(4), 387-405.

Quagliana, H. L., King, P. E., Wagener, L. M., & Quagliana, D. P. (2012). Spiritually oriented interventions in developmental context. In D. F. Walker & W. L. Hathaway (Eds.), *Spiritually oriented interventions in child and adolescent psychotherapy.* Washington, DC: American Psychological Association.

Quamma, J. P. G., & Greenberg, M. T. (1994). Children's experience of life stress: The role of family social support and social problem-solving skills as protective factors. *Journal of Clinical Child Psychology, 23*(3), 295-305.

Querido, J. G., Bearss, K., & Eyberg, S. M. (2002). Theory, research, and practice of parent-child interaction therapy. In F. W Kaslow & T. Patterson (Eds.), *Compre-*

hensive handbook of psychotherapy, Volume two: Cognitive/behavioral/functional approaches (pp. 91-113). New York: Wiley.

Ramsden, S. R., & Hubbard, J. A. (2002). Family expressiveness and parental emotion coaching: Their role in children's emotion regulation and aggression. *Journal of Abnormal Child Psychology, 30,* 657-67.

Randour, M. L., & Bondanza, J. (1987). The concept of God in the psychological formation of females. *Psychoanalytic Psychology, 4,* 301-13.

Rapp-Paglicci, L. A., Dulmas, C. N., & Wodarski, J. S. (2004). *Handbook of preventive interventions for children and adolescents.* Hoboken, NJ: John Wiley.

Ratcliff, D., & May, S. (2004). Identifying children's spirituality: Walter Wangerin's perspectives, and an overview of this book. In D. Ratcliff (Ed.), *Children's spirituality: Christian perspectives, research, and applications* (pp. 7-21). Eugene, OR: Cascade Books.

Reichow, B., & Volkmar, F. R. (2010). Social skills interventions for individuals with autism: Evaluation for evidence-based practices within a best evidence synthesis framework. *Journal of Autism and Developmental Disorders 40,* 149-66.

Reiff, J. T. (1995). Nurturing and equipping children in the "public church." In N. T. Ammerman & W. C. Roof (Eds.), *Work, family, and religion in contemporary society* (pp. 199-218). New York: Routledge.

Richards, P. S., Hardman, R. K., & Berrett, M. E. (2007). *Spiritual approaches in the treatment of women with eating disorders.* Washington, DC: American Psychological Association.

Risdal, D., & Singer, G. H. S. (2004). Marital adjustment in parents of children with disabilities: A historical review and meta-analysis. *Research & Practices for Persons with Severe Disabilities, 2,* 95-102. doi:10.2511/rpsd.29.2.95

Rivers, J. W., & Stoneman, Z. (2003). Sibling relationships when a child has autism: Marital stress and support coping. *Journal of Autism and Developmental Disorders, 33,* 383-94.

Rizzuto, A. (1979). *The birth of the living God: A psychoanalytic study.* Chicago: University of Chicago Press.

Roben, C. K. P., Cole, P. M., & Armstrong, L. M. (2013). Longitudinal relations among language skills, anger expression, and regulatory strategies in early childhood. *Child Development, 84,* 891-905.

Robin, A. L., & Le Grange, D. (2010). Family therapy for adolescents with anorexia nervosa. In J. R. Weisz & A. E. Kazdin (Eds.), *Evidence-based psychotherapies for children and adolescents* (2nd ed., pp. 345-58). New York: Guilford.

Robin, A. L. (1998). *ADHD in adolescents: Diagnosis and treatment.* New York: Guilford.

Robinson, C., Mandleco, B., Olsen, S. F., & Hart, C. H. (1995). Authoritative, authoritarian, and permissive parenting practices: Development of a new measure. *Psychological Reports, 77,* 819-30.

Rodkin, P. C., Farmer, T. W., Pearl, R., & Van Acker, R. (2000). Heterogeneity of popular boys: Anti-social and prosocial configurations. *Developmental Psychology, 36,* 14-24.

Roehlkepartain, E., & Patel, E. (2006). Congregations: Unexamined crucibles for spiritual development. In E. Roehlkepartain, P. King, L. Wagener & P. Benson (Eds.), *The handbook of spiritual development in childhood and adolescence* (pp. 324-37). Thousand Oaks, CA: Sage.

Rogosch, F. A., Cicchetti, D., & Toth, S. L. (2004). Expressed emotion in multiple subsystems of the families of toddlers with depressed mothers. *Development and Psychopathology, 16,* 689-709.

Roque, L., Veríssimo, M., Oliveira, T. F., & Oliveira, R. F. (2012). Attachment security and HPA axis reactivity to positive and challenging emotional situations in child-mother dyads in naturalistic settings. *Developmental Psychobiology, 54,* 401-11.

Rose, A. J. (2002). Co-rumination in the friendships of girls and boys. *Child Development, 73*(6), 1830-43.

Rose, A. J., & Smith, R. L. (2009). Sex differences in peer relationships. In K. H. Rubin, W. M. Bukowski & B. Laursen (Eds.), *Handbook of peer interactions, relationships, and groups* (pp. 379-93). New York: Guilford.

Rose-Krasnor, L. (1997). The nature of social competence: A theoretical review. *Social Development, 6*(1), 111-35.

Rose-Krasnor, L., & Denham, S. (2009). Social-emotional competence in early childhood. In K. H. Rubin, W. M. Bukowski & B. Laursen (Eds.), *Handbook of peer interactions, relationships, and groups* (pp. 162-79). New York: Guilford.

Rosen, K. S., & Rothbaum, F. (2003). Parent-child relationships. In J. J. Ponzetti Jr. (Ed.), *International encyclopedia of marriage and family* (2nd ed., Vol. 1, pp. 103-11). New York: Macmillan.

Ross, H., & Howe, N. (2009). Family influences on children's peer relationships. In K. H. Rubin, W. M. Bukowski & B. Laursen (Eds.), *Handbook of peer interactions, relationships, and groups* (pp. 508-30). New York: Guilford.

Rothbart, M. K. (1981). Measurement of temperament in infancy. *Child Development, 52*(2), 569-78. doi:10.2307/1129176

Rothbart, M. K. (2004). Temperament and the pursuit of an integrated developmental psychology. *Merrill-Palmer Quarterly, 50*(4), 492-505. doi:10.1353/mpq.2004.0035

Rothbart, M. K. (2007). Temperament, development, and personality. *Current Directions in Psychological Science, 16*(4), 207-12. doi:10.1111/j.1467-8721.2007.00505.x

Rothbart, M. K. (2011). *Becoming who we are: Temperament and personality in development*. New York: Guilford.

Rothbart, M. K., & Ahadi, S. A. (1994). Temperament and the development of personality. *Journal of Abnormal Psychology, 103*(1), 55-66.

Rothbart, M. K., Ahadi, S. A., & Evans, D. E. (2000). Temperament and personality: Origins and outcomes. *Journal of Personality and Social Psychology, 78,* 122-35.

Rothbart, M. K., Ahadi, S. A., Hershey, K. L., & Fisher, P. (2001). Investigations of temperament at three to seven years: The Children's Behavior Questionnaire. *Child Development, 72,* 1394-1408.

Rothbart, M. K., & Bates, J. E. (1998). Temperament. In N. Eisenberg (Ed.), *Handbook of child psychology, Vol. 3: Social, emotional, and personality development* (5th ed., pp. 105-76). Hoboken, NJ: John Wiley & Sons.

Rothbart, M. K., & Bates, J. E. (2006). Temperament. In N. Eisenberg, W. Damon & R. M. Lerner (Eds.), *Handbook of child psychology, Vol. 3: Social, emotional, and personality development* (6th ed., pp. 99-166). Hoboken, NJ: John Wiley & Sons.

Rothbart, M. K., & Derryberry, D. (1981). Development of individual differences in temperament. In M. E. Lamb & A. L. Brown (Eds.), *Advances in developmental psychology* (Vol. 1, pp. 37-86). Hillsdale, NJ: Erlbaum.

Rothbart, M. K., Derryberry, D., & Posner, M. I. (1994). A psychobiological approach to the development of temperament. In J. E. Bates & T. D. Wachs (Eds.), *Temperament: Individual differences at the interface of biology and behavior* (pp. 83-116). Washington, DC: American Psychological Association.

Rothbart, M. K., & Posner, M. I. (2006). Temperament, attention, and developmental psychopathology. In D. Cicchetti & D. J. Cohen (Eds.), *Developmental psychopathology, Vol. 2: Developmental neuroscience* (2nd ed., pp. 465-501). Hoboken, NJ: John Wiley & Sons.

Rothbart, M. K., Sheese, B. E., Rueda, M., & Posner, M. I. (2011). Developing mechanisms of self-regulation in early life. *Emotion Review, 3*(2), 207-13.

Rubin, K. H., Burgess, K. B., Kennedy, A. E., & Stewart, S. L. (2003). Social withdrawal in childhood. In E. J. Mash & R. A. Barkley (Eds.), *Child psychopathology* (2nd ed., pp. 330-71). New York: Guilford.

Rubio, J. H. (2003). Three-in-one flesh: A Christian reappraisal of divorce in light of recent studies. *Journal of the Society of Christian Ethics, 23*(1), 47-70.

Rueger, S. Y., Malecki, C. K., & Demaray, M. K. (2010). Multiple sources of perceived social support and psychological and academic adjustment in early adolescence: Comparisons across gender. *Journal of Youth and Adolescence, 39,* 47-61.

Ruma, P. R., Burke, R. V., & Thompson, R. W. (1996). Group parent training: Is it effective for children of all ages? *Behavior Therapy, 27*(2), 159-69.

Rutter, M. (1979). Protective factors in children's responses to stress and disadvantage. In M. W. Kent & J. E. Rolf (Eds.), *Primary prevention of psychopathology, Vol. 3: Social competence in children* (pp. 49-74). Hanover, NH: University Press of New England.

Rutter, M. (1983). Stress, coping, and development: Some issues and some questions. In N. Garmezy & M. Rutter (Eds.), *Stress, coping, and development in children* (pp. 1-41). Baltimore, MD: Johns Hopkins University Press.

Rutter, M. (1989). Pathways from childhood to adult life. *Journal of Child Psychology and Psychiatry, 30,* 23-51.

Rutter, M., & Garmezy, N. (1983). Developmental psychopathology. In E. M. Hetherington & P. H. Mussen (Eds.), *Handbook of child psychology* (Vol. 4, pp. 775-912). New York: Wiley.

Ryan, A. M., & Ladd, G. W. (Eds.). (2012). *Peer relationships and adjustment at school.* Charlotte, NC: Information Age Publishing.

Ryan, V., & Edge, A. (2012). The role of play themes in non-directive play therapy. *Clinical Child Psychology and Psychiatry, 17*(3), 354-69.

Saarni, C. (1999). *The development of emotional competence.* New York: Guilford.

Salmon, K., Dadds, M. R., Allen, J., & Hawes, D. J. (2009). Can emotional language skills be taught during parent training for conduct problem children? *Child Psychiatry and Human Development, 40,* 485-98.

Sameroff, A. J. (1975). Early influences on development: Fact or fancy? *Merrill-Palmer Quarterly, 21*(4), 267-94.

Sameroff, A. J., & Chandler, M. J. (1975). Reproductive risk and the continuum of caretaking casualty. In F. D. Horowitz, M. Hetherington & S. Scarr-Salopatek (Eds.), *Review of Child Development Research* (Vol. 4, pp. 187-244). Chicago: University of Chicago Press.

Sameroff, A. J., Seifer, R., Baldwin, A., & Baldwin, C. (1993). Stability of intelligence from preschool to adolescence: The influence of social and family risk factors. *Child Development, 64,* 80-97.

Sameroff, A. J., Seifer, R., Barocas, B., Zax, M., & Greenspan, S. (1987). IQ scores of 4-year-old children: Social-environmental risk factors. *Pediatrics, 79,* 343-50.

Sanders, M. R., Markie-Dadds, C., & Turner, K. M. (2001). *Practitioner's manual for standard triple p.* Queensland, Australia: Triple P International.

Sandstrom, M. J., & Coie, J. D. (1999). A developmental perspective on peer rejection: Mechanisms of stability and change. *Child Development, 70,* 955-66.

Sanson, A., & Prior, M. (1999). Temperament and behavioral precursors to oppositional defiant disorder and conduct disorder. In H. C. Quay & A. E. Hogan (Eds.),

Handbook of disruptive behavior disorders (pp. 397-417). Dordrecht, Netherlands: Kluwer Academic Publishers.

Santrock, J. W. (2011). *Life-span development* (13th ed.). New York: McGraw-Hill.

Santucci, A. K., Silk, J. S., Shaw, D. S., Gentzler, A., Fox, N. A., & Kovacs, M. (2008). Vagal tone and temperament as predictors of emotion regulation strategies in young children. *Developmental Psychobiology, 50,* 205-16.

Sasayama, D., Hayashida, A., Yamasue, H., Harada, Y., Kaneko, T., Kasai, K., Washizuka, S., & Amano, N. (2010). Neuroanatomical correlates of attention-deficit hyperactivity disorder accounting for comorbid oppositional defiant disorder and conduct disorder. *Psychiatry and Clinical Neurosciences, 64*(4), 394-402.

Sasso, G. M., Garrison-Harrell, L., McMahon, C. M., & Peck, J. (1998). Social competence of individuals with autism: An applied behavior analysis perspective. In R. L. Simpson & B. S. Myles (Eds.), *Educating parents and youth with autism* (pp. 173-90). Austin, TX: PRO-ED.

Satir, V. (1983). *Conjoint family therapy.* Palo Alto, CA: Science and Behavior Books.

Sattler, J. M. (2006). *Assessment of children: Behavioral, social, and clinical foundations* (5th ed.). San Diego: Jerome M. Sattler.

Saudino, K. J. (2005). Special Article: Behavioral Genetics and Child Temperament. *Journal of Developmental and Behavioral Pediatrics, 26*(3), 214-23.

Sauter, F. M., Heyne, D. A., & Westenberg, P. M. (2009). Cognitive behavior therapy for anxious adolescents: Developmental influences on treatment design and delivery. *Clinical Child and Family Psychology Review, 12*(4), 310-35.

Sayger, T. V., Horne, A. M., & Glaser, B. A. (1993). Marital satisfaction and social learning family therapy for child conduct problems: Generalization of treatment effects. *Journal of Marital and Family Therapy, 19,* 393-402.

Scarr, S. (1993). Biological and cultural diversity: The legacy of Darwin for development. *Child Development, 64,* 1333-53.

Scarr, S., & McCartney, K. (1983). How people make their own environments: A theory of genotype → environment effects. *Child Development, 54*(2), 424-35.

Schaff, P. (1890–1900). *The Nicene and Post-Nicene Fathers,* Series 2. (Vols. 1-14). Buffalo, NY: Christian Literature.

Scharff, D. E., & Birtles, E. F. (Eds.). (1994). *From instinct to self: Selected papers of W. R. D. Fairbairn, Volume 1: Clinical and theoretical papers.* Northvale, NJ: Jason Aronson.

Scharff, D., & Scharff, J. (1987). *Object relations family therapy.* New York: Jason Aronson.

Schermerhorn, A. C., D'Onofrio, B. M., Turkheimer, E., Ganiban, J. M., Spotts, E. L., Lichtenstein, P., & Neiderhiser, J. M. (2011). A genetically informed study of associations between family functioning and child psychosocial adjustment. *Developmental Psychology, 47,* 707-25.

Schofield, T. J., Conger, R. D., Donnellan, M. B., Jochem, R., Widaman, K. F., & Conger, K. J. (2012). Parent personality and positive parenting as predictors of positive adolescent personality development over time. *Merrill-Palmer Quarterly, 58,* 255-83.

Schoon, I., Parsons, S., & Sacker, A. (2004). Socioeconomic adversity, educational resilience, and subsequent levels of adult adaptation. *Journal of Adolescent Research, 19,* 383-404.

Schore, A. N. (2003). *Affect regulation and disorders of the self.* New York: W. W. Norton.

Schore, J. R., & Schore, A. N. (2008). Modern attachment theory: The central role of affect regulation in development and treatment. *Clinical Social Work Journal, 36,* 9-20.

Schrodt, P., Ledbetter, A. M., & Ohrt, J. K. (2007). Parental confirmation and affection as mediators of family communication patterns and children's mental well-being. *Journal of Family Communication, 7,* 23-46.

Schroeder, C. S., & Gordon, B. N. (2002). *Assessment and treatment of childhood problems: A clinician's guide* (2nd ed., pp. 115-58). New York: Guilford.

Schwartz, D., Dodge, K. A., Pettit, G. S., & Bates, J. E. (2000). Friendship as a moderating factor in the pathway between early harsh home environment and later victimization in the peer group. *Developmental Psychology, 36*(5), 646-62.

Schwartz, D., & Proctor, L. J. (2000). Community violence exposure and children's social adjustment in the school peer group: The mediating roles of emotion regulation and social cognition. *Journal of Consulting and Clinical Psychology, 68,* 670-83.

Schwartz, C. E., Wright, C. I., Shin, L. M., Kagan, J., & Rauch, S. L. (2003). Inhibited and uninhibited infants 'grown up': Adult amygdalar response to novelty. *Science, 300*(5627), 1952-53.

Schwartz, J. A. J., Gladstone, T. R. G., & Kaslow, N. J. (1998). Depressive disorders. In T. H. Ollendick & M. Hersen (Eds.), *Handbook of child psychopathology* (3rd ed., pp. 269-89). New York: Plenum Press.

Schwartz, K. D., Bukowski, W. M., & Aoki, W. T. (2006). Mentors, friends, and gurus: Peer and nonparent influences on spiritual development. In E. C. Roehlkepartain (Ed.), *The handbook of spiritual development in childhood and adolescence* (pp. 310-23). Thousand Oaks, CA: Sage.

Schwarz, B., Stutz, M., & Ledermann, T. (2012). Perceived interparental conflict and early adolescents' friendships: The role of attachment security and emotion regulation. *Journal of Youth and Adolescence, 41,* 1240-52.

Sears, W. (1985). *Christian parenting and childcare.* Nashville: Thomas Nelson.

Seegobin, W., Reyes, J. R., Hostler, H., Nissley, G., & Hart, A. (2007). Relationship with parents, God concept, self-esteem, and relationship intimacy. In P. Hegy (Ed.), *God images and the religious imagination.* Lewiston, NY: Edwin Mellen.

Seifer, R., Gouley, K., Miller, A. L., & Zakriski, A. (2004). Implementation of the PATHS curriculum in an urban elementary school. *Early Education and Development, 15,* 471-85.

Seifer, R., Sameroff, A. J., Baldwin, C. P., & Baldwin, A. L. (1992). Child and family factors that ameliorate risk between 4 and 13 years of age. *Journal of the American Academy of Child & Adolescent Psychiatry, 31,* 893-903.

Seifer, R., Sameroff, A. J., Dickstein, S., Keitner, G., Miller, I., Rasmussen, S., & Hayden, L. C. (1996). Parental psychopathology, multiple contextual risks, and one-year outcomes in children. *Journal of Clinical Child Psychology, 25,* 423-35.

Semrund-Clikeman, M. (1995). *Child and adolescent therapy.* Boston: Allyn and Bacon.

Sexton, T. I., & Alexander, J. F. (2005). Functional family therapy for externalizing disorders in adolescents. In J. L. Lebow (Ed.), *Handbook of clinical family therapy* (pp. 164-94). New York: Wiley.

Shadish, W. R., & Baldwin, S. A. (2009). Meta-analysis of MFT interventions. *Journal of Marital and Family Therapy, 29*(4), 547-70.

Shapiro, J. P., Friedberg, R. D., & Bardenstein, K. K. (2006). *Child and adolescent therapy: Science and art.* Hoboken, NJ: John Wiley & Sons.

Shaw, D. S., Criss, M. M., Schonberg, M. A., & Beck, J. E. (2004). The development of family hierarchies and their relation to children's conduct problems. *Development and Psychopathology, 16,* 483-500.

Shedler, J. (2010). The efficacy of psychodynamic psychotherapy. *American Psychologist, 65*(2), 98-109.

Shields, A., & Cicchetti, D. (1998). Reactive aggression among maltreated children: The contributions of attention and emotion dysregulation. *Journal of Clinical Child Psychology, 27,* 381-95.

Shields, A., & Cicchetti, D. (2001). Parental maltreatment and emotion dysregulation as risk factors for bullying and victimization in middle childhood. *Journal of Clinical Child Psychology, 30,* 349-63.

Shields, A., Dickstein, S., Seifer, R., Giusti, L., Magee, K. D., & Spritz, B. (2001). Emotional competence and early school adjustment: A study of preschoolers at risk. *Early Education and Development, 12,* 73-96.

Shiner, R., & Caspi, A. (2003). Personality differences in childhood and adolescence: Measurement, development, and consequences. *Journal of Child Psychology and Psychiatry, 44*(1), 2-32.

Shipman, K. L., Schneider, R., Fitzgerald, M. M., Sims, C., Swisher, L., & Edwards, A.

(2007). Maternal emotion socialization in maltreating and non-maltreating families: Implications for children's emotion regulation. *Social Development, 16,* 268-85.

Shirk, S. R. (1988). *Cognitive development and child psychotherapy.* New York: Plenum Press.

Shirk, S. R. (1999). Developmental therapy. In S. W. Russ & T. H. Ollendick (Eds.), *Developmental Issues in the Clinical Treatment of Children* (pp. 60-73). Boston: Allyn and Bacon.

Shirk, S. R., Karver, M. S., & Brown, R. (2011). The alliance in child and adolescent psychotherapy. *Psychotherapy, 48,* 17-24.

Shirk, S.R., & Russell, R. L. (1996). *Change processes in child psychotherapy: Revitalizing treatment and research.* New York: Guilford.

Shirk, S., Talmi, A., & Olds, D. (2000). A developmental psychopathology perspective on child and adolescent treatment policy. *Development and Psychopathology, 12*(4), 835-55.

Shults, F. L. R., & Sandage, S. J. (2006). *Transforming spirituality: Integrating theology and psychology.* Grand Rapids, MI: Baker Academic.

Siegel, D., & Hartzell, M. (2004). *Parenting from the inside out.* Los Angeles: Tarcher.

Siegel, D. J. (2001) *The developing mind: How relationships and the brain interact to shape who we are.* New York: Guilford.

Siegel, D. J., & Bryson, T. P. (2011). *The whole-brain child: 12 revolutionary strategies to nurture your child's developing mind.* New York: Delacorte Press.

Siegel, D. J., & Hartzell, M. (2003). *Parenting from the inside out: How a deeper self-understanding can help you raise children who thrive.* New York: Penguin Group.

Siegel, R. S., La Greca, A. M., & Harrison, H. M. (2009). Peer victimization and social anxiety in adolescents: Prospective and reciprocal relationships. *Journal of Youth and Adolescence, 38*(8), 1096-109.

Silk, J. S., Shaw, D. S., Forbes, E. E., Lane, T. L., & Kovacs, M. (2006). Maternal depression and child internalizing: The moderating role of child emotion regulation. *Journal of Clinical Child and Adolescent Psychology, 35,* 116-26.

Silk, J. S., Shaw, D. S., Prout, J. T., O'Rourke, F., Lane, T. J., & Kovacs, M. (2011). Socialization of emotion and offspring internalizing symptoms in mothers with childhood-onset depression. *Journal of Applied Developmental Psychology, 32,* 127-36.

Silk, J. S., Shaw, D. S., Skuban, E. M., Oland, A. A., & Kovacs, M. (2006). Emotion regulation strategies in offspring of childhood-onset depressed mothers. *Journal of Child Psychology and Psychiatry, 47,* 69-78.

Silk, J. S., Steinberg, L., & Morris, A. S. (2003). Adolescents' emotion regulation in daily life: Links to depressive symptoms and problem behavior. *Child Development, 74,* 1869-80.

Siman-Tov, A., & Kaniel, S. (2011). Stress and personal resource as predictors of the adjustment of parents to autistic children: A multivariate model. *Journal of Autism and Developmental Disorders, 41,* 879-90.

Simpson, R. L., de Boer-Ott, S., Griswold, D., Myles, B., Byrd, S., & Ganz, J. (2005). *Autism spectrum disorders: Interventions and treatment for children and youth.* Thousand Oaks, CA: Corwin Press.

Sisemore, T. A., & Moore, R. L. (2002). Embracing the call to the least of these: Welcoming children in Jesus' name. *Journal of Psychology and Christianity, 21,* 318-24.

Skinner, B. F. (1938). *The behavior of organisms.* New York: Appleton-Century.

Slee, N., Spinhoven, P., Garnefski, N., & Arensman, E. (2008). Emotion regulation as mediator of treatment outcome in therapy for deliberate self-harm. *Clinical Psychology and Psychotherapy, 15,* 205-16.

Smith, C. (2003). Theorizing religious effects among American adolescents. *Journal for the Scientific Study of Religion, 42,* 17-30.

Smith, C. L., Calkins, S. D., & Keane, S. P. (2006). The relation of maternal behavior and attachment security to toddlers' emotions and emotion regulation. *Research in Human Development, 3,* 21-31.

Smith, P. K., Mahdavi, J., Carvalho, M., Fisher, S., Russell, S., & Tippett, N. (2008). Cyberbullying: Its nature and impact in secondary school pupils. *Journal of Child Psychology and Psychiatry, 49,* 376-85.

Smith, S., & Hamon, R. R. (2012). *Exploring family theories.* New York: Oxford University Press.

Smith, T. (2010). Early and intensive behavioral intervention in autism. In J. R. Weisz & A. E. Kazdin (Eds.), *Evidence-based psychotherapies for children and adolescents* (2nd ed., pp. 312-26). New York: Guilford.

Snow, D. J. (1992). Marital therapy with parents to alleviate behavioral disorders in their children. *Research on Social Work Practice, 2,* 172-83.

Snyder, J., Schrepferman, L., McEachern, A., Barner, S., Johnson, K., & Provines, J. (2008). Peer deviancy training and peer coercion: Dual processes associated with early-onset conduct problems. *Child Development, 79*(2), 252-68.

Snyder, J., Schrepferman, L., Oeser, J., Patterson, G., Stoolmiller, M., Johnson, K., & Snyder, A. (2005). Deviancy training and association with deviant peers in young children: Occurrence and contribution to early-onset conduct problems. *Development and Psychopathology, 17*(2), 397-413.

Sobanski, E., Banaschewski, T., Asherson, P., Buitelaar, J., Chen, W., Franke, B., . . . Rothenberger, A. (2010). Emotional lability in children and adolescents with attention deficit/hyperactivity disorder (ADHD): Clinical correlates and familial prevalence. *Journal of Child Psychology & Psychiatry, 51,* 915-23.

Southam-Gerow, M. A., & Kendall, P. C. (2000). A preliminary study of the emotion understanding of youths referred for treatment of anxiety disorders. *Journal of Clinical Child Psychology, 29,* 319-27.

Spence, S. H., Donovan, C., & Brechman-Toussaint, M. (1999). Social skills, social outcomes, and cognitive features of childhood social phobia. *Journal of Abnormal Psychology, 108*(2), 211-21.

Spiegler, M. D., & Guevremont, D. C. (2010). *Contemporary behavior therapy* (5th ed.). Belmont, CA: Wadsworth Cengage Learning.

Spilka, B., Hood, R. W., Jr., Hunsberger, B., & Gorsuch, R. (2003). *The psychology of religion: An empirical approach* (3rd ed.). New York: Guilford.

Spirito, A., & Kazak, A. E. (2006). *Effective and emerging treatments in pediatric psychology.* New York: Oxford University Press.

Spotts, E. L., Prescott, C., & Kendler, K. (2006). Examining the origins of gender differences in marital quality: A behavior genetic analysis. *Journal of Family Psychology, 20,* 605-13.

Sprenkle, D., & Blow, A. (2004). Common factors and our sacred models. *Journal of Marital and Family Therapy, 30*(2), 113-29.

Sprenkle, D. H., Davis, S. D., & Lebow, J. L. (2009). *Common factors in couple and family therapy.* New York: Guildford.

Spritz, B. L., Sandberg, E., Maher, E., & Zajdel, R. T. (2010). Models of emotion skills and social competence in the Head Start classroom. *Early Education and Development, 21,* 495-516.

Sroufe, L. A. (1995). *Emotional development: The organization of emotional life in the early years.* New York: Cambridge University Press.

Sroufe, L. A. (1997). Psychopathology as an outcome of development. *Development and Psychopathology, 9*(2), 251-68.

Sroufe, L. A. (2009). The concept of develop in developmental psychopathology. *Child Development Perspectives, 3*(3), 178-83.

Sroufe, L. A., & Rutter, M. (1984). The domain of developmental psychopathology. *Child Development, 55,* 17-29.

St. Clair, M. (2000). *Object relations and self psychology: An introduction* (3rd ed.). Belmont, CA: Wadsworth/Thomson Learning.

Stanley, S. M., Markman, H. J., & Whitton, S. W. (2002). Communication, conflict, and commitment: Insights on the foundations of relationship success from a national survey. *Family Process, 41,* 659-75.

Stansbury, K., & Sigman, M. (2000). Responses of preschoolers in two frustrating episodes: Emergence of complex strategies for emotion regulation. *Journal of Genetic*

Psychology: Research and Theory on Human Development, 161, 182-202.

Stark, K. D., Simpson, J., Schnoebelen, S., Hargrave, J., Molnar, J., & Glen, R. (2007). *'Action' workbook: Cognitive-behavioral therapy for treating depressed girls.* Ardmore, PA: Workbook Publishing.

Stark, K. D., Streusand, W., Krumholz, L. S., & Patel, P. (2010). Cognitive behavioral therapy for depression: The ACTION treatment program for girls. In A. Kazdin and J. Weisz (Eds.), *Evidence-based psychotherapies for children and adolescents* (2nd ed., pp. 93-109). New York: Guilford.

Starr, P. (1981). Marital status and raising a handicapped child: Does one affect the other? *Social Work, 26,* 504-6.

Stedman, J. M. (1977). Behavior therapy strategies as applied to family therapy. *Family Therapy, 4,* 217-24.

Steege, M. W., Mace, F., Perry, L., & Longenecker, H. (2007). Applied behavior analysis: Beyond discrete trial teaching. *Psychology in the Schools, 44*(1), 91-99. doi:10.1002/pits.20208

Stein, M. B., Fuetsch, M. M., Muller, N., Hofler, M., Lieb, R., & Wittchen, H. (2001). Social anxiety disorder and the risk of depression: A prospective community study of adolescents and young adults. *Archives of General Psychiatry, 58,* 251-56.

Steinberg, L. (2001). We know some things: Parent-adolescent relationships in retrospect and prospect. *Journal of Research on Adolescence, 11*(1), 1-19.

Stifter, C. A., & Jain, A. (1996). Psychophysiological correlates of infant temperament: Stability of behavior and autonomic patterning from 5 to 18 months. *Developmental Psychobiology, 29,* 379-91.

Stifter, C. A., & Spinrad, T. L. (2002). The effect of excessive crying on the development of emotion regulation. *Infancy, 3,* 133-52.

Stifter, C. A., Spinrad, T. L., & Braungart-Rieker, J. M. (1999). Toward a developmental model of child compliance: The role of emotion regulation in infancy. *Child Development, 70,* 21-32.

Stiles-Shields, C., Hoste, R., Doyle, P., & Le Grange, D. (2012). A review of family-based treatment for adolescents with eating disorders. *Reviews on Recent Clinical Trials, 7,* 133-40.

Stone, L. B., Hankin, B. L., Gibb, B. E., & Abela, J. R. (2011). Co-rumination predicts the onset of depressive disorders during adolescence. *Journal of Abnormal Psychology, 120,* 752-57.

Stonehouse, C., & May, S. (2010). *Listening to children on the spiritual journey: Guidance for those who teach and nurture.* Grand Rapids, MI: Baker Academic.

Stortz, M. E. (2001). "Where or when was your servant innocent?": Augustine on childhood. In M. Bunge (Ed.), *The child in Christian thought* (pp. 78-102). Grand Rapids, MI: Eerdmans.

Strain, P. S., & Odom, S. L. (1986). Peer social initiations: Effective intervention for social skill development of exceptional children. *Exceptional Children, 52,* 543-52.

Strain, P. S., & Schwartz, I. (2001). ABA and the development of meaningful social relations for young children with autism. *Focus on Autism and Other Developmental Disabilities, 16*(2), 120-28.

Strain, P. S., Young, C. C., & Horowitz, J. (1981). Generalized behavior change during oppositional child training. *Behavior Modification, 5*(1), 15-26.

Sturge-Apple, M. L., Cicchetti, D., Davies, P. T., & Suor, J. H. (2012). Differential susceptibility in spillover between interparental conflict and maternal parenting practices: Evidence for OXTR and 5-HTT genes. *Journal of Family Psychology, 26,* 431-42.

Sullivan, T. N., Helms, S. W., Kliewer, W., & Goodman, K. L. (2010). Associations between sadness and anger regulation coping, emotional expression, and physical and relational aggression among urban adolescents. *Social Development, 19,* 30-51.

Suveg, C., Kendall, P. C., Comer, J. S., & Robin, J. (2006). Emotion-focused cognitive-behavioral therapy for anxious youth: A multiple-baseline evaluation. *Journal of Contemporary Psychotherapy, 36,* 77-85.

Suveg, C., Sood, E., Barmish, A., Tiwari, S., Hudson, J. L., & Kendall, P. C. (2008). 'I'd rather not talk about it': Emotion parenting in families of children with an anxiety disorder. *Journal of Family Psychology, 22,* 875-84.

Suveg, C., & Zeman, J. (2004). Emotion regulation in children with anxiety disorders. *Journal of Clinical Child and Adolescent Psychology, 33,* 750-59.

Swanson, K., Beckwith, L., & Howard, J. (2000). Intrusive caregiving and quality of attachment in prenatally drug-exposed toddlers and their primary caregivers. *Attachment & Human Development, 2,* 130-48.

Swearer, S. M., Espelage, D. L., & Napolitano, S. A. (2009). *Bullying prevention and intervention: Realistic strategies for schools.* New York: Guilford.

Swords, L., Heary, C., & Hennessy, E. (2011). Factors associated with acceptance of peers with mental health problems in childhood and adolescence. *Journal of Child Psychology and Psychiatry, 52,* 933-41.

Swords, L., Hennessy, E., & Heary, C. (2011). Adolescents' beliefs about sources of help for ADHD and depression. *Journal of Adolescence, 34,* 485-92.

Szapocznik, J., Hervis, O. E., & Schwartz, S. (2003). *Brief Strategic Family Therapy for Adolescent Drug Abuse* (NIDA Therapy Manuals for Drug Addiction Series). Rockville, MD: NIDA.

Szapocznik, J., Murray, E., Scopetta, M., Hervis, O., Rio, A., Cohen, R., . . . Kurtines, W.

(1989). Structural family therapy versus psychodynamic child therapy for problematic Hispanic boys. *Journal of Consulting and Clinical Psychology, 57*(5), 571-78.

Tan, P. Z., Forbes, E. E., Dahl, R. E., Ryan, N. D., Siegle, G. J., Ladouceur, C. D., & Silk, J. S. (2012). Emotional reactivity and regulation in anxious and non-anxious youth: A cell-phone ecological momentary assessment study. *Journal of Child Psychology and Psychiatry, 53,* 197-206.

Tan, S.-Y. (2001). Integration and beyond: Principles, professional, and personal. *Journal of Psychology and Christianity, 20,* 18-28.

Tan, S.-Y., & Johnson, W. B. (2005). Spiritually oriented cognitive-behavioral therapy. In L. Sperry & E. P. Shafranske (Eds.), *Spiritually oriented psychotherapy* (pp. 77-103). Washington, DC: American Psychological Association.

Tarabulsy, G. M., Provost, M. A., Deslandes, J., St-Laurent, D., Moss, E., Lemelin, J., . . . Dassylva, J. (2003). Individual differences in infant still-face response at 6 months. *Infant Behavior & Development, 26,* 421-38.

Target, M., & Fonagy, P. (1994). The efficacy of psychoanalysis for children: Prediction of outcome in a developmental context. *Journal of the American Academy of Child and Adolescent Psychiatry, 33*(8), 1134-44.

Teicher, M. H., Andersen, S. L., Polcari, A., Anderson, C. M., Navalta, C. P., & Kim, D. M. (2003). The neurobiological consequences of early stress and childhood maltreatment. *Neuroscience and Biobehavioral Reviews, 27*(1-2), 33-44.

Teugels, L. M. (1994). "A strong woman, who can find?": A study of characterization in Genesis 24, with some perspectives on the general presentation of Isaac and Rebekah in the Genesis narratives. *Journal for the Study of the Old Testament, 63,* 89-104.

Teyber, E., & McClure, F. H. (2011). *Interpersonal process in therapy: An integrative model* (6th ed.). Belmont, CA: Brooks/Cole.

Thomas, A., & Chess, S. (1977). *Temperament and development.* Oxford, England: Brunner/Mazel.

Thomas, R., & Zimmer-Gembeck, M. J. (2011). Accumulating evidence for parent-child interaction therapy in the prevention of child maltreatment. *Child Development, 82,* 177-92.

Thomassin, K., Morelen, D., & Suveg, C. (2012). Emotion reporting using electronic diaries reduces anxiety symptoms in girls with emotion dysregulation. *Journal of Contemporary Psychotherapy, 42,* 207-13.

Thompson, R. A. (1994). Emotion regulation: A theme in search of definition. In N. A. Fox (Ed.), *The development of emotion regulation: Biological and behavioral considerations. Monographs of the Society for Research in Child Development, 59*(2-3, Serial No. 240), 25-52.

Thompson, R. A. (2008). Early attachment and later development: Familiar questions, new answers. In J. Cassidy & P. R. Shaver (Eds.), *Handbook of attachment: Theory, research, and clinical applications* (2nd ed., pp. 348-65). New York: Guilford.

Thompson, R. A., & Calkins, S. D. (1996). The double-edged sword: Emotional regulation for children at risk. *Development and Psychopathology, 8,* 163-82.

Thorndike, E. L. (1911). *Animal intelligence: Experimental studies.* New York: Macmillan.

Timmer, S. G., Urquiza, A. J., Zebell, N. M., & McGrath, J. M. (2005). Parent-child interaction therapy: Application to maltreating parent-child dyads. *Child Abuse & Neglect, 29,* 825-42.

Torres, J. B., Solberg, V. S. H., & Carlstrom, A. H. (2002). The myth of sameness among Latino men and their machismo. *American Journal of Orthopsychiatry, 72,* 163-81.

Toth, S. L., & Cicchetti, D. (1999). Developmental psychopathology and child psychotherapy. In S. Russ & T. H. Ollendick (Eds.), *Handbook of psychotherapies with children and families* (pp. 15-44). Dordrecht, Netherlands: Kluwer Academic Publishers.

The Treatment for Adolescents with Depression Study (TADS) Team (2007). The Treatment for Adolescents with Depression Study (TADS): Long-term effectiveness and safety outcomes. *Archives of General Psychiatry, 64,* 1132-44.

Trentacosta, C. J., & Shaw, D. S. (2009). Emotional self-regulation, peer rejection, and antisocial behavior: Developmental associations from early childhood to early adolescence. *Journal of Applied Developmental Psychology, 30,* 356-65.

Trible, P. (1984). *Texts of terror: Literary-feminist readings of biblical narratives.* Philadelphia, PA: Fortress Press.

Trommsdorff, G., & Cole, P. M. (2011). Emotion, self-regulation, and social behavior in cultural contexts. In X. Chen & K. H. Rubin (Eds.), *Socioemotional development in cultural context* (pp. 131-63). New York: Guilford Press.

Trommsdorff, G., & Kornadt, H. (2003). Parent-child relations in cross-cultural perspective. In L. Kuczynski (Ed.), *Handbook of dynamics in parent-child relations* (pp. 271-306). Thousand Oaks, CA: Sage.

Tronick, E. Z., & Cohn, J. F. (1989). Infant-mother face-to-face interaction: Age and gender differences in the coordination and the occurrence of miscoordination. *Child Development, 60,* 85-92.

Trosper, S. E., Buzzella, B. A., Bennett, S. M., & Ehrenreich, J. T. (2009). Emotion regulation in youth with emotional disorders: Implications for a unified treatment approach. *Clinical Child and Family Psychology Review, 12,* 234-54.

Tseng, V. (2012). The uses of research in policy and practice. *Social Policy Report, 26,* 1-16.

Tsibidaki, A., & Tsamparli, A. (2009). Adaptability and cohesion of Greek families:

Raising a child with a severe disability on the island of Rhodes. *Journal of Family Studies, 15,* 245-59.

Tunali, B., & Power, T. G. (2002). Coping by redefinition: Cognitive appraisals in mothers of children with autism and children without autism. *Journal of Autism and Developmental Disorders, 32,* 25-34.

Twardosz, S., & Nordquist, V. M. (1987). Parent training. In M. Hersen & V. B. Van Hasselt (Eds.), *Behavior therapy with children and adolescents: A clinical approach* (pp. 75-105). New York: Wiley and Sons.

Underwood, M. K. (2004). Gender and peer relations: Are the two gender cultures really all that different? In J. B. Kupersmidt & K. Dodge (Eds.), *Children's peer relations: From development to intervention* (pp. 21-36). Washington, DC: American Psychological Association.

U.S. Census Bureau. (2011). *Statistical abstract of the United States.* Retrieved from www .census.gov/compendia/statab/2011/tables/11s1335.pdf

U.S. Department of Education. (2009). *WWC evidence review protocol for dropout prevention interventions, version 2.0.* Institute of Education Sciences, National Center for Education Evaluation and Regional Assistance, What Works Clearinghouse.

Valdez, C. R., Lambert, S. F., & Ialongo, N. S. (2011). Identifying patterns of early risk for mental health and academic problems in adolescence: A longitudinal study of urban youth. *Child Psychiatry and Human Development, 42,* 521-38.

Valiente, C., Eisenberg, N., Fabes, R. A., Shepard, S. A., Cumberland, A., & Losoya, S. H. (2004). Prediction of children's empathy-related responding from their effortful control and parents' expressivity. *Developmental Psychology, 40,* 911-26.

Van Lier, P. A. C., & Koot, H. M. (2010). Developmental cascades of peer relations and symptoms of externalizing and internalizing problems from kindergarten to fourth-grade elementary school. *Development and Psychopathology, 22,* 569-82.

VanderGast, T. S., Post, P. B., & Kascsak-Miller, T. (2010). Graduate training in Child-Parent Relationship Therapy with a multicultural immersion experience: Giving away the skills. *International Journal of Play Therapy, 19,* 198-208.

Verduyn, C., Barrowclough, C., Roberts, J., Tarrier, N., & Harrington, R. (2003). Maternal depression and child behaviour problems: Randomised placebo-controlled trial of a cognitive-behavioural group intervention. *The British Journal of Psychiatry, 183,* 342-48.

Vernberg, E. M., Abwender, D. A., Ewell, K. K., & Beery, S. H. (1992). Social anxiety and peer relationships in early adolescence: A prospective analysis. *Journal of Clinical Child Psychology, 21*(2), 189-96.

Vernberg, E. M., & Biggs, B. K. (Eds.). (2010). *Preventing and Treating Bullying and*

Victimization. Oxford, England: Oxford University Press.

Verstraeten, K., Bijttebier, P., Vasey, M. W., & Raes, F. (2011). Specificity of worry and rumination in the development of anxiety and depressive symptoms in children. *British Journal of Clinical Psychology, 50,* 364-78.

Viana, A. G., Gratz, K. L., & Rabian, B. (2011). Cumulative versus multiple-risk models in the prediction of anxiety symptoms. *Journal of Experimental Psychopathology, 2,* 354-70.

Vismara, L. A. (2009). Pivotal response training (PRT) for children and youth with autism spectrum disorders: Online training module. Sacramento: University of California at Davis Medical School, National Professional Development Center on Autism Spectrum Disorders. In Ohio Center for Autism and Low Incidence (OCALI), *Autism Internet Modules,* www.autisminternetmodules.org. Columbus, OH: OCALI.

Vitaro, F., Brendgen, M., Pagani, L., Tremblay, R. E., & McDuff, P. (1999). Disruptive behavior, peer association, and conduct disorder: Testing the developmental links through early intervention. *Development and Psychopathology, 11,* 287-304.

Vujeva, H. M., & Furman, W. (2011). Depressive symptoms and romantic relationship qualities from adolescence through emerging adulthood: A longitudinal examination of influences. *Journal of Clinical Child & Adolescent Psychology, 40,* 123-35.

Vygotsky, L. S. (1978). *Mind in society: The development of higher psychological processes.* Cambridge, MA: Harvard University Press.

Wachtel, E. F. (2004). *Treating troubled children and their families.* New York: Guildford.

Walden, T., Lemerise, E., & Smith, M. C. (1999). Friendship and popularity in preschool classrooms. *Early Education and Development, 10,* 351-71.

Walker, D. F. (2012). Applied clinical integration in psychotherapy with children and adolescents: A look ahead. *Journal of Psychology and Theology, 40,* 136-40.

Walker, D. F., Ahmed, S., Milevsky, A., Bagasara, A., & Quagliana, H. (2012). Sacred texts. In D. F. Walker & W. L. Hathaway (Eds.), *Spiritual interventions in child and adolescent psychotherapy* (pp. 155-80). Washington, DC: American Psychological Association.

Walker, D. F., & Hathaway, W. L. (2013). *Spiritual interventions in child and adolescent psychotherapy.* Washington, DC: American Psychological Association.

Walker, D. F., & Quagliana, H. (2007). Integrating Scripture with parent training in behavioral interventions. *Journal of Psychology and Christianity, 26,* 122-31.

Walker, D. F., Quagliana, H. L., Wilkinson, M., & Frederick, D. (2013). Christian-accommodative trauma-focused cognitive-behavioral therapy for children and adolescents. In E. L. Worthington Jr., E. Johnson, J. Hook & J. Aten (Eds.), *Evidence-*

based practices for Christian counseling and psychotherapy (pp. 101-21). Downers Grove, IL: InterVarsity Press.

Walker, D. F., Reese, J. B., Hughes, J. P., & Troskie, M. J. (2010). Addressing religious and spiritual issues in trauma-focused cognitive behavior therapy with children and adolescents. *Professional Psychology: Research and Practice, 41,* 174-80.

Walker, D. F., Reid, H., O'Neill, T., & Brown, L. (2009). Changes in personal religion/spirituality during and after childhood abuse: A review and synthesis. *Psychological Trauma: Theory, Research, Practice, and Policy, 1,* 130-45.

Walker, E. F., Grimes, K. E., Davis, D. M., & Smith, A. J. (1993). Childhood precursors of schizophrenia: Facial expressions of emotion. *American Journal of Psychiatry, 150,* 1654-60.

Ward, T. (1995). Introduction. In J. C. Wilhoit & J. M. Dettoni (Eds.), *Nurture that is Christian: Developmental perspectives on Christian education* (pp. 7-18). Wheaton, IL: Victor Books.

Warren, A. E. A., Lerner, R. M., & Phelps, E. (Eds.). (2011). *Thriving and spirituality among youth: Research perspectives and future possibilities.* Hoboken, NJ: John Wiley & Sons.

Waters, S., Virmani, E., Thompson, R. A., Meyer, S., Raikes, A., & Jochem, R. (2010). Emotion regulation and attachment: Unpacking two constructs and their association. *Journal of Psychopathology and Behavioral Assessment, 32,* 37-47.

Watson, J. B. (1913). Psychology as the behaviorist views it. *Psychological Review, 20,* 158-77.

Watson, J. B., & Raynor, R. (1920). Conditioned emotional reactions. *Journal of Experimental Psychology, 3,* 1-14.

Webster, R. S. (2005). Personal identity: Moving beyond essence. *International Journal of Children's Spirituality, 10,* 5-16.

Webster-Stratton, C. (2011). *The incredible years: Parents, teachers, and children's training series: Program, content, methods, research and dissemination.* Seattle: Incredible Years.

Webster-Stratton, C., Reid, M., & Stoolmiller, M. (2008). Preventing conduct problems and improving school readiness: Evaluation of the Incredible Years Teacher and Child Training Programs in high-risk schools. *Journal of Child Psychology & Psychiatry, 49*(5), 471-88. doi:10.1111/j.1469-7610.2007.01861.x

Weems, C. F., Silverman, W. K., Rapee, R. M., & Pina, A. A. (2003). The role of control in childhood anxiety disorders. *Cognitive Therapy and Research, 27,* 557-68.

Weersing, V. R., & Brent, D. A. (2010). Treating depression in adolescents using individual cognitive behavioral therapy. In J. R. Weisz and A. E. Kazdin (Eds.), *Evidence-based psychotherapies for children and adolescents* (2nd ed., pp. 126-40). New York: Guilford.

Weinberg, M. K., Beeghly, M., Olson, K. L., & Tronick, E. (2008). Effect of maternal depression and panic disorder on mother-infant interactive behavior in the face-to-face still-face paradigm. *Infant Mental Health Journal, 29,* 472-91.

Weisz, J. R., & Kazdin, A. E. (Eds.). (2010). *Evidence-based psychotherapies for children and adolescents* (2nd ed.). New York: Guilford.

Weisz, J. R., Ugueto, A. M., Cheron, D. M., & Herren, J. (2013). Evidence-based youth psychotherapy in the mental health ecosystem. *Journal of Clinical Child and Adolescent Psychology, 42,* 274-86.

Weitzman, M., Rosenthal, D. G., & Liu, Y.-H. (2011). Paternal depressive symptoms and child behavioral or emotional problems in the United States. *Pediatrics, 128,* 1126-34.

Wells, K. C. (2005). Family therapy for attention-deficit/hyperactivity disorder (ADHD). In J. L. Lebow (Ed.), *Handbook of clinical family therapy* (pp. 42-72). New York: Wiley.

Wells, K. C., Lochman, J. E., & Lenhart, L. A. (2008). *Coping power: Parent group facilitator's guide.* New York: Oxford University Press.

Wendel, R., & Gouze, K. R. (2010). Family therapy. In M. K. Dulcan (Ed.), *Dulcan's textbook of child and adolescent psychiatry* (pp. 869-86). Washington, DC: American Psychiatric Publishing.

Wentzel, K. R. (2009). Peers and academic functioning at school. In K. H. Rubin, W. M. Bukowski & B. Laursen (Eds.), *Handbook of peer interactions, relationships, and groups* (pp. 531-47). New York: Guilford.

Wentzel, K. R., Donlan, A., & Morrison, D. (2012). Peer relationships and social motivational processes. In A. M. Ryan & G. W. Ladd (Eds.), *Peer relationships and adjustment at school* (pp. 79-105). Charlotte, NC: Information Age Publishing.

Werner, E. E., & Smith, R. S. (1992). *Overcoming the odds: High risk children from birth to adulthood.* Ithaca, NY: Cornell University Press.

Werner, E. E., & Smith, R. S. (2001). *Journeys from childhood to midlife: Risk, resilience, and recovery.* Ithaca, NY: Cornell University Press.

Westerhoff, J. H., III. (1976). *Will our children have faith?* New York: Seabury Press.

Westermann, C. (1984). *Genesis 1-11: A Commentary* (J. J. Scullion, Trans.). London: SPCK.

Westhues, A., Hanbidge, A., Gebotys, R., & Hammond, A. (2009). Comparing the effectiveness of school-based and community-based delivery of an emotional regulation skills program for children. *School Social Work Journal, 34,* 74-96.

Whaley, S. E., Pinto, A., & Sigman, M. (1999). Characterizing interactions between anxious mothers and their children. *Journal of Consulting & Clinical Psychology, 67,* 826-36.

Whitcomb, S. A., & Merrell, K. W. (2013). *Behavioral, social and emotional assessment of children and adolescents* (4th ed.). New York: Routledge.

Whitman, T. L., Bokowski, J. G., Keogh, D. A., & Weed, K. (2001). *Interwoven lives: Adolescent mothers and their children.* Mahwah, NJ: Lawrence Erlbaum Associates.

Widiger, T. A., & Clark, L. (2000). Toward DSM-V and the classification of psychopathology. *Psychological Bulletin, 126,* 946-63.

Wiebe, S. A., Sheffield, T. D., & Espy, K. A. (2012). Separating the fish from the sharks: A longitudinal study of preschool response inhibition. *Child Development, 83,* 1245-61.

Wieland, N., & Baker, B. L. (2010). The role of marital quality and spousal support in behaviour problems of children with and without intellectual difficulties. *Journal of Intellectual Disability Research, 54,* 620-33.

Wilcox, W. B. (1998). Conservative Protestant childrearing: Authoritarian or authoritative? *American Sociological Review, 63,* 796-809.

Wilson, K., & Ryan, V. (2005). *Play therapy: A non-directive approach for children and adolescents* (2nd ed.). London: Elsevier Science.

Winnicott, D. W. (1953). Transitional objects and transitional phenomena. *International Journal of Psychoanalysis, 34,* 89-97.

Winnicott, D. W. (1957). *The child, the family, and the outside world.* Cambridge, MA: Perseus.

Winnicott, D. W. (1958). Anxiety associated with insecurity. In *Collected papers: Through pediatrics to psychoanalysis* (p. 97-100). London: Tavistock.

Winnicott, D. W. (1965). *The maturational processes and the facilitating environment.* London: Karnac Books.

Woodhouse, S. S., Dykas, M. J., & Cassidy, J. (2012). Loneliness and peer relations in adolescence. *Social Development, 21*(2), 273-93.

Yancey, P. (1987, February). The crayon man. *Christianity Today,* pp. 14-20.

Yangarber-Hicks, N., Behensky, C., Canning, S. S., Flanagan, K. S., Gibson, N. J. S., Hicks, M. W., . . . Porter, S. L. (2006). Invitation to the table conversation: A few diverse perspectives on integration. *Journal of Psychology and Christianity, 25*(4), 338-53.

Yap, M. H., Allen, N. B., & Sheeber, L. (2007). Using an emotion regulation framework to understand the role of temperament and family processes in risk for adolescent depressive disorders. *Clinical Child and Family Psychology Review, 10,* 180-96.

Yarhouse, M. A., Butman, R. E., & McRay, B. W. (2005). *Modern psychopathologies: A comprehensive Christian appraisal.* Downers Grove, IL: InterVarsity Press.

Young, M., E., & Fristad, M. A. (2007). Evidence based treatments for bipolar disorder in children and adolescents. *Journal of Contemporary Psychotherapy, 37,* 157-64.

Yust, K. M. (2004). *Real kids, real faith: Practices for nurturing children's spiritual lives.* San Francisco: Jossey-Bass.

Zahn-Waxler, C., Cole, P. M., Richardson, D. T., Friedman, R. T., Michel, M. K., & Belouad, F. (1994). Social problem solving in disruptive preschool children: Reactions to hypothetical situations of conflict and distress. *Merrill-Palmer Quarterly, 40,* 98-119.

Zalewski, M., Lengua, L. J., Wilson, A. C., Trancik, A., & Bazinet, A. (2011). Associations of coping and appraisal styles with emotion regulation during preadolescence. *Journal of Experimental Child Psychology, 110,* 141-58.

Zimet, D. M., & Jacob, T. (2001). Influences of marital conflict on child adjustment: Review of theory and research. *Clinical Child and Family Psychology Review, 4,* 319-35.

Zimmer-Gembeck, M. J., Lees, D., & Skinner, E. A. (2011). Children's emotions and coping with interpersonal stress as correlates of social competence. *Australian Journal of Psychology, 63,* 131-41.

Zimmermann, P. (1999). Structure and functions of internal working models of attachment and their role for emotion regulation. *Attachment & Human Development, 1,* 291-306.

Zinnbauer, B., & Pargament, K. I. (2005). Religiousness and spirituality. In R. Paloutzian & C. Parks (Eds.), *Handbook of the psychology of religion and spirituality* (pp. 21-42). New York: Guilford.

Zuckerman, M. (1991). *Psychobiology of personality.* New York: Cambridge University Press.

Zuckerman, M. (2008). Personality and sensation seeking. In G. J. Boyle, G. Matthews & D. H. Saklofske (Eds.), *The SAGE handbook of personality theory and assessment, Vol. 1: Personality theories and models* (pp. 379-98). Thousand Oaks, CA: Sage.

Zwierzynska, K., Wolke, D., & Lereya, T. S. (2013). Peer victimization in childhood and internalizing problems in adolescence: A prospective longitudinal study. *Journal of Abnormal Child Psychology, 41,* 309-23.

Subject Index

....

*An Association for Christian Psychologists,
Therapists, Counselors and Academicians*

CAPS is a vibrant Christian organization with a rich tradition. Founded in 1956 by a small group of Christian mental health professionals, chaplains and pastors, CAPS has grown to more than 2,100 members in the U.S., Canada and more than 25 other countries.

CAPS encourages in-depth consideration of therapeutic, research, theoretical and theological issues. The association is a forum for creative new ideas. In fact, their publications and conferences are the birthplace for many of the formative concepts in our field today.

CAPS members represent a variety of denominations, professional groups and theoretical orientations; yet all are united in their commitment to Christ and to professional excellence.

CAPS is a non-profit, member-supported organization. It is led by a fully functioning board of directors, and the membership has a voice in the direction of CAPS.

CAPS is more than a professional association. It is a fellowship, and in addition to national and international activities, the organization strongly encourages regional, local and area activities which provide networking and fellowship opportunities as well as professional enrichment.

To learn more about CAPS, visit www.caps.net.

The joint publishing venture between IVP Academic and CAPS aims to promote the understanding of the relationship between Christianity and the behavioral sciences at both the clinical/counseling and the theoretical/research levels. These books will be of particular value for students and practitioners, teachers and researchers.

For more information about CAPS Books, visit InterVarsity Press's website at www.ivpress.com/cgi-ivpress/book.pl/code=2801.

Finding the Textbook You Need

The IVP Academic Textbook Selector
is an online tool for instantly finding the IVP books
suitable for over 250 courses across 24 disciplines.

www.ivpress.com/academic/textbookselector